Year	Candidates	Party	Popular Vote	Electoral Vote
1836	**Martin Van Buren**	Democratic	761,549	170
	William H. Harrison	Whig	549,567	73
	Hugh L. White	Whig	145,396	26
	Daniel Webster	Whig	41,287	14
1840	**William H. Harrison**	Whig	1,275,017	234
	(John Tyler, 1841)			
	Martin Van Buren	Democratic	1,128,702	60
1844	**James K. Polk**	Democratic	1,337,243	170
	Henry Clay	Whig	1,299,068	105
	James G. Birney	Liberty	62,300	
1848	**Zachary Taylor**	Whig	1,360,101	163
	(Millard Fillmore, 1850)			
	Lewis Cass	Democratic	1,220,544	127
	Martin Van Buren	Free Soil	291,263	
1852	**Franklin Pierce**	Democratic	1,601,474	254
	Winfield Scott	Whig	1,386,578	42
1856	**James Buchanan**	Democratic	1,838,169	174
	John C. Frémont	Republican	1,335,264	114
	Millard Fillmore	American	874,534	8
1860	**Abraham Lincoln**	Republican	1,865,593	180
	Stephen A. Douglas	Democratic	1,382,713	12
	John C. Breckinridge	Democratic	848,356	72
	John Bell	Constitutional Union	592,906	39
1864	**Abraham Lincoln**	Republican	2,206,938	212
	(Andrew Johnson, 1865)			
	George B. McClellan	Democratic	1,803,787	21
1868	**Ulysses S. Grant**	Republican	3,013,421	214
	Horatio Seymour	Democratic	2,706,829	80
1872	**Ulysses S. Grant**	Republican	3,596,745	286
	Horace Greeley	Democratic	2,843,446	66
1876	**Rutherford B. Hayes**	Republican	4,036,572	185
	Samuel J. Tilden	Democratic	4,284,020	184
1880	**James A. Garfield**	Republican	4,449,053	214
	(Chester A. Arthur, 1881)			
	Winfield S. Hancock	Democratic	4,442,035	155
	James B. Weaver	Greenback-Labor	308,578	

Dedica

To: Egg Ribs
and Spare Rolls,
and Everything in Between

AMERICAN POLITICS

DIRECTIONS OF CHANGE, DYNAMICS OF CHOICE

RICHARD E. MORGAN
JOHN C. DONOVAN
CHRISTIAN P. POTHOLM
BOWDOIN COLLEGE

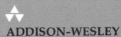
ADDISON-WESLEY
Publishing Company
READING, MASSACHUSETTS
MENLO PARK, CALIFORNIA
LONDON ★ AMSTERDAM
DON MILLS, ONTARIO ★ SYDNEY

Sponsoring Editor: *Stuart W. Johnson*
Production Editor: *Melissa P. Hodgson*
Designer: *Robert A. Rose*
Illustrator: *Oxford Illustrators Ltd.*
Cover Design: *Robert A. Rose*

PREFACE

We undertook this work in the conviction that today's beginning students of American politics are more and more in need of basic instruction about the institutional structures of our polity and how they work. At the same time, many texts are providing less and less such instruction, leaving students confused and adrift.

In addition to the failure to supply basic informational material on Congress, courts, parties, and the like, we find that many of the present introductory texts are highly theoretical or "gimmicky." For most beginning students this is disastrous. Freshmen or sophomores who do not know what OMB does, or how cases get to the Supreme Court, simply are not excited by repeated invitations to consider the relevance of eight structural-functional categories to an American reality they only dimly perceive, and are equally unlikely to be drawn into an extended consideration of whether our system is more elitist than pluralistic.

We shall be focusing on institutions and on political process. Our treatment of institutions will cover both the formal (legislatures, courts, and so on) and informal (parties, interest groups, media, and so on), and will focus on how these aspects of the system are *changing*. Thus, rather than the static 1950s portrayal of American politics, we hope to convey a series of pictures of institutions in motion.

Also, we feel that today's students are not receiving adequate exposure to the importance of *choice* in both society and government. Too few students are aware that every political, economic, or societal choice involves possible payoffs, possible risks, possible costs, and the closing off of alternatives. In fact, the organizing theme of the book is that the American political system is in a constant state of change and that change forces choices. We feel that students should be exposed to the dynamics of this process by the exploration of specific examples so that they can see that our system is in a continual state of becoming—and that choice—collective and personal—is what shapes that becoming.

Our book is distinctive in several other respects:

1. We illustrate institutional realities with reference to current policy issues. This may sound banal, but, on checking, we find that few texts leaven generalizations with examples more than occasionally.

2. Our book pays far more than the usual attention to foreign and defense policy making, and the impact of the international environment on American politics. We do this in part because we feel that this is a vital, overlooked area in terms of how the American political system will be able—or not able—to function in the 1980s. We also depart somewhat from the traditional by presenting civil rights and civil liberties as policy areas, not as gifts brought to America by the stork. And we include a full chapter on the media because we believe that mass media are transforming American politics. Our students sense this yet often lack perspective. Our treatment of bureaucracy not only describes the organization of the federal executive branch but also introduces the student to the actual workings of bureaucracy as an active force in shaping public policies.

3. Finally, we work to draw the students into the text, asking them questions; not simply about the material, but about their reaction to the various aspects of the topics. We feel that today's students want greater involvement in the material and that their *participation,* albeit imaginary, in the choices confronting the American system will enhance their learning experience and stimulate their interest.

We have attempted nothing radical. Rather our objective throughout has been to cover the basics in a very readable way. Above all we have sought to convey the varied flavors of American politics as we have savored them ourselves over many years as political scientists and participants. Our best hope is that our readers will find few "textbook treatments" in the pages that follow.

In bringing the book to publication we have accumulated a long list of debts. First, Mrs. Grace Lott and Mrs. Gladys Peterson invested time and love beyond anything that can be conveyed by the word "typing."

Further, we are very grateful to a number of fellow political scientists for reading portions of the manuscript and for offering us the benefit of their advice, which we heeded far more often than they may realize. They are:

Everett C. Ladd, Jr., University of Connecticut
Erwin C. Hargrove, Vanderbilt University
Richard F. Fenno, Jr., University of Rochester

Howard W. Hallman, Center for Governmental Studies
Larry Elowitz, Georgia College
Robert Keighton, Curry College

Clement E. Vose, Wesleyan University
Charles A. Joiner, Temple University
Sidney Wise, Franklin and Marshall College
Byrum E. Carter, Indiana University
Howard Bliss, Vassar College
David A. Baldwin, Dartmouth College
David R. Manwaring, Boston College
G. Calvin Mackenzie, Colby College
Arthur H. House, Office of Senator Abraham Ribicoff

William G. Munselle, University of Florida
Victor L. Profughi, Rhode Island College
John W. Smith, Henry Ford Community College
Robert E. Johnston, Georgia State University
Karen Lindenberg, Eastern Michigan University
Gregory Casey, University of Missouri—Columbia
David Kovenock, University of Maine
James S. Young, Columbia University

Special thanks go to our student assistants: Marianne Russell, Beth Cantara, John Campbell, Pamela Gray, Gail Hines, Julie Horowitz, and Joanne Golden.

We are also very grateful for editorial and technical advice and assistance from our friends and colleagues at Addison-Wesley, especially Stuart Johnson, Elizabeth Hacking, Karen Guardino, Will Buddenhagen, and Melissa Hodgson.

Finally we thank our wives for their forbearance during this time-consuming collaborative effort.

Brunswick, Maine
January 1979

R. E. M.
J. C. D.
C. P. P.

CONTENTS IN BRIEF

CONTENTS

PART II   POLITICS AND SOCIETY   91

CHAPTER 7

THE MEDIA: POLITICAL IMAGEMAKERS _____ 213

PART III · OUR CHANGING INSTITUTIONS _____ 247

CHAPTER 8

PRESIDENTIAL PARADOX: POWER AND WEAKNESS _____ 249

IN CONGRESS, JULY 4, 1776

The unanimous Declaration of the thirteen united States of America

CHAPTER 1 INTRODUCTION

This book is intended to provide you with the basic information you need to understand the elaborate institutions of American government and to follow the swirling maze of activity called American politics. In addition, the authors hope that by studying the various aspects of our public life treated in these chapters, you will come to appreciate two very important facts about our process of government: first, that governing involves *choice* between different things wanted by different people; and second, that our political system is in a constant process of *change*. Choice and change, therefore, are the themes of this book.

CHOICE

There are very few easy and "correct" options open to the participants in a sprawling and diverse political setting such as ours. Every decision involves sacrificing something to get something else; helping group X at the expense of group Y. Usually the choices facing political actors are quite distasteful. (That's why they so often postpone or try to avoid making them.)

Choices can be made one way or another, or even avoided, but they always involve gains and costs. *There is no such thing as a free lunch.* This is true for two fundamental reasons: first, people and groups in America want conflicting, mutually exclusive things; and second, there are never enough resources to go around. These are facts of life, and no amount of effort to gloss them over will make them go away. A candidate for office who spends money on television time will not have it to spend on direct mail appeals. Choice. A senator who votes for an affirmative action program will be helping women and blacks, but hurting white males. Again choice.

CHANGE

The American political system is continually changing. Like a great river, it is never the same any two times you look at it. Despite powerful currents of continuity, new eddies are forming and crosscurrents developing. And from time to time a crisis—a flood in the river—changes the location of a channel or even alters the course of the river.

We shall be concerned not only with the origins of the American political system, and how it functions today, but *where it is going*. You will be invited to speculate along with us about the direction this system may take in the future.

It is important to understand, for instance, what political parties have done in America; but it is also important to ask whether parties are still doing it. It is important to understand what the Supreme Court does for us; but it is also important for you to think about whether the Supreme Court's role is changing and whether that change is for the good.

Most changes come on the political system by surprise. This, as we shall presently see, was the case with the economic decline of the older cities, which in turn forced changes in city government. Sometimes government action (policy) triggers change—often in ways not intended by those who pressed for the governmental action.

For example, the limitations on presidential campaign spending that were imposed in 1976 were intended by supporters to reduce the possible influence of large givers on future presidents. But an important effect of these limitations has been to force candidates to concentrate more on attracting the attention of the free medium of television news, as opposed to more direct and traditional approaches, such as recruiting armies of local canvassers, or purchasing air time for speeches in which their views are developed in a systematic fashion. A premium is placed on glamor and the ability to be "newsworthy"; as a result, the way candidates run for office is significantly changed, and this in turn will surely influence the kinds of presidents we will get in the future. In the meantime, the large givers have greatly increased their contributions to congressional candidates.

To illustrate the approach we are inviting you to take to the study of American government, we will start with a short description of one major political issue. The issue we have chosen for this introduction is the "urban crisis." By exploring its complexities and seeing the dilemmas it creates for policy makers in government, we can clarify the purposes of the book, and illustrate our basic themes of choice and change.

THE URBAN CRISIS

The Carter administration found a number of serious issues confronting it when it took office, among which was the "urban crisis." Large city mayors have besieged the White House with demands for new, "meaningful" federal action. Even medium-city mayors clamored to be heard. Janet Frey, Mayor of San José, California, declared that "We are coming to you not as beggars, but as elected officials of the places where 75 percent of the people are. We've got a disproportionate share of the problems and we lack the resources."[1] President Carter pledged a major new approach, and set his aides to work on it in the spring of 1977. What did these aides find themselves facing?

[1] The *New York Times*, February 13, 1978.

A Nation of Cities

Over the last decade there has been great and justified concern in America over the condition of many of our cities. There has also been much talk about dramatic actions to save the cities. In the mid-1970s, the ludicrous but terribly real financial plight of New York City alternately horrified and entertained the nation. We often hear from the news media and politicians that we are "a nation of cities" and that the twentieth century has seen a transformation of America from a rural to an urban nation.

There is truth in these generalizations, but there is also exaggeration. One must remember the great variety of American cities. It is all too easy, given the media concentrations in New York and Los Angeles, to assume that most other cities are simply smaller versions of financial chaos and smog. But not all cities have all "urban problems." Traffic, for instance, is a very serious problem for New York and Los Angeles, but not so serious for Philadelphia or Atlanta. And, as Professor Daniel Elazar has pointed out, "of the more than 6,000 legally constituted cities in the nation, only five have populations over one million, and only fifty-one have populations over 250,000."[2]

The notion of America as an urban nation, with its suggestion of high-density crowding and dangerous streets, was given a great boost by the 1960 census reports, which announced that over 70 percent of all Americans lived in "urban places." The problem with these reports was that the Census Bureau's definition of an "urban place" was any settlement of 2,500 or more. Now, to most of us, such a settlement is really a small town, and even a "city" of 25,000 would not fit our mental picture of "urban area."[3] Thus, as we shall show elsewhere in this book, appearances and realities are not always identical.

In fact, despite the movement off the farms that took place early in this century, the American population is still very widely distributed. Ours is a low-density society and becoming more so by the year. Most of the cities over one million are, in fact, losing population. Far from becoming a nation of urbanites, we have become a nation of *suburbanites* and dwellers in small "regional cities." Only around 9 percent of us live in cities of over one million.

This is not to say that the urban crisis is not real, that it is not a problem the nation will have to cope with for years to come. Particularly the larger, older cities of the East and the Midwest—gigantic cities such as New York and Chicago, medium-sized cities such as Hartford and Youngstown, Ohio, and smaller mill cities such as Patterson, New Jersey,

[2] Daniel J. Elazar, "Are We a Nation of Cities?" *The Public Interest* (Summer 1966): 47–48.
[3] Elazar, "Are We a Nation of Cities?"

and Lewiston, Maine—do share a set of problems that have common causes.

Causes of the Crisis

One of the central functions of the older American cities was to serve as staging areas for waves of new immigration into the country. As the immigrants were organizing themselves within the cities, they provided

willing hands for certain labor-intensive manufacturing and transportation industries. Thus the cities contributed to the national economy, and the immigrants had work (even at very low pay) that enabled them to "make a stake" and move out of the city into other economic slots of the society. The older cities were also important because of the necessity of concentrating economic activity—buying, selling, and record keeping—in compact spaces.

In the decades since World War II, these functions of the traditional American city have been seriously disrupted by four socioeconomic developments.

First, and most damaging, is that the core areas of most of our older cities are rapidly losing their economic value. There simply are not enough things being produced or serviced or modified in the older cities that other Americans want to buy. The more labor-intensive sorts of industries, which provided work for immigrants in the past, have declined. They have been automated, or they have moved to the rural South, or they have moved to a suburban industrial park, or they have disappeared entirely in the face of more cheaply made products now coming from Japan, Korea, Taiwan. The importance of this decline in the economic value of the older cities can hardly be overstated in a discussion of their plight today.

Second, the requirement of geographical proximity for doing business, so important to the initial growth of cities around harbors and railheads, is also declining in importance. Transportation is becoming more and more automated and requires fewer and fewer hands. And the interstate highway system allows warehouses to spread out all over the countryside. Even more significantly, the development of computers has made it possible for individuals to engage in complicated commercial transactions, and keep perfect records of these transactions, while one participant sits in Vail, Colorado, and the other in Princeton, New Jersey. There are certain kinds of businesses that continue to require (or desire) geographic proximity, but high finance, publishing, and the performing arts provide relatively few unskilled jobs.

Third, the most recent immigrant wave into the older cities has been composed largely of black people, many of them from the rural South. In seeking to use the city as their entry to a better life, these late arrivals have labored under more severe burdens than their predecessors. Not only have they arrived to find the traditional pool of manufacturing and transportation jobs drying up, but blacks especially have been impeded in their upward and outward mobility by pervasive social racism. Other immigrant groups suffered from handicaps on their arrival in American cities, but none bore the burden of two hundred years of enslavement.

Finally, the impairment of the functions of the older cities has come at a time of rising expectations. Urban Americans of the post–World War

II generation take for granted the desirability of increasing municipal services. Public higher education, day-care for children, and a network of welfare and human development programs have been added to the staples of fire protection, police protection, and sanitation. Thus, for over two decades, many of the older cities have faced the necessity of offering more and more services to their citizens with less and less money to pay for these services. As the economic plight of the citizenry worsens, the need for public expenditure, especially on welfare, increases. As physical conditions and public safety within areas of the inner core of the older city deteriorate, more middle-class taxpayers flee to the suburbs. The mayors of the core cities are left in the unenviable position of having to appeal to voters who want and need more and more and are producing less and less.

The Political Dimension

It is small wonder in these circumstances that hard-pressed urban political leaders are mildly amused when nonurbanites tell them they must help themselves out of their plights. The mayors of the decaying older cities have no choice but to appeal endlessly to Washington and to their state capitals—trying to persuade presidents, governors, and legislators that more money must flow in their direction if they are to stay alive.

But it is also easy to see why the troubled cities encounter such opposition when they seek resources from the "outside." The substantial majority of the voters who choose the national and state officials are not immediately afflicted by the problems of the decaying older cities. Indeed, their ability to move themselves away from hard-core urban problems is one factor making these problems worse. How can these voters be persuaded that they should contribute substantial sums to help areas they perceive as doing very little for them? Humanitarian appeals are not without effect in American politics, but they are short-run approaches at best.

And presuming that the argument for greater aid could be made convincingly on moral grounds, or in terms of the long-term self-interest of nonurbanites, how would these resources most effectively be applied to the problems of the older cities?

Would you spend the money to support the human-services budgets of troubled cities? This would make life somewhat easier for the urban poor today, but would it do much to help tomorrow?

Or would you use these funds to attempt to reverse the decline of the older cities? This approach certainly is more uplifting of the spirit, but does anyone know how to do it?

Is it, in fact, within the power of government, even with lots of taxpayers' money to spend, to reverse this decline? Can manufacturing

and other labor-intensive industries be brought back to New York? Can government provide sufficient incentives for businesses, which technology has enabled to live apart, to move back to Cleveland? These were the questions that confronted President Carter's aides while they were formulating his urban-policy package.

There is no single answer to these complex questions. The crisis may at times be overstated, but it is nonetheless very real. Not all cities are affected, but many are. The decline of the older cities results from certain basic social and economic changes that nobody planned and that may be beyond the power of government to control. It is not beyond the power of government to ease the living conditions of the poor in the afflicted areas, but building a political consensus for such relief is not an easy job. How can one persuade the majority of voters, who live in suburbs, small towns, and new cities, that older cities deserve this special help?

The Carter Response

Well into its second year in office, after many months of work, the Carter administration had yet to unveil what was referred to as its "master plan" for the cities. To some extent this delay resulted from the strong position taken by Joseph Califano, Secretary of Health, Education, and Welfare.

Califano argued that the administration's program should not be directed at cities at all, but at the poor wherever they lived.

Califano reasoned, first, that this approach would be more fair: "We should place our primary emphasis on people in distress rather than places in distress." He also reasoned that this approach was good politics, since most members of Congress come from nonurban areas and a sizeable cities program "flies in the face of political reality."[4] And it was no accident that one of Califano's principal opponents, arguing for a cities-focused approach, was Patricia Roberts Harris, Secretary of Housing and Urban Development. The more place-oriented the Carter program, the more of it would likely fall to Harris's department to administer; the more people-oriented, the more would go to Califano's department.

By March of 1978, a year after work had begun, pressure had built up on President Carter to announce his program. The president was due to leave for South America and Africa at the end of the month, and he had committed himself to disclosing his package for the cities before departure. This self-imposed deadline, however, worked to embarrass rather than vindicate the administration.

A presidential press conference was called for March 27, and two days before, administration aides submitted the policy package to the president for final approval. Carter was dismayed, but went to work deciding "up or down" on the variety of programs put before him. The "master plan" that emerged was a collection of *already existing*, ongoing federal efforts that could be said to benefit the cities and in which various elements of federal bureaucracy had vested interests. On top of this collection were superimposed three new initiatives: a national urban-development bank to make low-interest loans as inducements for businesses to return to cities; tax credits for businesses to stay in distressed areas; and a program to create constructive jobs for the chronically unemployed. The total "new money" called for by this package was $4.4 billion—a far cry from the $50 billion "Marshall plan" for cities that some urban advocates (especially black leaders) had been talking about a year earlier.

Confronted with the destructive economic and social change that has overtaken many cities, governments can channel the limited resources available into attempts either to revive the cities or to lessen the suffering of people in the cities, or the higher levels of government can attempt a bit of both to the detriment of both efforts. Government can choose (or choose not to choose). What government cannot do is "the right thing." In its urban package the Carter administration chose a little of both. Its choices may, given all the factors involved, be wise. But they have been popular with no one.

[4] The *New York Times*, January 25, 1978.

Lessons to Be Learned

In short, the urban crisis, when it is looked at from inside the government, is not nearly as simple as it might look from outside.

If it were simple, it probably would have been dealt with already. But this is a matter about which "experts" disagree, about which there is no political consensus in the country, and with regard to which there is no clear course of government action guaranteed to make things better. The need for some sort of action is real; there are demands for action, and pressures are brought to bear on different parts of the governmental apparatus to do things. Frequently, of course, these demands and pressures are for different and contradictory things.

To understand the urban crisis in all its complexity, it is necessary to gain a working knowledge of the various components of the American political system, and to develop a feel for how these components—parties, interest groups, public opinion, state and local governments, the president, Congress, executive agencies, and the courts—relate to one another in taking the variety of actions (taxing, spending, and regulating) that we call public policy.

THE PURPOSES OF THIS BOOK

This book is designed to help you see issues from the "inside" perspective, and to appreciate that the American system, while complicated, is comprehensible.

First, we want to help you develop a clear understanding of how our governmental system developed. How did we become what we are today? What fundamental choices are embodied in the Constitution, and how have these original choices been altered by succeeding political generations? If ours was not a country committed to limited government and free internal movement of the population, it would not be as difficult to deal with obsolescent older cities.

Second, we hope to offer you a vivid introduction to the nongovernmental structures that are so very important to the way in which our system operates. Political parties, public opinion, and the pattern of interest-group activity affect not only elections but the entire policy-making process. If a coherent and supportive public opinion existed for aid to the troubled cities, the governmental response would also be more coherent.

Third, we shall explore with you the intricate organization and workings of the formal institutions of government in America. While concentrating on the national level, we shall also be noting the ways in which national institutions are involved in interactions with institutions at the state and local government levels. Policy outputs are always, at least in part, determined by the internal requirements of the particular governmental agency responsible for them. Remember the Califano (HEW) versus Harris (HUD) example!

Fourth, we shall let you see the formal and informal institutions in action. In three different areas of policy making—foreign policy, domestic policy, and civil liberties—we will explore how the parts of the system interact, slowly and painfully, to produce new policy results.

Fifth, and finally, we will be returning you, as we go along, to our basic themes of choice and change. Where have we been; what kind of people are we; where are we going? How would you make the trade-offs; how would you call the shots? This is the approach you are invited to take.

SUGGESTED READINGS

ABRAMS, CHARLES, *The City is the Frontier* (New York: Harper & Row, 1965).

A colorful critique of our cities, and an affirmation of hope for their future.

DAHL, ROBERT A., *Who Governs? Democracy and Power in an American City* (New Haven: Yale University Press, 1961).

A classic study of the inner politics of a medium-sized American city. Very readable, and available in paperback.

MUMFORD, LEWIS, *The City in History: Its Origins, Its Transformations, and Its Prospects* (New York: Harcourt, 1961).

A statement of the utopian idea of the "classical city."

WOOD, ROBERT C., *Suburbia: Its People and Their Politics* (Boston: Houghton Mifflin, 1958).

An analysis of the suburbs, stressing the flight from urbanism as a retreat into a "politics of nostalgia."

The framers of the Constitution, who distrusted democracy, deserve much credit for the success of our democracy. . . . The framers insisted in 1787, and their document insists today, that law is the price of liberty, duty of happiness, communal order of individual development, deliberation of wise decision, constitutionalism of democracy. Their Constitution, conceived in this tough-minded philosophy, has made it possible for a restless race to have its stability and its progress, too. It has been perhaps the most successful conservative device in the history of mankind, and the Americans, a singularly conservative people for all their restlessness, have adored it with good reason. It has been their king and church, their ark and covenant, their splendid sign of freedom and unity; it has been all these things because, first of all, it has been their tutor in ordered liberty.

Clinton Rossiter

CHAPTER 2 FOUNDING THE REPUBLIC: THE ORIGINAL CHOICES

What does it mean to "make a constitution"? And what is "constitution-alism" anyway?

Sometime in 1768 a small group of woodsmen adventurers from Virginia penetrated the Appalachian barrier into the hostile Indian country of the upper Holston Valley, and settled along Watauga Creek. They had passed beyond all signs of civilization, but thought they were still in Virginia. They were wrong. Several years after their arrival a new survey of state boundaries placed them in the governmental great beyond. There would never be any help from Williamsburg, the capital of Virginia. Thus, "on a forgotten day in 1772," a small group of these woodsmen, armed with Pennsylvania rifles, met on the banks of the Watauga to drink raw whisky and talk. They wanted government for mutual protection and they gave it to themselves. They drafted a written agreement, formed an association, and elected an executive committee.

This was the beginning of what would become the State of Tennessee.[1] More importantly, it was an example of the American commitment to **constitutionalism**, the specification in writing of the structure, functions, and limitations of government. It was an idea bred into the bones of Americans long before the Revolution or the birth of our present United States. Whether woodsmen or tidewater aristocrats, Americans made limited governments to serve specific purposes through a written constitution.

The purpose of this book is to help you understand the American political system as it operates today. However, it is impossible to understand how things work today without knowledge of how our governmental institutions were formed, and how our basic attitudes about politics developed. Throughout this text, therefore, we will focus on those aspects of our past that are necessary to an understanding of the present. In this chapter we shall identify certain basic choices made early in our political history that powerfully affect our politics today. At every crisis in our politics, we Americans explore anew the meaning of our Constitution and the intention of those who wrote it. Nothing illustrates this more dramatically than the Watergate crisis, in the course of which the relationship of the president to Congress was re-examined.

We seem to have less and less respect in recent decades for the great figures of American political history. Although this trend is regrettable, it is not hard to understand. In the light of the enormous scientific and technical achievements of the twentieth century, these men seem to us primitive in their understanding of the natural universe; therefore, we find it hard to take seriously (at least between crises) their insights into government and society. In addition, our heightened moral sense en-

> Constitutionalism, the creation of written documents outlining the structure, functions, and limitations of government, was an idea bred into the bones of the American people.

[1] Roy F. Nichols, *American Leviathan* (New York: Atheneum, 1963), pp. 52–53.

courages a certain contempt for the social views of previous generations of Americans. What can we learn from men who owned slaves, believed bleeding a treatment for fever, routinely subjugated women, and believed that intercourse with a virgin would cure venereal disease? Washington insisted on absolute secrecy at the Constitutional Convention, and was arrogant and domineering in his personal relations; Hamilton was capable of seriously considering monarchy as a form of government for the United States; and Jefferson was given to attacks on the press that would make Spiro Agnew blush. But the history these men helped make, far from being our adversary, is a source of strength and guidance.

It is possible to have certain attitudes that are old-fashioned by today's standards and yet still have a shrewd understanding of the potentials and limits of politics. The men who made the American Revolution, wrote the Constitution and Bill of Rights, and set the institutions of our national government in motion were, to a unique degree, *thoughtful* politicians. They may seem to us somewhat backward in their physics, but they were superbly educated by any standards in history and philosophy. These men were constantly reflecting on the revolution they were making, on the causes of their postwar discontents, and on the future prospects of the constitution they were hammering out. It may be debated whether they have left us a burdensome tradition, a rich heritage, or a frustrating mixture of both. What is not debatable is that they gave us the basic vocabulary and rules within which our civic life is continued to this day.

The men who made the American Revolution, wrote the Constitution and the Bill of Rights, and set the institutions of our national government in motion gave us the basic vocabulary and rules within which our civic life is continued today.

THE PHILOSOPHICAL FRAMEWORK

Many scholars have attempted to describe and summarize the thinking of the framers of the Constitution. Some have stressed their political philosophy; some their capacity as practical politicians. In this chapter we shall examine the *process* by which they made the Constitution, and will stress six related but distinct principles that guided them throughout this process. By shrewd politicking, they hammered these principles into the language of the Constitution, and in the first years of the new nation they struggled to develop institutions based on these principles. These principles combined philosophical insights with practical accommodation to the needs of the times. Although we will be discussing them in detail later on in the chapter, we will summarize these principles briefly here.

The first of these overriding principles was **federalism**—the division of power between a central and regional government. During the period between the American Revolution and the ratification of our present Constitution in 1788, the thirteen states existed together under a weak form of central government known as the **Confederation**. The individual states were fiercely jealous of their independence—they existed before the union and had been the building blocks of the nation. So although there was interest in a stronger, more efficient central government, it was thought essential to **states' rights** that power be divided equally between the national government and the states.

A second important principle, which would result in a difference between the new Constitution and the Articles of Confederation, was the need for a *vigorous executive*. The conduct of both domestic and foreign policy was becoming too complicated to be managed by a legislative branch alone. A chief executive was needed. The framers knew full well the potential dangers of concentrating too much power in one person, but were confident they could avert this danger by building checks and balances into the constitutional arrangement of institutions.

A third principle, to which many of the more influential framers were committed, was the necessity for a *supreme national court* to police the constitutional structure they were erecting. The written Constitution would be treated as the highest law of the land, and would be enforced by the Supreme Court against the other branches of national government and the states.

Fourth was the principle of **checks and balances**. A vigorous executive was needed and important powers were to be vested in Congress, but abuses of these powers had to be prevented. One way of doing this was through the creation of the Supreme Court. Another way was to provide for a sharing of functions between the executive and legislative branches. Thus, for instance, the president was to be commander in chief of the armed forces, but had to rely on Congress to raise and supply these forces.

Fifth, the framers were deeply committed to the idea that the central government they were creating was to be a *limited government*. It was to legislate for the national community in some ways, but was to respect the primacy of private institutions and freedom of individual action in other spheres. This idea went beyond the division of power between states and nation dictated by the principle of federalism. For the framers, all government was to be limited. The national government was to respect the rights of the states, and both states and nation were to respect the primacy of the private sector (especially in economic matters) and the liberties of the people.

Sixth, and last, the framers intended to create a *mixed government*. They were convinced that pure democracy was an unstable political arrangement that inevitably degenerated into tyranny. These politicians of the late eighteenth century had seen a lot of war, revolution, and political turbulence. They appreciated that liberty and governmental stability depended on one another. There were thus to be oligarchical elements of the Constitution (such as the Supreme Court) that would check the excesses of democracy.

These six principles represented basic political choices made by the framers. In the two hundred years since these choices were made, vast changes in the nature of the American nation have forced us to modify these principles in various ways. In the remainder of this chapter we will see how the framers come to make their choices, and in subsequent chapters we will examine the choices made by later generations. In the course of this exploration of American constitutionalism, you must continually ask yourself to what extent you agree with the choices made by those in power. What would *you* have done if faced with these same choices?

THE BACKGROUND OF THE CONSTITUTION

Many different ideas and experiences were brought into sharp focus by the American Revolution and the necessity of setting up new institutions of government. But through all the passion and turbulence of late-eighteenth-century America, we must not lose sight of two prevailing characteristics of the founding fathers—they were at home in the language and culture of England, and their expectations about how governmental power should be exercised were also based on over a century of experience as semi-independent colonies and on lessons painfully learned in the struggle for independence.

Before we discuss the making of the Constitution of the United States and the launching of our institutions, we will try to identify these ideas and experiences that went into the founding of the Republic.

Two important characteristics of the founding fathers of our Constitution were that they were at home in the language and culture of England, and their expectations about how governmental power should be exercised were also based on over a century of experience as semi-independent colonies.

The English Inheritance

The most important thing about the various small groups of immigrants and adventurers who landed on the eastern coast of North America in the late 1500s and early 1600s was that they were English. However much some of these settlers may have felt themselves to be refugees from England, rejecting the particular leaders then in power, their basic attitudes about politics and government were shaped by the experience of *their* forefathers. What does this mean in terms of our own history?

We have all been bored more than once by the ease with which Robin Hood and his Merry Men foiled the wicked Sheriff of Nottingham and the bad King John while romping about in Sherwood Forest. But tired legend tells us something about the evolution of politics in feudal England. From the beginning of their country's evolution as a single kingdom (after the Norman Conquest in 1066), the English resisted the establishment of absolute, centralized governmental power.

Today we tend to think of **feudalism** as a sort of political tyranny. But in England it also involved a division of political power, or, more accurately, an institutionalized struggle for political power.[2] Out of the feudal political struggles emerged England's constitutionalism and its parliamentary institutions. The evolution of these institutions was long and sometimes painful, but it was marked throughout by instances of successful resistance by the nobility (the lords and barons of the realm, who held regional power) against claims by the king to absolute centralized power.[3]

In the course of time, the class of political leaders was broadened to include other, lesser local leaders. The institutional forms that evolved, through which members of the nobility and the local leaders came to exercise their check on the monarch, were the Houses of **Parliament**—Lords and Commons. In the feudal economy, moreover, there was an expectation that the relationship between lord and vassal would be reciprocal, with rights and legitimate claims to respect of those rights running both ways in the relationship. And there was constant political struggle over the particulars of the mutual obligations that limited concentrations of social power.

The continuing governmental tension between political leaders (first nobles and then elected commoners) and the monarch produced a set of documents and a powerful tradition of written basic law. The first of these documents was the Magna Carta (1215), in which the barons, gathered on the plain at Runnymede, forced the real King John to affirm in writing that the past customs of feudalism were the law of the land—that the king's power was limited and that the rights of the barons had to be determined by the judgment of their peers.[4]

Another document, the Confirmation of Charters (1295), established the principle (which was to be asserted persistently and with fateful consequences by the American colonists) that important new taxes required the consent of spokespersons of the people.

The Habeas Corpus Act of 1679 provided a written prohibition against imprisonment without a legal basis, and while law never guarantees justice, it is a great deal better than the momentary whim of those in power. Between the Magna Carta and the Habeas Corpus Act, a system of law was developed that became the basis of the American legal system. This **common law** was made by judges deciding actual cases. Over the years, the courts followed the best of the previous decisions in similar cases. These decisions became **precedents** to be followed by other courts. As we

---

[2] Helen Cam, *Law-Finders and Law-Makers in Medieval England* (New York: Barnes and Noble, 1963), pp. 44–58.

[3] Elwin Lawrence Page, *The Contributions of the Landed Men to Civil Liberty* (Williamstown, Mass.: Department of Political Science of Williams College, 1905).

[4] See William Holdsworth, *Some Makers of English Law* (London: Cambridge University Press, 1938), pp. 15–16.

shall see in Chapter 11, the way in which the United States Supreme Court makes constitutional decisions is a direct outgrowth of this common-law tradition.

Of all the English documents that were imprinted on the American political tradition, perhaps the most important was the Bill of Rights of 1689. In the mid-1600s, England's national evolution had been disrupted by a savage religious and civil war. The reigning king (Charles I) was put to death and Parliament decayed into insignificance under a "commonwealth" created by the brilliant fanatic, Oliver Cromwell. After Cromwell's death the monarchy was restored, but with more severe limitations than before on the prerogatives of the king.[5] From this point on it is proper to speak of Great Britain as a **constitutional monarchy**. The Bill of Rights of 1689 gave members freedom of debate in Parliament; it gave the people the right to petition the Crown for redress of grievances and the right to bear arms. It was typical of a tradition of written guarantees of civil liberties, a tradition that was to manifest itself powerfully in American constitutional development.

The evolution of the English parliamentary system was marked throughout by instances of successful resistance by the nobility against claims by the king to absolute central power. Out of this continuing tension evolved a tradition of written guarantees of civil liberties that was to manifest itself powerfully in American constitutional development.

The Colonial Experience

As a result of their English inheritance—a background of divided power and of great documents specifying rights and limitations on central authority—the American colonists were quick to write charters on which to base their civic affairs. The most famous of these colonial governmental

[5] See generally J. R. Tanner, *English Constitutional Conflicts of the Seventeenth Century: 1603–1689* (London: Cambridge University Press, 1928).

The tendency of early Americans to specify their rules of government in written documents is illustrated by the Pilgrims' adoption of the Mayflower Compact before even landing in Plymouth in December of 1620.

documents was our Mayflower Compact of 1620. This document went further than anything in the British experience and included two very radical ideas: first, that government should be rooted in the consent of the governed; and second, that people properly create government out of a **contract** among themselves.

These basic ideas were carried forward in the Cambridge Platform of 1630, the Fundamental Orders of Connecticut in 1639, the Massachusetts Body of Liberties of 1642, and a number of less famous colonial governmental documents.[6]

But the making of governmental documents (the penchant toward constitutionalism) was not the only aspect of the colonial experience that served as an important backdrop to the emergence of the nation. We all remember that there were, in the beginning, different kinds of colonies. Several, such as Massachusetts Bay and Virginia, were established by trading companies back in England. Several others, such as New York after the British takeover, were royal colonies with a governor appointed by the king. Others were proprietary in form (Pennsylvania and Maryland), having been given by the king personally to William Penn and Cecilius Calvert. What is remarkable about these colonies is the rapidity with which, whatever the original forms, they developed in parallel fashions.

In addition to written charters outlining basic features of government, the colonies formed legislatures, often bicameral (two-chambered), to check the appointed governors. In time, these assemblies came to assert powers to levy taxes, appropriate monies, and initiate legislation. Often colonial legislators bent an appointed governor to their will by refusing to appropriate funds for his compensation until a concession was forthcoming. Legislative representatives throughout the colonies were elected not by all the people, but by **freeholders** (those who owned land). But local communities, with their town meetings, became accustomed to substantial **autonomy**, and this autonomy would eventually become a powerful element of the American political culture.[7]

A final aspect of the colonial experience that was important for later American development was the division of power and functions between the colonial governments and the central government in London. The British Empire, by the middle of the 1700s, was in fact (but not in form) a *federal* system. The central government in London provided external defense, a uniform system of money and credit, and a large common

[6] See Richard L. Perry and John C. Cooper, *Sources of Our Liberties* (New York: New York University Press, 1972), pp. 61–221.

[7] See Clinton Rossiter, *The First American Revolution: Part One of Seedtime of the Republic* (New York: Harcourt, 1953) pp. 138–187.

marketplace for colonial goods. It spoke for the colonies in international affairs but, beyond that, allowed substantial autonomy to the colonies in taxing and running themselves. In many ways this was a comfortable arrangement. Little in direct taxes was extracted from the colonies to pay for the central services. The posture of London toward her North American colonies was described perceptively by William Pitt, one of America's best friends in Parliament, as one of "benign neglect."

All this was to change in the 1760s as London, in the wake of the expensive French and Indian Wars (1754–1763), sought to extract more taxes from the colonies and to subject them to greater central direction. The Stamp Act initiative of 1765 was the first of a series of measures aimed at integrating the colonies more closely into the Empire. But it was too late. The experience with loose union made a tighter control by London unacceptable.

What is important for us to understand is that the Americans had a rich experience with what we now call *federalism* before the Revolution. The gravitation toward federal union after independence, therefore, was a matter not of radical innovation but of seeking the familiar: a division of power between central and regional government.

The American movement after independence toward federalism—the division of power between central and regional governments—was not a matter of radical innovation but grew naturally out of the colonial experience.

The Revolutionary Experience

While it is important to appreciate the way in which English history and colonial development formed a backdrop to the founding of the Republic, it would be wrong to suppose this was the whole story. The break from England was terribly painful for many Americans. They thought and argued long about it, and the debates leading up to the Declaration of Independence in 1776 sharpened American ideas about how government should be organized. There was a rise in radical sentiment—a reaction not only against the English government, but against all government. The best expression of this new radicalism was in Tom Paine's famous pamphlet, *Common Sense*, published in 1776. There was, in addition, close scrutiny of the English politics of the day to determine what had gone wrong. There was an effort to identify strengths of the traditional English Constitution, which might be emulated, and weaknesses, which might be avoided. Finally, the problems of explaining independence, adopting constitutions, fighting the revolutionary war, and coping with the problems of the postwar period taught the Americans lessons that would loom large in the framing of the Constitution.

Radicalism

Although the upsurge of **radicalism** during the revolutionary period was antigovernment, it was at the same time democratic in its emphasis on

Colonial radicalism was given increased impetus in the crucial year of 1776 by the publication of Tom Paine's *Common Sense*. While Paine's egalitarianism and enthusiasm for democracy went beyond what most political leaders of the day would accept, his ideas became a part of the American political heritage on which future generations could draw for inspiration and arguments in further democratizing the system.

broader participation in government. While the principal leaders of the colonies still feared excesses of democracy, there was no question that the new America would have a democratic flavor. Sam Adams, arch rabble-rouser of the Revolution, thundered against any governmental interference whatsoever in the lives of the citizens; indeed, it is difficult to determine from Adams's tracts that human government had any legitimate functions at all. Adams also wrote eloquently of the equality of persons and the desirability of broadening the franchise. Such libertarian and egalitarian radicalism enjoyed only short-lived triumphs, but the later gradual movement of American institutions toward a more democratic system owes much to this surge of colonial radicalism, unleashed by the struggle against England. The radical-democratic spirit did not in the longer run dominate American politics, but after 1776 it would always be a part of the scene.

Social and economic (as well as ideological) consequences of the revolutionary struggle also helped make American society more democratic. The power of so-called aristocratic elements in America was diminished when many English loyalists (or **Tories**, as they were called) were driven out of new states by vigilante activity and mob terrorism. Much Tory property was confiscated, causing a transfer of wealth that also had consequences for land ownership, and political participation broadened.[8]

The breakdown of the English constitution

Why did the British cabinet abandon the policy of "benign neglect" for what the colonists regarded as a repressive policy on London's part? Why did they ignore the *de facto* federal nature of the Empire and, many felt, violate the colonists' rights as Englishmen? Some of those involved in the making of the Constitution perceived the answer as a corruption of English institutions—the king (the despised George III) had compromised the independence of Parliament. Through his own faction—the "King's Friends"—George had corruptly fused the executive and legislative powers. This was the road to tyranny, and explained why the colonies were so suddenly oppressed by Britain. The English constitution was perceived to have broken down, and oppression resulted.[9] Thus the determination of the framers of the Constitution to effect a clear separation of the executive and legislative branches was directly related to their perception of what had gone wrong in the mother country.

Explaining independence

The break from England was a traumatic experience for most American politicians. They were terribly torn between their loyalty to existing authority on the one side and, on the other, their basic human rights to form a new government that would respect citizens in ways the corrupted British system did not. What is difficult to appreciate today, through the fog of bicentennial romanticism, is the anguish felt by intelligent men over this choice.

John Adams finally opted for independence (or rebellion, as the British called it) at the last moment with a heavy heart. John Dickinson of Pennsylvania, one of the sharpest critics of British policy toward America, could not bring himself to approve independence at all. And although its opening passages make an eloquent plea for **natural rights**, even Thomas Jefferson's Declaration of Independence was actually a careful legalistic indictment of George III rather than an attack on the British constitution. In short, the basic justification for rebellion was that Britain had broken its own imperial and constitutional rules. The rights of which the colonies

[8] See Robert E. Brown, *Middle-Class Democracy and the Revolution in Massachusetts, 1691–1780* (Ithaca, N.Y.: Cornell University Press, 1955); and Elisha P. Douglass, *Rebels and Democrats: The Struggle for Equal Political Rights and Majority Rule During the American Revolution* (Chapel Hill, N.C.: University of North Carolina Press, 1955).

[9] See Bernard Bailyn, *The Origins of American Politics* (New York: Knopf, 1968).

were deprived were their traditional, and thus legal, rights as Englishmen.[10]

The state constitutions

Once the first steps toward rebellion were taken, however, the ex-colonies began to incorporate into their new constitutions the more radical political ideas generated during the struggle against Britain. **Majority rule** was formally recognized; and while voting was still assumed to be limited to property owners, property qualifications were lowered to allow more people to vote than formerly. Most of the new constitutions included a **bill of rights**. This guaranteed to the new state citizens the traditional English rights as well as certain distinctive colonial rights, such as protection against unreasonable searches, which were safeguards against encroachment by the new state governments. As might be expected, the legislatures of the new states predominated over the governors, and the powers of the central state governments were restricted in order to preserve, as far as possible, local self-government. Most of these original radical-democratic state constitutions were impractical, and had to be amended or replaced in the early years of the new nation. But in their original form they were among the most important documents of our political history.[11] They represented in pure form the political ideals of the original revolutionary assemblies that voted to go it alone in the new world.

Running the war

But the dream of going it alone, with highly decentralized institutions, quickly became a nightmare. The new states could not *banish* British arms from North America without concerted action. Central authority was necessary to raise money to supply the army, to decide on who should command where, and to pursue a uniform foreign policy. Yet the only central authority was the **Continental Congress**, which was very weak. There was no executive department. The direction of the war (such as it was) was done by the Congress. Victory was a near miracle of individual genius and luck considering the kind of national government that had been set up.

The **Articles of Confederation**, which were not formally ratified until 1781, had been in effect as the constitution of the United States from early in the Revolutionary War until they were replaced by the present Constitution in 1789. The Congress could not levy taxes directly, but only

[10] Carl J. Friedrich and Robert G. McCloskey, *From the Declaration of Independence to the Constitution: The Roots of American Constitutionalism* (New York: Liberal Arts Press, 1954).

[11] See Francis N. Thorpe, ed., *The Federal and State Constitutions, Colonial Charters, and Other Organic Laws* (Washington, D.C.: Government Printing Office, 1909).

through the states. Legislation required a two-thirds majority. Any amendment to the Articles required unanimity of the former colonies. This arrangement resembled an international organization (such as the present United Nations) more than it did a national government.

Replacing the empire

In peace, the Articles of Confederation served no better than they had in war. Trade barriers were thrown up between the states. The paper money issued by Congress during the Revolution (those famous continental dollars that were not worth a damn) had not been backed by a credible treasury, and the postwar experience was worse. There was no uniform money, and no general system of credit. The individual states frantically began maneuvering for economic preference with foreign countries. And militarily, the colonies were helpless. It had taken all available energies to hold on until the British gave up. After Yorktown, the Continental Army was disbanded, and in an international environment still hostile to the newly independent colonies, Congress was without resources. The states, in fact, began to conduct independent foreign policies, and it was widely supposed in Europe that the United States (the English called it the "national bantling") could not long survive. It was bound to be gobbled up piecemeal by the real great powers of the world.

The upsurge in radical sentiment, the scrutiny of the English system and its perceived corruption, and the problems of justifying the break with England, adopting state constitutions, fighting the revolutionary war, and coping with its aftermath were all part of the revolutionary experience. This experience taught the Americans valuable lessons that would loom large in the framing of a new Constitution.

THE CONSTITUTIONAL CONVENTION

The men who were the moving spirits behind the Constitution drafted at Philadelphia in the hot summer of 1787 and finally ratified in 1789 were politicians of wide experience. Many of them had taken part in opposing British colonial policy before the Revolution. Most of them had fought and suffered under the misrule of Congress during the war. And in peace they saw their dream of a new nation imperiled by confusion among the states and by weakness within a central government that was unable to establish order within the Union.

Historian Merrill Jensen has argued that the ills of government under the Articles of Confederation would have worked themselves out in time. But in the minds of the framers, as revealed in their extensive writings, they were facing serious external threats. It was clear to them that for the new nation to survive, the British Empire had to be replaced, and a reformed central government created that would perform the crucial functions of conducting orderly foreign relations, establishing uniform money and credit, and providing for national defense.

Political scientist Leonard D. White has provided probably the best short description of the end of the Confederation. When George Wash-

A New View of the Founding Fathers

Historian Merrill Jensen, whose views on the constitutional period are treated in this chapter, is presently at work on a projected fifteen-volume Documentary History of the Ratification of the Constitution.

In discussing his research with a New York Times *reporter a few years ago, Professor Jensen remarked that*

> *If these eighteenth-century figures were alive today, they could give cards and spades to any of our present-day politicians. . . . They could take the game away from any of them. When it comes to logrolling, dirty politics, hanky-panky, bribery—you name it—our founding fathers often behaved in a way that would* make many twentieth-century politicians look like saints.*

Jensen's favorite character was

> *. . . a New Hampshire Congressman who was always writing his children and exhorting them to lead moral lives, but when he lived away from home it seems his landlady rendered services beyond board and room—and he didn't pay up. Our researcher who found the letters about all this was so religious, and so shocked, that he didn't know whether he should take copies or not.*

*From Israel Shenker, "Dirty Politics in 18th Century—Sainthood in 20th," *New York Times*, March 15, 1978.

ington entered New York as first president under the new Constitution, there was almost nothing to take over from the old regime.

> There *was*, indeed, a foreign office, with John Jay and a couple of clerks to deal with correspondence from John Adams in London and Thomas Jefferson in Paris; there *was* a Treasury Board with an empty treasury; there was a "Secretary of War" with an authorized army of 840 men; there were a dozen clerks whose pay was in arrears, but an unknown but fearful burden of debt, almost no revenue, and prostrate credit. But one could hardly perceive in the winter of 1789 a government of the Union.[12]

The final straw for the Confederation, what moved these elite politicians we call "the framers" to launch their bloodless *coup d'etat*, was the outbreak in one state, and the threat in others, of civil disorder. Economic

[12] Leonard D. White, *The Federalists* (New York: Macmillan, 1948), p. 1.

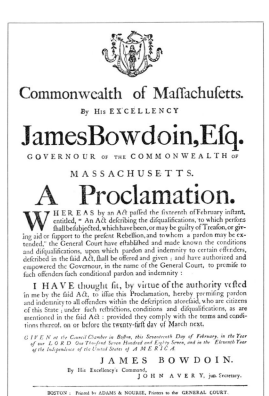

Commonwealth of Massachusetts.

By His EXCELLENCY

JamesBowdoin,Esq.

GOVERNOUR OF THE COMMONWEALTH OF

MASSACHUSETTS.

A Proclamation.

WHEREAS by an Act passed the sixteenth of February instant, entitled, " An Act describing the disqualifications, to which persons shall be subjected, which have been, or may be guilty of Treason, or giving aid or support to the present Rebellion, and to whom a pardon may be extended," the General Court have established and made known the conditions and disqualifications, upon which pardon and indemnity to certain offenders, described in the said Act, shall be offered and given ; and have authorized and empowered the Governour, in the name of the General Court, to promise to such offenders such conditional pardon and indemnity :

I HAVE thought fit, by virtue of the authority vested in me by the said Act, to issue this Proclamation, hereby premising pardon and indemnity to all offenders within the description aforesaid, who are citizens of this State ; under such restrictions, conditions and disqualifications, as are mentioned in the said Act : provided they comply with the terms and conditions thereof, on or before the twenty-first day of March next.

GIVEN at the Council Chamber in Boston, this Seventeenth Day of February, in the Year of our LORD One Thousand Seven Hundred and Eighty Seven, and in the Eleventh Year of the Independence of the United States of AMERICA.

JAMES BOWDOIN.

By His Excellency's Command,
JOHN AVERY, jun. Secretary.

BOSTON : Printed by ADAMS & NOURSE, Printers to the GENERAL COURT.

Among the events that convinced many members of the Constitutional Convention of the need for a stronger central government was Shays's Rebellion. Governor James Bowdoin responded promptly to the revolt with the proclamation shown, and state troops put down the disturbance. Shays's predicament was memorialized in the doggerel of the day: "My name is Shays/in former days/in Pelham I did dwell sir,/but now I'm forced/to leave that place/because I did rebel sir."

depression struck in 1785–1786, and debtor groups demanded a moratorium on debt collection. Antagonism grew worse between the poor and the well-to-do, between countryside and town, and between farmer and merchant. Things came to a head in July of 1786 in western Massachusetts, where a veteran of Bunker Hill, Captain Daniel Shays, led an agrarian revolt. Commanding a flying column of irregulars, Shays marched on the government arsenal at Springfield. Governor Bowdoin of Massachusetts sent the state's militia under Revolutionary War hero General Benjamin Lincoln, and **"Shays's Rebellion"** was put down.[13] But shivers ran through the country. It was clear that there had to be a better organized central government to back up the states and deal with disorders that threatened to sweep across state lines.

The need for a central government that could establish control over the Union and deal with civil disorder was brought to a head with Shays's Rebellion.

[13] Allan Nevins and Henry Steele Commager, *A Short History of the United States* (New York: Modern Library, 1942), pp. 118–123.

The "Calling" of the Convention

There is no ignoring the boldness with which the framers moved, first to reform and then to replace the Articles. The existing Congress was not anxious to be replaced. It grudgingly approved the call for a meeting of specially chosen state delegates to consider amendments to Articles. The product of these deliberations was, presumably, to be referred back to the Confederation Congress and then to the state legislatures as provided by the Articles.

The delegates chosen to consider amendments to the Articles of Confederation bypassed both the existing government and the state legislatures in engineering its adoption. As a result, they ensured that the new document would be a creation and creature of the people, rather than the states.

This did not happen. Meeting in secrecy with the revered Washington as presiding officer, the delegates quickly decided that their document would include the rules for its own adoption or rejection. Rather than going to the existing Congress and the existing state legislatures, they would refer it directly to conventions in the states delegated especially for that purpose. By doing this, the delegates were bypassing not only the enfeebled central governmental mechanism, but also the state legislatures. Should the new constitution be approved, it would be by specially chosen delegates of the people of the states. Thus the new central government would not be a creation and a creature of the states, as government under the Articles of Confederation had so clearly been, but a creation and creature of the *people*. This was a crucial distinction.[14]

The Philosophical Context

In addition to their English and colonial political legacies, the delegates who settled in the comfortable inns of Philadelphia that summer, and drank deeply and talked late at Benjamin Franklin's finely appointed house, shared something else—a knowledge of certain influential political writing and thought.

In the wake of the tumultuous events leading to England's adoption of the Bill of Rights in 1689, a thoughtful essay on government appeared from the pen of John Locke. In his *Two Treatises on Government* (1689), Locke expressed a set of ideas about government that quickly became the basis for a **liberal tradition**. His ideas powerfully influenced the men at Philadelphia, and through them, have influenced successive generations of American political leaders.[15]

John Locke saw government as a contract between free, consenting citizens and the state. His ideas became the basis for a liberal tradition that to this day exerts a powerful influence on our political system.

Locke saw government as properly resting on a contract between free, consenting citizens and the state. The primary purposes of government were the physical protection of humans, one from another, and the protection of their property, which was seen as an extension of themselves.

[14] See Clinton Rossiter, *The Grand Convention* (New York: Macmillan, 1966).

[15] On the importance of Locke's thought to the development of American politics, see Louis Hartz, *The Liberal Tradition in America* (New York: Harcourt, 1955).

To secure these protections, people agreed to give up certain of their natural rights to behave as they pleased, and bound themselves to the state—but only for so long as it delivered the protections. Government was to be limited and nontyrannical, operating through general rules announced in advance of their application—in other words, through law.

Another writer who influenced the thinking of the framers was the Baron de Montesquieu. In describing a desirable system of government in his *Spirit of the Laws* (1748), Montesquieu stressed the importance of separate executive, legislative, and judicial institutions if government were to remain free and open. Separating institutions with shared functions would result in checks and balances. No one branch of government could invade and dominate another branch, and out of the competition between them the liberties of the people were protected and governmental stability ensured.

To a generation that saw the root of its troubles with Britain in the compromising of the independence of Parliament (the legislature) by the king (the executive), this theory of checks and balances had obvious appeal. The first effort by the former colonists to avoid tyranny had been to allow only a weak legislature at the national level, and this had failed. But the doctrine of separation of powers offered a way of providing for the vigorous central government and the strong executive that they thought necessary, while ensuring against the development of tyranny.

In Baron de Montesquieu's doctrine of separate executive, legislative, and judicial institutions, the framers found a way to ensure against the development of tyranny while still providing for the vigorous central government and the strong executive they thought necessary.

While most of the delegates shared a common sense of the inadequacy of the Articles of Confederation, they disagreed about the particulars of how the new union should be organized. But if the Articles were to be swiftly and cleanly replaced, the convention had to work secretly and differences had to be hammered out quickly.[16]

Conflict and Compromise

There were a number of political splits that cut across the new states and were reflected by their delegates at Philadelphia. A major division was between those predisposed to a stronger union, and those who still associated strong central government with British oppression. Another was over the nature of the executive power—the "presidency"—that was to be created. (An early draft of the Constitution preferred the term "governor," but this was later changed to the stronger "president.") Still further disagreement was over the role to be played by the Supreme Court—whether it would pass on the constitutionality of acts of Congress. Finally, there was division over the extent of the powers of the new national Congress.

[16] See Max Farrand, *The Framing of the Constitution of the United States* (New Haven: Yale University Press, 1913), pp. 54–67.

The Constitutional Convention was marked by tension and deep political conflict, particularly between the large and small states. Breakdown was averted through compromise, which has since become the defining style of American politics.

Of all these, however, it was the tension between the large and small states over the composition of the legislature that threatened to deadlock the convention. For example, Virginia, populous and proud, led in the convention with a proposal that would have based representation in the new government squarely on population. New Jersey countered with a proposal that would have preserved for the most part the one-state, one-vote system that prevailed under the Articles of Confederation.

Breakdown was averted and in a fashion that was to become the hallmark, the defining style, of American politics—through *compromise*. It is easy to scorn compromise as a form of weakness. But without compromise in a thousand conflicts throughout our history, there would have been no nation. In one tragic instance in which our genius for political compromise failed us (in 1860–1861), the matter was settled in civil war; by a majority beating an intractable minority into submission.

Sometimes called the **Great Compromise** (sometimes the Connecticut Compromise in recognition of Oliver Ellsworth of that state, who proposed it to the delegates), the solution adopted by the convention to the conflict between the large and small states was the familiar two-chambered Congress, with the Senate based on the equality of the states (pre-existing building blocks of the union) and the House of Representatives based on population.

There were other, more subtle and less famous compromises, of course. There was a compromise in the mechanism of choosing the president (an "electoral college" composed of legally unbound electors chosen by the legislatures of particular states). And there was the compromise over how slaves were to be counted for purposes of representation in the House ("three-fifths of all other Persons"). Most importantly, there was compromise over the nature of the federal union itself. What, precisely, were to be the powers of the national government? Which were to be reserved for the states? Some of these questions were answered in the Constitution itself, but much was left to be unraveled by posterity.

The Perils of Ratification

Despite the inspired compromising and some calculated fudging of issues at Philadelphia; despite the final and decisive vote of the convention; and despite the well-kept secrecy of the convention (which allowed the proposed constitution to be set before the people as a unified proposal rather than "leaked" in bits and pieces), the outcome of the **ratification** conflict was very close in several key states. Anti-Federal elements (harking back to revolutionary radicalism) held sway in several state legislatures, and were strongly represented at the special state conventions elected to consider the draft charter.

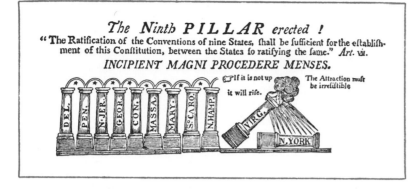

Shown is a 1787 cartoon stressing the political importance of Virginia's ratification of the proposed Constitution. Even though the document became technically ineffective after New Hampshire's ratification (the ninth state required by Article VII), had the two key states of Virginia and New York stayed out, the Union would probably never have gotten off the ground. The table below* shows the final results of the ratification process.

State	Date	Vote in the Ratifying Convention
Delaware	December 7, 1787	Unanimous
Pennsylvania	December 12, 1787	46–32
New Jersey	December 19, 1787	Unanimous
Georgia	January 2, 1788	Unanimous
Connecticut	January 9, 1788	128–40
Massachusetts	February 6, 1788	187–168
Maryland	April 28, 1788	63–11
South Carolina	May 23, 1788	149–73
New Hampshire	June 21, 1788	57–47
Virginia	June 25, 1788	89–79
New York	July 26, 1788	30–27
North Carolina	November 21, 1789	194–77
Rhode Island	May 29, 1790	34–32

* From Jonathan Elliot, *The Debate in the Several State Conventions on the Adoption of the Federal Constitution* (Philadelphia: Lippincott, 1836–1845).

One especially powerful criticism leveled at the proposed constitution was that it lacked a bill of rights after the fashion of the postrevolutionary state constitutions. Proponents countered that this omission could be remedied easily by adding amendments; eventually this was done by the adoption, in December 1791, of Amendments One through Ten—our present federal **Bill of Rights.**

The debates over ratification probed into all corners of the six articles produced at Philadelphia. What would be the relationship of the states to the new union? What, precisely, would be the powers of the new Congress under Article I; of the president, under Article II; and of the Supreme Court, under Article III? Different defenders and critics of the proposals

From Madison's *Federalist*, No. 10

The latent causes of faction are thus sown in the nature of men; and we see them everywhere brought into different degrees of activity, according to the different circumstances of civil society. . . .

It is vain to say that enlightened statesmen will be able to adjust these clashing interests, and render them all subservient to the public good. Enlightened statesmen will not always be at the helm.

The inference to which we are brought is, that the *causes* of faction cannot be removed, and that relief is only to be sought in the means of controlling its effects.

[Madison goes on to argue that the size of the new union, and the division of powers between the states and the national government, will create a situation in which factions counterbalance one another, with no one group successful in establishing tyranny. Thus, through federalism, will the effects of faction be controlled.]

gave different answers.[17] A product of this searching argument was a set of short essays, urging adoption of the Constitution, that appeared in newspapers under the pen name of Publius. In collected form, these became known as *The Federalist*. It is now generally agreed that James Madison wrote fourteen of the papers, Alexander Hamilton fifty-one, and John Jay five. The authorship of fifteen more is disputed as between Hamilton and Madison.

The Federalist is a series of essays urging adoption of the Constitution. These essays give us valuable information about the intentions of those who were framing the Constitution, and have been invaluable throughout history in helping us interpret the Constitution.

Not all of the papers are equally interesting, but they give us valuable information about what the framers were thinking about. Among the most important are Madison's *Federalist* No. 10 (in which the advantages of the federal nature of the union were emphasized) and Hamilton's *Federalist* No. 78 (in which the future role of the Supreme Court was foretold). *The Federalist* constitutes the most important contemporaneous comment on what the terse, sometimes ambiguous sentences of the Constitution were meant to mean. Throughout our history we have relied on *The Federalist* to help us interpret the Constitution.

[17] See Elliot, *The Debate in the Several State Conventions on the Adoption of the Federal Constitution.*

James Madison.

PRINCIPLES OF THE CONSTITUTION

The outcome was close in several of the states. But the Constitution was adopted on June 21, 1788, after the favorable vote of the New Hampshire convention. It was adopted on its own terms, as set down in Article VII, which required that only nine of the original thirteen states assent. What were the basic principles of this new Constitution? What generalizations can be made about the kind of government the framers thought they were establishing? Earlier in this chapter, we summarized six basic principles that represented the fundamental political choices made by the framers. Let us now examine these principles in more detail.

Six basic political principles—those of a federal government, a vigorous executive, a constitutional court, a system of checks and balances, a limited government, and a mixed government—represent the fundamental political choices made by the framers of the Constitution.

Federal Government

Most importantly, it was to be a federal government. Certainly it has never been, at any point in our history, precisely clear what powers would be exercised by the states and what by the national government. But it was clear from the beginning that the central government was not simply a creature of the states. There were real governing powers vested in Congress, the president, and the Supreme Court, which set the new government apart from the old Confederation.[18]

Under Article I, Section 8 of the Constitution, the new central government would have the power to levy taxes directly on its citizens by majority vote of Congress and without the consent of the states. There was power here also to coin money and regulate interstate commerce, as well as to enact legislation "necessary and proper" to the discharge of powers enumerated in Article I, Section 8.[19] This was to be interpreted in later years as a very broad authorization. But, and this is important to note, there was no *general* grant of legislative power to the national Congress. It was assumed that the states would adopt and administer most of the laws needed to protect the health, welfare, and (in those early days) morals of the citizens. This was the so-called police power of the states, which was guaranteed them by the Tenth Amendment. The national legislature was to act only on matters of national concern. There were, however, several great unanswered questions.

First, were the powers granted in Article I, Section 8, to be construed narrowly or broadly? Were there any areas in which national power could never override the states, whatever the national need? This would be a recurring source of controversy throughout our political history and would eventually put Franklin Delano Roosevelt and the Supreme Court on a collision course, as we shall see in Chapter 11.

Second, could state governments interpose their authority between their citizens and a national law if the state opposed that law? And was ratification of the Constitution final? Could a state, once it had entered the Union, secede if it believed that the national government was violating the original understanding of the Constitution? The questions of interposition and secession were finally settled in blood in the Civil War.[20]

The most important thing to understand about the Constitution is the constantly evolving relationship between the federal and state governments. The framers of the Constitution suggested the basic outline of federalism, but left great leeway for future adjustment. Choices were left open, and we shall see in Chapter 3 how conflict developed around these choices.

A Vigorous Executive

To many of the framers who sweated through the Philadelphia Convention and later politicked in the state ratifying conventions for the new Consti-

The federal government was given real governing power in matters of national concern, while the administration of most of the laws needed to protect the health and welfare of citizens was left to the individual states. Many questions, however, were left for posterity to answer.

[18] See Alpheus T. Mason, *The States-Rights Debate: Anti-Federalism and the Constitution* (Englewood Cliffs, N.J.: Prentice-Hall, 1964).

[19] On the theory of federalism, see K. C. Wheare, *Federal Government* (London: Oxford University Press, 1951).

[20] Aaron Wildavsky, *American Federalism in Perspective* (Boston: Little, Brown, 1967).

Section 8. The Congress shall have Power To lay and collect Taxes, Duties, imposts and Excises, to pay the Debts and provide for the common Defence and general Welfare of the United States; but all Duties, Imposts and Excises shall be uniform throughout the United States;

To borrow money on the credit of the United States;

To regulate Commerce with foreign Nations, and among the several States, and with the Indian Tribes;

To establish an uniform Rule of Naturalization, and uniform Laws on the subject of Bankruptcies throughout the United States;

To coin Money, regulate the Value thereof, and of foreign Coin, and fix the Standard of Weights and Measures;

To provide for the Punishment of counterfeiting the Securities and current Coin of the United States;

To Establish Post Offices and Post Roads;

To promote the Progress of Science and useful Arts, by securing for limited Times to Authors and Inventors the exclusive Right to their respective Writings and Discoveries;

To constitute Tribunals inferior to the supreme Court;

To define and punish Piracies and Felonies committed on the high Seas, and Offenses against the Law of Nations;

To declare War, grant Letters of Marque and Reprisal, and make Rules concerning Captures on Land and Water;

To raise and support Armies, but no Appropriation of Money to that Use shall be for a longer Term than two years;

To provide and maintain a Navy;

To make Rules for the Government and Regulation of the land and naval Forces;

To provide for calling forth the Militia to execute the Laws of the Union, suppress Insurrections and repel invasions;

To provide for organizing, arming, and disciplining, the Militia, and for governing such Part of them as may be employed in the Service of the United States, reserving to the States respectively, the Appointment of the Officers, and the Authority of training the Militia according to the discipline prescribed by Congress;

To exercise exclusive Legislation in all Cases whatsoever, over such District (not exceeding ten Miles square) as may, by Cession of particular States, and the Acceptance of Congress, become the Seat of the Government of the United States, and to exercise like Authority over all Places purchased by the Consent of the Legislature of the State in which the Same shall be, for the Erection of Forts, Magazines, Arsenals, dock-Yards, and other needful Buildings;—And

To make all Laws which shall be necessary and proper for carrying into Execution the foregoing Powers, and all other Powers vested by the Constitution in the Government of the United States, or in any Department or Officer thereof.

tution, one of the major faults of the old Confederation was the lack of an executive.[21] Indeed, in a reaction against the colonial governors and the British monarch, the executive function had disappeared from American government in the immediate postrevolutionary period. The state governors were mostly weak officials, restricted by "executive councils" that had to approve their smallest acts. The governor of Virginia complained that he could not even buy a pair of pants for a state militiaman without asking the council for permission! Not many state governors could have responded as decisively as Bowdoin did in putting down Shays's Rebellion, and there was only a Congress at the national level.

This void was to be filled by the "presidency" created under Article II. It is interesting that Hamilton took pains in *Federalist* No. 70 to attack the idea "which is not without its advocates, that a vigorous Executive is inconsistent with the genius of republican government." Quite the reverse was true, said Hamilton, who went on to argue that "energy in the Executive is a leading character in the definition of good government." The protection of the community against foreign attacks depended on it, as did "steady administration of the laws." And Hamilton explained the reasons why Article II would create an "energetic" president: (1) unity (one man, not a committee), (2) duration (four-year terms), (3) adequate provision for support (through the Congressional power of direct taxation), and (4) "constant powers."

[21] For excellent treatment of the political skills of the framers, see John P. Roche, "The Founding Fathers: A Reform Caucus in Action," *The American Political Science Review* LV, No. 4 (December 1961).

Alexander Hamilton.

> ARTICLE II, *Sections 1 and 2*, United States Constitution
>
> **Section 1. The executive Power shall be vested in a President of the United States of America. . . .**
>
> **Section 2. The President shall be commander in chief of the army and navy of the United States, and of the militia of the several States, when called into the actual service of the United States; he may require the opinion, in writing, of the principal officer in each of the executive departments, upon any subject relating to the duties of their respective offices, and he shall have power to grant reprieves and pardons for offenses against the United States, except in cases of impeachment. . . .**

But what were these "constant powers"? The "executive power" was vested in the president, who was given certain duties: to take care that the laws were faithfully executed; to act as Commander in Chief of the armed forces; to appoint and commission all officers of the government; to recommend to Congress "such measures as he shall judge necessary and expedient"; and to report periodically on the state of the nation.

The framers clearly intended to create a vigorous executive office, although its exact dimensions were left to future generations to define.

Far from conveying complete powers, Article II seemed only to suggest the dimensions of the office. Nevertheless, the intent of the framers to create a "spacious" office was clear from the essays in *The Federalist*. And as we shall see in Chapter 3, a succession of strong incumbents ultimately shaped the presidency into the vigorous executive office *The Federalist* envisioned.[22]

A Constitutional Court

This pattern of suggestive constitutional language, contrasted with the clearer intent expressed in *The Federalist*, occurs again in the case of Article III, which outlines the role of the Supreme Court. Did the framers intend the Supreme Court to have the power to declare acts of other branches and of the states unconstitutional? Certainly Hamilton, in *Federalist* No. 78, foresaw such power for the judicial branch. His argument was that the Constitution's limitations on government would be meaningless unless enforced by the courts. And this argument would later be used by John Marshall in formally claiming the power to review acts of Congress. This also we shall explore in Chapter 3.

[22] See Rexford G. Tugwell, *The Enlargement of the Presidency* (Garden City, N.Y.: Doubleday, 1960).

> ### From Hamilton's *Federalist*, No. 78
>
> Some perplexity respecting the rights of the courts to pronounce legislative acts void, because contrary to the Constitution, has arisen from an imagination that the doctrine would imply a superiority of the judiciary to the legislative power. It is urged that the authority which can declare the acts of another void, must necessarily be superior to the one whose acts may be declared void. As this doctrine is of great importance in all the American constitutions, a brief discussion of the ground on which it rests cannot be unacceptable.
>
> There is no position which depends on clearer principles, than that every act of a delegated authority, contrary to the tenor of the commission under which it is exercised, is void. No legislative act, therefore, contrary to the Constitution, can be valid. To deny this, would be to affirm, that the deputy is greater than his principal; that the servant is above the master; that the representatives of the people are superior to the people themselves; that men acting by virtue of powers, may do not only what their powers do not authorize, but what they forbid.

The Constitution vests "judicial power" in the Supreme Court. The Court has since interpreted this to mean judicial review—the power to declare acts of Congress, the president, and the states unconstitutional.

But should we accept Hamilton's views as final? Article III clearly vests the "judicial power" in a Supreme Court. But how many of the framers would have agreed with Hamilton that the judicial power naturally included what has become known as **judicial review**—the power to declare acts of Congress, the president, and the states, void as unconstitutional?

There is no certain answer. Charles Beard, disturbed by what he regarded as an abuse of the power of judicial review by the Court in the late nineteenth and early twentieth centuries, set out to do research that he thought would prove that most of the framers had not intended that such power be accorded the judiciary. He concluded just the opposite.[23] Furthermore, many important figures of the Philadelphia Convention never expressed themselves at all on the role of the Supreme Court. The best that can be said is that the balance of the evidence indicates that at least some of the most important framers favored judicial review. James Wilson of Pennsylvania, for instance, was even clearer than Hamilton on

[23] Charles A. Beard, *The Supreme Court and the Constitution* (New York: Macmillan, 1912).

ARTICLE III, *Sections 1 and 2*, United States Constitution

Section 1. The judicial Power of the United States, shall be vested in one supreme Court, and in such inferior Courts as the Congress may from time to time ordain and establish. The Judges, both of the supreme and inferior Courts, shall hold their Offices during good Behavior, and shall, at stated Times, receive for their Services a Compensation, which shall not be diminished during their Continuance in Office.

Section 2. The judicial Power shall extend to all Cases, in Law and Equity, arising under this Constitution, the Laws of the United States, and Treaties made, or which shall be made, under their Authority;—to all Cases affecting Ambassadors, other public Ministers and Consuls;—to all Cases of admiralty and maritime Jurisdiction;—to Controversies to which the United States shall be a Party;—to Controversies between two or more States;—between a State and Citizens of another State;—between Citizens of different States;—between Citizens of the same State claiming Lands under the Grants of different States, and between a State, or the Citizens thereof, and foreign States, Citizens or Subjects.

In all Cases affecting Ambassadors, other public Ministers and Consuls, and those in which a State shall be a Party, the supreme Court shall have original Jurisdiction. In all other Cases before mentioned, the supreme Court shall have appellate Jurisdiction, both as to Law and Fact, with such Exceptions, and under such Regulations as the Congress shall make. . . .

the matter. And the future, although not without a fight, decided they were right. The Supreme Court is the monitor of American constitutionalism.

Checks and Balances

Notwithstanding their desire for a stronger national government, the framers took great care to set up an internal system of checks and balances among the legislative, executive, and judicial branches to ensure that their national government could not come under the tyrannical control of one branch. The original postrevolutionary state constitutions had elevated the legislature to a position of dominance. The Articles of Confederation provided little other than a legislature to serve as the central governmental mechanism. In both cases the intention was to protect against the growth of **tyranny**, which was then associated with executive figures—the king and his colonial governors. Legislatures were thought closer to the people and thus naturally more virtuous and less tyrannical. But, unhappily, they were also inefficient.

The framers were sadder and wiser men, who had watched the legislatures fail, and they were ready to seek other ways of hedging against the development of tyranny. They had the option of creating a parliamentary system, with a prime minister chosen by (and responsible to) the majority of the legislature. They rejected this option. In their eyes the parliamentary system, as they were familiar with it in Britain, could be too easily perverted into an instrument of centralized despotism. They wanted none of a single **faction**, or clique (such as the "King's Friends"), controlling both the executive and legislative functions.

To guard against the tyranny of any one branch of government, the framers set up an internal system of checks and balances. These were based on the separation of institutions that shared and competed in the exercise of power.

What they did want, as we have noted, was a vigorous executive. But as a hedge against tyranny, they created separate legislative and executive institutions that were interdependent in the process of governing. They also created a constitutional court. The result was not really a separation of powers, but a separation of institutions that shared and competed in the exercise of power. The president may propose taxes and expenditures, but must wait for Congress to provide them. He is chief spokesman for the nation in foreign affairs, but two-thirds of the Senate must concur. He may veto legislation, but his vetos may be overridden by two-thirds votes of both chambers.

The consequences of this decision to opt for separate institutions, and for a sharing of power in such a way as to encourage checking and balancing, are apparent in almost every aspect of the operation of the American national government today. We shall note the consequences again and again in studying Congress, the president, and the processes of domestic and foreign policy making.

Limited Government

Related to the concepts of federalism, judicial review, and checks and balances, is the concept of limited government. The English and colonial roots of American constitutionalism are important to understanding how deeply the framers felt about limiting the scope of governmental activity. Not only was the federal government denied any general legislative power, but the Bill of Rights, which established some quite specific limitations on the national government, was quickly added after the adoption of the original seven articles.

Nor did the framers conceive that the sphere of federal activity and control could be extended limitlessly. They may not have been specific about the bounds on federal power, but clearly not even Hamilton regarded these bounds as infinitely flexible. (Twentieth-century Americans would change that, however; we discuss the radically altered nature of our federalism in Chapters 10 and 13.) Defense, foreign affairs, an orderly marketplace, and sound monetary arrangements—these were the great objectives of the new federation. Beyond these, the less the new government did, the safer would be the liberties of the people.

The framers of the constitution were strong central government men by the standards of the day—especially in comparison to many members of state legislatures and prominent local politicians, who favored retaining the weak Confederation. But the framers desired only to overcome the disunity of the Confederation. They assumed that most needs of most people would be satisfied in what we today would call the private sector.[24] Indeed, the existence of strong private institutions represented for them an even stronger bulwark against tyranny than checks and balances. Of all the original constitutional principles, this, perhaps, has been most altered by America's changing needs.

The framers felt strongly that most of the people's needs would be satisfied by private institutions. Therefore, they intended the new government to be limited, with sufficient power only to overcome the disunity of the Confederation.

Mixed Government

Finally, the government established by the Constitution of 1789 was intended to be a *mixed* government. The framers, schooled as they were in Locke, Montesquieu, and Greek and Roman political philosophies, rejected pure democracy as a basis for the new government. Along with Plato and Aristotle, they saw pure democracy as inherently unstable and susceptible to rapid degeneration into demagoguery and mob rule.

In fact, *no* pure form of government was thought stable; pure monarchy decayed into personal tyranny, and virtuous aristocratic regimes degenerated into vicious oligarchies. The secret of governmental stability—and thus the preservation of liberty—lay in mixing aspects of rule by the one, the few, and the many. This is what the framers attempted to do.[25]

The House of Representatives was to be popularly elected; the Senate was, originally, once removed from the electorate. Until the adoption of the Seventeenth Amendment, in 1913, Senators were chosen not at the polls but by the state legislatures. The Senate was (and is still referred to as such) the "Senior Chamber." Thus, according to legend, when Washington was asked by Jefferson (who had not been present at the Philadelphia convention) why a second, less "popular" legislative chamber was thought necessary, Washington asked his fellow Virginian why he was in the habit (common in the eighteenth century) of pouring his coffee into the saucer and back into the cup before drinking it. When Jefferson replied, "to cool it, of course," Washington was supposed to have concluded, "even so we pour legislation into the Senate—to cool it."

---

[24] See David C. Smith, *The Convention and the Constitution* (New York: St. Martin's Press, 1965), p. 54.

[25] An excellent study of the thought of the framers concerning mixed government is Paul Eidelberg, *The Philosophy of the American Constitution* (New York: The Free Press, 1968).

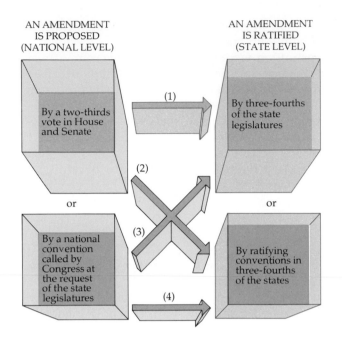

AN AMENDMENT
IS PROPOSED
(NATIONAL LEVEL)

AN AMENDMENT
IS RATIFIED
(STATE LEVEL)

By a two-thirds
vote in House
and Senate

By three-fourths
of the state
legislatures

or

or

By a national
convention
called by
Congress at
the request
of the state
legislatures

By ratifying
conventions in
three-fourths
of the states

Fig. 2.1
Traditional and alternative ways of amending the
Constitution. Article V of the Constitution provides several
different means of constitutional amendment. The common
practice throughout our history, however, has been for the
Congress to propose amendments to be acted on by the
legislatures of the several states.

Originally, the presidency itself would be twice removed from the
voters. Under the electoral college arrangement provided for in Article II,
each state chose electors who would then meet to elect the president and
vice-president. The method of choosing these electors is not specified by
Article II, and in our early presidential elections they were often appointed
by the state legislatures. There is no doubt that the framers intended the
electors to be "leading characters" of the states; people of property and
wisdom and experience would gather in privacy and quiet, apart from the
babble of the political marketplace, and make their choice. They were not
meant to be mere counters, reflecting an outcome at the polls.

Rapidly, however, this aristocratic element of the United States Constitution was reversed by events. By the election of 1828, as we shall see

in Chapter 3, the rising tide of democratic sentiment had forced the states to choose their presidential electors by popular election. One of the many interesting ironies of American development is that the presidency has developed into the primary democratic institution of our system. The president is the only public official elected by a national constituency, and the electoral college has now only a numerical effect—in that the popular winner takes all the electoral votes allotted to a particular state.

However, one powerfully aristocratic element of the original constitutional arrangement has not only survived, but grown in importance as the republic has developed. The Supreme Court is composed of nine lawyers, appointed, in effect, for life, who happened to appeal to a president enough to be nominated, and were confirmed by the Senate.

The essence of the Court's function is **countermajoritarian**. Quite simply, the justices tell the rest of government—federal, state, and local— what basic rules they must play by. These few men, interpreting and building on the lean sentences of the original Constitution and the Bill of Rights, have spun out an elaborate body of constitutional law that controls much of our public life. Almost all major questions of public policy are, in the American system, translated into constitutional questions. What should be the government's posture toward abortion? How much regulation may be placed on the spending of political candidates? Should the death penalty be retained? All such matters are decided in the cool and quiet privacy of the "Marble Palace," the Supreme Court's building on Capitol Hill.

Sooner or later, almost all really important political conflicts in America involve opposing interpretations of the Constitution. Issues of race, religion, economic regulation, war, and even sex relations have, to varying degrees, constitutional dimensions. This does not mean that the Supreme Court will always make the most important decisions, for most issues also have more immediately political dimensions involving electoral politics, legislative dynamics, and presidential choice. It *does* mean that the constitutional component is a crucial factor in our political system, to a degree that is unique among political systems of the world.

The principles and particulars of the Constitution, modified and added to over the years, are crucial to understanding how things work in America. The framers continue to cast a long shadow. Richard Hofstadter, among the shrewdest students of our history, once observed that the framers "did not believe in man, but they did believe in the power of a good political constitution to control him."[26]

The framers felt that no pure form of government was stable; therefore, the answer lay in mixing all the aspects of rule. For example, while the House of Representatives was to be popularly elected, the Senate, the presidency, and then finally the Supreme Court were to be progressively further removed from the electorate. Today, the only surviving aristocratic element of the original arrangement is the Supreme Court.

---

[26] This theme is beautifully developed by Richard Hofstadter, in *The American Political Tradition* (New York: Knopf, 1948), pp. 4–17.

SUMMARY

In our discussion of the founding of the republic, we have focused on the Constitution of 1789. It embodied certain major choices that, while modified over time, continue to bind and guide us today. We have examined the background of the Constitution: how it grew out of the English cultural inheritance, and the American colonial and revolutionary experiences. We have discussed the actual framing of the constitutional document at the Philadelphia convention, the rough political road over which it had to pass to ratification, and the way in which philosophy of government was accommodated to the political realities of the time. Finally, we studied each of the six major organizing principles of the Constitution in turn: (1) federalism, (2) a vigorous executive, (3) a Supreme Court to interpret the Constitution, (4) checks and balances of one institution by another, (5) limited government, and (6) mixed government. While each of these has been much tried over time, each remains operative today. We concluded by stressing the unique extent to which our system translates its major conflicts into constitutional issues, and seeks to resolve them within the framework of its great principles and general language. Our constitutionalism provides for change within a context of controversies.

KEY TERMS

constitutionalism
federalism
states' rights
Articles of Confederation
feudalism
Parliament
Magna Carta
Habeus Corpus Act
common law
precedent
radicalism
Shays's Rebellion
Bill of Rights

Constitutional Convention
Great Compromise
electoral college
ratification
The Federalist
judicial review
checks and balances
limited government
mixed government
countermajoritarian

SUGGESTED READINGS

BEARD, CHARLES A., *An Economic Interpretation of the Constitution* (New York: Macmillan, 1961).

> The most powerful statement of the argument that the most influential members of the Constitutional Convention acted out of economically interested motives.

Brown, Robert E., *Charles Beard and the Constitution* (Princeton, N.J.: Princeton University Press, 1956).

Brown takes Beard to task for his cavalier use of evidence and his reckless generalizing in attributing economic motives to the framers.

Corwin, Edward S., *The Constitution and What it Means Today* (New York: Atheneum, 1963).

A very valuable guide to the meaning of the various clauses of the Constitution. A good purchase for the library of any serious student.

Farrand, Max, *The Framing of the Constitution of the United States* (New Haven: Yale University Press, 1913).

A classic, short history of the constitutional convention.

Friedrich, Carl, and Robert G. McCloskey, *From the Declaration of Independence to the Constitution* (New York: Liberal Arts Press, 1954).

A valuable and very readable study of the evolution of early American political ideas.

Hartz, Louis, *The Liberal Tradition in America* (New York: Harcourt, 1955).

A very influential essay, stressing the ways in which the political ideas of the founding period continued to affect American politics.

Hofstadter, Richard, *The American Political Tradition* (New York: Knopf, 1948).

An excellent set of essays on the contributions to the theory of American government made by our greatest political leaders from Hamilton to FDR.

Rossiter, Clinton, *The Federalist Papers* (New York: Mentor, 1961).

No student of American politics should be without a copy of *The Federalist*. This abridged edition by Rossiter is excellent and inexpensive.

Smith, David C., *The Convention and the Constitution* (New York: St. Martin's, 1965).

A good, short study of the process of Constitution-making. Available in paperback.

On October 25, 1794, the President of the
United States was returning from
Bedford, Pennsylvania, to the seat of
government. While crossing the
Susquehanna River, his coach became
lodged between two boulders in
midstream, and there he was forced to sit
in the rain until it could be extricated.
Such misfortunes were common
annoyances of the time, and we may
presume that Washington, a constant
traveler, was philosophical in the face of
this unwelcome delay. He may well have
seized the occasion to reflect upon the
great changes which had occurred since
the spring day in Philadelphia in 1787
when he was chosen to preside over the
work of the Constitutional Convention.
He might have taken deep satisfaction in
the accomplishments of these few years,
despite his anxieties about the outcome of
the expedition then on foot to subdue the
rebellious whiskey distillers of western
Pennsylvania.

Leonard D. White

CHAPTER 3 POLITICAL
DEVELOPMENT
IN THE NEW NATION

On the further slopes of the Appalachian Mountains in Pennsylvania, in and around the settlement of Pittsburgh, it was the custom of the small farmers to convert substantial portions of their grain crop into whisky. This was a matter not so much of choice as of necessity. Transportation in the eighteenth century did not allow for the carting of bulky grain back through the Appalachian passes to the markets of the East coast. Therefore, for its value to be redeemed, the grain had to be converted into some more compact and easily moveable product. Since the predominant ethnic background of the settlers of the area was Scottish, the answer was obvious.

When the new federal government enacted a tax on whisky, these western Pennsylvania farmers strenuously resisted. It was not that they had been singled out (the distillery, or still, was a feature of early American farms), but simply that they converted *more* of their crop into whisky than did their fellows east of the Appalachians. The Pennsylvanian reaction to the tax evoked memories of Shays's Rebellion less than a decade before.

Robert Johnson, a federal tax collector in western Pennsylvania, was seized by an armed mob; his hair was cut off, and he was stripped, tarred, and feathered, robbed of his horse and money, and left to make his way back East as best he could. The Deputy United States Marshal sent by the federal court in Philadelphia to arrest rebel leaders quickly returned to the judge protesting that to have tried to do so would have cost him his life. Another mob of farmers compelled one Captain Faulkner, who had merely rented an office to a federal revenue inspector, to pull out of the transaction or be scalped. After meeting in Pittsburgh, the farmers sent a protest to Congress saying that if the tax were not lifted they would withdraw from federal officials all friendship, trade, assistance, and comforts of life, "and upon all occasions treat them with that contempt they deserved."

Alexander Hamilton, Secretary of the Treasury and thus chief collector of the whisky tax, wrote to George Washington at Mt. Vernon urging decisive action. Hamilton also asked Attorney General Edmund Randolph whether any of the activity at the Pittsburgh meeting had been treasonable. Randolph assured Hamilton that "To assemble, to remonstrate, and to invite others to assemble and to remonstrate to the Legislature, are among the rights of citizens."

Hamilton was bitterly disappointed that Washington would not authorize him to personally lead a military force against the defiant farmers. What was finally agreed upon was a curious expedition that included (1) elements of the Virginia, New Jersey, and Pennsylvania militias commanded by Governor Henry (Lightfoot Harry) Lee of Virginia; (2) the United States District Attorney for Pennsylvania; (3) the federal Circuit Judge for Pennsylvania; and (4) Alexander Hamilton, in the capacity of chief revenue collector with a predominant interest in the outcome.

The reaction of provincial Americans to centrally imposed taxes ranged from sullen acceptance to sometimes violent action, such as the tarring and feathering of an excise officer pictured here.

News of the expedition's progress through the mountains moved ahead of it. Most of the leaders of what history has come to know as the *Whisky Rebellion* scattered before the arrival of Lee, Hamilton, and the Judge. There were a few arrests, a few midnight searches, a few scuffles, and that was that.

What is interesting about the Whisky Rebellion is that very little violence took place. The expedition sent to punish the rebels neither destroyed property nor remained in occupation very long. And Washington eventually pardoned the few persons who were arrested. Yet the expedition succeeded. The authority of the new government (its capacity to enforce its laws) was maintained, and without bloodshed, despite Hamilton's saber-rattling rhetoric.[1]

Such an exercise of authority would have been far beyond the capacity of the old Confederation, and vividly illustrates the fact that the new

The Whisky Rebellion showed that the new government could use force to enforce its laws directly against citizens.

[1] This account of the Whisky Rebellion is based on Homer Cummings and Carl MacFarland, *Federal Justice* (New York: Macmillan, 1937), pp. 29–51.

federal government could back up its laws with measured force. But all was not easy sailing for the new central government. In today's world we are all too familiar with the dangers that beset new nations. Political scientists sometimes refer to a **crisis of legitimacy** through which all new nations must pass. An unfamiliar government is naturally regarded as somewhat alien and strange by its citizens, and must quickly generate confidence and respect if it is to establish itself. As with any young organism, surviving the early period of life is particularly difficult.[2]

The Constitution was merely a collection of words in the winter of 1789. The real government had to be created by the men who set the provisions of the new document in motion. In fact, if the "Godlike Washington" had not assumed its leadership and lent it his own vast prestige,[3] it is unlikely that the "national bantling" would have survived. And perhaps equally important were the contributions of Hamilton as chief policy maker of Washington's administration, Thomas Jefferson as creator of an opposition party, John Marshall, who secured the power of judicial review for the Supreme Court, and James Madison, the principal architect of the Bill of Rights.

In this chapter we shall examine how the major institutions of American government were *actually formed,* and briefly trace the ways in which they developed in the nineteenth and early twentieth centuries. The basic organization of some of these institutions (such as the Congress) was specified in the Constitution; other important institutions (such as our political parties) grew up altogether outside of the framework sketched at Philadelphia in 1787. But whether constitutionally based or not, our development during the first few decades contributed as much to the *shape* of our institutions of today as did the framers.

We shall also note the ways in which federalism—the division of power between the national government and the states—came to be defined and redefined in governmental practice. The framers of the Constitution had drawn the outline of federalism, but left it to succeeding generations to struggle over the particulars, and to adapt the federal system to changing circumstances.

Finally, we shall note the ways in which the new government was progressively democratized—during its initial formative period and through its growth to maturity in the nineteenth and early twentieth centuries. The framers had envisioned a limited representative democracy. But pressures of a growing population and the growing popularity of

[2] See Seymour Martin Lipset, *The First New Nation* (New York: Basic Books, 1963), pp. 15–60.

[3] For examples see Marcus Cunliffe, *George Washington, Man and Monument* (New York: Mentor Books, 1960).

egalitarianism soon broadened participation and involved voters more directly in the process of governing.

In reading each of the three sections of this chapter you should ask yourself how our political institutions might have developed differently, and whether the ways in which they did develop leave them more or less able to cope with tasks of governing in the latter third of the twentieth century.

INSTITUTIONAL DEVELOPMENT

In a widely quoted essay on political development, Samuel P. Huntington defined *political development* as "the institutionalization of political organizations and procedures." Huntington went on to define **institutionalization** in this way:

> Institutions are stable, valued, recurring patterns of behavior. Organizations and procedures vary in their degree of institutionalization. Harvard University and the newly opened suburban high school are both organizations, but Harvard is much more of an institution than is the high school. The seniority system in Congress and President Johnson's select press conferences are both procedures, but seniority is much more institutionalized than are Mr. Johnson's methods of dealing with the press. *Institutionalization* is the process by which organizations and procedures acquire value and stability. The level of institutionalization of any political system can be defined by the adaptability, complexity, autonomy, and coherence of its organizations and procedures.[4]

Let us see how this relates to the growth of our government in the formative years after its birth in 1789.

The Presidency

Initially, of course, the presidency was shaped by Article II of the Constitution; but the institution was also shaped by the precedents set by successive incumbents. Some contributed much, some little, but later presidents were able to do things, to assume powers, because their predecessors had done so before them, had used the office creatively. The institution of the presidency has been more deeply imprinted by the personal styles of its incumbents than either the Supreme Court by its famous chief justices or Congress by its foremost leaders.[5]

The office of the presidency is to a large extent shaped by the personal styles of the incumbents.

[4] Samuel P. Huntington, "Political Development and Political Decay," *World Politics* 17 (April 1965): 386–430.

[5] An interesting description of this process is Rexford Tugwell, *The Enlargement of the Presidency* (Garden City, N.Y.: Doubleday, 1960). Also interesting is Louis W. Koenig, *The Chief Executive*, 3d ed. (New York: Harcourt, 1975).

Abraham Lincoln, Franklin
Roosevelt, and Theodore
Roosevelt are three examples of
charismatic leadership.

Perhaps the most important thing to happen to the presidency was George Washington. Today we are familiar with the term *charismatic*, used to describe leaders of such transcendent popularity that their leadership in itself, especially in new nations, helps to establish the authority of that government, contributing to its **legitimacy**. Nkrumah was such a figure in Ghana in the 1950s, as was Gandhi in the emerging Indian nation. The danger in new nations is that such leaders will evolve into dictators—that their popularity will become a cult of personality and democratic development will be frustrated as their rule becomes personal and permanent. Excellent examples of this were Sukarno in Indonesia and Touré in Guinea. There is always a fine line between the political charismatic and political criminal. But America was lucky in Washington.

The prestige was certainly there. It was almost treasonable to criticize the "Godlike Washington." As early as 1873, President Ezra Stiles of Yale effused in a sermon, "How do I love thy name! How often have I adored God, for creating and forming thee, the great ornament of humankind!" But Washington had more than just prestige. Although not a great policy leader (the policy of his administration was largely shaped by Alexander Hamilton, the secretary of the treasury), he had the capacity to contain conflict. To offer the most striking example, during his administration a bitter dispute broke out between Hamilton and Thomas Jefferson, the secretary of state, that led eventually to the development of the first political parties. The emerging conflict between "Hamiltonians" and "Jeffersonians" compelled Washington to serve a second term, although he had wished to serve only one. But because of his presence the party system evolved peacefully, without disrupting the fragile institutions of the new republic in their vulnerable beginnings.

Immensely popular, George Washington was able to contain conflict and to establish the dignity and importance of his office as policy-initiating institution.

The way Washington conducted himself as president established the dignity and importance of the office as a coordinate branch of government equal to Congress. By sponsoring Hamilton's policies, he established the presidency as a policy-initiating institution. In addition, certain of his smaller gestures projected the idea of executive power as an important and natural aspect of good government. For instance, Washington made it his practice to deliver his State of the Union message (required by Article II) to Congress in person. This unmistakeably echoed the British practice of the monarch addressing the opening session of Parliament from the throne.

Certain of Washington's behaviors were obviously too regal for Jefferson and his followers. For example, Washington also adopted the practice of declaring national holidays. While trivial itself, this practice was enough to inflame the passions of states righters, who opposed the idea of national power. But Washington's popularity prevented the Jeffersonians from openly attacking him. They were forced to concentrate their fire on Hamilton, while Washington went majestically on, behaving as an elected king.

What is fascinating is that Jefferson, who bitterly opposed expansive notions of executive power while he was in opposition to Hamilton and Washington, did little to detract from the growth of the presidency after he himself was elected to that office in 1801. He may have refused to issue a Thanksgiving Day proclamation, but he more than made up for this in (1) his vigorous leadership from the White House of his party's majorities in the House and Senate; (2) his audacious use of executive power in pushing through the Louisiana Purchase; and (3) most especially, his use of the foreign affairs and war-making powers of the presidency in preparing the nation for the embargo (prohibition on trade) and the resumption of war against Great Britain.

This pattern of strong presidents adding to the prestige and power of the office continued throughout the nineteenth century. One thinks of Abraham Lincoln's use of the war powers in particular: He imposed a blockade on the rebelling states before Congress declared war, and he unilaterally suspended ordinary legal procedures to deal with disloyalty in the North.

Jefferson, Lincoln, and the Roosevelts all added to the prestige and power of the presidency.

An example from the early twentieth century comes in the presidency of Theodore Roosevelt. Roosevelt's accession to the presidency coincided with the appearance of truly national news media. The development of the telegraph services tied the newspapers together as never before. It was Theodore Roosevelt's genius that he sensed the existence of an instantaneous national audience and strove to take advantage of it. For him the presidency was a **bully pulpit**—an office to be used to educate and lead the nation. While it remained for TR's cousin, Franklin Delano Roosevelt, to perfect the techniques of the presidential use of the media through use of the radio and development of the press conference, the birth of this new source of presidential power came in the administration of TR.

In Chapter 9, we shall examine the modern presidency in detail and note how the precedents set by institution-shaping incumbents in the past are clearly visible in the institution of today.

The Federal Bureaucracy

That part of the federal government to develop the most slowly was the **bureaucracy**—the administrative agencies of the nation.

There were only four officers in the original cabinet. The secretary of state presided over a few clerks and sustained correspondence with ambassadors abroad. The secretary of war presided over a few clerks and an almost nonexistent army. The attorney general was not even a full-time government employee. Edmund Randolph, who got the job only because he was George Washington's personal lawyer, was expected to advise the president and other cabinet officers about legal matters and make up the rest of his income through private practice. A Department of Justice—a bureaucracy for administering federal laws—did not come into existence until 1870!

It was in Alexander Hamilton's Treasury Department that the first model of a policy-making bureaucracy developed. While tiny by modern standards, composed of Hamilton himself, an assistant, and a few close aides, the department quickly developed programs that tied the interests of the American financial community in the various states tightly to the new federal government. Political scientist Seymour Martin Lipset reminds us of how important it is that new regimes establish themselves by demonstrating effectiveness—by delivering "payoff" to important groups within the country. This is precisely what Hamilton's Treasury Department did.[6]

From the Philadelphia convention on, Alexander Hamilton's vision of the American future was of a great commercial Republic. He and his Federalist supporters were very conscious of the threats to the new Republic from the international community, and were determined that the new nation would take its place as quickly as possible as a major actor on the world stage. In contemporary terminology, this meant rapid economic development. Rapid economic development, as we are all too well aware today, depends on capital. Where was it to come from? The Congress of the old, feeble Confederation had barely scraped through the revolutionary war by issuing worthless money. The various states had raised their contributions to the war effort by issuing bonds that they were now unable or unwilling to redeem. Reams of worthless paper floated about the country and it was unlikely that in these circumstances the banks of London and Amsterdam would be much interested in making loans to facilitate American economic development.

Hamilton's answer was for the federal government to move swiftly to ensure the commercial credit of the new United States. The government assumed the revolutionary war debt of the states, and laid plans for the creation of a central bank of the United States to stabilize the currency and provide a stable system of credit. These policies created a national debt that caused both fearful and scornful reactions from anti-Federalists. But they accomplished their purpose: Those financial interests in the nation that looked to interstate and international markets perceived their future as bound up with the prospering of the national government.

Of the other bureaucratic elements of the new regime, the one with the greatest impact on the lives of Americans was the Post Office. This agency, today almost disowned by the federal government and the object

As secretary of the treasury, Alexander Hamilton worked to make the new nation into a great commercial republic. He moved swiftly to stabilize the currency and provide a solid system of credit.

[6] Koenig, *The Chief Executive.*

of scorn for its inefficiency, was the one federally provided public service that most Americans used. It was terribly important to them; they admired it, and depended on it, and in its own humble way, the early federal post certainly had something to do with confirming the legitimacy of the new central government of the period, if only because of its efficiency. (So important was this federal service to early-nineteenth-century Americans that Jefferson considered it an outrage that non-Christians should be deprived of mail service on Sundays—he thought that the system should function seven days a week.)

While the bureaucratic structures established in the new nation were insignificant and primitive by today's standards, they did work to the immediate benefit of many Americans, and to that extent aided the success of the new national enterprise.[7]

The Congress

The institutionalization of Congress was a fascinating process. In the early years of the nineteenth century, Congress operated in a state of chaotic disorganization. While the Senate and House are often pictured as heroic places where giants walked the earth, the reality was one of individual brilliance but institutional weakness. Webster and Calhoun did indeed hold forth in the Senate, and Henry Clay in the House, but their achievements were personal, made despite the disorganization of the chambers.

Yet by 1885, when Woodrow Wilson, a young political scientist at Princeton, published his famous book *Congressional Government*,[8] the process of institutionalization of rules, customs, and structures of power within Congress had progressed to a point where essentially all the features of the modern institution were present. In a period of weak presidents in the latter decades of the nineteenth century, Congress, and particularly the Senate, emerged as the predominant branch of the national government.[9] What had happened in the years between 1800 and 1884 to cause this change? To answer this question, it is helpful to understand the character of Washington and its people during those early years.

A frontier capital

Until 1800, the government of the United States had enjoyed an itinerant existence. First set up in New York, it moved to Philadelphia, and finally

[7] For a detailed description and analysis see Leonard D. White, *The Federalists* (New York: Macmillan, 1948).

[8] Woodrow Wilson, *Congressional Government* (Boston: Little, Brown, 1885).

[9] On the period in the history of the Senate, see David J. Rothman, *Politics and Power in the United States Senate, 1869–1901* (Cambridge, Mass.: Harvard University Press, 1966).

Washington, D.C., in 1851 and 1978.

to its permanent location where the Potomac and the east branch of the Anacostia converged. America was the first nation in history to create a national capital from nothing. Furthermore, what was described by many visitors as a "low and malarial swamp," insect-ridden and wild, seemed an improbable location for the capital of a great republic. While plans were being laid for a marvelous city of broad avenues and gleaming buildings, the reality of Washington, D.C., at the accession of Thomas Jefferson to the presidency, was a drafty and unfinished White House, and a capitol building consisting of two squat wings (for House and Senate) connected by a boardwalk. The road that has become Pennsylvania Avenue wound down to a swamp that bogged carriages in the rain and sent up choking dust in dry weather. Primitive accommodations were the rule.

In one respect only did the capital of 1801 resemble Washington today. It acted, as James Young has pointed out, "as a magnet for society's idle and society's unwanted: people sick in mind or body, imagining conspiracies against them, imploring help, or bent upon revenge; . . . small-time confidence men; needy pamphlet-writers—, selling their talents for calumny for the price of a public printing contract; . . ." [10] All these were drawn to the District of Columbia.

No man in his right mind would, given the local conditions and the lack of amenities of the transportation system of the day, bring his family to Washington. So members of Congress lived in frame boarding houses, and at very close quarters indeed. Tempers flared often both in the boarding houses and in the chambers of Congress, and more than one duel was fought in the scanty woods along the Potomac.

Such tension was hardly surprising given the diversity of the men involved. The dominant style was of the slave-holding South. Entertainment was hard to come by, and hunting and fishing along the Potomac attracted many of the southern senators and representatives. Bird dogs and whisky were some diversion from the interminable, mind-deadening speeches in the chambers. Refreshment was lavishly provided in the cloakrooms of both houses, and hunting whips and pistols were a familiar sight on the floor. Another group of Congressmen came from the frontier hinterlands—men such as David Crockett, uncut gems, brash and boastful, accustomed to the woods and drunken barbecues, but suspicious of the tidewater aristocrats with their social airs and expensive horses and English guns. Finally, there were the New Englanders, cultural outcasts in the upper southland, ill at ease, inward turning, men who kept to themselves and to their lodgings. They longed for when they could return north to "civilization."

[10] James S. Young, *The Washington Community: 1800–1820* (New York: Columbia University Press, 1966), p. 25.

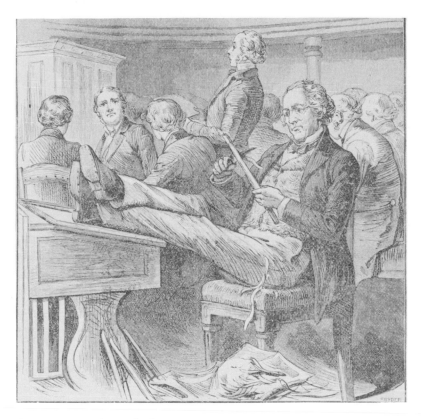

Sam Houston whittling in the Senate.

The system for the orderly transaction of congressional business was slow in emerging. Any representative or senator could bring forward a measure at any time, and other legislators could postpone action on a measure "by the simple expedient of talking." Debates were endless and boring. There was no Rules Committee in the House to control the flow of business to the floor, nor was there any way of stopping debate (a "cloture rule") in the Senate. The committee system for parceling out business was just beginning to develop, and party discipline was weak. President Jefferson did manage, for the first several years of his first administration, to exercise some control over the fractious Republican members on the Hill. This was one of his greatest achievements. But his system, while significant for the future development of relationships between president and Congress, was short-lived. James Madison could not duplicate it, and James Monroe did not even try.

The system for the orderly transaction of business emerged very slowly in Congress. By the late 1800s, however, it had reached a high degree of institutionalization. Two leading factors in this development were the emergence of party leadership and the growth of the committee system.

But somehow the congressional system progressed from this chaotic state to the high degree of institutionalization it displayed by the late 1800s. Two leading factors in this development were the emergence of party leadership and the growth of the committee system.

Party leadership and the committee system

It is interesting to note that in every Congress since 1861 there has been a majority able, on its own, to organize each house of Congress. While party discipline in the Senate and House of Representatives has never approached the level of, say, the British Parliament, it was important for the development of the institution that session after session Congress was organized along party lines without the necessity for forming intricate, unstable coalitions.

Even more important than the growth of party leadership, however, was the development of the committee system. Although present in a primitive form in the Congresses of the late eighteenth and early nineteenth centuries, committees were relied on much less than they came to be later on. As we have seen, it was the early custom for bills to be introduced directly onto the floor and discussed there. Only after the initial free-for-all was there referral to the committee, and in many cases

Thomas Jefferson.

this was a specially created committee, which disbanded after dealing with that single matter, and not a standing committee at all.[11]

The committee took on increased importance in the first two years of Thomas Jefferson's administration. Jefferson, through his Speaker of the House, exercised considerable influence over committee appointments, and was heavily involved in work of the more important committees, especially the Ways and Means Committee chaired by John Randolph. Because he could use the committees as instruments of his party control, within the chambers, Jefferson contributed to their strength. And although the Jeffersonian system of party control was short-lived, this initial emphasis on committees contributed to their development as part of the congressional system.

So while the party leaders (who were elected by the party members, meeting in what were called "caucuses") assumed the formal leadership positions on the floor of the House and Senate,[12] taking responsibility for fixing the agenda and allocating time for debate, a second set of leaders soon emerged—the powerful committee chairmen. They were only occasional allies of the party leaders—the Speaker of the House or the majority leader in the Senate. For instance, the chairman of the powerful House Ways and Means Committee regarded himself as slightly less important than the Speaker himself. Also in the House, the Rules Committee, which evolved after the Civil War as an instrument for managing the flow of legislation to the floor, eventually forced the Speaker to share the agenda-setting function.[13]

Furthermore, the development in both houses of the seniority custom over the latter part of the nineteenth century and the early years of the twentieth century had contributed to an increasing independence of committee chairmen from the party leadership. If they served as chairmen by virtue of their years, why should they subject themselves to leadership discipline?

In this fascinating way, the Congress of the United States moved from the chaotic disorganization of the early decades to a period of extensive institutionalization by the late 1800s. But, as Wilson observed, the process of institutionalization resulted in a *decentralized* power structure. We will see the continuing effects of the "institutionalized decentralization" when we examine Congress in Chapter 9.

Jefferson used the committees as instruments of party control, thus contributing to their strength.

[11] On the early history of the committee system, see DeAlva Stanwood Alexander, *History and Procedure of the House of Representatives* (Boston: Houghton Mifflin, 1916).

[12] For a treatment of this development in the House, see George B. Galloway, *History of the House of Representatives* (New York: Crowell, 1961), pp. 129–159.

[13] For an excellent study of this process see Nelson Polsby, "The Institutionalization of the U.S. House of Representatives," *The American Political Science Review* LXII (March 1968): 144–168.

Biography
Thomas Brackett Reed: "Czar" of the House

Thomas Brackett Reed, the great Speaker of the House in the late nineteenth century, sent out no questionnaires to the folks back home. Instead, he followed his own convictions, even defying, at times, majority sentiment within his own party. After unsuccessfully opposing American expansion in the Pacific, including annexation of Hawaii and acquisition of the Philippines, Reed startled the political world in 1899 with the announcement that he would not be a candidate for reelection as Speaker. Shortly afterwards he announced his decision not to run again for Congress.

Reed offered no public explanation for his going. To his constituents in Maine's first district who had supported him for more than two decades, however, he explained in a farewell letter, "Office as a 'ribbon to stick in your coat' is worth nobody's consideration." Joe Cannon, his successor as Speaker, years later offered this assessment: "His was the strongest intellect crossed on the best courage of any man in public life that I have ever known." Henry Cabot Lodge considered Reed "the ablest running debater the American people ever saw."

Historian Barbara W. Tuchman offers this portrait of Reed:

A physical giant six feet three inches tall, weighing almost three hundred pounds and dressed completely in black, out of whose collar rose an enormous clean-shaven baby face like a Casaba melon flowering from a fat black stalk, he was a subject for a Franz Hals with long white fingers that would have enraptured a Memling. Speaking in a slow and exasperating drawl, he enjoyed dropping cool sarcasm into the most heated rhetoric and watching the ensuing fizzle with the bland gravity of a New England Buddha. ("Czar of the House," American Heritage, *December 1962, p. 33)*

The Judiciary

Unlike the other major institutions of the national government—the presidency, the bureaucracy, and Congress—the Supreme Court did not assume its distinctive role in American government immediately after 1789. Political scientist Robert G. McCloskey, in fact, has suggested that the Court seemed almost to be marking time awaiting the arrival of its first great leader—the third chief justice of the United States, John Marshall.[14]

[14] Robert G. McCloskey, *The American Supreme Court* (Chicago: University of Chicago Press, 1960), p. 30.

For instance, when a wordy colleague was declaiming to the House his passionate preference for being right rather than president, TBR interjected: "The gentleman need not be disturbed; he will never be either."

When another member, notorious for fuzziness of thought and a halting manner of speech, opened his remarks with "I was thinking, Mr. Speaker, I was thinking . . ." the Speaker expressed the hope that "no one will interrupt the gentleman's commendable innovation."

"Russell," Reed once said to a Massachusetts representative, "you do not understand the theory of the five-minute debate. The object is to convey to the House either information or misinformation. You have consumed several periods of five minutes this afternoon without doing either."

After verbally silencing one opponent, Reed, looking about him sweetly, continued: "Having embedded that fly in the liquid amber of my remarks, I will proceed."

Reed was no admirer of President Benjamin Harrison, noted for his coldness of manner. Reed dubbed him, "the White House iceberg." McKinley he considered an "emperor of expediency." When Bryan campaigned a second time in 1900 on a platform of free silver, Reed quipped: "Bryan had rather be wrong than president."

In all of this Reed drew upon the resources of a cultivated mind. He had an excellent private library. He enjoyed reading Carlyle, Goethe, Macaulay, and Thackeray. He read and spoke French. At forty he started a diary in French "for practice."

Czar Reed was an uncommonly able person, whose leadership contributed significantly to the House of Representatives.

This judgment may be a little severe. In fact, the Supreme Court decided several important cases before Marshall became Chief Justice in 1801. In these decisions the Court made reference to the power of **judicial review**—the capacity to declare acts of Congress and of the states void because of unconstitutionality. In addition, Associate Justice James Wilson, one of the principal architects of Article II and a disappointed aspirant to the chief justiceship, delivered widely read lectures on the Constitution in which he delineated a theory of judicial review similar to one he had described at the convention and that Alexander Hamilton had further refined in *The Federalist* No. 78. It was, however, with John Marshall's opinion for the Court in the famous case of *Marbury* v. *Madison,* in 1803,[15] that the doctrine of judicial review by the Court of acts of Congress became firmly fixed in American constitutional law.

Marbury v. *Madison*

The origins of this case are a fascinating study in the politics of the time. John Marshall was a middle-class Virginian. He had been a revolutionary war officer, and had studied law in the informal fashion of the period. He was a devout supporter of the new national government, and (by 1800) a faithful partisan of Hamilton's Federalist party. His social background was quite similar to Thomas Jefferson's, but there the similarity ended. These two sons of Virginia, both ambitious, neither members of the tidewater aristocracy, hated one another with a passion.

Marshall served as secretary of state in the Federalist administration of John Adams. In that capacity, he was responsible in the waning days of the Adams administration for delivering some hastily signed commissions to newly created justices of the peace in the District of Columbia. These new appointees were, of course, also loyal Federalists. They were being rewarded with office just as the Federalist administration gave way to the Republican administration of Thomas Jefferson. The situation was further complicated by the fact that Adams had already nominated Marshall for chief justice. The outgoing secretary of state, and chief justice of the United States designate, forgot to deliver several of the commissions entrusted to his care. One was intended for William Marbury.

When the Republicans assumed office in 1801, James Madison, as Jefferson's secretary of state, found on his desk the signed commission for Marbury. But why should a Republican administration deliver this commission to an active Federalist? Madison refused Marbury his commission even though, as Marbury pointed out, it had been legally executed by the previous president.

Marbury went to court; moreover, he went directly to the Supreme Court of the United States. Proceeding under a provision of the Judiciary Act of 1789 that provided, among other things, that the Supreme Court might issue **writs of mandamus** (orders to public officials to perform required legal functions), Marbury asked John Marshall to order James Madison to deliver the commission that Marshall had so carelessly forgotten.

Marshall found himself in a dilemma. He certainly believed Marbury was entitled to his commission. And he was certainly prepared to lash out at Jefferson and Madison for their refusal to deliver it. But the matter was

[15] 1 Cranch 137 (1803).

Chief Justice John Marshall.

not that simple. The Jeffersonians were outraged (none more than Jefferson himself) at the number of Federalist judicial appointments that had been made in the waning days of the Adams administration. Jefferson and his supporters felt that the Federalists had attempted to pack the judiciary with propartisans in an effort to frustrate the will of the country, which had been so clearly expressed by Jefferson's election in 1800. None of the Federalist judicial appointments was more resented by the hot-tempered man in the White House than John Marshall's appointment to the chief justiceship. The newly empowered Jeffersonians were eager to impeach any Federalist judge, and particularly John Marshall, if halfway plausible grounds could be found.

Thus, if Marshall ordered Jefferson and Madison to deliver the commission, he would risk having his order disobeyed. In addition, it was certain that such an order would provoke the new administration to some sort of aggressive action against the judiciary—perhaps even an attempt at impeaching John Marshall himself. What was Marshall to do?

His exit from the maze was masterful: First, in the early pages of his opinion, Marshall hammered home the point that Marbury had a right to the commission and that Madison was behaving illegally in denying it. He went on to affirm that a court order to Madison requiring him to perform his legal duty would be an appropriate remedy for Marbury's wrong. But, in a neat turnabout, Marshall pointed out that such an order could not issue from the Supreme Court. The reason for this was that the act of Congress that purported to give the Court power to hear applications for writs of mandamus in **original jurisdiction** (not as appeals but with the case actually beginning before the Supreme Court) was unconstitutional.

The original jurisdiction of the Court, said Marshall, was explicitly delineated in Article III. It could neither be subtracted from nor added to by an act of Congress, and to the extent that Section 13 of the Judiciary Act sought to add to that jurisdiction it was unconstitutional and without legal effect.

In the case of *Marbury* v. *Madison*, John Marshall firmly established the doctrine of judicial review by the Court of acts of Congress.

At one stroke, John Marshall read Thomas Jefferson a stinging public lecture, escaped having to issue an order that would be disobeyed, and unambiguously asserted for the Court the power to declare acts of Congress unconstitutional. Not, one must admit, a bad day's work. And Marshall's opinion was well grounded in precedent—not the precedent of prior judicial decisions, but the precedent of Hamiltonian and Wilsonian ideas about judicial review that were familiar to the first generation of American political leaders. From a Federalist point of view, the only loser was poor Marbury, who never received his commission.

It is interesting to note that during John Marshall's long tenure on the Court (three decades after *Marbury* v. *Madison*), the Court never again exercised the power of declaring an act of Congress unconstitutional. But the power, once claimed, was there, and future Courts used it lavishly. And in other areas, the Marshall Court was extremely active. It is not exaggerating to say that in the years between 1800 and 1830, the Supreme Court was the principal institutional force in protecting and enhancing the power of the national government.

Political Parties

All too often the emergence of political parties in America is presented as a function of a personal conflict between Alexander Hamilton and Thomas Jefferson. True, the two men despised one another. Hamilton thought Jefferson to be "tinctured with fanaticism, crafty, not scrupulous nor very mindful of the truth, and a contemptible hypocrite. . . ." For his part, Jefferson thought Hamilton, "A man whose history, from the moment at which history can stoop to notice him, is a tissue of machinations against the liberty of the country. . . ." But there was much more to the dispute between the two men than personal enmity. They disagreed profoundly as to the nature, purposes, and future of the new central government. Their positions on issues became standards around which the party politics of the period were organized. And the two men were, in different ways, great leaders: Hamilton in his capacity to persuade and Jefferson in his organizational genius.

Hamilton and Jefferson disagreed profoundly as to the nature, purposes, and future of the new central government. Their positions on issues became standards around which the party politics of the period were organized.

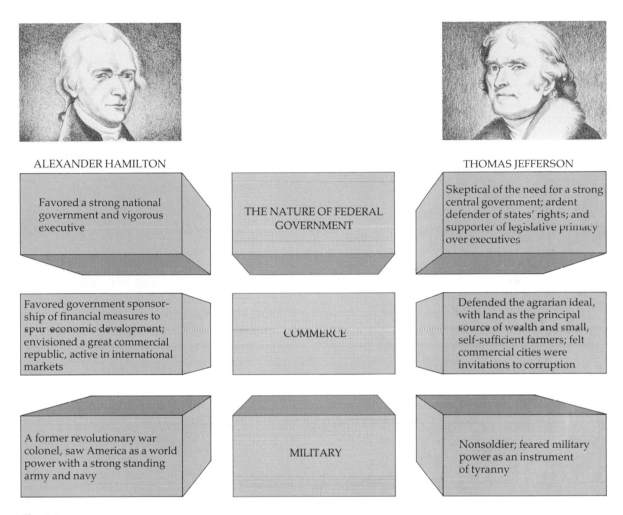

ALEXANDER HAMILTON

THOMAS JEFFERSON

THE NATURE OF FEDERAL GOVERNMENT

Favored a strong national government and vigorous executive

Skeptical of the need for a strong central government; ardent defender of states' rights; and supporter of legislative primacy over executives

COMMERCE

Favored government sponsorship of financial measures to spur economic development; envisioned a great commercial republic, active in international markets

Defended the agrarian ideal, with land as the principal source of wealth and small, self-sufficient farmers; felt commercial cities were invitations to corruption

MILITARY

A former revolutionary war colonel, saw America as a world power with a strong standing army and navy

Nonsoldier; feared military power as an instrument of tyranny

Fig. 3.1
The political-ideological confrontation between Alexander Hamilton and Thomas Jefferson. The conflict between Hamilton and Jefferson, the two most commanding figures of the formative period, was bitter and complicated. This chart portrays, in very general terms, the major disagreements between these two men, whose ideas still survive as contrasting threads in the weave of American political ideas.

The first two-party system

The most basic difference between Hamilton and Jefferson concerned the nature of the federal union. Jefferson had not been a supporter of the new Constitution. He had been out of the country at the time of its adoption, and while the historical record is skimpy as to his opinion of it, there is

The most basic difference between Hamilton and Jefferson concerned the nature of the federal union.

no doubt he was skeptical of the need for stronger national power. As we have already noted, the product of the Philadelphia convention was vigorously opposed by many powerful forces within the states who also feared the creation of a more powerful central government. Thus, by the time George Washington organized his first administration, there was already a division of opinion between **Federalists**—those who had vigorously argued for ratification of the Constitution and believed in strong central government—and **anti-Federalists**—those who had actively opposed or remained skeptical about the Constitution and were opposed to the notion of a strong central government.

At first, these divisions in the country did not constitute parties in the modern sense. They lacked organization, they did not propose candidates for office (Washington had been chosen by almost universal acclamation), and they were without leaders. But Jefferson's return from France, and his taking up office in the new government, gave the anti-Federalists a focus for their concerns.

A second policy difference between Hamilton and Jefferson involved government sponsorship of financial measures to spur economic development. Jefferson, in addition to his suspicion of central government, was inclined to **agrarianism** in his economic views. That is, he saw the principal source of wealth as land, and the model American as the small farmer—owning his own acres and largely self-sufficient. For Jefferson the commercial city was a source of trouble and corruption. Complicated arrangements of banking for commerce were to him invitations to corruption. And most of all, the notion of America as a world "power," flexing its muscles and maintaining a standing army and navy to protect its interests, seemed to him a horrible assault on the purses as well as the liberties of the people.

Thus, we have, locked up together in Washington's first cabinet, the arch-defender of the Constitution and strong central government, and the emerging theoretician of states rights. Hamilton was the brilliant policy innovator, pursuing his vision of a commercial republic active on the world scene. Jefferson was the agrarian Virginian philosopher, despising the very notion of complicated commerce. Hamilton was the revolutionary war colonel (he led the final bayonet charge at Yorktown) who yearned for a strong army and navy. Jefferson was the nonsoldier who feared a national military force as an instrument of tyranny.

The formation of an opposition organization around Jefferson was not long in coming. On May 17, 1791, Jefferson set out from Philadelphia on a long trip through the Northeast. The purpose of his journey was supposedly to collect material for the American Philadelphia Society, at that time the leading scientific body of the country. The notes that Jefferson finally produced for the Society proved to be largely indecipherable and

A second policy difference between Hamilton and Jefferson involved government involvement in the economic development of the country.

insignificant, but no matter. In the course of his journey, Jefferson met with editors and politicians, including Aaron Burr, whom they recruited to their cause. Very soon a Jeffersonian newspaper—a *Republican* paper, as it was called then—was functioning in Philadelphia. Hamilton responded to these oppositional initiatives by urging Washington to run for a second term in order to defeat the mischievous factionalism that was developing in the country. Hamilton also became more active in organizing the political forces within the various states that supported his position.

In addition, during this period, Jefferson was winning a spectacularly important convert to the states-rights cause—James Madison. A great deal has been written about Madison's move from support of strong central government and vigorous executive leadership in 1787, to opposition to these Federalist policies in the mid-1790s, and finally, in 1798, to authorship of the Virginia Resolution, which represented a direct challenge to the authority of the new central government. The coauthor of *The Federalist* became the cofounder of the anti-national opposition party.[16]

The Hamiltonian Federalists coasted to a second term with Washington in 1792, and in late 1793 Jefferson resigned from Washington's cabinet to formally assume leadership of his Republican Party. The Federalists won a bitterly contested election with John Adams in 1796, but it was clear that the organization of the Jeffersonian Republicans was superior. The Republicans reached down into the electorate, going after votes and attempting to mobilize electoral support. It was a new kind of instrument of democratic politics. The Federalists remained in the older, aristocratic tradition of politics. Hamilton was a brilliant intellectual leader, but his organization was made up of prominent leaders from the various states. There was little attempt to reach outward and downward toward an electorate that, by the end of the eighteenth century, was beginning to expand rapidly.[17]

The Alien and Sedition acts But the development of an opposition party in the new America was not without peril and pain. By the middle of the 1790s, another issue had arisen that divided Jeffersonian Republicans from the party of Hamilton and the new president, John Adams. In 1787 revolution swept France—a very different sort from that which had occurred in the American colonies a decade earlier. Not only was the existing form of government, the absolute monarchy of Louis XVI, swept away, but new slogans about revolutionizing the whole of society in the name of

---

[16] With great sympathy for Madison, Richard Hofstadter discussed this intellectual transition in *The Idea of a Party System* (Berkeley: University of California Press, 1969), pp. 82–85.

[17] See William Nisbet Chambers, *Political Parties in a New Nation, 1776–1809* (New York: Oxford University Press, 1963), pp. 53–74.

liberty, equality, and brotherhood, were exported from Paris. Such ideas struck receptive chords in Jefferson and his copartisans. Hamilton, Adams, and the other Federalists, on the other hand, tended to view the French Revolution as a barbaric excess to be regretted by civilized people. They identified the Jeffersonian Republicans as *Francophyles*—literally, "friendly to the French." They were considered if not actively treasonous, then certainly potentially treasonous in their dabbling in revolutionary ideas.

There is irony here, though only superficial. The same Alexander Hamilton who had trained in a militia company at King's College (later Columbia) to resist the British occupation of New York, and the same John Adams who had written brilliantly in defense of home rule for the colonies, were very comfortable in opposing what they saw as foreign subversion of a popularly based government. Apparently, opposing these revolutionary ideas was not at all the same thing as revolting against England.

This conflict in attitude toward one of the most powerful realigning events in modern history deepened the rift between the government and the opposition still further. In 1798, the Adams administration, branding the Republican party as infiltrated with foreigners and illegitimate, moved to prepare to expel French "agents" from the country and to repress "false, scandalous, and malicious" statements against the government.[18] This legislation, known as the **Alien and Sedition acts**, laid the legal foundation for suppression of political opposition.

If the Adams initiative had succeeded, a stable electoral process might never have developed. The reasons it did not succeed are not entirely clear. Perhaps the Federalists, and especially Adams himself, despite their violent anti-French and anti-Jeffersonian rhetoric, were psychologically unprepared to engage in full-scale repression. After all, they all shared generally the Lockean, liberal ideals of the revolutionary and constitutional periods, and simply may have stopped short of widespread jailings of journalists and politicians. Or it might be, as Leonard Levy has suggested, that American ideas concerning free speech were going through an important development in the decade of 1790–1800, and that by the end of that period the climate of opinion simply would not support vigorous enforcement of the new laws.[19] Or it might simply have been that the Jeffersonian opposition had grown too strong.

Whatever the reasons, the effort at repression failed. The Alien and Sedition laws mercifully expired, and within a very few years they came

---

[18] For a detailed description of this sorry episode, see James Morton Smith, *Freedom's Fetters* (Ithaca, N.Y.: Cornell University Press, 1956).

[19] Leonard W. Levy, *Legacy of Suppression* (Cambridge, Mass.: Harvard University Press, 1960).

to be viewed as a symbol of unacceptable governmental interference with the American political process. It is a pleasant irony of our political tradition that this most blatant and serious attempt at political policing developed a "reverse English" that has operated to restrict future leaders. No one would ever ask Congress again for the sort of "blank check" for suppressing opposition that Adams had sought and received.

There is always a great temptation for the government of the founders of a new state to stigmatize opposition as disloyal, to put down the emerging opposition party, and to establish themselves in rule.[20] The number of political systems in which this original ruling elite has peacefully surrendered the positions of governmental authority to an opposition is small indeed. The fact that the Federalists under Adams did ultimately yield some of their authority to the Jeffersonians, after the election of 1800, is of first significance for the development of the nation.

The disintegration of the Federalists The downfall of the Federalist party after 1800 had much to do with the nature of the party. It simply was not "popular." It did not attempt to organize at the grass-roots level. There is no escaping the conclusion that the Federalists, in the aristocratic tradition, regarded appeal to the voters as vulgar and dangerous in the long run. In this sense, the Jeffersonian Republicans were the first modern political party not only in America, but in the world.

Also important to the decline of the Federalists was the demise of Alexander Hamilton. While secretary of the treasury in the early 1790s, Hamilton became involved in a tawdry affair with a high-class whore. The lady, Maria Reynolds, was married to a former Revolutionary War officer, an unscrupulous blackmailer. Once Maria had Hamilton enjoying her favors, her husband, James, moved in and began systematically extorting money from the secretary of the treasury. Hamilton, like a lamb led to the slaughter, continued to see the lady and to pay. James Reynolds, of course, communicated this information to the Jeffersonian opposition. Madison, Jefferson, Monroe, and Burr all became involved in an effort to use Hamilton's embarrassment as a weapon against him, and eventually succeeded in forcing Hamilton's withdrawal from a leading role in politics.

However, the final blow to the Federalists as a party was their abandonment of the nationalist vision—the ideological cement Hamilton had used in building the coalition in the first place. The cause of this turnabout was conflict with Great Britain in the War of 1812, and the embargo on foreign trade that preceded it. Throughout Jefferson's second term and in both of Madison's, the largely Federalist commercial interests of New England felt intolerably victimized by the Republican foreign policy. They

The Alien and Sedition acts have become a symbol of unacceptable governmental interference with the American political system.

One reason for the downfall of the Federalist party is that it made no attempt to organize at the grass-roots level. The Jeffersonian Republicans, on the other hand, appealed to the populace, and in this sense were the first modern political party.

[20] See Chambers, *Political Parties in a New Nation*, pp. 113–126.

began to denounce national power as tyrannical, and to speak increasingly in a states-rights idiom. And in 1815, an unofficial convention of representatives of Federalist towns in New England met at Hartford and called for a revision of the Constitution to *lessen* the power of the national government.

The reversal was fatal. There was nothing left to distinguish Federalists from the antiwar elements within the Republican Party. By 1816, the Federalists were no longer a nationally competitive party, and the Republican coalition swelled to include nearly all serious politicians in the land. It was in this limited sense only that the administration of James Monroe (1817–1825) constituted an "era of good feeling." It was not that political conflict had been eliminated, but that for a brief period it was contained within a bloated coalition still formally referring to itself as Republican.

The second two-party system

The second two-party system was composed of Democrats and Whigs. The Democrats represented the small farmers and the immigrant workers of the cities, while the Whigs were the party of commerce and nationalism.

The result, in hindsight, was inevitable. The swollen Republican party, unable to encompass all of the political divisions within the growing country, finally broke apart into two new party formations. After a period of quickly shifting coalitions, a second two-party system emerged in the 1830s, composed of **Democrats** and **Whigs**. This new alignment was similar in certain respects to that of the Republicans and Federalists, but it differed in others.[21] The Democrats, identified with the towering figure of Andrew Jackson (much as the old Republicans had been with Jefferson), reached out to the small farmers of the rural countryside, and the immigrant workers of the cities. The Whigs were a party of commerce and nationalism, but without the aristocratic cast of the Federalists. Whig leaders such as Henry Clay were quite capable of organizing for democratic electoral politics and reaching out to the expanding electorate. The Whig presidential campaign of 1840 (with the ticket led by General William Henry Harrison and John Tyler—"Tippecanoe and Tyler too!") was a model of loudness, vulgarity, and overstatement ideally suited to the prevailing egalitarian sentiment of the day.

Harrison, a man of very considerable wealth, was presented as a plain son of the frontier living in a log cabin. The opposition Democratic candidate, Martin Van Buren, a man of very modest means, was presented as a champagne-sipping eastern aristocrat![22]

---

[21] See Richard P. McCormick, "Political Development and the Second Party System," in William Nisbet Chambers and Walter Dean Burnham, eds., *The American Party Systems: Stages of Political Development* (New York: Oxford University Press, 1967), pp. 90–116.

[22] Robert G. Gunderson, *The Log Cabin Campaign* (Lexington: University of Kentucky Press, 1957).

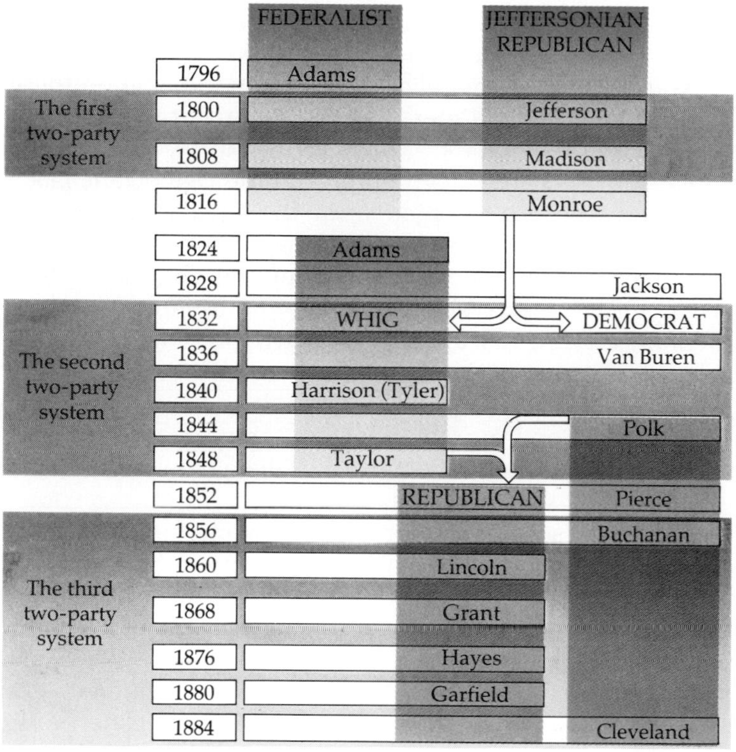

Fig. 3.2
The evolution of political parties in the nineteenth century. American politics has a strong tendency toward two-party alignment. This chart shows, in very simplified form, the development of political parties in the nineteenth century.

The third two-party system

It was the issue of extending slavery into the territories that led to the disintegration of the Whig party. In the 1850s, southern Whig planters ("Cotton Whigs") found it increasingly difficult to make common cause with the northern, antislavery elements of the coalition ("Conscience Whigs").

As the Whigs dissolved into a number of minor, localized parties in the late 1850s, a new coalition emerged. Opposed to extending slavery into the territories and to succession and other extreme states-rights claims by the South, this "Free Soil" party quickly evolved into the new Republican party. The Republicans elected Lincoln in 1860, presided over the war against the rebellious South, and oversaw the attempted "reconstruction" of southern society that followed the war.

The Whig party dissolved over the issue of slavery. In the late 1850s the new Republican party emerged, and elected Abraham Lincoln president.

What is remarkable about this realignment of our political parties is that the Democratic coalition *survived* the traumas of the slavery issue and the Civil War. It is true that the Republicans cut into traditional northern Democratic support among small farmers (getting some, but by no means all). But it is also true that the "ethnic" voters of the North, especially in large cities such as New York, remained faithful to the Democratic label.

The third two-party system emerged from the Civil War with the Republicans enjoying only a slight numerical advantage in the country. The two coalitions remained closely competitive until the election of 1896. In that year the Republicans were able to portray the Democratic candidate, William Jennings Bryan, as a dangerous economic radical. As a result, the Republican party gained a majority position that they held until Franklin Roosevelt's election in 1932. (The Republicans lost the White House to the Democratic Woodrow Wilson in 1912, but only because the party split that year between the candidacies of William Howard Taft and Theodore Roosevelt.)[23]

Since 1932, the Democrats have clearly been the dominant political party in America.

Since 1932, as we shall see in Chapter 5, the electoral fortunes of the Republicans have had their ups and downs. But the pattern has been one of Republican decline, with the Democrats now clearly the dominant coalition and a rapidly growing number who refuse to be identified with either party.[24]

Thus, while *tending* toward a competitive two-party alignment, our party politics have been changing continually. The recent decline in the Republican party and in interest in politics generally may signal the approach of another major change. We will discuss this further in Chapter 5.

EVOLVING FEDERALISM

In Chapter 2 we defined *federalism* as a system in which official power is divided between a central government and multiple provincial governments. These regional governments possess certain inherent powers and are not dependent for their authority to act on the central government (as would be the case in a *unitary* system such as that of Great Britain or France, where the counties and *départements* are created by the national government).

But how powerful was the new United States government to be? And

[23] For the evolution of Republican and Democratic coalitions after the Civil War, see Walter Dean Burnham, *Critical Elections and the Mainsprings of American Politics* (New York: Norton, 1970).

[24] See Norman H. Nie, Sidney Verba, and John R. Petrocik, *The Changing American Voter* (Cambridge: Harvard University Press, 1976), pp. 47–73.

what precisely were the autonomous powers of the states? The Constitution left a lot of room for argument and conflicting interpretation. During the nation's first century, bitter political conflicts developed over clashing conceptions of what the federal relationship was or should be, conflicts that led finally to civil war. It was through struggle that the federalism *evolved* as a system in our history.

Federalism in the Formative Period

From the beginning, Thomas Jefferson's attachment to the new national government was a matter of doubt. During the period of the convention and the ratification debates, Jefferson, as we noted earlier, was abroad. Although kept informed of developments at home, he declined to associate himself with either the supporters or opponents and was surprised by ratification.[25] He was later capable of drafting the extremely antinational Kentucky Resolution of 1798. In office, however, Jefferson did not proceed to dismantle or weaken the central government. In a few respects, the Louisiana Purchase being the outstanding example, he enhanced national power.

But it was the Supreme Court that, during the early nineteenth century, emerged as the principal defender of nationalism.[26] In 1816, in the case of *Martin* v. *Hunter's Lessee*,[27] the Marshall Court asserted the supremacy of the federal judicial decisions over those of the states. And in 1819, in *McCulloch* v. *Maryland*,[28] John Marshall defended the constitutionality of the Bank of the United States. In doing so, he gave an expansive reading to the powers of Congress under Article I, Section 8. The words "necessary and proper," which allowed legislation in exercise of these powers, were not, according to Marshall, to be narrowly interpreted; instead "necessary and proper" should be construed to allow any method appropriate to carrying out one of the enumerated powers of Congress.

While *McCulloch* was undoubtedly the Court's most important contribution to the growth of the power of the national government, the decision five years later in the New York Steamship case *(Gibbons* v. *Ogden)*[29] was also instrumental. In this case, the state of New York had granted a monopoly on steamboat navigation in the state's waters to a company originally headed by Robert Fulton. The steamboats of New Jersey were

---

[25] Robert Hendrickson, *Hamilton II, 1789–1804* (New York: Mason/Charter, 1976), pp. 98–99.

[26] See Leonard D. White, *The Jeffersonians* (New York: Macmillan, 1951).

[27] 1 Wheat. 304 (1816).

[28] 4 Wheat. 316 (1819).

[29] 9 Wheat. 1 (1824).

Fig. 3.3
The Louisiana Purchase and western exploration, 1803–1807. Prior to his election, Thomas Jefferson was known for his antinationalist sentiments. During his administration, however, he made a number of contributions to national power. The most notable of these was the Louisiana purchase, which doubled the size of the country.

barred from New York. Article I, Section 8, conferred on Congress the power to regulate interstate commerce. But what was interstate commerce? And what were the implications for the powers of the states of this grant to Congress?

Marshall's answer to these questions was broadly nationalistic and Hamiltonian: Commerce included the transportation between the states, and even though Congress had not moved to regulate this particular type of commerce, its power was such as to tolerate no interference by the states. The power of Congress, wrote Marshall, extends to "every species of commercial intercourse, . . ."

Along with the power to tax and spend for the general welfare, also included in Article I, Section 8, the commerce power became the opening through which national government eventually moved into nearly every aspect of American life. Beginning in the latter decades of the nineteenth century, and continuing with a rush after 1937, Congress adopted national policies on everything from the minimum wage to the hiring of women and the prohibition of loan sharking. This later extension of the power of central government took place on the foundation laid by Marshall.

At Marshall's death in 1835, President Andrew Jackson nominated Roger B. Taney to succeed him. Taney was a Marylander who had begun life as a Federalist, but whose opinions, by 1830, had taken on a states'-rights cast. For instance, Taney was a staunch opponent of the Bank of the United States—as staunch an opponent as Marshall had been a proponent. There was considerable concern among nationalists that the great achievements of the Marshall Court might be swept away. Daniel Webster wrote that "Judge Storey [Marshall's ablest lieutenant on the Court] thinks the Supreme Court is *gone,* and I think so, too."

But while the Taney Court moderated a few positions taken by the Marshall Court, it did not really alter the strongly nationalistic principles Marshall had imbedded in the structure of constitutional law. In fact, Marshall continued to cast a long shadow over the Court. While he was alive, many regarded Marshall as a bitterly partisan Federalist. In death, he became a secular saint, whose opinions were reverently quoted. As much as Washington or Hamilton, we have him to thank for the creation of a powerful central government.

In the tradition of John Marshall, the Supreme Court has emerged as a staunch defender of nationalism and strong central government.

The Civil War and the "Second American Constitution"

Of all the changes in the government and politics of the United States, from the ratification of the Constitution to the beginning of the modern period, none was more important than the breakdown of politics that led to the Civil War, and the constitutional changes (new basic choices) that came about as a result of that breakdown.

Secession and interposition

Of first importance is the fact that the war settled several basic questions of American federalism. During the years between Philadelphia and Appomattox, the nation had been troubled over the issues of **secession** (whether a state could withdraw from the Union) and **interposition** (whether a state could "interpose" its authority between its citizens and the commands of the national government if it believed those commands to be unconstitutional).

While there is no doubt as to the essentially nationalist disposition of the framers of the Constitution, the text of the document itself does not specifically foreclose on either secession or interposition. These fundamental questions lay unresolved, like submerged logs just below the surface, until the events leading to the Civil War. The issue of secession was settled once and for all by the Supreme Court when, in a famous decision in 1869, it held that the Constitution "looks to an indestructible Union composed of indestructible States."[30] As for interposition, while feeble attempts were made in the years after 1865 to revive this extreme states'-rights position (especially in the school integration struggles of the late 1950s), in practical terms it perished with the Army of Northern Virginia.

Two fundamental constitutional questions—secession and interposition—were settled once and for all by the Civil War.

The antislavery amendments

Just as profound for the future constitutional development of the country were the three constitutional amendments adopted in the immediate post-war period. The reason for these amendments was, of course, to define and protect the status of the newly freed black people of the South. In the first months of peace, the southern states moved quickly to establish so-called black codes, which denied black people state citizenship and other legal rights. Congress, tightly controlled by the more radical elements of the new Republican party, was determined to frustrate this effort and to provide federal protection for the "freedman." The result was the Thirteenth, Fourteenth, and Fifteenth Amendments. The Thirteenth Amendment, ratified in 1865, forbade the existence of slavery and empowered Congress to enforce that constitutional command by legislation. The Fifteenth Amendment, ratified in 1870, provided that the right of citizens to vote could not be denied or abridged by a state on account of race, or color. The most important of the trilogy, however, was the Fourteenth Amendment, ratified in 1868.

The Thirteenth, Fourteenth, and Fifteenth Amendments to the Constitution were designed to define and protect the status of the newly freed black people of the South. These amendments had profound effects on our future constitutional development.

Section 1 of the Fourteenth Amendment established that all persons born and naturalized in the United States are citizens of the United States *and* citizens of the particular states in which they reside. The amendment

[30] *Texas* v. *White* 7 Wallace 700 (1869).

then went on to address prohibitions directly to the states, a fact that is especially significant when one remembers that the prohibitions of the first eight amendments to the Constitution were addressed exclusively to the central government.

First, the states were commanded to make no laws abridging the "privileges or immunities of citizens of the United States; . . ." While seemingly pregnant with possibilities, this command is relatively unimportant. Other than traveling to the nation's capital, the Supreme Court has identified few distinct privileges and immunities connected exclusively with federal citizenship.

Second, however, the states were directed not to "deprive any person of life, liberty, or property, without due process of law; . . ." This proved a provision of mighty importance. As we shall see in Chapter 11, in our discussion of the Supreme Court, this *due-process clause* became a channel through which the specific commands of the first eight amendments eventually were extended to apply to state governments as well. As a national check on the powers of the states, the due-process clause has, in the twentieth century, been the basis for substantial change in the nature of American federalism.

Third, Section 1 of the Fourteenth Amendment commanded the states not to "deny to any person within its jurisdiction equal protection of the laws." This provision proved just as important as the due process clause. In the 1950s and 1960s, the *equal-protection clause* became the constitutional instrument by which the federal courts dismantled the structure of governmental racial segregation and went to to require racial balance in many school districts. It is also used to extend federal guarantees of sexual equality to the states, as we shall see in our discussion of civil liberties in Chapter 14.

Thus federalism, the roughly defined and seemingly fragile arrangement of divided sovereignty as established in 1787, not only survived a bloody conflict over its meaning, but emerged modified and strengthened as well.[31]

Federalism and Industrialization

Coming hard on the adoption of the post–Civil War amendments were certain changes in the American economy and society that placed new strains on the system of federalism, and forced further redefinition of the relationship between the national government and the states.

The 1870s and 1880s saw the American economy transformed from a pattern of small firms and individual manufacturers to one of domination

---

[31] Daniel J. Elazar, "Civil War and the Preservation of American Federalism," *Publius* 1, No. 1: 39–58.

The industrialization of the American economy forced a new relationship between the national government and the states.

by industrial giants. New technologies made possible a very rapid expansion of all industrial sectors, including transportation and manufacturing. The culmination of this was the development of the easily available automobile in the early 1900s.

Americans became much more mobile, and the great population shift from the countryside to the cities and finally the suburbs began. The business of the country, as President Coolidge was later to remark, was business. To build was good and to encourage enterprise was virtuous.

But the benefits of this period of rapid industrialization were not evenly distributed within the population. New waves of immigration from Ireland and from southern and eastern Europe provided bodies for the industrial labor force, but these people were poorly compensated and often worked in unhealthy and unnecessarily dangerous conditions. On the eve of the Civil War, America was a predominantly middle-class agrarian nation. By the opening of the twentieth century, it was a vastly richer industrial country, but with a large and very poor working class. In short, industrialization brought serious social costs and human suffering. There was mounting pressure for the national government to act to regulate the economic giants and improve some of the harsher conditions of economic growth. To do this, however, required further modification of the federal system, resulting in a vast extension of national power into areas previously reserved for the states.

In the first decades of the twentieth century, the Supreme Court, constitutional umpire of federalism, refused to make such modifications. Federal laws on such matters as regulating monopolies and banning child labor ran into trouble with the justices. Where the Marshall Court expanded national power, the Court under Chief Justices Fuller, White, and Taft was grudging as to further expansion.

The crisis came with the great economic depression of the 1930s and the accession to the presidency of Franklin Roosevelt. Armed with a popular mandate to use the central government to improve the economy, Roosevelt found himself hamstrung by the Court's insistence on traditional delimitations of federalism. The way in which the Court came to change its course in 1937 is treated in Chapter 11; here we will point out simply that the result was a modification of federalism as important as those effected by John Marshall's early landmark decisions and by the Civil War.

What emerged was a much larger and more important national government, which now interacts with the states and local government in a flexible, freewheeling fashion that would have been unimaginable fifty years ago. The states and localities remain important, vigorous governments, but much regulation and innovation is now undertaken directly by "the feds." The description of contemporary American federalism by Morton Grodzins (see box) is one of the best ever written.

"The American form of government is often, but erroneously, symbolized by a three-layer cake. A far more accurate image is the rainbow or marble cake, characterized by an inseparable mingling of differently colored ingredients, the colors appearing in vertical and diagonal strands and unexpected whirls. As colors are mixed in the marble cake, so functions are mixed in the American federal system. Consider the health officer, styled "sanitarian," of a rural county in a border state. He embodies the whole idea of the marble cake of government.

"The sanitarian is appointed by the state under merit standards established by the federal government. His base salary comes jointly from state and federal funds, the county provides him with an office and office amenities and pays a portion of his expenses, and the largest city in the county also contributes to his salary and office by virtue of his appointment as a city plumbing inspector. It is impossible from moment to moment to tell under which governmental hat the sanitarian operates. His work of inspecting the purity of food is carried out under federal standards; but he is enforcing state laws when inspecting commodities that have not been in interstate commerce; and somewhat perversely he also acts under state authority when inspecting milk coming into the county from producing areas across the state border. He is a federal officer when impounding impure drugs shipped from a neighboring state; a federal-state officer when distributing typhoid immunization serum; a state officer when enforcing standards of industrial hygiene; a state-local officer when inspecting the city's water supply; and (to complete the circle) a local officer when insisting that the city butchers adopt more hygienic methods of handling their garbage. But he cannot and does not think of himself as acting in these separate capacities. All business in the county that concerns public health and sanitation he considers his business. Paid largely from federal funds, he does not find it strange to attend meetings of the city council to give expert advice on matters ranging from rotten apples to rabies control. He is even deputized as a member of both the city and county police forces.

"The sanitarian is an extreme case, but he accurately represents an important aspect of the whole range of governmental activities in the United States. Functions are not neatly parceled out among the many governments. They are shared functions."

* From Morton Grodzins, "The Federal System," in Aaron Wildavsky, ed., *American Federalism in Perspective* (Boston: Little, Brown, 1967), p. 257. Reprinted by permission.

The Governmental Rainbow

EXPANDING DEMOCRACY AND INDIVIDUAL RIGHTS

The dictionary defines *democracy* as "power exercised by the people." But according to this simple definition, no large, modern nation could possibly be democratic. The "people" (if the population is large) cannot exercise governmental power themselves—they must *authorize* a relative few to exercise power *over them*. This is the basis of the representative or **indirect democracy** that the framers built into the national Constitution. And despite the experiments of some of the states from time to time with direct democracy (the device of the **referendum**—putting a particular policy issue up to popular vote—is a way of actually allowing the people to decide on a particular issue), the indirect democracy remains the general rule throughout the United States.

But who shall vote for officeholders? And which of these shall be elected directly and which indirectly? Initially, these questions were answered quite conservatively by the framers. But in Chapter 2 we noted a radical impulse (stressing equality in political participation), which had flourished during the revolutionary years but diminished during the 1780s. This impulse flowered again in the 1830s, becoming known as **Jacksonian democracy**.

The Democratic Surge

We have seen how the framers carefully adjusted the machinery of the national government so as to balance democratic elements with aristocratic elements. However, one important element in the operation of the government that was left entirely up to the states was the question of the extent of the **franchise**—the right to vote. And through the critical formative period from 1790 to 1801, these states slowly but surely broadened the electorate. Property qualifications, which in 1790 barred many, if not most, adult males from the ballot box, were reduced and in some cases eliminated. It was this broadened electorate to which the Jeffersonian Republicans with their electioneering and local societies reached out.

One reason for the speed and force of democratization during the revolutionary decade was that the American Tories (those who remained loyal to the English crown) were forced to leave the country in large numbers. These were precisely the sort of local power holders who could have been counted on to support the Federalist party in the 1790s and oppose in their respective states the extension of the franchise. In addition to sharply reducing the numbers of such people in the new nation, their expulsion also had the effect of making a considerable amount of land and property available to humbler men who had been supporters of the revolutionary cause. Thus, expulsion and expropriation created a precondition favorable to democratization and unfavorable to the survival of the Federalist party, no matter how brilliant its leaders.

The democratizing trend begun in the 1790s picked up momentum in the first three decades of the nineteenth century. Between 1816 and 1821, six new states entered the Union—Indiana, Illinois, Mississippi, Alabama,

One of the great battles of Andrew Jackson's political life was against the institution of the second bank of the United States, which Jackson, who styled himself a man of the people, saw as the instrument of an exploitive financial elite. Whigs, on the other hand, saw the bank as a necessary institution in the development of a productive economy in a wealthy nation. This cartoon shows Jackson as the victim of an antibank nightmare. Downing, representing the public, tries to haul him back to bed by his suspenders. The cartoon appeared when people were tired of the bank war.

Missouri, and Maine. All of their constitutions provided for universal white male suffrage.[32]

Other factors also operated during the early nineteenth century to democratize the new national political process. First, the population steadily increased. Thus, as qualifications for franchise diminished, there were more and more white males around to become voters. Second, more and more of the states were adopting the practice of electing the presidential electors directly. As a result, one of the most important checks on democracy built into the Constitution by the framers was being overridden in political practice. The framers had conceived of the electoral college as a coming together of leading figures from the states to *deliberate* on the choice of the president. How these electors were to be chosen was left altogether to the states. When the states chose electors, the elector became a simple arithmetical unit rather than a statesman making a choice.

An increasing voting population, an evolving electoral system, and changes in the method of choosing presidential candidates were among many contributors to the democratization of the American political process.

Another sure mark of increasing democratization was a change in the way in which presidential candidates were selected. In the first few decades after the adoption of the Constitution, candidates were chosen by party caucus within Congress. The Republican senators and representatives decided on a national standard bearer and the Federalists likewise.

But by the mid-1820s, pressures were building for broader participation in the nominating process. State and even local politicians were less and less satisfied to participate only indirectly through their congressional copartners. "King Caucus" came in for more and more criticism.

By 1832 the major candidates were nominated by "public national conventions."[33] These nominating conventions represented a much more open forum than the congressional caucus, but the evolution was, and is, incomplete. By the twentieth century, the convention has come to be supplanted in some states by direct presidential primaries for choosing or instructing delegates to the conventions. And in Chapter 6 we shall examine arguments for replacing the conventions altogether with a national presidential primary.

Many more examples of progressive democratization remain: the direct election of senators (Amendment Seventeen in 1913); the enfranchisement of women (Amendment Nineteen in 1920); and the eighteen-year-old vote (Amendment Twenty-six in 1971). So while some of the aspects of the "mixed government" envisioned by the framers remain, successive generations of Americans have, for better or worse, extensively modified the "original choice" made at Philadelphia.

---

[32] See Merrill D. Peterson, ed., *Democracy, Liberty, and Property* (Indianapolis, Ind.: Bobbs-Merrill, 1966), p. xv.

[33] Paul T. David, Ralph M. Goldman, and Richard C. Bain, *The Politics of National Party Conventions* (New York: Vintage Books, 1964), p. 40.

The Bill of Rights

Another aspect of democracy is the protection of individual rights and of minorities from majority tyranny. Here as well, important changes and developments came *after* the ratification of the Constitution, and have continued throughout history.

One of the principal criticisms made by critics of the proposed constitution (in 1787) was the absence of a bill of rights—a set of specific restraints on the power of the new central government. This, the anti-Federalists suggested, would protect both the liberties of the people and the integrity of the state governments.

The Bill of Rights set specific restraints on the power of the new central government. It was designed to protect both the liberties of the people and the integrity of state governments against the new national government.

Although a few of the framers (Hamilton, for instance) initially resisted this suggestion, arguing that such a bill of restraints was not necessary, supporters of the Constitution quickly bowed before the demand for a bill of rights. By the time the ninth state (New Hampshire) ratified, there was widespread agreement that a first order of business for the new Congress would be to propose to the states certain limiting amendments to the original charter.

The leading role in advocating the amendments was taken by James Madison, then at mid-passage in his ideological voyage from nationalism to states-rights-fundamentalism.

The First Amendment, familiar to us all today and destined to become a symbol of American liberty, forbade Congress from interfering with freedom of religion or of speech. Its interpretation by the Supreme Court in the twentieth century has been and continues to be a matter of heated political controversy, as we shall see in Chapters 11 and 14.

It is interesting to note that the First Amendment, by its own language, applies only to the national government. The Senate rejected a proposal that would have commanded that no state interfere with freedom of speech. (This congressional decision of 1790 was to be reversed in 1925, when the Supreme Court extended the First Amendment speech guarantee to the states.[34]) Also, it was proposed by the House, but rejected by the Senate, that the First Amendment exempt conscientious objectors from military service. In the mid-twentieth century such exemption would be provided for by an act of Congress that was in turn generously interpreted by the Supreme Court.[35]

The second of the amendments, while of little significance throughout most of our history, has lately become the focus of controversy. "A well-regulated militia, being necessary to the security of a free state, the right of the people to keep and bear arms shall not be infringed." In the next

[34] *Gitlow* v. *New York*, 268 U.S. 652 (1925).

[35] *U.S.* v. *Seeger*, 380 U.S. 163 (1965).

chapter we examine the savage political infighting that now swirls around the issue of gun control. One dimension of this controversy is the question as to whether the Second Amendment creates an individual right to bear arms or only that of organized state and military forces (then called the Militia, now called the National Guard).

Amendments Three and Four were addressed to particular outrages suffered by the American colonists in the period leading up to the break with Britain in 1776. The Third Amendment prohibits the quartering of soldiers in homes without the consent of the owner, and has not been of significance in our later national development. The Fourth Amendment, by contrast, protects "the right of the people to be secure in their persons, houses, papers, and effects, against unreasonable searches and seizures. . . ." This provision constitutes a substantial limitation on police practices, and in the mid-twentieth century was extended by the Supreme Court to apply to the states.

Amendments Five through Eight guaranteed certain rights to citizens accused of federal crimes. Of particular importance, especially after the Supreme Court extended these guarantees to the states, are the protection against self-incrimination in Amendment Five, the guarantee of trial by jury and assistance of counsel in Amendment Six, and the protection against unreasonable searches and seizures in Amendment Four. Amendments Nine and Ten have never been of much legal significance. They are, however, from time to time, invoked in political debate and occasionally referred to in the Supreme Court's opinions to enhance arguments that rest (supposedly) on other specifics of the Constitution.

SUMMARY

In this chapter we have focused on certain important changes and developments in the American political system that took place in the formative period of 1788–1800, and followed certain of these processes of change through to the twentieth century.

The initial development of our major national institutions was described—the presidency, the Congress, the Supreme Court, the bureaucracy, and political parties. We are now ready to examine the contemporary functioning of each.

The evolution of American federalism has been briefly traced, and in the chapters that follow we shall often have occasion to note the complicated ways in which state and local levels are intertwined with "the feds" in the governing of America.

Finally, we examined the way in which democratic participation expanded in the early nineteenth century and the way in which certain individual rights came to be secured by the Bill of Rights. In Chapters 11 and 14 we will return to the Bill of Rights and study the changes it has recently undergone, and certain choices facing the Supreme Court in defining its meaning for the future.

KEY TERMS

Whisky Rebellion
crisis of legitimacy
institutionalization
bureaucracy
committee system
judicial review
Marbury v. *Madison*
Federalists
anti-Federalists
agrarianism
Jeffersonian Republicans

Alien and Sedition acts
Democrats
Whigs
McCulloch v. *Maryland*
secession
interposition
due-process clause
equal-protection clause
industrialization
indirect democracy
franchise

SUGGESTED READINGS

BINKLEY, WINFRED E., *American Political Parties: This Natural History*, 4th ed. (New York: Knopf, 1964).

A standard treatment of the evolution of political parties in the United States.

BINKLEY, WINFRED E., *President and Congress* (New York: Knopf, 1947).

An excellent treatment of the varying conceptions of the presidency in American political development. Available in paperback.

CHAMBERS, WILLIAM NISBET, *Political Parties in a New Nation* (New York: Oxford University Press, 1963).

A brilliant treatment of the development of the first two-party system in America. Available in paperback.

ELAZAR, DANIEL J., *American Federalism: A View from the States* (New York: Crowell, 1966).

A good study of federalism in America, with emphasis on directions of change.

LEVY, LEONARD W., ed., *Judicial Review and the Supreme Court* (New York: Harper & Row, 1967).

A collection of excellent essays on the history, evolution, and contemporary practice of judicial review by the Supreme Court.

LIPSET, SEYMOUR MARTIN, *The First New Nation* (New York: Basic Books, 1963).

This is a very provocative analysis of the formative period of American institutions. Highly recommended.

MASON, ALPHEUS T., *The States Rights Debate: Antifederalism and the Constitution* (Englewood Cliffs, N.J.: Prentice-Hall, 1964).

A study of the roots of American federalism from the late colonial period to the adoption of the Bill of Rights.

PART II POLITICS AND SOCIETY

The public! The public! How many fools
does it take to make up a public?

Chamfort

Democracy is based upon the conviction
that there are extraordinary possibilities in
ordinary people.

H. E. Fosdick

The public! why, the public's no better
than a great baby.

Thomas Chalmers

All the ills of democracy can be cured by
more democracy.

Alfred E. Smith

CHAPTER 4 PUBLIC OPINION AND INTEREST GROUPS

It is mid-1975.

There is a bill before the United States Senate that would permit a single striking union to close down an entire construction project no matter how many other, nonstriking unions were involved. Called the **Common Situs** bill, it stirs intense debate in Washington. Organized labor, particularly the AFL-CIO, lists it as a major priority and urges that it be passed. Organized business, particularly the National Chamber of Commerce and the construction industry, feels that the bill is nothing less than a national disaster.

Both sides bring considerable pressure to bear. Letters are written to members of Congress. Phone calls are generated. Campaign contributions are offered. Past campaign contributions are brought to the senators' attention. Threats of opposition in the next election are heard. Delegations from labor and business groups pay frequent visits to the individual senators. Sometimes calmly, sometimes with great agitation, sometimes even with threats, both sides try to make sure their wishes are heeded. By the time the vote approaches, the pressures on uncommitted senators are intense.

Let us say you are an uncommitted senator. There is no place for you to hide. This is not an issue where you can "waffle," or come down a little on both sides. You have to vote yes or no (or abstain and be blamed by both sides). Either you are in favor of the bill or you are against it. Either way, you are bound to irritate a powerful political force. Unlike members of Congress, who may represent districts that are substantially for or against labor unions, senators represent larger constituencies with both groups well represented.

Would you vote on the basic principles involved?

Would you vote on the basis of the likely impact, positive and negative, on our national society and economy? On your state's society and economy?

Would you vote the way labor wanted you to?

Would you vote the way business wanted you to?

Would you carefully weigh your chances for reelection in light of how the people felt in your state?

Or would you, as one prominent senator did, take a step back. Tired of trying to see the political consequences of his vote, tired of being badgered by both groups, he summoned his legislative assistant and, throwing up his hands in frustration and irritation, exclaimed,

"What the hell, I'm just going to vote my conscience."

To most Americans, Common Situs was an unknown issue in 1976. To many other Americans, whatever their feelings on other public issues, Common Situs was thought to be of little consequence, falling far down on their list of priorities. Yet to some Americans this was an issue of enormous consequence, or so representatives of labor and business claimed. For some, Common Situs meant more power for the working person; for others, a severe curtailment of private enterprise; and for some small and medium-sized construction firms, possibly the end of their existence.

How can this be? How can an issue that is so important to some segments of the American public be ignored by others? More important, since this is only one issue among many, how can it be dealt with by the political system? How are the wishes, hopes, and demands of 220 million Americans achieved through the political process?

In Chapters 2 and 3, we traced the development of the American political system from its small-scale beginnings to its present sprawling complexity and gigantic size. In this chapter, we seek to examine the elusive something called "public opinion," to see what it is and how it influences the political process. We also examine the segments of organized public opinion known as interest groups, and suggest what they do in our society, and how they affect the political process.

As we examine these aspects of American politics, we shall be touching on fundamental questions about the rights of individuals and of groups in a free and democratic society. We shall be looking at conflicting demands and the competing pressures they create within the political system. Between the relative apathy of many Americans on most issues (or most Americans on many issues) and the frenzy of intense concern over controversial issues, there remains a working system of politics based on majority rule. Yet how this majority will can be ascertained is quite another matter.

"PUBLIC OPINION"

What is **public opinion**? The respected political scientist V. O. Key perhaps put it best when he noted that public opinion consists of "those opinions held by private persons which governments find it prudent to heed."[1] In other words, relevant public opinion is that which has some influence on policy-makers within the government. If a person in Tennessee is unhappy that the weather is too hot in August, this opinion is of little consequence for the conduct of government. This same citizen's concern about government regulation of the tobacco industry, however, may have more relevance, depending on a number of other factors.

But how much relevance, of course, depends on the *intensity* with which the opinion is held and the number of people holding that opinion,

Public opinion consists of those opinions that have some influence on government policy-makers. How much influence depends on the intensity of the opinion, the number of people holding the opinion, and where these people are located in the social structure.

[1] V. O. Key, Jr., *Public Opinion and American Democracy* (New York: Knopf, 1961), p. 14.

Public opinion is made up of many individual opinions. How does one distill these into one "public opinion"?

as well as where they are located within the social structure. We shall be dealing with these aspects—as well as the complicated notion of how to measure public opinion (no matter how defined)—in a later section. But first, we will attempt to define what public opinion is.

For Key, there is a difference between the mythical Public Opinion often referred to by politicians and the media ("The people want price controls"), and the actual sets of different public opinions. In truth, except for the tiniest, small-scale communities, an organic agreement, a single public opinion, is impossible. There are only the opinions of a variety of special "publics."[2] And this of course makes sense. There is not one American, but many. There are millions of Americans who live in rural areas, millions more who live in cities. There are Americans who work for a living, there are those who do not. There are Americans who are black and white and brown. There are Americans who are economically "poor" and those who are economically "well off." Some are religious, some are not. There are 220 million of us spread across a huge continent, coming from a vast variety of backgrounds. We want different and often conflicting things, and because of our different wants we perceive events differently. This is precisely why choice is the essence of government—to respond to the "want" of one group is to ignore another.

America is a complex culture. The more than fifty million people who have immigrated to this country since 1820 have brought with them ideas, attitudes, and cultural heritages from the far corners of the earth.[3] From the boatloads of early English pilgrims in the 1600s to the hundreds of thousands of Vietnamese refugees in 1975–1977, these people have come to America seeking a better life while bringing with them attitudes and skills from their native lands. Moreover, despite many claims to the contrary, it now appears that many ethnic groups were not as completely blended and homogenized as had once been assumed.[4]

What is an American? Boyd Schaefer suggests, "Nationalism is a set of learned responses."[5] We are not born an American—or Chinese, or Russian—we are made into one. This process is called **political socialization**.

Diversity remains an intrinsic, fundamental part of American life. The various public opinions are shaped by several powerful influences—the home, church, schools, the media, and people's life experiences. Amid this diversity there is something that can be called an *American culture*, a set of common experiences with which most of us can identify. Though the 1970s and 1980s have witnessed divergent life-styles and "counter-culture" responses, movies, cars, television, and McDonald's hamburgers remain as intrinsic parts of the American life. Therefore, on a variety of levels and in a certain materialistic sense, millions share a common experience. Holiday Inns boast of providing "no surprises" to the American family who travels from coast to coast (and even throughout the world).

Diversity is a fundamental aspect of American life. Amid this diversity, however, there is an American culture, a set of common experiences with which most of us can identify.

---

[2] See the various essays in Norman Luttberg, ed., *Public Opinion and Public Policy: Models of Political Linkage* (Homewood, Ill.: Dorsey Press, 1968).

[3] Oscar Handlin, *The Uprooted* (New York: Grosset and Dunlap, 1951).

[4] Michael Novak, *The Rise of the Unmeltable Ethnics: Politics and Culture in the Seventies* (New York: Collier Macmillan, 1971). See also Nathan Glazer and Daniel P. Moynihan, *Beyond the Melting Pot* (Cambridge, Mass.: MIT Press, 1963).

[5] Boyd Schaefer, *Nationalism and Beyond* (New York: Harcourt, 1955).

A Burger King is made of the same ingredients and tastes the same whether sold in Nome, Alaska, or Washington, D.C. Texaco gasoline, in and of itself, may not be recognizable to most Americans, but the Texaco logo and "the man who wears the star" are.

In addition to the interactions among the various factors making for diversity and those making for commonality, between differing heritages and common experiences, between the present realities and future (or past) dreams, there are many other forces at work on individual Americans and their political system.

Now, in some sense, the way in which our political process works depends on such gross features as the diversity and range of backgrounds, hopes, and achievements of so many different Americans. When students read in political science or political philosophy textbooks about alternative political forms, it is easy to gain the impression that any political system can be superimposed on any society, that people are always free to pick a particular political system.

This impression is probably incorrect. People, at least in the abstract, may be able to choose what sort of economic arrangements they want or what kind of ideology they wish to pursue. But once having chosen these goals, they cannot have any sort of *politics* they want. Politics can affect society, economics, and even, perhaps, basic beliefs. But politics is, itself, to some extent a contingent activity, that is, dependent on the society in which it takes place. In Chapter 6, we shall be looking at the economic and social contexts as they influence elections. Here, we are concerned with looking at the ways groups of people, through interest-group activity and the expression of the public opinions outlined above, influence the course of their lives. These societal aspects will be dealt with before we look at the precise ways individuals try to make their voices heard.

Views of Society

Given the diverse nature of American society and the great variety of American public opinions, it is natural that conflicts of interest arise. Clearly, assembly-line workers at General Motors view the minimum-wage figures differently from their counterparts in management, who see job performance in terms of keeping costs down and profits high. The baker who employs three people in Peoria, Illinois, may look with hatred on yet another set of federal forms designed to ensure that rolls and bread are of uniform standards throughout the United States. How people try to influence the political system is based on a number of individual factors, but in part is a result of how they view society. Not surprisingly, social scientists, in attempting to describe what kind of society America "really" is, tend to assert that it is "democratic" and that "the people" rule.

C. WRIGHT MILLS

ELITIST MODEL

America is run by a small group of people who control economic, political, and military power.

Fig. 4.1
Projected models of American society.

ROBERT DAHL

PLURALIST MODEL

Power is dispersed throughout American society, with a variety of groups influencing public policy.

THEODORE J. LOWI

COMBINED MODEL

American society has pluralistic elements, but some groups are more equal than others, giving society an unbalanced if not totally elitist cast.

There are three major schools concerning what American society is "really" like. The **elitist model** suggests that America is really run by a small group of people. These are the people who control economic, political, and military power. C. Wright Mills and G. William Domhoff, for example, argue that individual citizens lack control over their lives, and that members of a small elite make the basic political and economic decisions that affect all Americans.[6] Thus, for them, America is an organized hierarchy, with power coming from the top leaders (the elite) and going down to the rest of society (the nonleaders).

Many political scientists find this view too simplistic. They see political and economic power in the United States as being widely diffused and dispersed throughout the society. The political system is essentially *pluralistic*, with a variety of groups actively influencing public policy. Robert Dahl and David Truman feel that despite "blockages" and "bottlenecks," leaders of the country are responsive to the nonleaders.[7] Adherents to the

[6] C. Wright Mills, *The Power Elite* (London: Oxford University Press, 1956) and G. William Domhoff, *Who Rules America?* (Englewood Cliffs, N.J.: Prentice-Hall, 1967).

[7] Robert Dahl, *Who Governs?* (New Haven, Conn.: Yale University Press, 1961) and David Truman, *The Governmental Process* (New York: Knopf, 1958).

pluralist model have been accused, by E. E. Schattschneider among others, of illustrating the very upper-class bias that some earlier writers accused the entire society of displaying.[8]

There are three major views of American society. The elitist view suggests that America is controlled by a small group of powerful people. The pluralistic view feels the power is dispersed throughout society, with many groups influencing public policy. The third view is that American society and politics combine elements found in both the elitist and pluralist interpretations.

Still others say that neither the pluralist nor the elitist views in and of themselves tell the whole story. Theodore J. Lowi, for example, asserts that while the pluralist point of view is correct to the extent that American society is made up of many diverse groups with many conflicting options and goals, it is incorrect in its assertion that these various groups are equally effective. For Lowi, society has pluralist elements, but the elements have different degrees of political impact. Nonwhites, the poor, the less well educated, and many other groups are simply not able to compete in the policy-making process with other more powerful groups. Some groups are more "equal" than others and this gives American society an unbalanced if not totally elitist cast.[9] Yet Lowi also argues that in the American political system, government as we know it cannot function without the interaction of various interest groups.[10]

[8] E. E. Schattschneider, *The Semi-Sovereign People* (New York: Holt, Rinehart and Winston, 1960).

[9] See Theodore Lowi, *The End of Liberalism* (New York: Norton, 1969) and William E. Connolly, *The Bias of Pluralism* (New York: Atherton Press, 1969).

[10] Theodore J. Lowi, "American Business, Public Policy: Case Studies and Political Theory" *World Politics* VI (July 1964): 677–715.

Ralph Nader wields enormous influence in the name of the public good. Does he really represent the public interest?

The thousands of issues that arise within the political system, the diverse views of our citizenry, and the intermingling of class, ethnic, and geographical factors do suggest that American society and politics combine elements found in *both* the elitist and pluralist interpretations. Certainly American society is pluralistic enough so that those citizens who wish to participate in politics or in the influencing of political decisions can do so by joining with others of similar persuasion in interest groups or in political-party activity. But it seems foolish to argue that whatever pluralistic characteristics American society exhibits, there are not certain people who, by their wealth, position, or expertise, influence the course of political events. Nelson Rockefeller probably would not have been such a central figure for three decades had he been living on sales clerk's wages. Nor would his brother, David, who has not held public office. On the other hand, Ralph Nader is probably more "influential" in terms of policy-making than some millionaires or thousands of socially prominent people. Also, why should policy-makers care what people who don't care think?

Whichever view one takes of society, within the public at large there are certain people who are **opinion-makers**. This is as true in politics as it is in fashion or theater reviewing: Certain individuals carry more weight with their peers. In Chapter 6, we shall be looking at one category of opinion-maker, the candidate for office. In Chapter 7, we shall examine the role of another group of opinion-makers, members of the national and local media. In this chapter we are not concerned with particular types of opinion-makers. Rather, we are attempting to answer the following questions:

1. How do public opinions affect the political process?
2. How do individuals join with other individuals with similar interests and preferences to form an interest group?
3. What are the major interest groups that currently affect our lives and that are most likely to influence them in the future?
4. What are the limits on interest-group activity; should these limits be increased or decreased?

In the discussion and analysis that follows, the underlying theme will be the role of public opinion in policy formation.

Public Opinion and Politics

Let us assume that you represent a congressional district in Connecticut that includes about 700,000 people. Let us also assume that you are not interested in leading your **constituents**—the people you represent—toward any particular goal, and that you are not overly concerned with reelection. You simply want to represent the people to the best of your ability. You want to vote for measures that the majority favor and against those the majority oppose.

These are, of course, large assumptions, but let us just say for the moment that you are there, an ideal and well-intentioned representative, who is anxious to do the people's bidding.

How do you find out what that bidding is? As Richard E. Dawson and others have suggested, it is very difficult to actually reflect the diversity of opinions in even a small political universe such as yours.[11]

Do you listen to the people who call you on the telephone? If you do, then you are not listening to those who do not call you, either because they do not know your telephone number or because they do not want to spend the money or because they do not want to take up your time, assuming (quite rightly, perhaps) that you have better things to do.

Do you listen to the people you meet when you return home to your district? If so, then you are not listening to the vast majority of your constituents whom you do not encounter in a weekend of public events—those who stay at home, those who live at the other end of your district, those who see you but would not want to give you their opinion in public.

Do you pay attention to your mail? If so, how? Do you count the letters for and against a particular bill? Do you discount the intensity of feeling for or against an issue in order to count simply the volume of letters? If so, you may be ignoring the vast majority of your constituents who never write you letters or feel so excited they cannot calm themselves enough to commit their emotions to paper.

What about **polling**? Since the methods described above are likely to be unscientific and are not likely to let you determine with assurance exactly what the majority of your constituents actually believe on a given issue, why not just conduct a series of polls to determine how you will vote?

Most people seem to have a bias against polls, feeling either that they do not work or that their results are suspect. Widespread polling was initiated in the United States in the 1930s, when George Gallup formed the American Institute of Public Opinion (AIPO). Gallup was joined by a number of other famous polling operations, such as Elmo Roper and his Roper Survey, Louis Harris and his Harris Survey, and the University of Michigan's Survey Research Center. Since then, polling has been the subject of recurring controversy.

Over the years, polling has become more refined and sophisticated. Now, with the use of computers, polls have come to have, if properly

---

[11] Richard E. Dawson, *Public Opinion and Contemporary Disarray* (New York: Harper & Row, 1973).

done, considerable predictive value. Still, many people ask, how can the pollster, by questioning 600–800 voters in a state, predict how two million voters react? Can a sample of 1,600–2,000 people interviewed throughout the United States actually reflect the sentiments of 220 million Americans?

The fact is that the best polling firms, using carefully worded questionnaires and proper techniques, may predict with reasonable accuracy the opinions of the public. "Reasonable accuracy," of course, depends on what you want to know. There are five major "ifs" associated with polling that drastically affect the accuracy of the results—these are sample size, timing, sample makeup, the nature of the questions, and cost.

If properly done, polls can predict the opinions of a selected group with reasonable accuracy.

Sample size

The first major "if" associated with polling is the size of the sample. In a "universe" of one million people, a proper sample of 600 will yield a sampling error of plus or minus 5 percent. So if you asked the people of southern Illinois whether they preferred nuclear power to higher electrical bills and the answer came back 40 percent yes, 35 percent no, and 25 percent undecided, you could not be sure the high electrical bill side was ahead. This, then, would be an opinion "too close to call." With a sample of 300 you raise the sample error possibility to 6 percent, and with a sample of 200, it increases to 7 percent.

The size of the sample is an important factor in the accuracy of a poll.

On the other hand, if you wanted to find out whether the people in your district favored federal aid to parochial schools, and the result came back 75 percent yes, 20 percent no, and 5 percent undecided, you could be quite sure that a majority of people in your district favored such a course of action. You might or might not have reached the same conclusion from your mail and district visits.

Timing

A second major "if" associated with polling is the timing of the polltaking operation. Polls do not tell you what is going to happen. In fact, they do not even tell you what is happening at the moment you are reading them. They can tell you only what happened at the time the poll was taken. Therefore, polling data can become outdated if public opinion is changing. Many of the celebrated polling failures can be traced to changes in public opinion that took place following the actual interviews. Given the fact that a major poll involving 600 interviews may take a week or more and the computer analysis an equal amount of time, the situation may already have changed by the time you get the results to read. Public opinion on most issues does not change that rapidly, however, and a series of polls taken at, say, monthly intervals, should give you a good sense of which way public opinion is moving—if in fact it is moving at all.

Timing is also a key to a poll's accuracy. Polling data can become outdated if public opinion is changing.

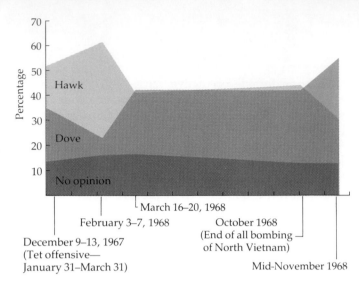

Fig. 4.2
The decline in American support that accompanied the deterioration of our war efforts in Vietnam, showing the effect of timing on poll taking. (Source: Charles W. Roll, Jr. and Albert H. Cartrid, *Polls: Their Use and Misuse in Politics* (New York: Basic Books, 1972.)

March 16–20, 1968

February 3–7, 1968

October 1968
(End of all bombing of North Vietnam)

December 9–13, 1967
(Tet offensive—
January 31–March 31)

Mid-November 1968

Dates of interviewing

Sample makeup

A third major "if" associated with polling, and perhaps the most important one in terms of accuracy, is the makeup of the voter sample. More critical than the number of people interviewed is the nature of the people interviewed. If your pollster called 600 people and 375 of them were senior citizens, the answers you received concerning their opinions on free prescription drugs for those over 65, or free college tuition for all wishing to go to college, would be heavily weighted, or slanted, in terms of the interests of this particular population group.

Therefore, it is vital that any polling sample accurately represent the **demographic** makeup of the population in your district. If 17 percent of the people in your district are over sixty-five, then the sample should have 17 percent of the respondents from this group. Likewise, you would want to have other age, sex, and ethnic groupings well represented in terms of their actual portion of the population. If you represented a district with a large number of union members you would want them accurately represented; the same would hold true for other income categories.

> The polling sample must accurately reflect the demographic makeup of the population.

It is not necessary that the actual sample correspond exactly to the demographic pattern as long as the end product is made statistically accurate. In other words, if your sample consists of only 15 percent senior citizen responses while the actual population is 17 percent, you can weight the 15 percent by adding an additional 2 percent to the final outcome. This matching of responses with the actual population "grid" or mix is very important if your polling results are to accurately represent the population whose opinions you are sampling. The Arab-Israeli conflict is of critical concern to many Americans, but of greater concern to American Jews than to American Indians. Depending on the relative number of each in your district, you will want to make sure the proper number of each is asked the questions.

The nature of the questions

A fourth major "if" associated with polling is the questions themselves. Some questions are easy to understand and ask. For example, you might be interested in knowing whether or not your constituents think President Carter is doing a good job. You could phrase the question as follows: "Do you approve or disapprove of the job President Carter is doing?" This question would likely give you a more accurate set of answers than if you asked: "Considering all the wonderful things he promised, don't you think President Carter is not doing as good a job as he should?"

Or, if you were interested in finding out how a majority of your constituents felt about a proposed dam, you would want to say, "Do you favor the building of the Cherokee dam?" rather than, "Do you favor the building of the Cherokee dam, which will flood 54,000 acres of our precious state and cost a billion dollars?" In other words, polls are not designed to educate the public or to give them your views on issues, but to find out the public's views on the issues; consequently, you do not want to "skew," or slant, the answers in one direction or another (although you may want to skew your own answer the next time you answer positively on the question of the Cherokee dam after finding that 65 percent of your constituents oppose it and only 15 percent favor it).

The questions asked in a poll must be carefully worded so that they do not slant the answers in one direction or another.

Also, if the issues are complex (such as welfare or tax reform), it is imperative that a series of carefully worded questions be asked. For example, in an extensive poll conducted by CBS news for the *New York Times* in 1977, 58 percent of the respondents said they disapproved of "most government-sponsored welfare programs." But when the pollsters went on to ask about a package of programs falling in the area of human welfare, a majority of the people approved of most of them. Thus, many were hostile to welfare as a concept but approved what it does.

Likewise, throughout the United States, if you ask people, "Do you favor property-tax reform?" a majority in most locations are likely to answer, "yes." But if you then ask, "In order to lower the property tax it is necessary to raise one of the following taxes; do you approve or disapprove?" a majority will oppose increasing the income tax, the sales tax, and most other taxes, leaving the representative to conclude that people really do not want property tax reform, but simply tax relief.

In much the same way, most people favor tax relief or tax reduction, *but* not at the expense of existing programs and services (particularly as they affect the various age/sex/occupational groups). No wonder representatives age rapidly on the job!

Cost

The final "if" that concerns you as a representative will undoubtedly be the cost of polling. Good polls, the kind of quality "scientific" operation

Good polls, based on sound sampling techniques, are expensive.

outlined above, are expensive. A decent 600-person sample taken on a statewide basis will cost about $10,000 for approximately 25–30 questions. This is an expensive, if effective, way to find out what the majority of people in your district feel about specific issues. You will have to have a great deal of money in order to employ the sampling technique on a regular basis. (And where you get that money may very well influence your vote as much as the polling results.)

Think of the thousands of issues that exist: How many will you be able to sample in any given poll (especially considering that perhaps ten of the questions on every poll are devoted, not to issues, but to demographics)? Not very many! Properly run polls can be effective, but their utility is limited beyond sampling a few key issues at regular intervals.

Where, then, are you? How can you as a representative sample opinion widely? What can you rely on? Your own "guestimate"? Your mail? Your constituent calls and meetings? Your polls? Clearly, you will need a mix. Public opinions are varied and complex, even in a limited political universe. People who have studied public opinion in considerable depth have developed a set of variables to describe characteristics of public opinion. Although this is not the place for a detailed discussion of the theoretical implications of each characteristic, you as a prospective representative (or more likely as a citizen) will want to be aware of the many aspects of public opinion that we have only hinted at. For example, Robert Lane and David Sears have developed a number of concepts that should enable you to see better the complexity of public opinion.[12] We summarize them as follows:

1. The **distribution** of an opinion; that is, how widespread it is. If there are 100 people in your district who oppose federal aid for abortion, this may not give you the same cause for reflection that 100,000 would.

2. The **structure** of an opinion; that is, are the opinions on a particular subject distributed evenly throughout the general population or do they appear more randomly, some here, some there, without any clear pattern? If there are 200 people in your district who oppose the building of a dam, it matters where they are located. Are all 200 near the site, or are they randomly scattered throughout the district?

3. The **saliency**, or relevancy, of an opinion. How important is the opinion? Is it generalized in tone, and lacking relevance to particular

---

[12] Robert Lane and David Sears, *Public Opinion* (Englewood Cliffs, N.J.: Prentice-Hall, 1964). Other interesting studies include Robert Erikson and Norman Luttberg, *American Public Opinion: Its Origins, Content and Impact* (New York: Wiley, 1973), Allen Wilcox, *Public Opinion and Political Attitudes* (New York: Wiley, 1974) and John Mueller, *War, Presidents and Public Opinion* (New York: Wiley, 1973).

legislation (for example, the opinion that government ought not to be corrupt), or is it sharply focused (for example, the opinion that the government definitely ought—or ought not—to provide money for abortions for poor women)?

4. The **fluidity**, or changeability, of an opinion. When the Watergate hearings began, the vast majority of Americans did not believe that President Nixon should be impeached. Eight months later, opinion was reversed, a majority believing that he should be. Public opinion on Nixon's impeachment proved to be fluid. The general shift toward more liberal thinking about discrimination against homosexuals is another example of fluidity of opinion.

5. **Volatility**, or how rapidly an opinion changes. Public opinion on impeachment was fluid, but not volatile. The change took place slowly over a long period of time. A volatile opinion, on the other hand, is one that changes rapidly and may even contradict itself. Opinions on so-called bottle bills, that is, proposed legislation calling for the banning of nonreturnable containers, have proved to be very volatile. In some states, public opinion has favored such legislation by margins of 10 to 1, only to reverse itself in a short period of time; or has been opposed by margins of 3 to 1, only to be overcome.

6. **Latency**, or the potential for additional people holding the same opinion. As an issue first breaks into the public's consciousness, the number of people holding any position, pro or con, may be quite low. But as the public awareness increases, so too can the number of people who

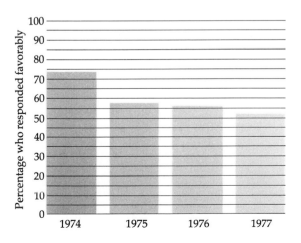

Fig. 4.3
The decline in support for the Equal Rights Amendment over time shows the fluidity of public opinion. (Source: Surveys by American Institute of Public Opinion (Gallup) and NBC news.)

care about it. There is an "upside potential" for most issues, within limits. Concern for whales and their preservation, initially high in the 1880s and then virtually forgotten for decades, has come back into vogue in the 1970s. But the potential concern over whales does not have the latency of, let us say, pollution control.

There are many other characteristics of an opinion that must be considered. Among them are its distribution, structure, saliency, fluidity, volatility, latency, and intensity.

7. There is also (and most important) **intensity**; that is, how strongly people hold an opinion. We are not simply concerned with how many people hold an opinion, or what the structure of that opinion is, but how intensely they care. As we shall see in Chapter 6, sometimes a single issue may turn a voter against (or for) a candidate, but only if the voter cares intensely about the issue.

Gun control is an area that illustrates vividly how a majority-held position may be checked by a smaller number of people who care intensely. Polling data suggest, at least in the abstract, that a majority of Americans approve of something called "gun control." But a majority of this majority do not care very strongly about it. To this majority, gun control as an issue simply does not rate with unemployment, crime, inflation, or other passionately held opinions, such as abortion, the Equal Rights Amendment, and so on. But to those who oppose gun control, it is, if you will pardon the pun, a life-or-death issue. They care and they organize, and they make it clear to public officials that they care very much. In politics, as in love, intensity often overrides passive resistance.

INTEREST GROUPS AND AMERICAN DEMOCRACY

If the representative has a hard time in ascertaining the majority position on an issue, how do you, as an individual who feels strongly about the issue, make your opinion known? You can write, you can call, or you can make an appointment to see the representative. But you are only one person; even if you urge your friends to do the same, you will probably not have much impact in a universe of 700,000. How, then, do you make the government responsive to your feelings and views?

One of the ways Americans have traditionally tried to give their individual opinions greater impact has been to join together with others of the same persuasion. They form interest groups, linked by a common opinion about a particular subject. Those who oppose abortion join with others who also oppose it. Those who favor construction of a national highway network join with others who also favor such an allocation of governmental resources.

In the classic work on groups in American politics, David B. Truman defined an **interest group** as a collection of people who share some particular attitude and who, as a group, make "certain claims upon other

Construction workers demonstrating for the Common Situs picketing bill and Indians protesting social and economic inequality. In recent years, many groups have become more vocal and visible in promoting their interests.

groups in the society for the establishment, maintenance or enhancement of forms of behavior that are implied by the shared attitudes.'' What makes an interest group different from a **categorical group** is emotion and action. Black cab drivers are a categorical group—they share several countable characteristics. But only if those shared characteristics give rise to a shared attitude—something the people involved feel strongly about—and only if

An interest group is a collection of people who share a common interest and work together to promote that interest.

the people begin to work together to do something, does an interest group form.[13]

In the case of a categorical group, you have no choice; you are in it by your very nature. You are a woman, or a black, or a Franco-American; you do not choose to be one. And being in a categorical group does not mean that you will automatically form an interest group. Not all blacks are in the Congress of Racial Equality (CORE) or the National Association for the Advancement of Colored People (NAACP).

The United States has always been a nation of interest groups. Foreign observers have long commented on America as a nation of "joiners."[14] At the present time, there are over 18,000 voluntary associations in the United States, ranging from labor unions to the antievolutionary league. Political scientists Sidney Verba and Norman Nie report that over 62 percent of all Americans belong to at least one interest group.[15] Abraham Holtzman found that more Americans belonged to more groups than did their counterparts in Great Britain and Italy.[16] Some are apolitical, like The American Society of Dowsers, The Burlington Liars Club, and the Society of Connoisseurs in Murder. Others are more concerned with the political process.

In the sections that follow, we shall discuss the different types of interest groups, and the pros and cons of their activities and their impact on politics.[17] Interest groups are really people combining for political purpose. An intrinsic feature of our political system, the combination of people to push for their self-interest, is basic to our democracy.

After all, why should people who feel the same way about an issue not attempt to voice their concerns to the government either through their representatives or through various governmental agencies? Is it not true that a banker in California will have more in common with a banker from North Carolina than with a grape picker (especially if the bank holds the mortgage on the farm that pays the grape picker's salary)? Conversely, the grape picker may be anxious to see an increase in the federal minimum wage (and thus share a common interest with the tobacco picker in North Carolina), while the bankers may well favor no increase.

---

[13] David B. Truman, *The Governmental Process*, 2d ed. (New York: Knopf, 1971).

[14] See, especially, Alexis de Tocqueville, *Democracy in America* (New York: Knopf, 1951).

[15] Sidney Verba and Norman Nie, *Participation in America* (New York: Harper & Row, 1972), p. 176.

[16] Abraham Holtzman, *Interest Groups and Lobbying* (New York: Macmillan, 1966).

[17] Grant McConnell, *Private Power and American Democracy* (New York: Knopf, 1966); V. O. Key, Jr., *Politics, Parties and Pressure Groups* (New York: Crowell, 1964); Harmon Ziegler, *Interest Groups in American Society* (Englewood Cliffs, N.J.: Prentice-Hall, 1964); and R. Joseph Momsen and Mark Canno, *The Makers of Public Policy: American Power Groups and Their Ideologies* (New York: McGraw-Hill, 1965); also, Robert Salisbury, ed., *Interest Group Politics in America* (New York: Harper & Row, 1970).

Types of Interest Groups

There are several major types of interest groups currently active in national politics. Let us look at some of the more important in terms of their total membership and their pursuit of broad aims.[18]

Organized labor

If this book had been written one hundred years ago, organized labor would not have loomed very large as an interest group. In fact, the question of whether or not there ought to be labor unions was hotly contested in the nineteenth century. Today, organized labor is the most populous of all interest groups, with over twenty-two million Americans belonging to trade unions (thirteen million in the AFL-CIO alone).

There are 130 national unions and more than 80,000 local unions. The American Federation of Labor–Congress of Industrial Organization (AFL-CIO) consists of dozens of large unions, such as the United Steel Workers, the United Auto Workers, the International Association of Machinists, and the International Association of Carpenters. Its Committee on Political Education (COPE) is one of the most important political forces in electoral politics. COPE's involvement in an important race may well mean the difference between defeat and victory. In 1974, for example, COPE moved hundreds of volunteers and hundreds of thousands of dollars into New Hampshire to support the election of John Durkin, who upset the incumbent senator, Louis Wyman, in a hotly contested runoff election after the two had finished in a virtual tie. George Meany, the portly, aging head of the AFL-CIO, has been actively courted by every president from Kennedy to Carter. It would be hard to believe that their interest derived from his ability to play the piano.

[18] See L. Harmon Ziegler, *Interest Groups in American Society* (Englewood Cliffs, N.J.: Prentice-Hall, 1964).

George Meany.

The largest of all the interest groups is organized labor. It is probably active on more issues than any other group, and has considerable power over international decisions.

In addition to the AFL-CIO, there are several independent unions that carry substantial political and financial clout. The International Brotherhood of Teamsters, the United Mine Workers, and the railroad brotherhoods have historically been especially active in electoral politics. Organized labor keeps a careful watch on how members of Congress and senators vote. COPE, in particular, rates national legislators on an ongoing basis. Not surprisingly, Senator Durkin has had a virtually perfect voting record as rated by COPE. Organized labor is probably active on more issues than any other interest group. Its powers over international decisions (such as tariff quotas or aid to Israel) is considerable.

Organized business

If labor is well organized and active politically, so is the business community. President Calvin Coolidge in 1927 reflected the reality of business power when he declared that "the business of America is business."

The National Association of Manufacturers, which dates back to the nineteenth century, now has over 15,000 member firms. The United States Chamber of Commerce, originally formed in 1912 to represent the business community on a local level, has over 4,000 local and state branches and represents 34,000 firms with over five million people. In addition (although there is obviously some overlapping membership), there are 14,000 trade associations, of which approximately 2,000 are national in scope. There are, finally, a variety of trade associations, such as the United States Brewers' Association, the American Trucking Association, the National Association of Real Estate Brokers, and many others. A visitor who strolls through the northwest section of Washington will see the offices of hundreds of them.

There is a tendency on the part of some to see the business community as a single enormous unit. But business, like organized labor, is often divided on specific issues and policies. The AFL-CIO is opposed, as are many Americans, to the organization of police and firefighters by the Teamsters. Likewise, the railroads are not unhappy about a rise in the federal or state tax on gas, which would hurt their competitors in the trucking industry. And the trucking industry, together with the construction industry, moved heaven and earth to have the United States pour over $100 billion into a highway system that the railroads thought was at the very least redundant.

The business community, though often divided on specific issues, has a major impact on elections primarily through the money it raises for favored candidates.

The business community, and the thousands of individual firms it contains, has a major impact on elections, primarily through the money it raises for favored candidates. In recent years, most national business associations have developed their own "Political Action Committees." Not surprisingly, many of these PACs supported Senator Wyman, who had a probusiness rating and a very low COPE rating.

Agricultural groups

A third category of interest group consists of those involved in agricultural matters. Although the number of farmers has steadily decreased in this century (by 1978 it was down to 2½ million), agricultural interest groups continue to be a vibrant and influential force in national and state politics.

The first agricultural interest group to gain national prominence was the Patrons of Husbandry, established in 1867. Subsequently known as the Grange, this organization was founded to help educate people in rural America and to give the often isolated farmers a sense of community and togetherness. In the 1870s and 1880s, however, it became more and more political in character, essentially in reaction to the monopoly of rail transportation and in protest against the high rates farmers had to pay to get their produce to market.[19] Because farmers had to use the railroad and there was only one railroad serving their area, there was no competition.

[19] See Philip Taft, *Organized Labor in American History* (New York: Harper & Row, 1964).

Capitol Hill police keep their eyes on a group of goats as they graze on the steps of the Capitol. Farmers turned about fifty of the animals loose on the Capitol grounds as part of their protest against government inaction on farm price supports.

The Farm Bureau, established in 1902, with approximately 1.3 million members, is active in supporting specific commodities, especially wheat, corn, tobacco, and cotton. Most farm products also have their own interest groups, such as the American Cattlemen's Association, the National Co-operative Milk Producers, and the National Apple Institute. Often, these groups will work together in an attempt to influence policy. An interesting coalition has worked to thwart legislation designed to remove tobacco from the Food for Peace program. For a number of years, Congress has approved price supports ($44 million annually) for the tobacco growers and insisted that the Food for Peace program distribute tobacco abroad. Critics have argued that since the Surgeon General has proven that tobacco smoking is harmful to one's health, and another branch of the federal bureaucracy, HEW, is engaged in an energetic campaign to get Americans to stop smoking, the federal government ought not to be in a position of either (1) promoting further production of the crop or (2) virtually giving away to foreigners (and encouraging them to consume) a product considered harmful to the health of Americans (and thus presumably harmful to Turks or Spaniards or Algerians).

In 1977, an effort was made to remove tobacco from the Food for Peace program and to begin a process of gradually eliminating price subsidies for tobacco. The tobacco industry, which provides employment for approximately 600,000 families, strenuously objected and was joined by other agricultural interest groups. The measure was defeated.

At other times, the agricultural interest groups may be divided in their views. The American Cattlemen's Association, for example, opposed the price supports paid to grain producers, the cost of grain being the single most expensive item in the production of beef. The producers of wheat, corn, and soybeans, on the other hand, fight to keep price supports for these products.

The agricultural groups possess considerable political clout (in terms of numbers) in such states as Iowa, Nebraska, Wisconsin, and Indiana. At the national level, their primary activity is lobbying in Washington. They also supply campaign funds to likely candidates. The American Milk Producers Association has been particularly noticeable—even infamous—in this activity, dispensing millions of dollars to dozens of candidates, including a highly questionable payment of $600,000 to former President Nixon's 1972 campaign. Nixon overruled his secretary of agriculture and increased federal price supports for milk.

Agricultural interest groups are most influential in the midwestern farming states such as Iowa, Nebraska, Wisconsin, and Indiana. They also are active lobbyists in Washington.

Professional groups

Professional groups form another category that has grown in importance in the past several decades. If organized labor is generally thought to be "blue collar," then the professional-interest groups may generally be characterized as "white collar." Teachers, doctors, and lawyers have formed powerful interest groups. The National Education Association (NEA), with over one million members, has become increasingly vocal in recent years and, especially on the state level, important politically. Its operation in Washington consists of over 600 people.[20] The American Federation of Teachers, the American Association of University Professors, the American Dental Association, and the American Trial Lawyers Association are other examples.

Of all the white-collar interest groups, the one that has probably had the greatest impact on public policy over the longest period (whether positive or negative, depending on one's point of view) is the American Medical Association. Established in 1901, its membership now includes nearly 80 percent of all M.D.'s licensed in the United States. The AMA spends more than $30 million annually on its lobbying efforts while its political-action arm, the American Medical Political Action Committee (AMPAC), dispenses campaign funds to candidates at the state and local level as well as to national politicians.[21]

> Professional groups, the most powerful being the American Medical Association, have gained in importance in recent years.

Public interest groups

The so-called **public interest groups** are another category that seems to be growing in importance. One of the most influential is Common Cause, founded by John Gardner, former Secretary of Health, Education, and Welfare; also in this group are Americans for Democratic Action (ADA) and Conservative Union. Common Cause has over 350,000 members and has focused on such "public interest" concerns as campaign practice abuses, and full disclosure of political finances and sources. Ralph Nader's Public Citizen, the American Civil Liberties Union, and the League of Women Voters are groups that consider themselves as representing the total public rather than any occupation, class, or ethnic group. All would argue that they are seeking to better society and would insist that they are acting for the greater good, rather than for a special or narrow interest.

> Public interest groups see themselves as representing the total public rather than any occupation, class, or ethnic group.

By and large, many of these claims are valid. But some have argued that the "public interest" does not exist and that these groups represent one public interest among many possible versions. Most Americans would agree that elections should be fairly and honestly run and that money should not be used to corrupt the political system. But not every public-spirited citizen would agree with the League of Women Voters that United

---

[20] See the interesting L. Harmon Ziegler, *The Political Life of American Teachers* (Englewood Cliffs, N.J.: Prentice-Hall, 1967).

[21] See Oliver Garceau, *The Political Life of the American Medical Association* (Cambridge, Mass.: Harvard University Press, 1941).

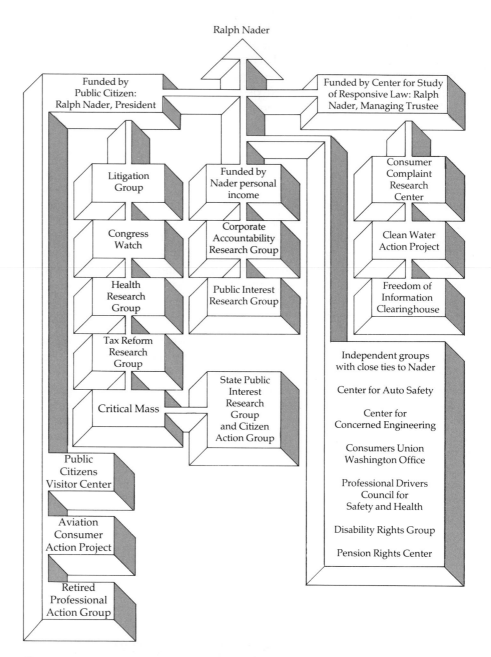

Fig. 4.4.
Ralph Nader's public interest empire. (© 1978 by The New York Times Company.
Reprinted by permission.)

States participation in the United Nations and its ancillary organizations is in the best interest of the entire country. And how many Americans would agree with Common Cause that people ought to be able to register to vote by mail? Likewise, do a majority of Americans support every effort on the part of the Civil Liberties Union to press certain individual rights to the point where they may well threaten the individual rights of others (see Chapter 14)? These are complex issues, and the public interest groups have every right to strive to make their points; but some of their activities put them very close to other, more highly politicized groups who also claim to speak for the "real" America.

Ideological groups

This brings us to still another category: **ideological groups,** of the right and the left, that seek the restructuring of American society, sometimes by violent means. The John Birch Society, the Ku Klux Klan, the American Nazi Party, all urge that Americans work to make their society something other than it is. The John Birch Society, founded by Robert Welch in 1958, probably stands as the symbol of the radical right (although the more hardware-oriented Minuteman Society is more extreme in its techniques).

Ideological groups, of the right or left, seek to restructure society, sometimes by violent means.

On the other side, the radical left reemerged in the 1960s as a set of important (albeit ephemeral) interest groups. Students for a Democratic Society (SDS) met at Port Huron, Michigan, in 1962 and drafted a statement asking for a reformed America focused on injustices in American society, such as poverty, racism, and war in Vietnam. Splinter groups used more radical methods, including street protests and demonstrations. Some SDS members condoned violence, while the Weathermen faction finally went underground and crossed the line from useful dissent into terrorism. The New Left challenged the pluralistic view of American society and argued that you had to get outside the system in order to achieve social reform.[22]

"Cause" groups

There are a number of important interest groups that do not fit conveniently into any of the above categories. The National Association for the Advancement of Colored People (NAACP), the Urban League, and the Congress of Racial Equality (CORE), for example, seek to improve the lot

---

[22] See Edward J. Bacciocco, *The New Left in America: Reform to Revolution 1956–1970* (Stanford, Calif.: Hoover Institution Press, 1974). For the radical right, see David Bell, ed., *The Radical Right* (Garden City, N.Y.: Doubleday, 1964) and Robert Schoenberger, *The American Right Wing* (New York: Holt, Rinehart and Winston, 1969); and for the radical left, Paul Jacobs and Saul Landau, *The New Radicals* (New York: Random House, 1966).

Both Mrs. Ford and Mrs. Carter, shown here at the National Women's Conference in Houston, Texas, in 1977, fought hard for women's causes during their husbands' administrations.

of black Americans.[23] Others seek to improve society through the emancipation of women, urging their acceptance into society on the basis of achievement, not sex. The National Organization for Women (NOW), formed in 1966, and the National Women's Political Caucus, formed in 1971, are prime examples of this kind of activity.

A number of groups are frequently lumped together as "environmentalists." Organizations such as the Sierra Club, with 140,000 members, Ducks Unlimited with 180,000, and the Wilderness Society with 70,000,

---

[23] See August Meier and Elliot Rudwick, *CORE: A Study in the Civil Rights Movement, 1942–1968* (New York: Oxford University Press, 1973).

enjoy the generalized support of a broader community. Their increasing activities in the past decade are shown in specific governmental decisions. Other groups include the Environmental Defense Fund and Friends of the Earth. The environmentalists played a key role in halting the construction of the supersonic transport plane, the SST, lobbying Congress to drop its support of the project. They also delayed construction of the Alaskan pipeline and added to its additional cost by insisting on improved safety features. A steadily growing cluster of groups, recently joined by Ralph Nader, opposes the spread of nuclear power plants.

And there are thousands of other "cause" groups, ranging from the 1,050,000-member National Rifle Association, which has been extremely effective in preventing additional gun-control legislation, to the miniscule Florida-based Fair Education Foundation, which fights the teaching of evolution as scientific fact. Other examples among thousands are the American Legion, the National Council of Churches, B'nai B'rith's Anti-Defamation League, the General Federation of Women's Clubs, the Knights of Columbus, the Fellowship of Christian Athletes, Boy and Girl Scouts, the Public Library Association, World Pen Pals, and the American Bottle Collectors Association.

There are many other interest groups, concerned with a variety of issues including racism, sexism, the environment, and individual causes.

Governmental interest groups

A final category worthy of our attention and one that is often overlooked is the governmental, or bureaucratic, interest group. The Army Corps of Engineers acts as an interest group supporting additional dams, canals, and flood-control projects, as does its principal bureaucratic rival, the Bureau of Reclamation.[24] Similarly, the civil service, which protects most bureaucrats from arbitrary dismissal, tends to protect them also from political pressure. Some have argued that this has created a "new class" beyond the control of the general public. We shall be returning to this theme in Chapter 10, but it should be mentioned that the federal bureaucrats have a vested interest in the size and budget (the organizational "health") of their organization. They are able to exert pressure on various points within the decision-making process.[25]

Techniques of Interest Group Action

Thus the United States today remains a nation of interest groups. Tens of thousands of groups with hundreds of thousands of opinions and millions

[24] See Arthur Maass, *Muddy Waters* (Cambridge: Harvard University Press, 1951); see also Elizabeth Drew, "Dam Outrage! The Story of the Army Engineers," *Atlantic* (April 1970), 51–62.

[25] See Randall Ripley and Grace Franklin, *Congress, the Bureaucracy and Public Policy* (Homewood, Ill.: Dorsey Press, 1976).

of members—clearly, the various groups disagree with one another. Clearly, each group strives to make its opinions felt in the political process. What are the techniques they use to make their opinions effective?

In a subsequent section, "Lobbying and Lobbyists," we shall be examining the process by which interest groups employ individuals to influence the course of lawmaking in the United States. But first we shall look at the broader-gauge approaches groups may employ on a society-wide basis to influence the general public as well as legislators.

Membership drives and publicity

For interest groups, there is strength in both dollars and numbers. Therefore, one of the most typical techniques is simply to expand membership. For Ducks Unlimited and Common Cause, membership drives are very important. Members are recruited to pay dues, to maintain the group's solidarity, and to educate the public about the group's beliefs and activities.

In order to increase membership, interest groups seek publicity. This may be "free," in terms of getting news stories that have the effect of promoting their cause. For example, the Save Whales group gets free publicity by making media events out of their efforts to stop whaling expeditions. If the media fail to cover the events, interest groups may engage in molding public opinion by purchasing advertisements. The International Ladies Garment Workers Union buys air time to explain how much better off garment workers are, now that the industry is unionized. The Save Our Schools Society and the League to Restore Decency invest money in TV commercials to call attention to what they consider the insidious influence of pornography in our society. It is perfectly legitimate under our system for interest groups to propagate their views by purchasing newspaper space or radio and TV time.

Public protests

It is also perfectly legitimate under our system for these interest groups to engage in public protests, as long as these protests do not infringe on the rights of others or inflict bodily harm on others. Public protests may take the form of mass rallies, marches, and other group activities to dramatize the point of view represented by the particular interest group.

In the 1960s, civil-rights activists staged marches all over the United States to dramatize the plight of the American blacks, who had been denied full participation in our economic and political systems. Public protests by antiwar groups helped to turn the tide of national opinion against the war in Vietnam. In the late 1970s and early 1980s, women's-rights and gay-rights protests helped to raise the level of public consciousness over these areas of discontent.

George McGovern is an elected representative of the people, but does he really represent the views of the majority? Here he is seen on a trip to Cuba, a country that many Americans feel is an enemy of the United States.

Election campaign activity

We have already alluded to another way in which interest groups may work for or against change—through involving themselves in election campaigns. For example, interest groups frequently assist candidates by donating money and by providing logistical support and volunteers. On the other hand, if candidate X does not appeal to a particular group, it can support his or her opponent. In 1976, Ralph Nader's group identified a dozen members of Congress who, they felt, opposed the public interest on a wide range of issues and donated money, time, and volunteer support to seek their removal.

Interest groups may also try to stimulate public support for—or opposition to—particular legislators by "rating" their performance. They perform this rating by selecting a number of issues important to them, and then ranking the individual on the basis of her or his vote on these items. The Americans for Democratic Action, for example, rates Senator George McGovern as a "good" senator because he usually votes for positions they support and against positions they oppose. The American Constitutional Union (ACU) believes that Senator McGovern is a "bad" senator because he votes against positions they support and for positions they oppose. On the other hand, the ACU feels that Senator Strom Thurmond from South Carolina is a "good" senator, while ADA says he is a "bad" senator.

Although the interest groups using them obviously feel that these ratings are important, and the individual representatives do pay some attention to their overall ratings, there is little evidence that these ratings hold much interest for the general public or that the individual voter is likely to make up his or her mind on the basis of one interest group's rating. There is also the question of how the test issues are selected. For a number of years, a representative's or senator's vote on the appropriation for the B-1 bomber was an important test of that person's "liberalism" or "conservatism." Voting for the B-1 was considered "conservative." Yet if one stops and thinks about it, what is "conservative" about spending $100 billion for a plane that may or may not be able to penetrate the Soviet Union's sophisticated air-defense system by the middle 1980s, the time of its deployment?

Legal action

Among the techniques used by interest groups to make themselves heard are membership drives and publicity, public protests, election campaign activity, and legal action.

Interest groups may also attempt to use the courts to overturn unfavorable laws or to impede execution of these laws. The NAACP used the courts in 1954 to bring about major school desegregation, in the famous *Brown* v. *Board of Education* case. More recently, various environmental groups have taken to the courts to stop dams and to protest everything, from black ducks to wolves and mustangs.[26]

Interest groups also intervene on behalf of governmental appointments. They may testify that a potential appointee is "opposed to labor" or "propollution" or "antiblack" or "probusiness," depending on their point of view and the particular instance. While it is seldom the case that a single interest group's opposition is central to the approval or disapproval of a particular appointment, several interest groups may have impact.

Finally, interest groups may seek to influence legislation at the state or national level. They may seek to have their representatives promote, oppose, alter, or clarify pending legislation. This complex set of influences and aspects is worthy of a separate section.

LOBBYING AND LOBBYISTS

Lobbying is a term referring to any intentional effort to influence legislation.

To many Americans, the term **lobbying** suggests smoke-filled rooms, intimidation, bribery, and excess influence exerted on the legislative process. Actually, the term is far more neutral, meaning any intentional effort to influence legislation. Originally, the term evolved because much of this effort to influence legislation took place in the lobbies of the various state houses. The public (and this included lobbyists) was not allowed on the floor of legislative assemblies.

[26] Clement E. Vose, "Litigation as a Form of Pressure Group Activity," 319 *The Annals* 20 (1958).

In recent years, Americans have been told about efforts by International Telephone and Telegraph not only to influence legislation but also to encourage the overthrow of the government of Chile. Other reports have indicated that millions of dollars were spent by the government of South Korea and its central intelligence agency in efforts to influence congressional voting on matters important to the government of South Korea. These stories indicate abuses that have occurred in the American political system and Americans are justified in being indignant. (We note with some irony, however, that much of the opposition to Korean intelligence operations in the United States is by the good citizens who condone American intelligence operations in other countries.[27])

Of the thousands and thousands of lobbyists who are active in Washington and the fifty state capitals, most of them routinely try to influence legislation in perfectly legal fashion, exercising their basic rights under the United States Constitution. The National Fertilizer Association has legitimate goals, as do the Veterans of Foreign Wars, the Citizens for Control of Federal Spending, the Committee of Copyright Owners, the United States Savings and Loan League, and the Disabled American Veterans. These groups and thousands more simply seek to ensure that the views of their members are represented in the lawmaking process. These lobbyists urge support for legislation that is favorable (or less unfavorable) to their interests.

Despite its normally routine activity, however, the lobbying process remains a fascinating one that has stimulated a number of recent books.[28]

Lobbyists may be divided into a number of categories, depending on how they operate. At the financial and influential top of the profession stand the Washington lawyers, sometimes referred to as the "super-lawyers." They dispense advice to legislators, to government officials, to other lobbyists, to the interest groups, and to large corporate enterprises. They represent their clients before various federal agencies and generally stay "in the know." They deal principally in information, advice, and counsel. In *The Best and the Brightest*, David Halberstam illustrates perfectly the super-lawyer in full surge as he describes Clark Clifford in action.[29]

---

[27] For an overview of work dealing with corruption and other irregularities, see Larry Berg, Harlan Hahn, and John Schmidhauser, *Corruption in the American Political System* (Morristown, N.J.: General Lenz Press, 1976); Jethro L. Berman, *How the Government Breaks the Law* (New York: Stein and Day, 1974); Theodore Becker and U. G. Murray, eds., *Government Lawlessness in America* (New York: Oxford University Press, 1961).

[28] See Lester Milbrath, *The Washington Lobbyists* (New York: Rand McNally, 1963); Donald Hall, *Cooperative Lobbying* (Tucson: University of Arizona Press, 1969); Lewis Dexter, *How Organizations Are Represented in Washington* (New York: Bobbs-Merrill, 1969); Joseph C. Goulden, *The Super Lawyers* (New York: Weybright and Talley, 1972).

[29] See David Halberstam's *The Best and the Brightest* (Greenwich, Conn.: Fawcett, 1972), pp. 790–791.

Bert Lance turned to super-lawyer Clark Clifford in a desperate but unsuccessful attempt to save his job when called before a congressional committee to explain questionable financial practices.

Most lobbyists are more deferential and modest. There are the company lobbyists, who simply represent their firms in Washington. Congoleum, Computer Controls, Alcoa Aluminum, and thousands of other firms simply keep a representative in Washington to look out for their interests. Other lobbyists represent interest groups as a whole (or an entire industry), while still others freelance, taking on client X in 1979 and client Y in 1980. The Washington super-lawyers do well. Joseph Califano, presently secretary of HEW, reported an income in excess of $500,000 in 1976.

Then there are lobbyists who represent federal bureaucracies. We have previously called attention to the Army Corps of Engineers, which lobbies for dams and other major projects. The Pentagon has become famous (or infamous) in recent years for its lobbying efforts on behalf of expensive weapons systems (see Chapter 10). The United States Postal Service, with over 700,000 employees and a budget of $1.5 billion, is one of the largest bureaucracies in the United States; it periodically fights a successful battle for pay raises. The Maritime Administration lobbies for increased subsidies for American merchant marines, and not coincidentally was instrumental in pushing through legislation requiring that a certain percentage of imported oil be carried by American ships, a law that certainly aids the American fleet if not the American consumer.

What do they do?

But what do lobbyists do? Actually, they do a lot of things, frequently providing a number of services that may not be readily apparent. Let us assume that you are the new representative from the seventh district of

Texas. You are now in Washington and anxious to do a good job for your constituents. You undoubtedly know a good bit about how the voters in your district feel about certain issues, such as the oil-depletion allowance, but you know very little about a great many of the other things.

One of the first services the lobbyists (as a group) perform is providing you with *information*. Now, of course, much of this information is designed to help you understand their particular position, but much of it will be useful to you no matter how you end up voting. Many of the better lobbyists are more informed than many members of Congress and/or their staffs. Often they appreciate the nuances and possible ramifications of potential legislation better than even Capitol Hill veterans. With tens of thousands of bills being tossed in the hopper every session, you and your staff will simply be unable to cope with all of them. Lobbyists also provide some information about how a particular bill will affect your voters. Naturally, they will try to exaggerate how unhappy or happy your constituents will be, but they often will understand ramifications of particular bills better than you. The good lobbyist is a close student of legislative detail.

In addition to providing information, skillful lobbyists also enjoy access to influential groups or people. Many have been around long enough to know how to get something out of the Veteran's Administration or the Department of Labor. Many lobbyists are retired or defeated members of Congress, who know how the bureaucracies work and how Congress works; when to offer your pet amendment; when to lean heavily on the VA; when to be polite with HEW; or which committees will be most useful.

Let us say you want very much to get a hardship case in the military settled. One of your constituents joined the navy and is now stationed in Japan. His father dies and he has become the sole supporter of his mother and younger brother. He needs to come home to run the family farm. As a freshman member of Congress, you may not know what official to call at the Pentagon, let alone what to say when they say, "no way."

The lobbyist from Boeing, who has been anxious to get your vote on the B-1 bomber, is a retired three-star Air Force general. Chances are, he will be able to help you get the attention of the person who can transfer your constituent home, probably within the week. Of course, he may be back again right before the vote on the B-1 appropriation to ask a favor of you, but that is another aspect of the situation. In reality, the leading lobbyists are more secure in their jobs than many legislators, and have larger staffs, more operating expenses, and more legislative experience.

Lobbyists also may assist in the drafting of legislation. In fact, many prefer to be called *legislative counsels*. If you want to introduce a bill that will give people tax credits for insulating their homes, thereby saving fuel, you may not be familiar enough with the economics of the insulation industry to know what form of credit is most likely to stimulate the new

Lobbyists provide information, enjoy access to influential groups or people, and assist in the drafting of legislation.

demand. And if you are interested in trying to introduce a bill to deregulate the price of natural gas, a lobbyist for the industry will certainly be able to help you do that.

The crunch obviously comes to you as a freshman in Congress, when (1) the lobbyist who has helped you returns and wants your help on a particular vote, or (2) when lobbyist #2 shows up in your office and suggests that lobbyist #1 not only represents the wrong industry and the wrong constituency, but also does not know what he or she is doing. The crunch may also come when (3) a lobbyist really wants your vote on a particular issue and either reminds you of past contributions to your campaign or, not so subtly, suggests that you will receive more (or less) campaign support in your next election bid. Then you will prove—to yourself, if to no one else—just who you really want to represent.

Checks on Lobbying

Why not reduce the level of lobbying? Many have argued that lobbyists are too powerful, that they constitute a major force, one that often undermines the faith and trust of the American people. In partial response to this, Congress passed the **Regulation of Lobbying Act** in 1946, designed to make the identity of lobbyists and the amounts spent on lobbying activity a matter of public record. Lobbyists are required to register with the Clerk of the House of Representatives and to file periodic reports showing sources and amounts of money received and spent ("all who give $500 or more and all who receive $10 or more"). Failure to do so is supposed to result in a $10,000 fine and/or a five-year prison term and banishment from further lobbying for three years. Banishment from lobbying for three years could thus mean the loss of tens of thousands of dollars worth of commissions.

The law is vague. The widespread abuses of the 1960s and 1970s, for example, occurred in spite of it, although it did lead to some convictions. After all, a lobbyist would look a little silly putting down $10 every time he or she bought a senator two drinks and a shrimp cocktail.

In the final analysis, a very thin line runs between curtailing excess lobbying efforts and abridging First Amendment rights. Under our Constitution, people may combine to express their opinions and are free to attempt to influence the course of legislation. Let us consider the case of a young woman who recently graduated from a large midwestern university, majoring in history and English.

She now works for a firm of lobbyists in Washington, D.C. After preliminary training and orientation, she was assigned to work on the Westinghouse account. Westinghouse makes, among other things, large generators used in nuclear power stations. Therefore, it is concerned that the United States continue to build atomic power stations. This is all right

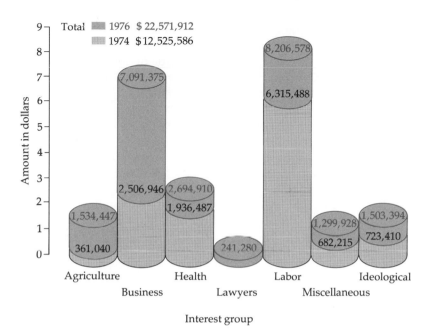

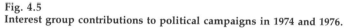

Fig. 4.5
Interest group contributions to political campaigns in 1974 and 1976.

with the young woman lobbyist-to-be. She was active in environmental groups on her home campus and sent numerous letters opposing the Alaskan pipeline. She also feels that fossil fuels are running out and that the United States must find alternative sources of energy.

Although initially skeptical, she has come to believe that nuclear energy is America's best hope for meeting the increased energy demands during the rest of this century. She is convinced that the problem of nuclear wastes is soluble and minor, compared to the pollution aspects of other fuels, such as coal. She is enthusiastic about nuclear energy in general and Westinghouse's participation in particular. She is enraged at President Carter for attempting to shut down the nation's only plutonium breeder reactor.

So there she is, in Washington, getting paid for doing a job she thinks is important and working for a company and an industry in which she believes. Let us say that you are that young woman. Why should you not be allowed to work for legislation favorable to what you believe in? Why should you not be allowed to work against legislation harmful to the industry you believe in? As long as you stay within the law, why should you not have the right to try to educate people, including members of Congress, so that they will more fully appreciate your position?

The lobbying system has both advantages and disadvantages in our society. Although the system is abused, and does not always operate in the interests of society "as a whole," it does help our political system to embrace a diversity of interests and viewpoints.

Sometimes known as the "Third House" (after the two houses of Congress, the House of Representatives and the Senate), the informal society made up of lobbyists is an imperfect mirror of society. Often the specific wishes of lobbyists (and the opposition) stand in the way of legislation that might (or might not) theoretically benefit "all of the people." Nevertheless, interest groups and their lobbyists help to stir debate, thus focusing attention on conflicting views of societal change. They allow the major political parties to embrace a variety of interests and viewpoints so that our major parties remain broad-gauged and philosophically diverse. They also represent countervailing interests—pluralism, if you will—in the American political process.

Perhaps "Mr. or Mrs. or Miss or Ms. Everyperson" is not qualified to decide about the "safety" of nuclear power. Perhaps proponents will overstate their case. Perhaps their case will be opposed by those who favor coal, or gas, or solar, or tidal, or wind power. Given the complex and bewildering nature of modern society, the overwhelming aspects of technology, perhaps it is desirable to have diverse interest groups and their lobbyists fight it out. What obviously should be avoided, of course, is a situation where the multinational corporations control not only oil, natural gas, and coal, but also nuclear fuel and solar panels. But this problem takes us beyond opinion and interest groups.

In the last analysis, the choice rests with the American voter. He or she is the ultimate authority within the political process, and if a particular representative seems to be too concerned with particular interests, too supportive of a particular lobbying effort, then that representative may be turned into a lobbyist at the next election. This assumes that voters know enough, care enough, and are organized enough to win the next election.

SUMMARY

We have been concerned in this chapter with public opinion, its changes and its constants. We have also examined a variety of views of American society that have been put forth to explain political behavior. Finally, we examined the nature of interest groups: how they are formed; how they seek to influence the political process; and how they interact with one another and the people's representatives.

In the process, we have tried to stress the complex nature of American society, and the variety of economic, regional, and general interest differences that affect the response to the question, "Are interest groups good or bad?" Our answer is that they exist and will continue to do so. They are an intrinsic part of the American political process as we know it. Each reader, depending upon his or her viewpoint, will want to see interest group activity increased or decreased, more freedom for groups or less, more individual participation in the lawmaking process or less. But with interest groups as with so many other aspects of the American political system, as Aldous Huxley put it in his foreword to *Brave New World*, "You pays your money and you takes your choice." [30]

KEY TERMS

Common Situs	**interest group**
public opinion	**public interest group**
political socialization	**ideological group**
elitist model	**lobbying**
pluralist model	**Regulation of Lobbying Act**
polling	

SUGGESTED READINGS

DEXTER, LEWIS, *How Organizations are Represented in Washington* (New York: Bobbs-Merrill, 1969).

> An excellent short study of Washington lobbying by a political scientist who has seen the process from the inside as a participant.

GLAZER, NATHAN, and DANIEL P. MOYNIHAN, *Beyond the Melting Pot* (Cambridge, Mass.: MIT Press, 1963).

> A classic study of the persistence of ethnicity as a factor in American politics.

KEY, V. O., Jr., *Public Opinion and American Democracy* (New York: Knopf, 1961).

> Perhaps the best overview of the subject of public opinion.

LIPPMANN, WALTER, *Public Opinion* (New York: The Free Press, 1922).

> Early, but very sensitive, study of American public opinion by one of the most acute journalistic observers of our politics. Available in paperback.

NIE, NORMAN H., SIDNEY VERBA, and JOHN R. PETROCIK, *The Changing American Voter* (Cambridge, Mass.: Harvard University Press, 1976).

> The most up-to-date accounts of the influence of public opinion and interest group activity on American voting behavior.

TRUMAN, DAVID, *The Governmental Process*, 2d ed. (New York, Knopf, 1971).

> The best comprehensive account of the operation of interest groups in the American system.

---

[30] Aldous Huxley, *Brave New World* (New York: Bantam Books, 1966), p. xiv.

No force acting on mankind has been less
carefully examined than Party, and yet
none better deserves examination.

Sir Henry Maine

The political parties created democracy
and modern democracy is unthinkable
save in terms of the parties. As a matter
of fact, the condition of the parties is the
best possible evidence of the nature of
any regime.

E. E. Schattschneider

The governmental system is not working
because the political parties are not
working. The parties have been weakened
by their failure to adapt to some of the
social and technological changes taking
place in America. But, even more, they
are suffering from simple neglect: neglect
by Presidents and public officials, but,
particularly, neglect by the voters.

David S. Broder

CHAPTER 5 AMERICAN POLITICAL PARTIES: REALIGNMENT OR TRANSFORMATION?

It is November 1976. Jimmy Carter, almost unknown outside the South a year before the election, has just been chosen as the nation's thirty-ninth president. His election race against incumbent Gerald Ford was a close contest. Carter ran well in his home region, while dividing the industrial Northeast with Ford. West of the Mississippi was Ford territory. When it was all over, Carter held a slight edge in both total popular vote and in the special arithmetic of the electoral college. A peaceful transition from one era to the next was under way.

How much of Carter's political success story was attributable to the Democratic party? How much should we credit to the personality, ambition, organizational skills, and good fortune of the candidate and his small circle of political assistants, most of whom were under thirty-five years of age and unknown outside Georgia prior to the 1976 campaign? What does the Carter victory tell us about the strengths and weaknesses of American political parties today?

The Democratic party, as an organization, did not go out and handpick Jimmy Carter as its prime standard-bearer to capture the presidency after the Nixon-Ford years. Organizational Democrats, given their preference, might have selected Senator Henry Jackson of Washington or the late Senator Hubert Humphrey of Minnesota as their candidate in 1976. As noted in Chapter 6, Carter, like most candidates today, built his own personal organization. He also skillfully utilized the mass media in establishing himself as an authentic national candidate. In effect, Carter captured control of the nominating procedures of the Democratic party by using a series of presidential primary elections.

A presidential election affords one view of American parties. It is not the only view. Although there were a number of promising newcomers to the two houses of Congress, the 1976 elections continued the normal pattern of Democratic control. In gross numbers, in fact, the new distribution of Democrats to Republicans was almost the same as before. But this time (January 1977), for the first time since 1968, both the executive and legislative branches of the national government were controlled by the same party. Does this make any difference in terms of policy-making? Is party government possible in the United States? How much influence do political parties exert in setting or changing the course of public policy? What is the effective role of party politics in the national government of this country? Before we seek answers to these questions, we should examine the general situation in which our political parties find themselves.

Political scientist Frank Sorauf observes: "A great deal has turned sour for the American parties in the last few years. The late 1960s saw the decline of their prestige; along with other institutions of American government and politics, they have borne a good deal of the blame for the general malaise and the decline in public confidence that beset American society."[1] Is this correct? Are American political parties in any sense agents of change? Or do they merely reflect more profound economic and social changes taking place within the society? Did the parties bring about the public mood or are they its unintended victims?

American politics is not a simple thing. Our political parties are so complex that even the most carefully trained observer is probably seeing them only partially. How else are we to explain the sharp disagreements among knowledgeable people about the present condition of American political parties? If scholars and politicians are unsure of the present condition, how certain are their views of future trends?

Among leading authorities, views range all the way from the notion that "the party is over" to the more conventional and reassuring interpretation that finds the basic American party system remaining pretty much intact. A third possibility is that our political parties are being transformed before our eyes as they adapt to the changing needs and demands of our society. This chapter explores each of these various interpretations. Our aim is to provide you with a basis for forming your own informed judgment about the current condition of our political parties. Ordinary citizens by their actions (or inaction) are likely to have a lot to say about the future of American political parties.

Suppose our party system is deteriorating. So what? Would this make much difference to us, as citizens? If our parties are being transformed, as some observers believe, what effect, if any, might changes in the party system have on government in relation to our daily lives? How may Jimmy Carter, the "head" of the Democratic party, use the Democratic majority in Congress to help bring about the changes in policy he talked about during his drive for the White House? In short, what are our parties supposed to do, and what, in fact, are they doing?

WHAT IS HAPPENING TO PARTIES?

Walter Dean Burnham, a political scientist, and David Broder, a leading journalist, are among those who believe that American political parties have reached an advanced stage of deterioration (or "decomposition"). Burnham traces the process of party breakdown all the way back to the election of 1896, an election that, as we noted in Chapter 3, realigned politics in a fundamental way. The election of 1896 turned aside a growing farmer protest movement and helped create a powerful probusiness Republican majority party.

[1] Frank Sorauf, *Party Politics in America,* 3d ed. (Boston: Little, Brown, 1976), p. 414.

1896: Prelude to Deterioration?

At the same time, the post-1896 party system actually *reduced* participation in our national elections.[2] In 1896, 79 percent of the electorate voted. This level has never been reached since then. After falling to 49 percent during a period of Republican domination in the 1920s, voter turnout increased again during the age of Franklin D. Roosevelt, but it never reached the level of the late nineteenth century. In recent decades, the tendency has been steadily downward, reaching 54 percent in 1976. Paradoxically, as more Americans are eligible to vote, the percentage doing so has declined.

David Broder has gone so far as to suggest that "the party is over." He stresses a variety of factors that discourage the development of "responsible" (that is, disciplined to support a party program) parties in the United States.

[2] See Walter Dean Burnham, *Critical Elections and the Mainstream of American Politics* (New York: Norton, 1970) and David Broder, *The Party's Over* (New York: Harper & Row, 1970). A brief statement of Burnham's thesis appears as "The End of American Party Politics" in *Transaction* (December 1969), pp. 12–22. On the importance of 1896 as a "critical" election that effected a basic political realignment and depressed voter participation, see E. E. Schattschneider, *The Semi-Sovereign People* (New York: Holt, Rinehart and Winston, 1960).

Fig. 5.1
Is the party over? Surveys show a marked decline in partisan affiliation, as shown.
(© 1977 Congressional Quarterly, Inc. p. 717 Weekly Report, March 18, 1978. Reprinted with permission.)

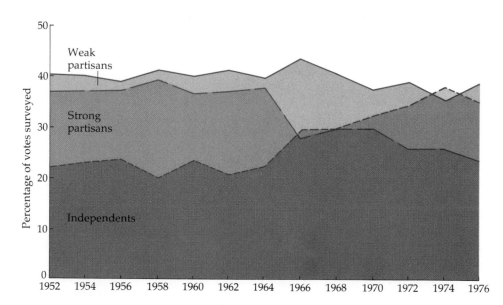

One very important factor is the cost of running a political campaign. In the face of widespread voter apathy, modern electioneering requires huge sums of money in order to exploit fully the seductive charms of the electronic tube. Candidates for high office are "packaged" and "sold" to a mass audience in much the same fashion as automobiles and deodorants are. The skillful use of the mass media requires the resources of advertising and public-relations firms, not political-party organizations. Candidates often depend more on the "image" they project than on their faithfulness to a party program only dimly perceived by many citizens. (We discuss these aspects more fully in Chapters 6 and 7.)

Political parties experience great difficulty in raising the huge amounts of money that modern campaigning requires. Therefore, most presidential candidates have created their own fund-raising organizations. For example, the Committee to Reelect the President (CREEP), which raised some $40 million for Mr. Nixon's 1972 campaign, functioned almost wholly independently of the Republican National Committee. The new election laws, first applied in 1976, which provide for public financing of presidential races, also served to reduce the importance of party fund-raising. These laws greatly assisted the cause of Jimmy Carter, an "outsider."

A number of other factors have also had the effect of weakening American political parties. The rise of the modern civil service and the accompanying decline of **patronage** (political jobs) as a form of organizational "glue" is an obvious example. Equally important today is the increasing reliance on professional (public relations, especially), rather than political, skills in political campaigns.

Our parties appear to be declining in importance, then, because a number of the functions they formerly performed in nominating and electing candidates for public office have been taken over by nonparty organizations. Burnham argues that the struggle between the parties has been a vital ingredient in making this a "democracy." The parties, as he views them, have been the single most important instrument available to ordinary people for exerting some influence on the makers of public policy. In contrast, the interest-group system, described in Chapter 4, serves as an instrument of power and privilege. The decline of parties, in this view, threatens to make our system less "democratic" (that is, less subject to popular control).[3] Burnham concludes:

> It seems fairly evident that if this secular trend toward politics without parties continues to unfold, the policy consequences will be profound. To state the matter with utmost simplicity: political parties, with all their well-known human and structural shortcomings, are the only devices thus far invented by the wit of Western man which, with some effectiveness, can generate countervailing collective power on behalf of the many individually powerless against the relatively few who are individually—or organizationally—powerful.[4]

According to one theory of American political parties, the party system is over because it no longer provides the functions it once did.

The "party is over," so the argument runs, because the party no longer provides the functions it once did. How are ordinary citizens to exert any leverage on Big Government if the party system is further weakened?

Party Realignment?

Other observers are not so pessimistic about the condition of the party system. They see the party system in a gradual process of realignment. These observers see a cyclical process at work. As we have noted, 1896

[3] See especially Burnham's essay, "The End of American Party Politics."

[4] Burnham, "The End of American Party Politics."

was a year that produced a fundamental realignment of American politics. Later in this chapter we discuss the New Deal party coalition ushered in during the early 1930s: another example of realignment. Following this pattern, we seem to be overdue in terms of another important realignment. This line of analysis has recently been given an impressive statement by James Sundquist, who places principal emphasis on the cyclical process at work in the historical evolution of American political parties. A combination of great public figures, significant crosscutting issues, and shifts in public mood are among the factors that alter the direction of politics.

For example, in the 1930s, the emergence of Franklin D. Roosevelt as champion of the masses, the need for action in the face of prolonged economic depression, and a supportive public mood produced the New Deal programs and a new party alignment. Sundquist argues that the old New Deal **coalition** (or something very similar to it) still undergirds the Democratic majority. So long as this coalition holds together, a fundamental realignment of our parties is not likely to take place.

Writing in 1973, Sundquist observed:

> In the long run, the prospect may well be for a further gradual decomposition of the two-party system. But there is at least as much reason to believe that in the shorter run the headlong march toward decomposition that marked the late 1960s will be checked or even reversed, the New Deal party system will be re-invigorated, and most of those who ceased identifying with one or the other major party in the recent turmoil will reidentify.[5]

Please note that Sundquist offered this interpretation before Jimmy Carter gained his ascendancy in national politics. Is President Carter the beneficiary of the post–New Deal party system, or is he the product of sweeping changes in American politics and voting patterns?

Another view is that our political parties are undergoing a period of re-alignment. This theory sees a cyclical process at work in the historical evolution of American political parties.

The center holds

In a book published in 1968, when some thought America was likely to shift to the political left in the aftermath of Vietnam escalation and domestic unrest, Richard Scammon and Ben Wattenberg argued that a majority of Americans remained located near the political center, as noted in Chapter 6. Scammon and Wattenberg's "real majority," as they labeled it, was "unpoor, unblack and unyoung." Noting that at least 60 percent of the potential electorate declared a preference for the Democratic party, Scammon and Wattenberg maintained that "success" for Democratic candidates in national politics lay in staying as close as possible to the center within this post-FDR setting.[6]

[5] James L. Sundquist, *Dynamics of the Party System* (Washington, D.C.: The Brookings Institution, 1973).

[6] Richard Scammon and Ben Wattenberg, *The Real Majority* (New York: Coward-McCann, 1970).

Biography
Louis Howe

Louis Howe was a forty-year-old, seasoned political reporter working for the New York Telegram *covering the New York Legislature in Albany when he first laid eyes on freshman Senator Franklin D. Roosevelt of Hyde Park, a twenty-nine-year-old patrician and political novice who chose to challenge the party bosses during his first session. Howe, a tiny, chronically ill, gnarled, and truculent man was strangely mesmerized by the young Roosevelt, scion of the Hudson River squirearchy and a product of Groton and Harvard.*

Mrs. Howe tells the story. It was the summer of 1911. She and her husband were entering church on Sunday morning. Suddenly Louis grabbed her arm. "See that tall fellow in front of us?" he asked, "That's Franklin D. Roosevelt. Some day that young man will be president of the United States. You wait and see." *

The story may seem apocryphal, but Howe wrote a friendly social letter to Roosevelt the next year (1912) that begins, "Beloved and Revered Future President". And this to a thirty-year-old rookie state legislator who had offended the party's bosses!

The Howe-Roosevelt relationship may be unique in American history because Howe, with singular tenacity, worked for twenty years thereafter with one overwhelming goal in mind: to

* Source: Lela Stiles, *The Man Behind Roosevelt: The Story of Louis McHenry Howe* (New York: World, 1954), p. 32.

The nomination of Senator McGovern in 1972 would seem an implausible tactic, given this interpretation. McGovern's disastrous showing in the election, indeed, seems to confirm this view. So, perhaps, does Jimmy Carter's impressive triumph in 1976, with this exception: Carter's powerful attraction for black America. Jimmy Carter held slight appeal for McGovern's "new-liberal" issue-activists. He appealed to the Democratic center *and* the blacks. This voting support made possible a narrow victory over Gerald Ford, the nonelected incumbent.

The Transformation of Parties

A third line of interpretation argues that the nation has moved away from the New Deal party system, not through a fundamental realignment, but *see Franklin D. Roosevelt in the White House. When FDR went to Washington during World War I as assistant secretary of the navy in President Wilson's administration, Howe went along as his assistant. When Roosevelt was crippled by polio, Howe and Mrs. Roosevelt played the decisive role in convincing FDR that he could still have a political career. Louis Howe was at FDR's right hand all the way to the White House in 1932.*

On the night of April 18, 1936, while President Roosevelt was delighting the Washington press corps at the annual Gridiron Club dinner at the Willard Hotel, a few hundred yards away Louis Howe gently passed away in his bedroom in the White House.

The president received the news as soon as he returned to the White House. He went immediately to his study, canceled all engagements for the next week, and ordered the White House flag lowered to half mast.

Louis Howe was accorded a state funeral in the East Room of the White House, attended by cabinet members, ambassadors, and the great names of the nation.

FDR went all the way to Fall River, Massachusetts for the burial services.

Among FDR's personal papers there is a little memo addressed to Mrs. Roosevelt: "I suggest the following be put on Louis's tombstone: 'Devoted friend, adviser, and associate of the President,' FDR."

Louis Howe (center) with Roosevelt and James Farley, Chairman of the Democratic National Committee.

through a continuing process of adaptation to social and economic change. Our parties "transform" themselves. Everett C. Ladd, Jr., the principal proponent of this view, concludes that we have developed a party system that is quite different from the old FDR coalition; and we have done so without having undergone a so-called realigning election. Ladd notes a number of conditions that have led other observers to the deterioration theory. They include the rise of ticket splitting, the increasing reliance on the mass media in political campaigns, and the tendency of the mass electorate to judge in terms of personality rather than issues. Both parties are "porous," Ladd argues, but they also are far from being dead, precisely *because they adjust to the process of social change!* While the Republicans have seen their support weaken, the Democrats have become an "Establishment" party. By this, Ladd means that the Democratic party, which has

The third theory of American political parties is that they continually transform themselves through a gradual process of adaptation to social and economic change.

One of the most important factors in Jimmy's Carter's success in 1976 was his very strong showing among black voters. Here he is shown with Dr. Martin Luther King, Sr. during a rally in downtown Atlanta in April 1976.

been viewed since the days of FDR as the party of the underprivileged, now contains "major segments of the high socioeconomic and political classes" of this country.

Ladd, with his associate, Charles Hadley, finds that Roosevelt's New Deal had the long-range effect of creating "a new middle class." The members of this class who are beneficiaries of the New Deal programs remain overwhelmingly favorable to the national Democratic party.[7] This

[7] See Everett C. Ladd, Jr., and Charles D. Hadley, *Transformation of the American Party System* (New York: Norton, 1975).

fact alone helps to explain the difficulty the Republican party faces in trying to move out of its position as permanent minority. It also helps to explain Carter's appeal in the South, where a new middle class is especially conspicuous. Indeed, isn't Jimmy Carter a spokesman for this new middle class?

Issue-activists

One of Ladd's more interesting findings is the appearance of a group of **issue-activists** in both major parties. These are individuals who are active in party politics and who think issues are important. To those who assert that there are no basic differences between Republicans and Democrats, Ladd discovers "issue-activists," who differ sharply. This is especially noticeable among the college-educated:

> There has been a decided trend toward polarization—with college-educated Republicans often more conservative than the general membership of their party, and college-educated Democrats regularly much more liberal than their party's rank and file.[8]

These college-educated issue-activists are less likely to be content with traditional, "center-of-the-road" consensus politics than are the rank-and-file voters. The rise of a new kind of activist increases the pressure within the parties to select candidates holding sharply different ideologies. The selection of Senator Goldwater by the Republicans in 1964 and of Senator McGovern by the Democrats in 1972 would fit this interpretation, assuming that the issue-activists captured the nomination machinery in both cases. LBJ's victory in 1964 and Nixon's in 1972 were of landslide proportions for the party that had *not* been captured by its issue-activists, although neither Johnson nor Nixon was generally considered an especially attractive or popular candidate. Ronald Reagan was an issue-activist candidate in 1976, but he failed to make it. In any event, Jimmy Carter's ultimate triumph appears a victory for pragmatic politics, rather than issue activism. On the surface, in fact, Carter's triumph appears to have been achieved in the face of the new Democratic issue-activists, most of whom would have preferred a more liberal candidate. Thus far, the new issue-activists do not seem to have had much success in getting their candidates into the White House.

THE NEW DEAL AND AFTER

In order to gain a better perspective on how this country got to where it is politically in the 1970s, we think it is advisable to trace briefly the

Issue-activists are individuals who are active in party politics and think issues are important.

[8] Ladd and Hadley, *Transformation of the American Party System,* p. 323.

political developments since Franklin Roosevelt. We do this because the changes inside the body of the American electorate—for example, the coming to maturity of your generation—are bound to have a profound effect on political parties, the chief agency for popular participation in our complex system.

Franklin D. Roosevelt, the Democratic nominee, a martini-drinking Episcopalian who regarded Georgia as his second home, carried every state west of Pennsylvania in 1932. The Republican party was almost wiped out in the midwestern heartland that gave it birth in the 1850s. FDR's victory reshaped the landscape of American electoral politics and created a new party alignment. His massive victory four years later brought with it one of the most authentic national mandates in our history.

Franklin D. Roosevelt campaigning.

Only Maine and Vermont resisted the New Deal tide in 1936. One wag mused that if the campaign had run a few more weeks, Roosevelt would have carried both of these bastions of Yankee conservatism and Canada as well! FDR was subsequently reelected to an unprecedented third term in 1940 and to a fourth in 1944.

This series of remarkable victories was made possible by the forging of a multigroup coalition that put an end to the post-1896 party system. In effect, the FDR–New Deal era produced a new party system that effectively reversed the earlier roles of the Republicans and Democrats.[9] Henceforth, the Democrats were to constitute the popular majority, with the Republicans assigned the role of a permanent minority. Far from suggesting the deterioration of parties, the Roosevelt era brought into being a new political coalition.

The New Deal Coalition

The political coalition that came together to support Franklin D. Roosevelt and his New Deal programs may have been the broadest in our history. FDR drew support from farmers, South and West; industrial workers, especially those of most recent immigrant background, such as Italian, Polish, Irish, and the northern blacks (few southern blacks had the vote); and academics and artists, as well as Main Street, U.S.A. The New Deal political "revolution" also altered the balance among the great interest groups. Under Roosevelt's friendly sponsorship, organized labor spread for the first time to the nation's mass-production industries—autos, steel, rubber, chemicals. Big Labor joined Big Business and Big Agriculture as a major force in Washington interest-group politics (see Chapter 4 for more detail). At the same time, organized labor developed a political-action arm that helped mobilize the vote for FDR on election day.

Harry S Truman, who succeeded to the presidency when FDR died in 1945, made a valiant effort to hold together the elements of this grand political coalition. Mr. Truman won a surprising upset victory over a confident Republican opponent, Governor Thomas E. Dewey of New York, in 1948, despite third parties on the left and right. The New Deal coalition proved its potency and durability even after the magic symbol "FDR" was gone from the ballot. The great broad center of the New Deal coalition held.

The Eisenhower Era: Divided Government

Dwight D. Eisenhower, Commander in Chief of American armed forces in Europe during World War II, dominated the political landscape during the 1950s in a manner that reminded some observers of Franklin D. Roo-

> Roosevelt and the New Deal introduced a new Democratic coalition that may have been the broadest in history. Since then, the Democrats have become the popular majority, with the Republicans apparently assigned the role of the permanent minority.

[9] See Everett C. Ladd, Jr., *American Political Parties* (New York: Norton, 1970) for a brief description of the development of the FDR coalition and its impact on the party system.

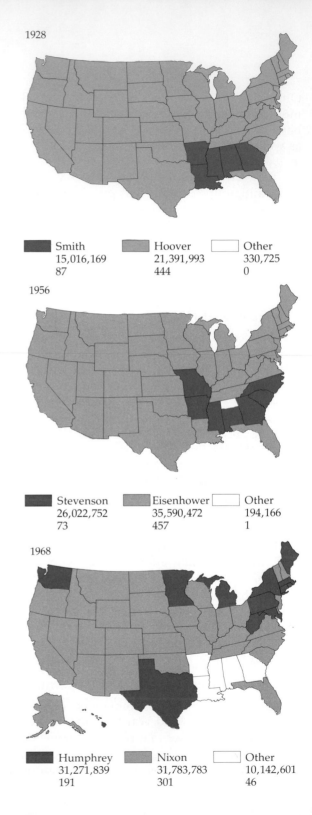

Fig. 5.2
Presidential election results from 1928 to 1976.

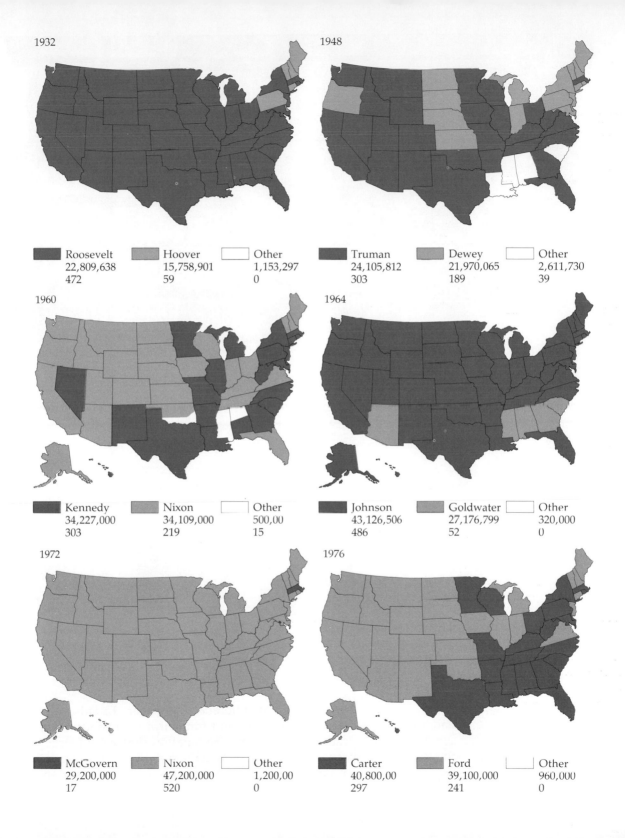

1932

Roosevelt
22,809,638
472

Hoover
15,758,901
59

Other
1,153,297
0

1948

Truman
24,105,812
303

Dewey
21,970,065
189

Other
2,611,730
39

1960

Kennedy
34,227,000
303

Nixon
34,109,000
219

Other
500,00
15

1964

Johnson
43,126,506
486

Goldwater
27,176,799
52

Other
320,000
0

1972

McGovern
29,200,000
17

Nixon
47,200,000
520

Other
1,200,00
0

1976

Carter
40,800,00
297

Ford
39,100,000
241

Other
960,000
0

The scoreboard shows:

	EISENHOWER	STEVENSON	
ALA.	149,329	209,564	
ARIZ.	90,338	51,878	
ARK.	35,123	48,991	
CALIF.	473,226	389,007	
COLO.	102,871	61,915	
CONN.	710,059	406,561	
DEL.	92,328	75,16	
FLA.	512,308	361,09	
GA.	136,097	227,	
IDAHO	39,270	26,	

President-elect and Mrs. Eisenhower during a Republican victory celebration in November 1956. With them are vice-president-elect and Mrs. Richard Nixon.

sevelt. There was an important difference, however. Eisenhower, who had a distaste for party politics, did not transform his extraordinary personal popularity into a new political combination that would strengthen the Republican party. The Democrats remained strong in Congress in the face of Eisenhower's presidential landslide victories. Eisenhower enjoyed the presence of a slim Republican majority in Congress only during the first two of his eight years in the White House. When Eisenhower returned to private life in 1961, the Democrats remained the party of the majority.

Eisenhower drew a large number (as many as 25 percent) of urban, Catholic voters away from their normal Democratic allegiance. To this extent, Eisenhower succeeded in cracking the New Deal coalition. His appeal to these voters in the northern cities appears to have been largely personal. In any event, most of them returned to the Democratic fold in 1960, helping to make possible John F. Kennedy's photo-finish victory over Richard M. Nixon, who had served as Eisenhower's vice-president.[10]

The 1960s: "Party Government" Restored

The Democratic majority party firmly controlled both the presidency and the Congress in the 1960–1968 period. Lyndon B. Johnson, who assumed the presidency following the assassination of Kennedy in November 1963, achieved a victory of landslide proportions against a Republican ticket headed by Senator Barry Goldwater, a staunch conservative. The propor-

[10] See Theodore White, *The Making of the President, 1960* (Boston: Atheneum, 1960) for a fascinating, behind-the-scenes account of the 1960 campaign. White has written similar accounts of each presidential election between 1964 and 1972.

Fig. 5.3
The Republican-Democrat balance in the House and Senate.

Congress	Years	House		President	Senate	
89th	1965–1967	295	140	Johnson	67	33
90th	1967–1969	248	187	Johnson	64	36
91st	1969–1971	243	192	Nixon	58	42
92nd	1971–1973	255	180	Nixon	55	45
93rd	1973–1975	244	191	Ford, Nixon	57	43
94th	1975–1977	291	144	Ford	61	39
95th	1977–1979	292	143	Carter	62	38

Democrat
Republican

There was a brief period of solid party government during the Johnson administration, out of which came the most substantial and expensive set of domestic programs since the days of the New Deal.

tions of this victory in 1964 also produced an unusually large Democratic majority in Congress. The result was the subsequent enactment of major domestic programs featuring aid to education, Medicare for the elderly, strong civil-rights legislation, urban renewal, and an array of job-training programs. Johnson's **Great Society** constituted the most substantial and expensive set of domestic programs since the days of the New Deal.

Do parties have an impact on public policy? The answer may depend in part on the kind of leadership emanating from the White House. In Eisenhower's case, there was relatively little interest in exerting party leadership, and Eisenhower, a Republican, had Democratic majorities in Congress during six of his eight years. With Johnson in the driver's seat, the Democrats in Congress greatly expanded our domestic programs during the 1960s and Johnson after 1964 enjoyed unusually large Democratic majorities in Congress. At the same time, the Kennedy-Johnson years also brought an expanding program of direct American military intervention in Vietnam. Vietnam soon divided the nation along lines of intense emotion. In March 1968, President Johnson announced that he would not seek his party's nomination for reelection. Vietnam helped bring an end to a brief period of party government, in which the Democratic majority party had controlled the White House and the Congress.[11]

The Nixon Years: Division and Stalemate (1969–1974)

Richard M. Nixon won a narrow victory in 1968 over Hubert H. Humphrey, the Democratic candidate who had served as LBJ's vice-president throughout the period of Vietnam escalation. Mr. Nixon's landslide triumph over Senator George McGovern four years later extended further another period of divided government. Throughout his White House years, President Nixon faced Democratic congressional majorities. Having served as Eisenhower's vice-president in the 1950s, Mr. Nixon was familiar with the special stresses and tensions that arise when White House and Congress are controlled by opposing political parties. Unfortunately, Mr. Nixon carried little of the immense personal popularity that Eisenhower enjoyed, nor did he convey Eisenhower's impression of benign, "above-the-storm," calmness. On the contrary, Mr. Nixon brought with him to the White House a reputation as a fierce partisan. This portion of his reputation was almost all that survived when he resigned from the presidency six years later.

The Nixon years were marked by a series of bitter struggles between the White House and the congressional Democrats, especially over budg-

[11] See John C. Donovan, *Politics of Poverty*, 2d ed. (Indianapolis, Ind.: Bobbs-Merrill, 1973) and *The Policy Maker* (Indianapolis, Ind.: Bobbs-Merrill, 1970) for elaboration of the themes touched on in this section.

etary issues. The revelations of the attempted Watergate coverup, as they unfolded in 1973–1974, worsened the situation. The circumstances of Mr. Nixon's resignation (the first presidential resignation in our history), followed by a pardon issued by his handpicked successor, Mr. Ford, left the federal government in a state of political stalemate on the eve of the nation's bicentennial.[12]

This brief review of recent party history suggests a number of possibilities for party activity in relation to making public policy depending on party strength in Congress and the kind of party leadership emanating from the White House. We turn next to a brief look at party organizations and functions to see in what ways they may be affected by the process of change.

The Nixon years were marked by bitter struggles between the White House and the congressional Democrats.

PARTY ORGANIZATION AND FUNCTIONS

As noted above, this country entered the twentieth century with a fully developed political party system. What were its important functions? The party system we inherited from the nineteenth century performed a number of vital functions. In addition to providing a body of elite leaders and establishing a public-policy agenda, the party system, in which Republicans contested with Democrats for control of the government, brought a large measure of political stability to a complex industrial society. The modern system of political parties does all this and provides a means of participation for the general citizenry. For most Americans, most of the time, the political party serves as the principal means of exerting some influence on the making of public policy. Because the party system has served these vital functions, any important changes in the nature of that system are likely to carry troublesome implications for the smooth functioning of our society.

Among other things, the political party system provides political stability and a means for the general citizenry to exert some influence on public policy.

Decentralization and the Party Platform

Organizationally, American national parties are not highly centralized, nor have they ever been. Our political parties are better described as being rather loose aggregations of strong state and local political groupings. Representatives (called party delegates) of these state and local party organizations come together in a national convention once every four years. There they bargain to form a coalition that will unite behind a candidate who appears to have some potential for capturing the White

American political parties are decentralized, loose aggregations of strong state and local political groupings.

---

[12] An excellent recent study of presidential elections since 1952 is Herbert Asher, *Presidential Election and American Politics: Voters, Candidates and Campaigns since 1952* (Homewood, Ill.: Dorsey, 1976).

House. Usually, the **party platform**, which presents the party's stand on the issues of the day, is hammered out *before* the delegates know who the candidate will be. (The Carter phenomenon in 1976 was an exception; his people played the decisive role in writing the final version of the Democratic platform.) The party's national committee, its only continuing central organization, exerts no disciplinary authority over the voting behavior of its party members in the Congress relative to the party platform. Often, candidates virtually ignore the party platform as they run their own campaigns, not wanting to be tied to all its specific positions. Carter a meticulous man, took care to see that the platform was written to meet *his* specifications.

Federalism and Party Organization

The basic organizational structure of the American party system has changed surprisingly little from when it was first put together by Andrew Jackson's organizers. Both major parties today contain a federal pattern of organization. Our parties mirror the national government in this respect. There are fifty state committees. Below the state committees stand the county committees. In some instances these are strong organizations; more often, they are not. The local level has its own layer of party committees and organizations. In the cities, important party organizations may be found at the precinct level. Some of these local party organizations are still run along lines that would remind one of the days of "boss" rule in the late nineteenth century. Then, urban "machines" (as they were called by the reformers) were assimilating hordes of European immigrants into the new American society; today, they are more likely to have supporters who are black or Spanish-speaking.[13]

Political scientist William J. Keefe summarizes the essentials of "boss"-led "machine" politics in the earlier period:

> In the late nineteenth and early twentieth century the best examples of strong party organization could be found in the large cities of the Northeast and Midwest—New York City, Boston, Philadelphia, Jersey City, Kansas City, and Chicago. Well-organized and strongly disciplined, the urban "machine" during this era was well-nigh invincible. Precinct and ward officials maintained steady contacts with their party constituencies, finding jobs for people out of work, helping those who were in trouble with the law, helping others to secure government benefits such as welfare assistance, assisting neighborhoods to secure government services, helping immigrants to cope with a new society, and facilitating merchants and tradespeople in their efforts to obtain

---

[13] Fred Greenstein, *The American Party System and the American People*, 2d ed. (Englewood Cliffs, N.J.: Prentice-Hall, 1970) has a strong section on urban political organizations.

contracts, licenses, and the like. The party organization was at the center of community life, an effective mediary between the people and their government. Party officials were "brokers," exchanging information, access, and influence for loyalty and support at the polls."[14]

The Jacksonian movement created this pattern of party organization in order to provide for mass participation in politics. The Age of Jackson also gave us the delegate convention system for making nominations, which is still the method by which candidates for the nation's highest office are chosen. Finally, the Jacksonians were the first to offer a national party platform.

The Primary

Probably the most important organizational "invention" since the age of Jackson is the **primary election** as a device for candidate selection. The primary was put forth early in this century by progressive reformers who fought against the "machines." They argued that the conventions were manipulated by the "bosses" (the heads of the powerful state and local organizations), who handpicked the candidates behind closed doors in smoke-filled rooms. The primary was seen as a means of reopening the candidate selection process to the votes of ordinary rank-and-file voters. Actually, the direct primary, in replacing the support of the party organization as a means of gaining nomination, has served to weaken political parties.

As disclosed further in Chapter 6, the 1976 election shows how important the presidential primaries may be, especially for an "outsider" like Jimmy Carter, who started the race virtually unknown as a national figure. Carter announced early that he would participate in all thirty primaries. He lost little time in establishing the image of "front runner," and his persistence and resilience in surviving the thirty contests (he did not win them all, by any means) and his mastery of the media meant that he went to the Democratic National Convention with the nomination in his hip pocket. An "outsider" had used the primary system with a strong assist from the media to gain his party's presidential nomination. Carter did this despite the candidacies of several better-known contenders, the opposition of a number of powerful organizations, and more-than-normal public apathy.[15]

The party system today has the same federal pattern of organization as when it was first put together under Andrew Jackson. The only important innovation since that time has been the primary election.

[14] William J. Keefe, *Parties, Politics, and Public Policy in America,* 2d ed. (Hinsdale, Ill.: Dryden Press, 1976), pp. 16–17.

[15] See Gerald Pomper, *The Election of 1976* (New York: David McKay, 1977) for an assessment by a team of political scientists anxious to compete with journalists in offering almost instantaneous post-election analysis.

Party Reform

Periodically, efforts are made to "reform" American political parties. Usually, these efforts have as their central purpose to increase *participation* in party affairs, although, historically, political activists have never constituted more than a tiny percentage of the voting populace. The most recent reform wave has been felt more strongly inside the Democratic party, which has since responded to the recommendations of the so-called McGovern Commission in 1970. As a result, the delegate selection process has been opened considerably to represent women, blacks, and young people, and the party now holds national policy conferences midway between presidential conventions. Whether these recent changes have effected "reform" within the majority party remains to be seen.

The Republican party, less given to reformist urges, struggles against the handicap of being a permanent national minority party, with no present prospect of gaining control of Congress and with a shrinking base in the electorate.[16] At present, only one potential voter in every five favors the Republican party.

Having examined briefly the changing functions of our parties, the growing influence of primaries, especially in presidential politics, and the reform urge, we turn next to an examination of what differences, if any, exist between our two major parties.

PARTIES OF COMPROMISE

American political parties have been held together historically by techniques of compromise. Conflicting viewpoints tend to be accommodated. There may be (and, as we shall soon note, are) differences of substance that separate most Democrats in Congress from most Republicans. Indeed, party ties count for more in the bulk of congressional voting than some critics seem to realize. Nevertheless, the differences between Republicans and Democrats are not those that would separate a "conservative" party from a "labor" (or Socialist) party, as in Great Britain.

Clinton Rossiter described our two major parties as follows:

> They are creatures of compromise, coalitions of interest in which principles are muted and often even silenced. They are vast, gaudy, friendly umbrellas under which all Americans, whoever and wherever and however-minded

---

[16] William J. Crotty has prepared a thoroughgoing study of party politics in terms of "the reform cycle" that includes the reform attempts of the late 1960s. See his *Political Reform and the American Experiment* (New York: Crowell, 1977). He examines registration and voting, money, and campaigns (including public funding) as well as presidential nominating methods. See also Austin Ranney, *Curing the Mischiefs of Faction* (Berkeley: University of California Press, 1975).

they may be, are invited to stand for the sake of being counted in the next election. The parties, moderate, and tolerant and self-contradictory to a fault, are interested in the votes of men, not in their principles. . . .[17]

This is not a new view of American parties, but it seems as valid today as it did when Rossiter wrote it many years ago.

Party Differences

Because our major parties are relatively nonideological, with a tendency to compromise, it is often assumed, inaccurately, that there are no important differences between them. In fact, the difference can be quite real—and important. The Republican party arose in the middle of the last century over one central issue: the expansion of slavery. Although the Republican party contained several elements—Free Soilers, Conscience Whigs, Know Nothings—it was originally a party opposed to the further expansion of slavery. The Democratic party in the days of Jackson carried a warm appeal for working people and agrarians.

In the contemporary era, the Republican party better represents the interests of the great private corporations while the Democratic party, since FDR, has proved to be a more reliable instrument for advancing the interests of organized labor. Black Americans now give Democratic presidential candidates their strong support. Naturally, Democratic administrations are more responsive to the policy demands of the black community than Republican administrations. (This is not to say that Democrats in power satisfy the demands of this constituency.) The Democratic party, with its labor and black constituencies, is somewhat more sensitive to the

Our party system has traditionally been marked by compromise and accommodation. Nevertheless, there are important differences between the two parties that cannot be discounted.

[17] Clinton Rossiter, *Parties and Politics in America* (Ithaca, N.Y.: Cornell University Press, 1960), p. 11.

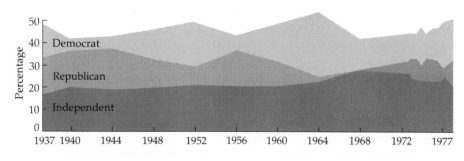

Fig. 5.4
Trends in party affiliation. (Source: *Public Opinion,* March/April 1978, based on AIPO (Gallup) Surveys. Reprinted by permission.)

issue of unemployment than the Republican party. The Republicans, on the other hand, are somewhat more sensitive to the inflationary threat and are, therefore, quicker to opt for deflationary policies. In all of this, however, the differences are matters of degree.

The differences between the major parties are not sharply ideological, but they are there and they have operational significance. A new generation of political scientists working on the frontiers of voting-behavior research is skillfully probing the meaning of American parties as perceived by the electorate in terms of the popular "images" of these parties.[18]

We mentioned earlier the emergence of new issue activists in both Republican and Democratic ranks. Miller and Levitin see a potentially powerful source of political change in what they call "the new politics" of the 1970s. They label one group of issue-activists "the new liberals" and the more conservative (also smaller) group "the silent minority." The differences between these groups in their nonpolitical attitudes and in their general support of the political system are negligible. Where they differ and differ profoundly is on questions of social value related to influence and power in our society: the stuff of serious politics.[19]

More "Responsible" Parties?

Some critics decry the American party system with its tendency to seek compromise. They wish the differences on matters of program were sharper. Some would prefer clearer distinctions between "liberal" and "conservative" positions. This, they claim, would make voters' choices mean something.

A "responsible" party system, in this view, would feature parties with sufficient cohesion, coherence, and discipline to formulate a detailed public-policy program and to enact it into law once the party controlled the executive and legislative branches. Such a party system would closely resemble the model offered by political parties in the British Parliament. American parties have usually fallen short of this conception. Instances of party government are not unknown—witness the FDR and LBJ periods— but neither are they common.

The case for more responsible parties received an authoritative statement in a report the American Political Science Association published in 1950. The report, entitled *Toward a More Responsible Two Party System*, represented the work of a distinguished committee of political scientists,

---

[18] See especially Richard J. Trilling, *Party Image and Electoral Behavior* (New York: Wiley-Interscience, 1976), p. 234.

[19] Warren E. Miller and Teresa Levitin, *Leadership and Change: Presidential Elections from 1952 to 1976* (Cambridge, Mass.: Winthrop, 1976).

chaired by E. E. Schattschneider. (Interestingly enough, Professor Schattschneider was the author of a major work describing the accommodationist and coalitional nature of American political parties.) It is generally assumed that the A.P.S.A. committee had in mind an idealized version of the British party system—with its tight party organizations and discipline—as a model for a "more responsible" American party system.[20] A quarter of a century later, American political scientists do not appear to have convinced political activists that a "responsible" party system is a live option in American politics. Does this mean that Americans prefer "irresponsible" parties? Where do we look for parties of "principle" in a system in which the major parties seek to compromise differences and conflicting viewpoints?

THIRD PARTIES: IDEOLOGY AND PRINCIPLE IN AMERICAN POLITICS

Political parties displaying ideological fervor and a will to fight hard for those issues that have been ignored or neglected by the two major parties appear with astonishing regularity in our national elections. We do, indeed, have ideological parties in this country. Like apple pie, they are as traditional as our major parties. **Third parties**, as they are called, provide an alternative within American politics to so-called accommodationist or compromise politics. The fact that we call them "third parties" suggests a qualitative difference from the two major parties. Third parties have a major disadvantage. They do not gain control of the Congress or elect their candidates to the White House. The reason is quite clear. Most American voters are not especially attracted to parties that draw sharp ideological and issue distinctions. This being the case, one may ask, What do third parties do? Why are some American voters attracted to them? Are third parties engaging in an exercise in futility?

The importance of third-party activity in American electoral politics is illustrated in the elections of 1912, 1932, 1948, and 1968.[21]

1912: Debs and Roosevelt Assist Wilson

In 1912, two third parties challenged the major parties. The Socialist party, led by Eugene V. Debs, scored its highest gains, polling nearly a million votes. But the largest and most successful third-party effort of the pre–

[20] E. E. Schattschneider, *Party Government in the United States* (New York: Holt, Rinehart and Winston, 1942).

[21] D. A. Mazmanian, *Third Parties in Presidential Elections* (Washington, D.C.: The Brookings Institution, 1974).

Theodore Roosevelt.

World War I period was launched the same year under the leadership of
Theodore Roosevelt, the former Republican President (1901–1909). When
the votes were counted, the Democratic ticket, headed by Woodrow
Wilson, had amassed 6.3 million popular votes (42 percent). President
Taft, the GOP standard bearer, received fewer than 3.5 million (23 percent), while Roosevelt, as Bull Moose Progressive, garnered more than 4
million (27 percent). Debs's 900,000 votes, representing almost 6 percent

of the total, proved to be the high-water mark for democratic socialism in this country. Roosevelt's candidacy split the normal Republican vote while Democrat Woodrow Wilson, also responding to progressive sentiment, went on to become a major figure.[22]

1932: Failure on the Left

The year 1932 seemed an ideal time for an impressive third-party showing. The conditions appeared to be ripe for a massive voter protest. As many as fifteen million able-bodied workers were unable to find any employment whatsoever. The Great Depression was a time of unprecedented despair for millions of decent Americans. Hoover, the Republican incumbent, seemed vulnerable to an attack from the political left because his party had hailed themselves throughout the 1920s as the "architects of prosperity." Now, the business-led economy lay in ruins.

But there was no strong showing on the political left in 1932. Norman Thomas, the Socialist candidate, polled fewer votes than Debs had in 1912. Thomas's percentage of the popular vote was a mere 2 percent. Foster, the Communist party candidate for president, polled exactly 102,875 votes—a quarter of one percent of the total, hardly the stuff that revolutions are made of. Franklin D. Roosevelt, a wealthy country squire, a graduate of the exclusive Groton School and Harvard University, who was also a victim of polio, was the Democratic standard-bearer. His ticket gained 57 percent of the popular vote. An ideological, issue-oriented party did *not* win. Furthermore, the nation passed through this moment of supreme economic crisis without an ideologically oriented party even gaining ground.[23]

1948: The Center Holds

American voters in 1948 faced their first opportunity since the death of FDR in 1945 to reshape national politics and, possibly, "undo" the New Deal. There were two important third-party efforts in 1948. Truman, the Democratic incumbent, faced a challenge on the left from a Progressive-Labor ticket headed by Henry Wallace, who had once served as FDR's vice-president. At the other extreme, Strom Thurmond, Governor of South Carolina, headed a States Rights–Dixiecrat ticket that was strenuously opposed to civil-rights legislation. Governor Thomas E. Dewey of New York, the GOP standard-bearer, was an Eastern "progressive" Republican.

[22] W. E. Binkley, *American Political Parties: Their Natural History,* 3d ed. (New York: Knopf, 1958).

[23] Binkley, *American Political Parties.*

Governor George Wallace of Alabama ran the most effective third-party candidacy in recent times. Paralyzed in 1972 in an assassination attempt, he was never again able to achieve the same success, although he continued to campaign from a wheelchair.

The third parties did not succeed in knocking Truman out of the ring, as it was supposed that they would. Instead, he won an upset victory over Dewey, the clear preelection favorite. Thurmond and Wallace each polled somewhat fewer than a million and a quarter votes. Their respective shares of the popular vote total were 2.4 percent and 2.37 percent.

Once again, the political center in American politics held firm against weak challenges from either extreme.[24]

1968: Running against Washington

This time, a third-party candidacy threatened to throw a national election into the House of Representatives. Governor George Wallace of Alabama, by appealing to the white South and to ethnic urban voting blocs elsewhere, hoped to gain enough votes in the electoral college to deny the election to either Richard Nixon, the Republican nominee, or Hubert Humphrey, the Democratic candidate. He failed in this strategy. Nixon edged out Humphrey in a close race. But Wallace, nevertheless, had polled ten million votes: a sizeable protest.

[24] Gerald M. Pomper, in his study of elections, finds 1948 representing another triumph for the new voting coalition put together first by FDR. 1948 was part of a realigning era, in this view. See his *Elections in America* (New York: Dodd, Mead, 1968).

Wallace posed a continuing problem for each of the two major parties. Neither was in a position to ignore his following. Wallace was the first American politician to successfully exploit the disenchantment stemming from Vietnam and the domestic turbulence of the 1960s. He struck upon themes in 1968—anti-Washington, antibureaucracy, "return government to the people"—that many mainstream politicians were to adopt in the 1970s. Our major political parties are not likely to ignore ten million voters for very long.[25]

By 1976, it was too late for George Wallace. Is it conceivable that George Wallace of Alabama made the candidacy of Jimmy Carter of Georgia feasible, if not inevitable? Do you agree that the voters appear to be

[25] Mazmanian, *Third Parties in Presidential Elections,* offers special treatment of the George Wallace phenomenon.

Fig. 5.5
Selected third-party vote totals 1832–1968.

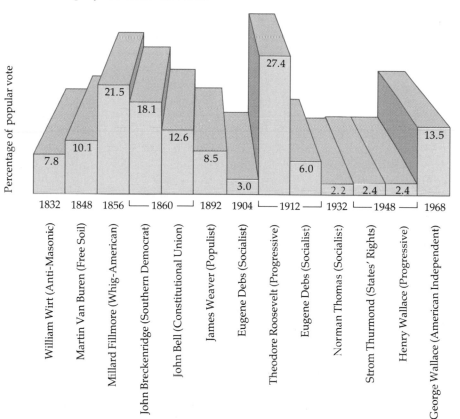

telling us that they feel most comfortable with people in the mainstream of American parties—even when they sound as if they are not?

What Third Parties Teach Us about Our Two-Party System

Why do we not have major parties of "principle" in this country? Why are American parties not divided along ideological lines, with "conservatives" in one party opposing "liberals" in the other?

Although they have never had a candidate elected to the White House, third parties offer an important alternative to the compromise politics of the two-party system, and help keep the system alive.

As we have noted, our third parties have often been parties of principle and ideology. They do not, however, win elections. But the examples cited above show that a third-party movement may affect the balance of forces in national politics.

Third parties are part of the American political tradition. We have a durable and adaptable two-party system, modified from time to time by third-party activity. Third-party activity, by blunting the ideological thrusts of the two major parties, helps explain the longevity of our so-called two-party system.

AN ASSESSMENT: STABILITY AND ADJUSTMENT

What kind of party system is this? Two major parties that have been with us since the Civil War (with the Democrats going back to the age of Jackson) continue to dominate national politics. From time to time, they are challenged, occasionally invigorated, and may even be modified by third-party activity. Nevertheless, the Democrats and Republicans control the turf. Academic authorities bemoan our parties' lack of "responsibility" and, as we have seen, the major parties display a ready tendency to seek compromise on divisive issues. The party system is variously thought to be deteriorating, realigning, or transforming itself. But this much is not subject to serious challenge: *Democrats and Republicans continue to share the capacity to govern the United States.*

Furthermore, this has been a central fact in American government for more than a century. We have a remarkably *stable* and *adjustable* party system. Endorsement by one of the two major parties offers the sole route to the White House. Only the Democrats and the Republicans have the capacity to enact national legislation. *No feasible political alternative exists.* Furthermore, the two controlling parties have worked out a unique relationship within Congress. Since the days of FDR the Democrats have come to constitute virtually a permanent congressional majority. There is no real possibility that the Republican party will soon seize control of Congress. The Republicans in Congress constitute an institutionalized minority. (The Republicans have organized the Congress for a grand total of four years—1947–1949 and 1953–1955 since 1930.) We now have a new political generation coming to maturity that has *never* witnessed a Republican-controlled Congress. You may never see one.

An important consequence is that the Democratic majority party finds itself covering such a broad range of interests and issues that its own cohesiveness is constantly threatened. The extremes pull away from the center. Some of the more interesting struggles of contemporary politics are fought out *within* the Democratic party. This aspect of our politics was noted back in the 1950s by Samuel Lubell. Lubell observed a pattern in American politics featuring a *dominant majority*:

> Thumbing back through history, we find relatively few periods when the major parties were closely competitive, with elections alternating between one and the other. The usual pattern has been that of the dominant majority party, which stayed in office as long as its elements held together, and a minority party, which gained power only when the majority coalition split.

Lubell went on to note that: "It is within the majority party that the issues of any particular period are fought out. . . ."[26]

President Carter was well aware that a potential source of opposition to his political leadership lay within his own Democratic party. The issue-activists, who supported McGovern with enthusiasm in 1972 and who worked hard for Udall during the 1976 primaries, lost little time in criticizing Carter's fiscal "conservatism."

Patrick Caddell warned President Carter about this wing of the Democratic party in his Working Paper on Political Strategy presented in December, 1976:

> *The liberal establishment*—Traditional liberals in the Democratic party in many ways are as antiquated and anachronistic a group as are the conservative Republicans. However, because of their representation in the establishment, the media and in politics they have a weight in public affairs far greater than their numbers. They have been openly hostile in the past to Governor Carter not only because he has a different set of national priorities, but also because of differences over style and approach.[27]

Caddell, who knew this wing of the party well, having served as pollster for Senator McGovern in 1976, pointed to Senators Kennedy and McGovern and Representative Udall as individuals who would see little risk in "challenging an incumbent President coupled with an overwhelming desire for doing so."

A large majority party may easily become too large to contain its internal differences. This is an ever-present reality inside the current Dem-

---

[26] Samuel Lubell, *The Future of American Politics*, rev. ed. (Garden City, N.Y.: Doubleday Anchor, 1956), p. 212.

[27] Patrick H. Caddell, *Initial Working Paper on Political Strategy*, December 10, 1976.

ocratic party. The inner tensions within the majority party encourage Republicans to think again of recapturing the White House.

Political Stalemate

A further consequence of the American party system is that it encourages and supports *divided government*. Many years ago, James M. Burns labeled this "the deadlock of democracy."[28] Since 1950, the Republican party, an entrenched minority in Congress, has nonetheless captured the White

[28] James M. Burns, *The Deadlock of Democracy* (with revisions) (Englewood Cliffs, N.J.: Prentice-Hall–Spectrum, 1963).

A recent and controversial example of two-party collaboration occurred during the Senate ratification of the Panama Canal treaties, in which the Republican and Democratic leadership collaborated to ensure passage of the treaty. Here Republican leader Howard Baker and Democratic leader Robert Byrd share congratulations after the Senate ratified the second Panama Canal treaty in Washington.

House no less than four times in seven contests. Contemporary American politics, therefore, always has to *assume* the possibility of divided government. Under these circumstances, party government (with so-called responsible parties) is bound to be difficult to achieve and almost as difficult to sustain once it has been achieved. There is a word for the common condition of American national politics: *stalemate. Stalemate* obviously serves best the interests of those who prefer no great changes in the way things are.

Prior to the Carter administration, political stalemate precluded reform of the welfare mess, any fundamental reform of the federal tax code, a resolution of the inflation-jobs dilemma, and a reassessment of spending priorities, to mention a few of the larger items that have figured prominently in political discussions in recent years. Since the same items loomed high on President Carter's agenda for action, he had little choice but to seek to break the stalemate. But the presence of Democratic majorities in the two houses of Congress did not guarantee Carter any easy victories in getting his elaborate program enacted into law. The political deadlock was not simply a matter of Democrats battling Republicans.

A fuller meaning of American politics is likely to be found when one gains an understanding of the American electorate. Our political parties are a reflection of us—who we are and what we want. Our parties respond to the demands we make upon them.

PARTY POLITICS AFTER CARTER

It is too early to know what effect the election of 1976 is to have on the future of American party politics. Jimmy Carter's nomination and election was a triumph in the skillful use of the mass media. At the same time, his margin of victory over Gerald Ford, the nonelected head of a caretaker administration, was narrow. Black voters supported Carter handsomely and he also did well among white southerners and among white Protestants in general. Labor union members were among his strongest supporters. On the other hand, Carter was viewed with great skepticism by the new-breed issue-activist so prominent in McGovern's 1972 campaign.[29]

In other words, Carter entered office with nothing like a clearcut national mandate. His support within his own party was mixed. Although the Democrats commanded overwhelming majorities in Congress, the internal divisions within this swollen majority were evident. In addition, Carter was very much an "outsider" who had gained office by challenging the Washington community. His attack on the bureaucracy and politics as

---

[29] Pomper, *The Election of 1976.*

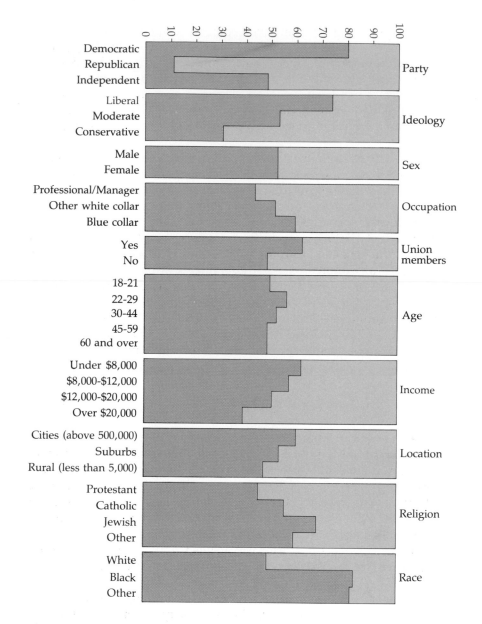

Fig. 5.6
How various groups voted in the 1976 presidential election. (Source: CBS Poll of 14,836 voters as reported in the *Times*. © 1976 by The New York Times Company. Reprinted by permission.)

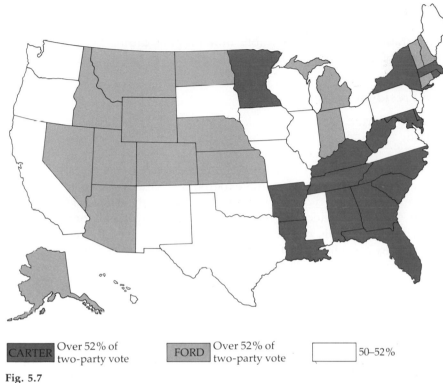

CARTER Over 52% of two-party vote   FORD Over 52% of two-party vote   50–52%

Fig. 5.7
1976 presidential election: a nation divided.

usual was frank enough. Furthermore, he promised wholesale reform: reform of the welfare system, taxation, the bureaucracy itself; a reorganization of our national security system; a comprehensive energy program; national health insurance; and a balanced budget! Little wonder, then, that President Carter in the White House continued his effort to project himself as a mass-media celebrity, much as President Kennedy did in the early 1960s. The personality and style were different, but the approach was much the same. Barry Jagoda, Carter's television advisor, boasted: "We've got the biggest star in television. Jimmy Carter may be the biggest television star of all time."[30]

Perhaps. But how does a "prime-time president" fare in dealing with a congressional majority containing legions of noncelebrities? What is the effect of television on the party system? Can the Republicans find a mass-media celebrity of their own who will give them another clean shot at the

[30] Quoted in Richard Reeves, "The Prime-Time President," The *New York Times*, May 15, 1977.

White House in 1980? Do not television stars shine with rare intensity and then fade with monotonous regularity? How else are we to explain Carter's deteriorating position in the public opinion polls during his first year and a half in office?

The President's Organization

President Carter was too shrewd politically to rely exclusively on image-building. Like all recent presidents, Carter got to the White House by building and by leading his own political organization of key operators and managers. Jody Powell and Hamilton Jordan, his top two White House assistants, were not media experts, but hard-working young political operatives. They did not work for the Democratic National Committee or the Georgia Democratic State Committee; they were organizers *for* Jimmy Carter. In this respect, they were very much like Amos Kendall, who played a similar role for Andrew Jackson, and Thurlow Weed, an organizing genius from Albany, New York, who helped create the Whig combination to compete with the Jacksonians. Only the political environment—and the society—had changed.

Once he had reached the White House, it was not likely that Carter would place his political future (looking ahead to 1980) in the hands of the Democratic National Committee. Carter originally placed Kenneth Curtis, a former Maine Governor and a Carter loyalist, in the position of national chairman, as well as a number of his own people, in the national party headquarters. After ten months, Curtis resigned after a continuing struggle with the people around Carter in the White House. The trick was to keep Carter's own personal organization in working order in 1980 without alienating the party regulars and without giving room to the party liberals to move their favorites forward so as to challenge Carter. This problem became even more pertinent as Carter came to be viewed by the media, his rivals, and his opponents as a potential one-termer.

A Vibrant Arm

Pat Caddell[31] put it nicely: "It is my belief that we should consider making the DNC more than it has been under past presidents: we should make it an active, vibrant political arm of the Carter White House."

Caddell specifically called for the selection of a national party chairman who would be a "loyalist" and an "insider," which he further defined as being a person willing to "take direction" from Carter's personal and political staff.

---

[31] Caddell, *Initial Working Paper on Political Strategy*.

His memo continues: "The DNC must build an operating organization for Carter. This means not only bringing in Carter activists into [sic] the structure of the DNC itself, but building strong organizations in states and cities for the future."

The Machiavellian public-opinion pollster left little to the imagination: "Utilizing the DNC in this way to reward supporters, co-opt adversaries, and merge other political organizations into aliances [sic]. One of the functions, particularly in 1978, should be identifying and hopefully co-opt [sic] the people who might help staff opposing presidential campaigns."

So that his point would be crystal clear: "One of the best ways, I think, to limit the potential opposition in the future is to remove from the job market as many of those with experience and talent in presidential politics as can be accommodated."

The Democratic National Committee in the Carter era did not fit the usual textbook description of a "national" party organization. Instead, the national headquarters of the majority party was an arm of a White House political organization, as it normally is. Carter and *his* people (and they were *his* people) wished to "maximize the incumbency," in the words of John Dean of Watergate fame. Like Nixon's men and LBJ's men and JFK's men, the people around President Carter were *presidential* loyalists, not *party* loyalists. This key fact tells us much about the nature of national politics in the United States. The presidential "party" is loyal to the president. Period.

Questions for Pondering

On the basis of our analysis in this chapter, what kind of a party system would you expect to find in the United States, given our two-party tradition and the kinds of voting behavior described above? Would you expect to find a party committed to socialism? Would you expect to find a party that took a firm stance for conservatism? Would you expect the Bull Moose party to make a comeback? Would you expect the Communist party to broaden its base of support and capture a significant number of seats in Congress? Do you think that we have the party system we desire?

SUMMARY

American political parties, resilient and adaptive perhaps to a fault, have performed important functions within the total political-governmental system. They provide one of the few links between the general public and policy-making officials. The major parties remain the single most important agency for asserting the aspirations of the general public. The parties appear to be changing. The skyrocketing costs of mass-media campaigns have overwhelmed the fund-raising capacities of regular party organizations. Public financing is on the rise, with unpredictable consequences to party organizations. The mass-media campaign brings advertising, public relations, and polling specialists directly into the strategy and direction of electoral politics, once considered the prime preserve of the professional, organizational, party politician. Contemporary electioneering activity combines the ancient art of doorbell ringing, the more modern art of telephone ringing at the local and precinct level, and the even more recent art of television and radio advertising. Nineteenth-century political campaigns, with their hoopla and torchlight parades, provided one of the few good shows of a lifetime for the ordinary guy. The candidate for public office today must use media that offer entertainment to a mass audience on a continuous basis. As we note in Chapter 6, it is not easy to project a candidate's "image" in competition with Charlie's Angels and The Fonz.

These are some of the reasons American political parties are thought to be in trouble. Their condition may even be as serious as the critics maintain. But no one has conceived an alternative for the strategic role of parties in providing and electing elite political leadership. Between them, the major parties continue to control the nomination of candidates for the presidency. The Democrats and Republicans share a century-long monopoly in electing presidents. The same two major parties continue to monopolize the membership of Congress. Does this suggest "decomposition" and "deterioration"?

On the other hand, even where there are signs that the traditional ties of party allegiance are definitely weakening, ticket-splitting is on the increase. Disenchantment with politicians and politics-as-usual runs high. The last members of the FDR political generation, which has provided the elite leadership since the end of the Second World War, are about to disappear from the scene. A new political generation rises to ascendancy in national politics. The party of apathy continues to enroll more loyal supporters than either the Democrats or Republicans. But the Democrats and Republicans between them control the presidency and the Congress, just as they have since the age of Lincoln.

KEY TERMS

deterioration theory
realignment theory
transformation theory
coalition
issue-activists
New Deal
party government
Great Society

party platform
primary election
third party
divided government

SUGGESTED READINGS

BRODER, DAVID, *The Party's Over* (New York: Harper & Row, 1972).

A critique of the party system by a well-respected journalist who laments the deterioration of parties and offers some ideas for reform.

BURNS, JAMES M., *The Deadlock of Democracy* (Englewood Cliffs, N.J.: Prentice-Hall, 1963).

An analysis of American politics that maintains that there are two centers of power (presidential and congressional) around which traditional parties are split. Argues that a more responsible party system is needed to break this political stalemate.

CHAMBERS, WILLIAM N., and WALTER D. BURNHAM, *The American Party System: Stages of Political Development* (New York: Oxford University Press, 1967).

A series of essays by political scientists and historians, who trace the development of national and local political parties in the United States.

KEY, V. O., Jr., *The Responsible Electorate* (New York: Vintage Books, 1968).

An impressive portrait of the American voter and an analysis of political behavior that suggests that American voters are considerably more rational than many of their critics have assumed.

LADD, EVERETT C., Jr., and CHARLES D. HADLEY, 2d ed. *Transformations of the American Party System* (New York: Norton, 1978).

A revealing study of party competition and conflict that traces the current period of instability to the unraveling of the coalitions that favored or opposed the New Deal programs of Franklin D. Roosevelt.

LOWI, THEODORE, *The End of Liberalism* (New York: Norton, 1969).

A critique of "interest-group liberalism" urging a return to public philosophy. Lowi's "Juridical democracy" prescriptions may leave political realists somewhat unsatisfied, to say the least.

MAZMANIAN, D. A., *Third Parties in Presidential Elections* (Washington, D.C.: The Brookings Institution, 1974).

Analyzes the role of third parties and traces their history, with special emphasis on the candidacy of George Wallace and the American Independent party in 1968.

SCHATTSCHNEIDER, E. E., *Party Government* (New York: Holt, Rinehart and Winston, 1942).

A study of political parties that posits the need for more centralized and disciplined parties.

SORAUF, FRANK J., *Party Politics in America*, 3d ed. (Boston: Little, Brown, 1976).

An impressive overall analysis of party politics.

SUNDQUIST, JAMES L., *Dynamics of the Party System* (Washington, D.C.: The Brookings Institution, 1973).

An analysis of three major realignments of the past—those identified with the critical elections of the 1850s, the 1890s, and the 1930s—that attempts to clarify the dynamics of the system.

You can fool all the people some of the
time, and some of the people all of the
time, and those ain't bad odds.

Political consultant

CHAPTER 6 ELECTIONS IN AMERICA: VOTER CHOICES, CANDIDATES, AND STRATEGIES

The congressional candidate was completing a hectic day of campaigning. As he went through a busy supermarket he stopped here and there to chat with shoppers. Young, energetic, and handsome, he moved easily from group to group. Seeing two elderly ladies nod and smile after he left them, the campaign manager came over to see what had pleased them.

"What do you think of him?" the manager asked.

"We like him, we like him a lot," said one woman while the other nodded in agreement.

Eager to find out what they liked, the manager asked, "Well, what do you like about him?"

"Oh," said one, "his stand on the issues."

"Which issues?" asked the manager, hoping to discover a stand that could be emphasized in the campaign.

"You know, *the* issues," reiterated the lady.

Puzzled, the manager turned to the second lady.

"What does she mean, 'the issues'?" he asked.

"She means," the second lady said, with only a trace of a smile, "she means the issues—like his blue eyes."

The first lady nodded vigorously, "That's what I said, 'the issues.'"

Why do voters choose one candidate over another? Do they make their selection on the basis of party affiliation? Or because one candidate stands for a specific point of view? Or do they, like the women in the campaign example, make up their minds on the basis of the candidate's personality or physical features? Which factors are most important in influencing the voter's choice in American politics?

These are not unimportant questions. Elections play a critical role in the successful working of the American political system. They present opportunities for voters to express their wishes and to choose leaders from among the candidates. In the United States, more than 500,000 public

TABLE 6.1
THE 1976 VOTE IN
RELATION TO "PARTY
IDENTIFICATION"

	DEMOCRAT		INDEPENDENT			REPUBLICAN	
	STRONG	WEAK	DEM.	IND.	REP.	STRONG	WEAK
Carter	73%	48%	50%	22%	10%	3%	16%
Ford	7	16	16	27	61	87	55
Other	1	3	5	4	3	2	2
No-Vote	19	33	29	47	26	8	27

From Warren E. Miller and Teresa Levitin, *Leadership and Change: Presidential Elections from 1952 to 1976* (Cambridge, Mass.: Winthrop Publishers, 1976).

officials at all levels of government are chosen by the people. In 1976 more than 105 million Americans registered to vote and more than 80 million voted in the presidential election, a record number. In terms of the number of people chosen and the number participating, elections offer important evidence as to how badly or how well our political system is working. They may also offer clues as to the direction in which it is going.

Some observers argue that elections are merely symbolic exercises designed to keep the great mass of the population tied to the system. They contend that the voters really have little choice between Tweedledee and Tweedledum. Others argue that voters are manipulated through advertising and packaging; that in effect, they are "tricked" into voting a certain way. Still others maintain that elected officials are not really bound

During his 1968 campaign for the presidency, the charismatic Robert F. Kennedy generated a tremendous degree of enthusiasm, which was cut off abruptly when he was killed by an assassin.

by the positions they take during a campaign—that because they are elected for fixed terms, nothing can be done about misrepresentation until the next election.

Other observers of the electoral process in the United States argue the reverse. They maintain that competing candidates do offer policy alternatives or choices. They maintain that if voters are unhappy with the choice of candidates during one election, they can put forward others. Some also suggest that the elections and the advertising that goes with them are exactly what most voters want. If elected officials are not true to their promises, they can always be voted out of office in the next election.

In this chapter, we have several objectives. First, we examine the rules of the game and the basic structure of elections. Second, we take a look at the voters of the United States, asking the important questions: "Who votes?" and "Why do they vote?". Finally, we discuss the campaigns themselves, looking at the many factors that come together in an election. We pay special attention to the practical side of campaigns, examining exactly what gets voters to the polls and persuades them to support a particular candidate. We also discuss the various choices candidates must make in choosing their campaign staff, their positions on the issues, and the ways in which campaign funds are spent.

THE ADMINISTRATION OF ELECTIONS

Since the ratification of the Constitution, there has been a gradual movement toward more popular participation in our electoral system.

As Chapter 3 suggests, the electoral framework of the American political system has been continually changing since the ratification of the Constitution. The framers of the Constitution feared the possibility of mob rule. Therefore, many of the original rules of the game were designed to reduce the power of the majority. Senators were originally elected by state legislatures, and the system of presidential electors was established precisely to prevent the popular election of the president. Since then, however, there has been a gradual, even hesitating movement toward more popular participation through elections.

Our federal system allows for a wide assortment of political rules and regulations depending on state, local, and regional differences.

Another change in our electoral framework has involved the development of many different rules and regulations depending on state, local, and regional differences. Both the original national Constitution and the various state constitutions set few definite rules. As a result, a great variety of electoral methods came into practice over the years. Our present federal system continues to allow for a wide assortment of political rules and practices affecting nominations and elections. These administrative details may seem dull and not very useful, but they underscore the changing nature of those rules as well as the costs and benefits of different approaches.

The way in which the ballot is arranged has varied from place to place. The **party column** *(or "Indiana")* **ballot** *lists candidates in rows under their party affiliation, while the* **office column** *(or "Massachusetts")* **ballot** *groups candidates by office with the party label following individual candidates. In many cases, the party ballot has a single, large box beside the party name so that a voter can, with a single mark, vote for all the candidates of that party.*

This "big box" form of the party ballot increases the likelihood of voting a straight party ticket. In a number of states, efforts to eliminate the big box have been hotly contested. Parties that are strong in a given state tend to oppose these efforts. While the form of the ballot may appear to be a purely technical matter, it can also have very practical effects on the outcome of elections. In the state of Maine, for example, the elimination of the big box is considered a factor that aided the election of two young Republican members of Congress, since it reduced the incidence of straight Democratic balloting in several key cities.

*Ballot
Arrangement*

Ballots

Early in our history, people registered their choice orally. Voters simply came to the polls on election day and voiced their preference. By the 1830s, a number of cities and towns switched to written **ballots**. These were often printed by individual candidates or their parties. Even then, the ballots were marked in plain sight of election officials and onlookers. Not surprisingly, voters were often pressured to vote a certain way and the practice of buying votes was widespread.

The *secret*, or *Australian ballot*, as it was known, was used first in Kentucky in 1888 and then in Massachusetts in 1889, although, surprisingly enough, it was not adopted everywhere in the United States until 1950! Voting machines, which enable individuals to register their votes by pulling levers rather than by making marks on paper ballots, were introduced in Pennsylvania in 1892. Even today, fewer than half of all votes cast in a national election are recorded on voting machines. Some communities are experimenting with computer cards, on which voters "punch out" their choices.

The Nominating Process

How do people get their names on the ballot? In a representative democracy, there must be some method by which individual aspirants come forward and put themselves up as candidates. The American system features a two-step process. The first step involves the nomination of a candidate. The second involves the selection of an individual to hold a particular office from among those who have been nominated.

In the early days of the republic, the nomination process was very simple. Individuals announced that they were running, in effect nominating themselves. This method is still quite common in small towns and rural areas, especially for local positions. As more and more people sought office, however, and communities grew in size, self-nomination became too burdensome and a caucus system developed. A **caucus** is simply an informal group of people who meet to nominate a candidate or to discuss ideas. In addition to putting up candidates for local and state elections, caucuses have also played an important role in selecting delegates to state and national conventions. (We saw in Chapter 3 how the national conventions replaced the congressional caucuses.)

Conventions arose with the steady growth of towns. The resulting expansion of the political arena made it impossible to have everybody present because it became too crowded. Therefore, local caucuses sent delegates chosen on the basis of geography or population to the state conventions. During much of the nineteenth century, state conventions did the bulk of the nominating for major political offices. When the conventions and their accompanying "smoke-filled rooms," where the party bosses handpicked candidates (see Chapter 5), became the targets of reformers in the twentieth century, they were replaced by **primaries** (that is, elections that precede elections). By and large, although state conventions have continued—either to nominate delegates to national conventions or to express a "preference" for candidates—their nominating functions for major offices have generally been replaced by primaries.

Today the most common method of nominating political candidates is the primary.

Primaries

The most widely used form is the **closed primary**; that is, one in which voting is restricted to party members. In Illinois, for example, Democrats may vote only in the Democratic primary, Republicans in the Republican primary, and Independents in neither. A voter must be a member of the party or must declare an affiliation at the polling place. The voter then receives the ballot of that party. Forty-two states now hold closed primaries and approximately three-quarters of all nominees are chosen in this fashion. Critics charge that only party members get to choose the candidates that all Americans, including large numbers of Independents, vote for in the general election. Also, since only 30–40 percent of the eligible voters turn out to vote in a primary election, those choosing the

TABLE 6.2
CARTER IN THE
PRIMARIES*

PRIMARY (DATE)	CARTER'S VOTE	PERCENTAGE	PLACE
New Hampshire (2/24)	23,373	28.4%	1
Massachusetts (3/2)	101,948	13.9	4
Vermont (3/2)	16,335	42.2	1
Florida (3/9)	448,844	34.5	1
Illinois (3/16)	630,915	48.1	1
North Carolina (3/23)	324,437	53.6	1
Wisconsin (4/6)	271,220	36.6	1
Pennsylvania (4/27)	511,905	37.0	1
Dist. of Columbia (5/4)	9,759	39.7	1
Georgia (5/4)	419,172	83.4	1
Indiana (5/4)	417,463	68.0	1
Nebraska (5/11)	65,833	37.6	2
Maryland (5/18)	219,404	37.1	2
Michigan (5/18)	307,559	43.4	1
Arkansas (5/25)	314,306	62.6	1
Idaho (5/25)	8,818	11.9	1
Kentucky (5/25)	181,690	59.4	1
Nevada (5/25)	17,567	23.3	2
Oregon (5/25)	115,310	26.7	2
Tennessee (5/25)	259,243	77.6	1
Montana (6/1)	26,329	24.6	2
Rhode Island (6/1)	18,237	30.2	2
South Dakota (6/1)	24,186	41.2	1
California (6/8)	690,171	20.5	2
New Jersey (6/8)	210,655	58.4	1
Ohio (6/8)	593,130	52.3	1
Totals:	6,227,809	39.0	

* Note that these are the only states that have primaries; Carter was the only candidate to enter every primary.

nominee may not be typical voters.[1] In 1976 Jimmy Carter became the Democratic candidate on the basis of a total primary vote of 6.2 million, while Jerry Ford beat out Ronald Reagan on the basis of less than 5 million primary votes.

The **open primary**, in which any qualified voter may participate, is held in eight states. Some think that because it allows all voters to participate, the open primary is more representative. Those who oppose the open primary point out, however, that participation is generally no higher than in closed primaries. In addition, open primaries give members of the opposition party a chance to vote for a weaker opposition nominee, thus making the general election more favorable for their candidate. In recent years, such states as Wisconsin and Texas have experienced difficulties with this type of "crossover."

[1] V. O. Key, Jr., *An Introduction to State Politics* (New York: Knopf, 1956).

Both open and closed primaries may lead to the selection of a nominee who has received a **plurality**, which means the largest number of votes but less than 50 percent. In fact, most states do not insist that a nominee receive 50 percent. Thus, a relatively small number of voters may actually pick the nominees. For example, in the 1976 Republican presidential primaries in Texas and North Carolina, less than 10 percent of the adult population chose the winner.

Eleven states do have laws requiring that the nominee have over 50 percent of the votes. In the event that no candidate receives a majority of the vote, a **runoff** is held, usually with the top two or three vote getters allowed to run. In districts and states in which gaining the nomination is often tantamount to winning the general election, runoffs may assume additional importance.

Finally, there is the **nonpartisan primary**. All voters are free to participate, and candidates are not required to declare their political affiliation. As a consequence, the voters are often unaware of the candidate's affiliation. This type of primary is used to elect such people as school board members, local judges, and some city and town officials who are chosen on a nonpartisan, or nonparty, basis. In such cases a nonpartisan primary may be followed by a nonpartisan general election.

General Elections

General elections must be held for federal offices such as president, senator, and member of congress. They always take place on the first Tuesday following the first Monday in November.

Unlike primaries and conventions, which may take place at any time during the year, general elections always take place on the first Tuesday following the first Monday in November. At this time, elections must be held for federal offices such as president, senator, and member of Congress.[2]

Administering elections involves supervising the voting and the adherence to campaign laws.[3] Since campaign laws differ from state to state, enforcement is usually local. A town clerk, board of election commissioners, or other designated officials provide a polling place (often a school), voting booths, ballot boxes, or voting machines. The polls are open on election day for a specified period (usually from 8 A.M. to 8 P.M.), although absentee ballots (for those who cannot come to the polls for reasons of health, travel, and so on) may be collected prior to election day. On election day, officials check off people who come to vote against the registration lists of eligible voters. Quite often representatives of the political parties will also be present to observe the process.

[2] Gubernatorial races, however, may be held at different times, as in the case of Louisiana, which elects its governor during February of the presidential year.

[3] Douglas Rae, *The Political Consequences of Election Laws* (New Haven, Conn.: Yale University Press, 1967).

As in so many other areas of American life, the federal government plays an increasing role in the supervision of elections, the registration of voters, the conduct of campaigns, and campaign financing. We shall cover a number of federal initiatives in the sections that follow. In terms of the administration of elections, federal involvement in the size and makeup of electoral districts is both recent and important. In 1964, for example, the Supreme Court ruled that both houses of state legislatures must be based on "substantially" equal numbers of people in each district.[4] The court also declared that great differences in the population of congressional districts were unconstitutional.[5] As a result, during the next two years over 250 congressional districts were redrawn, with the goal of having each member of Congress represent approximately 500,000 persons. Subsequent court decisions, most notably in 1971,[6] gave some leeway in reapportionment (the redistricting of political areas), but federal involvement seems to be continuing and expanding. Thus the federal courts have had a profound influence on the changing rules of the electoral game.

> The federal government has played a continuing and expanding role in the administration of elections.

Presidential Elections

The nomination and election of the president is a uniquely American experience. This vital phenomenon consists of (1) a nominating convention preceded by a series of primary elections, and (2) the competition for electoral college votes in a general election. The whole process is bewildering, complex, confusing, and, to those who participate, exhausting. R. W. Apple, Jr. of the *New York Times* has quite rightly labeled the process "exhausting, fragmented, irrational, superficial and ridiculously expensive."[7]

Political scientists who have examined the process in detail have also commented on its difficulties.[8] To make the process more understandable, we shall divide it into four sections: the delegates to the national convention, how these delegates are "won" by the candidates, the convention itself, and the workings of the presidential electoral college mechanism.

The delegates

As noted in Chapter 2, during the first three presidential elections, members of the electoral college met and agreed on George Washington (twice)

---

[4] *Reynolds* v. *Sims,* 377 U.S. 583 (1964).

[5] *Wesberry* v. *Sanders,* 377 U.S. 1 (1964).

[6] *Abate* v. *Mundt,* 403 U.S. 182 (1971).

[7] R. W. Apple, Jr., "There Must Be a Better Way," The *New York Times,* March 28, 1976.

[8] James Barber, ed., *Choosing the President* (Englewood Cliffs, N.J.: Prentice-Hall, 1974); Herbert Asher, *Presidential Elections and American Politics* (Homewood, Ill.: Dorsey Press, 1976).

Delegate Allocation

The allocation of delegates is a complex and confusing process. In 1976, for example, the Republican convention had 6 delegates at large from each state, 3 delegates for each House seat from that state, 14 at-large delegates from the District of Columbia, 8 from Puerto Rico, 4 from Guam, 4 from the Virgin Islands, 1 extra delegate for each state with a Republican governor, 1 extra delegate for each Republican senator from the state, 1 extra delegate for each state with a House delegation that was at least one-half Republican, and, for states that gave the Republican nominee their electoral-college votes in the previous election, 4½ delegates plus 60 percent of the state's electoral-college vote.

The Democratic delegates to the national convention are allocated by an equally complicated method. This formula gives equal weight to the total population of the state and to the average vote for the Democratic candidates in the two most recent presidential elections (thereby avoiding the full impact of the McGovern disaster, in which the Democratic nominee carried only one state, Massachusetts. Another formula gives equal weight to the average of the vote for the Democratic candidates in the two most recent presidential elections and to Democratic party registration or enrollment as of January 1, 1976. Still a third formula gives equal weight to the vote for the Democratic candidates in the most recent presidential and gubernatorial elections.

and John Adams. With the development of political parties after 1796, however, congressional caucuses were used to nominate candidates, from whom the electors chose the next several presidents. In the age of Andrew Jackson, a system of national conventions developed, with political parties nominating candidates who were then voted on in the general election. The candidate receiving the majority of electoral votes was declared the winner. (The candidate who earned a state's popular vote gained all of that state's electoral votes.)

We still choose presidential candidates through a convention system invented by the followers of Andrew Jackson. The methods used to select delegates to the conventions, however, have been altered with the changing times.

Although we still choose presidential candidates through a convention system invented by Jackson's followers, the methods used in selecting delegates to the conventions have been altered with the changing times. Since the national nominating conventions would be completely overrun if all delegates who wished to attend were free to do so, some form of proportional representation had to be developed. Each national party has adopted its own rules, although, generally, the representation from each state is based on the voting strength of the political party in that state.

The present system used by the Republican and Democratic parties is confusing. First of all, the numbers of delegates keep changing. In 1968 there were 1,333 Republican delegates and 2,622 Democratic. In 1972 there were 1,348 Republicans and 3,016 Democrats. In 1976 there were 2,259 Republicans and 3,011 Democrats. Second, the allocation of delegates is based on a complex formula (see box). This is just another example of how the political system of the United States keeps changing to meet new demands and new needs.

The winning of the delegates

As if these aspects of the electoral system were not confusing enough (and far removed from the daily lives of most of us), the methods of selecting individual delegates also differ from state to state. The result is a crazy patchwork quilt. Some delegates are chosen by state conventions, some are elected in state primary elections. In some states they run pledged to a particular candidate, and in others they run uncommitted. In some states they are bound by the outcome of a presidential primary; that is, they have been chosen on the basis of who actually won the primary. In others, the delegates may be elected even though they support candidates other than the person who won the primary. The arrangement is so complex that the Library of Congress guide, *Procedures for Selection of Delegates to the Democratic and Republican 1976 National Conventions,* was nearly two inches thick.

Thirty states held presidential primaries in 1976. They ranged in size from Vermont (11 Democratic, 18 Republican delegates) to California (280 Democrats and 167 Republicans). Some of the states, such as New Hampshire, held **binding primaries**; that is, the winner of the primary received a definite percentage of the delegates. In others, such as New York, the individual delegates were chosen, although the name of the candidate they were supporting appeared on the ballot. In still others, such as Vermont, the primary results were merely **advisory**; that is, the winner of the primary did not automatically get a percentage of the delegates. Further confusion in the presidential primary sweepstakes results from the fact that some primaries have a "winner-take-all" feature, while others employ a proportional method of allocating delegates.

In most of the remaining twenty states that hold primaries, the state party convention ultimately chooses the delegates. These states choose delegates by means of the caucus system at the local level before moving to regional (that is, county or congressional district) levels and then on to the state level. Iowa, Mississippi, and Connecticut were examples of caucus states in 1976. Fully one-quarter of all the delegates to both national conventions were chosen by this method. In five states, the delegates

Delegates are selected by a bewildering array of methods that differ from state to state.

Carter's Narrow and Ambiguous 1976 Victory

"Jimmy Carter's 1976 march on Washington can properly be described as an electoral tour de force—or as an indifferent showing. To come from so far back and capture the nomination of a major party (and then the presidency) is an extraordinary achievement, one that surely should not be dismissed lightly. But Carter also manifested striking weaknesses.

"He led the field by only 4,300 votes in New Hampshire, or by 5.5 percent. If Jackson, Wallace, Brown, or Humphrey had entered the New Hampshire primary, it is almost certain that Carter would not have attained the plurality which gave him a badly needed bit of early momentum. Carter had "right field" all to himself in New Hampshire, while the liberal vote was divided. *After getting only 14 percent of the Massachusetts vote and running fourth, Carter won Florida with one-third of the popular vote and a lead of only 4 percent over George Wallace. Humphrey was not entered. Neither was Brown. Jackson got going late. Carter then won the Illinois popular vote handily (with 48 percent of the total vote, and a 20 percentage point lead), but only Wallace, Shriver, and Harris were on the ballot with him. The* Times-CBS News Poll *indicated that Hubert Humphrey would have swept the Illinois primary had he been entered.*

"With all the momentum thus generated, Carter won Wisconsin by one percentage point, Michigan by two-tenths of a point. He lost in Nebraska, was trounced in Idaho, Nevada, and Maryland, was solidly beaten in Oregon, was defeated in the New Jersey delegate voting, was swamped in California. He had much earlier done poorly in the New York delegate race. Out of these raw materials

were chosen by the state party committees *without* a primary or a state convention!

As James Davis has pointed out, the effort to secure delegates is complicated further by **favorite sons**.[9] These individuals, who are popular in their home states, are not seriously running for president, but want their names presented at the national convention. They may run in primaries or caucuses in their home states in order to gain bargaining chips at the national convention, either to try for the vice-presidential nomination or to influence the party platform, or to get some publicity on national television. In 1976, favorite sons such as Governor Jerry Brown in California and Senator Adlai Stevenson III in Illinois sought to head off an early nomination victory for Jimmy Carter.

[9] James W. Davis, *Presidential Primaries: Road to the White House* (New York: Crowell, 1967); and *Springboard to the White House—Presidential Primaries: How They Are Fought and Won* (New York: Crowell, 1967).

one could easily build a hypothetical progression of early defeat, loss of momentum, drift back into the pack, and disintegration.

"There is also the largely forgotten fact that after Carter had acquired a lead during the primary season, he was typically unable to hold it. *Thus in state after state, from Florida through Michigan and Wisconsin, he saw his lead over contending Democrats weaken in the last days before the primary voting—a datum indicated by the surveys of the candidate's own pollster, Patrick Caddell—just as once his nomination appeared well nigh irresistible, he began to get beaten badly by a young California governor.*

"One may argue, still, that winning primaries is the best test of electability, and that Carter won more of those in 1976 than any other Democrat. The weakness of the claim that presidential primary victories indicated a popular mandate is revealed most clearly by the following:* only 20 percent of the voting-age public in the states which held presidential preference contests actually cast ballots in the Democratic primaries of 1976; *Carter received the votes of about* 8 percent—*and this in the context of crowded fields and a changing mix of possible alternatives from one state to another. This 8 percent was more than any other Democrat received, and as translated through the party's current delegate selection procedures it gave Carter the victory.* But it hardly indicates he was the choice of 'the people.'"

Selection is reprinted from *Transformations of the American Party System*, 2d ed., by Everett Carll Ladd, Jr., with Charles D. Hadley, with the permission of W. W. Norton & Company, Inc. Copyright © 1978, 1975, by W. W. Norton & Company, Inc.

A final confusing aspect of the present system is the way in which candidates get on the ballots in the primary states. In some states, all candidates are automatically listed. If they want to get off the ballot, they have to request removal (as Senator Edmund Muskie did in Florida in 1976). In other primary states, individuals have to ask to get on the ballot. In many instances candidates pick and choose the primaries in which they wish to run, basing their strategies on where they think they will do well. Senator McGovern did this with great effectiveness in 1972.

Jimmy Carter gambled in 1976 that his momentum from the early primaries would help him later on, as indeed it did. Henry Jackson picked his primaries carefully and discounted the others; still he failed. In much the same fashion and with the same result, Ronald Reagan chose to challenge President Ford only in specific primaries. Also, some primaries seem to carry more impact than others, regardless of the number of delegates involved. New Hampshire, as the first of the nation's primaries, gave George McGovern's candidacy a big boost in 1972 when he received

A dramatic example of the power of the press occurred in the 1972 presidential campaign. Senator Edmund Muskie had been the front runner but had been plagued by unfavorable news stories of questionable accuracy about his wife, which were published in the Manchester (New Hampshire) *Union Leader*. In attempting to refute the articles and denounce the *Union Leader* in a speech in front of their building, Muskie began to cry. This display of lack of control hastened his decline in the polls and signaled his eventual defeat.

36 percent of the vote, even though Senator Muskie gained 49 percent. John Kennedy's smashing defeat of Hubert Humphrey in the West Virginia primary in 1960 is regarded as the turning point in a race that finally gained Kennedy his party's nomination. Critics argue that the present system (or, as you can see, fifty different systems) is altogether haphazard and illogical. Some of these primaries are scheduled on the same day, thereby forcing candidates to be superficial in their appeals. Voters may catch a glimpse of candidate A getting on an airplane and candidate B

getting off, but that may be all they see. Some observers have suggested that a national presidential primary would be better, although that would certainly aid the better-known candidates. Vice-President Walter Mondale, who spent $100,000 and a year of his life only to drop out of the presidential sweepstakes a year early, argues that a set of six regional primaries, with their voting dates rotated by lot, would offer a much better way.

Indeed, the present *ad hoc* mixture of caucus and primary arrangement seems to need overhauling. Whatever replaces it should retain certain features. The very grueling nature of the present arrangement puts an exceptional stress on candidates for the presidency while exposing them to the harsh glare of the national media for long periods of time. It also tends to eliminate those who are not able to take this kind of pressure. George Romney looked like a very strong candidate in 1968 until he ran afoul of the primaries. Senator Edmund Muskie, the acknowledged front runner in 1972, failed to build the organization and to formulate a strategy necessary to sustain his original position.

The convention

The recent upsurge in interest in the primaries tends to overshadow the historical evidence that in most presidential nomination struggles in this century, primaries have not usually been decisive. Indeed, until recently, primaries were *not* all that decisive. Republican primaries left Thomas E. Dewey in 1948 and General Dwight D. Eisenhower in 1952 about where they had been before the primaries: almost sure bets to gain the nomination. Willkie in 1940, Stevenson in 1952, and Humphrey in 1968 each won the nomination without making a large or substantial effort in the primaries. As two major studies indicate, the candidate who stands highest in the national opinion polls generally has the best chance of winning the nomination.[10]

It may well be that the advent of television and the more media-oriented campaigns have given the primaries an added importance. George McGovern was virtually unknown in 1972 until he did well in a series of primaries, gaining national recognition in the process.[11] Jimmy Carter in 1976 was far down in the polls until he won caucuses in Iowa and Maine and primaries in New Hampshire, Vermont, Florida, and Illinois.

---

[10] Gerald Pomper, *Nominating the President: The Politics of Convention Choice* (New York: Norton, 1966); and James Davis, *Presidential Primaries: Road to the White House.*

[11] Interestingly enough, McGovern gained the nomination and won more of the primaries than any other candidate, but he did not win in the total primary vote. In seventeen primaries, he received 3.9 million votes to Hubert Humphrey's 4 million, George Wallace's 3.6 million, and Muskie's 1.8 million.

Participants in the 1976 national conventions.

By the time the delegates assemble for the national convention, the nomination is usually within the grasp of one candidate.[12] Only once in the last forty years have the Democrats gone beyond the first ballot in choosing a nominee, and only twice have the Republicans. By contrast, the Democrats took 103 ballots to choose their candidate in 1924, John W. Davis, and he proved to be a weak standard-bearer. The convention itself often proves to be a fairly dull affair so far as most Americans are concerned. The hoopla of demonstrations, the cheering delegates, the long, dull speeches soon take on a certain sameness. The picture of hordes of delegates wandering around apparently aimlessly during the late evening hours seems quite pointless. The ever-present journalists, eager to inject some life into the proceedings, eagerly search out any rumor, hoping it may lead to a tidbit of new information or, better still, potential crisis in convention politics.

[12] See, for example, James A. Michener, *Presidential Lottery* (New York: Random House, 1968); and Malcolm Moos and Stephen Hess, *Hats in the Ring: The Making of Presidential Candidates* (New York: Random House, 1960).

Once the presidential nominee has been selected by a roll-call vote, there is usually mild excitement and suspense over whom the nominee will choose as a running mate. Although there is often a good deal of talk about making the convention "open" (that is, letting the delegates decide on the running mate), presidential nominees normally pick their own candidates for vice-president.

Sometimes nominees will try to balance the ticket by picking a running mate from another part of the country (as John Kennedy of Massachusetts did in selecting Lyndon Johnson of Texas). At other times, they will try to select a running mate who offers contrasting temperament and appeal (as Hubert Humphrey did when he chose Edmund Muskie in 1968) or simply someone they feel comfortable with (as Barry Goldwater did in 1964 when he chose an amiable and obscure Congressman, William Miller).

In terms of impact on the electorate, there is not much evidence that the running mate usually makes a significant difference. Except in very close races (such as Kennedy's narrow victory over Nixon in 1960), the choice of a vice-presidential candidate is not critical. On the other hand, the way in which the vice-president is selected may occasionally have an important impact on the electorate, as in the case of Senator McGovern's selection of Senator Thomas Eagleton as his running mate in 1972. In selecting a man with a history of mental illness, then stating that he stood behind that man "1,000 percent" just prior to forcing him off the ticket, and, finally, scrambling around frantically for a replacement, Senator McGovern lost whatever tiny chance he might have had to be elected president. On election day, his position in the polls had finally inched back to about where it had been on the night he was nominated, and he lost badly.

Despite their drawbacks, the national conventions perform a number of important functions. First, they give national exposure to the party nominees. Second, the platform committee draws up the party platform that later is ratified by the convention. Third, the convention alters the rules under which subsequent conventions will be manned. Finally, the convention serves as a symbolic link between the nomination process and the general election, allowing time for the electorate to refocus attention on the coming competition for the single most important office in the entire political system.

National conventions give national exposure to party nominees, establish the party platform, and provide a symbolic link between the nominating process and the general election.

The electoral college

Once the parties' nominees have been selected, the long, hard run for the presidency is under way. Political scientists Nelson Polsby and Aaron Wildavsky and political journalist Theodore White have done superior work in describing the course of presidential elections.[13] White's eminently readable accounts of the presidential races in 1964, 1966, 1968, and 1972 take the reader inside these campaigns.

Central to the presidential election is the **electoral college**. The framers of the Constitution did not foresee modern campaigns and competing political parties. Their principal concern was to create a system that would not be dominated by mob action. Therefore, they established an electoral college, whose numbers have grown with the expansion of the United States until today it consists of 538 members (435 for the membership of the House, 100 for the Senate, and 3 for the residents of the District of Columbia).

The electors now actually choose the president (270 votes are now required to win), since voters in presidential elections technically select *slates of electors,* not the candidates themselves. The slate of electors is chosen by the party apparatus in each state. The electors then go to the state capitol on the first Monday after the second Wednesday in December to go through the ceremony of casting their ballots.

Most Americans think of the balloting as routine, but in 1972 one Republican elector from Virginia did not cast his vote for Nixon, who had won the state handily. Instead, he voted for the Libertarian party candidate. Since Nixon had the vast majority of electoral votes anyway, the vote was merely an empty protest. At the same time, it underscores the fact that electors are not *legally* bound to vote for the popular choice, although they are pledged to do so.

Another difficulty with the electoral college system is related to its **winner-take-all provision**. The candidate receiving the most popular votes gets all the state's electors. Thus, it is possible for a candidate to receive the majority of popular votes on a nationwide basis and still lose the election if his opponent has strength in states with large electoral votes. This has happened twice in our history and almost a third time.

Voters in presidential elections actually vote for slates of electors, chosen by the party apparatus in each state. These electors then choose the president. Under this system, it is possible, and has occasionally happened, that the candidate can win the popular vote and yet still lose the election.

In 1876, Rutherford B. Hayes, the Republican candidate, received 4,033,768 votes to the Democrat Tilden's 4,285,992, while carrying the electoral college 185 to 182. In 1888, Benjamin Harrison, the Republican candidate, took 5,439,853 to Grover Cleveland's 5,540,329, but Harrison carried the electoral college 233 to 168. In 1960, if a mere 9,000 people in Illinois and Missouri had voted for Nixon instead of Kennedy, Nixon would have won the electoral college vote, while losing the total popular vote by a narrow margin. As it was, only 112,000 popular votes separated the two candidates nationally in an election in which 69 million Americans voted.

[13] Nelson W. Polsby and Aaron Wildavsky, *Presidential Elections: Strategies of American Electoral Politics* (New York: Scribner's, 1968); and Theodore White, *The Making of the President: 1960, 1964, 1968, 1972* (New York: Atheneum, 1961, 1965, 1969, 1973).

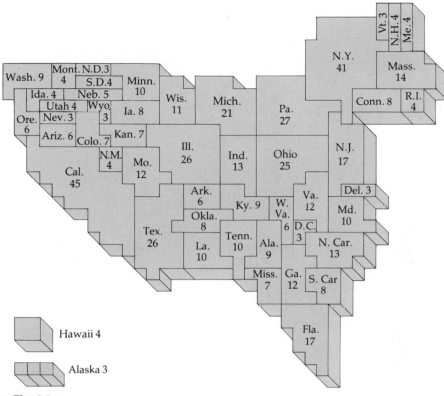

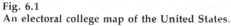

Fig. 6.1
An electoral college map of the United States.

If no candidate receives a majority of electoral votes, the election is forced into the House of Representatives, where each state delegation has one vote and a majority vote is necessary for election. If neither candidate receives a majority of electoral votes for vice-president, the Senate picks from among the top two candidates. Each Senator has one vote and a majority is required.

The election in 1968 showed how vulnerable the system is to strong third-party intrusion. If Hubert Humphrey, rather than Nixon, had carried a few more states, Governor George Wallace (who carried five states with 46 electoral votes) would have forced the contest into the House. This was generally thought to have been Wallace's prime objective. The 1976 presidential election was decided by only 56 electoral votes even though Carter's total vote was almost 1.6 million more than Ford's. A swing of 3,500 votes in Ohio and Hawaii would have thrown the election to Ford. The special arithmetic of the electoral college would have then read: Ford,

Jimmy Carter, shortly before the Democratic national convention, gets a hero's welcome in New York City.

270; Carter, 268, rather than Carter, 297; Ford, 241. As Ford's campaign manager, would you have been able to avoid second thoughts?

The very existence of the electoral college affects the strategy of the presidential candidates, encouraging them to allocate more of their time and money to the major industrial states, with their large blocs of electoral votes.

Richard Nixon kept his pledge to campaign in all fifty states in 1960. This turned out to be poor strategy, since the hundreds of thousands of travel-miles exhausted him, fragmented his resources, and cost him some critical states. In the closing hours of the campaign, while Nixon flew to Alaska, Kennedy was concentrating his efforts on the industrial Northeast. In a race as close as this one, a different strategy with regard to electoral votes might have brought Nixon victory. Four years later, Nixon campaigned entirely differently, concentrating on nine border states in the mid-Atlantic, the midwest areas, and the South. This time he won by 500,000 votes out of a total of 73 million.

Neal Pierce believes that the electoral college system ought to be scrapped and replaced by the direct election of the president.[14] This would reduce the importance of big, swing states such as Pennsylvania and Ohio, while increasing the value of others, such as Nebraska or the New England states. Other experts, citing the studies of Charles Sellers, have suggested that, given the remarkably equal distribution of votes between Democratic and Republican candidates for president, a change in the electoral system might be very upsetting, creating, in effect, a whole new political system.[15]

The system might be modified by having each state's electoral votes allocated on a proportional basis, reflecting each candidate's popular vote within that state. But as in so many other areas of our political life, people are divided about the desirability of significant change. Although there is sporadic interest in reforming the electoral system, the issue is complex and dimly perceived by most Americans. Yet it casts a shadow over presidential elections, influencing strategy and ultimately threatening a standoff, which would then be thrown into the House of Representatives.

As we have seen, the rules of the game, the basic structure of the American electoral system, do affect the way elections are conducted. Also, slow, gradual changes in the rules indicate that the system, while flexible, is also ponderous. In addition, the rules of the election game ultimately depend on voters and how voters behave.

VOTERS AND VOTING PATTERNS

As of 1976, more than 150 million Americans were eligible to vote. We call them the **potential electorate**. Virtually all American citizens over the age of eighteen—except those convicted of major crimes—are eligible to register and to vote. This constitutes the largest number of American adults eligible to vote in our country's history. With the elimination of literacy tests for federal elections and a sharp reduction in the residency require-

[14] Neal Pierce, *The People's President: The Electoral College in American History and the Direct Vote Alternative* (New York: Simon and Schuster, 1968).

[15] Charles Sellers, "Equilibrium Cycle in Two-Party Politics," *The Public Opinion Quarterly* 29 (Spring, 1965), 16–37; and Gerald Pomper, *Voters Choice* (New York: Harper & Row, 1975).

ments (to as few as thirty days), the opportunity to register has never been greater, nor more universal. Congress is considering legislation to enable persons to register by mail rather than, as is now the case, by appearing in person. The relative ease of registration and the eligibility of so many persons are relatively new features of our political system. We shall now trace the history of the right to vote, examine who votes and why, and explore the patterns of political participation in the United States.

The History of Participation

The extension of **suffrage**, or the right to vote, has taken place slowly over many years. The struggle to provide every adult American with the right to vote has been a long, hard effort, as we noted in Chapter 3. In the early days of the Republic, few could vote. Slaves could not. Women could not. Property qualifications prevented many adult males from voting. So, too, did literacy tests. So, too, did high poll taxes. There were so many restrictions that probably no more than one in every thirty-five persons was eligible to vote in eighteenth-century America.

The situaton changed only gradually. Reductions in the property qualifications came steadily during the first half of the nineteenth century and finally, following the Civil War, the slaves were freed. In the case of the freed slaves, however, their initial participation was soon checked by a combination of voting tests and intimidation. Not until the twentieth century did "popular participation" take on full meaning. The Nineteenth Amendment (1921) gave women the right to vote, thereby roughly doubling the number of eligible voters. The Twenty-fourth Amendment (1964) forbade poll taxes. The Twenty-sixth Amendment (1971) lowered the minimum voting age to eighteen. In addition, the Civil Rights Acts of 1964 and 1975 sought to protect the voting rights of all eligible voters—especially black Americans—and thus gave meaning to the Fifteenth Amendment.

In total, the expansion of voting rights has resulted in more Americans than ever before being eligible to vote. In terms of their ability to participate in the political process, Americans have never had greater opportunity to choose their political leaders.

And yet, ironically, many Americans do not vote. Forty million Americans failed to register in 1972. In addition, 23 million who were registered failed to vote. Of the 150 million Americans in the potential electorate in 1976, only 80 million voted, because they either failed to register or did not bother to vote after they had registered. In the 1976 presidential election, 45 percent of the potential electorate did not vote.[16]

[16] For some interesting insights, see Richard J. Carlson, ed., *The Issue of Electoral Reform* (New York: Municipal League, 1974). On the 1976 election see Gerald Pomper with associates, *The Election of 1976* (New York: McKay, 1977).

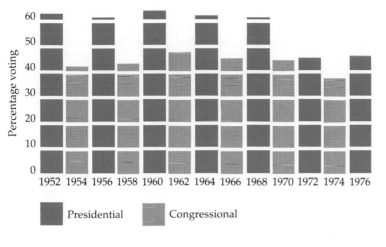

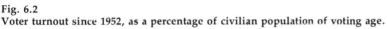

Fig. 6.2
Voter turnout since 1952, as a percentage of civilian population of voting age.

Typically, in congressional and gubernatorial races, 50–60 percent do not vote. In primaries, 70–80 percent may not. This is a far lower turnout than is experienced in most industrialized democracies of Western Europe. Although only white adult males were eligible to vote in the 1880s and 1890s, a large percentage of those eligible to vote did so. Along with an expanding electorate has gone a steady decline in participation rates. Under our political system, the voter, if he or she is to play a decisive role, must participate, at least to the extent of voting. Clearly, something is not working as it should. Before we seek possible reasons, let us examine who votes and who does not.

Voting rights have steadily expanded so that today more Americans than ever before are eligible to vote. At the same time, there has been a steady decline in participation rates.

The Nonvoter and the Voter

There have been a number of recent studies focusing on voting and voter behavior.[17] There is abundant empirical evidence answering the question, "Who is the nonvoter?" The nonvoter tends to be young (that is, between eighteen and twenty-five years old) or old (over sixty-five). The nonvoter is likely to be from a rural area, and poorly educated. The nonvoter is also

[17] See, for example, Angus Campbell et al., *The American Voter* (New York: Wiley, 1960) and *Elections and the Political Order* (New York: Wiley, 1966); David Kovenock and James Prothro, *Explaining the Vote, 1960* (Chapel Hill: Institute for Research in Social Science, 1973); N. H. Nye, S. Verba, and S. R. Petrocik, *The Changing American Voter* (Cambridge, Mass.: Harvard University Press, 1976); and Warren E. Miller and Teresa Levitin, *Presidential Elections from 1952 to 1976* (Cambridge, Mass.: Winthrop, 1976.)

more likely to be nonwhite and from the lowest socioeconomic group. In other words, a poor, black youth from the rural South is far less likely to vote than a high-income, white, middle-aged person from a suburb in the North or West.[18]

The typical voter, on the other hand, is more likely to be a middle-aged, white male, from suburban or urban areas, educated and relatively affluent. Or, as Richard Scammon and Ben Wattenberg put it, the typical voter is "unyoung, unpoor and unblack."[19] The voter, whether male or female, is also more likely to identify with a political party. (Those who belong to political parties are far more likely to vote than those who do not.[20] On the other hand, recent elections have brought an increase in ticket-splitting and independent voting. This change bears watching in the future.)

These observations have been supported by the evidence from recent elections. In the 1972 presidential election, for example, over 82 percent of the people with college education voted as against only 55 percent of those with a grade-school education. Those earning $10,000 a year or more had a 75 percent turnout, while those earning below $3,000 had slightly more than a 45 percent turnout. White-collar workers had a 76 percent voter effort; manual workers only 54 percent. Sixty-four percent of the white population voted in contrast with 54 percent of the black. Sixty-six percent of those living in the North and West voted versus 55 percent in the South.

Patterns of Political Participation

The high percentage of nonvoters also ties in with low levels of political activity in other respects. Lester Milbrath, in his pioneering study of political participation, indicates that less than 1 percent of the adult population run for office or solicit funds for candidates.[21] Only 4–5 percent attend caucuses or engage in other forms of party activity, while only 10 percent make financial contributions to political parties or work on behalf of candidates. Only 25–30 percent attempt to talk others into voting for or against a candidate. Political activism is by no means a common experience for most adult Americans. Is it any different for you?

[18] Sidney Verba and Norman Nie, *Participation in America* (New York: Harper & Row, 1972) and K. V. Mulcahy and R. S. Katz, *America Votes* (Englewood Cliffs, N.J.: Prentice-Hall, 1976).

[19] Richard Scammon and Ben Wattenberg, *The Real Majority* (New York: Coward-McCann and Geoghegan, 1970).

[20] Judson James, *American Political Parties in Transition* (New York: Harper & Row, 1974).

[21] Lester Milbrath, *Political Participation: How and Why People Get Involved in Politics* (Chicago: Rand McNally, 1965).

In addition to being apathetic and passive, many adults in our society remain glaringly ignorant about the basics of the political system itself. Fred Greenstein, for example, has indicated that less than 50 percent of the adult population know the length of the term of a member of Congress or can tell how many Supreme Court Justices there are or what the Bill of Rights is.[22] Forty-five percent of the adult population could not even recall the number of senators from their state, let alone know who they were.

Why do so many people lack a basic understanding of the political system? Why do so few people involve themselves in politics? Why do so few people vote?

These are very interesting questions, raising more questions about our "democracy." Unfortunately, few studies provide definite answers to them. Part of the reason may simply be the temper of the times. Although American electoral politics are probably less corrupt and more orderly than they were at the turn of the century, many people are turned off by politics. "Politics" and "politicians" are held in low repute by many citizens, including educated middle-class Americans. To these citizens the political system seems to have failed in recent years, or at least not worked properly. Voters' confidence in the government—that is, voters' willingness to say the government was doing a good job—slid dramatically in the 1960s and 1970s.

Widespread apathy may also be the result of a generalized sense that society is too complex and too confusing. The efforts of a single individual may seem futile. The political system involves so many millions of people and modern life itself is so overwhelming that individuals may feel a real sense of alienation. Also, those who vote and participate tend to be those who have been more "successful" (at least in terms of how Americans often measure success). Those who do not seem to be saying that since the system has not worked for them, why should they participate?

In view of these conflicting patterns of participation and nonparticipation, we are left with a puzzle: how to characterize the American political system. Just how "democratic" is it? Although this question has a number of aspects, in terms of *access* to political participation, the system is quite open and truly democratic. Whatever the case in the past, it is now open to virtually all adults. Placing undue emphasis on what percentage of people do not vote, or do not otherwise participate, may well cause us to miss this important point. Access, not participation itself, may be a far better test of the system's democratic potential.

Since more people are now able to participate than ever before and since, statistically, few people are prevented from participating, it then

In terms of access to political participation, our political system is truly democratic.

[22] Fred Greenstein, *The American Party System of the American People* (Englewood Cliffs, N.J.: Prentice-Hall, 1963); see also D. S. Ippolito, T. G. Walker, and K. L. Kolson, *Public Opinion and Responsible Democracy* (Englewood Cliffs, N.J.: Prentice-Hall, 1976).

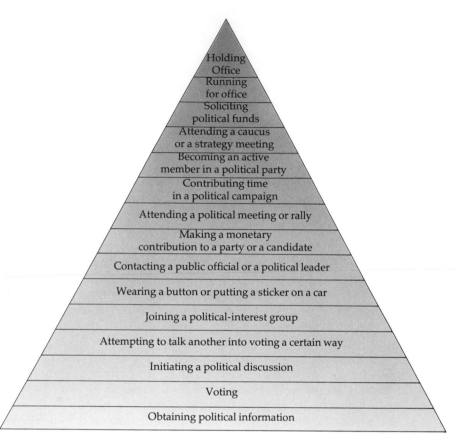

Fig. 6.3
Levels of political participation. (From *American Democracy in World Perspective*
by William Ebenstein et al. Copyright © 1976 by William Ebenstein, Henry A.
Turner, C. Herman Pritchett, and Dean Mann. By permission of Harper & Row,
Publishers, Inc.

becomes a matter of personal choice. Some choose to register, others do
not. Some register but do not vote. Millions of Americans register *and*
vote. In all cases, voting or nonvoting is left up to the individual. This
would seem to be one profoundly democratic element in the system itself.
Since getting people to the point of voting is one of the primary functions
of a political campaign, it is to this subject we now turn.

CAMPAIGNS

In the 1972 movie *The Candidate,* starring Robert Redford, a young attractive lawyer, Bill McKay, is approached by a political consultant to run for

the United States Senate. He is reluctant at first to challenge the incumbent senator, but gradually he is talked into running. Finally he agrees to run, but says "I want to go where I want, say what I want, do what I want." The professional consultant shakes his head and writes his reply on the back of a matchbook. It says simply, "You lose."

Although many Americans say they identify with the honesty and openness of the kind of campaign Bill McKay wants to run, in reality most campaigns for major public office are far more structured, far more organized, and far more controlled. People who become members of Congress, or senators, or governors, let alone presidents, simply do not go where they want, say what they want, or do what they want.

In this section we examine how modern campaigns are put together and how they work. Although we have drawn on the existing body of scholarly material,[23] we make a major effort to separate the practical from the theoretical and to concentrate on actual campaign situations and choices. While it is important for you to understand how campaigns are supposed to work, it is also important to learn how they in fact work, as well as the actual techniques and choices each candidate must face. These choices range from the basic campaign strategy to the raising of money and how it is spent.

The Candidate and the Strategy

Why does a person run for office, especially major office? Some candidates run to win, to be elected. Others run simply to feel important. Some candidates run knowing they will lose, but are anxious to stress a particular issue (such as opposition to abortion). Others run to help their party out, so that the election does not go to the opposing side by default. Some candidates run hoping that by doing so they will become better known and this will help their business. In the American political system, winning is not everything. Defeated congressional candidates sometimes become judges. Defeated gubernatorial candidates may go on to highly lucrative law practices. Defeated senatorial candidates may get appointed to important federal positions.

Let us assume you are going to run for a major office. Let us also assume you are running in order to get elected, not simply to have an opportunity to express your views. Now that you have decided to seek a

---

[23] Dan Nimmo, *The Political Persuaders: The Techniques of Modern Election Campaigns* (Englewood Cliffs, N.J.: Prentice-Hall, 1960); James Perry, *The New Politics* (Clarkson: Nother Potter, 1968); Ithiel de Sola Poole, Robert Abelson, and Samuel Popkin, *Candidates, Issues and Strategies* (Cambridge: Massachusetts Institute of Technology Press, 1965), Dan Nimmo and Robert Savage, *Candidates and Their Images* (Pacific Palisades, Calif.: Goodyear, 1976); James M. Perry, *The New Politics* (New York: Potter, 1968); and Joseph Napolitian, *The Election Game and How to Win It* (New York: Doubleday, 1972).

Ellen McCormack, despite her statements to the contrary, was essentially a one-issue candidate—anti-abortion—in the 1976 presidential campaign.

senate seat in Iowa or the governorship in Tennessee, you are immediately faced with a number of important decisions, not the least of which is deciding on your basic strategy.

Will you seek to engage the issues, contrasting your positions with those of your opponent? Will you attack your opponent's stand or will you run on your own, stressing your positions while ignoring those of your opponent? Will you concentrate on creating your image and try to say as little as possible in order to avoid alienating people? Whatever you decide to do, you will want to remember that in many elections, the person with the highest *name-recognition factor* (simply, the person who is best known) will win. And before the voters can identify with your positions, they have to know who you are.

Will you try to get out the vote of your party faithful? Or will you try to change the minds of the opposition? Or will you attempt to concentrate on the independents and ticket-splitters, assuming there are some voters you will never lose and some you will never get?[24]

Will you concentrate on television and the media? Or will you attempt to seek out the voters on a face-to-face basis, visiting them in their homes or walking their streets? Will you stress a message or personal contact, or some combination of the two?

These are not easy questions to answer, but you will have to do so early in your campaign. Much, of course, will depend on the specifics of your situation. But some of your initial decisions will determine how your entire campaign goes. Or does not go, as in the case of Birch Bayh's short, ineffective effort to become president in 1976. Senator Bayh was an attractive, articulate candidate with considerable potential support. Unfortunately for him, he adopted a disastrous strategy. In an election year when people were against "politicians," he spent over $200,000 telling the voters of New Hampshire and Massachusetts, "I am a politician." Most of the voters responded by voting for other candidates.

A sound basic strategy is a key element in any successful political campaign.

Organization

In *The Candidate,* Bill McKay begins his campaign by wandering around rather aimlessly, trying to do everything himself. Often candidates think they can do everything. But this is impossible. Candidates need a staff and an organization. To succeed, a campaign must have a structure.

In a major campaign, the candidate will need a campaign manager, to coordinate the many other people necessary to manage the "organized chaos" that is a part of a modern election. If you are running for Congress in Florida or the Senate in Pennsylvania, you will need someone to run the day-to-day affairs of the campaign. You will need someone to supervise volunteers. You will need a press aide. You will need an accountant to keep the campaign books and comply with the complex election laws. You will need a finance committee to raise money. You will need legal assistance to make sure the fund raising is, in fact, legal. You will need a scheduler, a driver, an advance person, a polling firm, and someone to do your advertisements. You will need researchers to find out about the hundreds of issues you never knew existed. You will need field people to organize your support all across the state.

At earlier periods in our history, candidates for major office did not need their own organization. The Democratic or Republican parties could usually provide the staff and personnel necessary to stage a campaign. But over the years state party organizations have become weaker and weaker. Usually the party's state committee can give the candidates some

[24] Walter DeVries and V. L. Terrance, *The Ticket-Splitter: A New Force in American Politics* (New York: William B. Erdmans, 1972).

help, raise some money, and generally be supportive. But in most situations candidates need to have their own organization. With as many as one-third of all voters belonging to no party, these organizations must find ways of attracting the independent voter.

Issues

When you have assembled your organization, you begin speaking to people. They will ask you questions about a variety of concerns they have. How you handle their questions is one of the primary reasons voters decide for or against you.

Oscar Ameringer has written, "Politics is the gentle art of getting votes from the poor and campaign funds from the rich, by promising to protect each from the other."[25] While this is a clever overstatement, it does indicate the real problem candidates have with "the issues." Most do not intend to mislead the voters. Many candidates make sincere efforts to speak their minds on the issues. But there are hundreds of issues, and many people entertain strong opinions on at least some of them. They may turn against a candidate on the basis of disagreement with a single position he or she takes, if they feel strongly enough about it.

Most voters are not issue oriented in the sense of rationally adding up all the stands candidates take and then judging them on their total. Emotional issues, such as abortion, gun control, or the 1978 Panama Canal treaty have great intensity and may turn a voter on or off in a hurry.

Candidates for major political office, therefore, frequently either try to ignore sensitive or controversial issues, or, if possible, appear to come down on both sides. This "waffling" or "blurring" of a candidate's position is often criticized but, to a certain extent, voters seem to get what they deserve. Many voters simply do not like to be upset. Or, as a successful politician once put it, "Candidates should stress familiar thoughts."

Candidates try to select the issues on which to take stands very carefully. If you are running for major office, you will want to pick the issues that are really important to you. To offer a stand on every conceivable issue is to court disaster. Whether elected officials *ought* to vote their conscience or the will of their constituents is a nice problem. Are you going to be a "leader" and vote any way you choose, or are you going to be a "representative," voting the way the majority of the people in your district want you to? In either case, you will be wise to listen to people as much as they listen to you.

Faced with the difficulties that stem from the issues, candidates often try to establish a personality image with which voters can identify. In

---

[25] Oscar Ameringer, *If You Don't Weaken* (New York: Greenwood Press, 1940), p. 393.

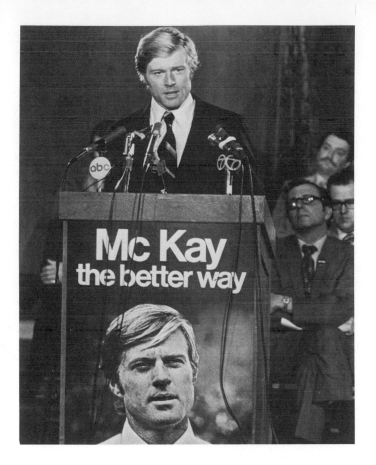

politics, as in so many other activities, *Peter's Placebo* is not without relevance: "An ounce of image is worth a pound of performance." Although Bill McKay starts out his campaign refusing to duck questions and taking a firm position on all the issues, he ends up winning with an innocuous and silly slogan: "Bill McKay: A Better Way." Slogans and media "packaging" of candidates are regular features of election politics and are likely to remain so.

Political candidates face enormous difficulties in deciding how to handle sensitive or controversial issues. Therefore, they often try to establish a strong personality image with which voters can identify.

The Media

The most glamorous and most expensive side of modern campaigning is located in the world of communications and advertising. The advent of television has revolutionized political campaigning in the United States.

One of the earliest races in which television proved to be important was the 1960 presidential race between Nixon and Kennedy. In the debates of that year, over 100 million persons watched the two candidates on television and nearly 60 percent of the voters said they thought the debates had influenced their decision. Since Kennedy won by only 112,000 votes, television may have had a definite impact.

As a result of the importance of the 1960 debates, subsequent presidents and would-be presidents have refused to debate and, instead, have turned to the massive use of television advertising. In 1972, almost $11 million was spent for television time in the presidential race alone. Much of the money was spent on short commercials designed to present the candidates in the most favorable of lights. Additional huge sums were spent on the actual production of the commercials.

Richard Nixon, who appeared tired, gaunt, and with a five-o'clock shadow in the first 1960 debate, returned in 1968 as a calm, serene, very carefully controlled candidate.[26] Candidates for major office almost always enlist the talents of advertising agencies and their "creative" people before presenting themselves to the American people.

Candidates also try to "make news," especially if what they do appears on the evening edition of the television report. There is great emphasis on what are called "pseudo" events or *media events*; that is, events created for television. Candidates go to nursing homes and tour factories, all with an eye toward media coverage and "free" advertising. The evening news subtly influences how many campaigns are run.

Of course, it is the job of the news media to report the political news, but the news media are not without their biases. For example, in a study of the 1968 election, Edith Efron found a good deal of evidence that during the last month and a half, CBS, NBC, and ABC gave far better coverage to Hubert Humphrey than to Richard Nixon.[27]

On the other hand, Nixon had the editorial support of over 75 percent of the 1,750 daily newspapers in the country. As stated in Chapter 7, in most American cities there is only one daily newspaper, and fully 60 percent of the total daily circulation in the United States is controlled by large newspaper chains. In addition, political reporters in general and those on the presidential train in particular have been severely criticized in recent years for shoddy reporting, laziness, and subjectivity.[28]

Political advertising is an important way for a candidate to get the message—whatever it might be—across to the public, no matter how the media handle the campaign. Numerous choices are available. There are thirty-second "spots" and sixty-second spots, two-minute commercials and five-minute commercials. People have argued that the thirty-second

[26] See Joe McGinnis, *The Selling of the President* (New York: Trident Press, 1969). For other examinations of the role of image making in politics, see Dan Nimmo, *The Political Persuaders: The Techniques of Modern Election Campaigns* (Englewood Cliffs, N.J.: Prentice-Hall, 1970); and Ray Hiebert, Robert Hone, John Lorenz, and Ernest Lotito, *The Political Image Merchants* (Washington, D.C.: Acropolis, 1971).

[27] Edith Efron, *The News Twisters* (New York: Mentor Books, 1972). For an interesting if episodic account of media "objectivity," see Robert Cirino, *The Power to Persuade* (New York: Bantam Books, 1974).

[28] Timothy Krause, *The Boys on the Bus* (New York: Random House, 1973). See also Harry Clar, ed., *Mass Media and Modern Democracy* (Chicago: Rand McNally, 1973).

advertisement is pure image, and viewers are given no opportunity to get more than a glimpse of the candidate's face and campaign slogan.

The short spot can backfire. Richard Ottinger won the New York Democratic senatorial primary in 1968 on the basis of superb short spots that carried the message, "Ottinger Delivers." In the general election, people expected him to; he failed to, and fell flat on his face.

Five-minute commercials carry both advantages and disadvantages. They are relatively cheaper than the shorter spots. For example, you may be able to buy five minutes of air time for the same price as two thirty-second spots. As a result, many television stations discourage the buying of five-minute commercials because they can make more money by selling that five minutes of time as *ten* thirty-second spots. And, although five-minute commercials are cheaper (if you can get them), they have a major disadvantage: Many viewers will not watch a political ad that long. Nevertheless, Jimmy Carter used a five-minute biography to great effect during the early 1976 primaries, and his handling of the longer ad fitted his image of a "different" candidate.[29]

As the candidate, you are faced with a host of media and media-related choices. How much of your budget should go for television? In some urban congressional districts, such as those around Los Angeles or New York, prime-time television may be too expensive. A single TV spot can cost $50,000 to make. How much should you spend on radio? Radio remains an overlooked medium that can be both inexpensive and effective in reaching some voters. How much should you spend on newspaper ads? You will want voters to learn that your staff will provide rides to the polls on election day. Weekly newspapers are important in rural areas. Their ads tend to be relatively expensive, but the weekly newspaper stays around barber shops, beauty salons, and bowling alleys for an entire week, thus giving the candidate very good exposure.

> Candidates are faced with a host of media and media-related choices. In recent years, huge sums of money have been spent on television advertising.

Then there is the choice between air time and production. Should you put your major effort into a superior set of ads, but show them less frequently? Or should you do simpler, less costly ads and show them more often?

Finally, there are the familiar campaign posters, buttons, and bumper stickers. Every campaign has them although there is no firm evidence that they have any effect on the voters whatsoever. At best, it can be said they keep up the candidate's morale.

Scheduling

There is no more important commodity in a campaign than the candidate's time. You can hire more staff, spend more money on advertising, or even

[29] Martin Schram, *Running for President, 1976: The Carter Campaign* (New York: Stein & Day, 1977).

raise more money with a greater effort. *But you cannot recover the candidate's time.* A carefully thought out, rationally arranged schedule plus a full-time scheduler who organizes the candidate's time will often do more than thousands of dollars worth of advertising.

Let us assume you are a woman running for Governor in Iowa. You have served in the state legislature, so you are already known in a number of towns. Your family comes from another part of the state, so you have a base in several other towns. Your task seems simple enough—visit the areas where you are unknown. Initially, you will accept almost any invitation, just to get going. But as the campaign develops, there will be conflicting events. Your scheduler will have to decide—do you attend the corn-harvest festival in Ottumwa or Des Moines? Do you address the Rotarians in Sioux City or the once-a-year meeting of the AMA?

It is crucial that a candidate's most important commodity—time—be scheduled efficiently.

One important principle is to concentrate on "one-time" events, those that occur only once in a campaign. The AFL-CIO convention, for example, may be your only chance to address a large group of labor leaders.

You should also dovetail your visits to locations with "media" stops. If you are campaigning in a town, take the time to visit the local radio station, appear on a talk show, or visit the local newspaper. Often weekly newspapers will not carry political news, but will print photos of the candidate talking with local residents.

Scheduling should also grow out of your basic strategy. In a primary, you will want to concentrate on the strongholds of your party, where the major sources of votes are. During the general election, you will want to reach out to other areas. If, for example, there are 954 towns in Iowa, and 285 of them have generally voted Republican during the last six or eight years, while 200 of them have generally voted Democratic, you, as a Democrat, will want to concentrate on those towns that are *swing,* that is, go Republican or Democratic depending on the election.

Finally, scheduling should be kept flexible during the final weeks of a campaign to allow you to take advantage of your opponent's weaknesses and to correct your own. It is unwise to accept invitations for the end of campaign unless you are sure it will be important that you appear. Sometimes areas you consider safe suddenly turn out to be trouble spots. For example, during the 1976 Democratic primaries, George Wallace assumed that he would do well in Florida and North Carolina. Therefore, he spent a month of valuable time campaigning in Massachusetts and Illinois. While Wallace was busy in these states, Jimmy Carter made major inroads in Florida and North Carolina, eventually winning both.

Polls

If scheduling is the most understated factor in modern campaigning, polling and polls may well be the most exaggerated. It is easy to see why polls hold so much attraction for candidates and reporters alike. Candidates like them for peace of mind. They may also be used to give encouragement to workers while spreading confusion among opponents. Reporters like them because they offer an easy story. Faced with conflicting signals as to who is "winning" and who is "losing," and the various claims of the candidates themselves, reporters may fasten on polling results as "facts."

Polls can, of course, be legitimate tools in political contests. Good polls, properly conducted, accurately measure voter sentiment.

But it is important to realize what polls do *not* do. As we mentioned in Chapter 4, they do not tell you, as a candidate, where you are now, or where you are going. They tell you only where you *were* at a given moment in the past. Even as the polling data are being assembled and analyzed, they are aging, often rapidly. Polls are merely snapshots, not motion pictures or images in crystal balls. A series of polls may reveal voter shifts and trends, but there are practical limits to polling. For one thing, polls are quite expensive to do properly, often costing $15,000–$20,000 for a single statewide survey.[30]

Observers of the use of polls distinguish between **structured polls**—that is, specific questions with choices—and **open-ended polls**, where the interviewee is asked for his or her opinion (for example, "Why do you like Miss Jones?). There is a difference between phone polling and home polling, where the interviewer visits the subject at home. Home polling is slightly more accurate in many cases, and the interviewer has a better opportunity to ask more questions without the subject losing interest.

The most useful polls not only indicate who is ahead or behind, but also show the basis of their support. You will want to know which groups support you. Why? Can you attract more people by doing something you are not now doing?

Closely related to polling data is the use of computers and direct mail to get at target voters. Computers can store a great deal of information; for example, the names and addresses of all dairy farmers in the state. That information can be readily retrieved and used. Let us say you want to send a letter to all dairy farmers. You have the letter printed, have the computer run off the names and addresses on the mailing labels, which volunteers can attach, and send out a mailing. For smaller groups, you can get various types of office equipment that automatically type out "individual" letters. These enable you to reach a number of potential supporters directly. Computers can also be used to provide voter lists for volunteer use in going door to door to deliver campaign literature.

---

[30] For an overview of polling techniques and their implications, see C. W. Roll and A. H. Cantril, *Polls: Their Use and Misuse in Politics* (New York: Basic Books, 1972); Leo Bogart, *Silent Politics* (New York: Wiley, 1972); Richard Dawson, *Public Opinion and Contemporary Politics* (New York: Harper & Row, 1973); and George Gallup, *The Sophisticated Poll Watcher's Guide* (Princeton: Princeton Opinion Press, 1976).

The use of direct mail may be helpful, especially in certain situations. If the airwaves are saturated with advertising, if the newspapers are reporting political stories day after day, you may possibly get underneath all this "noise" with direct mail. One outstanding example of this tactic occurred in the 1968 gubernatorial race in New York. The incumbent governor, Nelson Rockefeller, was in deep trouble and for a time it seemed unlikely that he would gain reelection. Everybody knew he was the governor, and many disliked the job he had done. By the use of sophisticated polling techniques and direct mail, the Rockefeller campaign was able to personalize his accomplishments. People with retarded children received letters from the governor outlining what he had done for them. State employees received letters indicating their pay raises. Governor Nelson Rockefeller was reelected. Of course, as in many Rockefeller campaigns, money constituted no problem.

Other Techniques

Much of politics still involves "pressing the flesh," shaking hands, getting out to see the voters. If you have loads of time but little money, you may turn this to advantage by letting the voters see you in person.

A highly effective variation is the state or district-wide walk. Dan Walker walked across Illinois right into the governor's mansion. Maine Congressman Bill Cohen walked over 1,000 miles in two campaigns to dramatize his candidacy, and was elected by large margins. In an age of gadgetry and advanced technology, voters apparently find it reassuring to see the candidate in person.

Finances

All of the above aspects in a campaign are related to the spending of money. Candidates and their campaign managers make difficult choices based on the money available and their judgments about how much money should be spent where. In recent years, there has been increasing concern about election spending and contributions. Campaign spending has risen to extremely high levels. Corrupt practices associated with raising these tremendous amounts have occasionally called into question the very nature of our political system.

In 1952, a presidential year, approximately $140 million was spent on all United States elections. That figure rose to more than $500 million in 1976. A single senate race may cost as much as $5 million. A congressional race typically costs several hundred thousand dollars. The 1972 presidential elections found Nixon spending $48 million and McGovern $25 million.

Congressman Bill Cohen of Maine walked over 1,000 miles to dramatize his desire to bring government back to the people.

Along with the skyrocketing costs of elections have come serious abuses. Corporations, such as Gulf Oil and Lockheed Aircraft, gave hundreds of thousands of dollars illegally. Organizations such as the Dairymen's Association poured in additional illegal monies. Robert Vesco, an international financier on the run, gave $200,000 to the Nixon reelection campaign—in $100 bills.

Widespread abuses of election financing and the resulting public disenchantment have led to a series of reforms. The 1971 **Federal Election Campaign Act** was signed in 1972 and led to the stiffer 1974 amendments to the Federal Election Campaign Act. It also set a limit of ten cents per voter on the amount any presidential candidate could spend on advertising. In 1976, every candidate who qualified took advantage of this, and the matching-funds provision is credited with opening up the presidential primary race to individuals who ordinarily would not have been serious candidates. A good example is Ellen McCormack, who ran in a number of primaries on an anti-abortion platform. All told, the fourteen people who ran for president in 1976 spent $70 million, an increase of one-third over

The Federal Election Campaign Act of 1971 was designed to prevent widespread abuses of election financing.

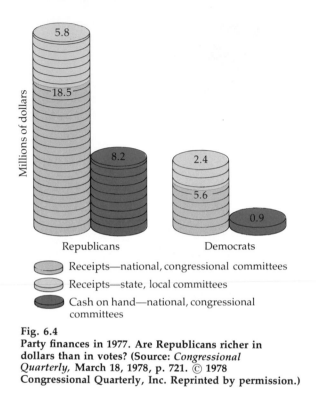

Fig. 6.4
Party finances in 1977. Are Republicans richer in dollars than in votes? (Source: *Congressional Quarterly,* **March 18, 1978, p. 721. © 1978 Congressional Quarterly, Inc. Reprinted by permission.)**

Election Reform

While the Supreme Court ruled in 1976 that some of the provisions of the 1971 Federal Election Campaign Act were unconstitutional, the following provisions of the law were upheld:

1. A $1,000 limit on individual contributions to any campaign (under the law, the primary and general elections each count as separate campaigns).

2. Tightened disclosure and reporting laws. Candidates must file reports listing virtually every contribution, and are required to do so on specific dates so that the reports will be made public as the election campaign progresses.

3. A limit of $5,000 on organizational contributions to campaigns and also specifications of the amounts the national and state party organizations can give to candidates.

4. Limits on presidential campaign spending if candidates take matching funds from the federal government. In what many regard as a first step toward public financing of elections, the law provided that any candidate seeking to receive matching funds had to raise $5,000 in each of twenty states, although no donation could be more than $250 to count toward the total.

that spent in 1972. Of this total, $24 million came from the federal Treasury.

Why do people contribute to campaigns? It is easy to give a cynical answer—they want something in return. The large company contributions, those of the large labor unions, and many individual donations are expected to produce favorable legislation or other political favors. But many Americans give for a variety of reasons. Some believe in the democratic process and want to give individual candidates an opportunity to get their message across. They believe in a particular issue and want the person favoring the issue to have their support. Some give money so that if the candidate is elected he or she will at least listen to their views. Some give money so that they can feel important.

Is it true that in the future only wealthy individuals will be able to run for office? Public financing would seem to be one of the few ways available to prevent this from becoming true. The costs would be surprisingly low, less than one-tenth of 1 percent of the total federal budget, and many Americans would say it was a bargain at that price.

But any comprehensive public-financing law must take into account the unconstitutionality of limiting the amount individuals can spend to get their views across. It must also deal with the problem of incumbency Any system of public financing that did not give the challenger additional monies would favor those already in office. As Common Cause and others have pointed out, the problem of incumbency is already there.[31] In 1976, for example, in both House and Senate races, many incumbents received more than twice as much as those opposing them.

For you, the candidate, there are other questions. Should you take money from organized groups, whether business or labor? Should you concentrate on trying to raise money through small donations, perhaps through direct mail? Or should you make an effort to raise as much as you can by concentrating on the $1,000 donors (often called the "heavy hitters")? How will you make it clear that donations to you will not mean political favors for those who give? Will you feel free to oppose bills even though their proponents gave you money?

Wherever the candidate turns, hard choices have to be made. This may help explain why relatively few Americans seek elective office.

SUMMARY

In this chapter we have examined the dynamics of elections in America. We have looked at how they are organized and who can, as well as who

---

[31] Alexander Heard, *The Costs of Democracy* (Chapel Hill: University of North Carolina Press, 1960). See also Herbert E. Alexander, *Money in Politics* (Washington, D.C.: Public Affairs Press, 1972) and *Political Financing* (Minneapolis, Minn.: Burgess, 1972).

does, participate in them. We have tried to give a sense of what it means actually to conduct a campaign while suggesting the various choices candidates must make in pursuing victory.

Elections offer the best opportunity for ordinary people to make choices in American politics. Elections are the people's expression. Elections determine who will represent the people and for how long. But governing is an ongoing process. People give their opinions not just at election time, but through mail, phone calls, telegrams, public opinion surveys, and the efforts of interest groups. In our complex, urbanized, modernized society, there remains a continuing need to make government responsible to the people on an orderly and ongoing basis.

Government is more than winning elections. Elections are the beginning, but only the beginning. They start something. They start a process in motion. They lead to governing. Most candidates are unprepared for governing, often having had no training whatsoever for it. You, as a candidate, will realize that the moment you are elected. As Robert Redford says in *The Candidate* when he learns he has won, "What the hell do I do now?" The voters have made their choice. Now the elected official faces a series of hard choices.

KEY TERMS

ballot	advisory primary
caucus	electoral college
primary	winner-take-all provision
closed primary	potential electorate
open primary	suffrage
plurality	structured poll
runoff	open-ended poll
nonpartisan primary	Federal Election Campaign Act
binding primary	

SUGGESTED READINGS

DeVries, Walter, and V. L. Tarrance, *The Ticket Splitter: A New Force in American Politics* (New York: William B. Erdmans, 1972).

> Focuses on the voter who does not vote the straight party ticket and emphasizes his importance to the winner in most close races. A key analysis of who actually decides the election in close races.

Key, V. O., Jr., *The Responsible Electorate: Rationality in Presidential Voting 1936–1960* (Cambridge, Mass.: Harvard University Press, 1966).

> Key declared that the voters are not fools and very often know exactly what they are voting for. This pioneering study indicates how important it is to know *why* people vote for a candidate or issue.

LANE, ROBERT E., *Political Ideology: Why the American Common Man Believes What He Does* (New York: The Free Press, 1962) and *Political Thinking and Consciousness: The Private Life of the Political Mind* (Chicago: Markham Publishing Company, 1969).

Two insightful studies of voters and their political conscience. Based in large part on specific interviews with voters. Lane is widely regarded as a leading American political scientist dealing with voters and their choices.

MILBRATH, LESTER, *Political Participation* (Chicago: Rand McNally, 1965).

A look at individuals and why they become involved in politics. Milbrath has done considerable work in the areas of political behavior and the formation of political attitudes.

POLSBY, NELSON W., and AARON B. WILDAVSKY, *Presidential Elections: Strategies of American Electoral Politics* (New York: Scribner's, 1972).

A comprehensive and substantial treatment of presidential elections and their political configurations. Looks at how and why certain candidates succeed and others fail in the presidential sweepstakes.

SCAMMON, RICHARD M., and BEN WATTENBERG, *The Real Majority* (New York: Coward-McCann, 1970).

A provocative and often criticized analysis of the voting patterns and political attitudes of "middle Americans." Indicates that much of the social engineering efforts of the 1960s have not had the support of a majority of Americans.

THOMPSON, HUNTER S., *Fear and Loathing on the Campaign Trail* (New York: Quick Fox, 1973).

An irreverent and outstanding description of the presidential primaries in 1972. Captures much of the insanity of the process. A disturbing, but exciting, look at what goes into a presidential race.

Our liberty depends on the freedom of
the press, and that cannot be limited
without being lost.

Thomas Jefferson

A popular Government, without popular
information, or the means of acquiring it,
is but a Prologue to a Farce or a Tragedy;
or, perhaps both.

James Madison

Truth is that which most contradicts itself
in time.

Lawrence Durrell

Get your facts first, and then you can
distort 'em as much as you please.

S. L. Clemens

CHAPTER 7 THE MEDIA: POLITICAL IMAGEMAKERS

In the popular, award-winning movie *Network,* a television network anchorman, Howard Beale, grows outraged and then deranged. In the midst of the nightly news, he jumps up, runs to the window, and yells out, "I'm mad as hell and I'm not going to take this any more." Millions of Americans find that exciting, follow his example, and the show becomes a smash hit. In fact, the program is so successful that the network is unwilling to take Beale off the air despite his bizarre antics, including threats to kill himself while on the air.

A thinly disguised critique of the major networks—ABC, NBC, and CBS—the film exaggerates many aspects of today's television. But it does express a growing concern about the power of television. As Beale himself puts it:

> Because the only truth you know is what you get over the tube! There is a whole and entire generation right now who never knew anything that didn't come out of this tube! This tube is the gospel! This tube is the ultimate revelation! This tube can make or break presidents, popes and prime ministers! This tube is the most awesome goddamned force in the whole goddamned world! And woe is us if it ever falls in the hands of the wrong people.[1]

In fact, *Network* makes a powerful argument that television has already fallen into the wrong hands. When Beale's ratings decline, United Broadcasting Systems hires radicals who assassinate the demented newscaster before the prime-time audience, again for high ratings.

Many Americans are confused and concerned about the role played in our society by the **media**, a term that includes any agency or means of mass communication. People complain that there is too much violence on television, or too much soap and not enough real sex. Some complain that news is almost always "bad news," never "happy." Others worry that television and radio have driven too many newspapers out of business by taking away advertising revenues. Still others feel that the advertising itself is somehow at fault, creating a climate of opinion and a hunger for a consumer-oriented life-style that perverts and distorts America. Many Americans suggest that the media taken together, especially the people who bring us the news, whether in print or over the airwaves, shape and mold our political perceptions. Finally, there are those who claim that our choice of those elected is in fact manipulated by slick advertising types and biased reporters.

In Chapter 6, we explored the electoral process and the role that the candidate's advertising and use of media coverage plays in campaigns and elections. Here we are concerned with the broader long-term way in which the media shape our politics, and with some of the questions now being

---

[1] *Network,* novelization by Sam Hedrin, screenplay by Paddy Chayefsky (London: Sphere Books, 1977), p. 97.

raised as to whether these effects are good or bad. We are concerned with how the conflicting demands of interest groups are portrayed; how Americans acquire their information on a daily basis; how the press and other segments of the media influence our lives; and how the basic constitutional freedoms of press and free speech have been enhanced or weakened by the growing weight of the mass media.

This chapter is central to our own themes of change and choice. Most basic works dealing with the American political system have avoided any discussion of the media, except in passing reference to their effect on elections or to presidential use of the media in communicating with the American people. This chapter addresses some of the central issues concerning the media as we know them and their changing role in the American political system.

First we ask, What is the role of media today? Then we concern ourselves with what various groups think it *should* be. Second we ask whether the media are biased. Do they play their role badly or well? Third we consider the very important question of access to information: Is too much information available? Do political and economic interests manipulate us by withholding information from the news? Do Americans have sufficient information on most subjects to make sensible economic and political choices? Fourth we ask, Is there too much concentration of power within the media? Should newspapers own television stations? If so, how many? This brings us to our final set of questions dealing with the regulation of the media. Does our society place too many restrictions on the media? Not enough? Should members of the public have access to the media in order to express their opinions? If so, how much access and who should provide it? And who pays the bill?

These questions relate to aspects of the American political system that we have covered in earlier chapters. They also touch on some subjects, such as foreign policy, that we cover in subsequent chapters. These are difficult, even perplexing, questions, as challenging as any in this book. To want to understand America requires knowing more about the media. For better or worse, the activities of the media affect many aspects of our lives. Whether the media serve as a mirror of, or as a manipulator of, the mass public, they remain an inherent link connecting the lives of 220 million Americans.

THE ROLE OF THE MEDIA IN SOCIETY

Taken together, the newspapers and the magazines we read, the radio we listen to, and the television we watch are intrinsic parts of modern industrialized society. In all modern societies, the media serve a key function in communicating information. If the media are controlled by a small group of people, or by the government, they may bring selective or official information to people; in a more open system, more divergent views are likely to be presented. But in either case, the media are an essential agency in a complex, modernized society.

The exact role of the media play varies from one society to the next and from time to time. But in a modern, technologically sophisticated society such as ours they loom as an important influence on public attitudes and moods.

There are more than 122,000,000 television sets in the United States. In 1976, an average of 24 million Americans watched the nightly news on the three major networks. Television has had an amazing growth. In August 1945, there were only 7,000 TV sets, of which 5,500 were in New York City. Only five American cities had any television at all. In 1976, CBS

In all modern societies the media serve a key function in communicating information.

enjoyed a viewing audience of 9.3 million, NBC another 8.6 million, and ABC 6.5 million.[2] When an American president chooses to address the American people on all the networks, no fewer than 100 million people are likely to watch him. There are 250 million radio sets in the United States, 50 percent of which are on at any moment. There are 950 television stations and more than 5,000 radio stations.

Each day, 1,750 daily newspapers are published in the United States. Major newspapers often reach more than half a million people. The *Los Angeles Times,* for example, has a circulation of over 1 million; The *New York Daily News,* 1.7 million; the *Chicago Tribune,* 650,000; the *Washington Post,* 550,000; and the *New York Times,* 800,000. National wire services such as United Press International (UPI) and Associated Press (AP) feed most of the remaining daily newspapers. There are 8,800 weekly newspapers in this country.

[2] Ron Powers, *The Newscasters* (New York: St. Martin's Press, 1977), p. 196.

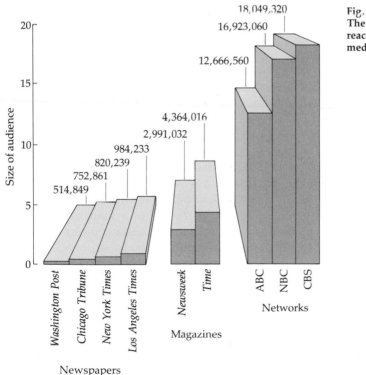

Fig. 7.1
The size of the audiences reached by major mass media.

Many Americans depend on weekly news magazines. *Time* reaches 4 million homes; *Newsweek*, 3 million; and *U.S. News and World Report*, 2 million.

Clearly, the print, radio, and television segments of the media are ubiquitous, bombarding individual Americans daily with thousands and thousands of impressions in word, sound, and picture. Many of these impressions carry political overtones. They contain "pitches" by public officials and candidates. They describe actions taken (or not taken) by people in public life. They subtly (sometimes not so subtly) tell Americans what is wrong (or right) with their lives, occasionally suggesting how things might be changed for the better (or worse). Not only do they bring to each of us a bewildering variety of opinions and sensations, but they also, for all their fragmentation and sensationalism, tend to bring Americans together in a common experience. At the very least, they bring groups of Americans together (often to be set against other Americans). Contemporary society could not function without the information brought collectively by the media. This vast, sprawling nation, with all of its groupings and tensions, is held together in part by its communications network.

> The various segments of the media not only bring to each of us a bewildering variety of opinions and sensations, but also tend to bring us together in a common experience.

The Fourth Estate

At the end of the eighteenth century, the distinguished British historian Thomas Carlyle quoted Edmund Burke as saying, "There were Three Estates in Parliament; but, in the Reporters' gallery yonder, there sat a Fourth Estate, more important far than they all." The three estates were the nobles, the clergy, and the peasants, and Burke's point was that the press, with its power to inform and criticize, to expose and prod, had become a **fourth estate**—a vital, even critical, force in the political process. Even as intrepid a general as Napoleon once remarked, "I fear three newspapers more than a hundred thousand bayonets." Allowing for Napoleon's exaggeration, there can be little doubt that various newspapers over the years have influenced the decline and fall of a number of world leaders. Press criticism played a major role in the abdication of Edward VIII of Great Britain. Carl Bernstein and Robert Woodward, young, unknown investigative reporters for the *Washington Post*, exposed the lies and coverup of the Nixon administration following the Watergate affair, thereby paving the way for the first presidential resignation in our history.

> Various newspapers over the years have influenced the course of history.

The media have a role to play in our American political system as **loyal opposition**—in other words, the newsmen and newswomen who cover the national, state, and local political scenes usually support the overall system, but at the same time are often highly critical of wrongdoing at any level. This is true of radio and television reporters as well as

Carl Bernstein (left) and Bob Woodward (right) compare impressions in front of the White House.

journalists.[3] Sometimes the press acts to support the government. For example, during the period prior to the American-sponsored invasion of Cuba in 1961, the *New York Times* uncovered the story but postponed its release following a request from President Kennedy. Over the years, some reporters have shared information they gathered overseas with various agencies of the United States government, including the Central Intelligence Agency.

Clearly the job of a conscientious reporter is not easy. Assume for a moment that you are an overseas reporter for the *Washington Post*. While on assignment in the Middle East, you discover that the United States is planning to recognize the Palestine Liberation Organization as the sole legitimate spokesman for the Palestinian refugees.

[3] For a fascinating overview of the interactions among politics, economics, and the changing social milieu, see Erik Barnouw, *A History of Broadcasting in the United States*, 3 vols. (New York: Oxford University Press, 1970).

Moreover, you further discover through your contacts that the United States has not informed the Israeli government, which remains completely in the dark. You are on to a major story, a major scoop that should provide a significant boost to your career. When you confront American officials in the area with the story, they immediately arrange for you to speak with the secretary of state. Calling from Washington, the secretary tells you point blank that by publishing the story at this point you would completely destroy a carefully orchestrated effort to achieve a lasting peace settlement in the area. The secretary promises that the Israelis will be told "at the proper time" and that you will be free to publish the story after that has happened.

What would you do? Would you send your story off to your editors in Washington and let them take the responsibility for publishing or not publishing it? Would you feel that you should go ahead and publish the story and let the chips fall where they may? Or would you feel that the interests of world peace are more important than your personal career advancement? Much would depend on your judgment as to whether this strategy was likely to lead to peace, and whether you trusted the secretary of state. But clearly you would be in a dilemma. How you resolved this ethical dilemma would have important consequences for your career, your paper, the United States, and perhaps the world.

Given the importance of their relationship with the press, most office holders and would-be office holders seek to establish a good rapport with reporters. As Jules Witcover demonstrates in *Marathon: The Pursuit of the Presidency*,[4] how reporters feel about a candidate influences the way they report the candidate's actions and words. On the national level, with a need to reach a mass audience, such a relationship may be critical. Television in particular plays a crucial role, for the way a candidate comes across in a television newscast may aid or impede that candidate's career.

During the 1976 presidential election, Jimmy Carter's skillful use of political advertising helped get his campaign going. Even more importantly, Carter's relationship with the national media and his appreciation of what television could and could not do for him helped him to project an image that Americans responded to. As Barry Jagoda, his media advisor, put it:

> We're different because we understand that television is more than journalism. No one in the White House before has ever treated television as a great American institution—like big labor or the auto industry. . . . My job is knowing what broadcasting wants and to a certain extent, making them think that what we want is actually their idea.[5]

Reporters are often placed in ethical dilemmas. How they resolve these dilemmas can often have important consequences for society.

[4] Jules Witcover, *Marathon: The Pursuit of the Presidency 1972–1976* (New York: Viking Press, 1977).

[5] Richard Reeves, "The Prime Time President," *New York Times Magazine*, May 15, 1977, p. 18.

Would pseudoevents such as Carter's fireside chats have been effective before the age of the media?

Once in office, President Carter went out of his way to create pseudo-events that enabled him to reach millions of Americans while casting a symbolic glow around himself. Town meetings and fireside chats, dutifully covered by the national media, enabled Carter to come across as president of all the people.

The intertwining of politics and the media tends to place successful politicians in the realm of show business, even after they leave office. Norman Brokaw of the William Morris Agency managed to sell former

How would Lieutenant General Ulysses S. Grant have fared as a presidential candidate in this age of the glamorous politician?

How the media feel about a political candidate can strongly influence the course of that candidate's career. The intertwining of politics and the media tends to place successful candidates in the realm of show business.

President Ford and his wife Betty to book companies and the television networks. Irving "Swifty" Lazar, Hollywood agent, was able to sell former President Nixon, despite his precipitous fall from favor, for millions of dollars to the networks and book publishers. The packaging and show-business aspects of contemporary politics make students of American history a trifle uneasy. Would Abraham Lincoln be a likely candidate in the age of television and national media?

THE BIAS OF THE MEDIA

How do the media shape the news? Do they favor one candidate over another? Do they feature one type of event over another? Do they present their own views in subtle ways? In this section, we seek to examine the various ways in which our society is portrayed by the media. We proceed by asking a number of questions.

Is Good News News?

The first question is a simple one, but it has great significance for our society. Will the print and broadcast media cover "happy" stories or good news? If one listens to the nightly news is one likely to see a series of stories about how smoothly life is going in Australia or how pleasant the summer has been in Chicago? It is quite unlikely that this will be the case. What constitutes most news is bad news—accounts of plane crashes, murders, insurrections, tornados, fires, uprisings, wars, conflicts, and disasters.

A majority of the big stories appearing in the media, in fact, suggest that good news is usually not news. Various defenders of the media argue that it is the public who decides what is news: The public, they argue, prefers news stories that have a preponderance of the "bad." This attitude, of "give the people what they want," is seen most clearly, not only in television programming, but in the more sensational of the daily papers. As Bill Grundy puts it in *The Press Inside Out*, "Unless a paper is financially successful (that is, has a large readership and ad revenues) it will not be politically important."[6]

In television, an enormous amount of time and effort has been devoted to the show-business aspect, including the news programs. The major networks have spent literally millions of dollars in order to discover what the public wants. Increasingly, they have discovered that the mass public wants the news to be entertaining. ABC, for example, spent $10 million to find out why "AM America" should be turned into "Good Morning, America" and thus provide more entertainment. "In many stations, television news has become too important to be left to the newspeople," reports Ron Powers.[7]

The news, when viewed as "entertainment," requires giving the audience visual stories that will hold their attention. As a consequence, political campaigns spend a great deal of time and effort trying to create **media events**—events tailored for media coverage—of the right duration and impact to qualify as "entertainment." Powers feels that this accent on entertainment has been detrimental to the news, since it means that the reporting of complicated and lengthy stories is often so oversimplified that it becomes misleading or even incorrect. Visual "excitement" is substituted for a dispassionate assessment of what is happening.

Recently news has been viewed increasingly as entertainment, a trend that many people feel has been detrimental to dispassionate, accurate reporting.

[6] Bill Grundy, *The Press Inside Out* (London: W. H. Allen, 1976), p. vii.

[7] Powers, *The Newscasters*, p. 18.

Do the Media Make News?

Related to the question of what constitutes "news" is whether the media, by their very presence, "make" news. Certainly this is not true in many everyday situations. Reporters cover a fire or a hurricane or a riot; they do not make these things happen. At the same time, the mere presence of television cameras and dozens of reporters may influence the course of events by encouraging the participants to act, because they can be sure their actions will be covered.

The mere presence of the news media may change the course of events, thus becoming a self-fulfilling prophecy.

A corollary to this aspect is the self-fulfilling prophecy that sometimes results when a network sends a crew to cover an event. In order to justify the expense and the initial decision to send the crew, an event of little consequence may be made to appear as if it were of substantial importance. In the spring of 1966, for example, George Wallace came to Dartmouth College in Hanover, New Hampshire, to give an address. Governor Wallace had spoken at dozens of other campuses, often with minimal coverage. Because there was some opposition on campus to his coming, and because Dartmouth College had connections with the national media and was anxious to get some publicity, a number of reporters and television crews were present.

As Wallace's car approached the lecture hall, a number of students converged on it and began to rock the car back and forth. Campus police soon appeared, the rocking stopped, and Wallace proceeded to give his speech. After the incident, which occurred in the full glare of the television cameras, the reporters streamed to the phones to call in the "story." One student, amazed at all the fuss over such a trivial and inconsequential incident, asked one of the reporters, "This isn't news, is it?" "You bet your ass it is, kid," was the reply from a well-known reporter on one of America's most respected newspapers. Sure enough, the next day's paper and the newscasts were filled with stories and pictures of the "riot" that had taken place on the Dartmouth campus. The presence of major news concentrations can, in fact, make news.

Are the Media Biased or Just the Reporters?

Some have argued that news reporters are biased, favoring one candidate or cause over others and therefore reporting the news in a slanted fashion. Many reporters disagree. As Dan Rather, CBS's TV journalist, puts it:

> My job is to inform, not persuade. At the same time I don't want to come across as some kind of Pollyanna. I do not subscribe to the idea of the reporter-as-robot. I can't walk into a room and say to you, look, every day that I went to the White House I left my emotions behind me. But one test of the professional is how hard he tries and how well he succeeds in keeping his own feelings out of a story. I tried.[8]

[8] Dan Rather and Mickey Herskowitz, *The Camera Never Blinks* (New York: Morrow, 1977), pp. 13–14.

Others are not so sure. Edith Efron claims members of the press are being self-serving when they say they are not biased. Her analysis of the TV news content of the 1968 presidential election led her to conclude that there was a strong bias for Hubert Humphrey and against Richard Nixon.[9] Less harsh critics of the media, such as Kurt and Gladys Lang, insist that the media do not present news straight, even if they want to: "Rather, they show that television, as well as radio and print, always introduces some element of refraction into the actuality it conveys."[10]

This refraction, or distortion, as the term is used here, may have a variety of sources beyond favoritism. The 1972 presidential election affords one example. Even assuming that the same bias against Nixon existed as in 1968, the press by and large came to the early conclusion that the Democratic nominee, George McGovern, could not win. This was due in part to the senator's incredible series of political blunders following his nomination, and in part to the skill with which Nixon used the office of the presidency in running for reelection. By the fall of 1972, the press treated McGovern the way one must approach a victim of terminal cancer—with a distant kindness symptomatic of an avoidance reaction.

The relationship between bias and press-media treatment is a difficult one to assess. Reporters are human beings who feel certain ways about issues, individuals, and actions. Yet professionally, they are supposed to rise above their particular foibles and concentrate on reporting "the facts." The problem of assessing the extent to which reporters in particular and the media in general manage to take a detached view of things is a continuing one.

> To what degree media reporters are able to take a detached view of the events and people they cover is an important question.

Too Much Information or Not Enough?

Does the American public lack the information to decide on issues? Does the government withhold too much information? Do its news media provide us with too much information or not enough? As Ben Bagdikian has written, "nothing in the world matches the communication power of American television networks."[11] Although Bagdikian cites a number of instances in which the American public was completely captured by the media (for example, 96 percent of all homes with television had them on for the period following President John Kennedy's assassination), he also indicates the extent to which sheer *information* is an important aspect of the situation.[12]

[9] Edith Efron, *The Newstwisters* (Los Angeles: Nash, 1971), p. 47.

[10] Kurt Lang and Gladys Engel Lang, *Politics and Television* (Chicago: Quadrangle Books, 1968), p. 290.

[11] Ben H. Bagdikian, *Information Machines: Their Impact on Men and the Media* (New York: Harper & Row, 1971), p. 294.

[12] Bagdikian, *Information Machines*, p. 295.

Interview
Walter Cronkite:

Walter Cronkite, the anchorman for the CBS evening news, is considered by many to be the best known and most respected newsperson in America. Time *Magazine has described him as "the single most convincing and authoritative figure in television news." The following are excerpts from a lengthy interview with Cronkite by* PLAYBOY *magazine. The issue being discussed here is the controversy surrounding the relationship between the Nixon administration and the press. The Nixon administration felt that the press has a liberal (and therefore hostile) bias; the press felt that the administration was trying to control the news.*

PLAYBOY: You are perhaps the most outspoken of all newsmen in defending broadcasters' rights against Government intimidation. In fact, you have used the word conspiracy in describing the Nixon Administration's efforts to discredit the press. How would you characterize this conspiracy?

CRONKITE: Let me say, first of all, that after I used the word conspiracy the first and only time, in a speech to the International Radio and Television Society in New York a couple of years ago, I began to regret the use of the word—only because I found that there were still people who equated conspiracy with some of the witch-hunts of the past. The word has nearly lost its true meaning. Having said that, I still feel that this is basically what has taken place: a well-directed campaign against the press, agreed upon in secret by members of the Administration. I can't see how it's possible to have such an orchestrated, co-ordinated campaign without some prior plan and agreement—which really comes out to be a conspiracy.

PLAYBOY: Can you trace it to one person in the Administration?

CRONKITE: I certainly think that the President has to be held accountable, since he's the boss. . . .

PLAYBOY: Nearly all politicians have felt the need to control the press to some degree. Is this Administration simply more sophisticated than its predecessors in the techniques of applying pressure effectively?

CRONKITE: I don't know that they're any more sophisticated, but they're the first ones who have deliberately set out to *use* those techniques.

PLAYBOY: What has been the chronology of this attack? Was Vice-President Agnew's 1969 Des Moines speech—in which he attacked the "tiny, enclosed fraternity of privileged men"—the start of it all?

CRONKITE: I think that was the open declaration in the battle. Before that, it was simply felt that this Administration's antagonism had been about like the antagonism shown by previous Administrations, Democratic as well as Republican—particularly Democratic—toward the press. An adversary relationship, we all agree, is a good thing. But the Agnew attack suddenly became a matter of Administration policy and, more than that, a threat to use Governmental weapons against the press. Then, following Agnew's speech, there was a tightening in attitudes on the part of press-relations people in the Government. It was a subtle thing.

PLAYBOY: Not being cooperative with reporters?

CRONKITE: Yes. And clearly displaying a feeling that they felt they were under pressure from the press but that they were going to be protected higher up. They took the hard line.

PLAYBOY: There have been private complaints by news executives of other networks about rather direct applications of this hard line. They say that staff aides of the FCC, and sometimes Administration staff people, upon hearing that a controversial documentary is in the works, will telephone the station managers of affiliate stations and remind them that their license is coming due for renewal in a few months. They raise that reminder in connection with whether the station manager is going to clear the documentary for broadcast or not. Has that happened at CBS?

CRONKITE: I haven't heard anything like that here at CBS, but that doesn't mean it doesn't happen.

PLAYBOY: In December of last year, Clay T. Whitehead, who is President Nixon's communications advisor, announced to a journalism fraternity in Indianapolis that a bill was in the works that would place a local station's license in jeopardy if the station couldn't "demonstrate meaningful service to the community." Whitehead said "the community-accountability standard will have special meaning for all network affiliates. They should be held accountable to their local audiences for the 61 percent of their schedules that are network programs." Whitehead used the words bias and balance in defining this accountability. What do you think is behind such a requirement?

CRONKITE: I think the Administration would like to deflate, if possible, the power of the network news programs. But I don't know how in the world local station owners could do that. I think it's impossible. On the basis of what knowledge are they going to edit locally what we broadcast nationally? They don't have the sources of information available at their finger tips, as we do. Are they going to challenge a statement made by a network news correspondent in Saigon? How are they going to do that? Are they simply going to decide it doesn't sound right to them? Or it doesn't sound fair to them? I think this is what Mr. Whitehead would like to impose. . . .

PLAYBOY: Whitehead's second argument is that a great deal of economic and social power is concentrated in the networks. CBS, for example, does research and development in military and space technology, owns two publishing houses and has phonograph-record, record-club and film-communications divisions.

CRONKITE: That's right. We're big. And we're powerful enough to thumb our nose at threats and intimidation from Government. I hope it stays that way.

PLAYBOY: But are you powerful enough to broadcast in your own interest, as opposed to the public interest?

CRONKITE: That danger probably exists. I couldn't deny it. But there are an awful lot of journalists who wouldn't work for networks if they did that. That's the first line of defense. The second line of defense, which I admit is a matter of trust, is that none of the network managements is as venal as that. At least they haven't shown that side to me. I've been here for 22 years and I just don't think that's likely.

Originally appeared in **PLAYBOY** Magazine; copyright © 1973 by **PLAYBOY**.

It has sometimes been alleged that Americans in the 1960s did not have enough information. They lacked concrete knowledge as to how the war in Vietnam really was going. They were not only not told about American actions in Laos and Cambodia, they were actually misled. They were not informed about the actions of the Central Intelligence Agency, which conducted illegal actions not only abroad but within the United States as well. They were unaware during the important 1972 presidential election of the extent to which the Nixon administration engaged in illegal activities and harassed political opponents.

By the mid-1970s, however, it appeared that the pendulum had swung in the other direction. Americans were deluged with information about the workings (or nonworkings) of various governmental agencies. Official secrets were leaked. Masses of almost extraneous materials were made available. The media, in a frenzy of activity, seemed to go from accepting what the government said in the 1960s to almost refusing to believe anything it said. The Carter administration, having been swept in on a wave of "openness" and "honesty," was soon engulfed in a serious problem concerning Bert Lance, the budget director and close friend of the president. Within a matter of months after the inauguration, the American people were overwhelmed with bits and pieces of Lance's previous financial dealings. His large bank overdrafts, his use of collateral, his lavish entertaining, his use of a corporate airplane for personal use—all were presented as a kind of major scandal. Finally Lance resigned, and the media immediately turned their attention elsewhere.

Another important question is the degree of information that should be available to the public.

The former director of the Central Intelligence Agency, Richard Helms, was subsequently indicted for lying to a congressional committee concerning the role of the United States in Chile a decade earlier. Helms had an interesting defense. Not only had previous directors lied to other congressional committees, he argued, but these lies were absolutely necessary to conduct foreign policy in the modern world. You could not, Helms insisted, tell everything you knew at all times and to all people. The result would damage the national interest. That this defense had some validity was recognized by the Justice Department in its decision to allow Helms to plead guilty to the minor offense of "not answering fully." Some people have argued that this should not be the case, and that public officials should be accountable.

Distortion: Ideology or Accident?

Thus emerges one of the major media questions for the 1980s: What precisely is the public's right to expect that the news it receives is accurate, fairly presented, and complete? Political reality is always very difficult to perceive accurately *in the short run*. The "facts" of a situation are rarely self-evident. The participants in political or military conflict situations will struggle to give their versions of events. But when the media reporters seek to penetrate the contradictory press releases they are handed, there is no guarantee that their information will be more accurate than that of the individuals, groups, or governments involved.

An excellent example of this is provided in a remarkable two-volume work by Peter Braestrup, who was chief of the *Washington Post* Saigon bureau during the latter part of the Vietnam War.[13]

The conclusion of this lavishly documented work is that the American press (print and electronics) seriously misrepresented the crucial events of the Tet offensive. With historical hindsight, it is now clear that the offensive was an enormous gamble on the part of the North Vietnamese. They committed their main force units to an invasion of many cities and towns in the expectation that these units would be able to stay in those cities and towns; the people would rise to support them, the South Vietnamese army would give way, and, finally, the Thieu regime would topple in humiliation and confusion. None of these things happened.

While the North Vietnamese and their allies in the National Liberation Front (Vietcong) inflicted great damage and high casualties in the attack, they were beaten back with greater loss to themselves and achieved none of their tactical objectives.

However, Tet was *reported* as an unmitigated disaster for the South Vietnamese army and their American allies. While the North Vietnamese were being painfully driven out of city after city, as much as a quarter of all Tet coverage focused on the siege of the United States Marine outpost at Khe Sanh. This episode was quite untypical of the rest of the battle (not, as Walter Cronkite put it, a "microcosm" of the entire war), and even it was wildly misinterpreted. Several networks were solemnly predicting the imminent fall of Khe Sanh at the very time the North Vietnamese were withdrawing from their positions, and one correspondent reported on the evening before the Marines moved out for mop-up operations that "there is really no end in sight."

Why did such a distortion occur? Braestrup suggests it was because too much reporting was done from Saigon and too little on the basis of firsthand experience in the field. In addition, the reporters were not experienced in military matters and had reason to distrust military sources. Other observers, however, have suggested that the explanation lies in an antiwar ideological bias on the part of reporters, which led them to interpret events positively for North Vietnam and negatively for South Vietnam and the United States. Truth, as is so often the case, probably lies some-

It is important to keep alert to possible sources of distortion in the news.

[13] Peter Braestrup, *Big Story: How the American Press and Television Reported and Interpreted the Crisis of Tet 1968 in Vietnam and Washington* (Boulder, Colo.: Westview Press, 1977).

Some people feel that the news reporting of the Vietnam War was distorted. Whether or not this is true, photos such as this, showing Vietnamese children fleeing from a napalm attack, certainly increased opposition to the war at home.

where in between. The more important point, perhaps, is to cultivate a healthy distrust of all sources of information, and to train ourselves to ask how the imagemakers' existing commitments and ideology may have affected the proffered image.

Ethical Choices

In addition to the problem of *accurately portraying* public events, the media must often decide what *is* a legitimate public event. The public may expect news, but the individuals who are part of the news story may have important needs as well. Take the following example: You are a reporter for one of the big weekly news magazines. You discover in the course of interviewing a number of former CIA agents that during the late 1960s one of your former college professors reported to the CIA on her findings when she traveled to Latin America. You discover that your former professor did not take any money from the CIA, nor was she sent abroad by them. The CIA simply wanted to know what she had found in Bolivia and Paraguay.

As a reporter, you may want to tell the entire story. But how will you balance the individual professor's right to privacy in terms of this situation with the need of the public to have all the information it can get? Will the country be better off if you "expose" the professor for acts that may be regarded as unpopular even though they are certainly not illegal? Will the general population appreciate your reluctance to withhold your sources in the interest of telling a good and important story without implicating the "innocent"? Or is the truth better served by laying out the entire story and letting the chips fall where they may, even if that means ruining other lives (or drying up sources)?

And what about the whole question of the ethics of encouraging the "leaking" of information to the media? The government official who opposes a certain policy is persuaded to leak adverse information by a reporter who also opposes it. The trading of information with reporters is one thing, but the attempt to actively intervene to cast unfavorable light on a policy simply because of personal bias is another. Jack Anderson maintains that the "whistle blowers" who leak information to him and other investigative reporters are doing a public service. But the reverse is also the case—it is often from base motives that leaks occur. And in a sense, reporters who use unidentified sources prevent those accused from being able to confront their accusers.

The whole question about information and how much the public should have, as well as the issue of how reporters come by their information, is related to yet another, even broader concern: To what extent do the media mirror society and to what extent do they mold it? How influential are the media in altering society and how much a prisoner of their own inhibitions and styles of operation are they? It is to these questions that we now turn.

> There are fundamental ethical considerations relating to how much information the public should have and how reporters should come by that information.

DO THE MEDIA MIRROR OR MOLD?

This question might seem to answer itself. We have a huge media industry that touches almost all our lives daily. We see the news. We hear the news. We read the news. The news influences us and the way we think about issues, about people, and about the world. Edward Epstein charges that the media, especially television, distort the realities of American society.[14] During the 1960s, the images were sharp, violent, and ugly. Campuses were in revolt; antiwar agitation was widespread. Several large cities were torn by racial turmoil. Images of a society coming apart at the seams overwhelmed the viewer. Of course, most campuses were not in revolt. Antiwar protesters were vastly outnumbered by those who passively accepted the war. Racial incidents, on a nationwide basis, was far less prevalent than one might have assumed by watching the evening news.

Epstein goes farther. He asserts that *by its very nature* television news is distorted:

> As long as the requisites remain essentially the same, network news can be expected to define American society by the problems of a few urban areas rather than the entire nation, by action rather than ideas, by dramatic protests rather than substantive contraductors, by rhetorical dialogues rather than the resolution of issues, by elite news-makers rather than economic and social structures, by atypical rather than typical views, and by synthetic national themes rather than disparate local events.[15]

So legitimate grounds remain for questioning whether the media present a true picture of society. The news as entertainment, requiring short, action sequences, certainly is a concept that affects us all. A half-hour news program with a series of visually interesting action stories may in fact be designed simply to hold our attention in between the explicitly entertainment programs:

> While the prime requisite is to maintain a mass audience, audience studies at all three networks consistently show that the vast preponderance of viewers whose attention must be retained for a half-hour of national news are watching television at that hour for the entertainment programs that either precede or follow the news, not for the news itself.[16]

Here is a dilemma. The various networks compete for the viewing public; gaining a greater share of the viewing public means greater advertising revenue. So why not give the public what it wants? The problem is that in making the news entertaining and in giving the public what it wants, reality may well be distorted, *at the very least.* In the scramble for ratings, the networks inevitably focus on those stories that will hold the attention of the mass public. The Public Broadcasting System is more likely to aim at a higher level of understanding. While the news there is far more thoughtful, it is much duller and relatively few people watch it. PBS says they accept this, that they are not in it for the mass audience. On the other

[14] Edward J. Epstein, *News from Nowhere: Television and the News* (New York: Random House, 1973).

[15] Epstein, *News from Nowhere*, p. 272.

[16] Edward J. Epstein, *Between Fact and Fiction* (New York: Random House, 1975), p. 203.

hand, the highly successful, award-winning "Sesame Street," put on by PBS, presents a situation quite similar to that of the major networks. In order to justify continued programming, "Sesame Street" needs to attract and hold a large audience. Thus, learning is made fun with dramatic incidents, cartoons, and lots of action even as the child learns. Surely it is a good thing that the children learn. At the same time, children are surely getting a distorted view of what learning is all about. Is all learning fun? Action filled? Visually oriented?

It may well be argued that the mass media do more than distort the news, that they alter our view of society. Advertising in magazines, in newspapers, and on radio and television portrays aspects of our society that definitely structure popular perceptions of ourselves. There are numerous examples that might be given. We shall concentrate on four: our attitudes about health, material possessions, violence, and old people.

Do the media simply reflect the realities of American society? Or do they distort the news, thereby altering our view of society? There are a number of indications that many of our attitudes are conditioned by what the media tell us.

The "Sick Society" and How to Cure It

Television in particular and the media in general influence the way we feel about health. Stop and think how many commercials have to do with sick people. Judging by the commercials, one would think that all Americans suffer from headaches, upset stomachs, constipation (or diarrhea), and aches and pains virtually all the time. How do these Americans manage to cope? They take pills. They rub salves and ointments all over themselves. A variety of packaged remedies make their colds vanish, give them superior bowel movements, and cure their deepest personal problems. The image suggests that the American public is miserable and decrepit—about to fall apart at the seams. Only by taking a vast array of tablets and liquids will Americans be able to cope with their physical miseries. Only by ingesting a variety of substances will they cope with the troubles of day-to-day living in an anxious world.

The Good Life and Happiness

The media depend on advertising for revenues and profits. This advertising invariably features items of a material nature. The assumption seems to be that the acquisition of material goods makes people happy. This may or may not be true. New cars may make people happy. Whizzing along on a snowmobile at fifty miles an hour may cure the winter blahs. New clothes may help a person get a good job. Furniture may turn a house into a home. On the other hand, all of these items may not help an individual at all. But people are made to think they will.

The competition of brand names, the seemingly endless variety of material goods, the fads that suddenly sweep the country (such as the "pet rock" craze, where rocks were sold to be kept as pets) are all borne in upon Americans by the media. The incessant pulse of advertising stimulates the economy while encouraging a life-style of conspicuous consumption. Seldom do the airwaves urge a vigorous examination of alternative life-styles. There is little suggesting that Americans might be better off with fewer material possessions. There is certainly not much in the way of a philosophy that declares that "small is beautiful" or that people should try to be as happy as possible with as little as possible.

It is difficult to pinpoint precisely the total impact of this socialization process on popular attitudes. Some have argued that the media's veneration of materialism and consumption has produced "cognitive dissonance" (meaning a sharp break between what people expect to have and what they actually end up by having). The gap between what people have and what they are socialized to accept as "the good life" may easily erupt in antisocial actions such as riots and lootings. Even in the best of circumstances, there seems little doubt that the way we think about ourselves is conditioned by what the media tell us.

Violence and More Violence

Many of the most popular television programs—the long-running westerns and police shows—involve violence. Each week hundreds, if not thousands, of people are "killed" on television. Some have argued that this accent on violence has conditioned our society to place less value on human life and to become callous about killings. Some critics have gone even further, asserting that television violence, especially the violence experienced by children watching cartoons, actually encourages real violence.

Psychologists and other examiners of this phenomenon remain divided as to the actual connection, if any, between television violence and violence in our society. Those who disclaim such a correlation argue that the situation is actually the reverse; namely, that our society is a violent one and that television merely reflects, or mirrors, the reality of American society. Yet in a 1977 murder trial, it was argued that television violence was responsible for "intoxicating" a young murderer, leading him to commit the crime. Dr. Margaret Hanratty Thomas, an associate professor of physiology at Florida Technological University who was not allowed to testify at this trial, maintained that television violence can cause aggressive behavior, particularly in children. A major set of questions concerning the direct relationship between media violence and actual violence remains unanswered. In 1972, after a three-year study, the Surgeon General's Scientific Advisory Committee on Television and Sound likewise reported:

> . . . a preliminary and tentative indication of a causal relation between seeing violence on television and aggressive behavior; an indication that any such

causal relation operates only on some children (who are predisposed to be aggressive); and an indication that it operates only in some environmental contexts.[17]

Although television may be overrated as a generator of social behavior, it may be seen as spreading that phenomenon by example. Presumably, people would commit assassinations anyway, or hijack aircraft, but seeing these events successfully practiced on national television seems to indicate the possibility of reproducing such events. At the very least, individuals learn that it can be done, and the media are in large part responsible for transmitting this information.

Old Folks as Caricatures

In addition to reinforcing certain kinds of behavior and mirroring others, the mass media also seem responsible for the distortion of societal views concerning certain groups of people, most notably the elderly. If your view of older people is formed, at least in part, by the portrayal of older people in the media, think of how they are usually represented.

First, old people are depicted as constantly needing drugs and pills. They take pills to wake themselves up and to go to sleep. They take pills to have bowel movements and to clean their dentures. Commercials constantly portray older people as sick, infirm, and feeble-minded. Sex apparently is completely nonexistent for anyone over sixty years of age. In both advertisements and regular programs, older people are depicted as either senile or quaint.

Second, older people are portrayed as dependent creatures. Despite the fact that the vast majority of people in the United States over the age of sixty are self-supporting and leading normal and healthy lives, the media dwells on the elderly in old-age homes and on those who are destitute.

Third, very little attention is focused on the accomplishments of older Americans. American society places a strong accent on youth. As a consequence, older people have been presented, not as the strong role models of earlier generations, but rather as the almost nonexistent, ignored, and pitiful stereotypes of today. Just as blacks and women have asserted themselves against stereotyping, so it seems likely that the older Americans will come to resist the media's portrayal of them, thus redirecting the attention of the media to the positive and ongoing accomplishments of older Americans. There are some signs that the political system is beginning to recognize the power of senior citizens. A major breakthrough came in 1977 with the passage of legislation raising the mandatory retire-

[17] Douglass Cater and Stephen Strickland, *TV Violence and the Child: The Evolution and Fate of the Surgeon General's Report* (New York: Russell Sage Foundation, 1975), p. 76.

ment age for many workers from sixty-five to seventy. Such legislation is overdue recognition of the ability of older Americans to play useful and constructive roles in our complex, ever-changing society.

CONCENTRATION IN THE MEDIA

If there are conflicting views concerning what the media do, the extent to which they influence rather than merely report, there can be little question as to what has happened to the media themselves. In recent years, there has been an increasing and accelerating trend toward media concentration. In the case of newspapers, for example, there were 2,600 dailies in 1909. By 1975, the number was down to 1,749. Today, most metropolitan areas in the United States do not have competing newspapers.

Far more ominous is the spread of what Kevin Phillips has termed the "media goliaths,"[18] in which media companies in one field—television, for example—expand into magazines, book publishing, and so forth. For example, Radio Corporation of America (RCA) had total sales of $5.2 billion in 1976, ranking as the 31st largest company on the Fortune 500 list. In addition to NBC, with its national network of television and radio outlets, RCA also controls a variety of publishing operations, including Random House, Alfred A. Knopf, Pantheon, Ballantine Books, Vintage Books, and Modern Library. Columbia Broadcasting System (CBS) ranks 102nd in the Fortune 500 and had sales of $2.2 billion in 1976. In addition to five television stations (in New York, Los Angeles, Philadelphia, Chicago, and Seattle) CBS also owns fourteen radio stations; Columbia Records; Holt, Rinehart and Winston; and a host of magazines, ranging from *Field and Stream* to *Astrology Today*.

Time, Inc., which publishes *Time, Fortune, Sports Illustrated,* and *People* magazines, also owns Little Brown, Manhattan Cable TV, seventeen weekly newspapers, and Home Box Office. The New York Times Company, with 1976 sales of over $450 million, publishes the *New York Times* and the *International Herald Tribune*; it also owns six daily and four weekly newspapers, Quadrangle books, Arno Press, Cambridge Book Company, and radio and television stations. The Washington Post Company, with sales exceeding $375 million in 1976, owns the *Washington Post,* the *Trenton Times*, the *Sunday Times Advertiser, Newsweek,* five television stations, and one radio station. Knight-Ridder, with 1976 sales of more than $677 million, owns forty-five newspapers, including two each in Charlotte, Columbus, Duluth, Lexington, Long Beach, Macon, St. Paul, San Jose, Wichita,

Media concentration has increased drastically in recent years. Many media companies have expanded into all fields of communication.

---

[18] Kevin Phillips, "Busting the Media Trusts," *Harper's*, July, 1977, pp. 23–34 and his *Mediacracy: American Parties and Politics in the Communication Age* (Garden City, N.Y.: Doubleday, 1975).

RCA
Rank: 31
1976 Sales: $5.32 billion

PRINCIPAL OPERATIONS:
Broadcasting
NBC: owns one TV station in Chicago, Los Angeles, Cleveland, New York City, Washington, D.C., and one AM and one FM station in Chicago, New York, San Francisco, Washington, D.C. (17.8% of total)

Publishing
Random House (Random House, Alfred A. Knopf, Pantheon, Ballantine Books, Vintage, Modern Library) (17.6% of total)

CBS
Rank: 102
1976 Sales: $2.23 billion

PRINCIPAL OPERATIONS:
Broadcasting
—owns five TV stations (New York, Los Angeles, Philadelphia, Chicago, St. Louis); seven AM radio stations and seven FM radio stations

Publishing
Holt, Rinehart and Winston; Popular Library (mass-market paperback)
W. B. Saunders—professional
NEISA—Latin American and Spanish books

Magazines
Field and Stream
Road and Track
Cycle World
World Tennis
Sea (to be combined with *Rudder*)
PV4
Popular Gardening Indoors
Astrology Your Daily Horoscope
Astrology Today
Your Prophecy
Psychic World
Popular Crosswords
Popular Word Games
Special Crossword Book of the Month
New Crosswords
Giant Word Games
The National Observer Book of Crosswords
Popular Sports: Baseball
Popular Sports: Grand Slam
Popular Sports: Kick-Off
Popular Sports: Touchdown
Popular Sports: Basketball
Fawcett Publications:
Mechanix Illustrated
Woman's Day
Rudder

THE NEW YORK TIMES COMPANY
Rank: 394
1976 Sales: $451.4 million

PRINCIPAL OPERATIONS:
Broadcasting
WREG-TV, Memphis, Tenn.
WQXR-AM/FM, New York City

Publishing
Quadrangle/NYT Book Co.
Arno Press, Inc.
Cambridge Book Co.

Newspapers
New York Times
International Herald Tribune (33.3%)
Six dailies and four weeklies in Florida:
Gainesville Sun
Lakeland Ledger
Ocala Star Banner
Leesburg Daily Commercial
Palatka Daily News
Lake City Reporter
Fernandina Beach News-Leader
Sebring News
Avon Park Sun
Marco Island Eagle
Three dailies in North Carolina:
Lexington Dispatch
Hendersonville Times News
Wilmington Star-News

Magazines
Family Circle
Australian Family Circle
Golf Digest
Golf World
Tennis
US
(Sold some eight professional magazines to Harcourt Brace Jovanovich in 1976)

THE WASHINGTON POST COMPANY
Rank: 452
1976 Sales: $375.7 million

PRINCIPAL OPERATIONS:
Broadcasting
WTOP-TV, Washington, D.C.
WJXT-TV, Jacksonville, Fla.
WPLG-TV, Miami, Fla.
WFSB-TV, Hartford, Conn.
WTOP-AM, Washington, D.C.

Newspapers
Washington Post, Trenton Times and *Sunday Times-Advertiser*. *International Herald Tribune* (30%)
Washington Post Writers Group (syndication and book publishing), L. A. Times–Washington Post News Service (50%)

Magazines
Newsweek
Books:
Newsweek Books

TIME INC.
Rank: 217
1976 Sales: $1.038 billion

PRINCIPAL OPERATIONS:
Films and Broadcasting
Time-Life Films
TV production and distribution, multimedia, TV books
Home Box Office
Manhattan Cable TV
WOTV—Grand Rapids, Mich.

Publishing
Time, Fortune, Sports Illustrated, Money, and *People* magazines account for 35% of total revenue
Time-Life Books
Little, Brown
New York Graphic Society (Alva Museum Replicas)
Minority interests in publishers in Germany, France, Spain, Mexico, and Japan

Newspapers
Pioneer Press, Inc.—17 weekly newspapers in suburban Chicago
Selling Areas-Marketing, Inc. (distributing marketing information)
Printing Developments, Inc. (printing equipment)

TIMES MIRROR COMPANY
Rank: 232
1976 Sales: $964.7 million

PRINCIPAL OPERATIONS:
Broadcasting
KDFW-TV, Dallas, Tex.
KTBC-TV, Austin, Tex.

Publishing
New American Library
Signet, Signet Classics, Mentor, Meridian paperbacks
Abrams art books
Matthew Bender law books
Year Book medical books
C.V. Mosby medical, dental, and nursing books and journals

Newspapers
Los Angeles Times, Newsday, Dallas Times Herald (Tex.). L.A. Times-Washington Post News Service (joint)

Magazines
Outdoor Life
Popular Science
Golf
Ski
The Sporting News
Ski Business
How to
The Sporting Goods Dealer

Fig. 7.2
Media Goliaths. (Ranking is in the Fortune 500 for 1976; sales figures are also for 1976.)

and Philadelphia. The Gannett chain, with sales of over $413 million, owns forty newspapers.

Martin Seiden, in an interesting and thought-provoking book, *Who Controls the Mass Media?* [19] vividly illustrates the loss of competition by describing how one city after another has lost its competing newspapers until at the present time only forty-three United States cities have competing major dailies. He also reveals the importance of the role played by the major **wire services**, United Press International (UPI) and the Associated Press (AP), in providing news for the giant news chains. UPI, which is privately owned by E. W. Scripps, was formed in 1907. It now employs some two thousand people and is a $60-million annual operation. AP, formed in 1848, is somewhat larger than UPI and is owned by a nonprofit association of newspapers. AP also employs some two thousand people and does a business of more than $70 million a year.

These wire services provide news to most newspapers in the country. In fact, many newspapers subscribe to both services. AP and UPI reports go to more than one hundred countries outside the United States. In addition, some three hundred domestic and foreign feature syndicates provide additional material for the papers. Seiden argues that competition in this area should be increased, having found that AP and UPI often tend to file much the same kind of story.

In addition to the problem of concentration, there is also the problem of control. Who determines what programs are to be seen? Seiden suggests that the media owners should be thought of as gatekeepers, past whom the content of the media must flow. He does not feel that advertisers in and of themselves control the content of the news, a view he considers simplistic. Clearly, the various media enterprises are in business to make money. Advertisers enable them to make money by buying space and access to the audience. But the rate advertisers will pay very much depends on the audience for the particular media, such as a newspaper. Seiden contends it is the audience, not the media, that ultimately produces revenues. If people follow one station, newspaper, or program rather than another, then they are, in effect, deciding what is popular and what is not. In this sense, the audience, not the advertisers or the media, "controls" things.

Who controls what is popular? The media? The advertisers? Or the audience themselves?

Seiden estimated a total advertising revenue of $15.3 billion for 1973, indicating that the daily newspapers received $7.7 billion; television, $4.5 billion; radio, $1.6 billion; and magazines, $1.5 billion.[20] Lester Brown suggests that "the freedom of the public, in fact, is the time bomb in

---

[19] Martin Seiden, *Who Controls the Mass Media?: Popular Myths and Economic Realities* (New York: Basic Books, 1974).

[20] Seiden, *Who Controls the Mass Media?* p. 22.

television."[21] The advertisers purchase shows the mass public will watch; freedom of choice determines which programs stay on the air and which go off; advertisers follow hit shows and shun losers. Thus, the argument goes, the public makes the final determination. What public chooses "The Gong Show" and what public prefers "60 Minutes"?

It would appear that the truth includes elements from both sides. Advertisers wish to sell products. They therefore wish to use the program or medium that gives them the most exposure among the groups they are seeking. But it is the public that makes certain shows, certain programs, and certain magazines and newspapers *more* popular than others.

CONTROL OVER THE MEDIA

In view of the media's economic, political, and social importance, does it make sense for the government to regulate them? Opinions on this crucial question differ widely. M. Stanton Evans is adamant that any governmental control over the media is wrong, and that whether the challenge to freedom comes from the right or the left, from one political group or another, the real danger is the fact that "the present level of government controls in our society is quite as hostile to political freedoms as it is to the freedom of the marketplace."[22] In this view, the First-Amendment guarantees of free speech and a free press should preclude regulation, and *any* government interference with the expression of ideas is wrong. Hence, government regulation has already gone too far.

Here we return to the already familiar theme of rights in conflict. In a free society, this conflict is inevitable. In the area of media and media control, the potential for conflict is particularly great. For example, the government, through the Federal Communications Commission, issues licenses for television and radio stations but not for newspapers or magazines. Is one mode of the media really "press" and the other something different? Does the First Amendment give the right to media conglomerates to establish monopolies over market areas by controlling both the morning and evening papers and perhaps a radio or television station as well? The government apparently thinks not, and has taken steps to prevent this sort of control.

Government Regulation through the FCC

Partly by default, partly by design, government regulation of the media has developed steadily over the years. The **Federal Communications Com-**

[21] Lester Brown, *Television: The Business Behind the Box* (New York: Harcourt, 1971), p. 365.

[22] M. Stanton Evans, *Clear and Present Dangers* (New York: Harcourt, 1975), p. 293.

mission (FCC) was formed in 1927 to grant licenses to broadcasters; originally this applied to radio, but it has since been extended to television. While initially licenses were rather freely given and almost never revoked, in recent years the Commission may refuse to renew a license if it decides the station is not complying with a variety of criteria. Licenses are renewed every three years. Some of these "criteria" are as follows.

First, the **fairness rule**, or **equal-time rule**, provides that a radio or television station that endorses or opposes a candidate for public office or attacks the "honesty, character, integrity or personal qualities of an identified person or group" must give the other side a chance to reply on the air and at no charge.

The fairness doctrine has had quite an impact on the political scene. It has meant that candidates should be given equal access to the media. On the face of it, this might seem desirable. But there are those who maintain that this rule disrupts the political process in at least two important ways. One, it penalizes the more active candidates, or those who actually have important things to say, by lumping them with their rivals even if their rivals are not doing as much. Two, the whole idea of "equal time," when carried to extremes, means that every candidate, no matter how frivolous, should enjoy equal access to the media. Thus, in an important Senate race there may be five people running, only two of whom have any chance of being elected. The voter in a sense will be penalized because the frivolous candidates occupy the time and space that could be used more fruitfully by giving the voters a closer and better look at the more serious candidates.

Why should radio and television be bound to the fairness rule or equal-time rule and the print media be exempted? Is the political process actually helped or hindered by this rule? Should the Yippies get the same coverage as the Republican party? Does the national vegetarian party really deserve equal time with the Democratic party? Some argue yes, some no.

Second, the FCC has developed a further rule having to do with monopoly: the **divestiture rule**, which requires that newspaper publishers may not own broadcasting franchises in the same city as their newspapers and that radio and television companies cannot own newspapers in the same city. Yet to tell a newspaper publisher that he or she cannot own a broadcast station would seem to be in direct violation of the First Amendment. Often called the "duo-poly rule," this criterion has meant in practice that one cannot own more than one type of property in each type of media in any one market. This applies only to cities or standard metropolitan statistical areas (SMSA).

Third, the FCC also restricts the number of hours of programming that stations may reserve from the national networks. This has been interpreted as being a way of keeping some programming local, thus reducing the power of the national networks and giving more expression to local viewpoints. This would seem to suggest that the FCC license is to be more than a license for making money, that it is more than just a right. There is tremendous variety in the forms local programming takes. Sometimes it is skillfully done, sometimes not. Popularity is also a consideration. The third time the local viewer is asked to engage "The Problem of Solid Waste Management" he is likely to turn to a national program or to shut off the set. Likewise, sponsors may be hard to find.

The fairness rule, the divestiture rule, and restrictions on the power of the national networks are all ways in which the FCC has sought to regulate the media.

Alternatives to Government Regulation

Assume that one accepts Martin Seiden's argument that "to call upon the government to control the mass media is to subvert the people's control placed over the government."[23] What are some alternatives to government supervision of the media? In 1973, the **National News Council** was founded to receive, examine, and report on complaints concerning the fairness and accuracy of news reporting and to defend the press against attacks on its freedom. The Council has fifteen members, nine of whom are chosen from the public and six from the news organization.

This self-policing body has been examined in some detail by Alfred Balk; from his study a number of conclusions have emerged.[24] There is a feeling that the scope of the Council should be expanded. Currently, the Council deals only with the major wire services, the national news magazines, and the radio and television networks. But it should also deal with individual newspapers, weekly as well as daily, and the individual radio and television stations. Balk offers as illustration a complaint in 1977 that was upheld against UPI for its coverage of the Senate Subcommittee on Health and Scientific Research on the arthritis drug Naprosyn. Syntex, who makes the drug, complained because the UPI story misquoted the committee, referring to Naprosyn as a "'borderline' cancer-causing agent," when in fact the committee was referring to another drug, not Naprosyn.

Before the Council can think seriously of expanding, two aspects of its situation would have to be clarified. In the first place, it can apply no legal penalties, so that its "punishment capability" is really quite limited. The Council's existence, therefore, may or may not inhibit people from making mistakes, but once mistakes are made, the penalties are not severe. Also, the Council is funded by various philanthropic foundations, so that it remains vulnerable to any cutoff of assistance.

[23] Seiden, *Who Controls the Mass Media?* p. 12.

[24] Alfred Balk, *A Free and Responsive Press* (New York: Twentieth Century Fund, 1973). See also, Daniel Schorr, *Clearing the Air* (Boston: Houghton Mifflin, 1977).

Would a movie star such as Ronald Reagan have been taken seriously as a presidential candidate before the age of the media?

Finally, the Council does not enjoy the whole-hearted support of the networks. Network officials argue that the internal censorship at ABC, NBC, and CBS is stricter than that of the FCC or the NNC, especially with regard to materials of a sexual nature. This kind of network policing is done "in house," where the public is less likely to see the outcome.

In short, the National News Council may be a start, but it is at best a slow and hesitant step. What about other alternatives to government regulation? Would competition improve the quality of the media? The Small Business Administration (SBA) announced in 1977 that it would soon propose a change in its regulations that would make it easier for women and members of minorities to buy radio and television stations. This, coupled with continuing controversy over divestiture and strong congressional opposition to media conglomerates gaining *more* power, suggests that sentiment may be growing in favor of more competition.

What is the impact of all this on American politics? Do you think it is a coincidence that as television has come to play an ever-larger role in campaigns and elections, we have also witnessed a steady increase in voter independence and ticket-splitting? What is the role of the media in influencing common attitudes toward "the new politics"?

There is a growing impression that television and the polls (see Chapter 6) have combined to transform the traditional structure of American party politics. As we noted in Chapter 5, our party organizations are in an advanced stage of decay. The steady decline of traditional parties gives rise to a politics organized around "political personalities." These personalities, in turn, rely on paid professionals, including media experts, whose loyalties are to the individual political personality who hires them, rather than to the party. Nixon's inner circle was comprised of this new breed and so, indeed, is Jimmy Carter's core of White House assistants.

Mendelsohn and Crespi, writing *before* Watergate, speculated that the result of this would be to produce a "cool" corporate style in American electoral politics. As they saw it, "This is 'the new politics' as it actually is today—purposefully analytic, empirically opportunistic, and administratively manipulative."[25]

Nongovernmental attempts at regulation include the National News Council, which has been only marginally effective as a self-policing body, and proposed changes that would increase competition.

SUMMARY

Where, then, are we? This chapter explores the growing power of the media in our society. We have looked at the ways the media involve themselves, both directly and indirectly, in many aspects of our lives. We have examined some of the hypotheses about the extent to which the media may manipulate reality as well as record it. While reasonable people may differ as to the precise impact of the media on specific behavior patterns (such as the effect of violence on television), there is widespread agreement that the media influence the way we look at life and ourselves.

[25] Harold Mendelsohn and Irving Crespi, *Polls, Television and the New Politics* (Scranton, Pa.: Chandler Publishing, 1970).

To some extent the media supplement the family socialization activities as they portray alternative views of human life and the universe. The media turn politicians away from the dictates of their parties to the demands of mass media. In doing so, they encourage a new style of politics and a new kind of politician.

Finally, we have looked at "rights in conflict" as represented by the issues of the freedom of the press versus government regulation. There is growing concern over increased concentration of power within the media. In all of the controversy and speculation, one fact stands out above the rest: The role of the media in American life is likely to grow, not diminish, in the years ahead.

KEY TERMS

media
fourth estate
news
media event
wire service
Federal Communications
   Commission (FCC)
fairness rule

equal-time rule
divestiture rule
National News Council

SUGGESTED READINGS

Bagdikian, Ben H., *Information Machines: Their Impact on Men and the Media* (New York: Harper & Row, 1971).

   A lively, easy-reading treatment of the media by a friendly critic.

Balk, Alfred, *A Free and Responsive Press* (New York: The Twentieth Century Fund, 1973).

   A plea for greater fairness, and self-policing of that fairness, on the part of newspapers.

Braestrup, Peter, *Big Story: How the American Press and Television Reported and Interpreted the Crisis of Tet 1968 in Vietnam and Washington* (Boulder, Colo.: Westview Press, 1977).

   A long, detailed, but very important study of the distorted reporting on the military side of the Vietnam War.

Cater, Douglass, *The Fourth Branch of Government* (Boston: Houghton Mifflin, 1959).

   Classic, beautifully written treatment of the growing importance of the press in American national politics.

EPSTEIN, EDWARD J., *News from Nowhere: Television and the News* (New York: Random House, 1973).

A fascinating look at how the evening news shows are put together by NBC, ΛBC, and CBS.

SEIDEN, MARTIN, *Who Controls the Mass Media?: Popular Myths and Economic Realities* (New York: Basic Books, 1974).

A somewhat dry, but very informative, study of the economic structure of the mass media.

WITCOVER, JULES, *Marathon: The Pursuit of the Presidency 1972–1976* (New York: Viking Press, 1977).

An excellent treatment of the importance of the media, especially the electronic media, in the last two presidential campaigns.

PART III OUR CHANGING INSTITUTIONS

The President is at liberty in law and conscience to be as big a man as he can. His office is anything he has the sagacity and force to make it.

Woodrow Wilson

We tend to think of the Presidency as a lonely place where a single leader hangs his various hats. In fact, it is a bureaucracy on top of a bureaucracy.

Douglass Cater

Goodness by itself is not enough. There must be a capacity for being active in doing good.

Aristotle

CHAPTER 8 PRESIDENTIAL PARADOX: POWER AND WEAKNESS

It is Inauguration Day, January 1977. The nation's capital is bitterly cold, the Potomac River frozen over. The new president, having taken the oath of office, and the First Lady, shunning the usual limousine, walk hand in hand the length of Pennsylvania Avenue from Capitol Hill to the White House.

The symbolism is apt. President Carter, the thirty-ninth president, wished to make a fresh start toward restoring public confidence, which had been badly shaken by the events of the previous stormy decade. This was to be a no-frills administration, and an "open" one.

Of course, it takes more than the manipulation of symbols to provide presidential leadership. You know that. And so did President Carter.

In this chapter we will explore with you the essential paradox of the American presidency: the fact that our central institution of policy leadership contains elements of both power and weakness. We want to discover the sources of both these elements.

Presidential leadership depends on the powers vested in that office by the Constitution, the cumulative precedents set by previous presidents, the degree of public support, the degree of cooperation by Congress, and the personality and character of the incumbent, to mention only the obvious. At the same time, the ability of a president to lead is constrained and limited by a host of factors. Prominent among these factors are constitutional limits, including the presence of an independent national legislature (Congress) with substantial powers of its own; the divisions and diverse interests within the nation; the opposition party; the tendency of huge bureaucracies to persist in doing what they have been doing; and the complexity of many of the problems facing a new administration.

The presidency, like its institutional rival, Congress, finds itself today in the throes of change. Although the presidential office in this century is one of awesome responsibility and power, it nevertheless rests on a fragile base of public confidence. Since the tumultuous events associated with our country's involvement in Vietnam and the resignation of President Nixon at the height of the Watergate crisis, public confidence in all major institutions, including the presidency, has remained thin. This fact alone places a major constraint on the president's ability to lead the nation.

As a result, our only truly *national* elective office is one in which official power and political necessity are combined in the task of persuading people to follow the chosen course of leadership. We will examine this paradox in the sections that follow.

> The essential paradox of our central institution of policy leadership—the presidency—is that it contains elements of both power and weakness.

THE PRESIDENT AS POLICY LEADER

Jimmy Carter, a born-again Christian, needed more than prayer to sustain his vision of greatness-to-be-restored. The nation's recent experiences included Kennedy's assassination, Johnson's virtual abdication of power, Nixon's humiliating resignation, and Ford's uneasy experiment in presidential caretaking: hardly the stuff that nourishes dreams of glory. But as apathy and cynicism soured the public mood, one central fact, beyond his own apparent self-confidence, encouraged Carter in his hope of restoring public confidence in the integrity of the system: The American government knows but one national policy leader, the president. No lofty senator, mighty congressional baron, entrenched bureaucratic chieftain, or ever-present commission enjoys any real capacity to lead the American people. Only the president enjoys this unique power. And when presidential leadership is weak, negative, or absent, we founder. So there is a natural craving for strong leadership.

The American government knows but one national policy leader, the president. At the same time, forces that resist strong central policy leadership are solidly institutionalized in our political system.

The trick, however, as Carter soon discovered, is to assert presidential leadership in a system where power is fragmented. In this system, the forces that resist strong central policy leadership—separation of powers, checks and balances, consensus politics—are solidly institutionalized in our Constitution and in our history.

The Setting

Not only was the Potomac frozen when Jimmy Carter took the oath of office as our thirty-ninth president, so was the national economy. Therefore, the first task before this "outsider" president and his team of advisers and assistants was to warm up the American economy. Seven and a half million workers, nearly 8 percent of the nation's work force, were jobless on Inauguration Day. Within a matter of weeks, the severest winter in years added another million to the jobless ranks. The administration's economic stimulus package, calling for more public service jobs and a tax rebate, its first legislative initiative, arrived on Capitol Hill just in time to be judged inadequate by those most likely to support it. Congressional critics, on the other hand, found the proposal inflationary. This was not simply a matter of congressional meanness, but reflected an honest difference of opinion concerning the proper ingredients.

Congress, staffed by a large Democratic majority and headed by a fresh group of leaders (albeit long-time Washington insiders), appeared willing to enjoy the traditional honeymoon period with the new chief executive, so long as it was a honeymoon between equal partners, and so long as it was brief! Carter, in turn, seemed aware that his greatest single source of presidential power lay in convincing the public that he was "for real." With public confidence restored, Carter might enhance his ability to persuade the leaders of the Washington community that a number of his program objectives served their interests as well. The Washington power brokers, in turn, would be more likely to follow his lead if it became clear that the new president enjoyed the support of an alert and attentive public.[1]

A president's greatest source of power is public confidence.

Image-building

In gaining his party's nomination and in winning the ultimate prize in American politics, Carter and his assistants displayed skill in the manipulation of symbols, which are vital to building an "image" via the mass media. While other presidents had recognized the importance of their image in an age of mass media, none had worked harder at the task of creating one than Carter and his staff. Now they were faced with the task

[1] Richard E. Neustadt, *Presidential Power* (New York: Wiley, 1960).

of matching "image" with actual performance in office. This required a **political strategy** for governing.

How much confidence do you have in presidential leadership? At the next presidential election, are you likely to feel that it is time to bring fresh leadership to the White House? Do you have the sense that the voting of ordinary citizens affects the direction of national policy? Do you think your choice will influence the outcome?

These were precisely the kinds of questions that troubled both the public and the political analysts while President Carter was eking out a narrow victory over Gerald Ford in 1976. Jimmy Carter and his immediate circle of political advisers were chiefly concerned to find ways of restoring public confidence once Carter entered the White House. They realized how limited his leadership role was likely to be if he failed to do so.

A Strategy for Governing: Pat Caddell's Memo

As it turned out, President Carter did come to office with a strategy for governing. Carter was in office less than six months when the press and the mass media got hold of an "Initial Working Paper on Political Strategy." This paper was the work of Patrick H. Caddell, Carter's public opinion polling expert during the successful campaign, who presented it on December 10, 1976, about six weeks before the inauguration. It offered an uncannily perceptive assessment of the reasons for Carter's victory and also presented a detailed strategy for governing, at least through the first year. The press immediately seized on Caddell's statements that "governing with public approval requires a continuing political campaign" and "too many good people have been defeated because they tried to substitute substance for style."[2] Carter had already made a number of symbolic gestures—the walk back to the White House following his swearing in, the fireside chat, the town meeting—all of which Caddell had suggested.

Presidential Public Relations

As soon as the Caddell memo hit the press, the charge was made that President Carter was placing public relations ahead of substantive issues. Actually, there was nothing new in this relationship among the presidency, the media, and the general public. Thirty years earlier, President Harry S Truman had written a letter to his sister stating: "All the president is, is a glorified public relations man who spends his time flattering, kissing, and kicking people to get them to do what they are supposed to do anyway."[3]

[2] Patrick H. Caddell, "Initial Working Paper on Political Strategy," December 10, 1976.
[3] An excerpt from this letter appears in *The People's Almanac*, 1975.

Initial Working Paper on Political Strategy

"The following memorandum is in response to your letter of November 29th. Obviously, this is only one perspective: it requires the additional perspectives of Jody, Hamilton and Stu—among others. A final plan must have input from the issues people, from the rest of our political advisers and, of course, your own goals and ideas.

"In devising a strategy for the administration it is important to recognize we cannot successfully separate politics and government. If the administration is to be successful, if it is to lead, it must move constituency groups such as Congress, special interest groups, the party, and the various factions in the general country. To do these things, it must operate from a strong political base. And, finally, to follow the logic to its end, the best way to ensure a political base is to run a successful government. In the end the people almost always recognize and reward good

performance and punish bad performance.

"Unfortunately, one of the pitfalls I have seen many 'executive' administrations succumb to is the desire to have 'good government' by divorcing government and politics. Following the early twentieth century 'reform' movement, many people instinctively feel that 'good' is necessarily apolitical. The result of this divorce is too often that the voters perceive that they unfortunately got a different person from the man they elected. Candidates fail to keep the implicit campaign promises they have made. Occasionally the result of 'apolitical' government is positive, but most times it leads to disappointing the voters and eventual political disaster.

"When politics is divorced from government, it often happens that the talented, well-meaning people who staff the administration act without understanding the reasons 'they all' were elected

---

An essential weakness of the presidency is the need for public relations, sometimes at the expense of complex substantive issues.

Mr. Truman was oversimplifying matters, however. The man who wrote these words also made the decision to drop A-bombs on two Japanese cities, launched a multibillion-dollar program of American assistance to postwar Europe, fired General Douglas MacArthur, led the nation in the Korean war, brought racial integration to our armed forces, and upset all expert opinion, including the pollsters, in defeating Thomas Dewey in the 1948 presidential election. A president must indeed flatter, kiss, and sometimes kick to get people to move in order to advance his objectives. This suggests the essential weakness of the office. At the same time, the destiny and the very lives of 220 million Americans rest on the hard choices required in presidential decision making.

It was not long before the new Carter administration found itself grappling with more difficult substantive issues than it could probably *and instead pursue policies which run contrary to public expectations and desires.*

"Essentially, it is my thesis that governing with public approval requires a continuing political campaign—though one conducted in a different framework. . . .

"One of the major reasons the Carter Administration must sell these themes [healing; restoring trust; giving a sense of purpose; a new ideology; new working relationships] is that it desperately needs to buy time! Most of the proposals Governor Carter has will require two or three years to implement. Without trust, the country won't be able to wait that long. We need a series of small promises and projects accomplished quickly that provide evidence that longer-term goals will also be realized.

"In presenting these themes to the American people Governor Carter has some unique strengths. We run the risk of losing these as we start worrying about the day-

to-day affairs of government. (The old cliché about mistaking style for substance usually works in reverse in politics. Too many good people have been defeated because they tried to substitute substance for style [*emphasis added*]; *they forgot to give the public the kind of visible signals that it needs to understand what is happening.)*

"I think some of the following stylistic points—along with their substantive counterparts—must be stressed:

1. President Carter is an open man: *He wants the public to see what he is doing, unafraid of press scrutiny, willing to share his ideas and proposals openly and with the American public.*

2. President Carter is different from other politicians: *President Carter is not tied to simply old answers and to the job."*

From Patrick H. Caddell, "Initial Working Paper on Political Strategy," December 10, 1976.

deal with. Little wonder that a number of Mr. Carter's most distinguished predecessors had complained about the job. Little wonder, too, that Carter soon found his standing with the public steadily weakening as the months wore on.

Consider the following items of expert testimony concerning the office:

1. George Washington wrote in 1789 as he was about to assume the office: "My movements to the chair of Government will be accompanied by feelings not unlike those of a culprit who is going to the place of his execution."
2. Thomas Jefferson referred to the presidency as "this splendid misery."
3. Abraham Lincoln, when asked if he "enjoyed" being president, replied that this reminded him of the fellow who was tarred and feathered and run out of town on a rail and who commented: "If it weren't for the honor of the thing, I would just as soon avoid all of this."

4. Harry S Truman, in a letter to his daughter, wrote: "It's a nice prison but a prison nevertheless. No man in his right mind would want to come here of his own accord."

How do we account for able, ambitious men, presumably in their right minds, going the hard route of electoral politics so that they might serve as president? Why does anyone seek this office with all its problems and frustrations? There is a mystery here worth unraveling. Let us turn first to the Constitution to see what grants of authority there are.

THE PRESIDENCY AND THE CONSTITUTION

The presidential office combines the functions of chief executive, policy initiator, commander in chief, and chief diplomat.

Obviously, there is enormous power in an office that combines the functions of *chief executive, policy initiator, commander in chief,* and *chief diplomat.* Let us look at each of these functions in turn.

Chief Executive

Article II in the Constitution states that "the executive power shall be vested in a President of the United States" who is to "take care that the laws be faithfully executed." This very generally describes the nature of the office, but specific presidential roles rest on other provisions of Article II.

Today the chief executive role also makes the president our chief bureaucrat, because he appears as the visible head of the huge administrative apparatus of the federal government. With nearly three million civil service employees, the federal executive branch, which is comprised of the cabinet departments, the independent regulatory agencies, and an ever-increasing array of operating programs, is ultimately headed by the president as chief executive. While the president's actual control of this vast and confusing set of bureaucracies remains diffuse and problematic (as we note in Chapter 10), our national government knows no other central administrative authority.

Policy Initiator

The president's modern role as policy initiator, that is, someone who begins the process of originating, stems from the provision that stipulates: "He shall from time to time give to Congress information of the State of the Union and shall recommend to their consideration such measures as he shall judge necessary and expedient."

The great bulk of modern legislation is originally put forward as part of the president's program. As we note in Chapter 9, Congress characteristically awaits the president's annual messages, tending to view these messages as establishing the national legislative agenda. This does not mean, however, that Congress feels disposed to give slavish support to the presidential program. As we note throughout this book, presidential policy initiatives are bound to encounter stiff resistance from a variety of sources.[4]

Commander in Chief

The text of the Constitution also prescribes for the president the role of commander in chief to the nation's military forces. Lincoln was the first president to see an inherent "war power" flowing to the president in his capacity as commander in chief. Lincoln's combining of an *inherent* executive war power with the commander-in-chief clause as a justification for extraordinary assertion of presidential authority marked the beginning of an important new presidential role. Edward S. Corwin observed:

[4] See also James Sundquist, *Politics and Policy* (Washington, D.C.: The Brookings Institution, 1968).

A dramatic illustration of the president's role as commander in chief was Truman's controversial firing of the tremendously popular General Douglas MacArthur because of disagreement over how the Korean War was being handled.

The sudden emergence of the "Commander-in-Chief" clause as one of the most highly charged provisions of the Constitution occurred almost overnight in consequence of Lincoln's wedding it to the clause which makes it the duty of the President "to take care that the laws be faithfully executed." From these two clauses thus united Lincoln proceeded to derive what he termed the "war power" to justify the series of extraordinary measures which he took between the fall of Fort Sumter and the convening of Congress in the special session of July 4, 1861.[5]

Thus the seeds of presidential warmaking power, which became the focus of such controversy during the Vietnam involvement in the 1960s, were sown more than a century ago by the president who perhaps best serves as the symbol of American "democracy."

Chief Diplomat

Article II invites a struggle between the president and Congress in foreign affairs. This struggle has grown increasingly visible in recent years. Nevertheless, negotiation with other nations is an executive, not a legislative, function. Although the Constitution says only that the president "shall receive ambassadors and other public ministers," the twentieth-century president plays a very large role as our chief diplomat. Woodrow Wilson saw this potential several years before he entered politics: "The initiative in foreign affairs, which the President possesses without any restriction whatever, is virtually the power to control them absolutely."[6]

The Supreme Court adopted a similar view in 1936. Justice Sutherland, a staunch conservative on domestic matters, speaking for an almost unanimous Court (there was one dissenting Justice) in the **Curtiss-Wright case**, drew a fundamental distinction between the president's power in domestic and foreign affairs. Sutherland referred to "the very delicate, plenary and exclusive power of the president as the sole organ of the federal government in the field of international relations—a power which does not require as a basis for its exercise an act of Congress."

President Carter was quick to seize on the potential of his role as world leader in attempting to place his own stamp on American foreign policy. He stressed human rights, thus causing a dampening of relations between the United States and the Soviet Union. Early in the year he flew off to Great Britain, junior partner in our "Grand Alliance," for a meeting with British, French, and German leaders. This initial visit proved to be a triumph in public relations, as many ordinary people on the other side of the Atlantic, evidently bored by the dullness of their own domestic

[5] Edward S. Corwin, *The President: Office and Powers,* 4th ed., revised (New York: New York University Press, 1957), p. 229.

[6] Woodrow Wilson, *Constitutional Government* (New York: Columbia University Press, 1908).

The president as chief diplomat: In this century, many presidents have preferred the foreign-policy aspects of their job. The best example of this is Richard Nixon, whose brilliant foreign-policy accomplishments were unfortunately overshadowed by his troubles on the domestic front. Here he is seen with Soviet leader Leonid Brezhnev.

politics, thought they saw a new kind of political leader in Carter. Before his first year was over, however, on another trip to foreign capitals, Carter found Sadat of Egypt and Begin of Israel had taken center stage away from him. In the meantime, by bringing the Panama Canal treaty to a head, he initiated a long struggle in the Senate while provoking a divisive political debate throughout the nation. These foreign policy initiatives and the response to them seemed to do little to increase his public stature at home.

Conflicting Constitutional Responsibilities

Our Constitution imposes a heavy burden on the president by requiring that he serve as the formal head of state as well as the operational chief executive. Most Western democracies have wisely divided these basic

Unlike the situation in most Western democracies, American presidents must serve as formal head of state as well as operational chief executive.

functions between two officials, as in Great Britain, where the Queen is the formal head of state while the Prime Minister serves as chief executive. Because the president serves as the head of state, his office automatically becomes a place of moral (that is, "morale") leadership. It becomes, in the words of Theodore Roosevelt, the "bully pulpit" (a good place to preach one's doctrines) from which to proclaim noble visions of the good society.

But the president as national preacher is engaging in a different role from the chief executive, who is busy with the complicated task of getting the job done. A president spends each day meeting with staff, briefing the press, entertaining party chieftains, consulting with congressional leaders, attempting to guide cabinet officers, and listening to the representatives of powerful organized groups; he must also find a few minutes to have his picture taken with Eagle Scouts and war heroes. Late at night, often following an official social function, the president may retreat to his upstairs rooms, there to face a pile of official papers thoughtfully provided by an attentive staff.

This "head of state" function of the office in turn conflicts with the president's role as the leader of his political party. How is the president to guard his image as the voice of the whole nation when he also speaks with the tongue of a partisan? But speak he must, because the only time an American party has one acknowledged leader is when it places him in the White House. In times of divided government, as during the Nixon-Ford years, this partisan role becomes even more troublesome since the president may not be speaking for a political majority, much less the whole people. A president who is busy giving the opposition hell is not likely to look like a statesman, especially to the millions of Americans who favor the opposition to begin with.

An Underdefined Institution

From the beginning, the presidency has been an underdefined institution.

Another difficulty inherent in the presidential office is that it has been an *underdefined* institution from the beginning. We have never been wholly clear about what was expected of the office. Right from the start, Americans have blown hot and cold on the subject of presidential authority. In times of economic crisis and war the country expects the White House to provide strong, assertive leadership, and we are not squeamish about the constitutional implications. We are quick, on the other hand, to react against executive authority when it is vigorously exercised in calmer times. The presidency is an office that is always too strong and always too weak, as Thomas E. Cronin has noted.[7] There is obvious strength in the hand that controls our nuclear weaponry. But the same presidential hand may

[7] Thomas E. Cronin, *The State of the Presidency* (Boston: Little, Brown, 1975), p. 2.

appear weak when it fails to "solve" the problem of unemployment or inflation (matters over which the president has only limited influence, as we discover in Chapter 12, and as Jimmy Carter learned during his early years in Washington).

The biggest problems the country faces are complex, long-term, and perhaps insoluble. This being the case, how is the president to gain the confidence of the people so as to have some fair chance of addressing these more basic difficulties? What would you say to the president of the United States if he were to seek your advice as to how he should approach his conflicting yet demanding responsibilities? You think you are too young to give advice? Patrick Caddell, while still a young man not long out of college, was asked this question by Jimmy Carter. Caddell's advice was:

> Carter needs to gain personal credibility and restore the trust of the people. If he can do this, he may convince them to give him a chance, to give him the time, to solve some of the long-term problems of the country. If we don't buy the time quickly, given their mood today, the American people may turn on us before we ever get off the mark.[8]

Time is of the essence, especially in the Oval Office of the White House. This was perhaps the most important lesson the Carter administration learned during its first two years in office. In the meantime, the dilemma persisted: how to restore confidence when the long-term problems resist easy solutions.

DOMESTIC VERSUS FOREIGN-POLICY PRESIDENCIES

The president's job is also complicated by the conflict between domestic and foreign-policy demands. Some find it useful in studying the presidency to separate the domestic presidency from the foreign-policy presidency. This distinction, of course, is drawn simply for the purpose of clarifying our understanding; it is, in fact, an arbitrary distinction. In the real world, whoever holds the office must deal with both aspects of presidential leadership at the same time. Furthermore, the more closely one examines the presidency the more intimately these two aspects of executive leadership are seen to intertwine. A failure abroad—for example, the failure of the United States's effort in Vietnam—can utterly destroy a domestic presidency, as Lyndon Johnson learned. A domestic crisis—for example, a serious economic recession—may call for a restricted role in world affairs, thus placing severe limits on presidential initiatives, as Gerald Ford soon realized.

Although they often conflict, the domestic demands and foreign-policy demands of the presidency are intimately intertwined.

[8] Caddell, "Initial Working Paper on Political Strategy."

Aaron Wildavsky, the political scientist who originated the **two presidencies theory**, has argued that the foreign-affairs presidency has the better of it. In his view, presidents enjoy greater success in controlling defense and foreign policies than they do in dominating domestic policies. Writing before Vietnam destroyed President Johnson's presidency, Wildavsky observed that "Even Lyndon Johnson has seen his early record of victories in domestic legislation diminish as his concern with foreign affairs grows."[9] The Johnson experience affords an unusual opportunity for examining presidential leadership in domestic and foreign affairs.

LBJ: A Case Study

Lyndon Johnson brought thirty years of national legislative experience to the White House. No previous president brought comparable credentials as a master legislator with him. Johnson's record of legislative achievement as a domestic president was impressive: civil-rights legislation, aid to education, Medicare, urban renewal, and anti-poverty legislation. Only Franklin D. Roosevelt, Johnson's one-time mentor, would be able to rival Johnson in this century as the architect of a major domestic program effectively enacted into law. (Woodrow Wilson would run third in this hypothetical race.) During his first two years in the White House, President Johnson won praise from the *Wall Street Journal* as well as the *New Republic* as a legislative miracle worker. Johnson's initial experience as domestic president, prior to military escalation in Vietnam, appears to have all the advantages over his foreign-affairs presidency. His tentative place among the successful presidents of this century took a sharp downward slide only *after* Vietnam became the focus of his administration.

President Johnson always displayed greater skill in the domestic legislative arena than in his handling of foreign and defense policies. More important, however, is that Johnson's course in Southeast Asia led to a crisis in public confidence that ruined his capacity to lead in the domestic field.[10] Ironically, it may well be that Johnson's unusual success on the home front caused him to push that much harder toward a massive involvement in Vietnam, thinking he had the country solidly behind him.

In any event, no matter how useful the concept of the two presidencies may be to political scientists, *in practice* these are not separate entities. Instead, both aspects of presidential leadership combine in a fateful blend of strength and weakness. No president finds it possible to concentrate on the aspect he prefers for the simple reason that both aspects are hopelessly intertwined. And both aspects of the job require tough choices among alternatives that are seldom clear.

[9] Aaron Wildavsky, "The Two Presidencies," *Transaction* (December 1966), p. 7.

[10] The collapse of the Johnson regime is examined in John C. Donovan, *The Cold Warriors* (Lexington, Mass.: D. C. Heath, 1974).

The Presidency during the Cold War

A number of recent presidents, mostly notably Eisenhower, Kennedy, and Nixon, displayed a marked preference for foreign affairs. This is partially explained, no doubt, by the nature of Cold War decision making. So long as they remained within the limits of Cold War policy assumptions, American presidents were able to gain substantial support in Congress for their foreign-policy activities. During this period, an effort was made to remove foreign-policy issues from politics by stressing a *bipartisan consensus.* Such a consensus in the foreign-affairs aspect of the office may give the president a sense of "control" that is often lacking in his dealings with domestic problems, where it is hard to find a consensus on *anything.* Foreign policy appears more attractive when viewed from the Oval Office because domestic issues are almost certain to lead to partisan debate, political struggle, and congressional opposition.

The fact that contemporary presidents often preferred to focus on foreign-policy matters does not mean that such a preference guarantees them lasting "success," however. In another fifty years, President Kennedy may be relegated to the footnotes alongside Millard Fillmore because his sole foreign-policy triumphs—a nuclear test ban treaty and facing down the Russians in a missile crisis—are likely to fade from view. The Vietnam debacle threatens to eliminate LBJ's chances of being ranked among our stronger presidents. And Nixon, despite his foreign-policy initiatives, seems likely to be assigned a position among our few tragic presidential failures.

THE PRESIDENT'S CABINET

Each president has a **cabinet** comprised of the various cabinet secretaries who head up each of the twelve executive departments. With few exceptions, recent presidents have found the cabinet not to be a terribly useful decision-making device. Formal cabinet meetings in most administrations are held with unpredictable frequency depending on the wishes of the president. The Carter administration, initially intending to restore the cabinet as a functioning institution, soon moved in the other direction.

We have never had cabinet government in this country in the sense of a group of senior advisers meeting formally with the president and arriving at collective decisions. In the contemporary era, the reality is that the secretary of state and the secretary of labor, for example, have policy-making and administrative responsibilities in subject matter areas that rarely overlap. The secretary of labor is not likely to have an informed basis for offering judgments on Middle East policy, while the secretary of state cannot be expected to be knowledgeable concerning joblessness and industrial safety.

Biography

LBJ: A Biographical Sketch

Lyndon Baines Johnson was twenty-three when he first went to Washington as an assistant to a Texas Congressman. The year was 1931. Six years later, before he was thirty, Johnson won election to the House in his own right in a special election filling an unexpired term of a former House member. The young Texan immediately won the favor of two powerful Washington figures: House Speaker Sam Rayburn, a fellow Texan, and President Franklin D. Roosevelt. LBJ supported FDR on the famous but unpopular Court packing bill. In later years, Johnson frequently told interviewers "FDR was like a daddy to me." So was Speaker Rayburn.

Johnson saw a chance to try for a seat in the Senate in 1941, an opening created by the death of an incumbent. When the votes were tallied, however, Johnson had lost to Governor W. Lee ("Pappy") O'Daniel by the thin margin of 1,311 votes out of more than 600,000 cast. Shortly thereafter, following the attack on Pearl Harbor, Johnson took a five-month leave of absence from the House, serving briefly as a United States Naval Reserve officer in the Pacific. Having thus established his credentials as a "fighting man," Johnson was reelected to the House in 1942, his fourth straight victory. He was thirty-five.

Johnson made his next try for a Senate seat in 1948. This time, running in a Democratic primary against a very conservative opponent, Johnson won his party's nomination by a mere 87 votes out of nearly a million cast, thereby gaining the nickname "Landslide Lyndon." This slim margin was provided by a late, late count that gave LBJ 202 additional votes from the ballot box in Precinct No. 13, in the tiny hamlet of Alice in Duval county on the Mexican border. But gaining the Democratic nomination in those years when the Republican party was woefully weak in Texas was tantamount to election in November. And so it was in this case. Thus, LBJ was launched on a career in the United States Senate that was to make him one of the most powerful officials in Washington.

In January 1953, Senator Johnson was elected floor leader of his party although he had been in the Senate only four years.

Forty-four years old, Minority Leader Johnson was the youngest floor leader of either party in either house of the 83rd Congress. The 83rd Congress, which was elected along with President Dwight David Eisenhower, provided a rare opportunity for the Republicans to control both the executive and legislative branches. (In fact, this hasn't happened since.)

When the Democrats recaptured control of both houses two years later, Senator Lyndon B. Johnson was embarked on his remarkable career as majority leader. In this role, he proved to be a masterful legislative tactician and manager of other legislator politicians. LBJ seemed to exult in the exercise of power. Nevertheless, Johnson gave all this up in order to join the Kennedy presidential ticket in 1960. Johnson's three years as vice-president (1961–1963) were almost surely among the least satisfying of his long Washington career. Although President Kennedy was correct in his relationship with his vice-president, senior White House staff members were less sensitive. Indeed, they allowed the Kennedy legislative program to founder without drawing on Johnson's extraordinary skills.

Kennedy's assassination late in November 1963 brought Johnson the ultimate prize he had long awaited: the presidency. He lost no time in driving a major domestic program through Congress. In winning a landslide victory over Republican Senator Goldwater in November 1964, President Johnson also gained additional voting strength in Congress. The Johnson legislative record is impressive: antipoverty, civil rights, aid to education, Medicare, and Model Cities stand high on the list. Unfortunately, the years 1965–1968 also brought the Americanization of the war in Vietnam, which was attended by bitter divisions at home. On March 31, 1968, addressing a national television audience, President Johnson took himself out of contention for his party's nomination for reelection and also halted the bombing of the north in Vietnam.

"The long hard effort was over now, and I was glad to see it end." This was Lyndon Johnson's feeling in January 1969 as he retired from public life, after nearly forty years of Washington policy making.

Theodore Sorensen, a top aide to President Kennedy, explained later how the cabinet was viewed during that administration:

> [Kennedy] had appointed his Cabinet members because he regarded them as individuals capable of holding down very difficult positions of responsibility. He did not want to have them sit through lengthy cabinet sessions, listening to subjects which were not of interest to them, not of importance to them, at least not of an interest to their primary duties and their primary skills. So he called Cabinet meetings as infrequently as possible, he called them only because he was expected to call them—tradition, the press, and public opinion being what it is—and he preferred to call Cabinet members to small or ad hoc meetings at the White House where the subject under discussion involved their departments or on which he wanted their particular judgments.[11]

Inner and Outer Cabinets

It is useful to think of two cabinets—the inner cabinet, which handles national security matters, and the outer cabinet, which is responsible for domestic programs.

Part of the explanation for the relative decline of the cabinet is that while cabinet members theoretically are equal, in reality some are more equal than others. Just as it serves an analytical purpose to think in terms of "two presidencies," today there are "two cabinets," an inner and an outer one. The **inner cabinet** handles national security matters, while the **outer cabinet** is responsible for domestic programs.[12] The inner cabinet meets frequently with the president and includes the secretaries of defense and state, and often the secretary of the treasury as well. Attorney General Robert Kennedy was also included in the inner cabinet during the Kennedy years, and Attorney General John Mitchell was a major insider during Nixon's administration.

The outer cabinet is usually comprised of those who head the domestic departments: Agriculture, Labor, Commerce, Interior, Housing and Urban Development, Transportation, and now Energy. Even the mammoth Department of Health, Education, and Welfare, with more than 100,000 employees and a budget that rivals that of Defense in size and complexity, is usually included in the outer ring.

The day-by-day operational significance of being a member of the inner rather than the outer cabinet is great. Those few cabinet officers who gain entrance to the inner cabinet enjoy access to the president and his principal staff assistants on a daily and even an hourly basis, if need be.

Members of the outer cabinet not only see the president far less frequently; they also customarily deal with the president's staff assistants, who serve as intermediaries between cabinet departments and the president. The practical consequence, obviously, is to elevate a few of the president's White House assistants *above* most cabinet officers and espe-

---

[11] Rexford G. Tugwell and Thomas E. Cronin, *The Presidency Re-appraised* (New York: Praeger, 1974), p. 250.

[12] Tugwell and Cronin, *The Presidency Re-appraised*, p. 236.

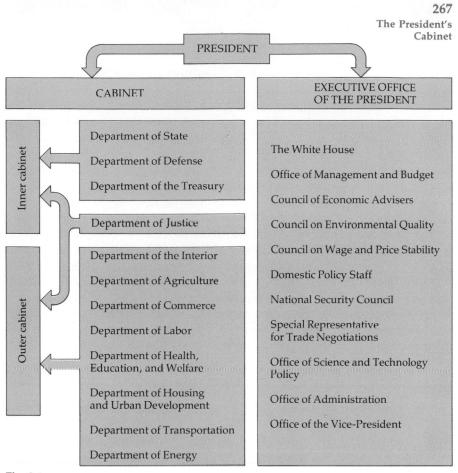

Fig. 8.1
The Cabinet and the Executive Office of the President.

cially those on the domestic side. In 1978, most observers placed presidential assistants Jody Powell and Hamilton Jordan in privileged strategic positions within the Carter White House. Their power depended on easy access to the president and the confidence he placed in them.

Presidential Priorities

The difference in status between inner and outer cabinet officers reflects a built-in sense of priorities at the presidential level. In terms of ready access to the president, there is little doubt that the inner cabinet officers enjoy distinct advantages over those who head the domestic agencies. On the other hand, you should not jump to the conclusion that one who heads a domestic department is simply performing a purely symbolic role. The cabinet officer who appears as a lesser figure than some of the top presidential assistants nevertheless remains a key actor in Washington politics simply because he heads a huge bureaucracy! In fact, some observers believe that bureaucracy today is almost as strong a rival to presidential policy leadership as is Congress. (In Chapter 10 we will explore the power of bureaucracy.) Thomas Cronin finds that "presidential relations with domestic cabinet officials have frequently been ambiguous, ill-defined and unsatisfactory."[13] A president may even try keeping his distance from many in his cabinet. But the issues, the interests, and the problems that these departments deal with will not go away.

Indeed, a president interested in protecting his own position from the shifting mood of a critical public may rediscover that the cabinet serves a useful purpose: that of a buffer. At a time when the general public displays an antibureaucratic bias, the cabinet officers will be there to take some of the heat, thus deflecting it away from the president.

One thing is certain: High-ranking White House assistants and cabinet officers remain rivals for presidential attention. The White House staff is likely to perceive the executive departments as narrowly self-interested bureaucracies with little sensitivity to the presidential perspective. Domestic cabinet officers, on the other hand, are likely to resent those White House aides who stand between them and the president. This inherent rivalry between White House staff and cabinet members adds still another dimension to the problem of presidential leadership.

We turn next to the rise of the "institutionalized presidency," a development that has brought into being a new and expanding group of White House assistants usually labeled "the president's men."[14] As presidential staff assistants grow in importance, they also grow in numbers.

> There is an inherent rivalry between the White House staff and cabinet members.

THE INSTITUTIONALIZED PRESIDENCY AND THE WHITE HOUSE STAFF

When Franklin D. Roosevelt entered the White House in 1933, in the depths of the Great Depression, he found the office organized approximately as it had been when his cousin Theodore had assumed it at the beginning of this century. There were secretaries, telephone operators, people to open the mail, and a household staff to prepare the meals and dust the furniture, but not much more. By the time of his death twelve years later, FDR had initiated steps that would give contemporary presidents a staff to assist them in dealing with the many-faceted substantive and administrative complexities of the job. An Executive Office of the President was created in 1939, along with the Bureau of the Budget, through which the annual budget would become a key instrument of presidential policy leadership. The president was also given a staff of his

---

[13] Cronin, *The State of the Presidency.*

[14] Patrick Anderson, *The President's Men* (Garden City, New York: Doubleday, 1969).

own, consisting of seven administrative assistants, to help him ride herd on the expanding executive bureaucracies.

Mr. Truman, who succeeded to the presidency when FDR died, was the first president to experience the steady expansion of the executive office as Congress continued to add presidential staff agencies. The Employment Act of 1946 created the Council of Economic Advisers to make professional economic advice available to the president. The National Security Council and the Central Intelligence Agency, created by an Act of Congress in 1947, were established to provide guidance in matters of foreign policy and national security policy. It is interesting that in both the management of the nation's economy and the carrying out of our global responsibilities, Congress saw fit to add to the professional and technical capacity of the presidency, its chief institutional rival. In each case, the growth of bureaucracy *inside* the presidency was a response to the growing and changing nature of the role of government in our lives.

> Since the 1930s the executive office has grown steadily in response to the growing and changing nature of the role of government in our lives.

The Swelling of the Presidency: A Mixed Blessing

This trend toward the increasing institutionalization of the presidency has continued with few interruptions ever since. As a result, it is now widely recognized that the presidency has become a complex bureaucratic institution, as well as being an office of policy leadership. The presidential office—a bureaucracy on top of the departmental bureaucracies—has expanded in order to cope with the complexities of making public policy. [15]

The increasing institutionalization of the presidency, often referred to as the "swelling of the presidency," creates problems for the president while aiming to help him. [16] Although each staff unit is created to assist the president, the point is soon reached at which the president, whoever he may be, finds it difficult to oversee his own expanding office. A president needs staff assistance, no doubt, but a highly placed staff assistant who enjoys frequent access to the president inevitably becomes a center of power in his own right. With the best intentions, the staff adviser is almost certainly going to have *his own* policy biases; at a minimum, he will have technical biases. Yet so far as other people in government are concerned, he speaks *for* the president.

The president has to assert his own policy leadership against the resistance of the "permanent government" (that is, the huge executive bureaucracies) and the forces of congressional opposition. He must also be alert to the possibility that his closest aides and assistants in the White House will be sorely tempted to go into business on their own. The

---

[15] See Dorothy B. James, *The Contemporary Presidency*, rev. ed. (Indianapolis: Bobbs Merrill, 1974).

[16] See Cronin, *State of the Presidency,* for more detail on the growth of the institutionalized presidency.

presidential staff agencies are also bureaucracies; all bureaucracies, large and small, have an institutional life of their own. The president must guard his own policy leadership, his own power of initiative, *against* the biases and the activities of his White House advisers.

Senator Daniel P. Moynihan, one of the few political scientists to have served at a high level within an executive department as well as as a White House staff assistant, has noted that "No collection of aides and high-ranking officials can ever be sufficiently sensitive to all the important political considerations the chief executive is swayed by."[17] But, as Moynihan also realizes, this does not stop these same advisers from acting on their own *for* the president. Furthermore, the president is in real danger of being isolated from unpleasant aspects of reality by his overzealous and overprotective staff.

Isolation of the President

George Reedy, a long-time staff assistant to Lyndon B. Johnson, put it this way: "A president's most persistent problem in staying in touch with reality lies in his own staff. It is the aspect of White House life that bears the most striking resemblance to a court."[18] As Reedy sees it, White House assistants have "only one fixed goal in life. It is somehow to gain and maintain access to the president." When this is turned around and examined from the president's viewpoint, the greatest staff problem, in Reedy's opinion, "is that of maintaining his contact with the world's reality that lies outside the White House walls."[19] Both the Watergate tapes and the Pentagon Papers reveal staff assistants "protecting" the president from a hostile outside world.

The increasing institutionalization of the presidency carries with it inherent dangers. Not only must the president assert his leadership against the power of the executive bureaucracies and the biases and activities of his advisers, he must also guard against isolation from an overprotective staff and the risks associated with group decision making.

Unless a president makes a real effort to remain accessible, he is in real danger of being overprotected by his own staff. The isolation of the president from unpleasant realities must be reckoned a distinct possibility in today's world. Furthermore, the swollen and institutionalized presidency not only carries the risk of presidential isolation, it also means that White House decision making takes on the characteristics of *group decision making*. As noted in Chapter 13 this was the case in the Cuban missile crisis (October 1962), when President Kennedy and a tiny band of advisers took the nation to the brink of nuclear war before the Russians finally backed off. This was also the case during the fateful years of military escalation in Vietnam.[20]

[17] Daniel P. Moynihan, *Politics of a Guaranteed Income* (New York: Random House, 1973), p. 547.

[18] George Reedy, *The Twilight of the Presidency* (New York: World Press, 1970), p. 85.

[19] Reedy, *The Twilight of the Presidency*, pp. 88 and 95.

[20] See Graham T. Allison, *Essence of Decision* (Boston: Little, Brown, 1971) for intimate detail on the decision-making aspects of the missile crisis. Compare Donovan, *The Cold Warriors*, on the period of Vietnam escalation.

Group Decision Making

Although the president retains the formal, ultimate authority of his office, very few White House decisions these days are solo decisions. When a president decides to veto a major item of legislation, as President Ford did on more than thirty occasions, he alone makes the formal decision. However, the structuring of the decision—the way in which the alternatives are posed—involves a complicated process in which political and technical advice are intermixed. By the time the question reaches the presidential desk, the options have often been greatly narrowed, sometimes to zero.

A classic example: When President Truman made the decision to drop an atomic bomb on Hiroshima in August 1945, he alone was in a position to make the ultimate, formal decision. In a very real sense, however, the decision had been made for him months earlier. The A-bomb was the product of a two-billion-dollar top-secret wartime project involving the leadership of the scientific community as well as the military. The use of the bomb, if it became a technical reality, was *assumed* almost from the beginning. The choice of the target city, also a technical matter, was the work of a high-level committee reporting to the secretary of war. The committee membership included the presidents of Harvard and MIT, but *not* the president of the United States! At no point in the process was any serious consideration given to the possibility of *not* using the A-bomb. President Truman's ultimate formal decision was made *within the set of assumptions* that governed the thinking of his advisers. It would have taken a lonely and extraordinarily self-confident hero to say in August 1945, "I have decided on my own *not* to use the bomb." In fact, let it be repeated, such a possibility was never contemplated.[21]

The Inner Circle and "Group Think"

The inner circle of executive decision making includes the president, a few of his highly placed White House assistants, and probably a cabinet officer or two. In national security matters it will usually include the secretaries of defense and state as well as the uniformed chairman of the Joint Chiefs of Staff. On rare occasions it may include a member of Congress or a senator. Occasionally, a private citizen may be included. The circle may or may not include the vice-president.

A real problem each president faces, assuming he wishes to face it, is that the inner circle readily becomes a circle of closed politics. By **closed politics** we refer to an atmosphere in which policy alternatives, dissenting views, and serious doubts are not encouraged. The period of Vietnam escalation and the Watergate episode demonstrate one of the principal weaknesses of inner-circle decision making. The inner circle is in danger

[21] Walter S. Schoenberger, *Decision of Destiny* (Columbus: Ohio University Press, 1969) presents the definitive account of the A-bomb decision.

H. R. Haldeman (seated), John Ehrlichman, and Henry Kissinger with President Nixon. Nixon worked so closely with these people to the exclusion of other input that his relationship with them was one of the best examples we have of closed politics.

of succumbing to "group think." **Group think** is a psychological mechanism by which members of small groups reinforce the consensus arrived at within the group by cutting off much of the reality outside the group— especially unpleasant reality![22] Do you find this hard to accept? Would you like to be the one person in the group to stand up and tell the president, the secretaries of defense and state, and the chairman of the Joint Chiefs of Staff they are wrong?

The Power to Persuade

How, then, does a president provide leadership in a governmental system in which power is shared among major institutions? How is a president

[22] Irving Janis, *Victims of Group Think* (Boston: Houghton Mifflin, 1972).

The Vice-Presidency

John Nance Garner, FDR's first vice-president, advised Lyndon B. Johnson in 1960:

"The vice-presidency isn't worth a pitcher of warm spit."

Thomas R. Marshall, Woodrow Wilson's vice-president:

"Like a man in a cataleptic state [the vice-president] cannot speak; he cannot move; he suffers no pain; and yet he is perfectly conscious of everything that is going on about him."

John Adams, who served as vice-president under President George Washington:

"My country has in its wisdom contrived for me the most insignificant office that ever the invention of man contrived or his imagination conceived."

Harry Truman, FDR's third vice-president:

"Look at all the vice-presidents in history. Where are they? They were about as useful as a cow's fifth teat."

Mr. Dooley (Finley Peter Dunne):

"It isn't a crime exactly. Ye can't be sint to jail f'r it, but it's a kind iv a disgrace. It's like writing anonymous letters."

Yet thirteen vice-presidents later served as presidents: John Adams, Thomas Jefferson, Martin Van Buren, John Tyler, Millard Fillmore, Andrew Johnson, Chester A. Arthur, Theodore Roosevelt, Calvin Coolidge, Harry Truman, Richard M. Nixon, Lyndon B. Johnson, and Gerald Ford. Evidently, the vice-presidency is one of the few routes open to the White House.

As usual, John Adams summed it up:

"I am vice-president. In this I am nothing, but I may be everything."

Of course, there is also the view of Spiro Agnew, who served as vice-president under President Richard Nixon before resigning in disgrace:

"Now I know what a turkey feels like before Thanksgiving."

to break away from the confines of the bureaucratic setting in which he finds himself? How does he move successfully against a variety of constraints? A president *must* find a way of persuading other powerful figures that their political (and bureaucratic) interests will be served by moving in the general direction he wishes to go. Whether he has any chance of succeeding in this supreme effort depends mightily on the degree of public support he is able to muster for his position. The president's ability to persuade, in short, is closely linked to his standing with the public. Let us assume the best—that the president enjoys strong public support. Where does he go from there?

As Neustadt reminds us, the president's ability to lead depends on his power to persuade. This, in turn, is influenced greatly by three interrelated factors: (1) the bargaining position of his office; (2) his professional

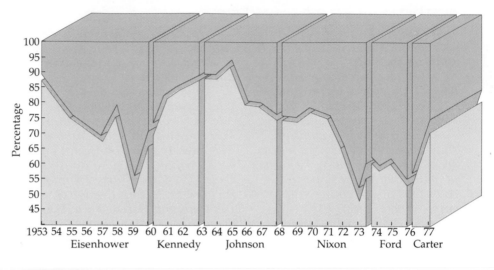

Fig. 8.2
Presidential success with Congress on votes from 1953 to 1977. The percentages are based on congressional votes on which the president took a position. (Copyright © 1978 Congressional Quarterly Weekly Report, p. 10. January 7, 1978. Reprinted with permission.)

The president's ability to persuade depends on the bargaining position of his office, his professional reputation in the eyes of other key politicians, and his public prestige.

reputation in the eyes of other key political actors, especially congressional leaders and bureaucratic chieftains; and (3) his public prestige.[23]

Our political process places a premium on the ability to bargain. The president is a powerful political figure facing other influential political figures. Entrenched bureaucratic chieftains and senior congressional leaders are likely to listen to a president who enjoys the solid support of an attentive public. They are just as likely to resist the same president once his administration shows signs of losing public confidence. The president alone is capable of maintaining this vital connection with *his* public.

A president's professional reputation in the Washington community depends on the way other power brokers perceive him and his administration. How effective is the president and his circle of key advisers and assistants in moving their program through the policy-making process? How are they viewed by the public? Do they know how to exercise power in a system featuring many constraints? Lyndon B. Johnson, an old and experienced Washington power broker, came to the White House enjoying a deserved reputation as an effective policy leader. Jimmy Carter, on the other hand, a Washington "outsider" when he assumed power, was viewed with skepticism by many other key actors in the system.

[23] Neustadt, *Presidential Power*.

Public opinion is also a rich basic source of presidential power, as Harold Laski, a perceptive British observer of American politics, noted many years ago. Laski found a two-fold source of presidential power in public opinion. The first flowed from the president's position as the one element in our government deriving from the nation as a whole. For this reason, the public looks to the White House for leadership in times of crisis. The second source is the public's natural interest in how things are going for us as a people.[24] In an age of complexity and high expectations, it is easy to assume that someone must be in charge.

Unfortunately, public opinion as a support for the exercise of presidential authority may rapidly vanish, as Presidents Johnson and Nixon discovered. A two-edged sword, public opinion also functions as one of the most important potential restraints on the exercise of executive power. In order to function, the system requires presidential leadership; presidents, however, find it increasingly difficult to live up to high public expectations about what they can do.

> Presidents are finding it increasingly difficult to live up to public expectations about what they can do.

Would you agree with the suggestion that a number of recent presidents—most notably Kennedy, Johnson, Nixon, and Ford—"failed" in the sense that widely held popular expectations concerning leadership and the effective functioning of our governmental system during their administrations were not met? Such a failure over a period of a decade and a half (or longer) is difficult to explain in personal or individual terms. It may be inherent in the system and it may diminish the *real* capacity of presidents to lead. If this is so, how are presidents likely to react? "Once presidents discover the embrace of the people is deadly, they may well seek to escape from it," is the blunt way Aaron Wildavsky has put it.[25]

Wildavsky is not arguing that the presidency is shrinking in importance. On the contrary, he believes that the office will be more important in relation to Congress and the bureaucracies. But as he sees it, the presidency is being transformed in its essential relationship with the public. Wildavsky concludes:

> In the future, Presidents will be more important but less popular than they are today. The Presidency will be more powerful *vis-a-vis* institutional competitors but less able to satisfy citizen preferences than it is now. Unwilling to play a losing hand, future Presidents will try to change the rules of the game. If they cannot get support from the people, they can increase the distance between themselves and their predators.[26]

This sounds plausible until one realizes that presidents have no way of hiding from the public in this age of the mass media. In the meantime, we face the harsh reality of the aggrandizement of presidential power.

[24] Harold Laski, *The American Presidency, An Interpretation* (New York: Harper & Row, 1940), pp. 144–145.
[25] Aaron Wildavsky, "The Past and Future Presidency," *Public Interest*, No. 41 (Fall 1975).
[26] Wildavsky, "The Past and Future Presidency," p. 57.

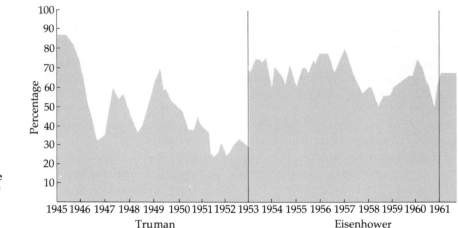

Fig. 8.3
Presidential popularity.
(Source: American Institute
of Public Opinion (Gallup)
Poll.)

THE IMPERIAL PRESIDENCY

The combination of Vietnam and Watergate presented us with a picture of the presidency close to running out of control. This, in turn, gave rise to what Arthur M. Schlesinger, Jr., entitled **the imperial presidency**. This commonly used term connotes an executive office that has assumed virtually autocratic power. Presidential power had grown to the point where none of the usual constraints—congressional, constitutional, political— seemed very effective, according to Schlesinger's view.[27]

The Pentagon Papers reveal a closed inner circle of policy making during the years of American military escalation in Vietnam. President Johnson and his small inner circle of top advisers met in an atmosphere that discouraged dissent and stifled serious criticism of the administration's course in Southeast Asia.[28] The same documents reveal that the Johnson administration stage-managed a minor naval incident in the Tonkin Gulf in August 1964 so as to win congressional approval (it was almost unanimous) of a resolution that the president then used to justify a vast expansion of our military effort in Vietnam. Time and again, official spokespersons in the executive branch deceived Congress, the press, and the American public about the course of the war in Vietnam.

The Watergate episode shows a similar pattern. An attempted obstruction of justice was planned in elaborate detail by the president and a small group of key White House aides. President Nixon and his associates came

[27] Arthur M. Schlesinger, Jr., *The Imperial Presidency* (Boston: Little, Brown, 1973).

[28] Donovan, *The Cold Warriors*. For an inside account see James C. Thomson, Jr., "How Could Vietnam Happen? An Autopsy," *The Atlantic* 221, No. 4 (April 1968): 47-53.

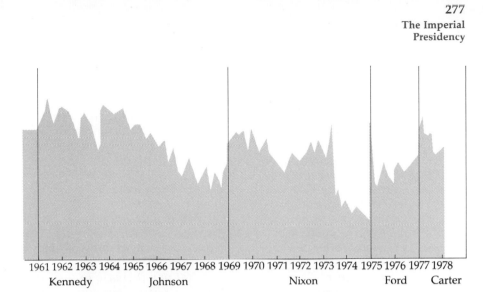

1961 1962 1963 1964 1965 1966 1967 1968 1969 1970 1971 1972 1973 1974 1975 1976 1977 1978

Kennedy   Johnson   Nixon   Ford   Carter

Many people feel that the Nixon administration symbolizes the height of the imperial presidency. Whether this is true or not, Nixon's decision to dress his White House guards in pseudo-Prussian uniforms increased this criticism of his presidency.

It was important to President Carter that his presidency be kept as "open" as possible. A decade and a half of essentially closed presidential politics, especially in matters of national security, demonstrated how vulnerable any president becomes when the White House inner circle encapsulates him. Furthermore, a sizeable segment of the attentive public was anxious to respond to an open presidency. Jimmy Carter's unprecedented two-hour radio conversation with the American people in March of 1977 provoked some nine million calls. The range of issues presented by the forty-two individuals whose calls went through to the president revealed a level of public concern that be-

lied endemic apathy. The callers were polite and respectful, but they were not servile, as the following excerpt from a conversation between President Carter and Gerald Anderson of Denver, Colorado shows:

Q. Mr. President.
A. Hi, Gerald.
Q. I'm wondering what is the justification with you trying to reduce the federal budget—the justification behind the $12,000 pay increase to the Congress? How can you lower the budget by giving them $12,000 and us $50 back?
A. Gerald, that's a hard question for me to answer.
Q. That's why I thought I'd throw it at you.

closer to getting away with the attempted coverup than most of us like to think.[29]

There is no point in minimizing the dangerous tendencies revealed by these recent experiences with executive abuse of power. But the expansion of presidential power began long before Vietnam or Watergate, as Professor Schlesinger's study also shows. The larger and more important issue is how the so-called imperial presidency grew out of fundamental developments within American society. What changes in our society encouraged the steady expansion of executive power?

Expanding Global Empire

Americans sometimes have a hard time accepting the facts about the history of our nation's expansion. We tend to gloss over the connection between the growth of the strong presidency in this century and the steady rise of the United States as a superpower. This century had barely opened when Theodore Roosevelt, an ardent expansionist, mounted the "bully pulpit" in the White House, there to preach a doctrine of vigor and

[29] See especially Carl Bernstein and Bob Woodward, *All the President's Men* (New York: Simon and Schuster, 1974).

strength. TR was an imperial-minded president who played the role openly and with contagious enthusiasm. He was roundly applauded for his efforts by many of his contemporaries.

Although neither Woodrow Wilson nor Franklin D. Roosevelt was as overtly an expansionist as TR, each led the nation into a world war in which American power proved to be the decisive factor. At the end of the second of these world wars, the United States, armed with nuclear weapons, found itself in the role of global policeman. The German and Japanese nations were reduced to rubble. The British Empire, grievously weakened, was about to be dismantled. The French empire, mostly a teasing illusion of past glory, engaged in a futile attempt for a while to hang on to the remnants in Algeria and Indochina. Only the Soviet Russian empire, largely landlocked and needing time to recuperate from the ravages of war and military invasion, appeared to pose any real threat to American global supremacy. The development of a permanent United States military establishment added a new dimension to executive leadership in world affairs.

The imperial presidency is a twentieth-century development that parallels the steady expansion of national economic, political, and military power. Since the days of Theodore Roosevelt, the United States has followed this course, interrupted only by a brief period of isolationism in the 1930s. As we approach the closing decades of this century, our position in the world is undergoing transformation, a transformation only partially seen and as yet imperfectly understood. The contemporary presidency, a mixture of strength and weakness, is being transformed, partly because we, as a people, are undergoing a process of change in our attitudes toward the presidency and toward our role in the world. The experiences of the past two decades have altered our expectations concerning presidential leadership. The balance of power in world affairs is very different from what it was in the early years of the Cold War.

> The growth of the imperial presidency is a twentieth-century development that parallels the steady expansion of national economic, political, and military power.

Today, the American empire shares the world stage with other great empires, most notably the Russian and Chinese. We are a powerful and rich industrial nation facing a third world of underdeveloped, nonindustrial nations. We profess to be a democracy in a world that recognizes only a few practicing democracies. Ours is the leading capitalist economy at a time when Western capitalism exhibits signs of hardening of the arteries. In short, the presidency is an institution in flux within a nation that is changing amid a world of confusing diversity.

Presidential Character

We face, finally, a basic dilemma in assessing the presidency. We look to the executive as the prime agency of policy leadership in a fragmented

*Four Types
of Presidential
Character*

*"The first baseline in defining Pres-
idential types is* activity-passiv-
ity. *How much energy does the
man invest in his Presidency? Lyndon Johnson went at his day like
a human cyclone, coming to rest
long after the sun went down. Calvin Coolidge often slept eleven
hours a night and still needed a
nap in the middle of the day. In
between the Presidents array themselves on the high or low side of
the activity line.*

"The second baseline is posi-
tive-negative affect *toward one's
activity—that is, how he feels about
what he does. Relatively speaking,
does he seem to experience his political life as happy or sad, enjoy-
able or discouraging, positive or
negative in its main effect. The
feeling I am after here is not grim
satisfaction in a job well done, not
some philosophical conclusion.
The idea is this: is he someone
who, on the surfaces we can see,
gives forth the feeling that he has
fun in political life? Franklin Roosevelt's Secretary of War, Henry L.
Stimson wrote that the Roosevelts
'not only understood the* use *of
power, they knew the* enjoyment *
of power, too . . . . Whether a man
is burdened by power or enjoys
power; whether he is trapped by
responsibility or made free by it;
whether he is moved by other peo-*

*ple and outer forces or moves
them—that is the essence of
leadership. . . .'*

*"The two baselines are clear
and they are also independent of
one another: all of us know people
who are very active but seem discouraged, others who are quite
passive but seem happy, and so
forth. The activity baseline refers
to what one does, the affect baseline to how one feels about what
he does.*

*"Both are crude clues to char-
acter. They are leads into four
basic character patterns long familiar in psychological research.
In summary form, these are the
main configurations:*

*"Active-positive: There is a
congruence, a consistency, between much activity and the enjoyment of it, indicating relatively
high self-esteem and relative success in relating to the environment. The man shows an orientation toward productiveness as a
value and an ability to use his
styles flexibly, adaptively, suiting
the dance to the music. He sees
himself as developing over time toward relatively well defined personal goals—growing toward his
image of himself as he might yet
be. There is an emphasis on rational mastery, on using the brain
to move the feet. This may get him*

into trouble; he may fail to take account of the irrational in politics. Not everyone he deals with sees things his way and he may find it hard to understand why.

"Active-negative: The contradiction here is between relatively intense effort and relatively low emotional reward for that effort. The activity has a compulsive quality, as if the man were trying to make up for something or to escape from anxiety into hard work. He seems ambitious, striving upward, power-seeking. His stance toward the environment is aggressive and he has a persistent problem in managing his aggressive feelings. His self-image is vague and discontinuous. Life is a hard struggle to achieve and hold power, hampered by the condemnations of a perfectionistic conscience. Active-negative types pour energy into the political system, but it is an energy distorted from within.

*"Passive-positive: This is the receptive, compliant, other-directed character whose life is a search for affection as a reward for being agreeable and cooperative rather than personally assertive. The contradiction is between low self-esteem (on grounds of being unlovable, unattractive) and a superficial optimism. A hopeful atti-*tude helps dispel doubt and elicits encouragement from others. Passive-positive types help soften the harsh edges of politics. But their dependence and the fragility of their hopes and enjoyments make disappointment in politics likely.*

"Passive-negative: The factors are consistent—but how are we to account for the man's political role-taking? Why is someone who does little in politics and enjoys it less there at all? The answer lies in the passive-negative's character-rooted orientation toward doing dutiful service; this compensates for low self-esteem based on a sense of uselessness. Passive-negative types are in politics because they think they ought to be. They may be well adapted to certain nonpolitical roles, but they lack the experience and flexibility to perform effectively as political leaders. Their tendency is to withdraw, to escape from the conflict and uncertainty of politics by emphasizing vague principles (especially prohibitions) and procedural arrangements. They become guardians of the right and proper way, above the sordid politicking of lesser men."

From James David Barber, *The Presidential Character,* 2d ed. (Englewood Cliffs, N.J.: Prentice-Hall, 1977), pp. 11-13. Reprinted by permission.

system. At the same time, our Constitution is based on a fear of concentrated power. Yet the president has access to enormous power, and this power may be abused, as we have been reminded in painful ways during the recent past. Louis Koenig has written that "the real presidency is what the presidency effectively is in the present, what it can do in a given situation."[30]

Nevertheless, we cannot be sure what any particular president will do in a given situation until he has done it, and then it may be too late, as in the case of Vietnam escalation, or almost too late, as in the case of the attempted Watergate coverup.

Obviously, the character and personality of the individual who occupies the Oval Office are critical ingredients. But how are these qualities to be assessed? Were not the "character" and "personality" of Richard M. Nixon well known to the general public prior to his election? James David Barber has focused the attention of political scientists on "presidential character" and has even worked out a typology for characterizing our presidents (see box).

Barber is suggesting that the public should pay more attention in advance to the kinds of individuals who seek the nation's highest office. He also implies that an active-positive president who seeks results is most appropriate in the contemporary era. While Jimmy Carter's "character" in the old-fashioned sense of the word remained elusive, he showed early signs of being an "active-positive" chief executive. More than this, Carter was the first president to acknowledge publicly his interest in Barber's theory. The second edition (1977) of Barber's book contains this testimonial on its cover: "I read Barber's book when it first came out. As far as an analysis of the presidents is concerned, *The Presidential Character* is the best book I've read."[31] Jimmy Carter.

Assuming that Jimmy Carter is indeed "active-positive," what does this tell us about his objectives and goals or his ability to meet them, given the constraints of his office? Does an "activist-positive" in the White House mean that we shall have welfare reform or a comprehensive energy program? In the final analysis, are not the morale and character of the American people at least as important as the character of the man in the White House when it comes to determining America's future?

The presidency is first and foremost a popular institution. It is a reflection of our political maturity. The historical record, we must admit, is decidedly mixed. We take justifiable pride in Washington, Jefferson, Lincoln, Wilson, and Roosevelt. The same society produced Pierce, Grant,

James David Barber has divided presidential character types into four general categories: active-positive, active-negative, passive-positive, and passive-negative. He implies that an active-positive president who seeks results is most appropriate today.

[30] Louis W. Koenig, *Chief Executive,* rev. ed. (New York: Harcourt, 1968), p. 3.

[31] James David Barber, *The Presidential Character,* 2d ed. (Englewood Cliffs, N.J.: Prentice-Hall, 1977).

Harding, and Nixon, each in his own way a tragic failure as president. The presidency in critical moments has proved hospitable to great men with noble visions. It has also endured at least its share of ordinary men with limited vision who all too often displayed little talent for leading a society of free people. The majority of the presidents the American people have chosen have escaped mediocrity without approaching true greatness. A government of men rather than of angels, as Madison described it, features a fallible instrument: the American presidency. Created by the people and continuously evolving in response to the changing demands of a restless society, the presidency reveals some of the strengths as well as a number of the weaknesses of American society.[32]

SUMMARY

The president of the United States has a tough job; some say the toughest in the world. It certainly is one of the biggest, providing executive leadership for a nation of 220 million people of diverse backgrounds. The American economy, the richest and most technically sophisticated in the world, is profoundly affected by the spending and taxing powers of the government. As head of state and also as the civilian commander in chief, the man in the White House, his finger on the nuclear trigger, can never avoid the awesome responsibilities of world leadership.

Nevertheless, as we have seen, the president is limited by powerful constraints: the independence of Congress, the persistent influence of huge bureaucracies in implementing programs, the questioning of a free press and the all-seeing eye of the TV camera, the changing moods of the American people, and the many ideological, economic, and political differences that make our politics chaotic.

The office has always severely tested the character of its incumbents. Some of our presidents were men of strong character: Washington and Lincoln are prime examples. Others have shown weakness under the pressures of office; neither Harding nor Nixon in this century, for example, was able to rise above the corruption of his administration.

In the present era, each president upon entering office inherits an institutionalized presidency—a bureaucracy on top of the huge executive bureaucracies. Whoever occupies the Oval Office finds that it takes unusual effort to keep the policy-making process open. There is a growing tendency for White House special assistants, especially the chosen few, to insulate the president, to isolate him from unpleasant reality.

[32] For a recent interpretation of presidential power that recognizes the weaknesses as well as the elements of strength, see Erwin C. Hargrove, *The Power of the Modern Presidency* (New York: Knopf, 1974).

In order to provide effective leadership in a system of fragmented power, the president must somehow *move* us. Without a sustained measure of public confidence in the man and the office, it is all too easy for the American national government to settle into a condition of political stalemate. And this is obviously not the ideal way for a great nation to address the difficult choices required in a rapidly changing world.

KEY TERMS

paradox of the presidency
political strategy
chief executive
policy initiator
Commander in Chief
chief diplomat
head of state
two presidencies theory
inner cabinet

outer cabinet
institutionalized presidency
group decision making
closed politics
group think
imperial presidency

SUGGESTED READINGS

ALLISON, GRAHAM T., *Essence of Decision* (Boston: Little, Brown, 1971).

Examines the Cuban missile crisis in terms of decision-making models. Sharply contrasts the "rational actor" and "bureaucratic politics" models.

ANDERSON, PATRICK, *The President's Men* (Garden City, N.Y.: Doubleday, 1969).

A popular study of the men around the president by a novelist who has had experience in the Washington community, including presidential speech-writing. Draws essentially on the careers of the men who served John F. Kennedy and Lyndon B. Johnson.

BARBER, JAMES DAVID, *The Presidential Character*, 2d ed. (Englewood Cliffs, N.J.: Prentice-Hall, 1977).

An important study of the psychological basis of presidential performance. Offers a typology for characterizing and assessing particular presidencies.

CORWIN, EDWARD S., *The President: Office and Powers*, 4th ed., rev. (New York: New York University Press, 1957).

A classic study based on the constitutional roots of presidential authority. A dated but still useful book.

CRONIN, THOMAS E., *The State of the Presidency* (Boston: Little, Brown, 1975).

A lively analysis of the contemporary presidency by a political scientist who has been sharply critical of "textbook" views of the presidency. Cronin is also critical of the "swelling" of the institutionalized Presidency.

DONOVAN, JOHN C., *The Cold Warriors* (Lexington, Mass.: D. C. Heath, 1974).

A series of case studies revealing the influence of a strategic elite in formulating, implementing, and perpetuating our Cold War policies. Emphasizes the closed nature of politics within the presidential inner circle of decision making.

JANIS, IRVING, *Victims of Group Think* (Boston: Houghton Mifflin, 1972).

A psychologist examines the nature of inner circle decision making, explaining the psychological mechanisms that operate to stifle dissenting views. Includes the Vietnam experience.

NEUSTADT, RICHARD E., *Presidential Power* (New York: Wiley, 1960).

An influential theory of presidential power stressing the bargaining nature of the office. Focuses on the relationship between a president's capacity to lead and his standing with the public as perceived within the Washington community of power brokers.

REEDY, GEORGE, *The Twilight of the Presidency* (New York: World Press, 1970).

Written by a long-time Lyndon B. Johnson assistant, this book argues that the contemporary president is likely to be isolated from harsh reality by a sycophantic staff.

WATERGATE CHRONOLOGY: JUNE 1972–AUGUST 1974

The Break-in During the early morning hours of Saturday, June 17, 1972, the offices of the Democratic National Committee, located in the Watergate Hotel, Washington, D.C., were burglarized by five professional "thieves," formerly employed by the CIA. A quick call by a security guard summoned the police, and all five men were arrested while still in the committee offices. Found to be using false names, the men carried with them several notes that were later to link them with prominent White House officials. The cover-up began immediately thereafter, when the news reached the White House.

Suspicion Grows Early in July, Watergate disclosures began piling up rapidly as connections were made between the burglars and the CIA, the FBI, and such White House aides as E. Howard Hunt, Gordon Liddy, James McCord, and Chuck Colson. United States District Court Judge John Sirica, the jurist assigned to oversee the grand jury investigation of the Watergate break-in, pushed to break the case wide open as he learned of other activities involving the Watergate criminals outside of Washington.

The Official Reply As plans got underway for the Republican Convention, President Nixon systematically denied any complicity on the part of the White House in the illegal Watergate activities. On September 17, the federal grand jury returned an eight-count indictment against seven men for conspiring to steal documents from and for eavesdropping on the Democratic Headquarters.

The *Washington Post* Investigates Two young *Washington Post* reporters, Carl Bernstein and Bob Woodward, who covered Watergate for months, began to piece together a story that exposed the involvement of the Committee to Re-elect the President in the Watergate bugging and burglary incidents, and in the sabotaging of Democratic presidential campaigns. The October 10 story opened a series of Woodward and Bernstein articles that revealed the involvement of former Attorney General John Mitchell and other prominent officials of the Nixon administration. The *Washington Post*, despite scathing attacks from the White House, continued to publish startling disclosures of illegal government actions, and on October 25, in another electrifying front-page story, Woodward and Bernstein traced the conspiracy to H. R. Haldeman, White House Chief of Staff. Only one step remained to the presidency.

Election Day On November 7, in the biggest presidential landslide ever, Richard Nixon was re-elected by 61.3 percent of the American voters. The overwhelming Nixon victory temporarily overshadowed Watergate.

The Watergate Seven On January 9, 1973, the trial of the seven men indicted in connection with the Watergate break-in began in the United States District Court in Washington, D.C., with Judge John Sirica presiding. On January 10, the first full day of the trial, a startling break came in the proceedings when E. Howard Hunt, precluding any testimony, pleaded guilty to the three counts of conspiracy, burglary, and illegal wiretapping. This guilty plea ensured Hunt's silence and made the calling of witnesses against him unnecessary. The Nixon Administration had succeeded temporarily in covering up

Emotional farewell speech before resignation.

Watergate. On January 30, the jury took only ninety minutes to find the only two defendants left to face prosecution, James McCord and Gordon Liddy, guilty on all counts.

The Senate Investigates The investigation of the Watergate break-in went into full swing when L. Patrick Gray, Nixon's nominee for director of the FBI, admitted during his confirmation hearing with the Senate Judiciary Committee to giving FBI files on the Watergate investigation to the White House. In further testimony, Gray revealed the involvement of the highest echelon of the White House in the cover-up, referring primarily to John Dean,

Chief White House Counsel to the President. Another break in the testimony came when Judge Sirica received a letter from James McCord admitting much of what people had been suspecting about Watergate: pressure from the White House to plead guilty, perjury during testimony, and much more. McCord later gave names, evidence, and documentation substantiating these charges to Senate lawyers. Early summer brought the testimony of former Attorney General John Mitchell and Special Assistant to the President Jeb Stuart Magruder; the resignation of Attorney General Kleindienst, Mr. Haldeman, and Domestic Adviser John Erlichman; and the firing of John Dean. President Nixon remained silent on his possible involvement in Watergate.

The Tapes On July 16, White House aide Alexander Butterfield added a new facet to the investigation by revealing the existence of an electronic eavesdropping system that allowed the president to record every conversation held in the White House. Requested by the Senate to submit the tapes for committee review, Nixon refused to honor the Senate subpoenas. Later in the month, John Dean implicated the president in the cover-up while giving testimony to the Senate. John Erlichman continued to deny his and the president's involvement.

Saturday Night Massacre The request for the tapes, which was advocated by Special Prosecutor Archibald Cox and supported by the Courts, made Nixon decide to end his problems by abolishing the office of Special Prosecutor. This led to the firing of Special Prosecutor Archibald Cox, Attorney General Elliot Richardson, and Deputy Attorney General William Ruckelhaus. Following this unorthodox

THE WHITE HOUSE

WASHINGTON

August 9, 1974

Dear Mr. Secretary:

I hereby resign the Office of President of the
United States.

Sincerely,

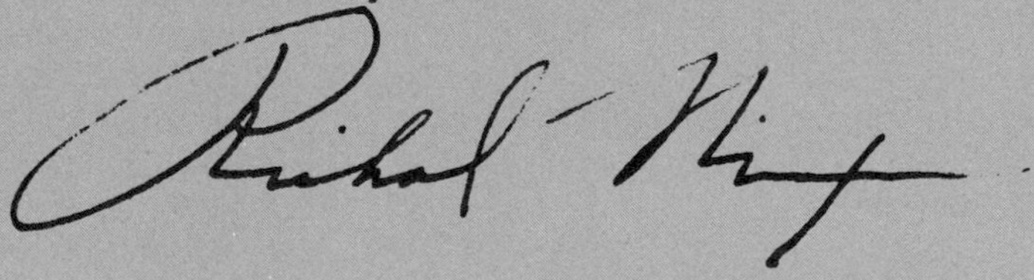

Richard Nixon

The Honorable Henry A. Kissinger
The Secretary of State
Washington, D.C. 20520

move, the House of Representatives was prompted to initiate resolutions of impeachment, and the House Judiciary Committee began to prepare for an impeachment inquiry. This process continued from October 22, the day after the firings, until February 1974, when the committee was ready to begin formal proceedings.

The Road to Impeachment On February 6, the House of Representatives formally granted the House Judiciary Committee power to investigate the conduct of President Nixon to determine whether there were grounds for his impeachment. The inquiry staff worked from February to May, collecting and assembling information and evidence relevant to the charges against Nixon. Beginning May 9, the assembled evidence relating Nixon's possible involvement in the break-in and cover-up was presented to the committee.

The Beginning of the End On July 24, the final stage of the impeachment inquiry began as the Judiciary Committee debate on impeachment opened. Another damaging blow was dealt to the Nixon defense when, on the same day, the Supreme Court ordered Nixon to yield the remaining tapes to the committee. On July 30, the House Judiciary Committee approved three articles of impeachment, recommending to the House that Nixon be impeached and removed from Office because he had violated his oath of office by obstruction of justice (Article I), by abuse of his presidential powers (Article II), and by contempt of Congress (Article III) in refusing to comply with the committee's subpoenas.

August—The End of the Road As the month of August began, the impeachment of President Nixon by the House of Representatives was considered a virtual certainty. Then, on August 5, the president announced that he was releasing the transcripts of three recorded conversations taped with Haldeman six days after the break-in. These transcripts clearly showed Nixon's involvement in the Watergate cover-up and break-in from day one.

The Final Step On August 9, 1974, in a nationally televised speech, Richard Milhous Nixon became the first president in American history to resign from office.

You can't use tact with a Congressman. A Congressman is like a hog. You must take a stick and hit him on the snout.

Henry Adams

The United States Congress is probably more powerful as a legislative body *vis-a-vis* the executive than any other legislative body in the world today.

Lewis A. Froman, Jr.

Fleas can be taught nearly anything a Congressman can.

Mark Twain

CHAPTER 9 THE CONGRESS: CHANGE AND CONTINUITY

When the Arab states imposed an embargo on oil shipments to the Western world during the winter of 1973, the United States imported 25 percent of its oil from foreign sources. Overnight, public attention was suddenly focused on "the energy crisis." At this point both President Nixon and congressional leaders called for a comprehensive plan to reduce this nation's dependence on foreign oil. Ironically, when President Carter entered office four years later, United States dependence on imported oil had increased from 25 percent to 50 percent, and yet Congress had not enacted a national energy policy. The development of such a policy absorbed a major share of President Carter's attention during his first two years in office. The energy issue engaged the Carter White House in an intense and prolonged struggle with Congress and major interest groups. The program that finally emerged from Congress, a partial one at best, was based on a bundle of compromises between the interests of producers and those of consumers.

How can this be? Given such an urgent national problem and the clear need to solve it, why had so little been done between 1973 and 1978? Why was there so much resistance to developing an energy policy for the United States? Was congressional slowness in responding to the crisis due to conflicting political pressures? To what extent was the fragmented

Fig. 9.1
The effect of the Carter administration's energy plan on petroleum imports. (Source: U.S. Budget in Brief, 1979.)

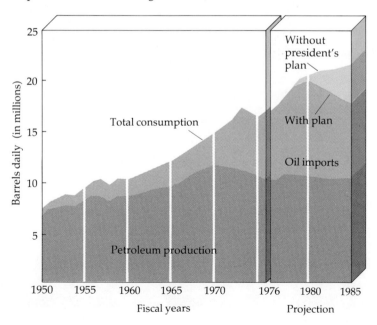

structure of Congress with its multiplicity of committees a factor? Is there some basic defect within the institution of Congress itself? How much fault lies with the American people, who cannot agree on what they want or need or what the problem is? Is it possible that Congress as a representative institution has difficulty solving problems when the diversity of opinion in our society is too great?

This chapter seeks to find answers to these questions by examining the nature of Congress in a changing world. This examination of Congress leads to still further questions: What is the nature of our national legislature? How did it develop its present form, and in response to which social forces? What is the basic relationship between Congress and the presidency? What does Congress do? How does it go about its work? What is the process by which it enacts laws? Who serves in Congress? How representative is it? Where is Congress heading in the immediate future? What changes are occurring in our society and in our governing institutions that seem likely to affect the choices we are forced to make in our own lives in the years that lie directly ahead?

The Congress of the United States is affected by the winds of change that are blowing through our society; probably to a greater extent than most citizens realize. The Congress of the late 1970s and early 1980s differs in important ways from the Congress of a decade earlier. Nevertheless, there are powerful elements of continuity in the institutional structure of Congress. Our aim in this chapter is to offer a balanced view of Congress—highlighting both the old and the new on Capitol Hill—as it responds to pressures of change.

DURABILITY AND POWER

Congress is one of the oldest—and hence most durable—legislatures in the world. In addition, it is one of the most powerful in its relation to the executive branch. The founding fathers specifically created a national legislature independent of the executive branch. By declaring that Congress was to have a major policy-making role along with the president, they clearly intended that the separate institutions of the national government would exercise powers jointly (the "separation of powers"). No single branch was to dominate the others. Subsequent political generations have bent the institution to fit the needs of their times, but Congress remains an independent institution of substantial power.

Political scientist Lewis Froman offers this assessment: "It is . . . undoubtedly true that in no other country has the legislature so much capacity for acting independently and for thwarting the will of the executive as in the United States."[1]

> The Congress of the United States is one of the most powerful legislatures in the world in its relationship to the executive branch of government.

[1] Lewis A. Froman, Jr., *The Congressional Process* (Boston: Little, Brown, 1967).

Structurally, Congress appears, on the surface, much as it did two centuries ago. It remains a bicameral legislature, with an upper house (the Senate) based on state equality and a lower house (the House of Representatives) based on population. But, as we saw in Chapter 3, major changes in the nineteenth century moved the important work of the two chambers from the floors to the committee rooms. Some critics have argued that Congress is outmoded, that we should not try to formulate public policy in the world's most powerful industrial democracy using an institutional framework designed to serve the very limited needs of a tiny, eighteenth-century, essentially rural republic. Although Congress has rapidly been adding to its professional staff (institutionalizing itself) and modernizing its procedures, such criticism persists.[2]

As we shall see, especially in our analysis of foreign-policy making in Chapter 12, much of the criticism of Congress's ability to make policy is legitimate. With the accelerating speed of events in the late twentieth century, Congress often appears ponderous and slow-moving. Nevertheless, in the aftermath of Watergate and Vietnam, the idea of a legislative branch strong enough to limit the power of the presidency at home and abroad seems to have gained in popularity. The presence of a strong Congress to check the initiatives of a strong presidency seems more important than ever.

It is ironic that this current emphasis on a strong Congress comes at a time when Congress itself does not enjoy widespread popularity. The shift in public mood of the late 1960s and early 1970s, revealing a profound erosion of public confidence in government, affected Congress as well. Indeed, Congress suffered the largest drop in confidence. Even though individual members of Congress are very popular and many are elected over and over, Congress itself is not held in high regard.[3]

How can one explain this situation? Why does the public say it wants a strong Congress when it places little faith in the one it has? No doubt part of the answer lies in the relationship between Congress and the president. The very principle of separated institutions sharing power involves shifting, changing relationships, depending on time and circumstance. We, the public, often misperceive this relationship. Which institutions are "up" and "down" in public esteem reflects, to some extent, the issues of the day. And all this happens within a traditional popular view of politics in America as a dirty business. Part of the problem also lies in the failure of many members of the public to give sustained attention

Today people are more than ever aware of the need for a strong Congress to check the initiatives of a strong presidency; at the same time, public confidence in Congress has been seriously eroded.

[2] For a comment on the institutionalizing process, see Nelson Polsby, "The Institutionalization of the U.S. House of Representatives," *American Political Science Review* 62 (1968): 144–168. For a critique, see Joseph S. Clark, *Congress: The Sapless Branch* (New York: Harper & Row, 1964).

[3] Walter DeVries summarizes the findings of several analysts, all of whom noted this sharp decline. See his essay "American Perceptions of Parties, Institutions, and Politicians," in *Voters, Primaries, and Parties* (Institute of Politics, Harvard University, 1976), p. 18.

to the serious issues of American national life. Hence Congress looms as an easy target and a plausible scapegoat.

CONGRESS AND THE PRESIDENT

A curious time cycle prevails in the relationship between Congress and the president; presidential assertions of authority alternate frequently with periods of congressional government. The Reconstruction period following the Civil War is an obvious example of the latter. Lincoln, who faced problems in governing unique to a civil war, had carried executive power to unprecedented extremes. Following Lee's surrender and Lincoln's assassination, however, Congress reasserted its powers swiftly, with the nearly successful impeachment of President Johnson, the imposition of military government in the states of the former Confederacy, and the writing of the Thirteenth, Fourteenth, and Fifteenth amendments. No one in the 1870s considered Congress a weak and impotent body.[4]

Woodrow Wilson, then a young political scientist, published his study *Congressional Government* in 1885 believing that Congress was the dominant partner in our national government. (He was to alter his views drastically after observing President Theodore Roosevelt in action.)[5]

Traditionally in our history, periods of congressional authority in government have alternated with periods of presidential authority.

[4] See Claude G. Bowers, *The Tragic Era* (New York: Blue Ribbon Books, 1929) for a classic study of Congress in the saddle during the era of Reconstruction.

[5] Woodrow Wilson, *Congressional Government* (New York: Meridian Books, 1956).

Fig. 9.2
**The precarious balance between the president and Congress.
(Reprinted by permission of George L. Rebh.)**

Strong Presidents and Congressional Resistance

Many of the conditions of the twentieth century have proved helpful to presidential initiatives in domestic and foreign policy, while placing Congress in a subordinate position. All over the globe this has been the "century of the executive." In America, strong presidents such as Woodrow Wilson and Franklin Roosevelt have dominated the politics of their time; so did Theodore Roosevelt, first of the "heroic" mold in this century.

But even the strongest of our heroic presidents find Congress soon reacting to assertions of executive power. Theodore Roosevelt engaged in a running battle with the leaders of his own party in Congress. Senate opposition shattered Wilson's dream of leading the United States into the League of Nations. Congress sharply rebuffed FDR when he tried to "pack" the Supreme Court, despite massive majorities of his own party in both houses. And FDR's leadership in world affairs was circumscribed in the decade before Pearl Harbor as Congress enacted a series of neutrality laws designed to limit the use of executive discretion in foreign policy.[6]

The struggle with Congress is not necessarily made easier for those chief executives who are more inclined to accept congressional constraints—so-called weak presidents. Taft, Theodore Roosevelt's handpicked successor, who did not share Roosevelt's notions of expansive presidential power, was outmaneuvered on the few things he wanted by the more conservative congressional leaders within his own party.

The Nixon years, 1969–1974, saw divided government in its classic (critics would say its worst) form. Nixon, a Republican, faced hostile Democratic congressional majorities from the day he entered the White House. His personal landslide victory in 1972 failed to alter Democratic control of Congress. The Nixon era was marked by an unusually intense struggle with these congressional majorities. This is explained partly by the Nixon administration's attempt to reorganize the presidency for strengthened executive policy leadership and partly by the extreme assertions of presidential prerogatives, particularly in budgetary matters, that preceded the revelations of Watergate. President Nixon challenged Congress as few predecessors had dared to do, and finally paid a price none of them had ever suffered before.

Gerald Ford (1974–1976) fared only slightly better than his predecessor, probably because, as the first unelected president in our history, he lacked a base in popular support—a vital factor in presidential leadership. A continuing battle between White House and Congress raged over virtually every major item of domestic legislation; at the same time, Congress asserted itself with exceptional vigor across the board in national security, foreign policy, and intelligence matters.

[6] James A. Robinson, *Congress and Foreign Policy Making*, rev. ed. (Homewood, Ill.: Dorsey, 1967).

Two Constituencies

Today, moreover, the congressional-presidential relationship is affected more powerfully than ever by the difference in electoral constituencies between the two institutions. The presidency is, after all, the one truly national office in the entire system. The president, whoever he may be, knows no serious rival as spokesperson for the nation. House members, on the other hand, are bound to a certain parochialism as representatives of 435 decentralized districts, and senators, no matter how officious their bearing, each come from one of fifty states. The senior senator from Wyoming may imagine he is speaking for all Americans when he offers his opinion on the Middle East, but most Americans will not see him that way. Indeed, they are not likely to hear him or even to know his name. As the nation has grown larger and more culturally interconnected and homogenous, the prestige of the single elected national leader has increased. The steadily increasing influence of the mass media, as discussed in Chapter 7, provides special advantages to the president as spokesman for the American people. "The national media," observes Richard Fenno, "is both Washington oriented and president oriented."[7]

Provincialism and Cosmopolitanism

In practice, Congress as a whole tends to represent the decentralized, particularized, provincial, diverse patterns of American society. The presidency, especially in this century, has evolved as the national institution most naturally suited to represent the more cosmopolitan, urban, and technically sophisticated aspects of American society. The presidency is directly linked to an American national electorate that watches the same TV news, whistles the same tunes, and reads the same issues of *Time* and *Newsweek*. This does *not* mean that every president will fit the cosmopolitan mold nor that a member of the House or Senate may not aspire to address other than parochial concerns. After all, there are leading congressional figures who represent constituencies other than just the folks back home. But this clash between national perspectives and the concerns of diverse local constituencies further complicates the struggle between presidency and Congress that is written into our constitutional system. At a time when Congress feels the need to reassert itself against the power of the presidency and is undergoing internal reorganization and reform, the institutional responses to the two differing constituencies add to the tension between the branches.[8]

> In general, Congress represents the decentralized, particularized, provincial, and diverse patterns of American society. The presidency, on the other hand, has come to represent the more cosmopolitan, urban, and technically sophisticated aspects of American society.

---

[7] Richard Fenno, Jr., "Strengthening a Congressional Strength," in Lawrence C. Dodd and Bruce I. Oppenheimer, *Congress Reconsidered* (New York: Praeger, 1977), pp. 264–265.

[8] See Lawrence C. Dodd's suggestive essay, "Congress and the Quest for Power," in Dodd and Oppenheimer, *Congress Reconsidered*, pp. 269–307.

Built-in Tension

The tension and competition between the executive and legislative branches of our government are an inherent part of our political system.

Many Americans do not understand that the tension and competition is part of our political system, the consequence of the constitutional choices made over two hundred years ago. By not altering the basic institutional aspects of the system, we *continue to choose* to reinforce these aspects. The distinguished constitutional scholar, Edward Corwin, once referred to the constitutional provisions regarding the conduct of foreign affairs as an "invitation to struggle" between Congress and the president. As we demonstrate, other policy areas (for example, economic policy making) fit this description as well. Would you think it wise to try to ease this struggle by allowing for more independent exercise of power by the various branches? Whose program would be adopted? Would a political stalemate be a likely consequence? Or would you think it preferable to adopt some parliamentary scheme uniting the two branches more closely?

OUR NATIONAL LEGISLATORS

The bicameral legislature was a compromise designed to protect the interests of the smaller states while reflecting also the weight of numbers.

As we saw in Chapter 2, the Constitutional Convention almost broke up over the issues of how this new national legislative body was to be organized and which interests were to be represented in it. The compromise arrived at was designed, in part, to protect the interests of the smaller states while reflecting also the weight of numbers. The House of Representatives was viewed by some with apprehension, however, because it might come to reflect popular opinion too directly; in other words, the House was feared for its democratic potential.

The Senate, on the other hand, was designed in part as a check on the lower House with its majoritarian potential. The 1787 Constitution provided that the senators were to be elected indirectly by the state legislatures, and this system prevailed until 1913, when the Seventeenth Amendment made it a direct election (in which senators are chosen by the voters in their states). The Constitution also provides that only a third of the Senate membership shall be elected every two years (along with the entire House). Senators serve six-year terms, three times the length of members of the House of Representatives. Although the founding fathers looked to the Senate to represent the interests of "the rich, the well-born, and the able," today both House and Senate respond in similar fashion to the voting power of their state and local constituencies.

Before examining the functions of Congress, we should first consider the kinds of people who are elected to our national legislature. What kinds of people would you expect to find representing you in Washington? Would you expect to find a perfect cross-section of the American populace?

Most members of Congress are white, middle-class males in their fifties. Representative Shirley Chisholm of New York and Senator S. I. Hayakawa of California are two prominent exceptions to this rule.

The Representatives and Senators: Who Are They?

Our national legislators—all 535 of them—are, on the average, "fiftyish," with senators running about five years older than House members. The 1970s brought larger numbers of younger people, especially to the House, and so the average age is declining. But Congress still, as with all American elites except athletics and the arts, has a distinctly middle-aged coloration.

Senators and representatives are drawn from the professional ranks, with lawyers predominating. One does not find dirt farmers, welfare mothers, or truck drivers among our national legislators. There are no carpenters, electricians, or machinists, and very few school teachers.

While the numbers of blacks, women, Jews, and Catholics are increasing, Congress remains, in its ethnic composition, a predominantly white, male, Protestant institution. It is also an affluent institution. CBS News reported that in 1978 the median net worth among senators was $531,000, while the median net worth among Senate committee chairmen (all Democrats) was $1,000,000. In addition, 25 of them, or 25 percent, are millionaires.

In short, the average member of Congress is by no means the average American. Representatives and senators are members of an elite. By background, training, and life experience, they identify with middle- and upper-middle-class society. They are professionals who have spent their adult lives in daily association with other successful and affluent Americans. What distinguishes our Washington legislators from their middle-class professional compatriots back home is their unusual preoccupation with elective politics. Most of their energies and talents are necessarily devoted to the special art of building and sustaining lengthy careers in Washington.[9]

Geographic diversity is, of course, automatically provided since representatives are residents of the districts they represent while senators must be residents of their states. It used to be argued that the rural areas were disproportionately represented in Congress. This is far less true today. Although less-populated areas may be overrepresented in the Senate, "all nonrural areas, including the largest cities, are over-represented" in the House.[10]

Our Washington legislators typically are political careerists (or, in common terms, "politicians"). The characteristic successful congressional career pattern reveals early experience in local and state politics and then a long period of service on Capitol Hill. In this century there has been a steady increase in **incumbency** among senators and representatives; once you are elected, your prospects for reelection are excellent, in most cases. It is not unusual for three-fourths of the total House membership to be reelected with wide margins of 60 percent or more.[11]

In the light of the above, one is not surprised to find that Congress in the twentieth century has perpetuated an internal pattern of leadership in which senior figures predominate. This pattern is being challenged by the new political generation entering Congress in ever larger numbers. When seventy-five new House Democrats banded together in January 1975, they

Our national legislators are typically members of an economic, educational, and professional elite.

[9] See Lewis Anthony Dexter, "The Representative and His District," in Robert L. Peabody and Nelson W. Polsby, *New Perspectives on the House of Representatives,* 3d ed. (Chicago: Rand McNally, 1976).

[10] See Leroy N. Rieselbach, "Congressmen as 'Small Town Boys': A Research Note," *Midwest Journal of Political Science* 14 (May 1970): 323.

[11] Albert D. Cover and David Mayhew, "Congressional Dynamics and the Decline of Competitive Congressional Elections," in Dodd and Oppenheimer, *Congress Reconsidered,* pp. 54–72. See also Mayhew's essay, "Congressional Elections: The Case of the Vanishing Marginals," *Polity* 6 (1974): 316–317.

were influential in unseating three senior committee chairmen. Nevertheless, both houses of Congress continue to be led by experienced Capitol
Hill career politicians who are as much an aspect of permanent reality as
are senior civil-service bureaucrats (in fact, they are likely to be neighbors
and to play at the same country club).[12]

How, then, does Congress change? Or, does it change? The answer
is yes, but slowly.

Internal Changes

First, we must remember that congressional elections normally produce
some turnover. Senior members do eventually retire or die in office. While
most House seats are considered "safe" (that is, relatively invulnerable to
successful political challenge), there are usually fifty to eighty seats that
are considered marginal. And the pull of presidential coattails may occasionally upset supposedly safe seats. LBJ's landslide victory over Senator
Goldwater in 1964, for example, helped some forty-five new Democrats
gain election, many more than would normally be expected. Since that
time the presidential coattail phenomenon has been weakening, as the
congressional vote appears to be growing increasingly insulated from the
presidential side.

It is also worth noting that congressional turnover has been relatively
substantial during the 1970s. More than half of the House members have
arrived in Washington since 1972. Much of this results from voluntary
turnover following retirements and resignations. Also, there appears to be
a growing interest in retirement among House members who have served
long terms and yet are not apparently in serious political trouble at home.
A very generous congressional pension plan may be encouraging this new
trend.

Second, the leadership corps of Congress is also subject to incremental change over time, especially as one political generation runs its
natural course, giving way to a new generation. This is very much the
case at the present time. The political generation that provided congressional leadership throughout the Cold War era is fading rapidly from the
scene. This new generation of Washington careerists in turn may be expected to produce its own patterns of leadership.

Each generation of political leadership has its own view of the world,
its own policy preferences. Richard Russell, Lyndon Johnson, John Stennis, John McClellan, Carl Albert, Wilbur Mills, Hubert Humphrey, Henry
Jackson, Wayne Hayes, and others occupied the congressional "command
posts" from the 1950s through the 1970s. But new potential leaders are

[12] See Richard E. Neustadt, "Politicians and Bureaucrats," in David B. Truman, *The Congress
and America's Future* (Englewood Cliffs, N.J.: Prentice-Hall (Spectrum), 1965).

emerging in both houses of Congress. Recent elections have brought dozens of new members to Capitol Hill.

Probably it is too early to say with any certainty what the Congress in the 1980s will be like. Congressional leadership will probably be somewhat younger than in the recent past. One also expects to see more minority representatives, more women, and possibly a few more mavericks in our future national legislatures. But Congress continues to attract the ambitious, upwardly mobile, middle-class professional politicians intent on making a career of it in Washington. Politicians today may find it useful to run "against" Washington, but that is where the action is.

THE FUNCTIONS OF CONGRESS

Congress performs three major functions: representation, lawmaking, and legislative oversight.

Congress as an institution performs several different functions in our political system. Each of these major functions—representation, lawmaking, and legislative oversight—carries with it implications for the ways in which Congress relates to the presidency. Each affects the way Congress and the presidency interact to make public policy. In addition, since many Americans fail to understand that Congress must perform all three functions simultaneously, they may be overly critical of the way in which Congress attempts to perform any single function. We shall examine each function in turn, indicating the ways in which each affects the system and our image of it. Congress, like the president, simply cannot be all things to all people.[13]

The Representative Function

Like all legislative bodies freely chosen, Congress has an important representative function to perform. For better or for worse, most members of Congress tend to represent the people who vote for them, or who they hope will vote for them. The working mother who wants a day-care center and the fiscal conservative who does not want to see money spent at all, let alone on a project he or she dislikes, simply cannot be represented at the same time on all issues. The representative must make hundreds of choices, both on the merits of the issues and on the people who count most in his or her political universe.[14] Is this necessarily bad? If so, what would you do about it?

---

[13] Randall B. Ripley, *Congress: Process and Policy* (New York: Norton, 1975). See especially Chapter 2, "Congressional Development."

[14] See Dexter, "The Representative and His District." See also Richard F. Fenno, Jr., *Home Style: House Members in Their Districts* (Boston: Little, Brown, 1978), for a brilliant new interpretation.

Popular
Congressman
plus
Unpopular
Congress

"If a member discusses the House as an institution in order to point out its institutional strengths, he or she runs the risk of being associated with an unpopular institution. So members tend their own constituency relations and even attack Congress from time to time to reenforce their customized political support at home. Whether or not such behavior contributes to the decline of confidence in Congress, it surely does nothing to balance the scales. It is a chicken-egg problem. It is also a problem of governance. Representative government requires more than accountability and responsiveness to constituents; it also requires the governing of constituents. From our home perspective it appears that most members of Congress have enough leeway at home, if they have the will, to educate their constituents in the strengths, as well as the weaknesses, of their institution. They have more leeway than they allow others—even themselves—to think. They can, in other words, identify themselves with their own institution even at the risk of taking some responsibility for what it does. They can, that is, if they will view the trust of their supportive constituents as working capital—not just to be hoarded for personal benefit but to be drawn on, occasionally, for the benefit of the institution. It will be a risk. But by taking that risk, they avoid a possibly greater risk: that Congress may lack public support at the very time when the public needs Congress the most. It would be a tragedy if its representational strength goes unrecognized and unused because the very representatives who make it strong are afraid to acknowledge that strength or use it to help govern the country."

From Richard F. Fenno, Jr., *Home Style: House Members in Their Districts* (Boston: Little, Brown, 1978), pp. 246, 247.

Competent political observers are far from agreement as to how well this representative function is being performed in the contemporary Congress. Some knowledgeable observers, most notably Richard Fenno, Jr., argue that Congress in recent years has become increasingly *more* representative of the diversities of our society than any other major governmental institution. Fenno believes that this transformation also helps in explaining the urge for reform in Congress. As he sees it, one stream of reform has focused on giving an increasing number of members "a piece of the action, by eliminating gross inequalities in internal influence." This broader distribution of influence inside Congress strengthens its representative nature. Fenno makes a similar argument about the reforms that have opened to public view portions of the legislative process that formerly lay hidden.

As is so often the case, these reforms carry costs. "If what we want from Congress is action, neither type of reform can be viewed as a blessing," Fenno continues. The greater the spreading of influence, the harder it is to develop or assert leadership inside Congress. This, in turn, makes the building of a consensus within the Congress on a complicated issue such as energy or welfare reform even more difficult to achieve. Consensus building in Congress is a very time-consuming process, but consensus-type decisions are also more likely to be regarded as fair decisions, so Fenno argues.[15]

Perhaps so, but there are others who feel that the contemporary Congress has become *too* representative; in other words, too easily influenced by local and particularized interests. Calvin Mackenzie has observed: "As members have become more sophisticated at communicating with and serving their constituents, and as interest groups have proliferated and improved their techniques of influence, the representative function has become more valuable to their self-interests (that is, gaining reelection) than the legislative function."[16] In this view, while Congress appears to be a more effective representative body than in the past, its ability to legislate in the national interest has suffered.

Some feel that Congress has become too representative of local and particularized interests, and that as a result its ability to legislate in the national interest has suffered. Others feel that Congress inadequately represents the poor and powerless in society.

There are others who criticize Congress for inadequately representing the poor and the powerless in our society. These critics insist that most career politicians, drawn largely from the privileged, affluent, upper-middle-class professional stratum, are likely to remain largely insensitive to the problems of those fellow citizens at the bottom layer in the social system. The question is not so much whether Congress represents local interests better than national interests, but whether the powerful groups in each locality receive disproportionate attention from most congressional politicians. Fenno, who considers its representational character as one of Congress's greatest institutional strengths, also believes that Congress does not adequately deal with people whose problems "lie at the core of the country's deep-seated social problems."[17] This is not to say that the affluent legislator will necessarily fail to take up the interests and causes of the poor. For example, Senator Kennedy of Massachusetts, member of one of the nation's wealthiest families, is frequently a prominent spokesman for the underprivileged.

The Lawmaking Function

If the first function of Congress, representation, is a very important aspect of its operation, its second, the lawmaking function, may be even more critical to the successful functioning of the American political system.

[15] Richard F. Fenno, Jr., "Strengthening a Congressional Strength," pp. 262-263.

[16] Calvin Mackenzie in a letter to the authors.

[17] Fenno, "Strengthening a Congressional Strength."

Article I of the Constitution states that "all legislative powers herein granted" are vested in Congress. Section 8 makes specific reference to these powers:

1. The power to appropriate funds from the national treasury
2. The power to tax for the common defense and the general welfare
3. The power to regulate interstate and foreign commerce
4. The power to provide for an army and navy
5. The power to declare war
6. The power to coin money
7. The power to create a system of federal courts
8. The power to override a presidential veto
9. The power to confirm major presidential appointments
10. The power to advise and consent in treaty making
11. The power to impeach the president and the vice-president

Whether the founding fathers intended Congress to dominate over the president is a matter of dispute. Whatever their original intent, with the increasing urbanization of America, the rise of industrialization, and the expansion to include fifty states and 220 million persons, legislative initiative is now firmly fixed in the executive branch.

Congress reacts to the president's program

Ever since the Great Depression of the 1930s, our presidents have taken the lead in legislative matters.

Congress now begins each session in January officially awaiting the presentation of the president's program, which will establish the legislative agenda for the year. This presentation, consisting of the State of the Union message, the budget message, and the economic message, has been prepared within the agencies of the institutionalized presidency. To this considerable extent, the Congressional role in lawmaking is one of reacting to policy initiative from the executive.

Nonetheless, the importance of those aspects of the lawmaking process that remain within the domain of Congress should not be underestimated. While the legislative *initiative* has largely passed to the executive, Congress still *disposes*. John F. Kennedy, who had served in House and Senate, found his perspective altered after viewing Congress from the Oval Office of the White House. "The Congress looks more powerful sitting here than it did when I was there in Congress," he commented. "But that is because when you are in Congress you are one of a hundred in the Senate or 435 in the House, so power is divided. But from here I look at the collective power of the Congress, particularly bloc action, and it is a substantial power."[18]

After nine months in office President Carter told a reporter: "My dealing with the Georgia legislature . . . didn't prepare me well for the

[18] Quoted by Neustadt, "Politicians and Bureaucrats," p. 118.

profound influence that Congress both warrants and asserts in defense and foreign matters." [19] He might have added in "energy, taxation, welfare, education, and health" matters as well.

The congressional lawmaking function is critical to the operation of our political system. Although the executive branch establishes policy framework, Congress has the capacity to amend, modify, delay, reduce, or reject major legislative proposals. This role gives Congress substantial power.

As previously noted, all presidents in this century, even the so-called strong presidents, have experienced the same reality. The institutionalized presidency (discussed in Chapter 8) establishes the policy framework; moreover, the president is ideally situated to propose the legislative agenda. Nevertheless, Congress retains the capacity to amend, modify, delay, reduce, or reject major legislative proposals. Congress also "incubates" policy ideas prior to the assertion of presidential initiative as some members of Congress manage to become policy experts who bring forth their own proposals. For example, Henry Jackson, Democratic Senator from Washington, is a leading congressional expert on arms control issues and energy. The Carter administration's initiatives in these fields drew on the ideas of Jackson and other key legislators.

The president's program is processed through a national legislature with substantial powers of its own, including taxation and appropriation, the "bottom line" of modern public policy making. As we note throughout this book, lawmaking in Washington takes place in the context of a continuing political struggle, a struggle that involves interest groups, parties, shifting coalitions, *and* the major governmental institutions. This incredibly complex legislative political process, involving as it does the interaction of the president, Congress, and executive bureaucracies, does not begin and end each calendar year as sessions of Congress do. The process is continuous, often requiring years, perhaps decades, for a major new program to make its way to final enactment. [20]

For example, Medicare, which technically took the form of an amendment to the Social Security law, finally emerged as much the creature of the tax-writing committees of Congress as it was the product of executive initiative. Originally proposed by President Truman, the bill finally managed to make its way through both houses of Congress during the administration of President Johnson, with a powerful assist from the chairman of the House Ways and Means Committee, who previously had opposed the bill. Indeed, this chairman was chiefly responsible for adding *Medicaid* (health care for the needy) as another amendment.

Actually, presidential initiative in relation to the congressional role in lawmaking is even more complicated when looked at closely. A detailed examination of several broad streams of domestic legislation in the period from Eisenhower through the mid-1960s reveals that even after so much of the legislative initiative has shifted to the White House, major legislative

[19] Saul Pett, "An Interview with the President," Associated Press, October 23, 1977.

[20] Charles E. Lindblom, *The Policy Making Process* (Englewood Cliffs, N.J.: Prentice-Hall, 1968).

proposals often find their way into a presidential program only after having first been introduced in an earlier session by individual members of Congress.[21]

The Legislative-Oversight Function

The framers wanted a strong legislative branch with significant lawmaking powers. They got it. They also wanted a legislature that would be representative (but not too representative). They got it. What the founding fathers did not anticipate (at least in its extent) was the legislative-oversight function of Congress. What is **legislative oversight**? Literally, it is the *overseeing* of various aspects of the massive federal administrative apparatus. Congress, through its committees and its power to tax and to appropriate money, looks over the shoulders of the many federal bureaucracies that have sprung up.

Of course, the framers of the Constitution also never anticipated such a tremendous growth in the number and size of the bureaucracies. Nor could they have envisioned the extent of congressional involvement with the bureaucracy, mainly resulting from the appropriation power vested in Congress. The steady expansion of the scope of governmental activity and the accompanying growth of bureaucracy virtually guarantees a strategic position for Congress in exercising legislative oversight over the administration of the federal government. This is a major change, largely brought about in this century.

When all is said and done, the key to congressional power vis-à-vis the chief executive lies in its control of the federal purse strings. For this reason, the most impressive academic studies examining congressional control of the administration focus on the Appropriation Committees of both houses. These committees and their subcommittees, in their annual and continuing examinations of the budgets of every executive bureau, come closer to the detailed operations of modern American government than do any other units of Congress.[22] This is not to say that they come close enough.

Congress has other devices available that have often proved useful in the exercise of its oversight function. Both houses number among their standing committees "Committees on Government Operations" (in the Senate, these are now called the Committee on Governmental Affairs),

> The oversight function of Congress—its power to oversee the operations of the executive branch—derives mainly from committees and its power to tax and to appropriate money.

---

[21] James L. Sundquist, *Politics and Policy* (Washington, D.C.: The Brookings Institution, 1968). Nelson Polsby has stressed this same theme in several of his writings.

[22] The definitive analysis of the congressional appropriations process is found in Richard F. Fenno, Jr., *The Power of the Purse* (Boston: Little, Brown, 1966). For detail on the relationship between appropriation committees and executive agencies, see Joseph P. Harris, *Congressional Control of Administration* (Washington, D.C.: The Brookings Institution, 1964), which remains the best study of congressional oversight.

The Senate Watergate Committee, with Sam Ervin in the center.

established shortly after World War II. Their purpose, as given in their principal charter, is to examine critically the operations of all government agencies covering the entire range of modern public policy. This means, in effect, that these committees have a roving commission to poke into the business of any federal agency. In addition, Congress displays a fondness for special committees, set up as opportunity dictates, to investigate anything that attracts interest in Congress. It was a special committee, headed by then Senator Ervin of North Carolina, that first opened the Watergate cesspool to public view.

Critics express concern that Congress has not been more zealous in oversight. The growth of a complex set of executive bureaucracies, the rise of the institutionalized presidency with its free-wheeling presidential assistants, the emergence of a permanent military establishment of vast size, the clandestine activities of a large intelligence community, the political manipulation of confidential data, and the use of the national security label to cover up the misuses of presidential power are developments of the past several decades that call for greater congressional scrutiny. The question is, did Congress fail to exercise its controls because it favored these developments or because it lacked the will to oppose and criticize? There is also the problem of demoralizing and impairing the efficiency of agencies by constant investigation—often by different congressional committees with different policy orientations. How would you make such trade-offs?

Whether the excesses revealed in the Watergate episode have encouraged Congress to make fuller use of its instruments of legislative oversight remains an open question. The activity of the so-called Church Committee, in investigating the CIA and the FBI in 1975 and 1976, represented the first hard look Congress had given either of these powerful agencies since their creation.

With its major functions of representation, lawmaking, and oversight, Congress looks on paper to be even more powerful than it probably is. If we are to understand why Congress is not as powerful in these areas as it might be, we must examine the styles adopted by members of Congress.

CONTRASTING STYLES

One of the aspects of Congress least understood by the general public is the matter of different styles members of Congress adopt. The manner in which Congress performs its institutional functions depends in part on how the individual members see themselves within the total American political system and how they act. Do they see themselves principally as representatives (looking after the particular interests of their constituents), as lawmakers, or as ombudsmen tracking down wrongdoing in government bureaucracy? Or do they see themselves doing all three? Do they leave initiatives to the White House, accepting the customary executive prerogatives? Or are they concerned with asserting the rights of Congress over and above the president and his agents?

Broadly speaking, a member of the House or Senate can choose his or her career pattern in Congress. Depending on which role individual members of Congress tend to emphasize, there are at least three major styles they can adopt: the service style, the legislative style, and the maverick style.[23]

[23] Roger H. Davidson, *The Role of the Congressman* (Indianapolis: Bobbs-Merrill 1969).

The Service Style

A member of Congress may decide to concentrate on serving the needs of local constituents back in the home district or the state. In this case, his or her congressional office will be organized to provide that service. For example, constituents want federal monies for their local housing and sewage disposal projects. Or they may seek help in dealing with the Social Security Administration and in processing complicated Medicare and Medicaid forms.

An ombudsman is a government official who investigates citizens' complaints against government and its employees, especially bureaucracy and bureaucrats. Ombudsmen originated in Scandinavia, but are becoming increasingly common in the United States.

As a part of the service style, the congressional office often functions as a kind of **ombudsman**, free-wheeling intermediary between the individual citizen and the many federal bureaucracies with their seemingly endless forms, delays, and apparent lack of concern for individuals.

Even the lowliest newcomer to Congress is given a sizeable staff these days. Therefore, each and every member finds it possible to provide this service function and every member does so, at least in part. The representative or senator usually maintains field offices back home in addition to a well-staffed office in Washington. These staffs and their offices are provided at the public expense. The proliferation of staff in recent years is a key element in the so-called institutionalization of Congress.

Deploying the staff: A matter of choice

A major element of choice is involved in the allocation of personnel and funds between Washington and the representative or senator's home base. By keeping the bulk of his or her staff in Washington, the member of Congress is assured of having the resources available to do a good job as legislator while keeping up on major issues. By placing the bulk of the staff back in the district, however, a member of Congress becomes better able to serve the needs of constituents.

Members of Congress do not necessarily choose the service function simply on humanitarian grounds—that is, on the theory that this is how the most people can be helped. The decision may also reflect concern about one's career in Washington. Members of Congress who seek long-term careers in Washington (as most do) will be sensitive to the relationship between the major economic interests of their state and the activities of the federal government. They will wish to see that these dominant interests are well served. It is hard to imagine any significant economic interest whose successful functioning is not related to the programs and structures of the federal government. Thus Louisiana, Texas, and Oklahoma representatives display a special zeal in promoting and protecting the interests of oil and natural gas, while the great fruit-growing combines of Florida and California look to their congressional representatives whenever legislative action is proposed to improve the wages and working conditions of migrant farmers.

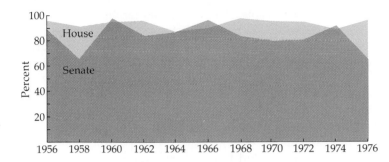

Service and incumbency

When people speak of the power of incumbency, they often mean that those in public office enjoy an advantage over their challengers at election time. The incumbent member of Congress may use the *frank*, or free mailing, to publicize "concern" for constituents. The incumbent enjoys easier access to the media; when a member of Congress speaks, he or she "makes news" more readily than challengers do. What is often overlooked, however, is the power that incumbents derive from service to the folks back home. When individuals are helped by their representative or senator, they tend to remember this and to vote accordingly. The widow whose son was given a hardship discharge from the Army because the senator from Iowa intervened with the Pentagon; the elderly pensioner whose Social Security check was "found" after it was sent to the wrong address; and the visiting teachers whose representative from Alabama got them places on a tour of the White House—all will have their special reasons for voting for the incumbent the next time around.

> A member of Congress who chooses the service style concentrates on the needs of his or her constituents.

The service style may help a member of Congress stay in power *or* move on to something else. Those who begin their Washington careers in the House sometimes wish to move to the Senate (and beyond in some cases). John F. Kennedy, Lyndon B. Johnson, and Richard Nixon were among those who started in the House before winning Senate seats. So too were Senators Henry Jackson and Robert Byrd. There does not appear to be a line running in the other direction, however. Between 1962 and 1974, fifty-eight House members tried for a place in the Senate. During the same period, no one left the Senate to run for the House.

The Legislative Style

At some point in their careers, members of Congress, having established a reasonably secure political base among their constituents, may seek to play a larger role as legislators. Some representatives who are so inclined find satisfaction in working within the legislative process and in helping it to function as smoothly as possible. These representatives may be less concerned about being identified with the substance of this proposal or that and more interested in occupying strategic positions where they may influence many items of legislation over long periods of time. Legislators who master the legislative maze thus find themselves in a position to assist other legislators with their bills. This will help if they later decide to seek one of the major leadership posts.

Some members of Congress manage to combine an interest in procedural aspects with the substance of legislation. The person chairing a standing committee is ideally situated to assist colleagues with their bills while retaining a large measure of influence in shaping major items of legislation reported by his or her committee. Chairing the House Ways and Means Committee, for example, affords ample opportunity for legislative leadership. Since this committee helps in writing all federal tax legislation, the person chairing the committee is in a position to help colleagues on and off the committee who wish to amend the federal tax codes; at the same time, legislative proposals having to do with Social Security, Medicare, and international trade legislation are likely to receive the benefit of the chair's personal influence. The head of Ways and Means is a legislative policy-maker *par excellence.* So too is the chairman of the Senate Finance Committee.[24]

The legislator as "opinion leader"

Some members of Congress choose to become involved with the substance and/or the procedural aspects of legislation. Those who choose the legislative style, however, risk becoming overidentified with controversial issues.

Inherent in the legislative style is the danger of becoming overidentified on one side or the other of controversial issues. Many people write to their representatives in Congress offering their opinions on issues or asking the representative's opinion. With the multiplicity of issues and the inherent danger of losing votes by coming down too firmly on one side or the other (as we noted in Chapter 6), some members of Congress may prefer giving the impression they are not "unalterably" opposed to either side. The answers constituents receive may be phrased so as to indicate what a good public servant the representative is without clearly taking a strong position.

As in other aspects of American life, when members of Congress display a need, an opportunity for some entrepreneur to make money may emerge. Thus, the "robo" service. Congressional representatives and senators may subscribe to a service that provides a set of answers to questions. The service will provide a "pro" answer, a "negative" answer, or something in between, depending on the need. These answers, designed to lose as few votes as possible, cover a wide range of subjects (they change monthly as new issues arise). Subscribers to this service get answers, and the machines to type them on, automatically. An office

[24] John F. Manley, *The Politics of Finance* (Boston: Little, Brown, 1970).

worker types the name of the addressee and a "personal" letter goes out to the citizen with a "personal" answer. In some offices, a human being, although seldom the member of Congress, may even sign a "real" signature (as opposed to a mechanical signer, which is widely used).

There is something a little bizarre about "robo" letters going out to real people, or about one "robo" machine communicating with another— for the bureaucrats and lobbyists have their own "robo" machines as well. A Senate computer, spewing out thousands of "personal" letters, written by "robo" machines, all signed by mechanical devices, to unsuspecting citizens should make us pause and wonder where we are all heading. To a member of Congress bent on publicizing his or her role as legislator, however, these may be necessary evils (if, indeed, they are considered "evils" at all).

The Maverick Style

In addition to concentrating on constituent service and/or legislation and issues, a member of Congress may choose to be a controversial "maverick," combining a flair for publicity with an unwillingness to "get along by going along." Every Congress features a few highly individualistic members, some of whom manage to build long careers in Washington. A leading example is Democratic Senator William Proxmire of Wisconsin, who began his Senate career by challenging Senator Lyndon Johnson, then the majority leader, over a committee assignment.[25] Senator Proxmire has stayed on to become a Senate fixture and to exercise considerable influence, as Chairman of the Banking Committee, senior member of the Joint Economic Committee, and member of the Appropriations Committee. Proxmire continues to dramatize himself as a special "watchdog" of the public interest. One of his favorite targets is special privileges for the Pentagon brass.

In discussing diverse congressional styles—service, legislative, maverick—we have been creating arbitrary categories in order to make the point that members of Congress exercise options in choosing their long-term career patterns. In reality, Congress is a complex human institution allowing more than one official "life-style." There is more than one way of becoming a part of the institution. We should also be clear that probably no real member fits just one category. But whatever the mix may be in individual cases, all new members, upon entering either house of Congress, soon discover that they are working within an institution with ancient patterns of behavior and complicated procedures for conducting official business.

So long as most members give a high priority to serving constituent needs in order to ensure long congressional careers, an uncritical public

[25] See David Mayhew, *Congress: The Electoral Connection* (New Haven, Conn.: Yale University Press, 1974).

Senator William Proxmire (right) chatting with Arthur Burns, then Chairman of the Federal Reserve Board, prior to Burns's appearance before Proxmire's Senate Banking Committee.

should not be astonished when Congress seems deficient as a lawmaking body or ineffective in controlling executive action. With the legislative workload increasing each year, most members of Congress are squeezed from all sides.[26]

HOW CONGRESS WORKS

The workings of Congress have never been easy for the outsider to understand. Woodrow Wilson concluded, almost a hundred years ago, that Congress was too complex and that "very few people do understand it, and its doors are practically shut against the comprehension of the public at large."[27] Wilson's perception remains valid today.

Because Congress is organized in such a way as to distribute power through committees, subcommittees, and the floor leadership, it is difficult to get a firm grasp on the institution in motion. Moreover, the very

[26] See Elizabeth Drew, "A Reporter at Large: Senator I and II," *New Yorker*, September 4–11, 1978.

[27] Woodrow Wilson, *Congressional Government*, p. 58.

fragmented nature of congressional power tends to make it move slowly. As Lewis A. Froman, Jr., has put it:

> I think it is clear that the decentralization of power within the Congress, the distribution of power within this decentralized structure, the many steps which bills must pass through, and the complexity of the rules and procedures which protect, quite closely, the rights of minorities, add up to a decision-making body which generally favors conservative interests and the *status quo*. [28]

In our exploration of the twisting corridors of congressional power, we begin with an examination of the formal positions of power; move to an analysis of the committee structure; and conclude with a study of how a bill becomes law.

Formal Positions of Power

The most important formal positions of power in Congress include the president of the Senate, the Speaker of the House, and the majority and minority leaders in the House and Senate. The House Speaker and the Senate majority leader are especially influential. Each house of Congress also uses a whip system.

The job of **president of the Senate** is filled automatically by the vice-president of the United States. The Senate president rarely exercises real influence in the Senate. Voting only in the case of a tie, the Senate president is not usually consulted by the Senate leadership when important decisions are made. Indeed, this role in the Senate is largely ceremonial. The majority party, in subtle recognition of this, provides a **president pro tempore** of the Senate—by custom, the senior senator—who serves as the official chair during the many expected absences of the vice-president. Since the day-by-day task of presiding over the usually almost empty Senate floor is a thankless chore, the presiding officer's chair is frequently occupied by junior members, who are said to be "logging in" their time—filling in for the president pro tem, who is filling in for the vice-president!

The **majority leader of the Senate** is a person of considerable influence within the body, but the degree of influence varies with the personality of the individual leader. To some extent, the job is what the leader makes of it. Lyndon Johnson, always the activist and builder-of-consensus, achieved a national reputation while serving as majority leader. Senator Mansfield, his successor, chose a less active role, one in keeping with his low-key style. [29]

---

[28] Lewis A. Froman, Jr., *The Congressional Process*, p. 3.

[29] See Rowland Evans and Robert Novak, "Lyndon B. Johnson: The Ascent to Leadership," and Andrew J. Glass, "Mike Mansfield, Majority Leader," in Norman J. Ornstein, *Congress in Change* (New York: Praeger, 1975).

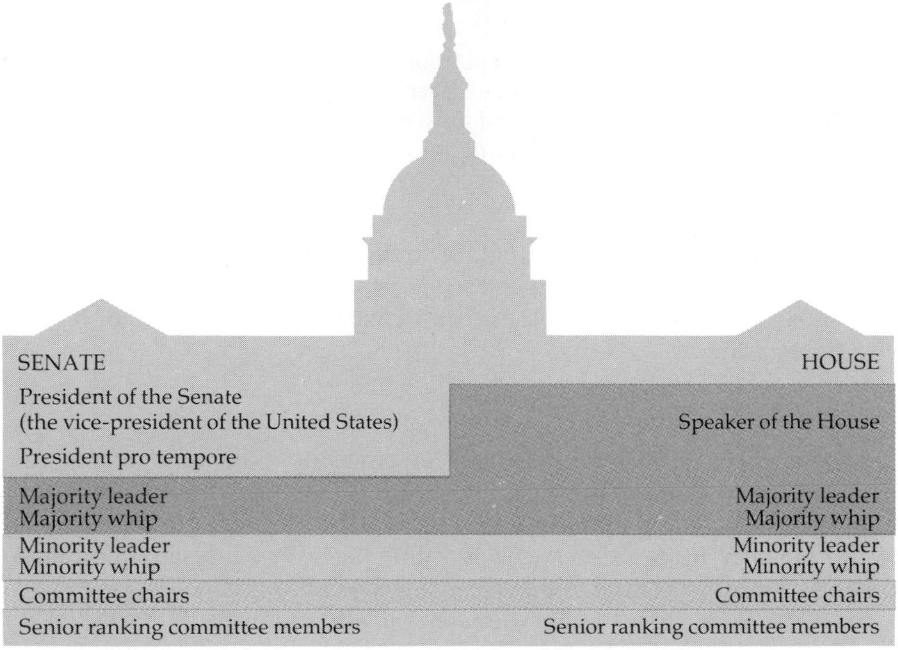

SENATE	HOUSE
President of the Senate (the vice-president of the United States)	Speaker of the House
President pro tempore	
Majority leader Majority whip	Majority leader Majority whip
Minority leader Minority whip	Minority leader Minority whip
Committee chairs	Committee chairs
Senior ranking committee members	Senior ranking committee members

Fig. 9.4
Leadership organization of Senate and House, majority and minority parties. Real majority leadership, shown in color, is different from the formal leadership.

Senator Robert Byrd, who became majority leader in 1977, functions as an efficient operator of a complex machine. He does not lead, as Mansfield did, by force of character, but is given his authority because his Democratic colleagues appear content to have the position in the hands of a Senate insider who will keep things moving along while much of the real power is wielded by such key chairmen as Russell Long, Henry Jackson, Edmund Muskie, Warren Magnuson, and John Stennis, among others.

The majority leader plays the key role in scheduling activity on the floor of the Senate, a notoriously slow-moving body. He has the right to be the first speaker heard on the floor at the opening of each legislative day. It is his responsibility to determine the Senate agenda, in consultation with the minority leader. This aspect of the Senate functions smoothly because in recent decades the minority leader has accepted a role as junior partner in the arrangement.

In this picture of President Carter shaking hands after the signing of a bill, we can see several powerful members of Congress. At the extreme left is Senator Russell Long (Democrat—Louisiana), and on the right are Representative Al Ullman (Democrat—Oregon), Chairman of the House Ways and Means Committee, and Senator Robert Byrd of West Virginia, Senate Majority Leader.

The **Speaker of the House** is the leader of the majority party in the House. The Speaker works closely with the majority leader. Together, they provide a more distinctly partisan approach than is typically found in the Senate.

The Speakership is not the dominant force it was when Thomas Brackett Reed in the late nineteenth century and Uncle Joe Cannon early in the twentieth century shaped the office into a position of almost autocratic power (albeit in the interests of a party majority). A revolt of rank-and-file members in 1910 against Speaker Cannon stripped the Speaker of much of his centralized authority. As a result, leadership in the House is shared by the Speaker and a group of senior colleagues.[30]

However, the Speaker remains, potentially, the most powerful member of the House. Speaker Thomas "Tip" O'Neill has shown signs of

[30] Neil MacNeil, *Forge of Democracy: The House of Representatives* (New York: McKay, 1963).

Biography

Speaker O'Neill: Shaper of Energy Policy

Congress was severely criticized in the mid-1970s for its inability to put together a coherent national energy policy. Sensitive to this criticism—and others—of Congress, the new House Speaker, Thomas ("Tip") P. O'Neill, Democrat of Massachusetts, went all out in support of President Carter's complicated and controversial energy package.

For three months, Speaker O'Neill kept the pressure on his fellow House Democrats in support of the bill. When the bill (HR8444) passed the House early in August 1977 by a 244–177 vote, it contained most of what the Carter administration wanted, except a tax on gasoline. O'Neill's forceful leadership of the Democratic majority left House Republican leaders unhappy. They charged that they had been virtually shut out on all decisions relating to national energy policy. With the assistance of the Carter administration, O'Neill beat back a determined effort by House Republicans and oil-state Democrats to end federal regulation of natural gas prices.

The Speaker's personal leadership was apparent from the outset, when he persuaded the House to create an unprecedented ad hoc committee on energy. This committee, chaired by Representative Ashley, Democrat of Ohio, reconciled the various versions of the bill as they emerged, piecemeal, from five standing committees. The Speaker also worked closely with veteran Representative Richard Bolling, Democrat of Missouri, his ally on the Rules Committee, so that a modified "closed" rule governed floor debate on the bill, making amendments difficult.

Finally, in a rare floor speech, the Speaker spoke out against the natural gas deregulation amendment.

"Slapping his hands together for emphasis, waving his arms, booming his Boston Irish voice, O'Neill exhorted his colleagues to vote against 'big oil.'

"'Never have I seen such an influx of lobbyists in this town,' the Speaker shouted. 'America is watching this legislation more than it has watched any legislation in years. Will the House fail? Can the House act? Can the House pull together on energy policy?'

"'Believe me, the future of this nation. . . . is at stake.' O'Neill concluded to applause." *

The deregulation amendment lost 199–227.

The Speaker had prevailed. Unfortunately for the Speaker, however, the Senate held quite different ideas on energy, leading to a long stalemate.

* *Congressional Quarterly* Weekly Reports LXXXV, No. 32 (August 1977), p. 1627.

offering a new style of personal leadership in a House that features a broader diffusion of influence than in the past. Since the 94th Congress, the Speaker has had the power to select the Democratic members of the Rules Committee, and the Rules Committee remains a key instrument in the scheduling of bills for House action. The Speaker also appoints members of select and conference committees, and grants recognition to those who wish to speak on the floor of the House. O'Neill has not hesitated to speak himself on critical issues when the vote is close. More than any other member, the Speaker is the director of floor activity; this helps explain his considerable influence among his colleagues in the majority.

The two most powerful members of Congress are generally thought to be the majority leader of the Senate and the Speaker of the House. However, these formal leadership positions may be overshadowed by the leaders of powerful committees on specific issues.

Both Houses of Congress have party **whips** who assist the leadership, majority and minority, in communicating with their rank-and-file colleagues and in getting accurate "nose counts" (advance intelligence on how members are likely to vote).

These formal leadership positions, dependent as they are on the personalities, character, and political skills of the individuals who occupy them, are sometimes overshadowed by the leaders of the committees. While the formal positions operate to centralize power and authority, the committee structure is a continual force leaning toward the decentralization and fragmentation of power. It is to the committees that we now turn our attention.

Congress: A Collection of Committees

A torrent of legislative proposals inundates every session of Congress, and each year the flood seems to increase. Each proposal is sent to an appropriate **standing committee**—an established committee in the congressional system designed to consider specific issue areas. The 435 House members devolve into twenty-two standing committees, while 100 Senators share positions on seventeen standing committees. These committees, and especially their subcommittees (of which there are more than 200), are the most important element in the congressional system. They handle the major burden of legislative work—separating wheat from chaff, and endlessly refining (coordinating), reworking, and modifying the one legislative item in twenty that is destined to become a public law.

So great is the tendency of Congress as a whole to accept the judgment of its committees in their areas of specialized competence that House and Senate may be viewed almost as collections of "little legislatures." Clem Miller, who once served in the House, put it this way: "Congress," he wrote to his constituents, "is a collection of committees that come together in a chamber periodically to approve of one another's actions."[31]

Just as standing committees form the nucleus of legislative activity, so do the people chairing these committees constitute, along with the formal

[31] Clem Miller, *Member of the House* (New York: Scribner's, 1962).

leaders, the core of congressional leadership. In this century, the heads of these committees have been selected on the basis of "seniority," a principle that is finally being modified at the insistence of a new political generation. Furthermore, the proliferation of subcommittees in recent years has served to broaden the patterns of influence within Congress.

Seniority: the controlling principle

The **seniority system** in Congress required that the important job of chairing a committee go *automatically* to the committee member of the majority party with the longest *continuous* service on the committee.[32] In recent years the newer generation of members of Congress challenged the seniority system as the sole principle for organizing Congress. In the House, the assignment of chairships is now subject to the approval by majority vote of the legislative party in caucus. In the first session of the 94th Congress (1975), a group of seventy-five new House Democrats added their weight to an existing liberal Democratic bloc and denied the chairships of three major committees to three senior members of long standing. What may be equally important, however, is that with one exception these chairships then went to the *next* senior members of those committees.

The most important elements in the congressional system are the committees, and the leaders of these committees occupy strategic positions within Congress.

The people chairing the committees, however selected, occupy strategic positions within Congress. They, often in working relationship with the ranking minority member, usually establish their committee's agenda and the subcommittee assignments. They, more than any other member, select the professional staff that is to serve the majority side of the committee (the senior minority members select the staff to serve their side). They also hold the initiative in scheduling committee hearings and in deciding the roster of witnesses to appear at hearings. After committee members have held hearings, heard testimony, consulted with staff members, and decided by a majority vote to report a bill favorably, the people chairing the committees normally manage the bill once it reaches the floor of the chamber. Here again we see important change at work. Today, those who chair the subcommittees are shouldering an increasing portion of the responsibility for managing legislation on the floor.

Especially in the House, where time for debate is sharply limited, even in the case of major bills, chairpersons decide which members of their committee shall have an opportunity to speak. If they are technically only the first among equals so far as their votes in committee are concerned, in fact, chairpersons who are worth their salt are likely to appear a lot "more equal" than their committee colleagues. They are likely to be aware of their preeminence, and so are their colleagues. Little wonder that mem-

[32] Barbara Hinckley, *The Seniority System in Congress* (Bloomington: Indiana University Press, 1971).

bers of the newer political generation entering Congress would like to either displace or please the people who chair the committees in which they are interested.

More powerful committees

Members of Congress display a keen interest in gaining assignment to the "right" committees. Some committees carry greater prestige—and more power—than others. Knowledgeable students of Congress, as well as members of Congress, disagree about the ranking of committees. But most would agree that Appropriations, Armed Services, and the tax-writing committees (Ways and Means in the House and Finance in the Senate) should be ranked as major committees.[33]

Assignments on Judiciary and the committees dealing with foreign affairs are also eagerly sought after. A member representing the coast of Massachusetts or Oregon is likely to find an assignment on Merchant Marine and Fisheries congenial. Conversely, virtually no one today would prefer serving on the District of Columbia Committee.

[33] Richard F. Fenno, Jr., *Congressmen in Committees* (Boston: Little, Brown, 1973).

The impeachment process of President Nixon began in the House Judiciary Committee, and the members of this committee were thrust into national prominence for a brief period in the summer of 1974.

Like college students, individual members go about their committee work with varying degrees of intensity. Those who gain reputations for being willing to labor long hours at the drudgery of committee work may be rewarded when subcommittee chairship vacancies occur. For example, the House Appropriations Committee enjoys a reputation for demanding hard work within an institutional life-style that is distinctly its own. Those who find work on such a committee congenial also enjoy a measure of prestige within the larger body.[34]

Special committees

Our discussion of committees has centered around those standing committees that deal with fairly well defined subject matters. These standing committees handle most of the day-by-day legislative work of Congress. In describing the congressional oversight function earlier, we noted the importance of **special committees**. These committees prove extremely useful when Congress wishes to react (or appear to react) quickly to some new, usually dramatic, problem.

The creation of special select committees has been useful to Congress when it wishes to examine a problem.

Normally, when a special select committee has completed its study or investigation, the committee issues its report and disbands. The so-called Church Committee (named for its chairman, Senator Frank Church of Idaho), established in the 94th Congress to examine the CIA, the FBI, and related activities, carried out a year-long investigation, recommended in its final report the creation of a permanent Senate committee to oversee the intelligence bureaucracies, and then promptly disbanded. The recommendation was acted on by the full Senate, and the new permanent committee was established. There have been occasions when special committees have hung on and then have become permanent, such as the committees on small business and aging.

The Congressional Maze: How a Bill Becomes a Law

Only one in every twenty bills becomes a law. The process has often been described as the "running of a maze" or "negotiating a labyrinth." This complex process is only dimly understood by most Americans.

Let us assume that you are a member of Congress. You have served two terms already and are now starting your third. You have done enough constituent service to be reelected by larger and larger margins, and now you feel you have more time to address the legislative functions.

Let us also assume that you have been a "good soldier" during your previous two terms. You have generally voted with your party and, more important perhaps, with whoever is chairing your committee. You have

[34] Fenno, *The Power of the Purse*.

not attacked Congress (at least, not in Washington and not back in your district if any national media were around), and you have not made a nuisance of yourself by arguing with your colleagues on the floor of the House.

You are from a district that has a number of senior citizens, and you are concerned about the difficulty many of them have in getting around. You would like to introduce a bill providing for federal tax credits to provide incentives to owners of commercial buildings to install ramps to bypass stairs.

Touching bases

First you sound out the leader of your committee, say Ways and Means. You ask his or her advice on whether this would make a good bill. If you can get your chairperson interested in your bill, you will have made considerable headway. If the chairperson is interested, and willing to keep an eye on the bill, you will want to get as many of your colleagues as you can to cosponsor the bill. Some will want to do so because they believe in the bill. Others will go along with you because you have helped them out in the past. Still others, although they do not particularly care for the bill, will go along because they like you personally. You would also be wise to check with the White House legislative liaison aides (especially if the president is of your party). You want presidential endorsement or, at least, neutrality.

The bill will be dropped into the "hopper," a box on the House floor, and will then be referred to a committee. At this stage, there is a certain amount of luck and/or politics involved. You will want your chairperson to try to steer it to your committee if the subject matter at all permits this. If some other committee grabs it, your chairperson may lose interest, and the other committee may change it in such a way as to defeat your purpose. The people chairing the committees and the formal (party) leaders are the key people in working out these assignments.

Let us assume your bill ends up in your committee and your chairperson maintains his or her interest in the project. It will then be assigned to a subcommittee (hopefully, the one on which you sit) for further drafting work and, possibly, hearings. Hearings these days are usually open and, since this is likely to be a popular bill, you will want them open. You will also want to hold all or part of those hearings back in your district, if possible. This will give you a good deal of publicity at home, thus alerting senior citizens to your efforts. On the other hand, every subcommittee cannot go traipsing around the country to Montana and Florida and Arizona for every bill, so you may well have to settle for an open hearing in Washington, which your press assistant can then bring to the attention of the voters.

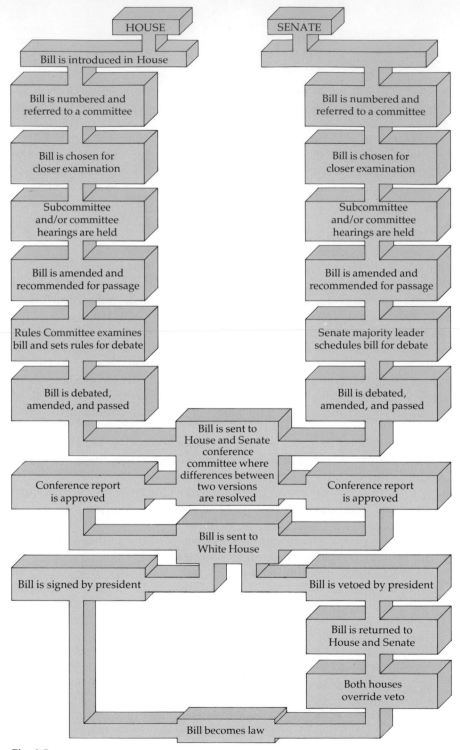

Fig. 9.5
Getting a bill through Congress.

Moving toward decisions

The subcommittee will then recommend to the full committee what course of action to take. Ordinarily, the recommendations of the subcommittee will carry considerable weight with the full membership (after all, they want *their* subcommittee reports respected), but the parent committee does have the power to rewrite the bill completely or to report the bill out to the House or Senate with or without amendments. On the other hand, the full committee may do nothing. If a bill is reported from committee, it is accompanied by a written report and often by a minority report as well. In the House, a bill is placed on one of several specialized House calendars. If it clears the House Rules Committee—a traffic-cop committee—it will then be debated on the floor of the House under the terms the Rules Committee has set for it. The terms include the times for debate and what amendments, if any, will be allowed.[35] In the Senate, a bill is placed on the calendar. It may be "called up" for debate and vote by unanimous consent (informal agreement to do so already having been arranged by the majority leader in consultation with the minority leader), or by a majority vote of the Senate.

Your bill is relatively noncontroversial (nobody really wants to appear to be against handicapped senior citizens), and, if there is no opposition from the White House, it may well pass the House with bipartisan support.

The other chamber

Once a bill is passed by one chamber, it is sent on to the other. Your bill is now out of your hands and it may be that this is the last you will see of it. The Senate has the option of passing it as it is, sending it to a committee, or ignoring it. Let us assume that a senator of the other party is worried about a possible challenge from you for his or her seat two years hence. He or she may not want you to get credit for such a bill. Or he or she may "redesign" the bill as if it were totally new and get it passed by the Senate.

Conference committee: critical stage

When there are major differences in bills that have passed their respective houses (as is often the case), a conference will be sought. In each house the formal leaders then name their conferees. A **conference committee** is typically composed of senior members of the standing committee that handled the bill, although these days token representation is often given to younger members as well. The conferees have the task of ironing out disagreements; their purpose is to find a compromise version that will muster majority support when taken back to the floor of both houses. In

[35] James A. Robinson, *The House Rules Committee* (Indianapolis: Bobbs-Merrill, 1963).

most cases, the conferees are able to reach some form of agreement and report back to their respective houses, but sometimes the conferees reach agreement only after important substantive changes have been made in the legislation. And it is perfectly possible that they may not be able to reach agreement at all.[36]

In this particular case, you may have taken care of your rival's concern by offering to share the credit and publicity surrounding the bill's passage. This may speed conference agreement, and the agreed-upon bill will be sent back to both houses. Each house has the power to approve or reject what the conference reports. If it is accepted, the bill in its final version is signed by the Speaker of the House and the president of the Senate before being sent to the White House, where the president may sign the bill into law, allow it to become law without his signature, or veto the bill.

If, as a junior member of Congress, you sponsor a bill that becomes a law, it will be a day to celebrate and remember. Who knows, it may even whet your appetite to play a more consistent legislative role.

CONGRESSIONAL REFORM

The slow workings of these committees, and their oligarchical internal power structures, are important reasons advanced for congressional reform. Suggested reforms run from radical reorganization of Congress along British parliamentary lines, to simply scrapping the seniority principle, to merely replacing the more aged and autocratic committee leaders.

With the 1974 elections, a number of freshmen members of Congress, riding a tide of reformist sentiment, assaulted the seniority principle. As we have noted, in the Democratic caucus of January 1975, they succeeded in dumping three aging chairmen. The freshmen were proud, excited, and sometimes verbal about their success in their zeal to assert liberal congressional authority against a conservative president.

At the same time a number of the more senior members of Congress felt the freshmen were becoming tiresome in their insistence on reform and their loud pronouncements about it. Thus, in the latter months of the 94th Congress, certain maneuvers were undertaken to blunt the liberal freshmen's sense of accomplishment. In what has become known as the "battle of the vetoes," President Ford sought to divide the reformers (many of whom were Democrats). Some senior members of Congress did little to prevent the president from teaching the freshmen the facts of political life. First, Ford vetoed the Emergency Farm Act of 1975, an antirecessionary move to assist farmers. This caused fifty urban Democrats

---

[36] Gilbert Y. Steiner, *The Congressional Conference Committee* (Urbana: University of Illinois Press, 1951).

to defect and uphold the veto (since they were for fiscal responsibility *and* had few farmers on their city blocks).

The rural members were angry and anxious to retaliate. When Ford also vetoed the Emergency Employment Act of 1975, they were only too happy to sustain the veto and defeat one of the pet projects of the urban members. Several more successful Ford vetoes followed, and a number of the freshmen, stunned and shocked, retreated into more familiar patterns of congressional activity.

Another reform movement emphasizes the opening of congressional activity to public scrutiny. Conference committees, the "marking," or revision, of bills, and House Appropriations Committee hearings were conducted for decades behind closed doors. With some exceptions, they are now open to public view. At the same time, there has also been a pronounced change in the attitudes of new members, many of whom reject the notion that a first-term legislator should be seen and not heard. Today power is undoubtedly shared more evenly within committees due to the strengthening of party caucuses, the weakening of the automatic succession of committee leaders, and the spreading of choice committee assignments more widely among junior members.

As we noted earlier in this chapter, these reforms, of course, have consequences, some of them at least partly unintended.

The costs of reform are illustrated by asking how some two hundred subcommittee chairships would be filled if the seniority principle were discarded altogether? The alternative of electing all chairpersons (and ranking minority members) in a party caucus would surely guarantee an intense internal political struggle. Perhaps there would be more "action," but it might be the only action Congress would have time for.

In any event, time-honored patterns of leadership do not give way easily. These patterns do change, but very few changes ever work quite the way the proponents intended. And, as we have seen, change in Congress carries costs. For example, the representatives of the old "white supremacy" South provided much of the leadership in a congressional bipartisan coalition during the period following World War II. This coalition, which was never formalized but was quite real, was often referred to as "the conservative coalition."[37] Only a few members of the coalition survived into the late 1970s as death and retirement took their toll. In their place come younger representatives from a new South, an area of the country that is changing possibly more than any other. The gradual demise of the conservative coalition involves changes in the structure of influence in Congress. This, in turn, reflects significant political and social changes

There have been various movements toward congressional reform, some of which have gradually changed the character of the congressional system. Today power is undoubtedly shared more evenly due to the strengthening of party caucuses, the weakening of the automatic succession of committee leaders, and the spreading of choice committee assignments more widely among junior members.

[37] See John F. Manley, "The Conservative Coalition in Congress," in Dodd and Oppenheimer, *Congress Reconsidered*, pp. 75, 95, and compare with John C. Donovan, *The Policy Makers* (Indianapolis: Bobbs-Merrill, 1970).

taking place within our society that are likely in time to bring changes in public policies.[38] The nature of these policy changes will be greatly influenced, no doubt, by the way this new political generation looks at and participates in American politics.

SUMMARY

We have been examining one of the oldest national legislatures in the world. It is a natural competitor against the executive branch. Yet the White House and the various bureaucracies *must* work with Congress—at least some of the time. How this mix of competition and cooperation is managed at any time may benefit the entire nation, or it may lead to stalemate and confusion.

Congress has a number of functions. We have looked at the most important: representation, lawmaking, and oversight. In addition, we have examined the internal workings of Congress; who is in Congress and why; and how members of Congress adopt differing styles of activity.

We have examined the making of laws; how the ideas of individual members of Congress get translated into laws that apply to all the people in the United States. We have also noted some of the ways in which a political career and its demands help determine which bills become law and how.

Today, as so often in the past, Congress finds itself the center of controversy. Many people criticize its inability to solve such problems as pollution, welfare, inflation, and unemployment. Still others object to the way Congress works: the modified seniority system, the slow pace of lawmaking, the far-reaching power of small and nearly anonymous subcommittees. Other Americans are appalled by what they take to be the abuse of power by some members of Congress and the way in which members of Congress seek to maintain themselves in office.

At the same time that Americans look to Congress to check the growth of presidential power, or to stop the excesses of such powerful institutions as the CIA and the FBI, they seem to lack faith in Congress as an institution. Some Americans will want to influence the directions in which Congress should move, and will support interest groups that lobby for reform. Others may want to support congressional candidates who are pledged to try to bring about change. Most Americans will not do anything to try to influence the course of change. Will those who so choose continue to have the right to hold Congress in low esteem? How does the indifference of many citizens affect the functioning of this long-lived and durable institution? How will Congress adapt to the changing demands and the shifting moods of American politics in the 1980s?

[38] See Norman J. Ornstein and David W. Rohde, "Seniority and Future Power in Congress," in Ornstein, *Congress in Change*, pp. 72–87.

KEY TERMS

incumbency

representation

lawmaking

legislative initiative

legislative oversight

ombudsman

service style

legislative style

maverick style

president pro tempore

majority leader of the Senate

Speaker of the House

party whip

standing committee

seniority system

special committee

conference committee

SUGGESTED READINGS

BOLLING, RICHARD, *House Out of Order* (New York: Dutton, 1965).

A personal account by a liberal congressional reformer of the workings of the House.

CLAPP, CHARLES L., *The Congressman: His Work As He Sees It* (Washington, D.C.: The Brookings Institution, 1963).

An attempt to portray the job of being a member of Congress as the member sees it. Based on extensive interviewing of House members. Unfortunately, this study does not include many senior members, and is now dated.

CLAUSEN, AAGE R., *How Congressmen Decide: A Policy Focus* (New York: St. Martin's Press, 1973).

An attempt to assess how members of Congress actually arrive at their decisions on policy.

DAVIDSON, ROGER H., *The Role of the Congressman* (New York: Pegasus, 1969).

A careful assessment of the congressional "role" by a political scientist who understands the inner workings of Congress better than most.

FENNO, RICHARD F., JR., *The Power of the Purse* (Boston: Little, Brown, 1966).

An examination of the appropriations procedure and its implications, with emphasis on its political characteristics. A classic study.

FROMAN, LEWIS A., JR., *The Congressional Process: Strategies, Rules, Procedures* (Boston: Little, Brown, 1967).

The standard work on Congress's elaborate procedures; argues that the procedures contain a conservative, status quo bias.

HINKLEY, BARBARA, *The Seniority System in Congress* (Bloomington: Indiana University Press, 1971).

Study of the seniority principle within the context of the congressional system.

MAYHEW, DAVID R., *Congress: The Electoral Connection* (New Haven, Conn.: Yale University Press, 1974).

A ground-breaking examination of the ways in which Congress is being reshaped institutionally so as to make the reelection of incumbents its central objective.

RIPLEY, RANDALL B., *Congress: Process and Policy* (New York: Norton, 1976).

A solid assessment of congressional decision-making procedures.

Men may come and men may go,
Secretaries of the Government
departments and Assistant Secretaries of
the Government departments may come
and may go, but the bureaucrats go on
forever. . . . No matter how zealous the
new Secretary, the Under Secretary, and
the Assistant Secretary may be, the civil
service bureaucrats will be all around
them. Even though the Secretary, the
Under Secretary, and the Assistant
Secretary take the wings of the morning
and fly to the uttermost parts of the sea,
even there the bureaucrats will be by their
side.

Senator Paul Douglas

Usually the social esteem of the officials
as such is especially low where the
demand for expert administration and the
dominance of status conventions are
weak. This is especially the case in the
United States; it is often the case in new
settlements by virtue of their wide fields
for profit-making and the great instability
of their social stratification.

Max Weber

CHAPTER 10 THE FEDERAL BUREAUCRACY: A FOURTH BRANCH?

"Bureaucracy."

"Bureaucrat."

These words are often heard in political campaigns these days, but never favorably. Politicians running for office use them as code words to exploit public disenchantment.

Young Americans are exhorted to prepare themselves for careers as doctors, lawyers, biochemists, meteorologists, urban planners, teachers, nuclear physicists, executives, and environmental engineers, among others. Seldom are they urged to prepare themselves to become "government bureaucrats."

Nevertheless, the likelihood is that one in every six of you reading this chapter will eventually find work on a public payroll, not a private one. This includes those entering all of the professions we have just listed.

It is easy to criticize "bureaucracy," but a lot more difficult to understand its all-pervasive reach or to find effective means of controlling its activities.

The federal bureaucracy has emerged as a principal rival of the president, Congress, and the courts in shaping national policy.

This chapter examines the growth of our public bureaucracies, especially the federal bureaucracy. This fourth branch of government has emerged as a principal rival of the president, Congress, and the courts in shaping national policies. We also note the rapid growth in recent years of public bureaucracies at the state and local levels. Indeed, in the two decades between Eisenhower and Nixon, during which the nation's population increased more than 30 percent, federal civilian employment was increasing by a modest 8 percent while the number of state and local public employees increased by a whopping 129 percent. Little wonder, then, that governors have often been among the severest critics of bureaucracy. This aspect of our changing federalism often goes unnoticed.

Shortly after he became governor of our largest state in 1975, Jerry Brown of California decreed a ban on state-issued briefcases for bureaucrats. Perhaps Brown's approach was slightly more sophisticated than the one suggested by former Governor George Wallace of Alabama, who repeatedly declared that if he were elected president, the federal bureaucrats' briefcases would be tossed into the Potomac River. But each governor in his own way was protesting the expansion of bureaucracy and the endless red tape that inevitably goes with it.

After two and a half years in the governor's office in Sacramento, Governor Brown conceded that he was not winning his battle with the bureaucracy: "All we can try to do is to cope with it, make it work better. I've tried to eliminate some agencies, but they keep coming back. Government is going to grow under right-wing, left-wing, or middle-of-the-road administrations. The question is at what rate and in which direction."[1]

[1] The *New York Times*, July 12, 1977.

Jerry Brown, Governor of California: "All we can do is try to cope with it . . . ."

Jimmy Carter, as presidential aspirant, also adopted an antibureau-cratic tone, making reorganization of the federal bureaucracy a major campaign theme. Yet one of Carter's first major proposals called for the creation of still another superbureaucracy, with enormous powers to reg-ulate and control: a Department of Energy, headed by a versatile super-technocrat, with nearly 20,000 civil service employees (bureaucrats) and an annual budget exceeding $10 billion. We shall examine the development of this new bureaucracy more carefully later in this chapter.

A quarter of a century earlier, while campaigning for the presidency, Dwight D. Eisenhower had been critical of the New Deal welfare pro-grams. Some naive conservatives had assumed that Eisenhower's land-slide victories in the 1950s foreshadowed the gradual undoing of the so-called welfare state (then in its relative infancy). On the contrary, rather

© Chicago Tribune–New York News Syndicate, Inc. Reprinted by permission.

than abolish the New Deal bureaucracies, Republican President Eisenhower, during his first year in the White House, elevated them to cabinet status with the creation of a Department of Health, Education, and Welfare. Today, HEW serves as a kind of bureaucratic holding company for a complex set of organizational structures reaching into just about every conceivable aspect of the daily lives of the American people. With 100,000 personnel and responsibility for administering a conglomeration of programs having a total annual expenditure in excess of $200 billion, HEW now exceeds the Department of Defense in size and scope.

Energy and HEW are examples of the steady growth of bureaucracy, especially as these organizations grow in power and influence within the federal government.

BUREAUCRACY: WHO, WHAT, AND WHERE?

Bureaucracy is by no means a Washington invention. It is a general phenomenon in today's world. The term bureaucracy refers to *any* administrative system, such as a government agency, that is permanent, that operates on standardized procedures, where the jobs performed have formal and specialized descriptions, and where direction and orders are supposed to come from the top down (hierarchical organization). General Motors is a large bureaucracy. In America today, "the federal bureaucracy" has come to designate the sprawling and diverse agencies of the executive branch of the national government.

This chapter offers a description and political analysis of the Washington bureaucracy. We are primarily interested in understanding how this bureaucracy functions within our governmental system; how it relates to the presidency and Congress; and the role it plays in making public policies, both domestic and foreign. Mark Twain's commentary on the weather may apply equally well to the federal bureaucracy: "Everybody talks about it, but nobody does anything about it." If this is true, we would like to know why.

How are we to explain bureaucracy's apparent ability to overwhelm the good intentions of ambitious politicians who *say* they would like to control it? Does bureaucracy have a momentum of its own? Is governmental bureaucracy, as Peter Drucker has suggested, moving beyond our ability to control it?[2]

Graham Allison, a student of bureaucratic politics, has stated the problem precisely:

> To be responsive to a wide spectrum of problems, governments consist of large organizations, among which primary responsibility for particular tasks is divided. Each organization attends to a special set of problems and acts in quasi-independence on these problems. . . . Government leaders can substantially disturb, but not substantially control, the behavior of these organizations.[3]

Are you bothered by the idea that government leaders may "substantially disturb" but "not substantially control" the behavior of HEW and the Pentagon? What does this suggest about the nature of our constitutional system and the condition of democratic politics? What are the implications for the future?

The Rise of the National Bureaucracy: A Response to Social Change

The huge administrative superstructure of the federal government grew largely out of profound changes taking place in our society and in the international arena since the 1930s. In Chapter 3 we noted the very small number and size of the original cabinet departments. In 1792 there were only 780 federal civil servants; at the end of John Adams's administration

A bureaucracy is any administrative system that is permanent, that operates on standardized procedures, where the jobs performed have formal and specialized descriptions, and where direction and orders are supposed to come from the top down.

[2] Peter F. Drucker, *The Age of Discontinuity* (New York: Harper & Row, 1969), p. 220.

[3] Graham T. Allison, *Essence of Decision* (Boston: Little, Brown, 1971), p. 67.

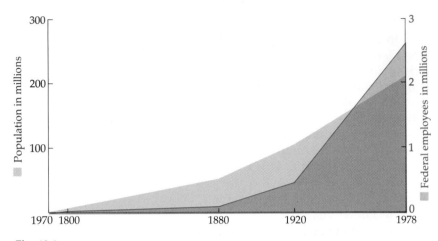

Fig. 10.1
The growth of the federal government as compared to population growth.

in 1800, there were 3,000. There were perhaps 95,000 federal civil servants when Grover Cleveland became president in 1885, and by 1925 there were nearly half a million. This was certainly steady growth, but it had taken a century and a quarter.

Over the *next half century*, however, the figure jumped to 2,700,000 civilian employees (as of 1978). Not all these employees work in Washington, of course. The federal establishment has now spread to all corners of the land.

World War II and its consequences produced vastly enlarged foreign affairs, defense, and intelligence agencies. The social and economic consequences of modern industrialism, brought into focus by the Great Depression, have produced large human-welfare agencies. And the growth of giant business corporations and large labor unions has given rise to large and diverse government agencies charged with regulating them.

The Washington executive bureaucracies constitute, in practice, a fourth branch of government, alongside the presidency, Congress, and the federal courts. The scope of this fourth branch was beyond the imagination of the founding fathers in 1787. Their intention was to create an efficient national government, but they left its particulars to Congress and future presidents. To George Washington, for instance, the very idea of a central governmental agency with millions of workers involving themselves in the daily lives of fellow Americans would have been horrible. But there is no going back to simpler times.

At present, these 2.7 million federal civilian employees live all around us (only one in ten of them works in Washington). They are our neighbors who work for the Post Office, for the Internal Revenue Service, in local FBI offices, as wage and hour inspectors for the Department of Labor, as weather observers, in the national parks and wildlife refuges, and, of course, on many military and naval bases. In fact, nearly a million federal civil servants are employed by the Defense Department; this is in addition to another two million Americans who wear the uniforms of the armed forces. (The latter are usually not called "bureaucrats," although they also are employees of the federal government.)

Not all the jobs held by these federal employees fit the stereotype of "bureaucrat." Some employees are clerk-typists, others are carpenters, plumbers, electricians, and so on. Still others, as we noted earlier, operate at the highest technical and professional levels: biochemists, architects, doctors, lawyers, and engineers, in a variety of specialties. And while they are termed "technicians," many of these people are engaged in making policy choices about what their agencies will do. Finally, there are the professional administrators—some fully protected by the civil service system, others appointed by the administration in power. These are the policy-making officials whose tribe has so rapidly multiplied in recent decades, and they are the most influential bureaucrats. Where are these influential shapers of policy located? Is it possible for the ordinary citizen to get to know "the names and numbers" of these important players of the bureaucratic game?

A Roadmap to the Federal Establishment

The president is head of the executive branch of the government, and in theory, all those in this branch work for him. In reality, however, the situation is quite different and more complex. There are some agencies and officials who are under the immediate control of the president, and are likely, at least most of the time, to be loyal to his priorities and purposes. Many more federal agencies, however, are quite unresponsive to presidential direction and a few seem virtually immune, as we noted in Chapter 8.

The Executive Office of the President

Let us begin our tour of the federal bureaucracy with the special group of agencies closest to the president—those contained in the **Executive Office of the President**. While some of these are quite small operations, others are quite large. They supposedly all function principally to support, inform, and aid the president, rather than to administer actual programs. In the language of bureaucracy, they are **staff agencies** and not **line agen-**

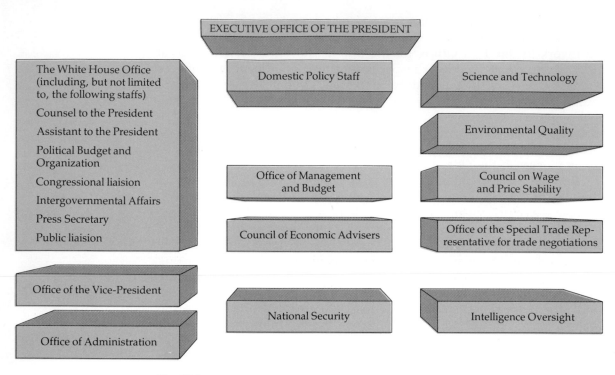

Fig. 10.2
The Executive Office of the President.

The Executive Office of the President was originally created to draw together a variety of advisers and assistants to support, inform, and aid the president, rather than to administer actual programs. In reality, the EOP is now an established bureaucracy composed of a variety of powerful agencies with a substantial degree of autonomy.

cies.[4] In at least one case, however, that of the Central Intelligence Agency, it is hard to accept the notion that line functions are not being performed. While the CIA aids the president by collecting intelligence, payments to the King of Jordan and programs to maintain anti-Communist Chilean newspaper editors (recently disclosed and obviously sensitive operations) are hardly staff functions. The "agency" clearly has its operational side.

The Executive Office of the President was created in 1939 in order to draw together a variety of advisers and assistants to the president. Perhaps the most important of the separate organizations that make up the Executive Office is the **White House Office** 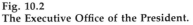. The president's closest aides have offices inside the White House itself. These are the people who offer him moment-to-moment and hour-to-hour advice, and who handle his scheduling, his press relations, his congressional relations, and his media relations and apologetics (indeed, President Carter established a new position: Special Assistant for the Media).

[4] For a brief history of the EOP, see James W. Davis, Jr., *The National Executive Branch* (New York: The Free Press, 1970), pp. 22–28.

The **National Security Council** (NSC) is also located in the Executive Office. The NSC itself is composed of the president, the vice-president, the secretaries of state and defense, and the chairman of the Joint Chiefs of Staff. The NSC meets from time to time and issues orders and approves position papers that represent the highest expression of national security policy.

Perhaps even more important than the NSC itself is the National Security Council staff, which is headed by the president's national security adviser. The council, after all, meets to consider what the staff has prepared, and the staff is the creature of the security adviser.

The **security adviser**—McGeorge Bundy to John Kennedy; Walt W. Rostow to Lyndon Johnson; Henry Kissinger to Presidents Nixon and Ford; and Zbigniew Brzezinski to Jimmy Carter—is part of the president's personal entourage. The security adviser has an office in the West Wing of the White House and is not encumbered by the day-to-day tasks of administering a department, as is the secretary of state. He may be the most important channel through which the president perceives the international arena in which the United States must operate. With a prestigious security adviser such as Henry Kissinger, the secretary of state takes something of a back seat in the formation of foreign policy. (Chapter 13 notes that Secretary of State Vance, as of 1978, has not appeared to be a policy initiator in the Carter administration.)

The National Security Council staff operates a "situation room" in the basement of the White House, where communication is maintained with the State Department, the Pentagon, the Central Intelligence Agency, and United States military commands abroad, so that the president may be apprised on a minute-to-minute basis of any important developments in the world.

Another important agency within the Executive Office of the President is the **Office of Management and Budget** (OMB). Long known as the Bureau of the Budget (and its director as "the budget director"), the OMB functions principally to supervise for the president the preparation of the annual budget of the federal government (see Table 10.1).

The respective agencies of the executive branch prepare their budget estimates, which are submitted to OMB for review, and OMB also reviews legislative proposals coming from the agencies before they are submitted to Congress. Thus, the budget director becomes the president's most important adviser and aide in prodding the vast federal bureaucracy into responding and performing as the president wants it. One reason Jimmy Carter so long resisted removing Budget Director Bert Lance in the summer and autumn of 1977 was Carter's strong need for a trusted old friend in the crucial OMB job.

The **Central Intelligence Agency** (CIA) is another presidential agency. The CIA not only collects and evaluates foreign intelligence for the NSC

TABLE 10.1
OFFICE OF MANAGEMENT
AND BUDGET

DIVISION	RESPONSIBILITIES
1. Budget Review Division	Budget instructions and procedures are developed, review of agency estimates coordinated, agency financial management plans are reviewed, and the budget document is prepared.
2. Economic Policy Division	Economic forecasts are developed as information is proposed about the economic outlook and the state of the economy.
3. Executive Development and Labor Relations Division	Programs to develop, deploy, recruit, and motivate career executives in the federal service are developed and wage and salary comparability studies are conducted.
4. Legislative Reference Division	Proposed legislation and agency reports on pending legislation and enrolled bills are reviewed for the President.
5. Management and Operations	Government-wide programs to improve organization, economy and management effectiveness are planned and implemented. Policy leadership and assistance are given to all agencies in information systems, statistical programs, planning, performance evaluation, and other management activities. Improved federal relations with state and local governments and public interest groups are developed including support of federal regional councils and federal executive boards.
6–9. National Security and International Affairs, Human and Community Affairs, Economics and Government, and Natural Resources, Energy and Science Divisions	Agency programs, budget requests, and management activities are examined, appropriations are apportioned, proposed changes in agency functions are studied, and special studies aimed at establishing goals and objectives that would result in long- and short-range improvements in the agencies' financial and operational management are conducted.
10. Director's Office	Executive direction and coordination for all Office of Management and Budget activities is provided. In this regard, staff support is provided in the areas of administration, public affairs, congressional relations, and legal affairs.

Source: Office of Management and Budget.

and the president; it also, pursuant to a secret directive from the National Security Council, engages in covert political operations abroad. Chapter 13 assesses the CIA policy role.

The head of the CIA is also the Director of Central Intelligence and is responsible for coordinating all the agencies of the federal government with either an intelligence-gathering or a counterintelligence mission. This so-called intelligence community includes, in addition to the CIA itself, the Defense Intelligence Agency and the National Security Agency (both located within the Defense Department), the Bureau of Intelligence and Research at the State Department, and the Federal Bureau of Investigation, which has responsibility for counterintelligence operations within the United States. The present Director of Central Intelligence, Admiral Stansfield Turner, has been given direct responsibility for coordinating both the programs *and the budgets* of these various intelligence agencies (including part of the FBI budget). It will be interesting to see whether Admiral Turner will be able to improve the performance of the community as a whole.

Other significant agencies within the Executive Office of the President include the Council of Economic Advisors and the Office of the Special Representative for Trade Negotiations.

The cabinet departments

Moving a step outward into the executive branch, we find the twelve cabinet departments. While there is a tendency to think of these as self-contained bureaucracies, with their central offices in Washington and field offices throughout the country, it must be remembered that many of the departments are themselves no more than rather loose holding companies of separate, specialized sub-bureaucracies. The Department of Transportation, for instance, includes such diverse agencies as the Federal Highway Administration, the Federal Railroad Administration, the Urban Mass Transportation Administration, the Coast Guard, and the Federal Aviation Administration.

Throughout our history, cabinet departments have been added to the original triumvirate of State, War, and Treasury as the federal government entered new areas of activity. Thus, Health, Education, and Welfare was established at cabinet level (bringing together a number of already existing independent agencies) in 1953. Housing and Urban Development was established in 1965, Transportation in 1966, and Energy in 1977.

The Departments of Labor and Commerce were created as a single department in 1903, and were separated into independent cabinet entities in 1913. The only cabinet department to be disestablished was, of course, the Post Office. In 1970, Congress abolished the Post Office and set up the United States Postal Service as a government-owned corporation.

Other executive agencies

This large group of agencies includes specialized bureaucracies, such as the Veterans Administration and the National Aeronautics and Space Administration (NASA), which are not part of any cabinet department. It

> Most of the twelve cabinet departments are simply umbrellas for a variety of separate, specialized sub-bureaucracies.

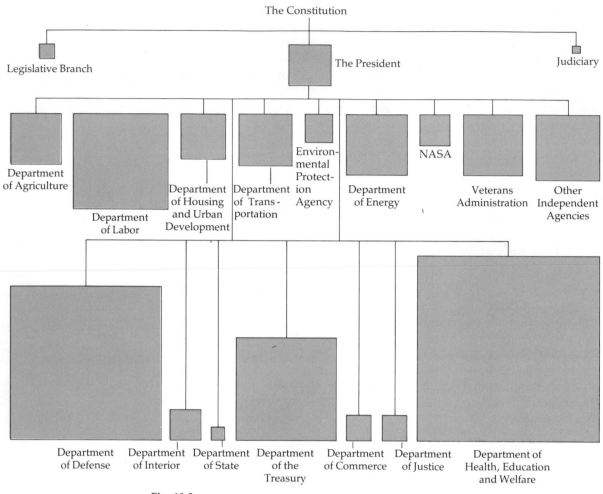

The Constitution

Legislative Branch

The President

Judiciary

Department of Agriculture

Department of Labor

Department of Housing and Urban Development

Department of Transportation

Environmental Protection Agency

Department of Energy

NASA

Veterans Administration

Other Independent Agencies

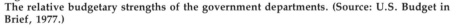

Department of Defense

Department of Interior

Department of State

Department of the Treasury

Department of Commerce

Department of Justice

Department of Health, Education and Welfare

Fig. 10.3
The relative budgetary strengths of the government departments. (Source: U.S. Budget in Brief, 1977.)

also includes a number of **government corporations**, such as the new United States Postal Service. The distinctive feature of the government corporation is that the revenues earned by its activities do not go into the national treasury, but remain as the operating revenues for the activities of the corporation.

Heads of these "unattached" executive agencies report directly to the president (in theory, at least), although they do not have cabinet status.

Juanita Kreps, Secretary of Commerce.

Patricia Harris, Secretary of Housing and Urban Development.

Some of them, such as the Veterans Administration with its thousands of branches across the country, are very large bureaucracies whose activities touch the lives of many citizens. Others, such as the United States Arms Control and Disarmament Agency, are small bureaucratic enterprises, but engage in activities that over the long run could be more important to the country than many things done within a Cabinet department.

The independent regulatory commissions

Independent regulatory commissions enjoy a peculiar status in the American governmental scheme of things. They do not have single directors, but are headed by multimember panels, or *commissions*, with one member designated chairperson. They are not directly responsible to the executive, the judicial, or the legislative branch of government. Commission members are appointed by the president with the consent of the Senate. But they do not report to the president; they do not serve at his pleasure

Independent regulatory commissions are not directly responsible to the executive, the judicial, or the legislative branches of government, on the theory that this would compromise their independence. However, they have tended to become too close to the private-sector interests they are supposed to be regulating.

(generally, they serve for fixed terms); and, by law, in most instances there must be a division of the commissionerships between members of the two major political parties.

The theory behind this semi-independent form of bureaucratic structure is that the commissions will not only make rules in accordance with the legislation setting them up, they will also adjudicate disputes arising under these rules; in doing so, they perform a quasi-judicial function. To have made such agencies directly responsible to the president would, so the theory goes, have compromised their independence. One result of this institutional independence, however, has been a tendency for the regulatory commissions to become too close to the private-sector interests they are supposed to be regulating. In the past, this has led, for instance, to considerable movement of persons from jobs in industry into the relevant regulatory agency and from the regulatory agency out into industry. The commission is highly sensitive to the needs of its "clients"; and they, in turn, rally to defend their commission.

The major regulatory agencies are the Interstate Commerce Commission, created in 1887, the Federal Trade Commission (1914), the Federal Power Commission (1930), the Federal Communications Commission (1934), the Securities and Exchange Commission (1934), the Civil Aeronautics Board (which fixes airline rates and routes) (1938),[5] and The Nuclear Regulatory Commission (1975).

The Civil Service System

Who are the men and women who fill the policy-making chairs in this bureaucracy? At the top, there are the cabinet officers themselves and perhaps 300–325 individuals who hold subcabinet rank or are heads of independent executive agencies. In addition, there are, at most, several thousand personal aides and assistants to the president, the cabinet officers, and the subcabinet officials and agency heads. This leaves the rest of the 2.7 million federal workers, some of whom hold policy jobs. These people are not in any real sense "the president's men," however, but are **civil service** appointees.[6]

For each incoming administration, a list is prepared of positions that can be filled by the new president. The list that the Carter administration worked from in 1976 had 2,200 positions. Things were not always so, and

---

[5] For the development of the theory of regulatory commissions, see Marver Bernstein, *Regulating Business by Independent Commission* (Princeton, N.J.: Princeton University Press, 1965); for a recent skeptical reappraisal, see James Q. Wilson, "The Dead Hand of Regulation," *The Public Interest* (Fall 1971).

[6] For a good discussion of this matter, see Herbert Kaufman, "The Growth of the Federal Personnel System," in Wallace Sayre, ed., *The Federal Government Service* (Englewood Cliffs, N.J.: Prentice-Hall, 1965).

it is interesting to reflect on the way in which the system of appointment to positions in the federal government has changed as the Republic has evolved. From the 1790s until the early 1830s, it was the custom for federal employees, except those at the highest levels such as cabinet officers, to remain in their places after the president who had appointed them had left office. This system resembled, on a very small scale, what we have today.

After Andrew Jackson's election in 1828, this system was replaced with what has come to be known as the **spoils system**. This term belongs to Senator Learned Marcy of New York, a leading Jacksonian, who earned his footnote in history with the ringing phrase, "to the victor belong the spoils." What is not remembered is that the spoils system, in its initial phase in the administration of Andrew Jackson, was a *progresssive* step, replacing the old practice of "to the vanquished belong the spoils." Much entrenched inefficiency, especially in the Post Office, was effectively attacked by replacing "permanent officials" with political appointees. But, as the nineteenth century wore on, the spoils system itself degenerated.

Rather than new administrations replacing deadwood with vigorous new people responsive to the wishes of the new president, positions came to be filled by political hacks with little interest in anything except collecting their salaries and maneuvering for better places. The continuing hassles that resulted began to strain the patience and energies of nineteenth-century presidents. Office seekers would crowd the White House day after day, and a climax of sorts was reached in 1881, when one such office seeker, Charles J. Guiteau, after failing to persuade President Garfield that he deserved to be Ambassador to Austria, shot the president down on the platform of Union Station in Washington, D.C.

The Civil Service Reform Act of 1883 provided for about 10 percent of the federal employees to be chosen through competitive examinations. Over the years, through successive amendments, the reach of the civil service system has been extended to cover more and more positions. In addition, other federal merit systems developed, such as the Foreign Service of the State Department and Special Agents for the Federal Bureau of Investigation.

The Civil Service Commission has acted as the principal recruiting agency for the federal government. The commission gives examinations to candidates at testing centers around the country. Individuals who pass examinations for various positions are placed on a "list of eligibles," and when a position opens in an agency covered by the civil service system, the commission provides the names of the three highest people on the eligible list. The agency is then obliged to choose one of the three names.

Under the civil service system, government employees are advanced through, and paid according to, eighteen government service ranks. Thus,

The assassination of President Garfield by a frustrated job-seeker.

a top administrator or professional—a GS-18—might be making as much
as $47,500 (before the 7 percent increase approved by President Carter in
the summer of 1977). A lively argument continues over the adequacy of
these rates of pay for federal civil servants, especially those in the top
professional policy-making jobs—roughly, GS-16 through GS-18.

With salary ranges roughly from $35,000 to $50,000, the compensation
is clearly not comparable to that which top administrators and professionals often receive in private industry or private professional practice. Some
commentators deplore this, suggesting that higher levels of competence
in the federal service could be achieved by making salaries more compa-

rable with those of the private sector. Other observers argue that when job security and the considerable fringe benefits of federal service, including a generous retirement pension, are counted in, and recognizing the likelihood that future presidents and Congresses are unlikely to allow federal salaries to lose ground to inflation, our bureaucrats are well remunerated, if not too well, for the services they perform.

Early in 1978, President Carter, as part of his larger bureaucratic reorganization effort, proposed to Congress a sweeping reform of the civil service system. The present Civil Service Commission is to be replaced by a new Office of Personnel Management. In addition, there will be a Merit Protection Board "to hear appeals and complaints from federal employees." A "fairer and speedier" set of disciplinary procedures is to be set up, and a special regulation adopted for senior federal executives, including a new system of incentive pay to encourage better performance. These proposals altering the comfortable life of the federal civil service passed the Congress with remarkably little change.

It is interesting to note that the federal civil service in America has been very much a middle-class career option. Persons of wealth and persons coming from the most prestigious universities and professional schools have usually not been attracted to civil service positions, with the exception of the foreign service and certain positions in the Department of Justice. This is in marked contrast to other democracies, especially Great Britain, where the career government service is sometimes considered more prestigious than private-sector employment.

> The Civil Service Commission is presently the principal recruiting agency for the federal government, but President Carter has replaced it with two new agencies—an Office of Personnel Management and a Merit Systems Protection Board.

Bureaucratic Policy Making

In the simple civics-book formula, the president initiates, the Congress enacts, and the bureaucracy obeys. Simple formulas tend to mislead, however. Bureaucracy, on closer examination, does not merely implement and administer; it often plays an important role in initiating programs and policies (see our discussion of employment and training programs in Chapter 12). The federal agencies have become a potent force in the incremental processes of policy making. Bureaucracy is a policy shaper and policy maker. It is not inert.

Those who hold positions of authority around the White House frequently complain about bureaucratic *momentum*. They find that the natural tendency of the huge bureaucracies is *not* to do nothing, but to keep on doing whatever it is they have been doing.[7]

---

[7] See Theodore Sorenson, *Kennedy* (New York: Harper & Row, 1965), pp. 301–302, for the view that the Bay of Pigs Project ". . . seemed to move inexorably toward execution without the President's being able either to obtain a firm grip on it or reverse it."

The bureaucracy plays an important role in initiating programs and policies. Although technically the president initiates policies and Congress enacts them, it is the bureaucracy that decides how Congress intended a program to be put into effect.

The president certainly proposes major policy innovations, and the Congress rejects or modifies them and finally passes a bill for the president's signature. But this is only the beginning of the policy-making process. The statute must be implemented. That is, some group of officials must decide what the words of the statute really mean and how Congress really intended the program to be put into effect.

Should you, for instance, wish to apply for participation in some new federal program, the chances are very high that the rules that would actually govern the way in which you applied and the details of your eligibility would be found, not in the statute, but in lengthy administrative guidelines written by a group of bureaucrats.

This would be true whether you were the superintendent of the school district applying to the United States Office of Education under the Elementary and Secondary Education Act of 1964, or whether you were a defense contractor seeking to bid for Air Force business. If individuals (or, more likely, interest groups) do not like the rules made by administrators, they may challenge them. They can go to the courts, arguing that the administrators had misread the intent of Congress, or they can return to Capitol Hill and seek to have the administrative agency's behavior corrected by subsequent amendment of the statute in question.

These are time-consuming procedures, however, and they require considerable resources and leadership skills to pursue successfully. Chief Justice Charles Evans Hughes once remarked about the Supreme Court: "We are ruled by the Constitution, but the Constitution is what the Judges say it is." This statement would well be modified to describe the situation that has developed within the administrative agencies. Congress makes laws, but the laws are what the bureaucrats say they are—at least, in the first instance.

So noticeable has this phenomenon become in recent years that Congress has taken to including in major pieces of legislation provisions for so-called **legislative vetoes**. In theory, such devices allow Congress to quickly correct, by simple or concurrent resolution, mistaken interpretations that the agencies make into rules. In fact, it is difficult to know whether the legislative veto will operate as a surer mechanism of congressional control than the traditional process of amending the statute in question. In effect, the legislative veto permits Congress only to acquiesce in or disapprove of executive actions.

Congress can, of course, exercise some control without either a legislative veto or a substantive amendment. Bureaucrats are regularly hauled before congressional committees and questioned and lectured about the rules they issue. But the fact remains that the bureaucrats are the permanent administrators of the statute and that even the more zealous congressional committees give only intermittent attention to the activities of the bureaucrats.

The Bureaucracy versus the President

Because the executive bureaucracies are so massive in terms of personnel and dollars, and because their influence on programs is so pervasive and their administrative activities so far-flung, presidents and their aides consider them a major constraint on presidential policy leadership. This attitude, common in all contemporary administrations, was well expressed by Arthur M. Schlesinger, Jr., historian and presidential assistant, in his lyric account of President Kennedy's "thousand days." Kennedy was determined "to restore the personal character of the office and recover presidential control over the sprawling feudalism of government." This central theme soon became a central frustration as presidential leadership clashed with the entrenched forces of bureaucracy:

> The presidential government, coming to Washington aglow with new ideas and a euphoric sense that it could do no wrong, promptly collided with the feudal barons of the permanent government, entrenched in their domains and fortified by their sense of proprietorship; and the permanent government, confronted by this invasion, began almost to function . . . as a resistance movement.[8]

President Nixon developed an almost paranoiac dislike for bureaucratic resistance to his policies during his years in the White House. As revealed in the famous White House tapes, the president and his inner circle of advisers were frequently frustrated by their inability to "move" the bureaucracy in directions deemed desirable.

At one point, President Nixon exploded when he learned that a regional administrator of HEW in California was not subscribing to the Nixon administration's policy. Nixon did not seem to realize that regional administrators, far removed from Washington decision making, are often loyal to earlier policies, especially when those earlier policies are favored by local political interests and local governmental bureaucracies.

This has long been the case, for example, within the United States Office of Education. Indeed, some observers feel that the Office of Education, a notoriously cumbersome and swollen agency, is incapable of being brought under the administrative control of the Commissioner of Education, much less the president and his staff.[9] This was no doubt one reason behind the Carter administration's proposal to establish a cabinet-level Department of Education.

Still, the president's sense of frustration when his policy leadership is ignored by a middle-level administrator is perfectly understandable. President Nixon could not understand why a regional administrator couldn't

[8] Arthur M. Schlesinger, Jr., *A Thousand Days* (Boston: Houghton Mifflin, 1964), p. 681.

[9] See Cheryl M. Fields, "Washington's Top Two in Education," *The Chronicle of Higher Education* (July 11, 1977).

An aide to Jimmy Carter displays a chart detailing the procedure for firing one government clerk for being absent from or late for work all the time. They are eighty-five necessary steps and each foot on the chart represents one month.

be fired or transferred to Micronesia (he *could* have been, but it takes time and a lot of effort). President Carter learned the same kind of lesson in an equally painful fashion. One good way of coming to a better understanding of the nature of the federal bureaucracy is to examine how a new administration addresses the bureaucracy. We now review President Carter's early efforts at reorganizing the federal bureaucracy.

CARTER REORGANIZES THE BUREAUCRACY

We noted earlier how President Carter came to Washington determined to challenge the bureaucracies. He promised reorganization and more reorganization. Patrick Caddell, Carter's pollster, stressed the reorganization theme in outlining a political strategy for the president. Noting that Carter was viewed by the voters as a potentially stronger and more decisive leader than his predecessor, Caddell suggested that this voter perception worked particularly well in two areas—". . . the desire for some kind of generalized 'change' and the idea that Carter as an 'outsider' would bring some kind of new approach to the Washington scene."

Caddell also pinpointed the importance of bureaucratic reorganization, which he saw as "the one strong *personal issue*" of Carter's campaign. Indeed, he felt that Carter had erred in not having made more of this issue toward the end of his campaign. Caddell put it this way:

Reorganization was unique among the issues of 1976 in that one candidate created it, nurtured it, and for all practical purposes, kept it as his own throughout the year. . . . It was a strong point not only because it was so personally connected to Jimmy Carter, but also because it played so well on voters' feelings about government and politics and "Washington."[10]

But while President Carter's emphasis on reorganization of the bureaucracies was central to his political strategy, why did the new president choose such a difficult area as energy to begin making his case? Once again, Caddell's memo is helpful:

> Energy. This is a vital area the president must face. He must convince the country not only that there is a real crisis but that the public can gain from supporting a real energy program. As I noted above, the public is skeptical about the actual seriousness of the problem and doubts the need to make sacrifices. To succeed, the president will have to propose an energy program that is both equitable and fits into a larger set of economic/social concerns. Announcing the Department of Energy might dramatize things in this area.[11]

Dramatize it, it did, but it also meant that presidential prestige would run high risks in an area of mounting public skepticism. There was also the risk of creating confusion by seeming to contradict the antibureaucratic thrust of his campaign by creating a new department rather than "getting rid" of anything. To combat bureaucracy by reorganization rather than elimination is harder for the voters to understand, but given the services the federal government is expected to deliver today, it may be the only practical antibureaucratic tactic open to a president.

To combat bureaucracy by reorganization rather than elimination may be the only practical antibureaucratic tactic open to a president.

Every president since Franklin D. Roosevelt has deemed it necessary to reorganize at least his own office. Most presidents in the modern era have entertained plans for a more extensive reorganization of the bureaucratic structures of the executive branch.[12] Few, if any, however, have so explicitly committed themselves in advance to this objective as Carter did. Having stressed the inefficiency, impersonality, and the unresponsiveness of Washington bureaucracies, President Carter lost little time in indicating this willingness to "take on" the federal bureaucracy.

The Department of Energy

Carter's first reorganization proposal called for the establishment of a new cabinet Department of Energy to be created from a cluster of eleven

[10] Patrick H. Caddell, "Initial Working Paper on Political Strategy," December 10, 1976, pp. 4-5.

[11] Caddell, "Initial Working Paper on Political Strategy."

[12] Harold Seidman, *Politics, Position, and Power: The Dynamics of Federal Organization*, 2d ed. (New York: Oxford University Press, 1970). Mr. Seidman was a long-time career official of the Bureau of the Budget.

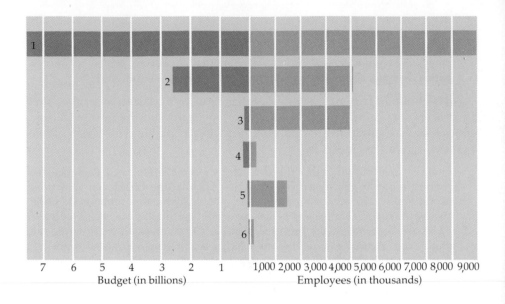

7   6   5   4   3   2   1   1,000 2,000 3,000 4,000 5,000 6,000 7,000 8,000 9,000
        Budget (in billions)   Employees (in thousands)

1 From Energy Research and Development Administration 2 From Federal Energy
Administration 3 From Department of Interior 4 From Department of Defense 5 From
Federal Power Commission 6 From other agencies

Fig. 10.4
The bureaucratic origins of the Department of Energy.
(Source: Fiscal 1978 budget figures.)

existing agencies (such as the Federal Energy Administration)—each with
a piece of the action (and with overlapping jurisdictions)—in the field of
energy resources. An unusually severe winter in 1977 provided the occasion and an atmosphere of urgency.

Dr. James Schlesinger, the president's Special Assistant for Energy,
was the principal architect of the Energy Department, and coordinated the
preparation of the national energy program, which in turn justified the
creation of the department. The existing agencies and programs that were
merged into the new department would, supposedly, work better and in
a more coordinated fashion. If Schlesinger and his colleagues could find
a way to make greater use of the nation's enormous coal resources, as well
as find workable methods for conserving energy, for developing new
technologies, *and* for preserving the environment, then the administration
could take credit for solving the substantive problem of energy and, also,
for knowing how to reshape bureaucracy for better results.

"Energy czar" James Schlesinger meets with Crown Prince Fahd of Saudi Arabia, presently one of the chief suppliers of oil to the United States.

Schlesinger: Super-Technocrat

Dr. Schlesinger entertained few illusions about the nature of his assignment or its difficulties. Indeed, he seemed to welcome a task that required a fundamental change in American assumptions concerning the nature of their affluent society: "Americans have never understood finiteness," Schlesinger declared. "They have believed in growth, expansion, limitless resources. In energy, all of these presuppositions must perforce change." [13]

The new "energy Czar" realized that the outcome depended mightily on the public. "The basic question that faces us on energy," he continued, "is not the particular techniques but whether we are serious. And the country has to be serious, because otherwise Washington will not be." [14] And while it is relatively easy to redraw lines of administrative responsi-

[13] Quoted by Anthony Lewis, *New York Times*, April 4, 1977.

[14] Lewis, *New York Times*, April 4, 1977.

Biography
James R. Schlesinger:
Cool Intellectual in Hot Dispute

"The eye of the energy industry is on James Rodney Schlesinger, sometimes arrogant, occasionally ingratiating and always intellectually imposing.

"President Carter's forty-eight-year-old Secretary of Energy not only presided over the creation of the Department of Energy but also assembled a team that is likely to influence energy policy long after his departure.

"Perhaps most important, it was Mr. Schlesinger's stature as the foremost intellectual in the Carter Administration and his closeness to the President that allowed the energy plan to be produced in relatively short order, with little of the usual interagency squabbling. Similarly, very little politics—some say too little—crept in to dilute the plan's potential impact.

"But Mr. Schlesinger has his drawbacks, principally his distaste for extensive social formalities. In the Capitol Hill world, which prizes such graces, Mr. Schlesinger's unadorned directness often compromises his effectiveness. What rescues him is his magnetism, a quality that led a national association of secretaries recently to vote him one of the 10 most exciting men in America, remarkable for a man rarely considered charismatic.

"Mr. Schlesinger's import has been bolstered by impressive credentials. After earning three degrees in economics from Harvard, he spent eight years teaching at the University of Virginia, followed by six years at the Rand Corporation. In 1969 he came to Washington as assistant director of the Bureau of the Budget and subsequently served as chairman of the Atomic Energy Commission, director of the Central Intelligence Agency and Secretary of Defense."

bility (and even to put a new chair in the Cabinet Room at the White House), it is vastly difficult, if not impossible, for government to change public attitudes.

If the assignment seemed to test the bureaucratic and political skills of Dr. Schlesinger, he was neither a rookie nor an "outsider." Schlesinger

is a super-technocrat, with a Ph.D. in economics from Harvard. Based
first with the RAND Corporation, an Air Force think tank, where he
applied the new management technique of systems analysis to weapons-
systems decision making, Schlesinger next served as a top defense analyst
in the Bureau of the Budget. In the Nixon-Ford era, Schlesinger served,
at one time or another, as Chairman of the Atomic Energy Commission,
Director of the CIA, and Secretary of Defense. Like the super-technocrats
of the Kennedy-Johnson years (McNamara, Bundy, Rostow, and others),
Schlesinger demonstrated how easily this new breed moves from one
"command post" to another astride the huge bureaucracies. In short,
Schlesinger possessed the intellectual ability, the administrative capacity,
and the Washington experience to tackle this enormously sticky problem.

The Dynamics of Reorganization

Schlesinger saw the task of establishing a Department of Energy as essential in developing a national energy policy. "The absence of organization
has contributed to the deficiency of policy," Schlesinger told a Senate
subcommittee. "Reorganization will help facilitate our decisions. But it
will not solve our energy problems."[15]

Plunging into this politically hazardous minefield with apparent relish,
Schlesinger and a team of assistants soon designed the blueprint for the
new Energy Department. The proposal called for the abolishment of the
Federal Power Commission (FPC), the Energy Research and Development
Administration (ERDA), and the Federal Energy Administration (FEA).
The functions of these agencies were to be consolidated with those of
other energy programs that had been scattered among at least nine other
federal agencies.

The "first front" in reorganization

Such a far-reaching proposal was bound to encounter resistance in Congress and from special interest groups. And so it did.

The Federal Power Commission, which regulated interstate natural-
gas prices and pipelines as well as some forms of electric power, was an
old-time regulatory agency. The FEA and the ERDA, on the other hand,
were newer agencies, created in order to separate the *regulatory* functions
from the *promotion* of energy. Indeed, they had only recently replaced the
old Atomic Energy Commission (AEC), which Dr. Schlesinger had once
headed! The AEC had been a prime example of an agency in which the
mixing of the functions of regulation and promotion had proved unfor-
tunate. Despite this, Schlesinger, always cool, calm, and deliberate, was

---

[15] *United Press,* March 9, 1977.

determined to combine the regulatory and development functions of his Department of Energy.

Once this issue was faced in House and Senate committee hearings, a knock-down, drag-out fight was underway over many of the bill's provisions. As a result, the *reorganization issue* remained unresolved when the Carter administration announced its energy *policy proposals* in the spring of 1977. These energy policy proposals proved even more controversial, precipitating a lengthy and passionate struggle in Congress and in the general arena of public debate.

Congress finally gave Carter and Schlesinger a Department of Energy that was substantially what they had asked for, although Congress did not agree that the Secretary of Energy should have the power to regulate natural gas and oil. But this proved to be only the opening phase of a prolonged struggle between president and Congress—with the bureaucracies in the middle—over reorganization.

A "second front" in reorganization

In the meantime, the Carter administration had won from Congress legislation giving the president broad authority to reorganize across the entire executive branch. Bert Lance, the ill-fated head of OMB, who had performed in a somewhat similar role during Carter's gubernatorial days in Georgia, was given the initial responsibility of leading the battle on this broad front.

The first objective was slimming down the president's own White House office, which had quickly developed a staff larger and more lavishly paid than Gerald Ford's. The second prong of this effort was a reorganization proposal that called for eliminating seven of the seventeen units in the Executive Office of the President. The units marked for extinction were the Office of Drug Abuse Policy, the Economic Opportunity Council, the Council on International Economic Policy, the Federal Property Council, the Energy Resources Council, and, lo and behold, the Domestic Council, which Nixon had created as a major innovation. President Carter's proposal called for the elimination of 250 of the 1,712 jobs in the EOP, including 134 of the 450 White House staff positions. In doing so, Carter said: "The ultimate thrust of the proposals is to strengthen Cabinet government. I'm very much opposed to having a concentration of people and authority in the White House staff." [16]

On closer examination, this Carter reorganization did little to change the concentration of people and authority in the White House staff. For openers, the cutback in immediate White House staff jobs was less than the 30 percent Carter had announced as his goal. Indeed, more than half

[16] *New York Times*, July 18, 1977.

of the cutback—or seventy jobs—would merely be shifted from the White House payroll to a new Central Administrative Unit within the Executive Office of the President! Presidential staff people were simply shifted from one payroll to another and from one unit to another within the institutionalized presidency. Furthermore, the disappearance of the Domestic Council, a Nixon creation, brought the establishment of a new Domestic Policy Staff, a Carter creation, headed by Stuart Eizenstat, Assistant to the President for Domestic Affairs. Eizenstat's influence rose steadily during Carter's first two years in office.

Further reinforcing the view that there was less here than met the eye, Bert Lance, while still Director of OMB in the summer of 1977, announced that eliminating staff positions under the reorganization plan would not mean laying off employees. "We have a pledge and a commitment that nobody will lose his job because of the reorganization process," Mr. Lance said, thus indicating the Achilles heel in most reorganization schemes. [17] (One of the first to lose his job was Mr. Lance, but not for reasons of reorganization.)

During his second year in office, President Carter gained Congressional support for an increase in the White House staff.

A "third front": Califano at HEW

There is another aspect of bureaucratic reorganization that does not require a commitment of precious presidential time and energy: reorganization at the department level initiated by the cabinet officer. Most cabinet officers give lip service to "reorganization"; few are willing to take it on directly. And for a very good reason: In reorganizing existing bureaus and divisions within an agency, the new head usually encounters fierce and often effective resistance. Reorganization requires an extraordinary amount of personal commitment on the part of the overworked cabinet officer and his personal staff. Willard Wirtz, Secretary of Labor in the Kennedy-Johnson era, effected a major reorganization of his department in establishing the Manpower Administration (See Chapter 12). A man of uncommon persistence, Wirtz spent six years engaging the resistance of sub-bureaucracies and their chieftains, client groups, and, at times, a congressional appropriations subcommittee.

Joseph A. Califano, Secretary of Health, Education, and Welfare in the Carter administration, also moved to bring about the reorganization of his sprawling bureaucratic complex. Created early in the Eisenhower administration, HEW, in a quarter of a century, had outgrown the Pentagon in terms of budget dollars and administrative complexity. With an annual budget exceeding $200 billion in fiscal 1979, HEW was actually

[17] *New York Times,* July 18, 1977.

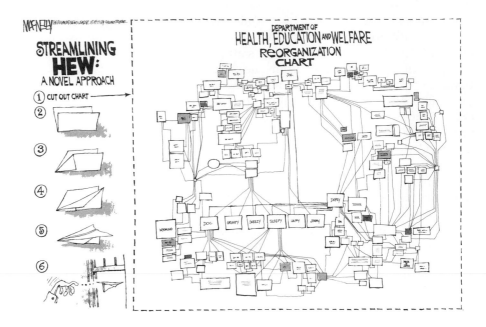

Chicago Tribune-New York News Syndicate, Inc. Reprinted by permission.

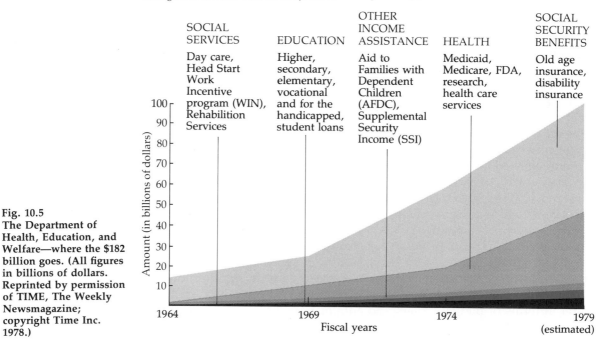

Fig. 10.5
The Department of
Health, Education, and
Welfare—where the $182
billion goes. (All figures
in billions of dollars.
Reprinted by permission
of TIME, The Weekly
Newsmagazine;
copyright Time Inc.
1978.)

outspending the Pentagon. No secretary of HEW had ever been able to bring the sprawling subagencies of HEW within a system of central control; many units—the National Institutes of Health, the Food and Drug Administration, the Office of Education—functioned as semiautonomous baronies. Moreover, as Elliot Richardson, former head of HEW, was fond of pointing out, the *existing* HEW programs far exceed anything understood by the public at large. He estimated that if all the Americans who were eligible for a particular program took advantage of their eligibility, the budget of HEW would have to be increased enormously.[18]

Like James Schlesinger, Joseph A. Califano, Jr., was an experienced Washington technocrat, who had served first in the Pentagon under Secretary Robert McNamara before moving in the mid-1960s to LBJ's White House, where he rapidly emerged as the president's principal assistant on domestic matters. Ironically, Califano, who helped inaugurate LBJ's expansive Great Society programs, under which HEW flourished, was now called upon to find a way of administering these programs more effectively. The task, in his own words, was "to make HEW the symbol of manageability—not the unmanageability—of Government."[19] In bold, swift strokes, Secretary Califano ordered a major realignment of agencies within his department *without* seeking congressional action. None was required because Califano brought about his realignment without abolishing any statutory program or agency. For example, Medicare and Medicaid, the government's principal health-financing systems, were placed under a single new agency to be called the Health Care Financing Administration. Previously, Medicare was under the Social Security Administration, while Medicaid had been a unit within the Social and Rehabilitation Service.

At the same time, Califano placed all cash assistance programs under the Social Security Administration. This agency, which had long administered the federal retirement and survivors' benefits programs as well as aid to the aged, blind, and disabled, was now assigned the multibillion-dollar Aid to Families with Dependent Children program previously administered by the Social and Rehabilitation Service.

The Social and Rehabilitation Service, stripped of all its functions, was abolished. Its day-care, family planning, and mental health programs were assigned to the Office of Human Development.

Califano was the first of Carter's cabinet officers to take decisive action aimed at fulfilling the campaign promise to reorganize the bureaucracy. The HEW secretary estimated that his administrative restructuring of the huge department would bring improved management savings of at least

[18] Elliot Richardson, *The Creative Balance* (New York: Holt, Rinehart and Winston, 1976), pp. 133–134.

[19] *New York Times*, March 9, 1977.

A/USSR/77 (H₁N₁) ACTIVITY AS OF JANUARY 26, 1978

Secretary of Health, Education, and Welfare Joseph Califano, here photographed at a news conference introducing the government's plan on how to protect the public from Russian flu.

one billion dollars during the first two years and at least two billion dollars annually by 1981.

Echoes from the past

In seeking to reorganize the institutionalized presidency—the White House staff and the Executive Office of the President—Carter came upon a set of problems that had fascinated and plagued President Nixon before him.

Richard M. Nixon, more than any other president since FDR, had made reorganization of the executive branch a prime objective of his administration. In his 1971 State of the Union message, Nixon declared: "Based on a long and intensive study, with the aid of the best advice obtainable, I have concluded that a sweeping reorganization of the executive branch is needed if the government is to keep up with the times and with the needs of the people."

After appropriate references to FDR's Brownlow Commission, which had originally recommended the creation of the Executive Office of the President in the late 1930s, and to the first and second Hoover Commissions in the late 1940s and early 1950s, which had commented adversely on the burgeoning federal establishment, Nixon said: "The time has come to match our structure to our purposes—to look with a fresh eye, to organize the government by conscious, comprehensive design to meet the needs of a new era."

And, indeed, the Nixon administration tried to reorganize. A Presidential Council was created, headed by industrialist Roy Ash, formerly of Litton Industries. The Council made many far-reaching recommendations, and Ash went on to become Director of OMB—the newly organized Bureau of the Budget. Other changes of names were made and lines of formal responsibility were altered. But the federal bureaucratic enterprise as a whole did not grow any smaller, nor was it dramatically more responsive to White House leadership after Nixon's reorganizing efforts than before.

Perhaps if Nixon's prestige had not fallen victim to Watergate he would have had greater impact on the "permanent government." And it is too early to pronounce with any confidence how much success may attend Carter's efforts to change it. Based on past experience, however, one's expectations should not be pitched too high.

BUREAUCRATIC POLITICS

In recent years political scientists have become increasingly curious about **bureaucratic politics**, especially how the bureaucratic structures and organizations enter the process of shaping policy. Scholars have come to realize what bureaucrats have known all along: Bureaucratic organizations have their own interests, which they vigorously pursue and protect.

There are two areas of special concern: organizational survival and perpetuation of organizational programs.

Survival

A bureaucratic organization will use every method available when fighting for its own survival. This is what makes reorganization so difficult to achieve; reorganization affects the career expectations and the egos of the officials involved, as well as altering the programs around which these career expectations are built.

Secretary Wirtz, in the example mentioned above, encountered special problems with the smallest bureau in his department, the Bureau of Apprenticeship and Training. BAT, as it was and is known, was marked for extinction in the 1960s as part of a reorganization plan that created the Manpower Administration. This would be a well-deserved extinction in

Attempts to reorganize the bureaucracy or existing bureaus and divisions within a bureaucratic agency usually encounter fierce and often effective resistance. Reorganization affects career expectations and egos of officials involved, as well as altering the programs around which these career expectations are built.

the eyes of BAT's critics, including the president's Bureau of the Budget. But BAT enjoys close ties with the building trades unions within the AFL-CIO. George Meany, the perennial president of the AFL-CIO, is a building trades man (plumbers' union). The middle bureaucratic levels of BAT traditionally house "alumni" of the building trades unions. When Wirtz attempted his reorganization, the head of BAT was a member of a family that provided much of the leadership in the bricklayers' union. Hence BAT, in resisting execution on behalf of a unified Manpower Administration, was able to draw on powerful support within the labor movement. A further complication favoring BAT's survival was the support it enjoyed from the chairman of the House Appropriations subcommittee (until his death in 1965). He, too, had once been a member of the bricklayers' union. Since the House Appropriations subcommittee is the most powerful unit in the congressional funding process, the subcommittee simply insisted that BAT survive or there would be no Manpower Administration. And it controlled the purse strings. More than a decade later, Wirtz's Manpower Administration (now called the Employment and Training Administration) continued to grow and flourish as more emphasis was placed on training and retraining jobless workers. BAT, still the special bureaucratic favorite of the building trades, also remained alive and well, and with the same bureau chief.

Program Perpetuation

A bureaucracy will fight almost as hard to preserve and protect one of its programs as to protect its organizational life. A program means personnel (more bureaucrats) and budget dollars; it can mean assured promotion and prestige. These are the basic facts of life in public administration. People (in the sense of personnel) and money (in terms of program dollars) are units in which bureaucratic success is measured. Of course, bureaucrats believe in their programs and are convinced they are good for the country. But given their intense personal interest in seeking to preserve and protect a program, bureaucratic politics requires reaching outside the bureaucracy to build a coalition of support for the program. If it is an antipoverty program that is threatened, bureaucratic politics may seek the support of an organization of welfare mothers who are clients of the program. The organization of welfare professionals administering the program are certain to be active participants in the struggle. Friendly members of Congress with local antipoverty programs in their districts will also be involved.

Some of the most famous cases of program preservation involve the defense of weapons systems. Perhaps because the dollars involved are so large, journalists prefer to write about them.

A bureaucracy will fight hard to protect its programs and its organizational life. A program means personnel and money, and may mean promotion and prestige for individual bureaucrats.

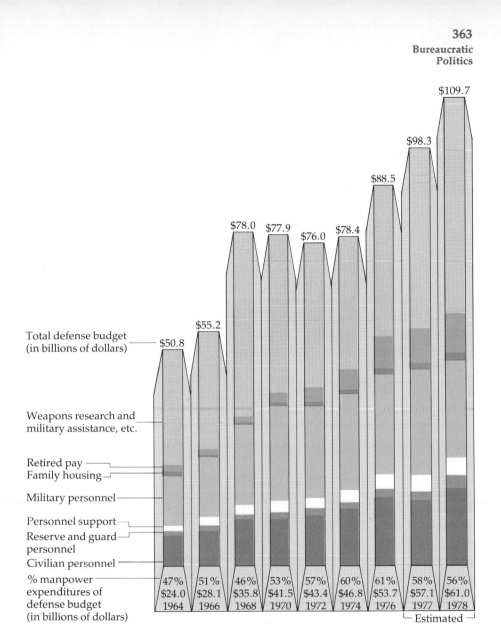

Fig. 10.6
The Department of Defense—where the money goes. Note that personnel account for more than half of Defense Department expenditures. (Source: U.S. Department of Defense. Reprinted by permission of *The New York Times.***)**

The F-18: reverse English

The F-18 is a remarkable airplane; it is also a threat to the Navy's favored F-14 program. Designed for the Navy by the Northrop and McDonnell Douglass Corporations, the F-18 is a "close-in" fighter, far smaller than its rival, the F-14, built by Grumman, the traditional builder of Navy fighter planes. The program called for building 800 F-18s, so as to create a "low-cost" fighter for carrier squadrons in the 1980s. Originally, the total cost of this program was projected at $12.8 billion; inflation increased the estimate to $14.5 billion in 1977.

The bureaucratic politics surrounding the F-18 have been intense. The Navy prefers the F-14 to the F-18. The F-14 is faster, flies farther and higher, and shoots more weapons at greater distances than the F-18. The F-18's advantages are its greater maneuverability and lower manufacturing costs. In 1977, the Navy decided in favor of the F-14. The tactic used was official Navy advice to Secretary of Defense Brown that it did not have the funds for the F-18 in the 1979 budget under the constraints imposed by the Carter administration. In budgetary jargon, the Navy went "above line," placing the issue in the lap of the defense secretary (a former secretary of the Air Force in the Johnson administration). The Navy informed the secretary that the Defense Department would either have to revise its "budgetary guidance" or limit some other program that it termed essential. In short, if the secretary wanted the F-18, he would have to fund it.

At this point, friends of the F-18 went into action. These friends included House Speaker Thomas P. O'Neill (Democrat), Senator Edward Kennedy (Democrat), and Senator Edward Brooke (Republican), all of Massachusetts. The F-18's engine is produced at a General Electric plant in Lynn, Massachusetts. Cancellation of the F-18 would mean the loss of 5,000–6,000 jobs in the Lynn area, already plagued by high unemployment.

Secretary Brown, under strong pressure from O'Neill and his colleagues, told the Navy to work out a budgetary "trade-off," but to keep the F-18 program alive—in other words, fewer F-14s would be produced. The compromise that was worked out proposed a one-year delay, from 1979 to 1980, in the start of procurement for the building of the F-18 fleet.[20]

In this case of "reverse English," the bureaucracy (the Navy) was maneuvered into retaining a program that did not have its full enthusiasm. But the Navy also kept its favorite plane, the F-14.

If you were in a position to make a decision on the future of the F-18, would you allow parochial concerns to influence your course of action? What strategic position do you think you would have to be in to play the decisive role in this?

[20] *New York Times,* June 22, 1977.

Bureaucracy and Congress

The federal bureaucracy and Congress, often locked in combat, are also to some extent dependent upon each other. The bureaucracy looks to Congress for programs and dollars. Congress looks to the bureaucracy to provide services to the citizenry and to assist the individual member of Congress in ways that will impress the folks back home.

Most members of Congress, as noted in Chapters 6 and 9, place a great deal of emphasis on service to their constituents. Congressional field offices are staffed with assistants whose prime task is to make the members of Congress look good by serving as an intermediary between the citizenry and the impersonal, slow-moving bureaucracies. Likewise, the executive bureaucracy will have special units whose essential task is "congressional liaison."[21]

These offices, going under a variety of labels, will have continuing working relationships with the congressional committees most closely related to the work of the agency. Invariably, this will include the relevant appropriations subcommittees as well as one or more substantive committees. The senior members of these committees will be special objects of attention and solicitude on the part of the congressional liaison staff. During the early years of the job training programs (the early and mid-1960s), the Department of Labor (the smallest of the departments) had *two* offices for congressional liaison: one headed by a special assistant to the cabinet officer, the other based in the department's budget office. A high-ranking career civil servant spent 90 percent of his time with the chairpersons and staffs of Senate and House appropriations subcommittees.[22]

The Role of the Bureau Chief: A Political Actor

The bureau chief, a key actor in bureaucratic politics, remains a neglected figure, in the literature of political science. Executive branch agencies are internally divided along functional lines into "divisions," and the divisions into "bureaus." These bureaus are thus the basic administration unit. The Federal Bureau of Investigation is a unit within the Department of Justice, although it often seemed autonomous in the days of J. Edgar Hoover. The Bureau of Roads is a unit within the Department of Transportation, and so on throughout the fourth branch of government.

The head of the bureau is usually called the bureau chief, although the official titles are endlessly varied, with director and administrator occurring frequently. There are bureau chiefs and bureau chiefs; most of

---

[21] See especially Randall Ripley and Grace Franklin, *Congress, the Bureaucracy and Public Policy* (Homewood, Ill.: The Dorsey Press, 1976).

[22] A. Holtzman, *Legislative Liaison: Executive Leadership in Congress* (Chicago: Rand McNally, 1970); also see J. Leiper Freeman, *The Political Process: Executive Bureau—Legislative Committee Relations,* rev. ed. (New York: Random House, 1965).

Although usually publicly anonymous, bureau chiefs often are responsible for administering programs of enormous expense and considerable social significance.

them remain publicly anonymous most of the time. Occasionally, a bureau chief will gain public notoriety, as J. Edgar Hoover did in his heyday while fighting mobsters and Communists. Anonymous or not, the bureau chief heads a complicated bureaucratic organization. In the federal bureaucracies, bureau chiefs often are responsible for administering programs of enormous expense and considerable social significance. They may have thousands of subordinate personnel in their organizations, many of them located outside of Washington, D.C. Their clientele typically reaches across the nation.

This obviously is a job calling for some combination of political and administrative skills. The bureau chief typically reports through an assistant secretary or an undersecretary to the cabinet officer. The bureau's annual budget, an element in the department's overall budget, is subject to the review and the ultimate control of the OMB, the staff arm of the institutionalized presidency. The bureau chief also faces a yearly review at the hands of congressional committees, especially appropriations subcommittees. These subcommittees often have detailed information (just as the OMB has) concerning the bureau's administrative operations. Presidents come and go, but the OMB staff is largely composed of career civil servants, while congressional staff members and senior congressional leaders also are long-term participants in the policy-making process. Naturally enough, the bureau chief is not likely to neglect these longer-term relationships; by preserving these he protects the bureau's program and personnel.

The Old-Boy Network

The permanent Washington community has been dominated for years by a network of "good ole boys." During the Cold War era, the national security side of government was heavily influenced by a social and economic elite in which the "old school tie" element was pronounced.[23] Thus, both domestic and national security policies have been subject to the influence of strategically placed individuals who have shared a common set of values (policy biases).

When a major policy leader, especially a president, arrives on the scene who seems prepared to pursue a new course, the old-boy–old-school-tie network grows apprehensive. James Kilpatrick, syndicated col-

[23] See John C. Donovan, *The Cold Warriors* (Lexington, Mass.: D. C. Heath, 1974), and Laurence H. Shoup and William Minter, *The Imperial Brain Trust* (New York: Monthly Review Press, 1977, with foreword by G. William Domhoff). A study of the influence exerted on United States foreign policy by the Council on Foreign Relations. Sees the CFR paralleling the Trilateral Commission in seeking the economic unification of the advanced capitalist world so as to create one world economy, with the so-called trilateral world at the center.

umnist, explained the initial reaction in Washington to the arrival of President Jimmy Carter and his group of political operatives:

> Much of Washington looks upon Mr. Carter as the Japanese looked upon MacArthur, as a proconsul governing by right of conquest. Ours is a city of good ole boys, of back scratchers, wheeler-dealers, fellows you can have a drink with. Mr. Carter is not a good ole boy. There is no small talk in him. He rarely kids around.[24]

The Washington community of notables might have preferred Billy Carter, the president's younger brother—a good ole boy—a wheeler dealer who enjoyed kidding around, small talk, and beer.

Jimmy Carter in the White House, with his strong distrust of this established Washington network, sent out an early signal that only the most dense should have missed. He challenged one of Washington's most skillful and experienced bureaucratic politicians, a man he had once worked for, Admiral Hyman Rickover, father of the Navy's nuclear fleet.

President versus admiral: chief executive versus a super–bureau chief

Carter's decision to challenge Rickover, secure in his unique power base, was taken early in his administration, and was perceived as a serious matter by both the president and the admiral.

As one knowledgeable critic explained some years earlier: "Many Senators have come to regard Rickover as another Senator." Knowing this, President Carter nevertheless cut out the funds for a fourth nuclear aircraft carrier, and also the funds required to convert the cruiser *Long Beach* to nuclear propulsion and to arm it with a new air defense weapons system. Specifically, Carter's revision of the Ford-initiated budget called for rescinding funds for the *Long Beach* conversion and for the nuclear carrier.

Since Carter had served on Rickover's personally selected staff as a young naval lieutenant, there was little doubt that the new president understood the importance of his challenge. For nearly three decades, Rickover had successfully taken on the traditional Navy establishment (which even FDR treated circumspectly), the civilian "brass" of the Defense Department, the OMB, and anyone else who resisted the development of a fleet based on nuclear power. In the process, Rickover, arrogant, driving, superbly competent, and tireless, proved himself to be one of the most effective bureaucratic politicians of the contemporary era. Skillfully weaving a web of influence with defense contractors, leading members of Congress, and the burgeoning nuclear giants (General Electric and Westinghouse, especially) Rickover seldom failed to get what he wanted by way of public funding for his pet projects.

---

[24] *Portland Press Herald*, April 29, 1977.

Jimmy Carter at the wheel of the nuclear-powered submarine *Los Angeles*. Admiral Hyman Rickover stands directly behind him.

Although the Congress at first seemed to support the president, within a matter of months it gradually became clear that Rickover was not prepared to surrender easily. Shortly thereafter, President Carter scored a mass-media presidential first by spending a day aboard a nuclear submarine in the company of Admiral Rickover, the first chief executive to do so. There was the president at the conning tower!

But Admiral Rickover, inscrutable and unbowed, remained the father of the nuclear Navy. If President Carter was to curb the further growth of nuclear-powered ships, he could expect a long and difficult struggle with Admiral Rickover and his allies in the years ahead. In the summer of 1978, Congress restored the funds for Admiral Rickover's fourth nuclear aircraft carrier, only to have the president's veto kill the carrier, presumably once and for all.

Bureaucratic Types

Admiral Rickover is not altogether an orthodox bureaucrat. Most career civil servants, including the highly placed ones, are much more content to operate within conventional limits.

Broadly speaking, senior career civil servants fall into two general categories: the orthodox and the change agents. Individual careers thrive in either category depending on the circumstances.

The **orthodox** (sometimes called "conservers"), who are certainly more numerous, take few risks along the way. They may be able, hard-working, and dedicated, and they help make the complex machinery of government work; but they tend to take a long-range view of the problems they deal with.[25]

Change agents, on the other hand, are prepared to gamble and are more impatient for results. They are just as able and hard-working, and no one doubts their dedication. But change agents are more willing to challenge the system; they tend to ruffle feathers along the way, as Admiral Rickover surely has. They are much more likely to join forces with reformist politicians and, in doing so, if all goes well, they move rapidly up the career ladder. If not, they tend to seek careers outside of government.

In-and-outers

Another, even more interesting bureaucratic type, is the *in-and-outer*. The American governmental establishment may be unique in its reliance on this special breed of bureaucrat called an **in-and-outer**. (Our British cousins, who do not have in-and-outers, are fascinated by this special American policy maker.) The in-and-outer has been well portrayed by former Assistant Secretary of State Roger Hilsman, himself a remarkable example

[25] For a typology of bureaucrats, different and more detailed than ours, see Anthony Downs, *Inside Bureaucracy* (Boston: Little, Brown, 1967), especially Chapter VIII.

of the type he describes: "They are the ones who kick and push and shove to get the government to recognize a problem and face up to policy choices rather than drift into indecision." [26]

Hilsman refers to those special operatives as *front men* as well as in-and-outers. Who are they? Where do they come from? What is their significance in shaping policy?

Bureaucrats can generally be classified as either orthodox or change agents. Lately, Washington has seen an increasing number of in-and-outers—people who come to Washington on behalf of the president for limited periods of time.

Characteristically, they come to Washington at the behest of the president and his staff for limited periods of time. They come from Wall Street, the huge corporations, leading law firms, and prestigious universities. They bring with them their technical expertise as well as a loyalty to the administration that has chosen them. They do not expect to stay in Washington indefinitely (although some do); they often have had almost no previous experience in national politics.

The selection of the front man is an important act in any national administration. Indeed, the collective decision in which a president and his staff choose the personnel to fill the top thousand positions in the executive branch may well be *the* most important decision they will make in office.

The reason is that the newcomers are a potential source of policy initiative within a complex system in which bureaucratic structures tend to link and in which most programs are resistant to other than marginal changes.

This does not imply that the newcomers are "better" than the permanent bureaucrats (or wiser) or that their policies are necessarily more humane. (Mitchell, Haldeman, Erlichman, and Dean, who figured prominently in Nixon's downfall, were front men and in-and-outers.) The difference is that these noncareer officials who come and go play a vital role that in other nations is often performed by permanent civil servants.

The in-and-out system has both advantages and disadvantages. It may correct for tired bureaucratic blood. The typical in-and-outer who expects to serve in Washington for a limited period is often willing to accept a lower government salary than his or her private profession or occupation affords. The pace at the higher levels of Washington decision making is grueling; bureaucratic exhaustion after a certain period is a near certainty. The in-and-outer may go at full tilt, knowing that he or she will return to his or her old job (after a brief period in a decompression chamber). In short, the in-and-outer is expendable, and this often proves to be an operating advantage.

The more glaring disadvantages are, as mentioned earlier, the relative lack of Washington political experience of most in-and-outers; their relatively long break-in periods; the difficulty of keeping a sustained policy drive underway; and the risk a president takes in choosing as primary

[26] Roger Hilsman, *To Move a Nation* (New York: Delta Books, 1964), p. 573.

change agents individuals who are often not well known to him or his men. President Kennedy, for example, had not previously met Dean Rusk, who was to serve as his secretary of state. Likewise, President Carter chose a cabinet composed almost entirely of people he scarcely knew.

In the Kennedy-Johnson years, Robert McNamara moved from president of the Ford Motor Company to secretary of defense to president of the World Bank; McGeorge Bundy from Harvard Dean to presidential special assistant for national security affairs to president of the Ford Foundation; William Bundy, his brother, moved from the higher echelons of the CIA and the Defense Department to editor of *Foreign Affairs.* Daniel P. Moynihan, a special assistant and subcabinet officer in the Kennedy-Johnson years, later served as domestic counsellor to President Nixon and as ambassador to India; President Ford appointed him as our ambassador to the United Nations. Mr. Moynihan was also a Harvard professor during most of these years. He is now a United States senator (and a Democrat) from New York.

Henry Kissinger was also presidential special assistant for national security affairs and later served as secretary of state in the Nixon-Ford era. He was also a Harvard professor who had served as sometime foreign policy adviser to Nelson Rockefeller. Since leaving public service, Dr. Kissinger has taken on a number of positions as professor (Georgetown University), television commentator, and writer of memoirs, and is well on his way to becoming a millionaire. He also now serves as a member of the board of the Chase Manhattan Bank, headed by David Rockefeller, and as a consultant to Goldman, Sachs & Company, Wall Street investment bankers. The successful in-and-outer may enjoy a lucrative career on the outside after gaining fame as an insider. This, too, is part of the reality of bureaucratic politics.

SUMMARY

In this chapter we have examined the structure of the federal bureaucracy, traced the Carter administration's attempts at bureaucratic reorganization, focused on the nature of internal bureaucratic politics (survival and perpetuation of programs), and, finally, suggested the difficulties all these pose for presidential policy leadership. We have emphasized that there simply is no sure way to provide comprehensive policy leadership in a system as complicated and as highly bureaucratic as ours. Small wonder that the sense of frustration at the center (the Oval Office of the White House) frequently is very real.

This perception of bureaucracy as a force in contemporary America raises several basic questions. In a governmental system of many separate bureaucracies, with presidential policy leadership sharply circumscribed on all sides, and with a Congress and political parties that adjust to change rather than lead the way, can clean decisions be made between carefully defined alternative policies? In a political system inclined to stalemate and in which public and private bureaucracies tend to interlock, where can central policy leadership be made more effective (if, indeed, such leadership is ever compatible with liberal democracy)?

In a total system that is both adjustable and durable—and, therefore, inherently resistant to drastic changes in public policy—the remarkable thing is not that policy innovation occurs so infrequently, but that it occurs at all! In a society where so much depends on adherence to the "rules of the game" and in which diverse interests actively seek to influence policy, should we really expect heroic political leadership?

In any event, bureaucracy is here to stay, a permanent feature of modern government. And bureaucrats are more than paper shufflers or inefficient automatons. Indeed, there are few career ladders in this country that provide better opportunities for upward mobility to able, ambitious young people than the Civil Service. And the people at the top clearly help in shaping the future of our country. Public bureaucracies, after all, won the Second World War, built the federal highway system, and put a man on the moon. Bureaucracy is a growing force to be reckoned with.

KEY TERMS

bureaucracy	spoils system
Executive Office of the President	legislative veto
White House Office	super-technocrat
National Security Council	bureaucratic politics
security adviser	congressional liaison
Office of Management and Budget	bureau chief
Central Intelligence Agency	old-boy network
government corporation	orthodox bureaucrat
independent regulatory commission	change agent
civil service system	in-and-outer

SUGGESTED READINGS

ALLISON, GRAHAM T., *Essence of Decision* (Boston: Little, Brown, 1971).

Examines the Cuban missile crisis in terms of decision-making models. A brilliant analysis of bureaucratic interaction on the national level.

BLAU, PETER M., *The Dynamics of Bureaucracy*, 2d rev. ed. (Chicago: University of Chicago Press, 1963).

An interesting examination of the interactions and power inside the bureaucracy.

Downs, Anthony, *Inside Bureaucracy* (Boston: Little, Brown, 1969).

An important study of a wide range of testable hypotheses on bureaucratic behavior, with emphasis on bureaucrats as "rational actors."

Fenno, Richard F., Jr. *The Power of the Purse* (Boston: Little, Brown, 1966).

A detailed case study of committee behavior in Congress that highlights the appropriations power of certain key committees. This is a classic study of the appropriations procedure, with emphasis on its political characteristics.

Rourke, Francis E., *Bureaucratic Power in National Politics* (Boston: Little, Brown, 1972).

A general, but interesting, study of the dynamics of bureaucratic power.

Wildavsky, Aaron, *The Politics of the Budgetary Process* (Boston: Little, Brown, 1964).

An insightful study of the federal decision-making process. Extends incremental models of bargaining to the budgetary process.

Has the Judicial Branch over-expanded its role in American government and over-politicized the process of constitutional adjudication? Nearly all the rules of constitutional law written by the Warren Court relative to individual and political liberty, equality, and criminal justice, impress me as wiser and fairer than the rules they replace. . . . In appraising them as judicial rulings, however, I find it necessary to ask whether an excessive price was paid by enlarging the sphere and changing the nature of constitutional adjudication.

Archibald Cox

CHAPTER 11 THE SUPREME COURT: AN IMPERIAL JUDICIARY?

President Nixon's first attempt to deal with the potentially damaging information contained in the Watergate tapes was to release an edited version in April 1974. As it turned out, the fact that crucial information was left off this edited version led to the court fight referred to in the text.

Wednesday, July 24, 1974, began as a typical Washington summer scorcher. But the weather was the only thing typical along the banks of the Potomac that day. In the "Western White House" at San Clemente, a shattered Richard Nixon, his reputation and his administration in a shambles, was struggling to cling to office. If he could stand off the impeachment effort of the House Judiciary Committee, and last out his term, perhaps something could be salvaged for the history books. After all, there were still many on Capitol Hill and in the country who were reluctant to condemn the president for the Watergate coverup on the evidence then available. These hard-core supporters asked for some direct, unambiguous evidence that Nixon had ordered an obstruction of justice. They wanted a "smoking pistol," and they had not found it in the edited transcripts of taped presidential conversations that the White House, under pressure from Congress and the news media, had thus far made public. Here was a slim hope for Richard Nixon.

But not for long. For on that hot Wednesday the Supreme Court of the United States voted 8–0 to require Nixon to turn over the tapes of over forty other conversations to the Special Watergate Prosecutor, Leon Jaworski. Three months before, Jaworski had sought **subpoenas**, legal orders, for all "tapes and the electronic and/or mechanical recordings" of sixty-four Nixon conversations that had taken place between June 20, 1972 and June 1, 1973—the critical coverup period.

The president and his lawyers had fought the issuance of the subpoenas all the way. They argued that the doctrine of **executive privilege** prevented courts from ordering the president to divulge his private conversations. Under our separations of powers, it was urged, each branch must respect the privacy of the others. The judicial branch could no more penetrate the Oval Office at the White House than Congress could demand transcripts of secret Supreme Court deliberations or the president demand to see notes of conversations between a member of Congress and colleagues.

It was a nice point. Informed opinion in the country was divided. Professor Charles L. Black, Jr., of the Yale Law School, wrote in the *New York Times* that "Mr. Nixon is dead right in refusing compliance with subpoenas. . . ."[1] Professor Black is generally considered a "liberal." Professor Arthur Schlesinger, Jr., the eminent historian of the City University of New York, replied that precedents running back to the presidency of James K. Polk and before "disposed of the extraordinary thesis propounded by Professor Black."[2] Professor Schlesinger is also generally considered a "liberal." Professor Alexander M. Bickel, Black's colleague at the Yale Law School, temporized and saw points on both sides.[3] The late Professor Bickel was generally considered a "conservative." And so it went.

But the justices had the final word. The question of the validity of subpoenas was quickly appealed to them, and in an opinion by Nixon's own appointee as Chief Justice, Warren Burger, the Court held that the need for crucial evidence for a criminal trial sometimes outweighs the need for confidentiality of presidential communication protected by the doctrine of executive privilege.[4]

The decision was a fatal blow to Nixon's hopes. Presidential assistants at San Clemente wondered, in the first minutes after the news was flashed from Washington, how to tell the president. Someone noticed that Nixon's Irish setter was wandering toward the door of the president's office, and suggested putting a sign around the dog's neck announcing "WE LOST." Nixon had previously suggested that he might not obey the subpoenas, even if their legality was upheld by the Court. Any impulse to do so, however, was quickly squelched by the president's chief attorney, distin-

[1] *New York Times,* August 3, 1973.

[2] *New York Times,* August 14, 1973.

[3] *New York Times,* May 23, 1974 and June 4, 1974.

[4] *U.S.* v. *Nixon,* 418 U.S. 683 (1974).

guished Boston lawyer James St. Clair, and by his Chief of Staff, General Alexander Haig. In a brief statement to the press, toward the end of that memorable Wednesday, St. Clair announced that Nixon would comply completely and immediately.

A few days later (August 5), knowing that the tapes being given to the Special Prosecution Force would soon be public, the president of the United States, on national television, admitted to the country that he had lied in denying an attempt to deflect the FBI investigation of the Watergate break-in.

The tape would later reveal that in the crucial conversations of June 23, 1972, with aide H. R. Haldeman, Nixon had entertained Haldeman's suggestion of using the CIA to side-track the FBI. Nixon said, "O.K., just postpone . . . . Just say (unintelligible) very bad to have this fellow Hunt, at, he knows too damned much, . . ." Had the Court flinched at deciding the issue, or decided the other way, Nixon might have hung on. But it did not, and for the first time in American history a president resigned in disgrace.

In forcing Nixon to turn over the Watergate tapes, the Supreme Court performed several of its classic functions. It redefined the relationship among the branches of the government; it vindicated the supremacy of law within the American governmental system; and it made some new constitutional law.

In this very dramatic incident we see the Court, under severe pressure, performing several of its classic functions. It successfully redefined the relationship among the coordinate branches of the federal government; it vindicated the supremacy of law within the American governmental system; and it made some new constitutional law. Most important, it demonstrated again its own uniqueness as an institution of government. Its decision, in effect, drove the combined head of government and head of state from office—and *no one seriously questioned* that the decision should and would be observed. The Court's action was almost instantly accepted as legitimate and binding. It is worth remembering that when another head of another democracy (India) tangled with her courts later that same year, the result was a three-year suspension of civil liberties and Mrs. Indira Gandhi's continuance in office.

In this chapter we shall (1) look at the way the Court works today; (2) briefly examine its various functions; and (3) trace the emergence of the "modern" Court and discuss how its work and policy-making direction have been changing. In conclusion, we will explore the costs and the benefits of the renewed activist course the Court has chosen to follow in recent years.

As we pursue this analysis, ask yourself from time to time where our political system would be *without* the Supreme Court. In what ways has the Court been changing recently, and are these changes for the good? You should also be sensitive to the difficulty of the choices the justices must make. In most important cases there is some merit to both sides of the question. And in addition to deciding which "right" to vindicate, the justices must decide whether the matter is appropriate for judicial resolution, and whether legal innovation is appropriate or not.

HOW THE COURT WORKS

Our usual mental picture of the Supreme Court is of the nine justices seated behind the bench in the "Marble Palace" (the Supreme Court Building) across the park from the Capitol Building. They are listening to lawyers' arguments and announcing opinions. But this, the public face of the Court, is only the tip of the iceberg. The real work takes place in the offices, the library, and the conference room—down corridors blocked by velvet ropes and uniformed guards where the public does not go.

In order to penetrate beyond the public face you should ask yourself how cases get to the Supreme Court. And how do the justices go about deciding on those that are accepted for consideration?

The Lower Courts

The Supreme Court reviews (except for one or two very special cases each term) decisions of law suits and criminal convictions made somewhere "below." Over 4,000 cases are docketed each year for some sort of consideration by the Supreme Court. Where do they come from? There is, first, the federal court system.

The federal courts

Article III provided for a Supreme Court and such inferior courts as Congress "shall from time to time ordain and establish." Under the Judiciary Act of 1789, which was discussed in Chapter 3, Congress established national courts in each state so that federal laws could be enforced in friendly forums, not in sometimes hostile state courts. Over the years, Congress has modified and expanded this system through successive amendments to the Judiciary Act. Since 1891 we have had a three-tiered system of federal courts: district courts, circuit courts of appeal, and one Supreme Court.

Our federal court system consists of district courts, circuit courts of appeal, and the United States Supreme Court.

The lowest level of the federal system, the **courts of first instance**, are the United States **district courts.** These courts are where trials in criminal cases and civil suits actually take place. There is at least one district for each state, and the large states, such as New York and California, are split into multiple federal district court jurisdictions. There are over five hundred district judges working in over ninety districts. These district judges characteristically sit alone. But in special cases, in which the constitutionality of federal law is at issue, district judges may sit together. In populace districts, such as the Southern District of California, there may be as many as thirty-three district judges.

At the intermediate level of the federal judicial system are the **circuit courts of appeal.** There are United States courts of appeal in eleven

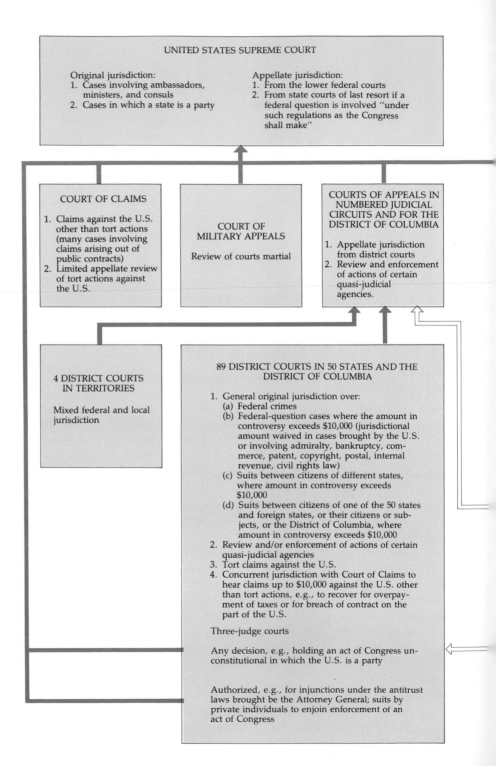

UNITED STATES SUPREME COURT

Original jurisdiction:
1. Cases involving ambassadors, ministers, and consuls
2. Cases in which a state is a party

Appellate jurisdiction:
1. From the lower federal courts
2. From state courts of last resort if a federal question is involved "under such regulations as the Congress shall make"

COURT OF CLAIMS

1. Claims against the U.S. other than tort actions (many cases involving claims arising out of public contracts)
2. Limited appellate review of tort actions against the U.S.

COURT OF MILITARY APPEALS

Review of courts martial

COURTS OF APPEALS IN NUMBERED JUDICIAL CIRCUITS AND FOR THE DISTRICT OF COLUMBIA

1. Appellate jurisdiction from district courts
2. Review and enforcement of actions of certain quasi-judicial agencies.

4 DISTRICT COURTS IN TERRITORIES

Mixed federal and local jurisdiction

89 DISTRICT COURTS IN 50 STATES AND THE DISTRICT OF COLUMBIA

1. General original jurisdiction over:
   (a) Federal crimes
   (b) Federal-question cases where the amount in controversy exceeds $10,000 (jurisdictional amount waived in cases brought by the U.S. or involving admiralty, bankruptcy, commerce, patent, copyright, postal, internal revenue, civil rights law)
   (c) Suits between citizens of different states, where amount in controversy exceeds $10,000
   (d) Suits between citizens of one of the 50 states and foreign states, or their citizens or subjects, or the District of Columbia, where amount in controversy exceeds $10,000
2. Review and/or enforcement of actions of certain quasi-judicial agencies
3. Tort claims against the U.S.
4. Concurrent jurisdiction with Court of Claims to hear claims up to $10,000 against the U.S. other than tort actions, e.g., to recover for overpayment of taxes or for breach of contract on the part of the U.S.

Three-judge courts

Any decision, e.g., holding an act of Congress unconstitutional in which the U.S. is a party

Authorized, e.g., for injunctions under the antitrust laws brought be the Attorney General; suits by private individuals to enjoin enforcement of an act of Congress

Fig. 11.1
The organization of federal courts. (Source: James MacGregor Burns, J. W. Peltason, and Thomas E. Cronin, *Government by the People,* 10th edition, Englewood Cliffs, N.J.: Prentice-Hall, Inc., 1978. Reprinted by permission.)

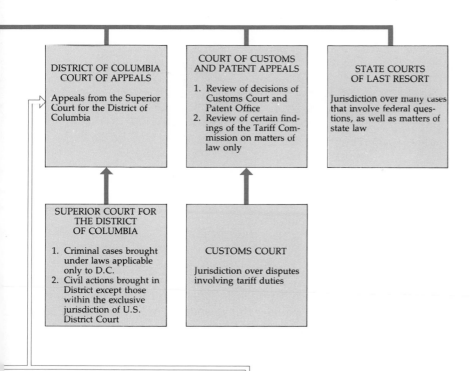

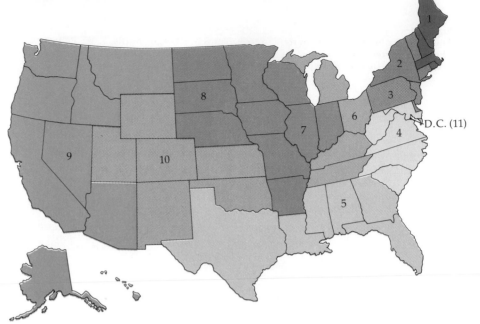

Fig. 11.2
The circuit courts of appeal of the United States.

circuits. Each circuit court, depending on the workload of the area it services, has between three and fifteen judges. Courts of appeal characteristically sit as three-judge panels. But on occasions, in highly charged cases, they may sit *en banc,* or altogether.

The jurisdiction of federal courts is based on the language of Article III of the Constitution. Cases involving federal statutes, claims under the Constitution, or treaties of the United States are appropriately brought in federal district courts. In addition, suits between persons residing in different states, where the amount at issue exceeds a minimum amount (presently $10,000), may be brought in federal courts.

In addition to these so-called **constitutional courts** established under Article III, Congress has, over the years, created a set of special-purpose courts dealing with particular types of cases, especially appeals relating to administrative decisions of the federal government. These include the Tax Court, the Court of Claims, the Court of Military Appeals, and the Court of Customs and Patent Appeals. These special **congressional courts** were created to handle disputes that begin within some element of the federal bureaucracy and may require special expertise on the part of the judge.

Consider, for example, the case of a college professor who writes books in her spare time. In the course of filling out her tax returns, the

Cases under the jurisdiction of federal courts involve federal statutes, claims under the Constitution, and treaties of the United States, as well as suits between persons residing in different states.

professor may claim as deductions from income expenses pertaining to the writing of these books. The Internal Revenue Bureau may challenge some of the expenses, such as the "writing off" of the cost of the maintenance of her study at home. Such a dispute might eventually make its way to the Tax Court.

The differences between these congressional courts and the regular constitutional courts (in addition to narrow specialization by subject matter) include the fact that the judges on congressional courts serve for terms rather than life. In addition, there are special procedures provided so that cases may move from the congressional courts to lower federal courts, or, in some cases, between different congressional courts.

The state courts

By far the largest part of the legal work of America, however, is done in state judicial systems. Most crimes and "causes of action" for civil suits are created by *state* laws and are the responsibility of state courts. As a generalization, it is fair to say that most state court systems are organized in a three-tier structure similar to that of the federal courts—trial courts, intermediate appellate courts, and a state supreme court. To illustrate the workings of these parallel but distinct federal and state court systems, and the way they relate to the national Supreme Court, let us take a typical criminal case. Cases in the state courts *must* proceed through the state system of appeal and review before the Supreme Court of the United States will consider them.

Let us say that our defendant was arrested at Coney Island after New York City narcotics detectives observed him selling a tiny plastic bag to a young woman. The bag was seized and found to contain heroin.

The day following the arrest, our defendant was brought before a magistrate (in this case, a judge of the New York City Criminal Court) and arraigned—that is, formally charged with a crime. He went to jail to await trial, as he could not raise the money for bail. His sister, who could sell some more of his heroin supply to raise bail money, sees it more to her benefit to leave him at the Riker's Island jail, having found dealing more profitable than prostitution.

In about a year, after a series of delays and defense motions to throw out the case because the detectives had insufficient reason to seize the plastic bag, our defendant is tried in the county-level court of Kings County, in Brooklyn, New York. The county-level courts in New York are called, frustratingly, supreme courts (in most places these are called superior courts).

After trial, verdict, and sentencing by the court in Brooklyn, the defendant could appeal his conviction in the intermediate-level appeals court of New York State—known as the Appellate Division. Should the result here still be disappointing to our pusher (now the **appellant**), and should

Most of the legal work in the United States is done in state courts. These consist of trial courts, intermediate appellate courts, and a state supreme court.

there exist some reasonable ground for further appeal, the next step is to the high court of New York, called, again frustratingly, the Court of Appeals. Only after losing there (and being sent to Attica) would our friend be able to join the long line asking the Supreme Court of the United States to hear his case.

As is clear from this brief example, the variety of names of state courts can be very confusing. Most states call their highest court the *supreme court*, but we have seen that New York departs from this practice, and a few states insist on supreme *judicial* court. In the majority of states, the intermediate appellate-level will be identified as courts of appeal, and the county-level courts *superior courts.*

A further complication is introduced at the state level because many states create special-purpose municipal or town courts at a level below the county courts to handle minor crimes, small civil suits, and specialized matters such as juvenile cases. Returning to our example in Brooklyn, the "supreme court" in King's County handles important civil suits and tries major felonies. The New York City Criminal Court handles misdemeanors and traffic offenses, and arraigns for some felonies. The county courts, however, are the workhorse courts of "first impression."

United States Supreme Court Review

Let us suppose that our erstwhile defendant from Brooklyn has lost an appeal all through the New York court system, and therefore has exhausted his state remedies. Let us further suppose that among his grounds for appeal was one which rested on the federal Constitution, or a federal statute—for instance, that the search that produced the incriminating heroin violated the Fourth Amendment's ban on unreasonable searches and seizures. Then our defendant (now our convict) may prepare a request for **Supreme Court review.**

The question at this stage, remember, is not whether he is a pusher (most assuredly he is), but whether the New York City detectives conducted an unconstitutional search. If they did, this would have the incidental effect (very pleasant for our friend in Attica) of voiding his conviction. New York could, of course, try him again, but without the heroin as evidence it probably would not be worth it.

Because he has been able to move speed (on a small scale) while in Attica, our pusher has been able to retain the services of an attorney to make his request for hearing to the United States Supreme Court.

Who are the justices?

So much for the background of our case. Now let us turn to the justices of the United States Supreme Court themselves. Who are they, and how do they work on cases such as that of our pusher?

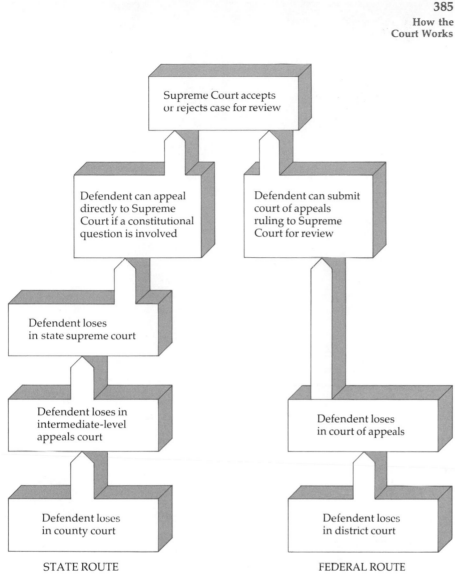

Fig. 11.3
The two most common routes to the Supreme Court.

Article II, Section 2 tells us that Supreme Court justices shall be nominated by the president and confirmed upon the consent of the Senate. Article III, Section 1 tells us that they shall "hold their offices during good behavior, and shall, at stated times, receive for their services a compensation which shall not be diminished during their continuance in office."

The blunt truth is that these few persons who interpret the laws of the United States and, even more crucially, its Constitution share minimal qualifications: endorsement at one time or another by a sitting president;

Supreme Court justices retire at their own discretion. They decide when they can or should no longer continue. Justice William O. Douglas, incapacitated by a stroke in 1977, first attempted to go on, but soon reconsidered and withdrew, opening the way for the nomination by President Ford of John Paul Stevens.

approval by the Senate; and, by iron bound *custom only*, some legal training. Once they commence their duties on the Court they are, except for serious, impeachable misbehavior, beyond the reach of political majorities and of the ordinary pressures of political life.

In its ethnic, religious, and socioeconomic composition, the United States Supreme Court has faithfully reflected the patterns of political leadership within the larger American policy (although like these larger patterns, this pattern is beginning to change). Of the over one hundred persons who have served as justices and chief justices all have been men, only one thus far has been black, and there have yet to be any appointees of Asian, American Indian, or Latin descent. The justices have been over-whelmingly white Protestant males of northern European extraction, with British and Scots-Irish ancestries predominating.

In making nominations for the Supreme Court, the president has, traditionally, considered region of the country an important factor. In addition, in the twentieth century, there has been an expectation that it was "good" to have a Roman Catholic on the Court. And beginning in 1916 with the appointment of Louis D. Brandeis, and running through the incumbencies of Benjamin Cardozo, Felix Frankfurter, Arthur Goldberg, and Abe Fortas (who resigned under fire in 1969), there was a Jewish justice on the Court. The important thing to observe about nominations is that while region and ethnicity are considerations, their importance increases and decreases at various periods. Certainly it can be expected that in the next few nominations, much more pressure will be exerted on the president to name a woman to the Court than to make up for the lack of a New Englander or a Jew.

Although some former poor boys have been nominated to the Court, most nominees have come from middle-class families, and most have received expensive university educations. Justices of the present Court range in age from seventy to fifty-two, and the average age of around sixty-five has changed very little over the past three decades. The nomi-nation of very young people is unlikely as it takes many years to build the sort of career that makes nomination politically plausible.

As to pre-Court professional and political backgrounds, appointees have varied widely. Some presidents have chosen to appoint men per-sonally close to them. Other presidents have attempted to make appoint-ments from the most distinguished membership of the legal profession—teachers, practitioners, and judges. Still other presidents have sought to nominate men whose views on important current constitutional questions agree with their own.

It is interesting to observe, however, that these presidential efforts to implant within the Court justices with views similar to their own have been largely unsuccessful. From Thomas Jefferson (who in 1804 appointed his copartisan William Johnson, only to see Johnson fall under the sway of Jefferson's arch enemy, John Marshall) through Dwight Eisenhower (who remarked of Earl Warren that the appointment was the "worst damn mistake I have ever made"), the record of presidents as court molders has been unimpressive. But there are always examples in American politics that contradict any generalization, and it is likely that Nixon remains pleased with his appointment of William Rehnquist, who has remained on the Court faithful to a conservative construction of the Constitution.[5]

---

[5] On the effects of preappointment background on judicial performance, see John R. Schmid-hauser, *The Supreme Court: Its Politics, Personalities and Procedures* (New York: Holt, Rinehart and Winston, 1961).

The steps of decision in the Supreme Court

Not only do the justices, like the president, do their most important work out of public view, they perform most of their work quite independently from one another. The Court sits *en banc*, together behind the bench, to hear all arguments several times each week during the term of the Court, which runs from October through the following June. The justices also meet in conference, usually once a week, to argue among themselves, vote, and make a variety of decisions about cases.

During conference deliberations no one but the justices is allowed in the conference room. If a book or a message must be sent in, the junior associate justice, just now John Paul Stevens, gets up, answers the knock, and takes the material. The secrecy of these conferences is almost never breached. A terrific flap resulted when, in the spring of 1976, Nina Totenberg, a public radio reporter, broadcast a story on a preliminary vote in conference. (She reportedly had social contacts with several of the law clerks.) However skeptical individual justices may be about secrecy in the other branches of government (Justice Douglas, for instance, was a persistent critic of secrecy as undemocratic), they support it as necessary for their own operations.

After a preliminary discussion that proceeds from the chief justice to the most junior associate justice, votes are taken on cases that have already been presented in open court. Voting proceeds from the most junior associate to the chief. After a particular case has been voted on, the task of writing an opinion is assigned by the chief justice, if he is with the majority on the case, or if not, by the senior associate justice within the majority. Justices desiring to write dissenting or concurring opinions may begin immediately after the conference vote, basing their opinions on their reactions to the discussion, or they may wait until the draft of the majority opinion has been circulated to them.

Of the over 4,000 cases that are docketed each year, the Supreme Court accepts only about 5 percent for full consideration. Justices are aided in their choices of what cases to consider by their law clerks.

Not all the decisions reached in the conference require opinions, of course. As we have noted, over 4,000 cases a year are **docketed**—that is, received for preliminary consideration. Most of these cases are subsequently rejected by the Court as not presenting questions sufficiently new or interesting to warrant taking up, a decision that must be made by vote of the justices in conference. It requires four votes to qualify a docketed case for oral argument and, presumably, decision. Only about 5 percent of docketed cases are voted for such full consideration.

The justices are assisted in their task of deciding what should be given full consideration by their law clerks, who are selected from the best and the brightest recent graduates of the foremost law schools. The chief justice enjoys the services of four clerks, while the associate justices have two apiece.

TABLE 11.1
FINAL DISPOSITION OF
CASES ACCEPTED FOR RE-
VIEW DURING THE 1976
TERM OF THE SUPREME
COURT

	DISPOSED OF	REMAINING ON DOCKET
ORIGINAL DOCKET	2	6
On merits	2	
Leave to file complaint denied	0	
APPELLATE DOCKET	1,929	395
On merits	309	
Appeals and petitions for review denied or dismissed (*Review Granted:* 147 (8.3%))	1,620	
MISCELLANEOUS DOCKET	2,075	323
On merits	62	
Appeals and petitions for review denied or dismissed (*Review granted:* 22 (1.1%))	2,013	
TOTAL	4,006	724

METHOD OF DISPOSITION

By Written Opinion (*Number of Written Opinions:* 142)	170	By denial or dismissal of appeals or petitions for review	3,633
By Per Curiam Decision	203	By denial of leave to file complaint—original cases	0
TOTAL			4,006

Source: *Harvard Law Review,* Vol. 91, November 1977. Reprinted by permission.

The request of our pusher for consideration by the Supreme Court would, therefore, be initially reviewed by a clerk for each justice. The clerk would then make a recommendation as to whether the heroin seizure at Coney Island was a Fourth Amendment violation. If four or more clerks think so, and four or more justices agree the case is worthy, the case will be voted up when its number is called in conference. Then briefs are called for (from the pusher's attorney and from the attorney general of New

York), and a date is set for oral argument. If only three justices (or no justices) are persuaded that the case is worthy, our Brooklyn friend must stick to his speed and wait on the state parole board.

Since 1975 the Supreme Court has enjoyed almost total discretion over which of the docketed cases to accept for argument and decision. Most requests for consideration come to the Supreme Court in the form of a petition for a **writ of** *certiorari* (an order to a lower court to send a case up). A small number of cases come to the Court on appeal. The Court is altogether at liberty to accept or reject cases coming on petitions for *certiorari*, but is technically obligated to take all cases that present valid appeals. To the distress of legal purists, however, there seems to be little operational difference between the way the justices handle *certiorari* and the way they handle appeal. It takes four votes to grant petition for *certiorari*, and four votes to confirm that an appeal is valid. Thus, if you persuade four justices you get review, and if after argument you persuade five (assuming the Court to be at full strength) you win your case.

FUNCTIONS: WHAT THE COURT DOES FOR US

It is probably true that the Supreme Court is, today, the most popular institution of American government. In a period in which the presidency has been tarnished and Congress is widely perceived as ineffectual, the Court seems to represent the elite corps above the sordidness of politics. But it is well to look beyond the glamor momentarily attached to the justices (at other times in our history, the Court has been profoundly unpopular), and ask what, over the long haul of our national development, this institution has really done for us. Is the Court really as important to our system? Is it really, as is sometimes suggested, the "most distinctive American contribution to the science of government"? Other democracies such as France and Great Britain operate without any precisely parallel institution. What *does* the Supreme Court do for us?

Policing the Federal Relationship

Justice Oliver Wendell Holmes, Jr., one of the most thoughtful of American lawyers and judges, once remarked that he thought the nation could have survived even if the Supreme Court had never developed the power to declare acts of the other branches of the federal government unconstitutional. But Holmes went on to observe that had the Court not been able to overturn acts of the individual states, legal chaos would have resulted. Different interpretations of the Constitution by state courts would have multiplied, and the uniformity necessary to the economic integration of the country could never have achieved the supremacy of federal law required by Article VI.

Furthermore, there has been recurring conflict in our history over what the states may do and what the federal government may do. Again and again tensions have exploded over federal power versus states' rights. In Chapter 3 we saw that the Federalists and the Jeffersonians had deeply differing interpretations of the respective power spheres of the nation and the states. It was John Marshall, however, who called the crucial constitutional turns, and encouraged the development of a strong national government. And it was Marshall's successor, Roger B. Taney, who encouraged some flexibility to allow for state innovation.

The Court, and Taney, failed tragically in attempting to resolve the crisis within the Union that led to the Civil War,[6] but in the later nineteenth and twentieth centuries, the Court did better at adjusting the federal relationship to the changing needs of different generations. The adjustment to expanding federal power at the time of the New Deal was difficult, but, as we will see later in this chapter, it was made.

Each year, cases come to the Court asking whether this or that state law infringes on an area of federal power, or whether some federal initiative intrudes unduly on the states. The Supreme Court continues to finely tune and modify American federalism. In the spring of 1976, for instance, the Court outraged the American labor movement by holding that the federal wages and hours law could not apply to the *governments* of the states as employers.[7] Congress, as a regulation of commerce, might require private employers to comply, but not the other American governments with which national sovereignty is shared.

> An important role of the Supreme Court is that of continually examining and redefining the relationship between the federal government and the states.

Umpiring Interbranch Disputes

The case of Nixon's White House tapes illustrates another function of the Supreme Court—settling disputes among the branches of the federal government. To return to Watergate, did the demands of the criminal justice process outweigh those of White House confidentiality represented by the doctrine of executive privilege? The Court decided they did.

If the checking and balancing of institutions envisioned by the framers is to work, there must be some basic power inherent in each branch that the other two are bound to respect. In the case of the Supreme Court, that power is in finally deciding constitutional questions about the powers of the other two! The president must respect the primary control of Congress over the appropriation of funds; and the Court depends on the president to enforce its orders when determined resistance arises (as when federal troops were needed to integrate Little Rock Central High School in 1957). The Court has neither troops nor dollars, but its prestige when making a constitutional decision is one to reckon with.

> Another important task of the Court is to settle disputes among the branches of the federal government.

[6] See *Dred Scott* v. *Sandford,* 19 How. 393 (1857).

[7] *National League of Cities* v. *Usery,* 426 U.S. 833 (1976).

In 1952, with the Korean war bogged down along the front line and the truce talks stalled at Panmunjon, the nation was hit with a potentially disastrous steel strike. President Truman hardly hesitated: He declared the steel mills nationalized, and the employees, now federal employees, were ordered back to work. But was it legal? General Van Fleet, the field commander in Korea, warned of the danger of his soldiers running short of ammunition and equipment replacements. Truman argued that in such an emergency his responsibilities as commander in chief justified his action. His plan was to give the workers a pay increase that the owners would find difficult to rescind when the mills were eventually returned to private control.

The matter, however, was not so simple. In 1947 Congress had enacted the Taft-Hartley Act. This provided a means by which the president, in the case of serious strikes, could go to a federal court for an order postponing the strike for eighty days *at the prevailing wages*. Before the passage of the act, Truman had denounced it as antilabor; he vetoed it, but it was reenacted over his veto. He had never used the law, and would not do so when faced by the steel strike.

The mill owners sought to have Truman's seizure declared illegal. The president relied on his inherent powers to respond to national emergencies under Article II. The case was speeded up so that in a matter of days it was before the Supreme Court.[8]

The justices were deeply divided. Chief Justice Vinson, along with Justices Reed and Minton, agreed with Truman that the context—the emergency circumstances—in which the president had acted justified his extreme measure. The majority opinion, however, which was written by Justice Black, was that the president lacked power to seize private property even to ensure continued production of vital war material. That power belonged, said Black, to Congress. Justice Douglas concurred. But for the three remaining Justices (one justice didn't participate), the matter was more complicated than was represented by either of these two sides. Justices Frankfurter, Jackson, and Burton thought that Truman was wrong because he *ignored the remedy that Congress had provided*. They would not say that the president could never have taken the action he had. Perhaps if Congress had not, by the Taft-Hartley Act, provided a way of dealing with strikes threatening national security, the president might have been justified in acting alone. But that was not the situation before the Court, and these justices cast their crucial votes against the constitutionality of Truman's act.

This famous case illustrates nicely the delicate question of power sharing among branches. The Court may not always deal with such questions

---

[8] *Youngstown Sheet & Tube Co.* v. *Sawyer,* 343 U.S. 579 (1952). For an excellent discussion of the case and the issues it raised see Alan F. Westin, *The Anatomy of a Constitutional Law Case* (New York: Macmillan, 1958).

easily, or to everyone's satisfaction, but it is hard to see how our separation of powers could survive without some umpiring.

Adapting to Changing Circumstances

In policing the federal relationship and umpiring the separation of powers—in saying what Congress can do, what the states may do, and, on rarer occasions, what the president may do—the Court has leaned in different ways at different times in our history.

During John Marshall's chief justiceship, national power was emphasized at a time when state divisiveness might have imperiled the survival of the new nation. In the late nineteenth and early twentieth centuries, on the other hand, the great period of industrial expansion was booming, and the Court's narrow interpretation of both federal and state power was in accord with the spirit of the times. But then, in the late 1930s, with the need for curbing the excesses of industrialization becoming painfully apparent to larger and larger numbers of Americans, the Court slowly moved to a broader interpretation of state and federal governmental power.

Also in the late 1930s, with dictators gaining power in Europe and the Far East, and the international area becoming increasingly dangerous for the United States, the Court gave an expansive reading to the power of the president in foreign affairs. Yet in 1974, when the presidency had swollen to what some called "imperial" dimensions and the corruption of Watergate threatened to destroy the faith of Americans in their leaders, the Court required the president to give way to the demands of the judiciary for criminal evidence.

It is vital to the survival of our constitutional structure that a mechanism exist to modify it, in a fairly rapid and flexible way, and to meet new challenges and changing circumstances. The amending process set forth in Article III is too cumbersome to be used more than occasionally. "We live under the Constitution," Chief Justice Charles Evans Hughes once remarked, "but the Constitution is what the judges say it is." This does not mean that the judges can say anything at all and get away with it. (We shall presently examine some constraints upon them.) It does mean that the Supreme Court functions, and necessarily so, as a kind of continuing executive committee of the Constitutional Convention.

Curbing the Majority

But of all the benefits we derive from the Supreme Court, none is more important than the way in which the Court defends the liberties of individuals and rights of minorities against what Alexis de Tocqueville called "the tyranny of the majority." The vindication of the civil liberties of criminals is (as Justice Holmes once observed) a test of the quality of a

The most important function of the Supreme Court is to defend the liberties of individuals and minorities against the tyranny of the majority.

civilization. But criminals will never be very popular with most people, and it is not an easy matter to define and defend their rights.

Similarly, those people most in need of the First Amendment's protection of free speech are often unpopular or genuinely offensive. The temptation to the majority to shut them up is ever present. After all, whose heart goes out to redneck members of the Ku Klux Klan who attach "Defend the White Race" signs to their pickup trucks? Or to Nazis desiring to march through a predominantly Jewish neighborhood? Political majorities can never be expected to be carefully and continually heedful of the value of basic civil liberties.

It is part of the genius of our system that we restrain the majority of the moment, and keep it from working its will, with respect to *certain fundamental matters* of individual liberty. Ours remains, in this respect, a qualified democracy—with certain types of questions placed outside the normal democratic process. We have a council of nine, hopefully wise, "guardians"; lawyers who decide from month to month, year to year, and generation to generation which particular matters shall be beyond majority control. Will one of them be abortion? At what stage of pregnancy? And what part of the constitutional text, in our history, or in our underlying idea of the Constitution, *justifies* making this one of the special questions that are beyond majority rule? The Court answered the first two questions, and wrestled with the third.

The Supreme Court wields a mighty power. Americans have accepted this power because what the Court decides is supposed to be grounded in our constitutional tradition. The Congress need not, and often does not, give formal reasons for what it does. It is free, within its power under Article I, to spend, tax, or not tax as the play of immediate political forces dictates. The Court is not free. It must explain itself in the language of the Constitution.

Nor can the Court preempt just any question of social policy. Questions must come to it as properly framed law suits or criminal appeals. And there are many kinds of public policy questions (such as whether to spend more on roads or on hospitals) that are very difficult to raise in law suits. In addition, the Constitution is a short document, which manifestly grants great discretion to the political, democratically responsible branches of government. Not every sort of perceived wrong, deprivation, or failing of the normal political process can be turned into a constitutional issue. What should be the minimum wage? Should the Air Force have a new bomber? Should there be more public funds for research into cancer or into heart disease? All are grist for Congress—not, at least under present understanding, for the Court.

But with all that said, the counter-majoritarian power of the Court is impressive, if not awesome. Because of its relatively good insulation from the heat of political pressure and public opinion, the Court has the capacity to resolve important questions of minority rights that have tied the "political branches" in knots. An excellent example of this sort of deadlock breaking is the decision on **legislative reapportionment** by the Warren Court. Here the justices created a new individual right ("one man, one vote") and forced action on the part of state legislatures, which for decades had been incapable of moving on their own.

Much of the Court's power to break deadlocks and protect minorities derives from its relative isolation from political pressure and public opinion.

These functions—policing the federal-state relationship, umpiring interbranch disputes, adapting our laws to changing circumstances, and curbing the majority—are important to the flexibility, the openness, and, indeed, the survival of our polity. But the Court is a fragile institution, an *oligarchic* feature of our otherwise democratic system. Its acceptance by us—its legitimacy—depends on our perception that it is limited in its decisions by the text and history of the Constitution, and that the justices take seriously their responsibility to explain what they do.

EMERGENCE OF THE "MODERN" COURT

In Chapter 3 we described the development of the Supreme Court from the formative years under John Marshall, and its role in establishing the authority of the new national government. We also noted how, by the late nineteenth century, the justices had developed a set of constitutional theories that protected private enterprise against government regulation at the federal and even the state level.

In the first three decades of our century, the Court remained firmly convinced that natural law and the Constitution forbade any extensive government interference with the free market. The economic philosophy, known as **laissez faire**, valued a free, uncontrolled market, and was read into the Constitution by the justices in order to limit the regulatory power of the states and the federal government.

Clearly these views do not represent dominant American opinion today. But it should be remembered that these views were held by most influential American political thinkers in the late nineteenth century. Much of what is now assumed about the right and obligation of the federal government to intervene at all levels of American life is very recent, much of it coming about as a result of the Great Depression and World War II.

The Nine Old Men

Franklin Roosevelt came to power in 1933 against the background of a ravished economy and rising expectations that the federal government would "do something" to remedy conditions. Millions of Americans were out of work. Many more had seen their life savings wiped out by the stock

A caricature of the "Nine Old Men." From left to right: Owen J. Roberts, Pierce Butler, Louis D. Brandeis, Willis Van Devanter, Charles Evans Hughes (Chief Justice), James C. McReynold, George Sutherland, Harlan F. Stone, Benjamin N. Cardozo.

market crash of 1929–1930. Many Americans lost their homes as banks failed or foreclosed on their home mortgages. Roosevelt's New Deal administration began to try to deal with this calamity. The conditions were unusual, and Congress was unusually ready to follow the lead of the chief executive.

A variety of statutes were enacted with remarkable speed in an attempt to revive the nation's economy. But almost as quickly as the Congress enacted the statutes, the Supreme Court struck them down.[9] The Court, composed in the popular phrase of the time of "Nine Old Men," placed itself on a collision course with Franklin Roosevelt and with the governors and legislatures of the more progressive states. In 1936, Roosevelt was reelected by the greatest landslide in American history. And his first order of business was to do something about the activist Court, which he believed was frustrating the democratic process.

Many Americans agreed with him that something had to be done. But the course Roosevelt embarked on soon brought him, at the height of his popularity, into deep conflict with the Congress and with public opinion. The president proposed that the Congress, acting under its Article III

[9] See Benjamin F. Wright, *The Growth of American Constitutional Law* (Chicago: University of Chicago Press, 1967), pp. 200-241. Decisions included: *Schecter Poultry Corp.* v. *U.S.*, 295 U.S. 495 (1935); *Railroad Retirement Board* v. *Alton Railroad Co.*, 295 U.S. 330 (1935); *Carter* v. *Carter Coal Co.*, 298 U.S. 238 (1936); and *U.S.* v. *Butler*, 297 U.S. 1 (1936).

powers, provide that a new justice would be appointed when any sitting justice failed to retire at the age of seventy. Roosevelt said this was necessary because the aging justices were getting behind in their workload. But everyone understood the real objective, which was to **pack the Court** and create a majority that would sustain New Deal programs.

Had this **Court Plan** been accepted by Congress, and had no sitting justice over seventy chosen to retire, Roosevelt would have had a total of six appointments to make. The majority of the new, larger Court might have swung the other way on the constitutionality of the New Deal and state regulatory legislation. However, the chief justice at the time, the able and energetic Charles Evans Hughes, shot the props from under the president's plan by informing the Senate Judiciary Committee that the Supreme Court was quite current in its work, and needed no supernumerary appointments.

Meanwhile, Roosevelt's Court Plan quickly came to be perceived by both the country and the Congress as dangerous. While it is clear that substantial majorities favored Roosevelt's legislative program, they rejected what appeared to be an attack on the independence of the judiciary. The excessive activism of the justices in defense of *laissez faire* was resented, but a remedy that threatened to alter the Court as an institution was perceived as going too far.

The Court Plan was not passed by Congress, and the fight for it cost Roosevelt prestige on Capitol Hill. But against the background of public dissatisfaction and congressional conflict, the Supreme Court in 1937 began to jettison the archaic *laissez faire* interpretations of the Constitution. Thus a more expansive reading was given to powers granted to Congress in Article I, Section 8—a reading that would have made John Marshall smile. By the early 1940s a mighty expansion of federal regulatory power was taking place with the Court's blessing.[10] New values came to loom larger for the justices than those of protection of property and limitations on federal power.

> A *laissez-faire* philosophy characterized Supreme Court rulings for the first three decades of our century. This gave way to more expansive interpretations of federal power after the Depression and Roosevelt's New Deal administrations.

The Roosevelt Court

Professor Wallace Mendelson has observed that "the Roosevelt Court abandoned one form of judicial activism, and toyed with another."[11] After the crisis in 1937, as the older of the nine old men began to leave the Court, Roosevelt made a series of appointments that changed the character of the institution. In 1937, Roosevelt named Senator Hugo Black (Alabama populist and loyal supporter of the ill-fated Court Plan) to fill the vacancy

[10] See especially, *Jones and Laughlin, U.S.* v. *Darby*, 312 U.S. 100 (1941); *Wickard* v. *Filburn*, 317 U.S. 111 (1942).

[11] Wallace Mendelson, "From Warren to Burger: The Rise and Decline of Substantive Equal Protection," *The American Political Science Review* LXVI (December 1972): 1232.

created by the retirement of conservative Willis Van Devanter. In 1938 Stanley Reed (another loyal New Dealer) was named, and in 1939 two law professors friendly to the New Deal, Felix Frankfurter and William O. Douglas, joined the Court. In the words of Professor Robert McCloskey, the new Court "made it plain that the *laissez faire* values of the recent past were no longer constitutionally viable, and that the humanistic values loosely described by the term 'civil liberties' were becoming a predominant judicial concern." [12]

The Warren Court

But the movement into this new field of constitutional development was slow. Throughout most of our national history, the first eight amendments to the Constitution, known as the Bill of Rights, applied only to the national government; before 1940 there were relatively few cases where these provisions had been authoritatively construed by the Supreme Court. In addition, the pre-1937 Supreme Court had given judicial activism a very bad name.

In the early 1940s, the liberal position with regard to the Court was that it should generally defer to legislative and executive judgments, intervening only to declare acts of the other branches and of the states unconstitutional in the clearest cases where such was specifically mandated by the language of the Constitution. It took over a decade and several false starts for the Court to settle on its new themes of equality and liberty. McCloskey concluded that "The years from 1940 to about 1943 were a period of irresolution marked by the alternate flowing and ebbing of judicial self-confidence." [13]

For example, in 1940 a deeply divided Court held that a state requirement that schoolchildren salute the flag was a constitutional exercise of the state's police power that interfered with neither freedom of speech nor freedom of religion. Three years later, with minor personnel changes, the Supreme Court reversed itself and held that the forced saluting of the flag was unconstitutional according to the First Amendment. [14] In another painful decision in 1944, in the middle of the Second World War, the Court upheld the authority of the federal government to order persons of Japanese descent to leave certain specified areas on the West Coast. It refused, however, to uphold the further detention of the Japanese after

[12] Robert G. McCloskey, *The Modern Supreme Court* (Cambridge, Mass.: Harvard University Press, 1972), p. 327.

[13] McCloskey, *The Modern Supreme Court*.

[14] In both *Minersville School Dist.* v. *Gobitis*, 310 U.S. 586 (1940) and *West Virginia State Board of Education* v. *Barnette*, 319 U.S. 624 (1943). On the tangled history of this case see David Manwaring, *Render Unto Caesar* (Chicago: University of Chicago Press, 1962).

their evacuation. The pattern is one of tentative development of a civil libertarian posture.[15]

Associating an important period in the history of the Supreme Court with the presiding chief justice at that time is an imprecise business at best. The complexion of the Court does not change automatically with a change of chief justice, and some chief justices exercise more influence over their fellow justices than others. But if ever the association is justified, it is during the years of Earl Warren's chief justiceship. While the commitment to innovation in civil liberties and civil rights that is associated with Warren's name began in the 1940s, and while the Court did not become superactivist all at once with Warren's appointment, there is no question that during the Warren years the self-restraining style that had characterized the Court since the late 1930s was abandoned. In its place a new **judicial activism** arose—this time an activism favored by liberals rather than conservatives.

The Supreme Court under Chief Justice Earl Warren was characterized by a new commitment to civil liberties and civil rights. The Court reinterpreted the Constitution in many areas of public law in order to maximize these values.

In area after area of American public law, the Warren Court majority reinterpreted the Constitution in an effort to maximize the values of political equality, social equality, and personal liberty (excluding personal rights of property). In the process, the Supreme Court as an institution loomed larger and larger as a national policy-maker at the expense of Congress and the state governments.

In Chapter 14, where we study how policy is made in the field of civil rights and liberties, we examine the impact of this new judicial activism in the areas of free speech, freedom of religion, racial and sexual equality, and restraints on law enforcement. Here we note briefly just a few examples of how the Warren Court "progressed" into activism.

Responding to McCarthyism

When President Eisenhower nominated Earl Warren to succeed Chief Justice Fred M. Vinson in 1953, the wave of national concern over subversive activities, particularly the operations of the Communist Party within America, was just receding. Senator Joseph McCarthy of Wisconsin had launched into his shameful exploitation of the fear of domestic Communism. An overreaction to that danger had touched all corners of American government. Both at the federal and state levels, this fear had resulted in a variety of new laws and administrative programs aimed at testing the loyalty of government employees in particular and of citizens generally. The Warren Court set out slowly to reverse this trend.

In considering constitutional challenges to government loyalty and security programs, the Supreme Court sailed a very careful course, tacking first one way and then another. In one instance, the Court relieved a

---

[15] *Korematsu* v. *U.S.,* 323 U.S. 214 (1944); *Ex parte Endo,* 323 U.S. 283 (1944).

Senator Joseph McCarthy, one of the most visible symbols of the wave of anti-Communism that swept the country in the years following World War II. McCarthy pursued his "witch hunts" against supposed subversives in the government to such an extreme that he was eventually censored by his colleagues in the Senate. As this picture shows, however, he retained the admiration of many Americans.

witness of the obligation of testifying before the House Un-American Activities Committee on the grounds that the Committee had not made clear how the questions asked were relevant to the matters under investigation.[16] But in a later case the majority concluded that if the relevance of the questions in a particular context of interrogation *was* sufficiently

[16] *Watkins* v. *U.S.*, 354 U.S. 178 (1957); *Barenblatt* v. *U.S.*, 360 U.S. 109 (1959).

clear, the inquiry by the House Committee into past beliefs and associations of witnesses was not forbidden by the First Amendment.[17]

The same careful approach is evident in the Court's dealings with cases arising under the Smith Act of 1940. This law made it a crime to advocate the overthrow of the government by force or violence. In 1951, under Chief Justice Vinson, the Court had decided in a split decision that this exercise of congressional power did not violate the First Amendment's guarantee of free speech.[18] That ruling, however, came in a case involving the top leadership of the Communist Party in the United States. The questions that faced the Warren Court in later cases involved lower level members of the CPUSA. In several carefully guarded opinions, the Warren Court made it clear that "mere membership" in an organization advocating violent overthrow of the government was not sufficient to indicate that particular individuals committeed the crime of advocacy.[19] If it were to convict persons under the Smith Act, the government was required to show active involvement in the advocating of force or violence.

By 1969, the Warren Court went even further, striking down an Ohio statute that made it a criminal act to advocate or teach the duty, necessity, or propriety of violence "as a means of accomplishing industrial or political reform."[20] The Court held the statute, which was quite similar to the Smith Act, unconstitutional because it failed to make the distinction between actively preparing a group for violence and simply advocating violence through abstract teaching. Their decision was based on the First Amendment, and made applicable to Ohio by the due-process clause of the Fourteenth Amendment.

In short, the Warren Court first accepted the basic validity of the Smith Act, but then, over the years, narrowed it through interpretation so that it could be applied only to a strictly limited class of situations. Finally, it virtually interpreted away the crime of advocating violent overthrow. This constituted an important, if incremental, change in the constitutional law of free speech.

Nationalizing criminal justice

The same pattern of gradually moving into an extremely innovative position was displayed by the Warren Court in its decisions dealing with the rights of criminal defendants. Throughout most of our history, the rights

---

[17] *Barenblatt* v. *U.S.*

[18] *Dennis* v. *U.S.*, 341 U.S. 494 (1951).

[19] *Scales* v. *U.S.*, 367 U.S. 203 (1961); *Noto* v. *U.S.*, 367 U.S. 290 (1961).

[20] *Brandenberg* v. *Ohio*, 395 U.S. 444 (1969). For an extended treatment of the speech cases, see Thomas I. Emerson, *The System of Freedom and Expression* (New York. Random House, 1970).

of criminal defendants in state criminal courts (where most of the prosecutions take place) were largely the business of the state. In a series of
cases beginning in the 1930s, however, the Supreme Court held that the
due-process clause of the Fourteenth Amendment required the states to
observe "basically fair" procedures in criminal proceedings.[21] What these
basic federal rights were the Court would say only in particular cases
brought to it. Thus the states could still adopt or experiment with whatever
procedures they chose; they would run afoul of the due-process clause or
the Fourteenth Amendment only when they abridged basic fairness as
defined by the Court from time to time.

At the federal level, of course, things were different. The specific
procedural guarantees of the Fourth through the Eighth Amendments
operated in federal criminal trials. These Bill of Rights provisions provided
greater protection for federal defendants than many states provided for
their criminal defendants. For example, as late as the 1950s, some states
did not require a court-appointed counsel in all serious criminal cases. But
this was required by Article VI at the federal level.

What the Warren Court did, over the period of almost ten years, was
to extend most of the specific guarantees of the Fourth through the Eighth
Amendments to state criminal trials (just as First Amendment rights had
previously been extended).[22] It did this by interpreting the due-process
clause of the Fourteenth Amendment as requiring more than basic fairness, and as incorporating the specific provisions of the Fourth through
Eighth Amendments. The old belief of minimum federal standards and
great leeway on the part of states gave way to a specific extension of
federal practices and guarantees to the states.

In 1963, for instance, the Sixth Amendment's right to counsel was
extended;[23] in 1964, the Fifth Amendment's privilege against self-incrimination was made applicable to state proceedings.[24] And in 1966, in perhaps the most famous of its criminal justice decisions, the Warren Court
extended the Fifth Amendment's privilege of self-incrimination not only
to state criminal trials but also to the interrogation of suspects by police
officers.[25] This resulted in the famous "Miranda warning" (familiar to all
TV watchers), by which suspects are advised of their right to remain silent
and the right to counsel.

The Warren Court not only extended the criminal justice guarantees
of the federal Bill of Rights to the states, it also engaged in a parallel
process of *expanding* and *redefining* these federal constitutional standards.

A notable innovation of
the Warren Court was that
it extended the criminal
justice guarantees of the
Bill of Rights to the states,
and also expanded and re-
defined these federal
standards.

[21] See especially, *Palko* v. *Connecticut,* 302 U.S. 319 (1937).

[22] *Gitlow* v. *New York,* 268 U.S. 652 (1925).

[23] *Mapp* v. *Ohio,* 367 U.S. 643 (1961).

[24] *Malloy* v. *Hogan,* 378 U.S. 1 (1964).

[25] *Miranda* v. *Arizona,* 384 U.S. 436 (1966).

One of the things the Warren Court was known for was its rulings protecting the rights of criminal defendants. These rulings, however, came to strike many people as inappropriate in the face of growing public concern over the rising crime rate.

The Fourth Amendment's prohibition against unreasonable searches and seizures had been extended to the states as a fundamental element of constitutional fairness in 1961; the Warren Court in 1961 also extended to the states the *federal* remedial rule that excluded from evidence material obtained in violation of this search and seizure guarantee.[26]

Furthermore, in 1967, the Court extended the search and seizure guarantee of the Fourth Amendment to cover the placing of telephone taps and microphones even in certain public places.[27] And in 1969, the Court

[26] *Mapp* v. *Ohio.*

[27] *Katz* v. *U.S.*, 389 U.S. 347 (1967).

limited significantly the sorts of searches that police officers could make after arresting individuals.[28]

While this trend was hailed by many, it was attacked by others. In fact, by the mid-1970s, doubts had grown as to whether the Court had gone too far. Were the justices protecting the rights of the accused to the point where guilty people were going free on technicalities? In paying so much attention to individual rights, was the Warren Court ignoring the rights of society in general? We shall return to this question in Chapter 14, but it is one you would do well to ponder here.

Civil rights

Other innovations by the Warren Court, however, seemed to come all at once, overcoming initial opposition. This was true of what is certainly the most memorable achievement of the Warren era—the 1954 decision in *Brown* v. *Board of Education*, the famous school desegregation case. This put the Court in the vanguard of American opinion on race relations. It gave life to the modern civil rights movement, and launched, in one stroke, a minor revolution in American law. Since 1896, it had been held that public facilities—such as schools—could be segregated as long as equal facilities were provided. Now that was revised.

In the years following the Brown case, the Supreme Court moved to ban all governmentally imposed racial discriminations, and finally, to require that schools be racially balanced as a remedy for past segregation. Equality—as expressed in the equal-protection clause of the Fourteenth Amendment—became a prime concern of the Warren Court.

The **equal-protection clause** was relied on by the Court for dismantling the apparatus of governmental racial segregation: It was also the basis for the Court's reapportionment decisions. Before 1962, it had been the practice and doctrine of the Court not to intrude into matters of legislative apportionment (how many voters elect how many representatives). Remedying the ills of the political process was thought to be a matter for the political process itself. In the famous phrase from an opinion of the 1940s, Justice Frankfurter had warned the Court against entering into the "political thicket" of reapportionment.[29] But after 1962, the Court plunged into the thicket and, striking out right and left, accomplished a minor revolution in American electoral law. The Court's newly discovered principle of "one man, one vote" was established as the law of the land, from which not even a school board election could deviate. This was a far cry from the traditional American practice whereby the matters of running elections, including apportionment, were left to the states.[30]

[28] *Chimel* v. *California,* 395 U.S. 752 (1969).

[29] *Colgrave* v. *Green,* 328 U.S. 549 (1946).

[30] For the culmination of this development, see *Oregon* v. *Mitchell,* 400 U.S. 112 (1970).

The integration of Little Rock High School, with the help of federal troops.

Many questions arose concerning this "revolution from above." Was American society so complex and its political leadership so fragmented that only the "nonpolitical" Court could make such sweeping changes? Might not citizens prefer that the president and the Congress, rather than the Court, lead in these important areas? Was there a danger that the Court (which, once appointed, is not answerable to any elected body) would continue to grow in power and strength until it overshadowed the legislative process? It was against such a background of controversy that Earl Warren retired in 1969 and President Nixon named Warren Burger as his choice for Chief Justice. Quickly thereafter, Nixon filled three other vacancies with Harry Blackmun (for Abe Fortas in 1970), Lewis Powell (for Hugo Black in 1972), and William Rehnquist (for John Marshall Harlan in 1972).

The Burger Court

From Warren to Burger

Much has been made, especially by journalists, of the differences between the Warren Court and the Burger Court. The Burger Court has been widely described as more "conservative." It has also been suggested that the Burger Court adheres to a judicial philosophy of **"strict constructionism"** (reluctance to make new interpretations of the Constitution). It is certainly true that the present Court has withdrawn from some of the more exposed forward positions taken by the Warren Court. But the style of its work continues to be activist and interventionist.

While the Court under Warren Burger has drawn back from several free-speech positions of the Warren Court era,[31] it generally continued the process of creating broader and broader protections for expression. In 1974, for instance, it overturned the conviction of a woman who repeatedly called a police officer a "mother-fucking-bastard" on the grounds that the statute under which she was convicted, which forbid "abusive language," was impermissibly vague.[32]

In the area of electronic eavesdropping, the Burger Court has extended the Fourth Amendment strictures beyond those developed during the Warren period.[33] And there has been no backing away from the central thrust of the reapportionment decisions, although the Burger Court has shown some tendency to show greater respect for some particulars of local election laws.

The Burger Court has also continued to extend the equal-protection clause of the Fourteenth Amendment to new situations. For instance, it held that the Cincinnati Public School System could not require pregnant teachers to take maternity leaves on a standard schedule—that is, after a set period in the term of pregnancy. Different teachers could teach different lengths into their respective pregnancies, the justices found, and each case had to be handled on its own terms.[34] And it was the Burger Court in 1971, in an opinion by the chief justice, that accepted mandatory school busing as an appropriate remedy for present racial imbalance in formerly segregated schools.[35] None of this is to say that the Burger Court is as "liberal" and egalitarian as the Warren Court. It is to say that the central thrusts of the Warren Court have been continued, and that in a number

> Although the Burger Court withdrew from some of the more extreme positions of the Warren Court, its work continued to be activist and interventionist.

---

[31] This has been especially true as regards the problem of censoring pornography. See *Pan's Adult Theatre* I v. *Slaton*, 413 U.S. 49 (1973).

[32] *Gooding* v. *Wilson*, 405 U.S. 518 (1972).

[33] See *U.S.* v. *U.S. District Court*, 407 U.S. 297 (1972). Commonly referred to as the *Keith* case.

[34] *Cleveland Board of Education* v. *LaFleur*, 414 U.S. 632 (1974).

[35] *Swann* v. *Charlotte-Mecklenburg Board of Education*, 402 U.S. 1 (1971).

of important instances the present Court has innovated broadly and strikingly in its own right. The best example is the abortion decision of 1974.

Roe v. Wade

In 1968, the Warren Court had decided *Griswold* v. *Connecticut*. In this case, a challenge was made to Connecticut's birth-control law. This law prevented not only the sale and dissemination of information about contraceptives, but also their *use*. The reasons that particular justices gave for finding the Connecticut law unconstitutional varied wildly, but Justice Black, in dissent, was clearly right in suggesting that what the Court was doing was finding in the due-process clause a right of privacy, which like the old liberty of contract, pre-1937, was not specified in the constitutional text. Black objected to this invention of a right to privacy as a throwback to the illegitimate innovation of the earlier period. Constitutional scholars studying the opinions in the Griswold case were not so sure. Did this really represent a willingness on the part of the Court to resurrect the old notion that the due-process clause embodied certain unspecific natural law guarantees that could be found there by sufficiently "sensitive" judges? Was the ultimate in judicial activism returning to fashion?

This question was answered affirmatively by the Court in *Roe* v. *Wade*. The case involved a challenge to the abortion laws of several states that prohibited abortions except for specified therapeutic purposes. The Court deciding the case was not the Warren Court of the 1960s; Chief Justice Warren Burger's name had now been given to a supposedly new period in Supreme Court decision making, and the justice who wrote for the majority in *Roe* v. *Wade* was Harry Blackmun, a Nixon appointee. Nonetheless, the abortion case fulfilled the promise of the birth-control case. Justice Blackmun found in the due-process clause an unspecific right of privacy that was held to prevent states from interfering at all with the free choice of women and their physicians concerning abortion in the first trimester of pregnancy. There was no effort in the Blackmun opinion to tie this holding to any particular language of the Constitution other than "due process."

The Warren Court began and the Burger Court completed the process of reviving the breathtakingly activist idea that certain fundamental but unwritten rights lurked in the due-process clause—the idea against which liberals had rebelled thirty years before when it was asserted by the Nine Old Men!

SUMMARY

In this chapter we have examined (1) how the Supreme Court works, (2) the important functions it performs in our political system, and (3) how the style of the modern Court has changed from judicial activism to judicial self-restraint and back again.

We have seen how the pace of innovation in the Warren and Burger years has raised questions about whether the contemporary Court, like its predecessor of the 1930s, is in danger of overstepping the proper bounds of the institution in the American system. Critics of judicial activism, such as the late Professor Alexander M. Bickel of the Yale Law School[36] and Professor Philip Kurland of the University of Chicago Law School,[37] point out that while judicial review is firmly and legitimately established in our political tradition, the Court should use this power as carefully and as infrequently as possible; to overturn the judgment of elected officials in a democracy, the argument goes, is a grave and risky thing. It should be done only when the action taken by a legislature, a president, or a governor is of a nature that contravenes a specific constitutional guarantee, or when the offending governmental action is of a nature intimately related to what the specific language and history of the Constitution forbid.

Defenders of judicial activism, on the other hand, such as Judge J. Skelly Wright of the United States Circuit Court of Appeals of the District of Columbia[38] and political scientist Martin Shapiro of Harvard,[39] suggest that the concern over the antidemocratic nature of the Court, and its vulnerability as an institution within our political system, are not causes for alarm. These commentators suggest that as long as particular Court decisions are progressive in *substance*, they will commend themselves to the more enlightened elements of the American population, and the Court will be safe and the country well served.

There is a continuing tension between the desire to see cases come out in particular ways and the discipline of constitutional form and structure in which the justices must work. The justices must constantly be choosing between those innovations that can be justified and those that cannot. Has the trade-off between activism and restraint been made well or ill by the Warren and Burger Courts? Are the fears of Archibald Cox expressed at the outset of this chapter justified or trivial? How would you decide?

[36] Alexander M. Bickel, "Notes on the Constitution," *Commentary*, August 1975, p. 53. But see especially his *The Supreme Court and the Idea of Progress* (New York: Harper & Row, 1970).

[37] See Philip B. Kurland, "Toward a Political Supreme Court," *University of Chicago Law Review* 19 (1969).

[38] J. Skelly Wright, "Professor Bickel—The Scholarly Tradition and the Supreme Court," *Harvard Law Review* 84 (February 1971): 769.

[39] Martin Shapiro, *Law and Politics in the Supreme Court* (New York: The Free Press, 1964), pp. 24-48.

KEY TERMS

executive privilege	*laissez faire*
district court	**Court Plan**
court of appeal	**Warren Court**
constitutional court	judicial activism
congressional court	**Smith Act**
trial court	due-process clause
intermediate appellate court	*Brown* v. *Board of Education*
state supreme court	equal-protection clause
appellant	**Burger Court**
docket	strict constructionism
writ of *certiorari*	*Roe* v. *Wade*
legislative reapportionment	

SUGGESTED READINGS

ABRAHAM, HENRY J., *The Judiciary: The Supreme Court in the Governmental Process,* 4th ed. (Boston: Allyn and Bacon, 1977).

An excellent primer on the Supreme Court and the judicial process.

BECKER, THEODORE, and MALCOLM FEELEY, eds., *The Impact of Supreme Court Decisions* (New York: Oxford University Press, 1973).

A good collection, bringing together studies of how Court decisions affect the real world.

BERGER, RAOUL, *Government by Judiciary* (Cambridge, Mass.: Harvard University Press, 1977).

A spirited attack on the lawmaking role of the modern Supreme Court. Highly controversial.

BICKEL, ALEXANDER M., *The Least Dangerous Branch* (Indianapolis: Bobbs-Merrill, 1962).

A very elegant argument that the Court should pursue a less ambitious course in American politics.

BICKEL, ALEXANDER M., *The Supreme Court and the Idea of Progress* (New York: Harper & Row, 1970).

A critical examination of the work of the Warren Court by one of the nation's most distinguished legal scholars.

ELLIOTT, WARD E. Y., *The Risk of Guardian Democracy* (Cambridge, Mass.: Harvard University Press, 1974).

A study of the influence of liberal interest groups on the Supreme Court's reapportionment decision. A "specialist" book, but very important.

PRITCHELL, C. HERMAN, and ALAN F. WESTIN, eds., *The Third Branch of Government* (New York: Harcourt, 1963).

An excellent set of short case studies of particular Supreme Court decisions.

VOSE, CLEMENT E., *Constitutional Change: Amendment, Politics, and Supreme Court Litigation Since 1900* (Lexington, Mass.: D. C. Heath, 1972).

A masterful study of American constitutional politics. A book for specialists, but so well written as to be accessible to beginning students.

One of the most awful truths about the
real world is that it is a muddle. Anybody
who is clear about it is under an illusion.
However carefully we refine our
techniques, we must never desert the
great tradition of muddling through. This
is the only realistic way to approach the
future of anything.

Kenneth Boulding (1978)

It is not that we lack the economic tools
to generate increased employment. The
real problem is that every time we push
the rate of unemployment toward
acceptably low levels, by whatever name,
we set off a new inflation.

Charles E. Schultze (1977)

CHAPTER 12 DOMESTIC POLICY MAKING: JOBS FOR AMERICANS

"Sitting around on a bench, waiting for the welfare check, and watching TV . . . . Got to be something better than that," said Dacida Williams, seventeen years old, black, and a high-school dropout from Bedford-Stuyvessant in Brooklyn. She is looking for a job.

She has not found one.

"Signing up, filling out applications, taking tests. I can type. I can file. They never called me," she added.

"That's where it be, sitting on the bench," said her boyfriend, Edwyn Blake, eighteen, "staring hard at the people going by. When the boredom gets bad, the violence comes. The young men 'go to the grass, trying to hurt each other. That's just working off frustration,'" he said.[1]

Why is unemployment among young urban blacks running at 40 percent? Why *doesn't* everybody have a job in the United States? Shouldn't the most powerful and richest country in the world be able to provide the opportunity to work to anyone who wants to work? To address these and related questions, we need to examine the hard choices involved in domestic policy making as it relates to achieving basic economic objectives in a rapidly changing society.

We have seen how Congress works, and how the president sets goals for the bureaucracy and attempts to set a direction for the nation. We have

[1] Jerry Flint, "Rising Unemployment Bewilders Young Blacks," *New York Times,* September 10, 1977.

Fig. 12.1
Black versus white unemployment. (Source: U.S. Department of Labor, Bureau of Labor Statistics.)

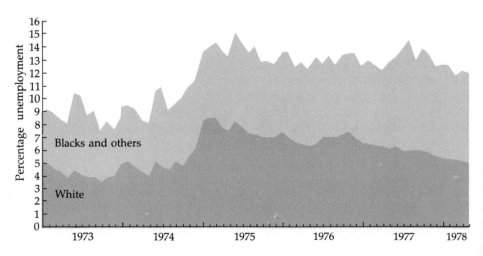

A Definition: Full Employment

*Ideally, **full employment** would mean a job for every able-bodied individual seeking work. In the United States, many economists and public officials would be prepared to accept an overall unemployment rate of 4 percent as approximating full employment. Some economists speculate that the changing composition of the United States labor force—for example, increasing numbers of younger and female workers—has probably raised the level of the "natural" rate of unemployment above 4 percent. In any event, the nation failed to achieve a 4 percent rate during the 1970s. Some would now argue for accepting a 5 percent rate—or higher.*

found that the bureaucracy is a forceful and influential participant in policy making. We have explained how people get elected and why. We have examined the basic legal structure of the country and how it operates.

But we need to know more. We need to know how domestic policy is made—or, as in the case of "full employment," how it has often not been made. Domestic policy making involves the interaction of institutions, interest groups, ideas, beliefs, and public opinion. Often it involves an interplay of the branches of the national government.

What are the connections between the policy struggle as described in earlier chapters and the kinds of policies followed by our government? Does the *how* (the way) of American policy making have important consequences for the *what* (the substance) of public policy? What is the relationship between process and substance? How do we account for the heavy incidence of joblessness among blacks and other minority groups? What is the government doing to solve the problems faced by Dacida Williams, Edwyn Blake, and the thousands of other Americans, many of them young, who are seeking to fulfill their hopes and dreams?

A LOT OF DIFFERENT NEEDS

Domestic policy making in the late twentieth century responds to a vast, and increasing, range of needs, especially in the areas of health, education, and human welfare. Environmental quality, transportation, agriculture, and natural resources are also obviously important. This chapter focuses on an aspect of policy making that is basic to all these issues: the relationship between the federal government and the functioning of the American economy. A sluggish or faltering economy makes the task of meeting public needs difficult and frustrating. It increases joblessness. A prosperous economy makes the task of policy making seem at least feasible.

A basic objective in a free society is the opportunity to work.

We will concentrate in this chapter on the *opportunity to work*, a basic objective in a free society that is of special concern for young Americans today. Without an opportunity to earn a living, citizens are deprived of an opportunity to fulfull their own personal development. Heads of families who are without work will naturally feel that they are depriving the members of their families of any chance to participate in the broader opportunities of our society. Without work, individual Americans are denied their chance to strive and to seek, to move ahead, and to feed and clothe their families without public assistance.

We are not talking about people too old, too ill, or too handicapped to hold a job, nor about those who do not want to work. We have in mind those individuals who are able to work, who are seeking work and cannot find it. While some people doubtless are content to collect unemployment insurance, obtain food stamps, and visit Medicaid physicians, most unemployed Americans feel frustration, anguish, and despair, the attitudes expressed by the two young people we met at the beginning of this chapter.

The Costs of Unemployment

Whatever the impact of unemployment on the lives of individuals, its cumulative impact on the federal budget is negative. The government will collect less as fewer workers pay taxes on their income. And as unemployment mounts, the government must pay out more and more for unemployment compensation, welfare payments, and aid to dependent children.

Many economists regard unemployment as a necessary trade-off in the fight against inflation. Its costs, however, are high, both for the individuals involved and for the federal government.

Among many economists, unemployment is regarded as a necessary trade-off in the fight against **inflation,** or rising prices. Furthermore, business enterprise is much more nervous about inflation than about unemployment. But productive workers who are put out of work in the trade-off against inflation cease to be taxpayers as long as they are out of work. Some public services may have to cease expanding or even be curtailed. An increase of one percentage point in unemployment nationally produces a $16 billion decrease in federal revenues. This is a lot of money even in today's inflated currency.

In addition to this loss of tax revenue, the government must pay out more to people who are out of work. In 1975, for example, during a period of unusually abrupt economic decline, unemployment compensation payments soon added $20 billion to federal spending. To put it bluntly, when some people lose their jobs, other people have to support them through their taxes. Or the government is forced to run a huge budget **deficit,** which occurs when expenditures exceed revenues, mortgaging the taxes of future Americans.

Unemployment Costs

Who Bears the Burden?

Who pays the price when our economy slows down? Certainly not the professional economists, who are well-paid professionals with an unemployment rate approaching zero. They are not among the innocent who

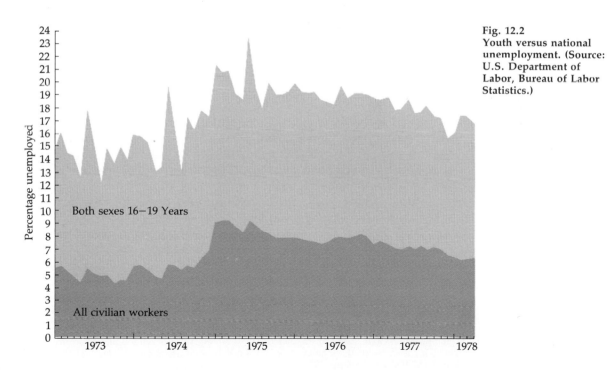

Fig. 12.2
Youth versus national unemployment. (Source: U.S. Department of Labor, Bureau of Labor Statistics.)

Unemployed youths lining up for summer jobs in Washington.

suffer when the economy skids into still another **recession.** In fact, the burdens of neither unemployment nor inflation are evenly distributed in American society. It is the young, and especially minority youth, who pay first and most heavily in joblessness. Unemployment rates among black Americans typically double those among white citizens. Even during our most prosperous times, the black community experiences high unemployment rates. Black Americans often say: "We are the last hired and the first fired." And indeed, when an economic recession begins, black workers are let go first; then, as the recession deepens, their unemployment rates reach catastrophic levels. For many black youths, joblessness is a permanent feature of life in the so-called affluent society.[2] The consequences for American society are frightful. Prolonged unemployment increases the

[2] Herman Miller's *Rich Man, Poor Man* (New York: Thomas Crowell, 1964), although dated, remains a definitive study of the disparities of American society. See also Warren Bloomberg, Jr., and Henry J. Schmandt, eds., *Urban Poverty: Its Social and Political Dimensions* (Beverly Hills, Calif.: Sage, 1970).

incidence of crime, drug abuse, and other forms of behavior that can ruin a person's chance of achieving a productive life in the future. The dollar costs of this pathology are enormous. The social costs are incalculable. Unfortunately, inflation also carries frightful social costs, cutting sharply into the living standards of the millions of Americans who are on fixed incomes. It is particularly harsh on many older citizens. Whichever way the policy makers lean in the trade-off between unemployment and inflation, large numbers of their fellow citizens will feel the consequences.

THE MESSY POLITICS OF POLICY MAKING

The making of domestic policy on matters as important as employment and inflation is directly influenced by a number of key factors: the goals of the president and his administration, the political makeup of Congress, the relative power of the various interest groups, and the continuing involvement of the permanent bureaucracy. Of equal importance is the disorganized condition of American politics. As we have noted before, American society addresses public policy issues, such as employment and inflation, through a messy political process in which numerous organized groups demand a piece of the action. This bureaucratic-political process involves the continuing interaction of the presidency, Congress, the bureaucracies, and the interest groups. These forces are not mere abstractions. All, in turn, are constantly looking for and are influenced by signals received from the public (usually a variety of publics), both allies and enemies. No one wants to be caught short when hard choices have to be made between conflicting objectives.

The bureaucratic-political process of domestic policy making involves the interaction of the presidency, Congress, the bureaucracies, and the interest groups.

Prevailing Moods

During a period of political stalemate and deadlock, the mid-1970s being a case in point, the general condition of American politics makes it harder than usual to bring new programs into being that will alter the direction of our society. In terms of dealing with the dilemma of jobs versus inflation, the prevailing public mood that accompanies a period of political deadlock makes it difficult to move sharply in *any* new direction.

In sharp contrast, the general mood of the early 1960s seemed to encourage changes in basic economic policies. John F. Kennedy, in running for the presidency, hit on a popular theme when he spoke of "getting the country moving again." There had been four economic recessions during the previous decade, each one leaving a higher level of unemployment. Kennedy's brief period in the White House brought marked improvement in employment without either substantially increasing inflation or incurring massive federal budget deficits.

President Johnson, an extraordinary legislative leader, found the public mood immediately following Kennedy's assassination supportive of strong leadership from the White House. Johnson took advantage of this mood as he drove his "Great Society" domestic programs through Congress in 1964–1966. The resulting shift in public priorities, as we shall see later, had profound consequences. At the same time, the Johnson administration began the long, fateful process of "Americanizing" the war in Vietnam. The additional federal spending required by the expanded domestic programs and the Vietnam war, accompanied by a large tax cut in 1964, combined to reduce joblessness dramatically. Unemployment was less than 3.5 percent when President Johnson left office, but the fires of inflation had also been ignited. In the meantime, a shift in public mood made it politically necessary for the Nixon administration to find a way to withdraw American forces from Vietnam.[3]

The Nixon years were also marked by an unsuccessful effort to keep the lid on inflation while allowing unemployment to rise only moderately. The Arab oil embargo in the winter of 1973 brought double-digit inflation combined with unusually high levels of unemployment. This economic bad news was soon accompanied by the sorry attempt to obstruct justice following the Watergate break-in. The precipitous decline in public confidence that ensued made it extremely difficult for President Ford to exert effective leadership from the White House. Mr. Carter, after a brief presidential "honeymoon," soon encountered the same obstacle, as his administration sought to address a lengthy agenda of difficult problems.

It is time now to examine the way in which employment and training programs developed during the 1960s and the 1970s in response to the jobs crisis.

EMPLOYMENT AND TRAINING PROGRAMS: THE 1960s AND 1970s

Certainly young people hanging around on the street corner or occupying the park bench today do not expect full employment to occur. Neither do many economists. Whatever people outside government may think, government economists maintain that the private sector, left to itself, simply is unable to provide jobs for all who need one. In order to keep up with an expanding work force, our economy needs to generate millions of additional jobs each year. In 1977, for example, about four million new jobs were created, most of them in the private sector, and yet unemploy-

---

[3] For more detail on this shift in mood as it affected Vietnam decision making, see John C. Donovan, *The Cold Warriors* (Lexington, Mass.: D. C. Heath, 1974) and Townsend Hoopes, *The Limits of Intervention* (New York: David McKay, 1969).

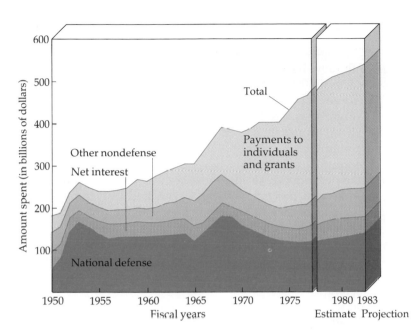

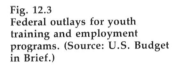

600

500

400

Amount spent (in billions of dollars)

300

200

100

Total

Other nondefense

Net interest

Payments to
individuals
and grants

National defense

1950   1955   1960   1965   1970   1975   1980 1983
Fiscal years   Estimate Projection

Fig. 12.3
**Federal outlays for youth
training and employment
programs. (Source: U.S. Budget
in Brief.)**

ment declined only a little more than one percentage point. Despite rapid growth in jobs, unemployment nationally in 1977 remained well above 6 percent while joblessness among young minority workers approached 40 percent.

Therefore, the government has the continuing responsibility of creating jobs both by stimulating expansion and growth in the private sector and by building public works, and by creating more and more **public service jobs**—jobs created to meet a specific need and funded with CETA (Comprehensive Employment and Training Act) dollars. The public service jobs programs and the government-sponsored training programs are broadly labeled **employment and training programs.** These programs, initiated first in the 1960s, have continued and expanded ever since, despite mounting criticism. The steady expansion of job-training programs has transformed the Employment and Training Administration in the Labor Department into the largest bureaucratic unit within the department. This administration did not exist prior to the Johnson administration. (In the Johnson years it was called the Manpower Administration.) The Carter administration requested $11.4 billion to support employment and training programs, including 600,000 public service positions, in fiscal year 1979.[4]

Initiated during the 1960s, government-sponsored employment and training programs have expanded steadily since then despite mounting criticism.

[4] See the *Congressional Quarterly Weekly News Report,* March 4, 1978, p. 592. Also see Roger Davidson, *The Politics of Comprehensive Manpower Legislation* (Baltimore: Johns Hopkins University Press, 1973).

The Kennedy Years

The first piece of "manpower" (now termed "employment and training") legislation, one of the few important items of domestic legislation enacted during Kennedy's famous 1,000 days, bore the unexciting title: The Manpower Development and Training Act of 1962. Designed by a small group of members of Congress assisted by a few technicians from the Labor Department, the bill subsequently was reworked by the staffs of the House and Senate labor committees.

Interestingly enough, the people who drafted the original bill were not thinking primarily of individuals like those we met in the introduction; that is, young people who had no skills and who had only rarely been employed. The principal concern of the lawmakers was retraining individuals who had experienced long periods of active work service, but whose jobs had disappeared in the onslaught of technological change. These were people who wanted to work, who had previously worked, but who found themselves out of jobs because of the forces of change at work within our own society.[5]

In the early 1960s, the image that struck many people was an unemployed white coal miner with a wife and several children, who had worked for many years only to find himself out of a job because new machinery did his job more quickly and efficiently, and because the demand for coal was shrinking in an era of cheap oil. The originators of the bill felt that it would be a relatively simple matter to retrain such a worker—say, by training him to run a bulldozer or steam shovel. It would be less expensive to retrain this individual and return him to the work force than to pay him unemployment compensation. The idea of retraining seemed simple, quick, and relatively inexpensive, as well as being socially useful.

Congress passed the legislation largely on these grounds, and the Labor Department was empowered to administer the program.

The new program had been in operation only a brief time when the Washington policy makers learned that job-training programs were merely touching the edges of a complicated problem that reached into every corner of the nation. Although federally funded, the job-training programs were carried out by two long-standing state and local bureaucracies: the public employment services and the vocational education system. The program concepts and dollars came from Washington, but the need for training and work was individual and local.

A universe of need: the other America

When the various state and local agencies began enrolling the "trainees," as they were called, they soon discovered that coal miners represented

[5] This early view of the problem is explained in greater detail in John C. Donovan's *The Policy Makers* (Indianapolis: Bobbs-Merrill, 1970). See especially Chapter 3.

Item: From 1947 to 1975, income disparity between blacks and whites narrowed by only eleven points. The average earnings of black families in the mid-1970s were 59 percent of the average earnings among white families.

Item: Economic conditions of the black poor worsened during the 1970s, not only relative to those of whites, but also relative to those of the growing black middle class, leaving a two-tiered black society.

Item: The movement of blacks from lower paying to better paying jobs slowed after 1970. A steady and encouraging decrease in the proportion of low-income black families during the mid-1960s was soon halted and has not improved since.

Item: In 1974, four out of ten black children were raised in poverty, against one white child in ten.

Item: The proportion of poor families headed by black women increased markedly in the early 1970s. By 1975, three-fourths of all poor black families headed by women received some or all of their income from public assistance.

These items are drawn from the 1978 annual report of the Carnegie Corporation. Alan Pifer, president of the Carnegie Corporation, warned that "We have arrived at a moment in history when both protest and conscience are dormant."

Pifer drew special attention to the horrendous situation in which young black Americans often find themselves.

"Poorly educated, untrained, heavily concentrated in urban slums, and ostensibly ill-suited for steady employment, the several hundred thousand youngsters who make up this group are an alienated, crime-prone element in our communities."

The unemployment rate for black youths—approximating 40 percent—is two and one-half that for whites.

Source: UPI, April 11, 1978.

Black Americans: Beyond Protest and Conscience

---

only a tiny portion of the jobless. The monthly reports reaching Washington showed that most people seeking retraining at the local level had very little previous work experience. Many of them were young. Many had no training at all. Many had never held jobs. Many were members of minority groups—blacks, Spanish-speaking Americans, Indians. Many were women. Most had experienced difficulty in finding, let alone holding, a job.

Within less than a year the job-training program activity revealed this vast universe of unemployed, discouraged Americans who lived in what Michael Harrington called "the other America." Here was a horde of Americans lacking skills, and often without previous work history; people who were the victims of racial discrimination, poor education, and poverty. Most were extremely ill prepared for what the technicians called "the

"The other America."

world of work." Simplistic retraining would not solve their deep-seated problems, which had their roots in the long-standing inequities of our society.[6]

A lengthy process of gradual alteration of job-training programs was now underway. Congress, the Department of Labor, and the Vocational Education Division of the United States Office of Education took the lead in encouraging the state and local agencies to take a fresh look at these problems. Endless hours of meetings and thousands of memorandums fed into this effort, aimed at altering the programs so as to meet this expanding need more efficiently. At the same time, state and local groups were demanding more federal dollars and more training programs. Members of Congress, upon learning of these demands, proved receptive.

[6] Michael Harrington, *The Other America* (New York: Macmillan, 1972).

THE WHITE HOUSE

WASHINGTON

December 23, 1963

MEMORANDUM TO: Secretary Wirtz

FROM: Theodore C. Sorensen

I would like a little elaboration of a point you made at the meeting today:

"takes $1250 to salvage a youth; otherwise would cost $40,000."

This elaboration should be no more than one page. I will need this information before 4:00 PM Thursday.

A memo from Mr. Sorensen, White House Counsel to President Kennedy, who was serving in a similar capacity to President Johnson. Sorensen was requesting more detail on a point made by the secretary of labor at a White House meeting late in December 1963, only a month after Kennedy's assassination. This was a very busy period when budget, State of the Union messages, and domestic program decisions were being put in their final form by the new president, his staff, and cabinet officers. Secretary Wirtz was making the point that it costs a lot less to train an unemployed youth for gainful employment than it does to keep him or her in a state of continuous joblessness.

LBJ Takes the Helm

President Kennedy's assassination sped the process of change. Lyndon B. Johnson, his successor, found himself in an excellent position to exert leadership in the wake of this national tragedy. As we stated earlier, the public mood was right. Johnson enjoyed widespread support in Congress as he moved ahead with the martyred president's unfinished legislative agenda. Johnson also saw the need for new approaches to the entire range of problems related to poverty. In January 1964, Johnson brought these problems to center stage when he dramatically declared "war on poverty."

*Political
Leadership and
Changing
Priorities*

Public priorities do *change, as they have throughout our two-hundred-year history. Sometimes they are changed because political leadership enjoys the necessary public and political support to effect the reordering of our national priorities. Indeed, a pronounced shift in public priorities occurred in recent years without most Americans clearly perceiving the change. Ironically, Senator McGovern, the unsuccessful Democratic presidential candidate in 1972, was advocating a shift in public priorities that* had already taken place.

President Lyndon Johnson greatly increased the human resources side of federal program activity and federal spending during the 1960s. His Great Society programs—the attack on poverty, federal aid to education at every level, urban renewal and model cities, an expansion of existing welfare programs, more vocational education, employment, and training activity, and the inauguration of Medicare-Medicaid programs pro-

viding health care for older Americans—all represented a major change. Despite the dollar costs of our military involvement in Vietnam during the Johnson years (calculated at some $100 billion overall), the defense portion of our national budget nevertheless began its relative decline, a decline that has continued steadily ever since. Because federal expenditures for human resources programs remained extremely modest through the Kennedy years, LBJ's domestic policy initiatives in the mid-1960s, combined with his extraordinary qualities as legislative leader, brought about a major shift in public priorities. The human resources side grew so as to overshadow the defense side, which gradually diminished as a proportion of federal spending. When Johnson left office, the forces of incrementalism that are built into the system took over and reinforced this changed set of priorities, despite two Republican presidents—Nixon and Ford—who might have preferred a different emphasis.

SPENDING TRENDS
(as percentage of total
budget outlays)

	1950[1]	1960[1]	1965[1]	1970[1]	1975[1]	1978[2]	1979[3]	1980[3]	1981[3]	1982[3]	1983[3]
National defense	29.1	49.0	40.1	40.0	26.2	24.0	23.9	24.2	24.6	24.7	24.6
Human resources	33.0	27.7	29.9	37.3	51.7	51.7	51.8	52.3	53.0	53.5	54.3
Net interest[4]	11.3	7.5	7.2	7.3	7.1	7.1	7.4	7.4	7.2	6.9	6.4
All other	26.6	15.8	22.8	15.4	14.9	17.1	16.9	16.1	15.2	14.9	14.6

Note: Totals may not add to 100% due to rounding

[1] Source: "Federal Government Finances," prepared by the Office of Management and Budget.

[2] 1978 Second Concurrent Resolution.

[3] Based on Congressional Budget Office projections of current policy projections. Source: "Five-Year Budget Projections: Fiscal Years 1979-1983," prepared by Congressional Budget Office.

[4] Total interest net of interest received by trust funds.

The table opposite reveals the changing trends in federal spending between 1950 and the 1980s. From the table, we see that just as John F. Kennedy was about to gain election to the White House in 1960, national defense accounted for a whopping 49 percent of all federal spending, with a mere 27.7 percent going to human resources programs. However, a shift in these proportions is underway as early as 1965, right in the midst of LBJ's Great Society initiatives (also the first year of Vietnam military escalation). By 1970, LBJ was gone from office and Richard Nixon, his Republican successor, occupied the White House. But in this year the human resources side continued to expand up to 37 percent, while defense remained at 40 percent, just as it did in 1965. And what happened during the Ford years? By 1975, national defense had shrunk to 26 percent while the human resources side exceeded 50 percent.

How is this to be explained? Shouldn't the Nixon and Ford administrations have been expected to reverse the Johnsonian priorities? Please bear in mind that Congress throughout this long period was controlled by Democratic majorities. Also, the incremental nature of the process carried the reordered priorities of the Johnson era through the 1970s. As our projections in the table suggest, these proportions are likely to hold well into the 1980s. Clearly, then, important changes in public policy do take place.

The centerpiece of Johnson's program was a bill designed inside the White House by a small group of technicians. The **Economic Opportunity Act,** as it was called, sailed through Congress. Johnson signed the bill into law in early August 1964. As with the earlier manpower and job-training programs, the emphasis was *not* on creating new jobs, but on training and retraining the unemployed. This time there was a difference, however, in that Johnson's new antipoverty program was directed at the young, the disadvantaged, and minorities. This new thrust continued until it was pushed aside by the war in Vietnam, which absorbed more of the president's time and energies. As the escalating war in Southeast Asia drew heavily on available resources in 1966, the attack on poverty failed to get funds for a large expansion of its program activity. Nevertheless, the program survived.

Johnson's antipoverty program, written in the White House, gradually gained the support of bipartisan congressional majorities. Congressional committees overseeing the program developed an interest in it. The appropriations committees especially played a leading role in the gradual process of reshaping the program and keeping it under control. The pro-

The 1964 Economic Opportunity Act, unlike earlier job-training programs, was directed at the young, the disadvantaged, and minorities.

grams were broadened in variety and scope, and Congress took a growing interest in the administrative details of the programs. In a similar fashion, those employed in these various programs—those who administered them as well as the clients served by them—also developed a vested interest in having them continued. The employment-training complex united members of Congress, clients, and bureaucrats (both federal and state and local) in a common undertaking, one that is here to stay.

Nixon Faces Incrementalism

By the time Richard Nixon assumed the presidency in 1969, hundreds of thousands of people were involved in job-training and antipoverty programs in every state and in most communities. Through the process of gradual and *incremental*—or step-by-step—adjustment, Congress and its committees, operating in the normal manner, had taken over the programs and revised and enlarged them, meanwhile uncovering a vast clientele. Naturally enough, Nixon was neither interested in, nor committed to, Johnson's domestic programs. In a number of cases, he was opposed to them. *But he was not able to eliminate them.* In fact, he had difficulty in cutting them back. Even following his 1972 landslide reelection victory, the Nixon administration found that it had perhaps slowed down the domestic programs of the 1960s, but had certainly not stopped them.[7]

Congressional interest was buttressed by the established bureaucracies, especially those in Labor and Health, Education, and Welfare, which now had under their control a series of massive operating programs enacted in the 1960s. And, as we have seen, these programs had been "federalized"; that is, implemented by state and local bureaucracies. Ironically, the Nixon years brought one major program addition in the form of the public service jobs mentioned earlier. Johnson originally had resisted this program, and Nixon certainly did not favor it, but his economic policies brought on a serious economic decline. Finally, the Republican president reluctantly accepted public service jobs as a further "answer" to chronic unemployment.[8]

When President Nixon left office in disgrace in August 1974, he left behind a bewildering array of employment and training programs and public service jobs programs costing billions of dollars annually. He had also turned over even greater operating responsibility to state and local bureaucracies.

[7] John C. Donovan, *The Politics of Poverty*, 2d ed. (Indianapolis: Bobbs-Merrill, 1974). This revised edition is the only study of Johnson's antipoverty program that examines the reasons for its survival during the Nixon years.

[8] By far the best account of this development is found in Howard W. Hallman, *Emergency Employment: A Study in Federalism* (University: University of Alabama Press, 1977).

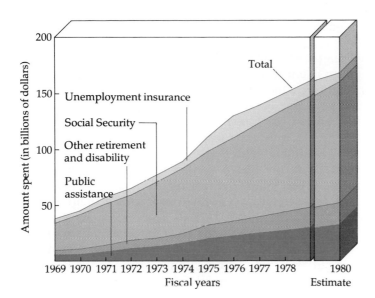

Fig. 12.4
Federal outlays for income security. (Source: U.S. Budget in Brief.)

So for more than a decade, Congress and the executive bureaucracies, in the face of the nation's inability to "solve" the problem of unemployment, carried the day against presidents who opposed the proliferation of these programs, who wished to cut them back. And after Nixon retired to San Clemente, this pattern of gradual growth continued under Ford.

Why is it that in spite of the efforts of some politicians and presidents such as Nixon to reduce these programs or eliminate some of them, they persist and in fact grow from one administration to the next? Is it because we are unable to find a feasible alternative? Is bureaucratic momentum or Congressional inertia a sufficient explanation? Do you see a connection between these programs and the failure thus far to find an answer to long-term unemployment?

Muddled or Muddling Through?

Why is making public policy so often such a gradual, incremental process? Why do pressing social problems take so long to be "solved"? Is it possible that some problems may prove to be insoluble?

We Americans seem to nibble away endlessly at joblessness, inflation, social security, welfare programs, and so forth. In a real sense, these basic problems are never completely solved, although we like to think of ourselves as a nation of "problem solvers." The basic issues, such as the lack of jobs or rising inflation, which usually involve basic dilemmas and difficult choices, are continuing items on the political agenda. Policy makers, especially the careerists (which includes most members of Congress and most bureaucrats), find themselves dealing with the same issues over and over again. They learn to live with them.

This may be inevitable in the messy politics of our democracy. The situation is not static, however. Policy changes do take place. A persistent nibbling away at basic and seemingly insoluble problems actually transforms the society over the longer haul.[9]

Lindblom and other believers in the theory of **incrementalism** argue that we Americans have made a virtue of "muddling through." While it is easy to talk glibly about "rational planning" and "going to the heart of the matter," doing so may prove too painful or too upsetting politically, especially for politicians, who are normally cautious people. Furthermore, Lindblom and other incrementalists believe that this slow, nibbling process produces striking new directions in policy *over time*. But it takes time. The Industrial Revolution did not take place overnight. Nor did the revolution for equal rights. We did not set out as a people to create a vast permanent military establishment, and yet we have one. The building of the welfare state, with its bewildering array of programs and the accompanying huge bureaucracy, is a product of a long evolution. As we have seen, the huge employment and training complex is a major development of the past two decades. Lindblom reminds us that these momentous program changes—and others—have frequently come about through "policy changes so undramatic as to obscure the magnitude of change."[10]

According to the theory of incrementalism, policy changes take place through a slow, nibbling process that eventually transforms the system over time.

How close is this view of the process to reality? Don't our most difficult social problems persist over long periods because the American people remain seriously divided about possible remedies? Welfare reform, for example, is likely to mean one thing to a resident of affluent suburbia, whose life-style precludes any real awareness of the condition of life in "the other America." The ghetto family, on the other hand, struggling to survive in a cold-water flat in the South Bronx, has quite a different view of welfare. Then there is the difficult matter of choice. President Carter pledged to bring about welfare reform during his administration. Nonetheless, when Joseph Califano, Secretary of Health, Education, and Welfare, presented an elaborate scheme for reform at a cabinet meeting in

[9] Lindblom, Charles, *The Policy Making Process* (Englewood Cliffs, N.J.: Prentice-Hall, 1968).

[10] David E. Rosenbaum, "Much More than Dollars Figure in Welfare Costs," *New York Times*, June 26, 1977.

"Incremen-
talism"

In a political system as large, diverse, and complex as ours, sweeping and drastic changes in public policy do not occur very often and seldom overnight. Changes in public policy are more likely to be achieved in *increments, in bits and pieces;* changes are usually made at the margins of existing programs rather than by bold new innovations. As Charles Lindblom expressed it:

Usually, though not always, what is feasible politically is policy only incrementally, or marginally, different from existing policies. Drastically different policies fall beyond the pale.*

The nature of the federal budgetary process also favors incremental decision making. The great bulk of the $500 billion federal budget is composed of ongoing programs whose dollar costs increase each year almost automatically. For example, Social Security expenditures mount as the older population increases in size and as benefit payments are raised in an effort to keep pace with inflation. The annual costs of the pension system for those retired from the armed forces approached $10 billion as this was written; these costs, like Social Security, will also increase steadily in the years ahead.

Even slight increases in the many programs included in the huge annual budget tend to produce a snowball effect, so that over a ten-year period a fair amount of change occurs.†

*Charles Lindblom, *The Policy Making Process*, (Englewood Cliffs, N.J.: Prentice-Hall, 1968), p. 26.

†The classic study of public policy making as reflected in the making of federal budgets is Aaron Wildavsky, *The Politics of the Budgetary Process*, 2d ed. (Boston: Little, Brown, 1974).

April 1977, the president exploded: "Are you telling me that there is no way to improve the present welfare system except by spending billions of dollars? In that case, to hell with it. We're wasting our time."

Welfare reform is expensive, so it conflicts with the budget-balancing objectives.[11] When the Carter administration presented its welfare reform proposal to Congress, it immediately encountered stiff resistance. Welfare reform never comes fully blown; instead, changes in the welfare system take place slowly and gradually. Here again, the role of central policy leadership is strongly constrained.

Do you find it acceptable that we make policy changes in small bits and pieces, slowly and gradually, rather than as the consequence of long-range planning? Is incremental policy making likely to prove adequate to the challenges of the late twentieth century?

[11] Lindblom, *The Policy Making Process*.

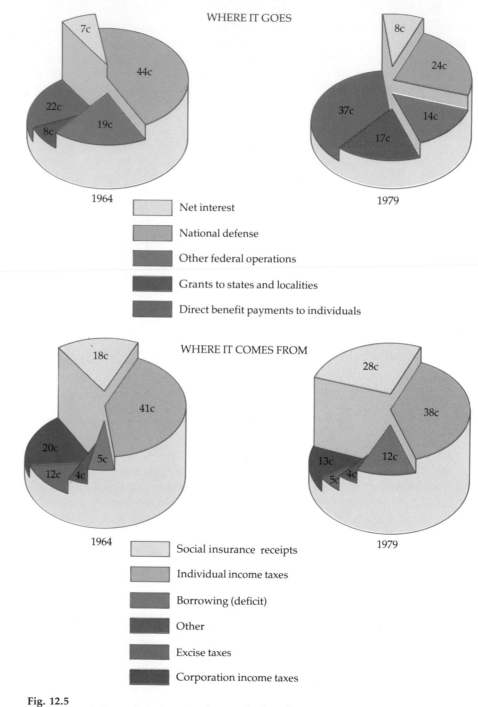

WHERE IT GOES

1964   1979

Net interest

National defense

Other federal operations

Grants to states and localities

Direct benefit payments to individuals

WHERE IT COMES FROM

1964   1979

Social insurance receipts

Individual income taxes

Borrowing (deficit)

Other

Excise taxes

Corporation income taxes

Fig. 12.5
The budget dollar—where it comes from and where it goes.

In seeking answers to questions of this magnitude, we should realize the difficult elements of *choice* involved in decision making and the complicated interrelationships among the various powerful actors involved in the messy bureaucratic politics of our democracy. Though it seems messy, muddling through offers a comfortable way of dealing with the onrush of eventful change. Alvin Toffler, in *Future Shock*, reminds us that human beings have difficulty in handling too much and too rapid change, whether in their work, living styles, or social mobility. Rapid and apparently unending change takes its psychological toll; it is profoundly upsetting and may even cause illness and accidents. This too may help us understand the durability of the "muddling-through" approach.[12]

Critics of the muddling-through approach, while not denying its validity as a *description* of the process, argue that Lindblom and other incrementalists seem too willing to accept the process *as it is*, with all of its inequities. Be this as it may, incremental policy making appears to be a feature of modern bureaucratic policy making in the United States. It fits nicely, for example, as a way of describing the way federal budget making takes place. (This bureaucratic basis of the muddling-through approach has been explained more fully in Chapter 10.)

Employment, unemployment, economic growth, and inflation are products of the functioning of the American economy. The economy in turn is affected by government's policies: public spending, taxation, and the manipulation of interest rates. And the president of the United States, naturally, is widely believed to be a key figure in managing the American economy. The performance of the economy in terms of jobs, prosperity, and prices, therefore, is critical in determining the success of any national administration.

Having examined, in a preliminary fashion, the partial response of the federal government to the presence of chronic joblessness, we turn now to overall presidential policy leadership in economic matters. President Jimmy Carter's experience during his first year in the White House serves as our case study.

JIMMY CARTER AND THE ECONOMY

The task of managing the world's leading industrial economy carries its own peculiar frustrations. The balancing of growth, employment, wages, and prices is shrouded in the mysteries of modern economic analysis. Only professional economists are thought to have control of the esoteric data, which are held to be beyond the grasp of ordinary mortals, especially politicians in the White House and Congress.[13]

---

[12] Alvin Toffler, *Future Shock* (New York: Columbia University Press, 1950).

[13] See Robert Lekachman, *Economists at Bay: Why the Experts Will Never Solve Your Problems* (New York: McGraw-Hill, 1975).

From left to right: outgoing Chairman of the Federal Reserve Arthur Burns, President Jimmy Carter, and the newly appointed chairman G. William Miller.

Each new president assembles his own team of economic advisers, starting with the Council of Economic Advisers, a White House staff agency created by the Employment Act of 1946. Every secretary of the treasury aspires to emulate Alexander Hamilton as a major architect of national policy. But this team does not necessarily include the chairman of the **Federal Reserve Board,** who has the nation's monetary policy as his special preserve. His long term renders him free of direct presidential control. President Carter, for example, inherited Dr. Arthur Burns, who at one time served as chairman of Eisenhower's Council of Economic Advisers, and was appointed to the Federal Reserve post by President Nixon. Burns consistently put the goal of controlling inflation ahead of the goal of full employment. Dr. Burns's prestige was too high for Carter to quarrel with him publicly, but when Burns's term as chairman ended in December 1977, Carter lost no time in replacing him with William Miller, a corporate leader thought to be more sympathetic to the administration's economic approach.

A president learns, some earlier than others, not to expect a clear consensus from his economic advisers concerning any specific course of action. The streams of advice are invariably muddy. There is an awkward reason for this. Every Western industrialized nation has experienced recurring bouts of inflation combined with high levels of unemployment, yet no major government in the Western world really knows how to achieve full employment without stimulating inflation. The United States, for example, has failed to achieve full employment at any time since World War II. It came close twice: briefly during the Korean War, and during the peak period of military escalation in Vietnam. These were periods of heavy additional federal spending and were, therefore, inflation prone.

> No major Western government knows how to achieve full employment without stimulating inflation.

President Carter came to Washington with pledges to get the economy moving, attack massive unemployment, curb inflation, and achieve a balanced budget—a very tall order including incompatible objectives. The last president whose administration came even close to meeting all these objectives was Kennedy. The decade and a half between Kennedy and Carter often featured high rates of inflation combined with unusually high rates of unemployment. After the nation achieved virtually full mobilization of the economy in 1966–1968 during escalation in Vietnam, the Nixon-Ford years brought with them a serious decline in economic growth and massive federal budgetary deficits.[14]

If Carter took strong measures to stimulate the economy he would surely encourage further inflation. On the other hand, if he failed to do so, there was little prospect for lowering the high level of unemployment.

Inheriting a Mess

In dealing with the state of the economy, President Carter found himself a captive of the recent past. Inevitably, each new administration coming to Washington takes off from a position bequeathed to it—and to the nation—by the outgoing regime. January 1977 was no exception, presenting a mixture of economic ingredients. Inflation appeared to have been slowed to about 6 percent after having soared to 12 percent two years earlier. But unemployment in an economy in which nearly ninety million Americans were working still hovered close to 8 percent when Carter took the oath of office. The housing industry remained stagnant on Inauguration Day. Detroit, after a good year, was jittery about the buying habits of American consumers, the new safety standards enforced by federal

[14] See "Inflation and Unemployment," *Congressional Quarterly* (Washington D.C.: 1975) for more detail.

Who Threw Us the Phillips Curve: A Trade-Off That Isn't Working

*A. W. Phillips, an English econo-mist, using data drawn from ear-lier British experience, drew a curve in 1958 showing an overall relationship between unemploy-ment and the rise in prices. Ac-cording to this curve, now widely known as the **Phillips curve**, the lower unemployment falls, the higher is the tendency toward in-flation. (In a tight labor market, where the demand for skilled labor exceeds the supply, employers will compete for the skills and in doing so will bid up the wages paid.)*

The policy conclusions com-monly drawn from Phillips's for-mulation was that we cannot choose an objective for unemploy-ment without regard for the price level. So we have to "trade off" un-employment against price stabil-ity, and vice versa. The dilemma thus posed for governments is dif-ficult: How many individual work-ers should be put out of work in order to maintain an "acceptable" rate of inflation? The moral impli-cations in the choice are obvious.

All Western industrialized na-tions have been plagued by this dilemma in recent decades. The British experience may shed some light on our own.

In the summer of 1966, the British economy was booming along, enjoying an unemployment rate of less than 2 percent com-bined with a modest rate of infla-tion. At this point, a Labour gov-ernment, following notions derived from Phillips's curve, decided to "deflate" the economy. The as-sumption was that the British economy could not be operated with less than 2 percent unemploy-

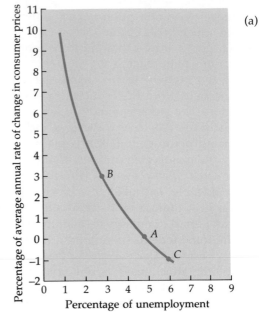

(a)

Figure (a) is a diagram of a hypothetical Phillips curve, showing the relationship thought to exist between inflation and unemployment. The Phillips curve in (b) is drawn from actual data of the U.S. economy. The line has been fitted to pass through as many points as possible, but still is not working; even at high unemployment levels, there is still inflation. Figure (c) shows this relationship in another way.

ment without risking serious infla-tion in prices and wages. Unfor-tunately, once a complicated in-dustrial economy is slowed down by government policy, it may prove difficult to start it again without overheating the economic engine.

Since 1966, through a series of governments and with many gy-rations in policy, the British have experienced steadily mounting un-employment and excessive rates of inflation. The trade-off between

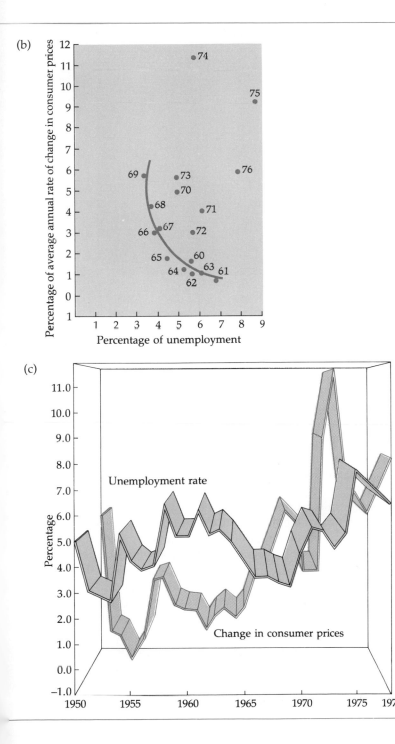

(b)

(c)

jobs and prices that is contemplated in the Phillips curve simply is not occurring in the United Kingdom. A decade after the original decision to deflate, there were nearly a million and a half unemployed workers in Great Britain, as against 200,000 in 1966, and a high rate of inflation.

Is the British example an exotic one? Not really. Today, every major Western industrialized economy experiences a similar dilemma.

In this country, for example, President Nixon entered office in January 1969 inheriting an unemployment rate of 3.5 percent, the lowest in decades, and an annual inflation rate of 6 percent. Fearful of further inflation fed by Vietnam spending, the Nixon administration (like the British government in 1966) chose to deflate the economy. Within a year, the huge American economic juggernaut had been slowed to a point of no growth, doubling unemployment, and yet the rate of inflation increased! A remarkable tour de force. Then the rapid escalation of energy costs following the 1973 oil embargo produced double-digit inflation in a sluggish economy accompanied by an 8 percent unemployment rate. Phillips's curve was left standing on its head.

Presumably, the Carter administration economists understood that the jobs versus prices trade-off had questionable validity. Still they faced the old dilemma of what to do, having inherited massive unemployment, high inflation, and sluggish growth, plus a huge budget deficit.

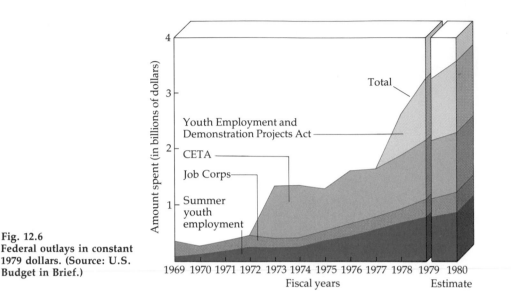

**Fig. 12.6
Federal outlays in constant
1979 dollars. (Source: U.S.
Budget in Brief.)**

law, and the future scope of Carter's energy policies. Meanwhile, energy costs continued their upward spiral. The nation's annual growth rate as Carter reached the White House stood at 4 percent, whereas a rate of 5 to 6 percent was necessary if substantial progress was to be made in reducing unemployment and the massive federal budgetary deficits. Women, blacks, and younger workers—key groups in Carter's constituency—continued to be the special victims of a sluggish economy. Their spokespeople were demanding action.

Low levels of economic growth also adversely affected the growth in federal revenues, thus guaranteeing a continuation of huge budget deficits, given the heavy costs of national defense and health, education, and welfare programs. Carter was pledged to balance the budget; the reality facing him showed that federal spending was exceeding $450 billion annually while revenues were running below the $400 billion mark. Thus Carter faced the unpleasant prospect of a $50 billion deficit during his first year in office, a level destined to carry into his second year as well. The fact that he had inherited the situation, and had very little room for maneuver, was likely to be lost among general public perceptions, especially as the months slipped away. The way in which the Carter administration managed the economy was bound to have a decided impact on his precarious standing with the public.

Conflicting Advice

As we have noted, each president inherits an ongoing economic situation. He also is certain to receive conflicting advice from his closest advisers. This is almost inevitable given the intractable nature of the country's economic problems and the lack of precision in economic forecasting. Bert Lance, a Georgia banker and Carter intimate, was brought in initially to head the Office of Management and Budget. Lance was a fiscal conservative, as many believed Carter to be also. Charles Schultze, on the other hand, Chairman of Carter's Council of Economic Advisers, had a track record as an economic expansionist, a reputation he may have wished to live down. (Schultze was a principal architect of LBJ's famous "guns and butter budget" of 1966, generally considered to have intensified inflationary pressures.) The secretary of the treasury, Michael Blumenthal, a modern corporate entrepreneur with a Ph.D. degree in economics, appeared to be a pragmatic realist capable of moving in either direction. Thus the Carter administration's economic policies were destined to represent compromise positions arrived at within the president's own inner circle of advisers. These positions were altered further by congressional and bureaucratic responses. And before the first year was over, Carter lost Lance, probably his closest and most trusted adviser.

Carter's own political situation required that he establish a base of popular support; this part of the task he seemed to handle well during his first few months in office. David Broder, a respected political reporter not known for exaggerated assessments, writing in March of that first year, considered Carter's initial performance "a triumph of communications in the arena of public opinion."[15] At that very moment, however, Carter and his advisers were grappling with the economic situation described above. And while many ordinary citizens may have been nodding approval of the president's performance in "opening" the processes of government, apprehension and skepticism colored the mood of Wall Street. During the first few months, as Carter's Gallup ratings moved slowly upward, the Dow Jones average (an index of the average prices of selected stocks, generally considered an indicator of investor confidence in the economy) drifted downward. Managing the nation's prosperity soon proved at least as problematic as handling the media. By the late summer and early autumn of the first year, the press and the media were labeling Carter an "inept" chief executive, and Washington president-watchers spoke increasingly of Carter as a one-term president. Wall Street remained apprehensive, and Carter's standing in the polls steadily declined.

In reality, the complex issues plaguing the president and his advisers defied simple solutions. There were no clear answers or obvious prescrip-

[15] *Washington Post*, March 5, 1977.

tions, even assuming Carter and his advisers were prepared to make hard choices. How much stimulus would it take to get the massive American economy moving? What form should the stimulus take in order to provide a maximum punch? How was it to be administered?

In the meantime, the president made other major decisions that were destined to have economic consequences. For example, his energy program, one of the first major initiatives during the early months, involved increasing taxes. So too did his firm decision to ask Congress to rescue the Social Security system from threatened bankruptcy. His decision in June 1977 to halt production of B-1 bombers meant unemployment for those who were building the bombers. (There were three B-1 bombers being tested when Carter made his initial decision.)[16] Wherever he turned, the president faced hard choices, most of which were bound to affect the national economy, for better or for worse.

Carter's First Economic Package

Carter's first economic package in 1977 provoked special interest because it signaled where his administration was placing its emphasis, at least during the first year in office. This first package contained tax proposals in addition to an expansion of public spending for public works and employment and training programs. The first Carter tax proposal stressed modest **rebates** for individual taxpayers and a restoration of the investment credit for corporations, rather than a permanent substantial tax cut. The tax program reflected a compromise between conflicting views; almost immediately an odd alliance of Republican legislators and the more liberal Democrats proclaimed it unacceptable. Secretary of the Treasury Blumenthal advised a group of Democratic senators to "hold their noses" and vote for the administration's proposal.[17] The public works spending program and the expansion of job-training programs were sure to gain widespread support in Congress, given their long-established acceptance.

But the tax-rebate proposal was in hot water from the outset. The AFL-CIO and Ray Marshall, Carter's secretary of labor, plus urban-based members of Congress, doubted that the modest tax rebate would carry a sufficient stimulus. In fact, Carter's economic advisers were not only divided on the issue but were uncertain what the effect of the stimulus might be. One anonymous administration economist admitted that "we're shooting in the dark a bit. We think we know within a broad range what our proposals would do in the way of creating jobs, but I'd be less than frank if I didn't say that our estimates could be way off."[18]

[16] "A Startling No: Mr. Carter Says the B-1 Isn't Necessary," *New York Times,* March 30, 1977.

[17] Quoted in *New York Times,* March 30, 1977.

[18] *New York Times,* February 13, 1977.

© 1976 Chicago Tribune-New York News Syndicate, Inc.

In the meantime, President Carter was having a hard time distinguishing friends and enemies. Senator Floyd Haskell, a liberal Democrat from Colorado, voted against the rebate saying, "It's like shoveling money out of an airplane." Freshman Democratic Senator Daniel P. Moynihan of New York supported the president's proposal. "The most important thing about the stimulus is that it should be stimulating, which means it should be soon. Let's not wait until February," Moynihan warned. Senator Russell Long, the powerful chairman of the Senate Finance Committee, who was personally unenthusiastic about the tax rebate, emphasized that the tax rebate was in danger unless the president asserted his personal leadership. "They are going to have to call in the top man if they are going to win this fight," he warned.[19]

Carter Kills His Rebate

President Carter, the top man, less than ninety days in office, proceeded to kill *his own* tax rebate. He then immediately prescribed a strong dose

[19] *New York Times,* April 2, 1977.

of nonstimulating economic medicine in the form of a comprehensive energy program calling for heavy additional taxation. The reasons for the sudden death of the tax rebate were complex. As noted, the proposal lacked support in the Senate, and the president risked some prestige if he were to fight for it and lose. But more important, Carter's economic advisers, buoyed by news of an improving growth rate and growing apprehension about inflation, found themselves arguing that the tax rebate was no longer necessary. (Forty-eight hours earlier, some of the same advisers had been publicly urging Senate support of the rebate.) As a result, the first Carter tax bill, as it finally emerged from Congress, offered only a modest tax reduction for some forty-seven million lower- and middle-class Americans, no tax rebate, and a few new concessions for business and industry. It was not by any means a very strong economic stimulant. Ironically, before his first year in office ended, Carter announced that a major tax cut would have top priority—in his second year! Getting this tax cut depended, of course, on getting the support of a majority in Congress.

But the first time around, the president decided to rely largely on the natural buoyancy of the economy and considerably expanded spending for public works, training, and job-creation programs. At the same time, he chose to make energy a central issue of his administration. This again was a difficult choice because a comprehensive energy program was certain to have economic consequences, not all of them helpful. An energy program designed to discourage the purchase and use of gas-guzzling autos was likely to put some American auto workers out of work unless affluent America was suddenly converted to smaller, domestic cars. Government action raising oil and gas prices meant further inflation. Carter seemed prepared to accept these consequences while attempting, without much success, to convince the public that he was offering "the moral equivalent of war." The White House viewed the energy crisis as a greater test of Carter's presidential leadership than any other single issue. But as we have noted before, a president seldom faces "single" issues. Energy is tied to taxes, prices, wages, and jobs: matters ordinary citizens care about very much. The connection among the pocketbook, market basket, and voting booth is close, and Congress approached the energy program warily. In fact, the incremental process by which Congress addressed the issue took two years to produce a modified program.

Back to Jobs and Training

With the abrupt removal of the tax rebate, congressional Democrats looked with renewed hope toward the other side of Carter's first economic package: those proposals calling for increased federal spending for public works, public service jobs, and job-training programs. In placing most of its original emphasis on this familiar area, the Carter administration remained well within the limits of conventional wisdom (and incremental policy making). The chief bureaucratic beneficiary of this additional largesse was the Labor Department, which passed the additional federal dollars on to the established bureaucratic structures of the state, county, and local governments. The Employment and Training Administration had accumulated an ever-expanding universe of job-training programs calling for total expenditures approximating more than $11 billion on an annual basis in fiscal year 1979.

Jimmy Carter also faced a youth unemployment epidemic that had been in danger of veering out of control for more than a decade. Here again, the incoming administration faced a bewildering array of ongoing program activity. Most Americans were unaware that some two million young Americans had taken part in a variety of youth programs during President Ford's final year in the White House. In 1976, there were 160,000 young Americans in public service jobs, 500,000 in work-experience programs, 200,000 in on-the-job training and classroom training programs, and 40,000 in the Job Corps. Another 1,135,000 participated in a variety of Neighborhood Youth Corps programs during the summer of 1976.[20]

The total cost of these youth programs approximated $2 billion annually, and the Carter administration was soon committed to raising this level of spending. But nagging questions persisted: Were these programs more than palliatives? Were there deeper ills in the world's most sophisticated industrial economy? Why is full employment experienced only in wartime? How does a society of widespread affluence explain the coexistence of chronic levels of joblessness, decade after decade? Is there something here that we are overlooking in this analysis? How has this nation addressed the issue of full employment in the recent past?

Let us examine next the way in which the struggle over full employment developed in this country.

FULL EMPLOYMENT: FDR AND HARRY TRUMAN

The Great Depression of the 1930s presented one of the most serious economic crises in our history. Indeed, the future of industrial capitalism and our constitutional system seemed threatened. But our World War II involvement, calling for total mobilization of resources, government controls, and jobs for American youth (ten million of them in the uniforms of the armed forces), "cured" the severe unemployment crisis of the Depression years.

[20] *Congressional Quarterly*, Almanac, 1976 (94th Congress, 2nd Session).

The unemployment crisis of the Depression was "cured" by World War II. Vast numbers of men were drafted into the armed services and the production of war materials dramatically increased the need for workers. Women filled many of the positions formerly held by men.

All American administrations face the same dilemma in formulating economic policy: How much employment is to be traded off to maintain reasonable stability in prices and wages?

Once the war was over, however, this country faced a critical dilemma: how to ensure jobs for all who were able and willing to work while maintaining a reasonably stable level of prices. Finding the proper policy mix did not prove easy.

The full employment issue in the United States has a history that burdens successive American administrations with the same hard choice in formulating economic policy: *How much employment is to be traded off to maintain reasonable stability in prices and wages?*

FDR's Economic Bill of Rights

The American economy's ability to perform postwar tasks emerged as an important concern in official Washington during the war. Could the economy, once it was demobilized, absorb the millions of young Americans who were serving in the armed forces? What would happen to wages, prices, and rents, all of which were subject to strict wartime controls, once those controls were lifted?

The **National Resources Planning Board** (NRPB), located in the Executive Office of the President, shared with the Bureau of the Budget a concern for the impact of governmental policy on the economy. These two presidential staff agencies were key actors in the struggle to use the federal budget as an instrument in achieving full employment. While the war continued to rage around the globe, President Roosevelt sent two NRPB reports dealing with postwar policy to Congress. *Security, Work and Relief Policies* (1943), the first of these planning documents, presented an elaborate domestic program that the president boldly labeled "a new bill of rights."

Unlike the original Bill of Rights in 1787, this document was the work of technicians and bureaucrats rather than political leaders. In this instance, the future of the economy was being planned from within the specialized bureaucracies of the new institutionalized presidency. (See Chapter 8 for more on the institutionalized presidency.) The document called for the following rights to be guaranteed to all Americans:

1. The right to work, usefully and creatively, through the productive years.

2. The right to fair pay, adequate to command the necessities and amenities of life in exchange for work, ideas, thrift, and other socially valuable service.

3. The right to adequate food, clothing, shelter, and medical care.

4. The right to security, with freedom from fear of old age, want, dependency, sickness, unemployment, and accident.

5. The right to live in a system of free enterprise, free from compulsory labor, irresponsible private power, arbitrary public authority, and unregulated monopolies.

6. The right to come and go, to speak and to be silent, free from the spying of secret police.

7. The right to equality before the law, with equal access to justice in fact.

8. The right to education, for work, for citizenship, and for personal growth and happiness.

9. The right to rest, recreation, and adventure, the opportunity to enjoy and take part in an advancing civilization.[21]

---

[21] See Stephen K. Bailey, *Congress Makes a Law* (New York: Columbia University Press, 1950), p. 27. Much of this thumbnail history of the battle over the Employment Act of 1946 is drawn from Bailey's book—now a minor classic.

These rights, the planners argued, could not be effective unless they were implemented by the federal government through a set of new programs. Such programs were to include the following:

1. A broad program of social security to ensure that all retired Americans had a stable source of income.

2. A national health program so that all Americans might have access to medical care regardless of economic circumstance.

3. A national education program to guarantee all Americans the opportunity to develop to their fullest, both in academic and technical situations.

4. A permanent program of large-scale public works to make it possible for every able-bodied American to work.

5. A new tax policy that would provide for relatively high taxes on income and inheritance combined with strong antimonopoly measures to ensure corporate responsibility. (This was deemed essential to pay for the national programs outlined above.)

It should be noted that these proposals were first put forth by President Roosevelt in 1943.

New Deal Planning: Congress Reacts

With the elaborate "welfare state" outlined by his 1943 economic bill of rights, FDR and his advisers were far too advanced for Congress and the general public.

In effect, a New Deal planning agency was advocating a postwar broadening of the New Deal, calling for greater federal intervention in the economy and in the society. By tying the new rights to specific programs, the government planners were seeking nothing less than a radical transformation of American society. In doing so, however, they had not consulted Congress, an oversight that was soon to cost them heavily in the heated debate that followed. The technicians and planners within the Executive Office of the President had moved far in advance of conventional thinking. They were ahead of both Congress and the general public, and indeed were ahead of most influential opinion makers. The proposed program was assailed as "outrageous" and a "giant step toward socialism" by its numerous critics, including a number of influential members of Congress, such as Republican Senator Robert Taft, Sr., of Ohio.

Within three months after the report was issued, Congress rose in righteous wrath and refused to give the NRPB any further appropriations. With its funding cut off, NRPB was finished. Congress had used its traditional power of the purse to show its displeasure with presidential economic planning. The more conservative elements in Congress, entrenched in the appropriations committees, simply refused to provide further funding to White House planning activity.

Although in killing the NRPB Congress had buried this form of planning, the problem of converting a mobilized wartime economy to a peacetime situation *without* substantial government intervention persisted.

American business enterprise had reason to worry. What would happen, businesspeople asked, when wartime contracts, running into the billions of dollars, were ended? Where were the jobs for the returning service men and women? Organized labor also felt the pressure. What would happen to members' jobs in a labor-surplus economy? What would happen to organized labor when unions were beset with large-scale layoffs? Where would we sell our surplus goods?

FDR's Sixty Million Jobs

President Roosevelt, as so often before, seized the initiative, calling for "the right to a useful and remunerative job," in his State of the Union address of January 1944. The Democratic platform adopted the following summer opened with these words: "The Democratic party stands on its record in peace and war. To speed victory, establish and maintain peace, guarantee full employment and provide prosperity. . . ."

During the autumn campaign, Roosevelt went further in calling for a postwar program to provide "close to sixty million productive jobs." Countering those who found this goal utopian, FDR insisted: "If anyone feels that my faith in our ability to produce sixty million peacetime jobs is fantastic, let him remember that some people said the same thing about my demand in 1940 for fifty thousand airplanes."[22]

In this fashion, the Democratic party under Roosevelt's wartime leadership was moving rapidly to endorse a new right—the right to a job—and to place the responsibility in the hands of the federal government. At the same time, the president was not committing his party to national economic planning. Nor was he clearly endorsing the elaborate welfare state envisioned in the NRPB's "bill of rights." Because his position seemed more moderate, Roosevelt's approach was politically more attractive. However, it also left unclear how sixty million jobs were to be created in an industrial economy largely dependent on market forces.

The focus of the Democratic party under Roosevelt was on the right of everyone to have a job. It placed the responsibility for this right in the hands of the federal government.

The Full Employment Bill

Encouraged by Roosevelt's lead, a small group of senators and a tiny band of Capitol Hill staff assistants went to work immediately to prepare a draft piece of legislation making full employment a national objective. Eschewing the usual legal jargon, the original draft of the bill stated simply and clearly that "The Congress hereby declares that every American able to work has the right to a useful and remunerative job in the industries, or shops, or offices, or farms, or mines of the nation."[23]

[22] Quoted in Bailey, *Congress Makes a Law*, p. 43.
[23] Bailey, *Congress Makes a Law*, p. 47.

Perhaps they were putting it too clearly and simply, because these were almost exactly the words FDR had used in several of his campaign speeches. With the benefit of full twenty-twenty hindsight, it appears that this close connection with the president did not aid the bill's chances of passage because conservative members of Congress distrusted presidential leadership. Aware of the fate of NRPB, the bill drafters designated the Bureau of the Budget as the appropriate agency to assist the president and Congress in shaping economic policy. At the same time, they called for creating a joint congressional committee on the Budget. It may have seemed a good idea to involve Congress in the process, but the proposed joint committee also represented a possible rival to the powerful taxation and appropriations committees.

Drafting the bill

Who were the people who drafted this ambitious legislative proposal, so potentially important to the future of this nation?

As it was introduced in January 1945, the full employment bill (S-380) had undergone no fewer than seven revisions in two weeks. These revisions were the work of a small staff hastily assembled in a dingy room on the subway floor of the Senate office building, opposite the men's room. Bertram Gross, the principal staff architect of this piece of legislation, was an assistant to Senator James Murray, Democrat of Montana, the bill's chief sponsor and a strong advocate of planned employment policy. A close observer described Gross as "the spark plug of enthusiasm who fired the staff with a passionate zeal for the cause of full employment."[24]

Gross represented a new breed on Capitol Hill at that time, the staff assistant with specialized technical competence who influences legislation by combining technical proficiency with attachment to a strategically placed legislator. These staff assistants have greatly multiplied in recent years.

The bill is rewritten

Both houses of Congress, operating in the normal manner through their standing committees, rewrote the full employment bill during the ensuing twelve months, often over the bitter objections of Gross and his associates. Interest-group activity, as suggested in Chapter 4, was intense. Organized labor pushed hard to keep the right-to-work concept intact and the commitment to full employment. Fearing undue governmental interference in the market economy, business groups were equally as active in trying to weaken the bill in vital respects. Farm groups were active on both sides of the struggle, with the American Farm Bureau Federation opposing the

[24] Bailey, *Congress Makes a Law*, p. 66.

bill while the National Farmers Union supported it. Legislation affecting jobs for Americans is bound to engage the activity of powerful economic groups.

Presidential leadership: missing ingredient

Unfortunately for the supporters of the bill, President Roosevelt was reaching the end of his resources. Physically and emotionally drained and close to death's door, Roosevelt concentrated his lagging energies on concluding the war and fulfilling his dream of establishing a United Nations organization to keep the peace. Although Bureau of the Budget personnel cooperated with Gross and his team, FDR never offered public endorsement of S-380. Steven K. Bailey offers this observation:

> Recognizing the importance of Congressional unity in terms of his dream for a United Nations Organization, the late President obviously felt that his endorsement of a specific full employment plan might muddy the water, and that specific plans for full employment had better come first from Congress itself. Roosevelt followed this hands-off policy until his death.[25]

Here is a classic example of the "two presidencies" we discussed in Chapter 8, in operation. Because he was so concerned with international matters, Roosevelt refrained from exerting his leadership as Congress proceeded to rewrite S-380. In this instance, national security issues took precedence over domestic priorities in the presidential view, initiating a trend that was to intensify during the next twenty-five years, as we also noted in Chapter 8.

Truman and full employment

Harry S Truman of Missouri assumed the presidency when Roosevelt died in April 1945. Some recent reappraisals of this period cast doubt on Truman's interest in governmental intervention in behalf of a full-employment policy.[26] The criticism seems harsh. Truman actually went further than FDR in supporting the cause of full employment once the issue entered the congressional arena. Truman established a four-man cabinet committee to coordinate the administration's efforts in dealing with the issue. Truman took to the airwaves (there was no commercial television at the time) to blast the committee's delaying tactics, after S-380 was bogged down in an unfriendly House subcommittee.

Because the forces opposing a commitment to full employment were so well represented in the congressional committee structure, Truman's leverage as president was limited. House Speaker Sam Rayburn, Truman's

[25] Bailey, *Congress Makes a Law,* p. 161.

[26] See especially Otis Graham, Jr., *Toward a Planned Economy* (New York: Oxford University Press, 1976).

close friend and ally, was tactical leader of the bill. Rayburn, preeminently a political realist, sensed that the underlying conservatism of the House made a strong bill unattainable. There was no majority sentiment on Capitol Hill, or probably in the country, for a statutory commitment to full employment. Hence, the House proceeded in due course to pass a greatly weakened version of S-380. The House action led to a conference committee selected to iron out the differences between the weakened House bill and a stronger version that the Senate had passed. As is so often the case, the conference committee held the key to the kind of employment legislation the nation was to have.

The conference on S-380

A twelve-member joint conference committee, with six members from either House, met late in February 1946. President Truman wrote in advance to the senior conferees as follows: "No bill which provides less than the Senate version can efficiently accomplish the purpose intended." The president followed this with a nationwide radio address asking for the enactment of full-employment legislation and urging the voters to let their representatives know their views on the issue. Two days before the first meeting of the conference, the White House sent a special message to Congress, reaffirming the president's desire for enactment of full-employment legislation.

The conference met in a situation of relatively balanced strength, but the more conservative House members were adamant in stating their unwillingness to accept any bill containing the words "full employment" or the "right to work."

In fact, the conferees wasted little time in settling upon a compromise. Bertram Gross was called in to juggle the words so as to make the compromise acceptable all around. Gross's technique required a willingness to sacrifice substance in seeking compromise. In juggling the words, Gross juggled out "full employment" and "right to work." The full-employment act, thanks to the thesaurus, was transformed into the employment act. The federal government was *not* committed to a goal of full employment. (Nor has it been at any time since 1946.)

The Employment Act of 1946

When the bill emerged from the conference committee, it was no longer a "full employment" act. Officially known as **The Employment Act,** the bill called for the promotion of "the maximum employment, production, and purchasing power." Rather than planning for full employment, the president was given responsibility for preparing an annual report on the state of the economy. This annual report, which goes to Congress each year, is prepared by the Council of Economic Advisers and staff (part of the institutionalized presidency). The report is in no sense a planning document that sets forth goals and objectives. Instead, it presents a report on the current condition of the United States economy.

This brief review of the origins of the Employment Act reveals the way in which a proposal to make full employment an objective of national policy was altered in Congress to something considerably less. The study illustrates a number of strands that are critical to our understanding of governmental decision making.

Lessons to Be Learned

First, the experience with the Employment Act *underscored the importance of presidential policy leadership when a major change in program is underway.* Neither Roosevelt nor Truman, for different reasons, chose to make full employment a major demand item on their congressional agendas. Truman did more than Roosevelt to support the bill, but his clout with Congress proved to be weaker.

Second, in the absence of strong presidential leadership, *congressional forces soon take over.* S-380 had an effective sponsor in Senator Murray, but it also faced the opposition of conservative legislators. Senator Taft, for example, one of the ablest senators in this century, was influential in derailing the full-employment concept. The pragmatic conciliatory style of Speaker Rayburn encouraged a watered-down version in order to gain House approval. As is usually the case, this important piece of legislation reflected a compromise between widely differing views of the role of the federal government in relation to our economy.

Third, *an economic issue of signal importance,* governmental planning versus a free market economy, *provoked intense interest-group activity.* Both sides enjoyed the support of a coalition of groups, and each worked hard at lobbying. But, as noted in Chapter 4, when conflicting interests fight over an issue of this importance, assuming the groups are fairly evenly balanced, *the prevailing mood* of the country will help shape the outcome. Planning by government to meet the objective of full employment was not a wildly popular idea in a nation anxious to abandon wartime controls and regimentation. This aspect also encouraged a political compromise.

Fourth, the enactment of this bill marks another early step in *the expansion of the institutionalized presidency.* The Bureau of the Budget, already an elite presidential staff agency, was an enthusiastic participant in the bureaucratic and political development of the Employment Act. And while the National Resources Planning Board of World War II days was an early casualty in the sharp infighting over full employment, the presidency was to gain a new staff agency, the Council of Economic Advisers, as a result of this law.[27]

The experience with the Employment Act of 1946 illustrates several important aspects of economic policy making.

[27] Edward S. Flash, Jr., *Economic Advice and Presidential Leadership: The Council of Economic Advisors* (New York: Columbia University Press, 1965). See also Walter Heller, *New Dimensions of Political Economy* (Cambridge, Mass.: Harvard University Press, 1966).

Finally, this case study illustrates the *growing importance of the staff technician in modern policy making*. Prior to the New Deal, most pieces of legislation were drafted by members of Congress, lobbyists, and close political advisers. Bertram Gross was a prototype of a new breed of political technician soon to proliferate on Capitol Hill and at the higher levels of the huge executive bureaucracies, especially the Presidency.[28] (This development is explained more fully in Chapters 8, 9, and 10.)

SUMMARY

In examining the way in which domestic policy is fought over in Washington, we have attempted to illustrate the necessity of making hard choices between several possibly conflicting objectives.

We have attempted to trace the debate of unemployment versus inflation from its origins during World War II to its policy consequences in our own time. In doing so, we have also had an opportunity to see how the institutionalized presidency, like Congress, has become the focus of conflicting demands. We have also noted instances in which bureaucratic input in the policy-making process has been important. And we have seen the ways in which complex issues attract the support and the opposition of powerful organized groups.[29]

Finally, we have stressed the way in which the essentially chaotic nature of American politics, as well as events in the international arena, influence the course of decision making. Those who argue that the American political system is inadequate to the challenges of a changing society may find support in the experience of the nation in approaching full employment. At the same time, those who believe that the system is generally successful note the absence of a consensus on the desirability of achieving one economic goal over others. Given that lack of consensus, the absence of a thoroughgoing full-employment policy may be seen as a natural consequence of our pluralist policies, our incremental process, and our messy politics.[30]

In these circumstances we continue to muddle through.

---

[28] For more on the technician as policy maker see Donovan, *The Policy Makers*.

[29] For a perceptive study of the ways in which the bureaucracies interact with congressional committees in shaping public policy, see Randall Ripley and Grace Franklin, *Congress: The Bureaucracy and Public Policy* (Homewood, Ill.: Dorsey, 1976).

[30] For a recent statement that considers what economic planning in the United States might be, by a former CEA chairman (under Nixon), see Herbert Stein, *Economic Planning and the Improvement of Economic Policy* (Washington, D.C.: American Institute in Public Policy Research, 1975).

KEY TERMS

opportunity to work

inflation

unemployment

full employment

recession

Great Society

public service jobs

employment and training programs

Manpower Development
   and Training Act of 1962

"the other America"

Economic Opportunity Act

incrementalism

National Resources
   Planning Board (NRPB)

economic bill of rights

full employment bill (S-380)

Employment Act of 1946

SUGGESTED READINGS

BAILEY, STEPHEN K., *Congress Makes a Law* (New York: Columbia University Press, 1950).

A classic behind-the-scenes case study of Congress writing the Employment Act of 1964. Bailey's participant-observer approach has served as a model for many subsequent case studies of congressional policy making.

DONOVAN, JOHN C., *The Politics of Poverty*, 2d ed. (Indianapolis: Bobbs-Merrill, 1974).

Another basic case study of policy making. Traces the formulation, evolution, and implementation of the Economic Opportunity Act of 1964 from its origins in the early hours of LBJ's presidency through the early Nixon years.

HALLMAN, HOWARD W., *Emergency Employment: A Study in Federalism* (University: University of Alabama Press, 1977).

One of the most knowledgeable experts in this field analyzes the development of emergency employment programs and shows how they are developed within our federal system.

LEKACHMAN, ROBERT, *Economists at Bay: Why the Experts Will Never Solve Your Problems* (New York: McGraw-Hill, 1975).

A distinguished economist known for his iconoclastic views is critical of the role of economists in public policy making.

HARRINGTON, MICHAEL, *The Other America* (New York: Macmillan, 1962).

A classic study of the poverty subculture in this country. Harrington's book is believed to have stimulated the interest of President Kennedy.

RIPLEY, RANDALL, AND GRACE FRANKLIN, *Congress: The Bureaucracy and Public Policy* (Homewood, Ill.: The Dorsey Press, 1976).

An excellent introduction to the complex interrelationships between Congress and the executive bureaucracies and how they affect public policy. Written with the undergraduate reader in mind while remaining faithful to the scholarly literature.

VIETNAM

American military and political involvement in Vietnam during the 1960s proved to be one of the most controversial and divisive episodes in our nation's history.

Official United States involvement in the Vietnam struggle began a decade earlier, in 1950, when the Truman administration decided that the military action then underway between the French army and the Viet Minh forces led by Ho Chi Minh involved vital United States interests. Our government made the hard choice to provide financial support for the French military effort. The Korean war broke out in June of the same year when the United States elected to resist an attack launched by North Korean forces. From that point forward, the situation in Vietnam was viewed as part of a broader United States effort aimed at opposing the spread of "Communism" in Asia.

The French military forces suffered a major defeat at the hands of Ho Chi Minh's army in the battle of Dien Bien Phu in 1954. At this point, the French government decided to seek a negotiated settlement in Vietnam. This settlement divided Vietnam (what was once French Indochina) at the seventeenth parallel. Ho Chi Minh's Viet Minh regime held the territory north of the seventeenth parallel. To the South, a Republic of Vietnam, headed by Ngo Dinh Diem, soon became a client regime directly dependent on United States assistance for its survival. Secretary of State Dulles, representing the Eisenhower administration and President Diem, in effect refused to accept the terms of the 1954 settlement, to which neither had been a party.

The intense and bitter political and military struggle inside Vietnam continued during the next decade. By 1963, it was becoming increasingly clear to United States advisers that the Diem regime was in serious trouble internally. It did not control the countryside and in the meantime had grown ever more repressive. In the summer of 1963, the Kennedy administration tacitly encouraged, and the CIA directly participated in, a plot on the part of the Vietnam army officers to get rid of Diem. In the *coup d'état* that followed, Diem and his brother were murdered.

Following the coup, the political situation in Saigon, the capital of the southern regime, grew increasingly precarious just as President Johnson was assuming the responsibilities of office following the assassination of Kennedy late in November 1963. At this time, United States military forces in Vietnam were limited to about 25,000 Special Forces army units (Green Berets, as they were called). The South Vietnamese army, the largest in Southeast Asia, was almost completely a United States creation, a client army that frequently depended on United States Army officers and noncoms for its leadership when engaged in battle. The United States was now financing the Vietnamese Republic's participation in the war with Ho Chi Minh's regime. (Total costs exceeded $100 billion during the Johnson era.)

In January–February 1965, shortly after his inauguration, Johnson, accepting the unanimous recommendation of his national security advisers, decided to escalate American military involvement in Vietnam by ordering large-scale United States Air Force bombing attacks on the North. Between March and November 1965, the number of United States Army troops in Vietnam increased from 25,000 Special Forces units to a total of 150,000. Before the fateful decision was made in 1968 to reverse course, this figure had swollen to more than half a million Americans.

During the first phase of the operation, the

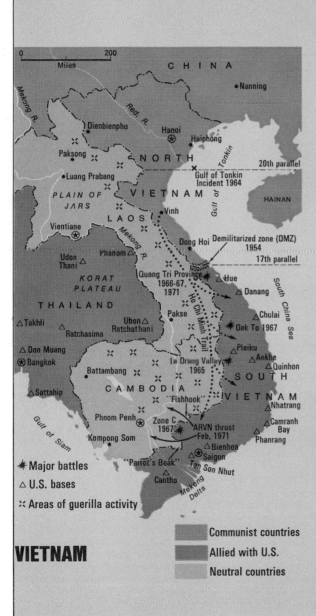

VIETNAM

0 ——— 200
Miles

* Major battles
△ U.S. bases
⋊ Areas of guerilla activity

Communist countries
Allied with U.S.
Neutral countries

American troops in Vietnam were professional soldiers. By 1966–1967, however, more and more of our soldiers were young men who had been drafted into the Army, often from college campuses. As the fighting continued year after year, and as more and more middle-class young Americans were drafted for military service, criticism of the war mounted steadily at home. When the military forces of the Northern communist regime, based in Hanoi, struck against United States forces during the so-called Tet offensive in February 1968, a battle that was seen at home on TV each night during the evening newscast, American public opinion turned sharply against our involvement.

In March 1968, President Johnson met with many of the advisers who earlier had supported escalation. This time the advice was split, with a number of key figures now urging him to halt the bombing and to reverse our course in Vietnam. On March 31, LBJ heeded this advice in a public announcement. At the same time, he announced that he would not seek reelection in November.

From 1968 to 1974, the American government participated in an excruciatingly slow but gradual process of military disengagement in Vietnam. President Nixon and Henry Kissinger, his key adviser, combined a program of slow reduction in United States military forces with an attempt at seeking a negotiated settlement with Hanoi. This process had gone a long way when suddenly the Saigon army in 1974 apparently lost the will to fight any longer. The United States Ambassador and his retinue escaped from Saigon by helicopter and ship only hours before Communist troops captured the city.

In this ignoble fashion, the direct United States involvement in Vietnam came to an abrupt end, bringing to a close one of the least edifying chapters in American history.

The political problems had become like a
thousand chess games, different from
normal chess games in that each was
played on a board with five different
levels and all games were interrelated. If a
good move was made on one board, it
might have a disastrous effect on two
hundred other games at one or more
levels and on the original game at two of
the other closely related levels. Thus it
had become too complicated and there
was no one total ending possible, and
truth had no bearing except on one game
at one level at one time.

James Barlow

CHAPTER 13 AMERICAN FOREIGN POLICY: HARD CHOICES IN CHANGING TIMES

The world probably does not appear to be as complex to most Americans as it does to Barlow. But with nearly 160 countries ranging in size from tiny islands with a few thousand people to huge, sprawling nations with hundreds of millions of people, international relations have become complicated indeed.

They also are more important to more Americans than ever before. A conservative sheik in a Middle East kingdom is assassinated. How will the new regime affect our lives? Will the regime raise the price of oil still further? What will be the impact—if any—on the millions of Americans who depend on oil for transportation, electricity, and heat? Will Americans be better off or worse off because of events in far-off and little-known places? Because of the importance of what happens beyond our borders, **foreign policy**—the way we deal with the rest of the world—is a matter of critical concern to Americans. Foreign policy poses issues requiring hard choices in an era of accelerating change.

COMPONENTS OF FOREIGN POLICY

What is foreign policy? How is it made? These deceptively simple questions concern and puzzle most Americans. In this chapter we will deal with these questions by looking at both the domestic and the international aspects of America's foreign policy. For the making of a particular policy depends on a complex mixture of internal, domestic concerns and international events over which we have little control, as well as some things we can do something about.

Understanding how foreign policy is made is not easy. Indeed, it is more difficult to explain the foreign policy process than it is to describe how a bill becomes a law or how a law is implemented. Also, Americans have traditionally felt uneasy with global power politics. As a people we have often sought relatively simple solutions to international problems. In a world of rapid change, we can no longer afford that luxury.

One of the reasons foreign policy making is so difficult to understand is that, in reality, foreign policy is made up of a number of components or parts. In fact, it is the sum total of the words and actions of one government in relation to other states. These governmental words and actions may be political or economic in nature. Or they may have to do with cultural events. Frequently they involve military issues. A government may begin a new trade policy by giving some countries better opportunities to acquire goods at cheaper prices. The countries of the European Common Market, for example, buy coffee and cocoa produced by the former French colonies at higher prices than they pay for the same products from Latin America. They do this in part to ensure a steady supply of these products, but also to ensure that the African countries that receive the subsidies take political positions at the United Nations and elsewhere that are favorable to the Common Market countries.

A government may also provide monetary or military support to another country in its conflict with a third party. Saudi Arabia sends millions of dollars every year to other Arab nations who are seeking to establish a Palestinian state in the territory held by Israel.

But foreign policy may also be simply a statement by which one country seeks to influence another. Leaders of the People's Republic of China, for example, speak out in support of "revolution," often without mentioning specific situations. The cliché that "actions speak louder than words" may be fairly accurate in many areas of human activities, but in foreign policy, words and symbols may carry considerable force in determining how actions are to be regarded. The way in which other states interpret a government's actions may be as important as the actions themselves. One person's terrorist is another person's freedom fighter.

Foreign policy usually includes a variety of actions. On the one hand, a state may respond to a specific situation with a particular reaction. For example, the Austrian government may become irritated over the way the Swedish government handles German terrorists in Stockholm. It may say things on the spur of the moment that run counter to its recent cooperation with Sweden. Many observers and commentators confuse this type of one-time, *ad hoc* reaction with policy. Generally speaking, what we term *foreign policy* presents a more definite pattern. A country may develop a program for a particular geographic region and in doing so may make a considerable effort to coordinate its policy toward the countries in that region.

For example, since the time of the Monroe Doctrine in the early nineteenth century, the United States has stated that, and generally has acted as if, Latin America is an area of primary interest, insisting that Latin America should be free of European "interference." Following this policy, the United States objected to the French presence in Mexico during the 1860s, to British activities in Venezuela at the turn of the century, and to Russian involvement in Cuba during the 1950s and 1960s. Whether the United States has any "right" to do so is not really the issue. The fact is that our foreign policy makers have behaved for over a century and a half as if they had that right.

Foreign policy may involve more than a reaction to specific episodes and the coordination of programs in certain areas of the world. It may also involve broad global designs or the preserving of certain basic values. For over 150 years, successive governments in Switzerland have based their international relations on the principle of **neutrality**; that is, the principle of not aligning themselves with either side during a war. Through two world wars and numerous European conflicts, the Swiss have remained

A cartoonist's view of Roosevelt's use of the navy to enforce the Monroe Doctrine in the Caribbean.

neutral, no matter which side they favored, and despite the specifics of individual situations.

Foreign policy may consist of a pattern of reactions to incidents and events, a series of programs and concepts, or a carefully thought out plan based on definite principles.

Foreign policy may thus be (1) a number of reactions to incidents and events, reactions that eventually form a pattern; (2) a series of programs and concepts; or (3) a carefully thought out plan based on definite principles. Or it may be a combination of all of these.

One word of caution: Most people tend to view foreign policy and its formation as being far more controlled than it frequently is. In actuality, much of the foreign policy of many nations of the world—including the United States—is often a case more of drift than of design, more a reaction to events than the controlling of them. With nearly 160 countries in the world, it is very difficult to structure all but a few of these relationships over a long period of time. Governments rise and fall. Old leaders die or are replaced. New leaders come to power. Alliances are formed. Wars break out. Wars are concluded. Alliances break down. Trade shifts occur. There are material shortages and material surpluses. As time is speeded by events, foreign policy may become merely a reflection of what has happened and what a country must respond to.

HISTORICAL PATTERNS OF AMERICAN FOREIGN POLICY

Just as it is difficult to determine such broad concepts as "national character" (the prevailing characterization of an entire people), so too is it often difficult to categorize a country's historical pattern of foreign policy making. A country may exhibit different patterns in its foreign policy at different times.[1] Or entirely different patterns may exist at the same time. In the case of the United States, several important themes have occurred over and over again until they have become a definite part of both our present and our future.[2]

Throughout our history, many Americans have urged a policy of **isolationism** and the avoidance of foreign commitments. From the days of Washington and Jefferson, with their fears of "foreign entanglements," through the current concern with disengagement and the scaling down of American commitments abroad, isolationism has been an important part of our domestic and diplomatic heritage. For over two hundred years, many Americans have urged that the United States turn its attention inward while avoiding involvement in the affairs—and wars—of other nations.

At the same time, from the very founding of the Republic, many Americans have believed in the principle of **expansionism,** urging that the United States spread outward to incorporate new lands and more people. Whether this line of thinking was based on the notion of **manifest destiny** (a nineteenth-century notion that America was destined to expand) or was simply a response to opportunities to expand, it has persisted as a dominant theme throughout much of our history. From the annexation of Texas in 1846, to the seizing of Guam, Puerto Rico, and the Philippines in 1898, and finally to the establishment of statehood for Alaska and Hawaii (also in the nineteenth century), expansionism stands out as an important feature of United States foreign policy.

Indeed, in somewhat different form, this expansionist impulse gave rise to armed intervention in such widely separated countries as Haiti, Mexico, China, the Dominican Republic, the Philippines, Cuba, Russia, and Nicaragua. During the brief period between 1904 and 1934, the United

A spirit of isolationism—the avoidance of foreign entanglements—has been an important theme throughout American history.

Along with the theme of isolationism has been the expansionist theme, which has given rise to United States intervention in a wide variety of countries.

[1] James Barlow, *One Man in the World* (New York: Simon and Schuster, 1967), p. 38.
[2] Ruhl Bartlett, *Policy and Power* (New York: Hill and Wang, 1963).

States intervened militarily no less than eight times in Latin America alone. This provides some historical perspective to the fact that during the last two decades, five different American presidents sent troops to intervene in five foreign countries—Korea, Lebanon, the Dominican Republic, Vietnam, and Cambodia.

It should be noted that any decision on the part of the United States to intervene (or not to intervene, in such recent cases as Angola, Yemen, and Bangladesh) has been accompanied by a clash of these isolationist and interventionist strands. Both isolation and intervention have been pro-

United States troops in Santo Domingo, the capital of the Dominican Republic, sent by President Johnson in 1965 on the grounds that rioting in the city was a prelude to a Communist coup.

moted on the basis of certain assumptions: either that the United States somehow can avoid involvement in the real world of international relations, or that by intervening, the United States could substantially alter the course of events in a given country over a long period of time. Many analyses of American foreign policy emphasize choices or alternatives, thus reinforcing the notion that the United States has merely to choose among different courses of action. Politicians and laypersons alike frequently ascribe to the United States power it does not in fact enjoy.

For example, following the rise to power of the Communist Party in China, it was widely alleged that the United States had "lost" China. How the United States could lose something it never had is not clear. What is clear is that while the United States often has considerable opportunity to exert influence in specific situations, it may also lack the power to stop broad historical movements such as nationalism or decolonization. Indeed, the very themes of isolation and intervention are too simple to be offered as answers to the problems of today.[3]

The central issues now facing the United States demand careful and objective analysis as well as considerable planning for the future. The persistence of change and the way we deal with change around the globe will profoundly shape United States foreign policy in the next decade.

What are some limits on action in international relations? What are the opportunities? What are the forces that endure? Which will recede? How can we choose our goals in the midst of onrushing events? Can we cope with the domestic and national demands of our own people as well as the aspirations and concerns of the rest of humanity with whom we share the earth? Americans cannot be all things to all people. But with our wealth and technology, our military power and the creativity of our ideas, the United States and its people are bound to exert influence on the future course of events.

Since foreign policy links us to the rest of the world, we should understand how it is made and why it is made in the way it is. Later we shall examine some of the issues that are likely to accompany us to the end of this century, and beyond. As we explore this complicated subject, ask yourself what you would do if you were in a position to directly influence the making of American foreign policy.

WHO MAKES FOREIGN POLICY?

American planes roar out of the skies in 1976 to attack Cambodian patrol boats, which have seized an American freighter. American foreign aid, which had been going to Zaire at relatively low levels until 1976, is in-

[3] S. F. Bemis, *A Diplomatic History of the United States* (New York: Holt, Rinehart and Winston, 1955).

creased dramatically. China, which has been on a list of countries denied trading rights with American firms, has now been granted the status of **most favored nation,** entitling it to trading advantages with the United States.

All three of these situations illustrate American foreign policy in action. Who made that policy and how? To many people the answer is simple: It is the president. Or it is the president and his secretary of state. To others, foreign policy is a result of manipulation by the Central Intelligence Agency (CIA) or the political actions of the multinational corporations. To still others, it is determined by Congress or the Department of Defense (DOD).

Regardless of who they think makes the final decision, most people assume that policy is made in a definite way, with the leaders—whoever they are—choosing courses of action based on alternatives and possibilities. This model assumes that the central figure, usually the president of the United States, receives information and advice from a number of groups and experts and makes his decision on the basis of this information. Once the decision is made, it is carried out by the various governmental bureaucracies.

As we shall see, the reality of foreign policy making is far more complex. Often a decision will result, not simply from a careful, rational choice, but also from political competition among various governmental organizations and groups within them. Those who seek a simple model to explain this ongoing series of interactions will be disappointed, for often different organizations or groups "take charge" in different situations. For example, Congress may have considerable influence in certain situations, as they did when they demanded that action be taken against the Cambodian government, which had seized the American freighter. On the other hand, the Central Intelligence Agency may have been the strongest advocate for increased aid to Zaire in 1977 because of its operations in neighboring countries. And the secretary of state and some large American firms may welcome the changed relationship with China, which the president proposed. But in all three instances, variety of groups and individuals influence the outcome, depending on the particular situation.

Often foreign policy will result not from a careful, rational choice, but from the influence of different organizations or groups, depending on the particular situation.

The President

Our examination of American foreign policy making begins with the president. He is the central figure, both in the Constitution and in fact. When many Americans think of foreign policy today, they think of President Carter sitting in his office "making policy."

The final responsibility for foreign policy is his. Under our Constitution, the president is both the chief executive and the commander in chief of the armed forces. He is also the chief diplomat. He sets the tone for the

President and Mrs. Richard Nixon standing on the Great Wall of China during their visit to China in 1972.

entire administration. He directs the nation's attention to one part of the world or another. He exchanges letters, messages, and telephone calls with other heads of state. He greets foreign dignitaries. He visits foreign countries. By his words and deeds, the president projects the American posture toward the rest of the world. He may continue an existing policy, as President Kennedy did in defending American interests in Berlin during 1961. Or he may act in ways that completely reverse recent history, as President Nixon did when he made his dramatic visit to China in 1972, or as President Carter did when he accepted the need for a Palestinian homeland in the Middle East.

As chief executive, commander in chief of the armed forces, and chief diplomat, the president has final responsibility for foreign policy.

A doodle made by John F. Kennedy during discussions about the Bay of Pigs invasion. Kennedy wrote "Decisions, Decisions, Decisions," obviously indicating the difficult situation he thought he was in.

The president appoints the major figures who oversee all aspects of foreign policy. He selects the secretary of state and the director of the Central Intelligence Agency (CIA), as President Carter did when he appointed Admiral Turner to head the CIA. His appointees also head the militarily important Joint Chiefs of Staff, and departments of Treasury, Commerce, and Agriculture, which also have foreign responsibilities. The president initiates and signs national treaties, either by formal agreement (which requires a two-thirds vote of ratification by the Senate) or, more commonly, by executive agreement (in which case no congressional approval is required).

The president's task in making foreign policy has increased in complexity and scope since the early days of the Republic. As more nations have emerged, the president has been forced to spend more time on foreign relations. And as the American political economy has spread its influence throughout the world, foreign events have had more direct impact on our internal affairs. The technological revolution, and the ensuing increased speed of communications, has altered the nature of diplomacy. For example, in the eighteenth century, President Washington gave Benjamin Franklin and other members of the peace delegation wide latitude to negotiate and sent them off to France. Since the delegation would be gone for long periods of time, the president could turn his attention elsewhere. Now, however, the president receives a constant stream of information flowing from all over the globe, and must often oversee even minor details of negotiations.

The increased complexity of the world serves to enhance the president's power.[4] Because of the volume of information flowing in and the tens of thousands of people involved in foreign affairs, the president is

The increased complexity of the world has enhanced the president's power, as he is often the only person with an overview of the whole situation.

[4] Thomas A. Bailey, *The Art of Diplomacy* (New York: Appleton-Century-Crofts, 1968).

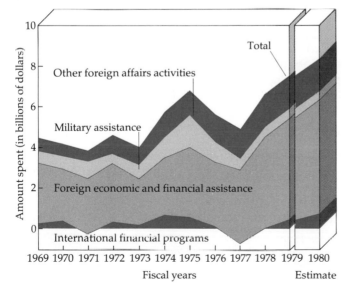

Fig. 13.1
Federal outlays for international affairs. (Source: U.S. Budget in Brief.)

often the only person able to claim an understanding of the whole situation. In addition, with huge bureaucracies to oversee and billions of dollars to allocate, the president may initiate policies without any particular agency knowing about it. With information, money, and secrecy adding to his power, the president is in a position of considerable advantage over others who would like to influence foreign policy.

In addition, the central role of the president has been heightened by various crises since World War II. With the dawning of the nuclear age and the presence of American military forces all over the world, the presidency is the focal point of national security decision making. When crises arise, as they did in Cuba during 1962 or Vietnam during 1965, the president's office becomes the center of both attention and power. Here decisions of enormous importance are made, often involving the lives or deaths of millions of people. Even when these crises are over, the president is left with increased power to act in future emergencies. Numerous observers have been concerned with the buildup of presidential power (as noted in Chapter 8), some going so far as to label this an "imperial presidency."[5]

There is a paradox here. For all his power, the president has only so many hours in his day. He is able to supervise only a tiny fraction of the information that pours into Washington from American diplomatic missions overseas, satellites, and other intelligence-gathering devices. With so many countries, he does well to know a little about a few. In addition to dedicated Americans who genuinely have the nation's interest at heart, he needs some advisers who disagree about policy. Since World War II, therefore, a vast set of bureaucracies has developed, bureaucracies that have considerable responsibility for the formation of various *aspects* of the foreign policy. What the president often needs most is a way to organize and coordinate these agencies. He needs to know how to limit their power; to make sure the information he receives is correct; and to prevent bureaucratic policy from becoming foreign policy.[6] All of this is easier said than done, as we have noted in Chapters 7 and 9.

The National Security Council

Each American president is confronted with a variety of bureaucracies, which all claim a share of foreign policy responsibility. How can he coordinate them? How can he ensure the orderly flow of information? How can he make sure that foreign policy is being based on valid assumptions? Since there are few, if any, neat and tidy lines of authority, the president

---

[5] Arthur M. Schlesinger, Jr., *The Imperial Presidency* (Boston: Houghton Mifflin, 1973). See also Raymond Aron, *The Imperial Republic* (Garden City, N.Y.: Doubleday, 1972).

[6] For an examination of bureaucratic politics, see Morton Halperin, *Bureaucratic Politics and Foreign Policy* (Washington, D.C.: The Brookings Institution, 1974).

must face lack of initiative, petty squabbling, and bureaucratic competition, in addition to dedicated Americans who genuinely have the nation's interest at heart but who also disagree about policy. Indeed, some have argued that many within the bureaucracies are often concerned more with the health of their organization—that is, the size of their budgets and number of personnel—than with what is best for the country. When the U-2 spy plane was developed and tested, months of debate followed as to who would fly it—the Air Force, the CIA, or some other agency. And during the Cuban missile crisis, despite a critical need for the U-2, inter-bureaucratic rivalry kept it grounded for more than a week.[7]

In an attempt to help the president coordinate foreign policy making, the National Security Council (NSC) was created during the Truman administration. Designed to bring together all the administrative heads involved in foreign policy (such as the director of the CIA) so that they could advise the president, the NSC has been headed by an assistant to the president and is part of the executive office.

The NSC was created by Truman to help the president coordinate foreign policy.

Each president has used the NSC in his own way. Under Truman it was a small group with limited responsibility. Although Eisenhower used the NSC staff extensively, critics said the process often produced consensus committee reports.[8] Under both Johnson and Kennedy, the functions of the NSC were often taken over by others, such as the president's adviser for national security affairs.[9] In the Nixon years, the NSC, then headed by Henry Kissinger, was the focal point for foreign policy formation.

Yet as Kissinger's influence grew and he was eventually appointed secretary of state, the NSC met less frequently. President Ford subsequently used the NSC as a counterweight to Kissinger after Kissinger was forced to relinquish his position as head of the NSC in 1975. Under several presidents, the NSC has been used to draw up a series of **National Security Study Memorandums** (NSSMs), which are designed to lay out the various choices or options available to the United States. Under President Carter, the crisis role of the NSC was reduced with the increased power of the director of National Intelligence, Admiral Stansfield Turner. As head of the NSC staff, Carter's national security adviser, Zbigniew Brzezinski, also played a role in reorganizing it. Brzezinski, a former Columbia University professor, and Turner, a classmate of Carter's at the United States Naval Academy, have worked well together during the Carter administration.

[7] Graham Allison, *Essence of Decision: Explaining the Cuban Missile Crisis* (Boston: Little, Brown, 1971); Elie Abel, *The Cuban Missile Crisis* (New York: Bantam, 1968); Robert F. Kennedy, *Thirteen Days* (New York: Norton, 1968); Klaus Knorr, "Failures in National Intelligence Estimates: The Case of the Cuban Missiles," *World Politics* (April 1969): 455–467.

[8] See Maxwell Taylor, *The Uncertain Trumpet* (New York: Harper & Row, 1959).

[9] See Lyndon Johnson, *The Vantage Point* (New York: Holt, Rinehart and Winston, 1971) and Roger Hilsman, *To Move a Nation* (Garden City, N.Y.: Doubleday, 1967).

The Department of State

The degree of influence carried by the State Department varies depending on the particular president and the particular secretary of state.

Traditionally, the United States Department of State has been a major partner in the formation of American foreign policy, although the exact extent of the department's influence has depended upon the particular president and the particular secretary of state. In the Eisenhower administration, the secretary of state, John Foster Dulles, wielded enormous power and shaped American policy in most parts of the world. Yet he often made personal decisions without extensive consultation with the department itself. In the first Nixon administration, William Rogers was almost powerless to effect policy as secretary of state because most decisions were made by Nixon and his special assistant, Henry Kissinger. President Carter's secretary of state, Cyrus Vance, is widely regarded as a professional diplomat who carries out rather than initiates foreign policy.

Jimmy Carter and Secretary of State Cyrus Vance in an impromptu conference on the veranda of the White House.

When most Americans think of the State Department, they think of the worldwide network of embassies, consulates, and missions. And since the secretary of state, whether powerful or weak, acts as the spokesperson on matters of foreign policy, most Americans tend to think of the department of state as playing an important role in foreign policy matters.

In terms of carrying out policy, this is true. The various missions and delegations attempt to accomplish what has been decided on. They assist Americans in their travel abroad. They collect information and pass it back to Washington (over a thousand cables come in daily). They also try to promote American business overseas. In fact, most American diplomatic missions will have one or more economic officers whose primary responsibility is the promotion of American business. Indeed, the American ambassador to one of the most important areas of Africa obtained his position in the late 1970s in large part because of his success in getting a major communist country in eastern Europe to buy American electrical generators.

In terms of actually *forming* policy, however, such as determining whether our government should do X or Y, the Department of State has lost influence over the past decade. In the case of the Cambodian seizure of the American freighter in 1975, for example, the department was simply told to defend United States action. It was not consulted beforehand. Moreover, State Department officials, including our Ambassador to Japan, found out about Nixon's proposed trip to China in 1972 when they read its details in the newspapers! And they were kept completely in the dark about the president's and Kissinger's ultimatum to the Soviet Union during the Yom Kippur War of 1974 between Israel and the Arab states.

Part of the State Department's difficulty is a function of its organization. It is divided both geographically and functionally. There are bureaus for African affairs, East Asian and Pacific affairs, European affairs, Inter-American affairs, and Near Eastern and South Asian affairs. In addition, there are bureaus for congressional relations, the United Nations, administration, consular affairs, and intelligence and research (INR).

Within the State Department, but remaining semiautonomous, is the Agency for International Development (AID), which administers various foreign assistance programs. These vary from roadbuilding in Colombia, to agricultural support in Sri Lanka, to the development of family-planning clinics in India. Two other agencies, the United States Arms Control and Disarmament Agency (ACDA) and the United States Information Agency (USIA), while separate from the Department of State, receive overall policy guidance from the secretary of state.

Many scholars and some former officials have argued that this compartmentalized organization, while good for carrying out policy, has made the department slow and ponderous in coming up with policy recommendations.[10] John F. Kennedy was anxious to have the State Department assert itself during the early days of his administration. When it did not, he called it a "bowl of jelly," complaining that it was too cautious in recommending policy changes. During the Johnson and Nixon years, the department was often ineffectual in presenting policy positions in opposition to those of the CIA or the Defense Department.[11] It may be that in the wake of criticisms of the CIA and the replacement of Henry Kissinger (who tended to run a highly personal operation), the State Department as a department can regain some of its former influence.

The Central Intelligence Agency

In contrast to the Department of State, the CIA developed in the postwar era as a primary determiner of American policy. Formed out of the old Office of Strategic Services (OSS), which operated during World War II, the CIA was established in 1947 to gather intelligence abroad. Its director is charged with coordinating the gathering of all foreign intelligence. Growing in size and importance during the 1950s and 1960s and employing tens of thousands of people, the CIA had an estimated yearly budget of nearly $2 billion in 1977.

Headed by the director of Central Intelligence, the "agency," as it is known, quickly developed as an important part of the foreign policy establishment. Divided into a number of functional bureaus called *directorates*, the CIA has divisions for intelligence (including current political, strategic, and economic research), science and technology, management (including communications and logistics), and, most controversially, operations. It is the *operations* directorate that has responsibility for the gathering of intelligence in the field, for counterintelligence, and for covert action, including "dirty tricks."[12]

---

[10] Dean Acheson has graphically illustrated this in his "The Eclipse of the State Department," *Foreign Affairs* (July 1971): 593–606.

[11] John F. Campbell, *The Foreign Affairs Fudge Factory* (New York: Basic Books, 1971).

[12] There are a host of books dealing with the CIA. Among the most notable are: Miles Copeland, *Without Cloak or Dagger* (New York: Simon and Schuster, 1974); A. Dulles, *The Craft of Intelligence* (New York: Harper & Row, 1963); S. Kent, *Strategic Intelligence* (Princeton, N.J.: Princeton University Press, 1966); Y. H. Kim, ed., *The Central Intelligence Agency: Problems of Secrecy in a Democracy* (Lexington, Mass.: D. C. Heath, 1968); Philip Agee, *Inside the Company: CIA Diary* (Baltimore: Penguin Books, 1975); L. Kirkpatrick, *The Real CIA* (New York: Macmillan, 1968); L. Kirkpatrick, *The U.S. Intelligence Community* (New York: Hill and Wang, 1973); Victor Marchetti and John D. Marks, *The CIA and the Cult of Intelligence* (New York: Knopf, 1974); P. J. McGarvey, *CIA: The Myth and the Madness* (Baltimore: Penguin Books, 1972); L. Fletcher Prouty, *The Secret Team* (Englewood Cliffs, N.J.: Prentice-Hall, 1973); H. H. Ransom, *Central Intelligence and National Security* (Cambridge, Mass.: Harvard University Press, 1958); H. H. Ransom, *The Intelligence Establishment* (Cambridge, Mass.: Harvard University Press, 1970); D. Wise and T. Ross, *The Invisible Government* (New York: Random House, 1964).

While most CIA intelligence estimates come from more or less open sources such as magazines, newspapers, and satellite photographs, some important information has been obtained from undercover or clandestine sources. Moreover, as the agency grew and involved itself in more and more countries overseas, it engaged in a number of activities that seemed to go beyond traditional methods of intelligence gathering. It bought or created companies overseas, ran airlines, trained and armed individuals and groups, attempted and succeeded in overthrowing governments, and involved itself in assassinations and attempted assassinations. Guatemala, Indonesia, Iran, the Congo, Iraq, Chile, Laos, and Cambodia are known to have been theaters of CIA operations.

In addition, the agency arguably went beyond the limits set by the National Security Act of 1947, especially those limits that stipulated no CIA involvement on the United States domestic scene. Various investigations, which resulted in the Rockefeller report of 1975, indicate that the CIA engaged in illegal wiretaps of American citizens within the borders of the United States, maintained unlawful files on American citizens, and supervised surveillance of the mails. Both Presidents Nixon and Ford attempted to limit some of these activities, while Congress in recent years has established a committee to supervise the CIA.

At the same time, it should be pointed out that a series of American presidents agreed with many of the agency's actions, particularly overseas. There are, and continue to be, many areas of the world where there are American interests and where uniformed Americans cannot go or cannot act effectively. There also are, and continue to be, tasks that other American agencies cannot carry out. The real test that the CIA poses for the American political system in the 1980s is the extent to which it can be controlled—in other words, allowed to perform the tasks for which it was created, and yet prevented from engaging in activities that go beyond its mandate. Even if the CIA has not become an "invisible government," in many instances it has *made* policy, rather than simply carried it out; and CIA attachments to foreign individuals and organizations have often run counter to the longrun best interests of the United States.

The CIA has become increasingly important in the area of foreign policy. The question now is the extent to which it can be controlled.

Ironically enough, it was during the Carter administration that the CIA gained new overview powers with the formation of the "National Intelligence Tasking Center," which was to act as a central clearing house for national intelligence estimates.

The National Security Agency

The CIA is not alone in the collection of information for intelligence. The National Security Agency (NSA), which is part of the Department of Defense, employs over 24,000 people, has an annual budget of over $1.2

billion, and operates more than $3 billion worth of complicated electronic gear. Formed in 1962, the NSA is primarily concerned with listening to the radio, electronic, and television and telephone transmissions of other countries.[13] For this purpose it uses over two thousand listening posts scattered all over the world and, together with the other agencies of the Defense Department, collects information by using spy-in-the-sky satellites (of which ten to twenty are launched every year).

Why was the NSA formed when the United States already had the CIA? The answer has several parts. In the first place, the Department of Defense was simply not anxious to have the CIA take over all aspects of intelligence gathering. In addition, the Defense Department controlled much of the classified "hardware" necessary to carry out the electronic surveillance of the Soviet Union and China. It had the rockets to launch the satellites. It had the ships and planes to monitor the borders of America's adversaries. It had trained manpower to operate the equipment and, like many organizations, it grew and grew.

Currently, the NSA is also responsible for the making and breaking of codes. Some of its "customers" include the Department of State, the Defense Department, and even the CIA. Although many codes cannot be broken, the NSA still makes efforts to keep track of "traffic patterns" in international relations, including the transfer of funds. In recent years, for example, it has begun to keep track of the location of **petrodollars,** funds that the Arab oil producers have invested in the United States.

While just knowing where foreign funds are located gives the United States an advantage in its dealings with other countries, the NSA faces a simple, but disturbing, problem: It simply collects too much information. So many data are accumulated on a daily basis that no more than 10–15 percent of the messages intercepted can be examined. The rest are often merely stored after "traffic patterns" are determined. The mere collection of information is not without important policy implications. The shooting down of a U-2 plane over the Soviet Union in 1960, the capture of the Pueblo spy ship by the North Koreans in 1968, and the sinking of a United States intelligence vessel by the Israelis during the 1967 war were all the result of our official electronic snooping.

The Department of Defense

The Department of Defense, the largest employer in the free world, also plays a prominent role in shaping our foreign policy.

If the State Department's role in foreign policy making has declined in recent years, and if the efforts of the CIA and the NSA have been questioned, there can be no doubt that the role of the Department of Defense (DOD) has increased sharply.[14] With over 1 million civilian employees and

---

[13] See generally Harvey Howe Ransom, *The Intelligence Establishment* (Cambridge, Mass.: Harvard University Press, 1970), pp. 126–133.

[14] Andrew Tully, *The Super Spies* (New York: William Morrow, 1969).

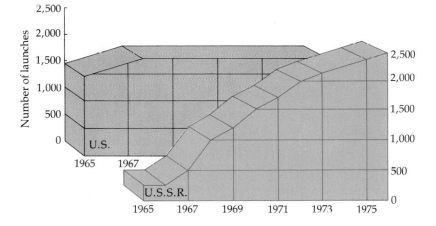

Fig. 13.2
Total missile launches by the United States and Russia, 1965–1975. (Source: *United States Military Posture Statement for Fiscal Year 1977*. Superintendent of Documents, U.S. Government Printing Office, Washington, D.C. 1976, p. 48.)

2.5 million persons in the armed forces, the DOD has become the largest employer in the free world. Its budget exceeds $120 billion per year, constituting more than a quarter of the federal budget in 1979. This fact alone helps to explain the prominent role played by the Defense Department in shaping our foreign policy.

A large slice of the department's budget goes for weapons. Helicopters cost over $1 million apiece, advanced bombers as much as $100 million, a single capital ship over $200 million, and super-carriers as much as $2 *billion*. In fact, since World War II, the United States has spent an incredible $1 trillion for a bewildering array of military technology and weapons systems. As Herman Kahn and others have pointed out, this means that in terms of technological "progress," we and the Russians have already fought World Wars III through VIII![15] Each new breakthrough by one side immediately leads to a countermeasure by the other, and now both sides have enough power to kill every person on the earth at least twelve times over. The constantly spiraling costs of weapons and weapons systems and the inconclusive nature of the arms race have even alarmed some members of the military establishment.[16] As a result, the United States and the Soviet Union have taken some tentative steps to slow down the arms race through the Strategic Arms Limitation Talks (SALT).[17]

The power of the Defense Department can also be measured by its worldwide network of bases. With literally *thousands* of bases and facilities

---

[15] Herman Kahn, *On Thermonuclear War* (New York: The Free Press, 1966). See also his *Thinking About the Unthinkable* (New York: Horizon Press, 1962) and *On Escalation: Metaphors and Scenarios* (New York: Praeger, 1965).

[16] Bruce M. Russett, *What Price Vigilance: The Burdens of National Defense* (New Haven, Conn.: Yale University Press, 1970); Ralph E. Lapp, *Arms Beyond Doubt* (New York: Cowles, 1970); Drew Middleton, *Can America Win the Next War?* (New York: Scribner's, 1975).

[17] John Newhouse, *Cold Dawn: The Story of SALT* (New York: Holt, Rinehart and Winston, 1973).

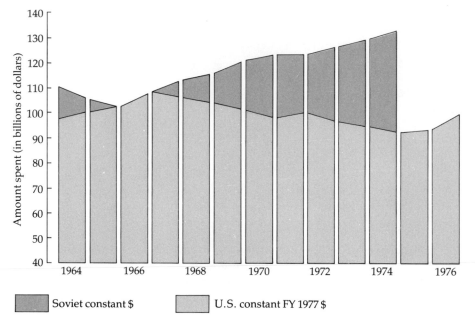

Fig. 13.3
Department of Defense baseline forces budget trends. (Source: *Department of Defense*
Appropriations for Fiscal Year 1977. **Committee on Appropriations, House of**
Representatives. 94th Congress, 2nd Session, Part I, p. 604.)

overseas (including over 120 in Japan alone), and with American troops
and technicians stationed in nearly thirty countries, the American military
presence itself often determines policy. Whatever the original reasons may
have been for sending troops to Korea, or the Philippines, or Turkey, or
Italy, or Iceland, or the Canal Zone, the fact that they are there now gives
the United States both a capability for action and a check on that action.
For example, during the 1960s and early 1970s, the United States supported a continuing Portuguese presence in Africa, even though most
Africans opposed that presence. Moreover, the United States did not
recognize the liberation movements in Angola, Mozambique, and Guine-
Bissau. Why? Because of the importance of our air and naval bases in the
Azores, bases our government leased from Portugal. In short, two decades
of American policy toward southern Africa was in large part determined
by a single (although important) base. Not surprisingly, when Africans
came to power, they did not think highly of our previous policy.

Congress

A final factor within the inner circles of foreign policy decision making is
Congress itself. Although its role has changed from decade to decade—

sometimes influencing policy on an almost daily basis, sometimes hardly influencing it at all—Congress has usually had the potential to greatly influence the decisions that shape American relations with the world.

Recent years have seen Congress taking both a passive and an active role in this area. During the 1950s and 1960s, Congress tended to leave most of the initiative to the executive branch. Following the disaster in Vietnam, however, Congress seemed anxious to assert its authority over the president. In one area, Congress has exercised its authority with some effect: The huge, bloated intelligence apparatus was reduced by nearly 40 percent between 1969 and 1976. The high-water mark of Congress's recent efforts occurred in 1974 with the passage of the **War Powers Act,** which limited to sixty days the time an American president could commit troops overseas without congressional approval.

Yet is Congress really suited to influence foreign policy beyond a certain point? As we have shown in Chapter 9, its workings are slow and ponderous. Its many committees with their overlapping jurisdiction and partisan concerns tend to fragment its impact. It lacks the staff necessary to oversee the many complex issues related to foreign policy. And since at least some foreign policy has to be made in private, the inability of Congress to keep a secret is often a drawback. In fact, one of the reasons both the executive branch and the intelligence agencies continue to resist further congressional supervision is that, as one wag has put it, "to tell anyone in Congress is to tell the world."

An additional difficulty in allowing Congress to play a major, ongoing role in policy formation lies in the nature of the institution itself. As we saw in Chapter 9, Congress is generally sensitive to the changing moods of the public. Few members of Congress get much mail on Afghanistan or Chad, so that except for high-visibility issues, those that really stand out, Congress institutionally is not greatly interested in our relations with most countries. Especially in the House, where members face reelection every two years, many members would prefer being safe rather than "right," and caution is the watchword. This may be prudent—and even necessary—politically, but it is not always the best way to make foreign policy. Also, although a good deal has been said about **bipartisanship** (Republicans and Democrats making policy without regard to political concerns), this concept is often ignored in day-to-day congressional politics.[18] But if you were a freshman member of Congress and there is heavy pressure on you to vote for a Republican position even though you feel it is the wrong position for the country, how would you vote?

One has only to look at the painfully slow evolution of something like an energy policy to see a persistent difficulty with Congress assuming additional responsibility in the field of foreign affairs. If Congress moves

[18] J. William Fulbright, *The Crippled Giant* (Garden City, N.Y.: Vintage, 1972).

slowly in grappling with a vital concern that affects virtually every American as well as our relations with many countries in the world, it is hardly in a position to be of much help in determining a prompt American response to a new government in Spain or Bolivia. Despite the large numbers of persons involved in the collection of information relating to foreign policy, the millions of Americans carrying out that policy in the armed forces and various bureaucracies, the actual formation of policy continues to be the work of a relatively small number of persons.[19] In fact, 435 representatives and 100 senators are no more likely to make foreign policy efficiently than they would a soup.

In addition, notwithstanding the expression, "politics stops at the water's edge," it seems clear that this is not usually the case. While Republicans and Democrats may rally to the president during a period of immediate crisis, by and large members of both parties often feel free to play politics with foreign policy. For example, when President Truman fired General Douglas MacArthur over his handling of the Korean War, many in Congress attacked the president's action. Even presidents often play politics with the affairs of state. President Kennedy told Senator Mike Mansfield in 1963 that he would get American troops out of Vietnam, but only after the 1964 election, apparently to avoid being attacked for "defeatism."

In short, although Congress is institutionally and politically at a disadvantage in dealing with complex foreign policy issues, it is likely to remain an influential participant in and an occasional critic of United States foreign policy.[20]

> Because of the slowness of its workings, as well as its political nature, Congress is at a disadvantage in dealing with the complex issues of foreign policy. Nonetheless, it remains an active and potentially influential participant.

Crisis Decision Making: A Case Study— Cuban Missile Crisis (1962)

We have described the principal actors in the foreign-policy-making process. Let us now examine that process in greater detail by focusing on the Cuban missile crisis of October 1962.

The Cuban missile crisis is a valuable study for several reasons. On the one hand, it involved the most significant confrontation between the United States and the Soviet Union in the nuclear age. In addition, the episode has been written about extensively, including some important observations by participants,[21] so we have a detailed picture of what took

---

[19] See Hilsman, *To Move a Nation*.

[20] A lot, of course, depends on House leadership. See Garrison Nelson, "Partisan Patterns of House Leadership Change," *American Political Science Review* LXXI, No. 3 (1977): 918–939.

[21] Abel, *The Cuban Missile Crisis*; Abram Chayes, *The Cuban Missile Crisis* (London: Oxford University Press, 1974); R. Divine, ed., *The Cuban Missile Crisis* (Chicago: Quadrangle Books, 1971); R. Kennedy, *Thirteen Days*; Arthur M. Schlesinger, Jr., *A Thousand Days* (Boston: Houghton Mifflin, 1965), pp. 796–830; Theodore Sorensen, *Kennedy* (New York: Harper & Row, 1965), pp. 752–809; Hilsman, *To Move a Nation*, pp. 159–252.

place. What emerges is an interesting portrait of the extent to which foreign policy decision making is the result of bureaucratic rivalry and politics, as well as the result of the "pulling and hauling" among individuals and groups.[22]

Indeed, the very fact that it took the American government so long to discover the presence of Russian missiles in Cuba is an indication of the influence of bureaucratic competition on policy. The CIA had been receiving numerous reports of Russian missiles in Cuba but tended to discount them, in part because the Russians had "never done that before." Badly burned by its handling of the abortive Bay of Pigs invasion the year before, the CIA was reluctant to press hard on the Cuban issue and yet seemed overeager in comparison to the Departments of State and Defense.

It was only after the Republican Senator from New York, Kenneth Keating, flatly stated that the Russians had built missile bases in Cuba that the CIA and Defense Department focused directly on the problem. Even then, ten days went by while the CIA and DOD argued over who would fly the U-2 planes.

When the U-2 brought back photographic evidence of the Russian missiles, President Kennedy assembled a small group of advisers to analyze the situation. It is instructive that he did not turn to the National Security Council, a body he thought was too unwieldy. Nor did he turn to Congress. In fact, congressional leaders were not included in the deliberations until after the decision to blockade Cuba had been taken. Instead, Kennedy formed an executive committee from NSC (called EXCOM). EXCOM was made up of the heads of the CIA, State Department, and Defense Department, as well as a number of other individuals including the president's brother, Robert Kennedy, and his close aide, Theodore Sorensen.

Although Kennedy wanted Dean Rusk, secretary of state, to lead the meetings, Rusk declined. The State Department's position changed from day to day; Rusk first advocated an air strike, then nothing, and finally a blockade. The United States representative to the United Nations, Adlai Stevenson, urged that the United States do nothing, or else "trade" its missile bases in Turkey and Italy for the Russian ones in Cuba. The head of the Joint Chiefs of Staff, Maxwell Taylor, presented the Defense Department's position—an all-out invasion of Cuba. Clearly the DOD wanted to redo the 1961 invasion, this time "properly." In fact, the battle plans had already been drawn up.

Not anxious to repeat its mistake of 1961, the CIA called for an air strike. Other individuals, including Secretary of Defense MacNamara and the president's brother, urged a course somewhere between a purely diplomatic response and an invasion or air strike. In the discussion that followed over the next several days, it became clear that many of the

[22] Graham Allison, *Essence of Decision: Explaining the Cuban Missile Crisis.*

Intelligence photo of Soviet freighter bound for Cuba in 1962. The assumption that the covered cargo on the deck was Soviet missile launches led to the Cuban missile crisis.

participants were reflecting the concerns of their respective bureaucracies and arguing for solutions that featured a major role for their organization. As Graham Allison has so vividly put it, in foreign policy making "where you stand depends upon where you sit."

It was, in fact, the nonbureaucratic participants such as Robert Kennedy and Theodore Sorensen who first advocated the eventual policy decided upon by the president, a blockade or "quarantine" of Cuba, which steered a middle course between the major bureaucratic extremes. Even after the policy was decided on and American ships began the blockade, there was considerable "pulling and hauling" between the secretary of defense, Robert MacNamara, and the Navy as to how to run the blockade.

In hindsight, it appears that the course of action chosen by President Kennedy was correct. But what would you have done in his position? Fearing nuclear war, would you have let the Russians stay? Or, anxious to follow your military advisers, would you have ordered an air strike?

WHO INFLUENCES FOREIGN POLICY?

If the president, State Department, CIA, Defense Department, and Congress play the most consistent, ongoing roles in the making of foreign policy, there are a number of other organizations and groups that affect that policy from time to time. While these do not carry much day-to-day responsibility for the making of foreign policy, they nevertheless may be of major consequence in specific areas. The Department of Justice's Bureau of Narcotics, for example, may be a major influence in the various treaties between the United States and such drug-producing countries as Turkey, Mexico, and Colombia.

Other Departments with Foreign Policy Assignments

The Department of Justice is only one of many government agencies that have personnel stationed overseas and that have some impact on specific policies. Altogether, there are at least thirty-four separate agencies in this category. They vary from the Veterans Administration and the Department of Health, Education, and Welfare to the National Science Foundation and the American Battle Monuments Committees.

Of this group, several are worth noting, since their role may be influential in some instances. The Department of Commerce is concerned with questions of international trade, especially the ability of American firms to do business abroad.

The Treasury Department, in addition to being involved with drug-related matters, is also concerned with the international monetary situation. In situations where international monetary agreements are to be negotiated, the Department of the Treasury is vitally concerned and may head up the actual negotiations.

The Department of Agriculture has generally played an important role in promoting agricultural products (such as tobacco or cotton) overseas. In the past, the department has also supervised the distribution of American surplus food abroad under Public Law 480 (1954), which was designed to reduce farm surpluses. The elimination of many of these surpluses has meant the phasing out of the program. Yet the Department of Agriculture continues to be involved in foreign aspects of the American agricultural situation and has often acted to structure foreign policy, as in the American-Russian wheat deals of 1973, 1975, and 1977.

The Multinational Corporations

In addition to a variety of government agencies that may influence policy in specific areas, there are also the **multinational corporations**; that is, companies with plants in more than one country. Over the past three decades, these giant firms have increased in size and impact.[23] This has been true not only in the United States, but elsewhere; such international giants as Unilever, Royal Dutch Shell, and Air France have offices in almost every country of the world.

The staggering global reach of the multinational corporations can be seen in some startling figures.[24] For example, the major multinational corporations—International Business Machines (IBM), General Electric, Polaroid, International Telephone and Telegraph (ITT), and Coca Cola— have total global assets exceeding $200 billion! Many of these companies are so vast that they dwarf the economies of entire countries. General Motors, for example, had sales in 1971 of over $28 billion. The entire gross national production of Switzerland—as well as virtually every single country in Africa—for the same period did not exceed $26 billion.

Although fully 60 percent of United States investment overseas is found in Canada, Great Britain, Germany, Australia, Venezuela, and France, its portion is growing in the **Third World** (which includes all countries save the United States, Europe, the Soviet Union, and Japan). Considering the size of the local economies, corporate American investment in Afghanistan or Ecuador may loom large indeed. Even in so large and modern a country as Brazil, nearly 50 percent of its gross national product is produced by foreign companies.

Multinational corporations, some of which are richer than the countries in which they operate, have acquired enormous importance throughout the world, and can have significant impact on the making of foreign policy.

Through the international transfer of knowledge, capital, and technology, these corporations are in the process of revolutionizing the world's economy.[25] Their sheer size gives them an enormous importance throughout the world and in specific countries. Not surprisingly, they often attempt to shape American policy as well as the domestic political situation in the host country. Over the past decade, Gulf Oil has paid tens of millions of dollars to influence politics in a wide variety of countries from Italy to Gabon (to say nothing of the United States). ITT not only tried to determine the outcome of the 1970 elections in Chile, when it was faced with expropriations of $500 million following the victory of President Allende, but also made a major effort to get the CIA to "destabilize" the government. When the CIA did not do all ITT wanted, the corporation went ahead and paid money to try and upset the government.

It is appropriate for these corporations to try to influence American policy through legal channels. And the multinationals also have a right to be concerned over their situations in foreign countries. Yet it is not always the case that what is good for, say, General Motors in South Africa is necessarily good for either South Africa or the United States.

[23] Abdul Said and Luiz Simmons, eds., *The New Sovereigns* (Englewood Cliffs, N.J.: Prentice-Hall, 1975). See also Anthony Sampson, *The Arms Bazaar* (New York: Viking, 1977).

[24] Richard Barnet and Ronald Muller, "Global Reach," *The New Yorker* (December 2–9, 1974).

[25] Samuel Huntington, "Transnational Organizations in World Politics," *World Politics* XXV, No. 3 (April 1973): 333–368.

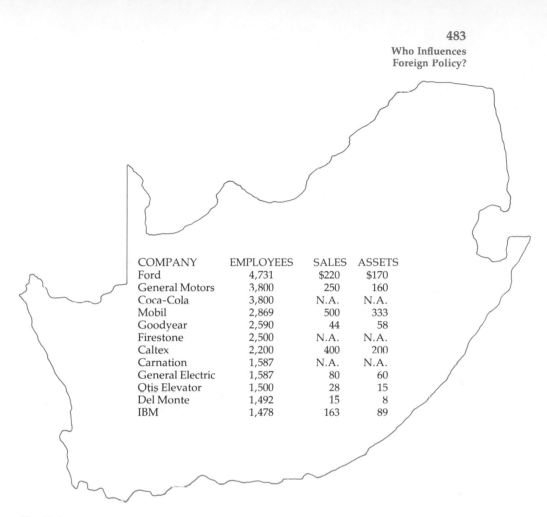

COMPANY	EMPLOYEES	SALES	ASSETS
Ford	4,731	$220	$170
General Motors	3,800	250	160
Coca-Cola	3,800	N.A.	N.A.
Mobil	2,869	500	333
Goodyear	2,590	44	58
Firestone	2,500	N.A.	N.A.
Caltex	2,200	400	200
Carnation	1,587	N.A.	N.A.
General Electric	1,587	80	60
Otis Elevator	1,500	28	15
Del Monte	1,492	15	8
IBM	1,478	163	89

Fig. 13.4
A dozen of the largest United States multinationals in South Africa.

Some major companies have also been singled out in recent years as having significant impact on the making of foreign policy. Companies that depend heavily on defense contracts seek to keep the defense budget high and, by extension, affect our foreign policy. Certainly such firms as Lockheed Aircraft, McDonnell Douglas, General Dynamics, Boeing, and American Telephone and Telegraph all have a stake in both the size of the defense budget and their share of it. Indeed, the executives of the companies, their stockholders, and their employees may all be anxious to continue the arms race for economic as well as strategic reasons. (We have noted some of the bureaucratic implications of this development in Chapter 10.)

Moreover, with so many former military personnel on their various boards of directors, the perspectives of these companies may be quite different from those with other backgrounds. In 1976, for example, Boeing Corporation, which did $1.56 billion of business with the Pentagon, had forty-eight former high-ranking officers on its staff. Rockwell International had thirty-six. Any proposed reduction in the arms race faces serious opposition from many of these companies.

The Media

No analysis of foreign policy making would be complete without a brief discussion of the role played by the media. Chapter 7 showed how newspapers, radio, and television influence the way we look at the world, although it is often difficult to say exactly how great their combined impact is in actual situations.[26] Consider, for example, the role of the press during the Vietnam war. As American involvement grew over the years, so too did the press coverage.[27] When President Eisenhower sent several hundred advisers to Vietnam, only an occasional American news reporter visited the area. With President Kennedy's 25,000 Special Forces troops came more of our press people. By the time President Johnson had enlarged the war to the point where half a million Americans were involved, the press representatives were there in the hundreds. And as we indicated in Chapter 7, the press clearly played an important role in misleading as well as informing the American public during the Tet offensive.

It would be hard to say just how influential the press was in determining the public's attitudes; there were many pros as well as cons concerning American involvement, and public opposition to the war tended to be accompanied by similar opposition on the part of the press. At the same time, there can be little question that the press coverage of Vietnam fed a mood of growing public disenchantment with the war.

In previous wars, what appeared in the press was heavily censored by the armed forces. By and large, in the case of Vietnam, censorship was comparatively light. Often unpleasant facts and situations were presented to those following the news. Also, as we have seen in Chapter 7, the sight of Americans dying in living color on the evening news undoubtedly brought the war home in unparalleled ways. What significance do you find in the fact that the Vietnam war—the first war to be fought on television—also proved to be an unpopular and divisive war?

The Public

A great deal depends on the public itself.[28] Generally speaking, the public is grossly ill informed about international relations. Few Americans could

---

[26] See John L. Hulteng, *The Messenger's Motives: Ethical Problems of the News Media* (Englewood Cliffs, N.J.: Prentice-Hall, 1976).

[27] David D. Halberstam, *The Best and the Brightest* (New York: Random House, 1972).

[28] See James N. Rosenum, ed., *Public Opinion and Foreign Policy* (New York: Praeger, 1960).

A scene from the Vietnam War.

name even a major portion of the 160 countries in existence today. The public's mood may be swayed by the press, by the president, and by events themselves. On the other hand, the public may make up its mind in ways that are not always understood at the time.[29] Some public support for the war in Vietnam may well have shifted to opposition for purely pragmatic reasons. After twenty years of struggle, $100 billion spent, and 45,000 Americans dead, the results appeared so meager as to make further sacrifices seem futile.

In any case, there is not one public, but many. In the field of foreign policy, this is an important distinction. There is the mass of people who have little sustained interest in international developments, and there are those who are relatively attentive to broad areas and specific policies.

[29] Gabriel Almond, *The American People and Foreign Policy* (New York: Praeger, 1960).

There is the general public, which tends to focus on problems only during moments of crisis or in the face of great events. There are numerous groups that care about and follow policy in particular areas. Jewish Americans, for instance, care about the Middle East, while Polish Americans are attuned to our policy toward Eastern Europe. And Catholic Americans care about our relations with the Vatican.

In fact, much of our historical interest in Europe can be traced to the fact that so many Americans originally came from that part of the world. Of the forty-six million immigrants who arrived from 1920 until 1974, more than thirty-five million, or over 76 percent, came from Europe. Perhaps this helps to explain why our Asian policy has been more open to debate than our commitment to the countries of Europe.

Some Americans favor our involvement as a global arbiter in a number of situations all over the world. Others would have us withdraw from the United Nations. Some feel we have the obligation to protect many of the smaller, weaker states from outside interference. Others feel that we ourselves are the greatest threat to those countries. Some feel our policy is too friendly toward the Soviet Union. Others feel it is not friendly enough.

This split in opinion is not surprising. The important thing is to ask ourselves why we should expect consensus and agreement on foreign affairs. We are a complex society of 220 million people, with diverse backgrounds, interests, hopes, and dreams. There is no uniformity of American opinion on most issues; why should there be consensus on foreign policy?

The important aspect in terms of the survival of the Republic is that the foreign-policy-making process be kept open. It is important that different opinions and positions be heard and encouraged. Individual citizens, groups, and companies have legitimate access to the process. The real challenge for the United States in the 1980s in this area will not be to create an artificial consensus but rather to ensure that diverse voices are heard. When foreign policy is heavily influenced by bureaucratic bargaining among large and complex organizations, it is important to seek policy alternatives that will serve national interests, not those of the bureaucratic leaders.

Can the American democracy encourage meaningful citizen participation in foreign affairs? Or, as in so many other countries, is foreign policy making to be the special preserve of a small number of elite leaders who deny the right and usefulness of public involvement? Can our political system function in times of crisis even as time is speeded up by events and when there is little opportunity to do more than react? Do we need long-range planning to ensure that the interests of the country as a whole are not to be trampled on in the name of expediency and crisis? What do you think?

THE ANATOMY OF CHOICE

In this section we are interested in presenting an important policy choice that will continue to confront the United States in the 1980s. As the reader, you are asked to think of yourself as having the deciding vote in the formation of policy in this area. You are also urged to consider the importance of the adage, "Where you stand depends on where you sit," since the problem area contains different points of view. This, of course, is invariably the case.

Should the United States Sell Weapons Overseas?

Recently a new debate has emerged in terms of American policy: Should the United States sell weapons overseas? This question is one that should be with us for a long time to come. What are the various points of view?

Since 1950, the United States has transferred over $86 billion worth of arms to various countries. While initially most of the arms were given away or leased, increasingly they are now sold. During 1974, for example, the Office of Munitions Control approved sales of over $8.3 billion to 136 countries. Total transfers exceeded $11 billion. Clearly, the arms business is big business and, with the new wealth concentrated in the rich but weak states along the Persian Gulf, it will become bigger yet. The United States is, of course, not alone in the arms trade. Russia has exported over $39 billion since 1950, including more than $5.5 billion in 1974. Recent years have seen a big increase in the Soviet effort. France, too, has gotten into the arms race in a major way, and is now the third largest supplier of weapons in the world.

Arguments against

Many arguments have been raised against American participation in the arms deals. One heard frequently is that the arms sent abroad under the various military assistance pacts cost the American taxpayer money. Another is that arms are usually accompanied by American technicians to train the armed forces of the host country in the use of those weapons, which involves the United States in a variety of potentially difficult situations. Still another argument is that sending arms abroad places the United States in the awkward position of supplying both sides in a conflict, even if no Americans are directly involved. American arms, for example, go to Saudi Arabia, Jordan, and Egypt as well as to Israel. In recent confrontations between Greece and Turkey, both sides drove American-made tanks and flew American-made aircraft.

People who oppose the sale of arms abroad also claim that massive purchases of sophisticated weapons actually put a drain on the American

Copyright, 1978, The Boston Globe/Distributed by Universal Press Syndicate.

military establishment. This is a relatively new development. Previously, most arms were second-hand weapons that had already been discarded by the armed forces. Now, however, Israel, Iran, and other countries insist on the most modern equipment in the field of supersonic aircraft, missiles, and radar systems, and the Yom Kippur War in 1973 used up over 600 aircraft and 2,700 tanks. And finally, the accent on arms and American participation in local arms races diverts countries from spending money on food and other badly needed development projects.

Arguments in favor

On the other side of the debate over selling weapons overseas, arguments are being made that America should continue to be an active participant in the arms race. For example, many feel that far from costing Americans money, the arms race is vital to the continuation of many companies. As noted in Chapter 10, Iran's purchase of eighty F-14 fighters from Grumman in the 1970s saved the company from bankruptcy. Furthermore, the sale of arms to various countries gives the United States some leverage over that country's policies, since once a country is committed to certain weapons systems it is difficult to switch. The Soviet Union, it is argued, by supplying Somalia, Guinea, Yemen, and Iraq, has gained a significant amount of influence over their foreign policies. And during the 1965 Indo-Pakistan conflict, the United States, by refusing to resupply both sides, did have an impact on bringing about a negotiated settlement. By 1976, Soviet deliveries of military supplies to the Third World reached their highest levels since the 1973 Middle East War.

Another argument in favor of selling arms overseas is that any drain on the United States military establishment can be overcome by expansion of plant facilities, thereby making the United States stronger in the long run. In addition, with America's balance-of-payment difficulties, we cannot afford to let billions of dollars go to other countries. A sale of a single jet fighter can earn as much foreign currency as a thousand autos. The General Dynamics A-15 fighter is expected to gross over $20 *billion* between now and 1990, and its acceptance by the major NATO buyers has been called "the arms deal of the century." Clearly, many American jobs and the future prosperity of entire communities rest on the continuation of selling abroad.

Finally, although the competition for arms sales may lead to countries buying weapons they do not need, there is little evidence that most countries, even in the poverty-striken Third World, would put their money into socially useful projects if the money were not spent on arms. Many leaders in the Third World bitterly resist the notion that sophisticated arms are only for the industrialized countries.

These are but a few of the arguments, pro and con, concerning the arms race and American participation in sales to other countries. Obviously, a worker in a helicopter factory will have a different point of view than someone whose job is in an insurance company or a liberal arts college. An economist concerned with the economic situation in the United States will view the situation differently from someone concerned about the incredible costs involved to countries that cannot afford the weapons. Someone who is against wars in general will find a monstrous logic in the notion of helping hundreds of countries to kill millions of people. Others will say the world cannot be changed by individual action. Perhaps the

An international exhibit of military hardware for sale.

arms trade is necessary to the continuation of nation states. Is this good or bad?

Where do you come down on this question?

SUMMARY

In this chapter we have discussed foreign policy making in America, identifying certain components and patterns in the substance of that policy. We have asked "who makes foreign policy," and have noted the variety of agencies involved in the process and the frequency of "crisis decision making." And we have attempted to answer the question, "Who influences foreign policy?" Finally, we have asked you, the reader, to consider the choices open to United States policy makers on one particularly difficult issue (arms sales abroad), and try to decide where you would stand.

As the example of arms export suggests, the present world situation is complex indeed. Throughout most of our history we have assumed that we could pick and choose the situations in which we wished to become involved. World War II, for example, seemed clear-cut. We knew the enemies, we knew the allies, and we proceeded accordingly.

But the emergence of these new forces in the 1960s and 1970s has complicated the world situation. With over 160 countries in existence, the United States must have a complex and sophisticated set of responses to the world. No simple formula will suffice. With our hundreds of military bases, embassies, consulates, and missions, and considering the interdependence of national economies throughout the world, we are engaged in the world. For better or for worse, we cannot withdraw from it.

Our challenge is to face the changed realities and cope with diversity. For the past two decades, American foreign policy has been rather like that of Austria following the Peace of Vienna in 1815—a major power concerned with preserving the status quo. As the most powerful country in the world, with numerous allies and ready access to raw materials, we have perceived that any change is for the worse, because change will affect the status quo. We have clung to outmoded world views long after the tide of history had begun to run the other way. We have supported colonial empires as nationalism has grown and overthrown them. We have supported the status quo in the face of popular movements.[30]

In the 1980s we can ill afford to make similar mistakes. We must face the fact that change is an important part of the world. We must assume that there are limits to American power, that we cannot accomplish all we would like. But at the same time we must face the reality that our economy, our political position, and our very lives are tied up with the rest of the world. It is a question not of avoiding all conflicts or of involving ourselves in all conflicts, but of picking and choosing those that are truly important.

The new generation of foreign policy makers must face this new complexity, dealing with change and diversity while recognizing the international arena for what it is. We must recognize opportunities and restraints, as well as goals, power, glory, and ideas and how they are related.[31] We must separate our primary interests from our secondary interests, and our secondary interests from our minor ones.

[30] See John C. Donovan, *The Cold Warriors* (Lexington, Mass.: D. C. Heath, 1974) for a view of the world between 1945 and 1968.

[31] Raymond Aron, *Peace and War* (New York: Praeger, 1966).

This requires courage and vision as well as patience and care. It will also take an "agreement to disagree" in the making of foreign policy and an understanding of the realities of international politics. International law in and of itself cannot keep the peace or ensure helpful interaction among states. The United Nations and other international organizations are themselves only partial reflections of the world as it is.[32] Power, whether economic, political, or military, always plays a large role in determining the shape of the world. How and where we choose to use our power—how America involves itself with the rest of the world during the decades of change that lie ahead—are the questions that confront us.

KEY TERMS

foreign policy	War Powers Act
neutrality	Cuban missile crisis
isolationism	EXCOM
expansionism	multinational corporation
manifest destiny	arms race
operations	

SUGGESTED READINGS

ALLISON, GRAHAM T., *Essence of Decision: Explaining the Cuban Missile Crisis* (Boston: Little, Brown, 1971).

A masterful core study of nuclear confrontation and foreign policy making. Brilliant analysis of bureaucratic interaction on the national level.

ARON, RAYMOND, *Peace and War* (New York: Praeger, 1966).

Aron is one of the best analysts of international relations, and his work is essential to an understanding of the global situation.

BEMIS, S. F., *A Diplomatic History of the United States* (New York: Holt, Rinehart and Winston, 1955).

An in-depth look at American foreign policy. Bemis puts America's foreign policy into its historical context.

FALK, RICHARD, *A Study of Future Worlds* (New York: The Free Press, 1975).

The future of humanity assessed from a variety of viewpoints. Attempts to see the United States as a major component, but yet a small part, of the total world order.

GURTOV, MELVIN, *The United States Against the Third World* (New York: Praeger, 1974).

A revisionist examination of American motives, foreign policy, and the Third World. Sets the case that America has done more harm than good.

---

[32] See Daniel P. Moynihan's engaging piece "The United States in Opposition," *Commentary* 59, No. 3 (March 1973): 31–44.

JOHNSON, LYNDON, *The Vantage Point* (New York: Holt, Rinehart and Winston, 1971).

A flat, often dull, effort by one of the most dynamic political figures of our time. Interesting more for what it does not tell than for what it does.

SCHLESINGER, ARTHUR M., JR., *The Imperial Presidency* (New York: Houghton Mifflin, 1973).

America in its 1970s and its overseas activities. Schlesinger rightly sees the rise of executive power in making the basic foreign policy decisions of the 1960s.

No one can say with finality just what rights Americans do possess. . . . Courts, legislators, presidents and governors must define our rights for us, and even though they often refer to constitutional language, the terms almost always require interpretation. . . . Ultimately, then, someone has to determine the course of American rights policies. Our rights do not exist as mere empty abstractions nor as a packaged kit of preformed protections available to every citizen at birth. On the contrary, like other public policies, rights policy formation is subject to the forces of politics and, consequently, to continual change.

Jay A. Sigler

CHAPTER 14 CIVIL LIBERTIES: STRUGGLE OVER CHOICES

The hero of Irving Wallace's recent pop novel, *The R Document*, is Chris Collins, a muddled but true-blue attorney general of the United States. Collins defeats a plot by the fascist director of the FBI to assassinate the president and abolish the Bill of Rights. Taking advantage of a massive national crime wave, the thinly disguised J. Edgar Hoover figure masterminds the movement for the adoption of a "Thirty-fifth Amendment" to the Constitution, which would allow suspension of civil liberties in time of internal emergency. Not only does the FBI director plan to create the emergency by blowing away the unsuspecting president, he also plans to regiment the country into carefully controlled, crime-free garrison towns. This arch-villain also orders the murder of the Chief Justice of the United States, and is foiled, of course, only at the eleventh hour. The Republic and the Bill of Rights are saved, and the grateful president pledges a new program to end crime through social improvement.

It is easy to say, "Why did people spend money for such bilge?" And yet the book (and the film that will inevitably follow it) reflects several very important aspects of civil liberties in America today.

First, the revelations of the mid-1970s concerning the FBI and CIA abuses of power have created at least a healthy skepticism about police practices in America; and there are those who would say the result has been a morbid readiness to believe the worst about government generally and law enforcement in particular.

Second, the country has been deeply afflicted in recent years by rising crime rates. And it is painful indeed to be afraid of crime at the same time as we are skeptical about our official protectors.

But third, and perhaps most important, Wallace's novel, in its own inept way, emphasizes the very real barrier that the Bill of Rights, as interpreted by the Supreme Court over the past several decades, places in the way of would-be architects of repression.

Wallace's fictional director must go to great lengths to subvert the Constitution. And the real J. Edgar Hoover, although he cheated from time to time when no one was looking, generally required a high level of compliance by the bureau to Supreme Court decisions. As long as we venerate the Constitution as we do, and as long as we, in the main, continue to regard most Supreme Court interpretations as legitimate exercises of judicial power, there are powerful levers of redress available to those individuals whom government has misused.

As we saw in Chapter 11, the Warren Court dramatically expanded **civil liberties** and **civil rights**—those rights belonging to individuals by virtue of their status as citizens or members of a civil society. And while the Burger Court is cutting back and tidying up in some areas, the core elements of the Warren Court policies are secure. In the meantime, the Burger Court has been adding some startling innovations of its own. So the rapid course of policy change seems likely to continue. What is not so apparent is that this course of change, this expansion of civil rights and liberties, is an intensely political process involving hard choices among competing values and among the desires of different groups of Americans. It is all too easy to assume that because the Bill of Rights is part of the Constitution, its meaning is fixed for all time. In fact, most of the specifics of the first eight amendments were given operational legal meanings only in the twentieth century.

Also, since the Supreme Court interprets the Constitution, it is too readily assumed that the evolution of American liberties is entirely a matter of **judicial construction.** The truth is that other institutions within our political process—Congress, the news media, interest groups, and so on— are also involved in struggling over definitions of the rights of Americans. In addition to **constitutional rights,** defined by the Supreme Court, a variety of **statutory civil rights** and liberties have been created. And these rights in some cases may be more important to ordinary citizens than constitutional rights. Examples examined later in this chapter are the provisions of the **Civil Rights Act of 1964,** which banned racial discrimi- nation in most public accommodations, and of the Privacy Act of 1974, which restricted the ways in which the federal government may obtain and retain information about citizens.

Rather than attempting to catalogue all the existing rights of Ameri- cans, in the first section of this chapter we introduce you to certain frontier issues of civil rights and liberties in areas ranging from free speech to sexual equality. These questions, which are presently being fought over in the political process, have no correct answers, in the sense of clear Supreme Court decisions or acts of Congress. You are invited to weigh the gains and risks of choosing one answer over another, and to decide what you would do.

In the second section of this chapter, in order to illustrate the process by which civil liberties are defined and expanded, we will focus closely on one evolving civil liberty—the emergence of a new, mixed constitutional- legislative "right to know." This new right has its foundation in the First Amendment, but its specifics have been filled in by legislation. In the course of this discussion you should ask yourself where the balance should be struck between the needs of the American people for information and the needs of government to protect sensitive materials. What new legis- lation would you have Congress enact in order to strike a better balance between secrecy and disclosure?

FRONTIER ISSUES

On the cutting edge of policy making in civil rights and liberties, activist lawyers play a leading role. Occasionally they work alone; more often they work for interest groups who want to advance their favored causes

Flo Kennedy, civil rights
lawyer.

through the courts as well as through congressional and administrative
lobbying and propaganda. An example of a legal loner is Florence Kennedy, a colorful eccentric, who delights in calling herself "Old Black Flo,"
and who has figured prominently in several important race and sex-
equality cases. A classic example of the interest-group lawyer is Jack
Greenberg of the NAACP Legal Defense and Educational Fund. Greenberg has been a prominent crusader for black interests for almost twenty
years.

Writing of the Warren Court years, Jonathan Casper perceptively distinguished "reformer" lawyers, who view "the law as a mechanism for
social change," from more "traditionalist" lawyers, who view the law as

"essentially a conflict-resolving mechanism."[1] And this pattern of activist lawyers urging judges to innovation (and legislators and bureaucrats to "positive action") is by no means a recent development. Clement Vose has identified the activist bar as crucial to the process of constitutional change in the early decades of this century,[2] and Benjamin Twiss made a similar observation of the late nineteenth century.[3]

Before there can be a right or a liberty that becomes defensible in court, someone has to decide that there *ought* to be such a right. This person or group, gathering supporters along the way, must develop arguments as to why judges should create the new right by decision, or why Congress should create it by statute, or why some otherwise obscure official in the bowels of the Department of Health, Education, and Welfare should create it by writing an administrative regulation. These governmental creations are what we regularly refer to as the **rights of Americans.** There are several different kinds (constitutional, statutory, and administrative), and different agencies of government become involved in formulating them. But first must come the argument and the efforts by the interest groups and the activists. Rights and liberties are not brought by the stork; they emerge only after prolonged and intensive political struggles.

> The rights and liberties we refer to as the rights of Americans emerge only after prolonged and intensive political struggles.

In the same way that presidents are criticized for not exerting (or for exerting too much) leadership in foreign or economic policy, they are frequently attacked over their civil rights and liberties performance. In the summer of 1977, the American Civil Liberties Union accused the new Carter administration of having "a poor civil liberties record," and of being "hostile when minority rights were under attack in Congress."[4] And this came after only a half-year in office.

Without attempting to cover every area (that would be a course in itself), let us examine several claims for new rights presently being fought over in our political process, and note the arguments for and against creating them.

Freedom of Speech

The First Amendment forbids Congress to make any law "abridging the freedom of speech, or of the press, or the right of the people peaceably to assemble, and to petition the Government for a redress of grievances."

[1] Jonathan D. Casper, *Lawyers Before the Warren Court: Civil Liberties and Civil Rights, 1957–1966* (Urbana: University of Illinois Press, 1972), p. 199.

[2] Clement E. Vose, *Constitutional Change: Amendment Politics and Supreme Court Litigation Since 1900* (Lexington, Mass.: Lexington/Heath, 1972).

[3] Benjamin R. Twiss, *Lawyers and the Constitution* (Princeton, N.J.: Princeton University Press, 1942).

[4] *New York Times*, July 19, 1977.

When we consider simply the text of the First Amendment as it bears on **freedom of speech,** an obvious question arises: Government may not abridge the right of free speech; fair enough, *but what is "speech"?* Much of the controversy within the Supreme Court and within our society over free speech has to do with how this question should be answered.

Over the years, the Supreme Court has held that commercial speech (advertising) is not entitled to the same degree of First Amendment protection as, say, political speech (an editorial or a news broadcast). In the same way, the Court has held that obscenity is not entitled to First Amendment protection. The justices have often tied themselves into knots attempting to determine what is obscenity and what is not, but when they can agree that it's looking them in the eye, they deny it protection. In the same way, "fighting words"—words likely to produce a physically violent response—are also unprotected; and those who use the public streets as a forum for airing their views may be prosecuted for disturbing the peace if they refuse to cease speaking in circumstances where the situation is about to get out of hand and the police can no longer protect the sidewalk orator from enraged listeners. Finally, **libel** and **slander** (verbal attacks on a person's character or reputation) are not protected by the First Amendment against civil suits by those who think themselves to have been damaged by something written or said about them.

Furthermore, First Amendment protection extends with its full force only to "pure speech." (*Pure speech* includes the written word and the spoken word, and closely allied media, such as pictures and films.) But when an action component is added to a particular expression—let us say, marching down the street—then the degree of protection must be adjusted in the interests of public safety and convenience, which may be threatened by large numbers of people milling about on the public ways. In the same fashion, "trashing" or sitting naked in the middle of Times Square can be viewed as forms of speech, but they are also potentially disruptive actions with which the organized community (through government) may concern itself.

How, then, would you deal with the problem of *Hustler* magazine? Some legal activists argue that all verbal and pictorial descriptions of sex should be protected by the First Amendment—that the obscenity exception should be eliminated. It is clear that there is no action component to *Hustler*—it's all words and pictures. But it is also hard to imagine that the publication possesses serious literary, artistic, or political value. Should it be protected throughout the country by the First Amendment, or should individual communities be able to decide whether *Hustler* should be sold within their borders?

Consider the problem of "chicken flicks." In these movies, children of seven to twelve years are pictured engaged in various sexual acts. There is no question that procuring minors for this purpose is illegal, but what about distributing the film product? If one takes a thoroughgoing libertarian position, and argues for *Hustler*, mustn't one then conclude that "chicken flicks" are protected by the First Amendment as well? Yet it is clear that if such materials can be legally marketed, ways will be found to procure victims to fuel the enterprise, and more and more children will be exploited.

In short, would you protect all expression dealing with sex, or would you retain some categories of nonprotected obscenity that the community could regulate? Again and again, free-speech issues resolve themselves into such choices. Is a particular utterance in or is it out; is it "expression" or is it bound up with some antisocial action that government may properly regulate?

Freedom of speech is a fundamental right guaranteed by the Constitution. Questions continually arise, however, as to what qualifies as speech. The issues of obscenity and of speech, combined with actions that may impose on others, are still very much subjects of legal controversy.

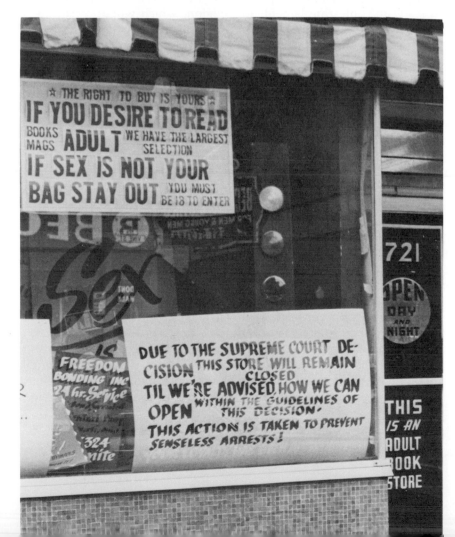

Adult book and film store in Cincinnati, Ohio.

Freedom of Religion

"Congress shall make no law respecting an establishment of religion, or prohibiting the free exercise thereof." This, the opening sentence of the First Amendment, makes two points: first, that the Congress (and the states) shall not aid "establishments of religion"; and that government shall not interfere with the "free exercise of religion."

Beginning in 1947, the Supreme Court has interpreted the **establishment clause** as prohibiting most forms of participation by churches, church schools, and religiously affiliated social service agencies (hospitals, orphanages, and so on) in government programs. While it is clear, for instance, that state governments can, as they see fit, aid nonpublic schools within their borders, they cannot aid nonpublic elementary and secondary schools *if they are affiliated with churches.* To allow such religious institutions to participate in governmental programs, the Supreme Court has held, would result in conferring benefits on religion, which would constitute a law respecting an establishment.[5] (But church-related colleges and universities may be aided on the theory that older students are less impressionable!)

It is interesting, however, that in cases dealing with the **free-exercise clause**—which forbids government interference with someone's religion—the Court has held that certain people are exempt for religious reasons from abiding by otherwise lawful government requirements. In a famous case decided in 1974, Chief Justice Burger wrote that the Wisconsin Amish, who did not believe in formal schooling for their young beyond the age of twelve, would not be required to obey the state school attendance law applying to all other Wisconsin children and parents. This was because the Amish sect objects to school attendance on sincere religious grounds.[6]

But if religious institutions must be kept from participating in governmental programs because that would constitute a benefit, how can one consistently give exemptions from otherwise valid community rules on the basis of religion? Don't these exemptions also constitute benefits to religion? This is not the end of the difficulty.

As government gets into the business of granting beneficial exemptions based on religious conscience, how is government to determine what is "religious"? When judges, and perhaps legislators and administrators, start making decisions about what is and what is not religious, doesn't this qualify as the kind of *"establishment of religion"* and governmental intermeddling with religion prohibited by the First Amendment? Thus far, the Court has been unable to resolve the contradiction between denying

Freedom of religion, another fundamental constitutional right, has also created legal ambiguities. For example, certain exemptions from federal laws granted under the free-exercise clause seem to violate restrictions outlined under the establishment clause.

---

[5] For a review of these decisions see Richard E. Morgan, "The Establishment Clause and Sectarian Schools: A Final Installment," *The Supreme Court Review,* 1973.

[6] *Wisconsin* v. *Yoder,* 406 U.S. 205 (1972).

benefits to religion under the establishment clause and conferring them under the free-exercise clause.

Some civil-liberty activists have been suggesting that part of the free-exercise problem could be avoided by reading the phrase "free exercise of religion" as free exercise of individual conscience. While this might get government out of the business of saying what was or was not religious, it would pose some difficult problems of its own. Should the state of Tennessee, for instance, be stopped from protecting the minority of its citizens who feel compelled on religious grounds to handle poisonous snakes as part of their church service? And what about the dangers posed to public health if a religious group in a particular state refused to be inoculated against a highly contagious disease?

People feel strongly about a number of things. Some are passionately opposed to sending their children out of the home to school, wishing to educate them themselves. Others are passionately opposed to paying all kinds of taxes. Disapproving of the ways in which public monies are spent, they would prefer to fend for themselves rather than consume the public services paid for by taxes. At what point does exempting persons from obeying on the grounds of conscience weaken the system of government under law?

If a four-family commune devoutly dedicated to the raising of pigs were to establish itself in your neighborhood, and demand that the zoning ordinance (which prohibited the keeping of livestock in a residential area) not be enforced against them, where would you stand? Would you grant them an exemption because they feel strongly, would you study them and test them to see if their conviction was of a religious nature, or would you tell them that the community's need for orderly land use and living patterns required that the law be consistently maintained?

And if you should decide to grant an exemption to the zoning law, either on grounds of conscience or because you were convinced that the commitment to rearing swine is genuinely religious, what would you say to the parents of the child next door who attends a Roman Catholic parochial school, which is excluded from federal educational enrichment programs because to allow its participation would benefit religion?

Racial Equality

In Chapter 3 we saw how the Fourteenth Amendment emerged from the period of Reconstruction after the Civil War. Although the requirements of the Fourteenth Amendment are directed specifically at the state governments, the Court has held that the rights and liberties that have been found to be inherent in its language apply to acts of the federal government as well.

We also saw how the Supreme Court, in the late nineteenth century, seized on the due-process clause of the Fourteenth Amendment to erect barriers against governmental regulation of the economy. And in Chapter 11 we noted how the Court, beginning in the 1920s and culminating in the 1960s, again used the due-process clause as a way of nationalizing the criminal-justice process. In approaching the law of race relations, however, it is not the due-process clause but the **equal-protection clause** (also found in the Fourteenth Amendment) that is crucial.

It was the equal-protection clause the NAACP relied on when it mounted its attack on **segregation** in public schools in the 1930s and 1940s, the campaign that finally led to the decision in *Brown* v. *Board of Education*, 1954. In 1896, the Supreme Court had decided that a state government could require racial separation in public facilities providing the facilities for the two races were substantially equal.[7] The lawyers for the NAACP, led by Thurgood Marshall, later an associate justice of the Supreme Court, argued against this interpretation. After their success in the Brown case, state-imposed racial segregation was wiped from the books.

Complex and painful questions remain, however. The *Brown* decision, and other equal-protection decisions that followed it, gave black Americans a right not to be discriminated against by government. But what about nongovernmental institutions that serviced the public? There was deeply entrenched segregation in many areas of the country in public accommodations and employment. But the equal-protection clause would not help here—it spoke only to the actions of states and not to the behavior of restauranteurs, hotel managers, and private-sector employers.

And even where public services were concerned, was it enough simply to stop segregating? What about the impact of past governmental discrimination, which could still have an effect into the future? A school district that had been segregated for seventy years might stop discriminating, but the effects of the past discriminations in school districting and school location would continue to produce the substantial effects and consequences of discrimination in the future.

Congress addressed itself to the subject of public accommodations and employment in the Civil Rights Act of 1964. Basing its action principally on the power to regulate commerce granted in Article I, Section 8, Congress forbade racial discrimination in theaters, restaurants, motels, and places of employment. And in response to the problem of the continuing structural impact of past segregation on school systems, the courts began to fashion remedies.

Where it was found that state-imposed discrimination existed in the past, school districts were required to do more than stop discriminating. They were required to achieve racial balance even if this involved massive

---

[7] *Plessy* v. *Ferguson*, 163 U.S. 537 (1896).

busing of pupils within the district. In addition, agencies of the executive branch began insisting on **affirmative action** (setting ethnic and sex quotas for employment and promotion) on the part of those receiving federal funds. Thus, national policy moved beyond nondiscrimination as a requirement of the equal-protection clause and of the Civil Rights Act of 1964, to a "color-conscious" use of quotas and an active reaching for balance.

What do you think of this? Are racially determined busing and the requirement of racial balance appropriate policies, or would you favor a "colorblind" policy, by which only racial discrimination would be forbidden?

The issue of racial equality also raises complex questions. National policy has now moved beyond simply nondiscrimination, which was required by the equal-protection clause and the Civil Rights Act of 1964, to an active use of quotas that some people feel goes beyond the bounds of the Constitution.

Sex Equality

In considering sex and the law in America, we encounter some of the same political actors and some of the same constitutional and statutory laws as in the question of racial equality.

At a constitutional level, the Supreme Court has again used the equal-protection clause to strike down certain legal distinctions between men and women that certain states and the national government had thought wise. For example, in 1973, the justices disallowed the practice of the military services whereby the "dependent allowance" automatically available to male members for their female spouse was not similarly available to female members for their male spouse.[8] Two years later, however, the closely divided Court rejected a due-process-clause challenge to the Navy's practice of maintaining separate promotion systems for male and female officers.[9]

What the Court seems to be saying in these cases is that when government makes distinctions based on gender, these distinctions must be *substantially rational*—that is, they must clearly serve some legitimate governmental end and not be matters of prejudice or mere convenience.

Following this approach, the Court, in 1977, struck down a provision of the Social Security Act whereby widowers, in claiming their wives' Social Security benefits, were required to show that they had, in fact, been dependent on their wives. Widows had never been required to show dependency on their husbands in order to collect; such dependency had been assumed. The Court found such a distinction between the sexes insufficiently "rational."[10]

As with race, the equal-protection clause in matters of sexual discrimination speaks only to governments, not private actions. But in the 1964 Civil Rights Act, Congress included sex discrimination as one of the be-

The Supreme Court has also used the equal-protection clause and the 1964 Civil Rights Act to strike down certain distinctions between men and women. In these cases, the government has indicated that the distinctions must be substantially rational, not just matters of prejudice.

[8] *Frontiero* v. *Richardson*, 411 U.S. 677 (1973).

[9] *Schlesinger* v. *Ballard*, 419 U.S. 498 (1975).

[10] *Califano* v. *Goldfarb*, 430 U.S.———(1977).

A woman cadet at the United States Naval Academy, formerly an all-male institution.

haviors forbidden to private interstate employers. Successive amendments to Title VII (the employment title) of the 1964 act have strengthened its provisions regarding sex discrimination. On the other hand, while it prohibits sex as a criterion in hiring (along with race, color, religion, and national origin), Title VII goes on to specify that sex (like religion and national origin) may be a legitimate criterion where there is "a *bona fide* occupational qualification reasonably necessary to the normal operation of that particular business or enterprise." In other words, sex is a valid criterion when there is some serious reason for hiring a woman over a man, or vice versa.

This, of course, brings the matter back to the courts. In the cases of both the government under the equal-protection clause and the private sector under the Civil Rights Act, courts must make the ultimate judgments concerning reasonableness. In 1971, the Court suggested that the exception for *bona fide* occupational qualifications extended only to "job situations that require specific physical characteristics necessarily possessed by only one sex."[11] Lower courts have generally followed this suggestion, rejecting employer practices of laying off women before men (because men usually are breadwinners and many women are second-income earners) while sustaining such things as limitations on jobs for women based on how much physical work they involve.

Once again, we encounter a frontier issue. Should government employers (under the equal-protection clause) and private employers (under the Civil Rights Act) be required to *individualize* physical-requirements tests? Is the military, for instance, justified in excluding *all* women from combat roles because many women are not physically up to them? There are, of course, exceptional women who could more than pull their weight. Should each individual applicant be tested? Should there be a rule of acceptance based on generalized differences between men and women? These questions are very much alive today and will remain so.

Restraints on Law Enforcement

In Chapter 11, we noted the way in which national procedural standards for the criminal-justice process were rapidly developed by the Warren Court; we also saw that this process has been slowed down, but not arrested, by the Burger Court. Public reaction to these stiffer national standards of search and seizure, self-incrimination, and so on, has been mixed. During the 1960s and early 1970s, however, there was little congressional involvement in making rules for the conduct of law-enforcement agencies—police, prosecutors, courts, and so on. The one major congressional effort during this period, the Omnibus Crime and Safe Streets Act of 1968, was principally concerned with protecting law enforcement from what congressional sponsors of the legislation saw as the "overrestrictive" tendencies of the Warren Court (see Chapter 11).

FBI abuses

In 1975, however, when a series of scandals broke concerning the way in which the Federal Bureau of Investigation had behaved toward blacks, the members of the so-called New Left, and other dissidents in the previous decade, Congress turned its attention to law-enforcement practices, at least at the federal level. Special committees were formed in both houses of Congress to investigate the behavior of the FBI, the CIA, and other federal intelligence gatherers. The investigative effort on the Senate side

[11] *Phillips* v. *Martin Marietta Corp.*, 400 U.S. 542 (1971).

Senator Frank Church, Democrat of Idaho, Chairman of the Senate Intelligence Committee, formed in 1975 to investigate alleged abuses by the CIA and the FBI.

was more impressive. A Special Select Committee, chaired by Senator Frank Church of Idaho, labored for over a year. The talented but hastily assembled staff of over ninety produced detailed documentation showing the abuses of power by the FBI in the closing years of J. Edgar Hoover's long regime as FBI director.

The FBI, with the knowledge of the director but without the knowledge of any attorney general (the responsible cabinet officer), mounted campaigns of political sabotage (called **counterintelligence programs**) against Communists, Trotskyites, and other persons, including the late Dr. Martin Luther King, who were regarded by the director and his confidants as being dangerous "subversives."

In addition, FBI agents engaged in tactics of questionable legality in seeking to apprehend real terrorists and criminals. Entries onto premises,

Date: 6/17/70

nsmit the following in _____

(Type in plaintext or code)

___AIRTEL_____ AIR MAIL – REGISTERED _____

(Priority)

TO: DIRECTOR, FBI

FROM: SAC, LOS ANGELES (P)

RE: COUNTERINTELLIGENCE PROGRAM
BLACK NATIONALIST-HATE GROUPS
RACIAL INTELLIGENCE
BLACK PANTHER PARTY (BPP)

Re Los Angeles teletype to Bureau, 6/15/70,
entitled "COMMITTEE UNITED FOR POLITICAL PRISONERS (CUPP),
IS-MISCELLANEOUS, THREAT AGAINST PRESIDENT NIXON".

Bureau authority is requested in sending the following
letter from a fictitious person to   Hollywood
"gossip" columnist for the "Daily Variety", who noted in his
6/11/70 column that JANE FONDA, noted film actress, was to be
present at the 6/13/70 Black Panther Party fund raising
function sponsored by CUPP in Los Angeles. It is felt that
knowledge of FONDA's involvement would cause her embarrassment
and detract from her status with the general public.

"Dear

I saw your article about Jane Fonda in 'Daily
Variety' last Thursday and happened to be present
for Vadim's 'Joan of Arc's" performance for the
Black Panthers Saturday night. I hadn't been
confronted with this Panther phenomena before but
we were searched upon entering Embassy Auditorium,
encouraged in revival-like fashion to contribute to
defend jailed Panther leaders and buy guns for
'the coming revolution', and led by Jane and one of
the Panther chaps in a 'we will kill Richard
Nixon, and any other M-----F----- who stands
in our way' refrain (which was shocking to say
the least!). I think Jane has gotten in over
her head as the whole atmosphere had the 1930's
Munich beer-hall aura.

"I also think my curiosity about the Panthers
has been satisfied.

"Regards

/s/ "Morris"

If approved, appropriate precautions will be taken
to preclude the identity of the Bureau as the source of this
operation.

Origin of a "letter plant" by the FBI's
Los Angeles office designed to
embarrass actress Jane Fonda as part of
a campaign against the Black Panthers.
Approval for sending the fake letter was
given by Bureau headquarters on June
25, 1970.

2 - Bureau (RM)   REC 16
2 - San Francisco (RM)
2 - Los Angeles   z JUN 19 1970

(6)

Appro   d: _____   Sent _____ M Per
            Special Agent in Charge

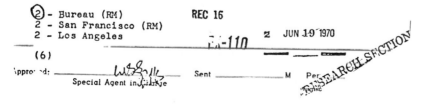

searches, and electronic eavesdropping were commonly used tactics, all conducted without warrants.

Another troubling, though not illegal, practice revealed by the Church Committee was the FBI's extensive use of informers, particularly during the disorderly 1960s. As every experienced policeman knows, informers are a notoriously unreliable lot. Sara Jane Moore, who bungled an assassination attempt on President Gerald Ford, was as inept at informing as she was with firearms. And the Detroit field office of the FBI was seriously embarrassed in 1976 when an informer within the Socialist Workers Party decided to curry favor with his FBI "control" by stealing a large number of the SWP's records. Not all informants are so unreliable or useless, but the display of the practice by the Church Committee raised questions as to the wisdom of the bureau's rather indiscriminate use of them.

In the wake of the Church Committee's disclosures, and under intense pressure from the Ford administration, Congress, the media, the FBI, and the Justice Department worked out a set of guidelines to cover future bureau investigations of anticipated crime in political contexts. By 1977, Congress was considering legislation to regulate the bureau and all intelligence agencies. This legislation would severely restrict the steps the FBI could take in advance of a crime being committed. If passed, it could become a model for the states in restricting the crime-prevention activities of their police forces. Critics of the legislation, however, argue that it does not go far enough. A coalition of groups led by the American Civil Liberties Union holds that the FBI and, by implication, all police forces should never undertake any investigative activity until the crime has been committed or is in progress.

In reaction to abuses by the FBI and CIA during the 1960s and early 1970s, Congress has taken steps to control law-enforcement practices. The crucial issue is whether one restricts investigation to post-crime detection, or whether one allows investigation aimed at prevention, especially as regards politically active individuals and groups. Either way, one sacrifices certain values.

In considering such restrictions, we are not, of course, talking about constitutional law. Legislation restricting the FBI is an excellent example of congressional policy making in the civil-liberties area. What do you think? Should police wait until the bloody bodies are littered about the airport waiting room, or should investigative activity of terrorist groups be undertaken on the basis of clues, hints, rumors, and anonymous "tips"?

There is no easy answer here. Either way one decides, one sacrifices certain values. If one restricts investigation to post-crime detection, society may be forced to endure certain outrages that might otherwise be prevented. But if one undertakes investigation aimed at prevention, especially as regards politically active individuals and groups, one involves agents of the state in political activity, most of which is completely innocent and is protected by the First Amendment.

THE RIGHT TO KNOW: A RIGHT IN THE MAKING

Events of the previous decade, especially those related to Vietnam and Watergate, have forced Americans to confront again a major question of democratic theory: "What measures may government properly resort to in preventing public disclosure of its internal documents?" This carries with it a related question: "What information is government justified in declining to disclose?" Legislation is being debated that would create new "information crimes." Judges, journalists, professors, members of Congress, and the Carter administration are scrambling to formulate new ground rules for secrecy and disclosure of government information. You should be following and participating in this debate, since the evidence will shape the future of our democracy and your role in it.

Our consideration of "the right to know" is organized around five issues:

1. To what extent can it be said that there is a *constitutional right* of access to government information, a First Amendment "right to know"?

2. What is to be done about the federal government's security classification system, which is perhaps the most important bar to citizens wanting access to government information at the national level?

3. Should there be any "information crimes" other than **espionage** (obtaining defense information and giving it to an enemy with the intention of injuring the United States)? More specifically, should we make the unauthorized disclosure of classified information a crime?

4. How good is the present mechanism of public access—the Freedom of Information Act—and what improvement might be made in it?

5. And, finally, should we pursue gradual, step-by-step reform of the existing patchwork of court decisions, statutes, and executive orders regarding public access, or is there something to be said for the idea of a single, comprehensive government information act?

A Constitutional Right to Know?

Until quite recently, litigation under the First Amendment was exclusively concerned with the right to speak or publish, and there was no mention of a right to have or seek information. However, by the mid-1960s, things were beginning to change. Today, the Supreme Court recognizes that the First Amendment's protection of speech carries with it some basic public right to information and also offers some degree of protection to journalists seeking news. However, these judicial opinions have been tantalizingly vague and unspecific; the dimensions of these constitutional rights have only been suggested. Here are the highlights of this gradual development.

In 1964, the Supreme Court created a special libel standard for public officials in the case of *New York Times* v. *Sullivan*.[12] Persons in this special newsworthy category had to show not only that what had been published about them was damaging and false (what ordinary citizens like you or

12 376 U.S. 255 (1964).

me would have to show) but also that it had been published with *actual malice*. This argument really rested on a right-to-know basis. The First Amendment value being protected by the justices was not so much that of free speech as it was the benefit to the public of unfettered discussion of the activities of public officials. Thus, it was more important that political debate be open and unrestrained than that public officials be able to protect themselves against lies and innuendo.

In May of 1965, Chief Justice Warren wrote for the Court in *Zamel* v. *Rusk*,[13] denying a person's claim of a First Amendment right to travel abroad (in this case, to Cuba) and inform oneself. Later that month, however, in *Lamont* v. *Postmaster General*,[14] the Court, speaking this time through Justice Douglas, upheld a First Amendment right to receive "communist propaganda" through the mails. Again the right to know, however, was not specifically mentioned; rather, Justice Douglas asserted a First Amendment interest in "uninhibited, robust, and wide-open debate" that echoed *New York Times* v. *Sullivan*.

In the famous *Red Lion*[15] case in 1969 the Court upheld the Federal Communications Commission's **fairness doctrine,** under which the Commission required radio and television stations to maintain an ideological balance in their programming. Here Justice White spoke approvingly of "the right of the public to receive suitable access to social, political, esthetic, moral, and other ideas. . . ." Yet in 1973 this interest was insufficient to sustain the claim of a paying advertiser for "access to the media" in *C.B.S.* v. *The Democratic National Committee*,[16] or the constitutionality of a state "right to reply" statute in the *Miami Herald* case a year later.[17] In both of these cases, Chief Justice Burger wrote that the primary First Amendment prohibition of governmental controls on the press outweighed the public interest in information flow.[18]

And there were several other cases over the years in which the questions of the public right to know and protection of the press arose. For example, *Branzburg* v. *Hayes*,[19] in 1972, saw the Court rejecting a First Amendment claim, resting on a public right to know, of a privilege for reporters to decline to testify about their sources before grand juries. Justice White reasoned that "the First Amendment does not invalidate

---

[13] 381 U.S. 1 (1965).

[14] 381 U.S. 301 (1965).

[15] *Red Lion Broadcasting Co.* v. *FCC*, 395 U.S. 367 (1969).

[16] 412 U.S. 94 (1973).

[17] *Miami Herald Publishing Co.* v. *Tornillo*, 418 U.S. 241 (1974).

[18] *Per contra* see Jerome Barron, *Freedom of the Press for Whom? The Right of Access to Mass Media* (Bloomington: Indiana University Press, 1973).

[19] 408 U.S. 665 (1972).

every incidental burdening of the press that may result from the enforcement of civil or criminal statutes of general applicability." Yet, in passing, White also remarked that news gathering was not without First Amendment protection.

Another case, *Stanley* v. *Georgia* (1969),[20] which tested a "possession of obscenity" statute, is one of several cases in which the Court has referred to a "now well established" constitutional right "to receive information and ideas." However, although this phrase may be well established, its meaning is anything but clear.

The best that can be said of the constitutional status of the right to know after examining such cases is that there have been repeated references to the right to hear and receive and seek information. However, these rights are of a substantially lower order of First Amendment magnitude than the right to speak, and must usually yield to "ordinary legal rules of general applicability." Furthermore, this opaque doctrine concerns only a *general* right to know, and has not been focused on the narrower issue of access to *government* information.

As one can see, the present law of public access rests on a rather shallow constitutional foundation. If the constitutional issues were clarified by the Court, Conrress and the bureaucracy would have some guidance in the shaping of legislation and administrative regulations. But this kind of clarification is likely to be a long time in coming.

There has been increasing recognition by the Supreme Court of a public right to know and to seek information. Present laws of public access to government information, however, rest on complex constitutional issues that have not yet been clarified by the Court.

The Security Classification System

There are some sorts of information that the federal government must keep secret because publication would impair something called "national security." This is widely agreed. But "national security" remains a terribly ambiguous term. Potential external dangers to the United States exist across a broad spectrum—from the classic case of disclosures endangering ships on the high seas,[21] to the disruption of our relations with another government because of the disclosures of exchanges conducted in expectation of confidentiality.

Unfortunately, "national security" is a label that may easily be used to cover governmental blunders,[22] as we learned in the recent past. It

---

[20] 394 U.S. 557, 564 (1969). The language was used in *Martin* v. *City of Struthers,* 319 U.S. 141, 143 (1943).

[21] This is sometimes supposed to be an imaginary horrible, but in 1942, in the wake of the Battle of Midway, the *Chicago Tribune* blew the fact that United States intelligence had broken an important Japanese naval code. United States naval vessels were then being deployed in accordance with information that the Japanese, had they realized their security had been breached, could have denied (by changing codes) or falsified. That the Japanese failed to pick up the leak does not mitigate its seriousness.

[22] See, generally, David Wise, *The Politics of Lying* (New York: Random House, 1973).

seems easy enough to say, "no more covering by classification," but this is too simple. The fact is that the disclosure of certain blunders may very well prejudice America's external security. In the real world of government (as opposed to the ideal, or make-believe, world of government so often projected by television and newspapers), hard information and human error, embarrassment to individuals, and damage to the international political position of the United States are often inextricably intertwined. Disclosing government information involves asking "which parts of which documents?" and "how much risk?" and "in whose judgment?" The problem is that our government may not be answering these questions very well at present.

Our formal **security classification system** is a twentieth-century creation. Until the second decade of this century, state secrets seem to have been kept by "gentlemen's agreements,"[23] and it was assumed that the internal documents of government were just that, and were not available to the public.

In 1911, Congress passed, and President Taft signed into law, a measure making certain unauthorized gathering and disclosure of information related to national defense a crime. This was followed, and replaced, by the **Espionage Act of 1917,** which provided severe penalties for the multiple offenses of obtaining and divulging defense information. At the same time, however, Congress refused to include criminal penalties for disclosure of material designated by the president to be sensitive. For there to be criminal liability, the material in question had to relate to national defense (still ambiguous, but narrower than simply "designated by the president"). There also had to be an *intent* (variously described in different subsections) to damage the interest of the United States.[24]

The evolving system

During World War I, the Headquarters of the United States Expeditionary Force developed an internal classification system employing the categories SECRET, CONFIDENTIAL, and FOR CIRCULATION ONLY. This system was carried over into the interwar years, becoming common throughout the Army and Navy. In 1940, President Roosevelt formalized the classification system in Executive Order No. 8381. Authority to classify documents SECRET, CONFIDENTIAL, and RESTRICTED was conferred on the secretaries of the war and navy departments.

Once more, during World War II, practice bounded ahead of the formal rules, as the classification TOP SECRET came to be used within

[23] 92nd Congress, 1st Session, *Security Classification as a Problem in the Congressional Role in Foreign Policy* (Comm. Print, 1971).

[24] See Harold Edgar and Benno Schmidt, "The Espionage Statutes and the Publication of Defense Information," *73 Col. L. Rev.* 929 (1973).

the uniformed services. This was the situation in February 1950, when President Truman issued Executive Order 10,104. TOP SECRET was authorized as a designation, but authority to classify continued to be restricted to the secretary of defense and the service secretaries.

However, on September 24, 1951, over a year into the Korean conflict, President Truman, by executive order, extended classification authority to nonmilitary agencies, broadening the scope from defense information to information requiring protection in the interest of national security. It was at this point that the classification system began to take on its contemporary form.

In 1953, President Eisenhower issued yet another executive order. This one was in response to criticism that too much material was being classified, that the authority to classify was too widely diffused, and that the guidelines for classification were unclear.

The Eisenhower order withdrew classification authority from twenty-eight federal agencies, and restricted that of seventeen others. It also included provisions for periodic review and declassification.

As a guideline for classification, the order referred to "national defense," but this was universally interpreted by bureaucrats to include "foreign relations." This document served as the framework within which the classification system operated for almost two decades.

Oddly enough, the classification system was never specifically approved by Congress, although it received tacit approval when its existence was recognized in the Atomic Energy Act of 1946, the National Security Act of 1947, the Internal Security Act of 1950, and, most importantly, the Freedom of Information Act of 1966.

The Nixon "reforms"

In 1972, following the furor over the publication of the Pentagon Papers and the prosecution of Daniel Ellsberg, President Nixon, on the advice of a Justice Department committee headed by William Rehnquist (soon to be appointed to the Supreme Court), issued a new Executive Order, No. 11,652. This order asserted national security as the criterion for classification, but it severely limited classification authority. Indeed, by the spring of 1975, it was reported that the number of personnel in all agencies authorized to classify material had dropped from 59,316 in June 1972, to 15,466 by December 31, 1974.[25] Executive Order No. 11,652 also provided an accelerated declassification schedule, but in its basic architecture the classification system went unchanged. (The Carter administration was soon at work on its version of the classification system, which is likely to appear in time as yet another executive order.)

[25] *New York Times*, June 16, 1976, p. 30.

Daniel Ellsberg, the former Defense Department employee who leaked the famous "Pentagon Papers" to the press.

The disjunction between the classification system and the espionage laws remained. Critics on one side were unhappy that so much was still being classified, while those on the other continued to worry that the system was enforced only with administrative and not, explicitly at least, with penal sanctions.

It does little good to haggle over this or that particular case of over-classification, as is so often the approach of would-be reformers in this area. Before we can choose intelligently between different ways of reforming the system, we might, perhaps, ask ourselves what we, the public, need to know in order to perform an effective role.

A new guideline

The principal problem facing us is how to redefine (or adequately define for the first time) precisely what is meant by a "national security" interest. We could define it as a "military secret." The practical effect of this would be to roll the system back through a series of executive orders to the Espionage Act itself.

On the surface, this is a logical approach. Military objects are fairly easily identified. And it can be argued that such a definition embodies the wisdom of our fathers. But why assume that information concerning military objects is *inherently more dangerous* than other sorts of information?

If the proper measure of the need for secrecy is external danger to the lives, property, and future well-being of Americans, then nonmilitary information, such as knowledge of our foreign-policy objectives and the intentions of key allies, may be as important as whether the location of a secret base or weapon has been betrayed by the CBS news.

Unscrewing the inscrutable

Here is the crux of the problem: External danger to the nation may arise from the disclosure of a wide variety of information. There is always some degree of speculation involved in determining what is *potentially* dangerous, and especially to what *degree* it is dangerous. There is no abstract, neat, purely logical way of drawing the lines. These are essentially political choices, and some free play must be allowed for what political theorist Michael Oakeshott has called "practical knowledge."[26] This practical knowledge develops from experience; it depends on intimate knowledge of the details of the situation that has given rise to the classification question. Of course, this means granting discretion to the people involved, and they are the very ones whose past misbehaviors have moved us to reform the system!

There may be no way of avoiding the danger of allowing some discretion to the very people who may abuse it. But it ought to be possible to formulate better guidelines for their behavior. To say that a system cannot be rationalized perfectly does not mean that it cannot be *improved*. To allow some discretion does not imply limitless discretion.

How would you define national security? What do the actual experiences of nations in the conduct of foreign relations (discussed in the preceding chapter) tell you about the sorts of information that should *not*

The Security Classification System has developed extensively since its creation early in this century. Still unresolved are the key questions of what is meant by national security interest: what sorts of information should not be released in the interests of national security versus what sorts of information are needed by the public for the proper functioning of the democratic process.

[26] Michael Oakeshott, *Rationalism in Politics* (New York: Barnes & Noble, 1974).

be released? Equally important is consideration of what sorts of information—especially what sorts of detail—are needed by mass publics, and the smaller attentive publics that, as we saw in Chapter 4, serve to lead opinion in America. What is required for the proper functioning of the political-adversary process we call democracy?

New Information Crimes?

Presuming for the moment that we are able to develop better classification guidelines, what punishments might be appropriate to ensure that material falling within such guidelines is not disclosed in unauthorized fashions?

The most extreme sanction available to government in protecting its legitimate defense and foreign-policy nondisclosure is **prior restraint** or forbidding publication. The sense of the majority opinions in *New York Times* v. *U.S.* (the Pentagon Papers case) is to strictly limit the circumstances under which this remedy may be invoked. In this situation, the *New York Times* and the *Washington Post* were in unauthorized possession of parts of a secret official history of American involvement in Vietnam. This had been supplied by Daniel Ellsberg, a former government employee and consultant, who had surreptitiously made photocopies of major portions of the history. The attorney general, speaking for the United States in federal court, asked for an injunction (a legal order) forbidding both newspapers to publish further installments. The Supreme Court held that only the gravest danger to national security could justify such an extreme remedy, and that was not present in the case of the Pentagon Papers.

A second approach is to punish by postpublication criminal penalty or by penalties directed against such necessary prepublication activity as unauthorized possession of material or failing to return such materials to proper authority. Right now, the only statutory basis for such prosecutions is in the espionage laws, which protect defense information and require that the persons making the disclosure have done so with a specific intent to harm the United States.

This leaves a third possibility—administrative sanctions against government employees. But presuming that we are able to achieve some new confidence that we are classifying the right things, can we be satisfied with a sanction that works *only so long* as the individuals subject to it are still interested in employment by the government? For that is precisely the case with the present reliance on administrative sanctions. Once the attractions of "going public"—more glamorous employment opportunities, ego gratifications, media attention, new sexual opportunities, and so on—come to outweigh the government career (in which one may have come to feel frustrated anyway), the system has no hold. Should disgruntled civil servants be in positions to attempt to "veto by leak" the policy initiatives of their bosses? Or is the cause of good government better served by keeping down the personal costs of going public?

Access and the Freedom of Information Act

So much for the ways in which government tries to keep certain things secret. What mechanism exists for us, as government outsiders, to gain access to official information? How much public access is available?

The **Freedom of Information Act (FOIA)** was signed into law by President Johnson in 1966, and amended (over President Ford's veto) late in 1974. At the heart of the Freedom of Information Act is a commitment to a policy of executive-branch disclosure—unless the requested materials fall within one of nine exempted categories of information.[27] The breadth and ambiguity of these exemptions, along with the cumbersome access procedures established by the act, have become the despair of its critics.

We now proceed to examine the following questions: Is the FOIA an adequate mechanism of public access? How does it relate to the classification system? To what extent does it protect sensitive materials which should be kept from disclosure? Where are its strengths and its weaknesses, and how can it be improved?

The first exemption

Of all of the exemptions, the first appeared most problematical. This exemption included anything considered by the "executive" to adversely affect "national defense and foreign policy interests."

In 1974, this exemption was amended to include only materials "specifically authorized under criteria established by an Executive Order to be kept secret in the interest of national defense or foreign policy." And it is added that materials must be "properly classified pursuant to such Executive Order."

By tying the secrecy exemption to the existing classification system, Congress presumably thought it was narrowing the exemption. This assumes that the guideline for classification is less ambiguous than the language used in the original act. But we have just seen that this is not so. Until we have a sharper definition of national security, we will continue to have a gaping hole in the Freedom of Information Act.

Protecting governmental privacy

Another weakness of the act involves the protecting of executive-branch privacy during the staging processes of policy development.

[27] It is worth asking whether it is odd that something called the "Freedom of Information Act," which nine out of ten Americans would probably describe as embodying a commitment to "governmental" openness, speaks only to *one* of the branches of the national government.

It is a fact of our political process, at all levels of government, that policy innovation (getting ready to do things) is very difficult. As we have seen, ours is a political system made up of competing interest groups. If the leaders of powerful oppositional groups (representing what may be very much minority interests) learn of a proposal in its formative state—before arguments, data, and support have been organized by the governmental innovator—the result may be frustrated initiative. In a period in which Americans generally are looking to government to take more initiative, especially in the area of domestic social policy, they would do well to ponder the desirability of giving policy makers some privacy for preliminary planning.

Political scientist Alan Westin has written of the need for organizational privacy, which governmental organizations, no less than private organizations, require in order to function and survive.[28] To deny certain spheres of organizational privacy to government agencies may put a weapon in the hands of opponents of the governmental action, and disrupt orderly policy development. Those within government must be able to express themselves freely, without fearing that their words will be turned against them. What does the FOIA do to protect such spheres of privacy for policy making?

The relevant provision of the FOIA is the fifth exemption, which protects "intra-agency memorandums or letters which would not be available by law to a party other than an agency in litigation with the agency." This exemption has been interpreted by the courts as including documents that embody opinions, subjective materials, or policy recommendations. Documents containing "essentially factual material" are not exempted. Only "opinion" is exempted.

But were the judges right in concluding that it is more disruptive to open and frank intragovernmental discussions to reveal "opinion" than to reveal "fact"? The premature disclosure of a set of empirical test results may be far more chilling to open discussion, frank airing of views, and orderly internal decisional processes than the disclosure of a tentative recommendation concerning some trivial aspect of a projected program.

In the real world of politics, it is usually difficult to separate fact and opinion cleanly. In the jungle of bureaucratic politics (which we toured in Chapter 10), these "factual" considerations are frequently subjective, and can be potentially just as disruptive as pure "opinion" (if it can be said that such a thing exists).[29]

[28] Alan F. Westin, *Privacy and Freedom* (New York: Atheneum, 1967), pp. 44–45.

[29] The literature on the policy-making processes of executive branch agencies is vast, but an excellent start toward an understanding of the subtlety of the business, and appreciation of the unsuitability of the fact-opinion distinction, would be Anthony Downs, *Inside Bureaucracy* (1967); the collection by Alan Altshuler, *The Politics of the Federal Bureaucracy*; and the classic article by Long, "Public Policy and Administration," in Norton Long, *The Polity* (Chicago: Rand McNally, 1962).

Protecting personal privacy

A final flaw of the Freedom of Information Act lies in its protection of personal privacy. The sixth exemption protects "personal, medical, and similar files" from disclosure. But this subsection further specifies that the disclosure might constitute a "clearly unwarranted invasion of personal privacy" in order to be covered. Thus for material to be protected against disclosure (in the interest of personal privacy), the governmental agency must bear the burden of demonstrating that it is personal, medical, or similar, *and* that the injury to privacy outweighs the gain in public information acquired by disclosure. The 1974 amendments did nothing to help on this point.

It may be that the passage of the **Privacy Act** in 1974 made this deficiency less worrisome than it otherwise might be. This statute, it can be argued, remedied the faulty privacy exemption of the Freedom of Information Act. Subsection (e) (10) of the Privacy Act provides that agencies shall

> establish appropriate administrative, technical, and physical safeguards to insure the security and confidentiality of records and to protect against any anticipated threats or hazards to their security or integrity which could result in substantial harm, embarrassment, inconvenience, or unfairness to any individual on whom information is maintained.

But precisely how will this provision affect the sixth exemption of the FOIA in actual practice? Between the Privacy Act's "inconvenience" and "embarrassment" and the FOIA's "unwarranted invasion," a gulf yawns. Furthermore, information about persons of the sort apparently contemplated by Subsection (e) (10) is certainly contained in files other than "personal, medical, or similar." Should the Privacy Act be read as modifying the FOIA? Or may the Privacy Act be relied on as independent grounds for refusal to disclose? Answers to these questions are yet to come either from the courts or from bureaucrats.

Perhaps the Privacy Act will fill the gap in privacy protection left by the FOIA, but on the face of the statutes at present, we seem to have mainly contradiction and confusion. Different officials within the Justice Department respond differently to the question of which act prevails. In fact, it is hard to find a better example of where congressional clarification is required.

Toward an Official Information Act?

Finally, we come to the question posed at the beginning of this section: Do we need a new law, and what sort? The present situation is confusing, as we have seen. In approaching reform, should we at least consider the advantages of replacing the current tangle of the FOIA, Espionage Act,

The Freedom of Information Act represented a fundamental commitment to a policy of executive-branch disclosure. But complex issues stem from the exemptions to the act, particularly in the areas relating to national security and organizational and individual privacy.

Privacy Act, and executive orders with a single comprehensive statute—a single law—that attempts to rationalize existing anomalies and provide clearer ground rules for all concerned, whether they be bureaucrats, the public, or the press?

Some observers argue that ambiguity and confusion concerning matters of secrecy and disclosure are an expression of the genius of our system. After all, if we had a single statute integrating and attempting to rationalize these matters, we might be worse off. Liberals would have to recognize that there are state secrets that should not be disclosed. Conservatives would have to recognize that there are strict limits on governmental secrecy, even where military and external affairs are involved. In short, it is to the advantage of those on both sides of the secrecy-disclosure dilemma to continue with the present confused arrangements—changing a bit here or a bit there, winning or losing at the tactical level, but never risking strategic engagement (just the sort of "incrementalism" we saw in our discussion of domestic policy making in Chapter 12).

Furthermore, the relevant model from the legal culture most similar to our own is unattractive. The British Official Secrets Act of 1911 has had many critics and few defenders on the American side of the water. Some Americans believe that the British arrangement stifles the press. To breathe the name "Official Secrets Act" is a sure way of inflaming any gathering of American journalists with fear of censorship.

But, should emotionalism be allowed to settle the matter? It need not be assumed that any governmental information act must follow the British model. Surely, there is no evil intrinsic to a single-statute approach, and no necessary virtue in confusion. At a more fundamental level, what evidence is there that the British press does badly whatever it is the press is supposed to do in a democracy?

It has been a constant theme of public-opinion research (discussed in Chapter 4) that the democratic process, at least in America, involves some public involvement in political choice on the basis of highly general sorts of information.[30] The crucial question, again, is: How much detail should the specialized communications elites have to use to get the attention of their less-attentive publics? And how much detailed information do elites need in framing an issue so that it may be perceived in some meaningful fashion by broader segments of the public?

The issue does not exist in a vacuum. In the real world, demands for more government information characteristically emanate from elites who oppose the policy of government and are seeking material useful to their cause. The elites understand the issue all along—that is why they are

[30] Angus Campbell et al., *The American Voter* (New York: Wiley, 1960); Vladimir O. Key, *The Responsible Electorate* (New York: Random, 1966); and N. Nie, S. Verba, and J. Petrocik, *The Changing American Voter* (Cambridge, Mass.: Harvard University Press, 1976).

seeking additional information. But although the oppositional activity of these elites is essential to democracy, it cannot be carried to the point of paralyzing the government. The critical information question is how much detail is healthy (in the sense of giving oppositional elites a fair opportunity to form issues sufficiently dramatically to gain attention) and how much will compromise the organizational privacy of government to the degree that it is debilitated by premature opposition.

The difference between vigorous opposition and destructive opposition is a hard one to perceive in particular cases, but as a long-term matter, as a pattern in our politics, there is no more important civic balance. (And we should not forget that one person's "vigorous" opposition is someone else's "destructive" opposition.)

It should also be remembered that, as we noted in Chapter 7, the news media in America are commercial enterprises.[31] To sell papers and attract viewers, they must entertain as well as inform. There is no civic virtue in disclosing early or in great detail just so that sales or Neilsen ratings may be increased.

It may be argued that the revelation of who said what to whom in an NSC meeting is "important" because it gets the attention of the public in the way a general discussion of the issue would not. Perhaps so. But the line between attention-getting and titillation is a fine one. In addition to the pathology of excessive secrecy, there is wisdom in recognizing the dangers of conducting government in a fishbowl. Again, making hard choices in a changing world is the essence of policy making. However we strike these balances, there may be advantages to be gained in a comprehensive government information act that are unlikely to be gotten piecemeal. What do you think?

SUMMARY

In this chapter, we have focused on several "frontier" issues in the area of civil rights and liberties, and have traced the evolution of the "right to know" as an example of recent civil-liberties policy making.

We have stressed that the courts, Congress, the executive branch, and interest groups are all active participants in policy making in this area, and that choices among conflicting values are as sharp and painful to make here as in any other policy area.

Whether we were discussing the problem of how to treat pornography under the First Amendment, or how to improve the Freedom of Information Act, we have shown that there are no self-evident "answers." Risk

---

[31] See, for instance, the observations of Edward J. Epstein, *Between Fact and Fiction* (New York: Random, 1975).

cannot be avoided. The legitimate desires of some Americans must inevitably be subordinate to the legitimate desires of others. To return to the example of *The R Document*, the Bill of Rights does constitute a considerable barrier against tyranny. It is especially noteworthy that our British cousins are increasingly troubled that they do not have one. But, having a Bill of Rights, and a Fourteenth Amendment with its "due process" and "equal protection" clauses, is only the base point—the starting line—for the continuing political struggle over civil rights and liberties in an age of big government and bureaucracy.

SUGGESTED READINGS

ABRAHAM, HENRY J., *Freedom and the Court* (New York: Oxford University Press, 1977).

A very good short introduction to the law of civil liberties and civil rights. In paperback.

BARKER, LUCIUS J., AND TWILEY W. BARKER, JR., eds. *Civil Liberties and the Constitution*, 3d ed. (Englewood Cliffs, N.J.: Prentice-Hall, 1978).

A useful volume of source material and helpful comments.

CASPER, JONATHAN D., *Lawyers Before the Warren Court: Civil Liberties and Civil Rights, 1957–1966* (Urbana, Ill.: University of Illinois Press, 1972).

A fascinating story of how lawyers and interest groups participate in making constitutional law.

DORSEN, NORMAN, *Discrimination and Civil Rights* (Boston: Little, Brown, 1969).

A useful, if now somewhat dated, casebook.

FORTAS, ABE, *Concerning Dissent and Civil Disobedience* (New York: Meredith, 1969).

The thoughts of a former Supreme Court justice on one of the most vexing questions of contemporary political theory.

KRISLOV, SAMUEL, *The Supreme Court and Political Freedom* (New York: The Free Press, 1969).

An excellent study of the implications of the First Amendment as interpreted by the Supreme Court.

LEVY, LEONARD W., *Against the Law* (New York: Harper & Row, 1974).

A spirited attack on the criminal justice decisions of the Burger Court by one of the most able American constitutional historians.

MORGAN, RICHARD E., *The Supreme Court and Religion* (New York: The Free Press, 1972).

A study of the Court's efforts to give coherent expression to the religion clauses of the First Amendment.

SIGLER, JAY A., *American Rights Policies* (Homewood, Ill.: The Dorsey Press, 1975).

Good study of rights and liberties evolving through a political process.

SKOLNIK, JEROME, *Justice without Trial* (New York: Wiley, 1975).

A call for greater regulation of police in dealing with criminal suspects.

VOSE, CLEMENT E., *Caucasians Only* (Berkeley: University of California Press, 1959).

A classic study of the role of the NAACP in bringing the school desegregation case (*Brown* v. *Board of Education*) to the Supreme Court.

WESTIN, ALAN F., *Privacy and Freedom* (New York: Atheneum, 1967).

A very important study of the emerging constitutional right to privacy.

APPENDIX: THE CONSTITUTION OF THE UNITED STATES

We the people of the United States, in Order to form a more perfect Union, establish Justice, insure domestic Tranquility, provide for the common defence, promote the general Welfare, and secure the Blessings of Liberty to ourselves and our Posterity, do ordain and establish this CONSTITUTION for the United States of America.

ARTICLE I

Section 1. All legislative Powers herein granted shall be vested in a Congress of the United States, which shall consist of a Senate and House of Representatives.

Section 2. The House of Representatives shall be composed of Members chosen every second Year by the People of the several States, and the Electors in each State shall have the Qualifications requisite for Electors of the most numerous Branch of the State Legislature.

No Person shall be a Representative who shall not have attained to the Age of twenty-five Years, and been seven Years a Citizen of the United States, and who shall not, when elected, be an Inhabitant of that State in which he shall be chosen.

Representatives and direct Taxes shall be apportioned among the several States which may be included within this Union, according to their respective Numbers, which shall be determined by adding to the whole Number of free Persons, including those bound to Service for a Term of Years, and excluding Indians not taxed, three fifths of all other Persons. The actual Enumeration shall be made within three Years after the first Meeting of the Congress of the United States, and within every subsequent Term of ten Years, in such Manner as they shall by Law direct. The Number of Representatives shall not exceed one for every thirty Thousand, but each State shall have at Least one Representative; and until such enumeration shall be made, the State of New Hampshire shall be entitled to chuse three, Massachusetts eight, Rhode-Island and Providence Plantations one, Connecticut five, New-York six, New Jersey four, Pennsylvania eight, Delaware one, Maryland six, Virginia ten, North Carolina five, South Carolina five, and Georgia three.

When vacancies happen in the Representation from any State, the Executive Authority thereof shall issue Writs of Election to fill such Vacancies.

The House of Representatives shall chuse their Speaker and other Officers; and shall have the sole Power of Impeachment.

Section 3. The Senate of the United States shall be composed of two Senators from each State, chosen by the Legislature thereof, for six Years; and each Senator shall have one Vote.

Immediately after they shall be assembled in Consequence of the first Election, they shall be divided as equally as may be into three Classes. The Seats of the Senators of the first Class shall be vacated at the Expiration of the second Year, of the second Class at the

Expiration of the fourth Year, and of the third Class at the Expiration of the sixth Year, so that one-third may be chosen every second Year; and if Vacancies happen by Resignation, or otherwise, during the Recess of the Legislature of any State, the Executive thereof may make temporary Appointments until the next Meeting of the Legislature, which shall then fill such Vacancies.

No Person shall be a Senator who shall not have attained to the Age of thirty Years, and been nine Years a Citizen of the United States, and who shall not, when elected, be an Inhabitant of that State in which he shall be chosen.

The Vice President of the United States shall be President of the Senate, but shall have no vote, unless they be equally divided.

The Senate shall chuse their other Officers, and also a President pro tempore, in the absence of the Vice President, or when he shall exercise the Office of the President of the United States.

The Senate shall have the sole Power to try all Impeachments. When sitting for that purpose, they shall be on Oath or Affirmation. When the President of the United States is tried, the Chief Justice shall preside: And no person shall be convicted without the Concurrence of two thirds of the Members present.

Judgment in Cases of Impeachment shall not extend further than to removal from Office, and disqualification to hold and enjoy any Office of honor, Trust, or Profit under the United States: but the Party convicted shall nevertheless be liable and subject to Indictment, Trial, Judgment, and Punishment, according to Law.

Section 4. The Times, Places and Manner of holding Elections for Senators and Representatives, shall be prescribed in each state by the Legislature thereof; but the Congress may at any time by Law make or alter such Regulations, except as to the Places of Chusing Senators.

The Congress shall assemble at least once in every Year, and such Meeting shall be on the first Monday in December, unless they shall by Law appoint a different Day.

Section 5. Each House shall be the Judge of the Elections, Returns and Qualifications of its own Members, and a Majority of each shall constitute a Quorum to do Business; but a smaller number may adjourn from day to day, and may be authorized to compel the Attendance of absent Members, in such Manner, and under such Penalties, as each House may provide.

Each House may determine the Rules of its Proceedings, punish its Members for disorderly Behaviour, and, with the Concurrence of two thirds, expel a Member.

Each House shall keep a Journal of its Proceedings, and from time to time publish the same, excepting such Parts as may in their Judgment require Secrecy; and the Yeas and Nays of the Members of either House on any question shall, at the Desire of one fifth of those Present, be entered on the Journal.

Neither House, during the Session of Congress, shall, without the Consent of the other, adjourn for more than three days, nor to any other Place than that in which the two Houses shall be sitting.

Section 6. The Senators and Representatives shall receive a Compensation for their Services, to be ascertained by Law, and paid out of the Treasury of the United States. They shall in all Cases, except Treason, Felony, and Breach of the Peace, be privileged from Arrest during their Attendance at the Session of their respective Houses, and in going to and returning from the same; and for any Speech or Debate in either House, they shall not be questioned in any other Place.

No Senator or Representative shall, during the Time for which he was elected, be appointed to any civil Office under the Authority of the United States, which shall have been created, or the Emoluments whereof shall have been increased, during such time; and no Person holding any Office under the United States shall be a Member of either House during his continuance in Office.

Section 7. All Bills for raising Revenue shall originate in the House of Representatives; but the Senate may propose or concur with Amendments as on other Bills.

Every Bill which shall have passed the House of Representatives and the Senate, shall, before it become a Law, be presented to the President of the United States; If he approve he shall sign it, but if not he shall return it, with his Objections, to that House in which it shall have originated, who shall enter the Objections at large on their Journal, and proceed to reconsider it. If after such Reconsideration two thirds of that House shall agree to pass the Bill, it shall be sent, together with the Objections, to the other House, by which it shall likewise be reconsidered, and if approved by two thirds of that House, it shall become a Law. But in all such Cases the Votes of both Houses shall be determined by Yeas and Nays, and the Names of the Persons voting for and against the Bill shall be entered on the Journal of each House respectively. If any Bill shall not be returned by the President within ten Days (Sundays excepted) after it shall have been presented to him, the Same shall be a Law, in like Manner as if he had signed it, unless the Congress by their Adjournment prevent its Return, in which Case it shall not be a Law.

Every Order, Resolution, or Vote to which the Concurrence of the Senate and House of Representatives may be necessary (except on a question of Adjournment) shall be presented to the President of the United States; and before the Same shall take Effect, shall be approved by him, or being disapproved by him, shall be repassed by two thirds of the Senate and House of Representatives, according to the Rules and Limitations prescribed in the Case of a Bill.

Section 8. The Congress shall have Power To lay and collect Taxes, Duties, Imposts and Excises, to pay the Debts and provide for the common Defence and general Welfare of the United States; but all Duties, Imposts and Excises shall be uniform throughout the United States;

To borrow money on the credit of the United States;

To regulate Commerce with foreign Nations, and among the several States, and with the Indian Tribes;

To establish an uniform Rule of Naturalization, and uniform Laws on the subject of Bankruptcies throughout the United States;

To coin Money, regulate the Value thereof, and of foreign Coin, and fix the Standard of Weights and Measures;

To provide for the Punishment of counterfeiting the Securities and current Coin of the United States;

To establish Post Offices and post Roads;

To promote the Progress of Science and useful Arts, by securing for limited Times to Authors and Inventors the exclusive Right to their respective Writings and Discoveries;

To constitute Tribunals inferior to the Supreme Court;

To define and punish Piracies and Felonies committed on the high Seas, and Offenses against the Law of Nations;

To declare War, grant Letters of Marque and Reprisal, and make Rules concerning Captures on Land and Water;

To raise and support Armies, but no Appropriation of Money to that Use shall be for a longer Term than two Years;

To provide and maintain a Navy;

To make Rules for the Government and Regulation of the land and naval forces;

To provide for calling forth the Militia to execute the Laws of the Union, suppress Insurrections and repel Invasions;

To provide for organizing, arming, and disciplining the Militia, and for governing such Part of them as may be employed in the Service of the United States, reserving to the States respectively, the Appointment of the Officers, and the Authority of training the Militia according to the discipline prescribed by Congress;

To exercise exclusive Legislation in all Cases whatsoever, over such District (not exceeding ten Miles square) as may, by Cession of particular States, and the acceptance of Congress, become the Seat of Government of the United States, and to exercise like Authority over all Places purchased by the Consent of the Legislature of the State in which the Same shall be, for the Erection of Forts, Magazines, Arsenals, dock-Yards, and other needful Buildings;—And

To make all Laws which shall be necessary and proper for carrying into Execution the foregoing Powers, and all other Powers vested by this Constitution in the Government of the United States, or in any Department or Officer thereof.

Section 9. The Migration or Importation of such Persons as any of the States now existing shall think proper to admit, shall not be prohibited by the Congress prior to the Year one thousand eight hundred and eight, but a tax or duty may be imposed on such Importation, not exceeding ten dollars for each Person.

The privilege of the Writ of Habeas Corpus shall not be suspended, unless when in Cases of Rebellion or Invasion the public Safety may require it.

No Bill of Attainder or ex post facto Law shall be passed.

No Capitation, or other direct, Tax shall be laid unless in Proportion to the Census or Enumeration herein before directed to be taken.

No Tax or Duty shall be laid on Articles exported from any State.

No Preference shall be given by any Regulation of Revenue to the Ports of one State over those of another: nor shall Vessels bound to, or from, one State, be obliged to enter, clear, or pay Duties in another.

No Money shall be drawn from the Treasury, but in Consequence of Appropriations made by Law; and a regular Statement and Account of the Receipts and Expenditures of all public Money shall be published from time to time.

No Title of Nobility shall be granted by the United States: And no Person holding any Office of Profit or Trust under them, shall, without the Consent of the Congress, accept of any present, Emolument, Office, or Title, of any kind whatever, from any King, Prince, or foreign State.

Section 10. No State shall enter into any Treaty, Alliance, or Confederation; grant Letters of Marque and Reprisal; coin Money; emit Bills of Credit; make any

Thing but gold and silver Coin a Tender in Payment of Debts; pass any Bill of Attainder, ex post facto Law, or Law impairing the Obligation of Contracts, or grant any Title of Nobility.

No state shall, without the Consent of the Congress, lay any Imposts or Duties on Imports or Exports, except what may be absolutely necessary for executing its inspection Laws: and the net Produce of all Duties and Imposts, laid by any State on Imports or Exports, shall be for the Use of the Treasury of the United States; and all such Laws shall be subject to the Revision and Control of the Congress.

No State shall, without the Consent of Congress, lay any duty of Tonnage, keep Troops, or Ships of War in time of Peace, enter into any Agreement or Compact with another State, or with a foreign Power, or engage in War, unless actually invaded, or in such imminent Danger as will not admit of delay.

ARTICLE II

Section 1. The executive Power shall be vested in a President of the United States of America. He shall hold his Office during the Term of four Years, and, together with the Vice President, chosen for the same Term, be elected, as follows:

Each State shall appoint, in such Manner as the Legislature thereof may direct, a Number of Electors, equal to the whole Number of Senators and Representatives to which the State may be entitled in the Congress: but no Senator or Representative, or Person holding an Office of Trust or Profit under the United States, shall be appointed an Elector.

The Electors shall meet in their respective States, and vote by Ballot for two Persons, of whom one at least shall not be an Inhabitant of the same State with themselves. And they shall make a List of all the Persons voted for, and of the Number of Votes for each; which List they shall sign and certify, and transmit sealed to the Seat of the Government of the United States, directed to the President of the Senate. The President of the Senate shall, in the Presence of the Senate and House of Representatives, open all the Certificates, and the Votes shall then be counted. The Person having the greatest Number of Votes shall be the President, if such Number be a Majority of the whole Number of Electors appointed; and if there be more than one who have such Majority, and have an equal Number of Votes, then the House of Representatives shall immediately chuse by Ballot one of them for President; and if no Person have a Majority, then from the five highest on the List the said House shall in like Manner chuse the President. But in chusing the President, the Votes shall

be taken by States, the Representation from each State having one Vote; a quorum for this Purpose shall consist of a Member or Members from two-thirds of the States, and a Majority of all the States shall be necessary to a Choice. In every Case, after the Choice of the President, the Person having the greatest Number of Votes of the Electors shall be the Vice President. But if there should remain two or more who have equal votes, the Senate shall chuse from them by Ballot the Vice President.

The Congress may determine the Time of chusing the Electors, and the Day on which they shall give their Votes; which Day shall be the same throughout the United States.

No person except a natural-born Citizen, or a Citizen of the United States, at the time of the Adoption of this Constitution, shall be eligible to the Office of President; neither shall any Person be eligible to that Office who shall not have attained to the Age of thirty-five Years, and been fourteen Years a Resident within the United States.

In Case of the Removal of the President from Office, or of his Death, Resignation, or Inability to discharge the Powers and Duties of the said Office, the same shall devolve on the Vice President, and the Congress may by Law provide for the Case of Removal, Death, Resignation, or Inability, both of the President and Vice President, declaring what Officer shall then act as President, and such Officer shall act accordingly, until the Disability be removed, or a President shall be elected.

The President shall, at stated Times, receive for his Services a Compensation, which shall neither be increased nor diminished during the Period for which he shall have been elected, and he shall not receive within that Period any other Emolument from the United States, or any of them.

Before he enter on the Execution of his Office, he shall take the following Oath or Affirmation:—"I do solemnly swear (or affirm) that I will faithfully execute the Office of President of the United States, and will, to the best of my Ability, preserve, protect, and defend the Constitution of the United States."

Section 2. The President shall be Commander in Chief of the Army and Navy of the United States, and of the Militia of the several States, when called into the actual Service of the United States; he may require the Opinion, in writing, of the principal Officer in each of the executive Departments, upon any subject relating to the Duties of their respective Offices, and he shall have Power to Grant Reprieves and Pardons for Offences against the United States, except in Cases of Impeachment.

He shall have Power, by and with the Advice and Consent of the Senate, to make Treaties, provided two thirds of the Senators present concur; and he shall nominate, and by and with the Advice and Consent of the Senate, shall appoint Ambassadors, other public Ministers and Consuls, Judges of the supreme Court, and all other Officers of the United States, whose Appointments are not herein otherwise provided for, and which shall be established by Law: but the Congress may by Law vest the Appointment of such inferior Officers, as they think proper, in the President alone, in the Courts of Law, or in the Heads of Departments.

The President shall have Power to fill up all Vacancies that may happen during the Recess of the Senate, by granting Commissions which shall expire at the End of their next Session.

Section 3. He shall from time to time give to the Congress Information of the State of the Union, and recommend to their Consideration such Measures as he shall judge necessary and expedient; he may, on extraordinary occasions, convene both Houses, or either of them, and in Case of Disagreement between them, with respect to the Time of Adjournment, he may adjourn them to such Time as he shall think proper; he shall receive Ambassadors and other public Ministers; he shall take Care that the Laws be faithfully executed, and shall Commission all the Officers of the United States.

Section 4. The President, Vice President and all civil Officers of the United States, shall be removed from Office on Impeachment for, and Conviction of, Treason, Bribery, or other high Crimes and Misdemeanors.

ARTICLE III

Section 1. The judicial Power of the United States, shall be vested in one supreme Court, and in such inferior Courts as the Congress may from time to time ordain and establish. The Judges, both of the supreme and inferior Courts, shall hold their Offices during good Behaviour, and shall, at stated Times, receive for their Services, a Compensation, which shall not be diminished during their Continuance in Office.

Section 2. The judicial Power shall extend to all Cases, in Law and Equity, arising under this Constitution, the Laws of the United States, and Treaties made, or which shall be made, under their Authority;—to all Cases affecting Ambassadors, other public Ministers and Consuls;—to all Cases of admiralty and maritime Jurisdiction;—to Controversies to which the United States shall be a Party;—to Controversies between two or more States;—between a State and Citizens of another State;—between Citizens of the same State claiming Lands under Grants of different States, and between a State, or the Citizens thereof, and foreign States, Citizens or Subjects.

In all Cases affecting Ambassadors, other public Ministers and Consuls, and those in which a State shall be Party, the supreme Court shall have original Jurisdiction. In all the other Cases before mentioned, the supreme Court shall have appellate Jurisdiction, both as to Law and Fact, with such Exceptions, and under such Regulations as the Congress shall make.

The trial of all Crimes, except in Cases of Impeachment, shall be by Jury; and such Trial shall be held in the State where the said Crimes shall have been committed; but when not committed within any State, the Trial shall be at such Place or Places as the Congress may by Law have directed.

Section 3. Treason against the United States, shall consist only in levying War against them, or in adhering to their Enemies, giving them Aid and Comfort. No Person shall be convicted of Treason unless on the Testimony of two Witnesses to the same overt Act, or on Confession in open Court.

The Congress shall have power to declare the Punishment of Treason, but no Attainder of Treason shall work Corruption of Blood, or Forfeiture except during the Life of the Person attainted.

ARTICLE IV

Section 1. Full Faith and Credit shall be given in each State to the public Acts, Records, and judicial Proceedings of every other State. And the Congress may by general Laws prescribe the Manner in which such Acts, Records and Proceedings shall be proved, and the Effect thereof.

Section 2. The Citizens of each State shall be entitled to all Privileges and Immunities of Citizens in the several States.

A Person charged in any State with Treason, Felony, or other Crime, who shall flee from Justice, and be found in another State, shall on demand of the executive Authority of the State from which he fled, be delivered up, to be removed to the State having Jurisdiction of the crime.

No Person held to Service or Labour in one State, under the Laws thereof, escaping into another, shall, in Consequence of any Law or Regulation therein, be discharged from such Service or Labour, but shall be delivered up on Claim of the Party to whom such Service or Labour may be due.

Section 3. New States may be admitted by the Congress into this Union; but no new State shall be formed or erected within the Jurisdiction of any other State; nor any State be formed by the Junction of two or more States, or parts of States, without the Consent of the Legislatures of the States concerned as well as of the Congress.

The Congress shall have Power to dispose of and make all needful Rules and Regulations respecting the Territory or other Property belonging to the United States; and nothing in this Constitution shall be so construed as to Prejudice any Claims of the United States, or of any particular State.

Section 4. The United States shall guarantee to every State in this Union a Republican Form of Government, and shall protect each of them against Invasion; and on Application of the Legislature, or of the Executive (when the Legislature cannot be convened) against domestic Violence.

ARTICLE V

The Congress, whenever two thirds of both Houses shall deem it necessary, shall propose Amendments to this Constitution, or, on the Application of the Legislatures of two thirds of the several States, shall call a Convention for proposing Amendments, which, in either Case, shall be valid to all Intents and Purposes, as part of this Constitution, when ratified by the Legislatures of three fourths of the several States, or by Conventions in three fourths thereof, as the one or the other Mode of Ratification may be proposed by the Congress; Provided that no Amendment which may be made prior to the Year One thousand eight hundred and eight shall in any Manner affect the first and fourth Clauses in the Ninth Section of the first Article; and that no State, without its Consent, shall be deprived of its equal Suffrage in the Senate.

ARTICLE VI

All Debts contracted and Engagements entered into, before the Adoption of this Constitution, shall be as valid against the United States under this Constitution, as under the Confederation.

This Constitution, and the Laws of the United States which shall be made in Pursuance thereof; and all Treaties made, or which shall be made, under the Authority of the United States, shall be the supreme Law of the Land; and the Judges in every State shall be bound thereby, any Thing in the Constitution or Laws of any State to the Contrary notwithstanding.

The Senators and Representatives before mentioned, and the Members of the several State Legislatures, and all executive and judicial Officers, both of the United States and of the several States, shall be bound by Oath or Affirmation to support this Constitution; but no religious Test shall ever be required as a qualification to any Office or public Trust under the United States.

ARTICLE VII

The Ratification of the Conventions of nine States shall be sufficient for the Establishment of this Constitution between the States so ratifying the same.

Done in Convention by the Unanimous Consent of the States present the Seventeenth Day of September in the Year of our Lord one thousand seven hundred and Eighty seven, and of the Independence of the United States of America the Twelfth. In Witness whereof We have hereunto subscribed our Names.

Articles in Addition to, and Amendment of, the Constitution of the United States of America, Proposed by Congress, and Ratified by the Legislatures of the Several States, Pursuant to the Fifth Article of the Original Constitution.

AMENDMENT I [1791]

Congress shall make no law respecting an establishment of religion, or prohibiting the free exercise thereof; or abridging the freedom of speech, or of the press; or the right of the people peaceably to assemble, and to petition the Government for a redress of grievances.

AMENDMENT II [1791]

A well regulated Militia, being necessary to the security of a free State, the right of the people to keep and bear Arms, shall not be infringed.

AMENDMENT III [1791]

No Soldier shall, in time of peace, be quartered in any house, without the consent of the Owner, nor in time of war, but in a manner to be prescribed by law.

AMENDMENT IV [1791]

The right of the people to be secure in their persons, houses, papers, and effects, against unreasonable searches and seizures, shall not be violated, and no Warrants shall issue, but upon probable cause, supported by Oath or affirmation, and particularly describing the place to be searched, and the persons or things to be seized.

AMENDMENT V [1791]

No person shall be held to answer for a capital or otherwise infamous crime, unless on a presentment or indictment of a Grand Jury, except in cases arising in the land or naval forces, or in the Militia, when in actual service in time of War or public danger; nor shall any person be subject for the same offence to be twice put in jeopardy of life or limb; nor shall be compelled in any criminal case to be a witness against himself, nor be deprived of life, liberty, or property, without due process of law; nor shall private property be taken for public use, without just compensation.

AMENDMENT VI [1791]

In all criminal prosecutions, the accused shall enjoy the right to a speedy and public trial, by an impartial jury of the State and district wherein the crime shall have been committed, which district shall have been previously ascertained by law, and to be informed of the nature and cause of the accusation; to be confronted with the witnesses against him; to have compulsory process for obtaining witnesses in his favor, and to have the Assistance of Counsel for his defence.

AMENDMENT VII [1791]

In Suits at common law, where the value in controversy shall exceed twenty dollars, the right of trial by jury shall be preserved, and no fact tried by a jury, shall be otherwise re-examined in any Court of the United States, than according to the rules of the common law.

AMENDMENT VIII [1791]

Excessive bail shall not be required, nor excessive fines imposed, nor cruel and unusual punishments inflicted.

AMENDMENT IX [1791]

The enumeration in the Constitution, of certain rights, shall not be construed to deny or disparage others retained by the people.

AMENDMENT X [1791]

The powers not delegated to the United States by the Constitution, nor prohibited by it to the States, are reserved to the States respectively, or to the people.

AMENDMENT XI [1798]

The Judicial power of the United States shall not be construed to extend to any suit in law or equity, commenced or prosecuted against one of the United States by Citizens of another State, or by Citizens or Subjects of any Foreign State.

AMENDMENT XII [1804]

The Electors shall meet in their respective States and vote by ballot for President and Vice President, one of whom, at least, shall not be an inhabitant of the same States with themselves; they shall name in their ballots the person voted for as President, and in distinct ballots the person voted for as Vice-President, and they shall make distinct lists of all persons voted for as President, and of all persons voted for as Vice-President, and of the number of votes for each, which lists they shall sign and certify, and transmit sealed to the seat of the government of the United States, directed to the President of the Senate;—The President of the Senate shall, in the presence of the Senate and House of Representatives, open all the certificates and the votes shall then be counted;—The person having the greatest number of votes for President, shall be the President, if such number be a majority of the whole number of Electors appointed; and if no person have such majority, then from the persons having the highest numbers not exceeding three on the list of those voted for as President, the House of Representatives shall choose immediately, by ballot, the President. But in choosing the President, the votes shall be taken by states, the representation from each state having one vote; a quorum for this purpose shall consist of a member or members from two-thirds of the states, and a majority of all the states shall be necessary to a choice. And if the House of Representatives shall not choose a President whenever the right of choice shall devolve upon them, before the fourth day of March next following, then the Vice-President shall act as President, as in the case of the death or other constitutional disability of the President.—The person having the greatest number of votes as Vice-President, shall be the Vice-President, if such number be a majority of the whole number of Electors appointed, and if no person have a majority, then from the two highest numbers on the list, the

Senate shall choose the Vice-President; a quorum for the purpose shall consist of two-thirds of the whole number of Senators, and a majority of the whole number shall be necessary to a choice. But no person constitutionally ineligible to the office of President shall be eligible to that of Vice-President of the United States.

AMENDMENT XIII [1865]

Section 1. Neither slavery nor involuntary servitude, except as a punishment for crime whereof the party shall have been duly convicted, shall exist within the United States, or any place subject to their jurisdiction.

Section 2. Congress shall have power to enforce this article by appropriate legislation.

AMENDMENT XIV [1868]

Section 1. All persons born or naturalized in the United States, and subject to the jurisdiction thereof, are citizens of the United States and of the State wherein they reside. No State shall make or enforce any law which shall abridge the privileges or immunities of citizens of the United States; nor shall any State deprive any person of life, liberty, or property, without due process of law; nor deny to any person within its jurisdiction the equal protection of the laws.

Section 2. Representatives shall be apportioned among the several States according to their respective numbers, counting the whole number of persons in each State, excluding Indians not taxed. But when the right to vote at any election for the choice of electors for President and Vice President of the United States, Representatives in Congress, the Executive and Judicial officers of a State, or the members of the Legislature thereof, is denied to any of the male inhabitants of such State, being twenty-one years of age, and citizens of the United States, or in any way abridged, except for participation in rebellion, or other crime, the basis of representation therein shall be reduced in the proportion which the number of such male citizens shall bear to the whole number of male citizens twenty-one years of age in such State.

Section 3. No person shall be a Senator or Representative in Congress, or elector of President and Vice President, or hold any office, civil or military, under the United States, or under any State, who, having previously taken an oath, as a member of Congress, or as an officer of the United States, or as a member of any State legislature, or as an executive or judicial officer of any State, to support the Constitution of the United States, shall have engaged in insurrection or rebellion against the same, or given aid or comfort to the enemies thereof. But Congress may by a vote of two-thirds of each House, remove such disability.

Section 4. The validity of the public debt of the United States, authorized by law, including debts incurred for payment of pensions and bounties for services in suppressing insurrection or rebellion, shall not be questioned. But neither the United States nor any State shall assume or pay any debt or obligation incurred in aid of insurrection or rebellion against the United States, or any claim for the loss or emancipation of any slave; but all such debts, obligations, and claims shall be held illegal and void.

Section 5. The Congress shall have the power to enforce, by appropriate legislation, the provisions of this article.

AMENDMENT XV [1870]

Section 1. The right of citizens of the United States to vote shall not be denied or abridged by the United States or by any State on account of race, color, or previous condition of servitude—

Section 2. The Congress shall have power to enforce this article by appropriate legislation.

AMENDMENT XVI [1913]

The Congress shall have power to lay and collect taxes on incomes, from whatever source derived, without apportionment among the several States, and without regard to any census or enumeration.

AMENDMENT XVII [1913]

The Senate of the United States shall be composed of two Senators from each State, elected by the people thereof, for six years; and each Senator shall have one vote. The electors in each State shall have the qualifications requisite for electors of the most numerous branch of the State legislatures.

When vacancies happen in the representation of any State in the Senate, the executive authority of such State shall issue writs of election to fill such vacancies: *Provided*, That the legislature of any State may empower the executive thereof to make temporary appointments until the people fill the vacancies by election as the legislature may direct.

This amendment shall not be so construed as to affect the election or term of any Senator chosen before it becomes valid as part of the Constitution.

AMENDMENT XVIII [1919]

Section 1. After one year from the ratification of this article the manufacture, sale, or transportation of intoxicating liquors within, the importation thereof into, or the exportation thereof from the United States and all territory subject to the jurisdiction thereof for beverage purposes is hereby prohibited.

Section 2. The Congress and the several States shall have concurrent power to enforce this article by appropriate legislation.

Section 3. This article shall be inoperative unless it shall have been ratified as an amendment to the Constitution by the legislatures of the several States, as provided in the Constitution, within seven years from the date of the submission hereof to the States by the Congress.

AMENDMENT XIX [1920]

The right of citizens of the United States to vote shall not be denied or abridged by the United States or by any State on account of sex.

Congress shall have power to enforce this article by appropriate legislation.

AMENDMENT XX [1933]

Section 1. The terms of the President and Vice President shall end at noon on the 20th day of January, and the terms of Senators and Representatives at noon on the 3d day of January, of the years in which such terms would have ended if this article had not been ratified; and the terms of their successors shall then begin.

Section 2. The Congress shall assemble at least once in every year, and such meeting shall begin at noon on the 3d day of January, unless they shall by law appoint a different day.

Section 3. If, at the time fixed for the beginning of the term of the President, the President elect shall have died, the Vice President elect shall become President. If a President shall not have been chosen before the time fixed for the beginning of his term, or if the President elect shall have failed to qualify, then the Vice President elect shall act as President until a President shall have qualified; and the Congress may by law provide for the case wherein neither a President elect nor a Vice President elect shall have qualified, declaring who shall then act as President, or the manner in which one who is to act shall be selected, and such person shall act accordingly until a President or Vice President shall have qualified.

Section 4. The Congress may by law provide for the case of the death of any of the persons from whom the House of Representatives may choose a President whenever the right of choice shall have devolved upon them, and for the case of the death of any of the persons from whom the Senate may choose a Vice President whenever the right of choice shall have devolved upon them.

Section 5. Sections 1 and 2 shall take effect on the 15th day of October following the ratification of this article.

Section 6. This article shall be inoperative unless it shall have been ratified as an amendment to the Constitution by the legislatures of three-fourths of the several States within seven years from the date of its submission.

AMENDMENT XXI [1933]

Section 1. The eighteenth article of amendment to the Constitution of the United States is hereby repealed.

Section 2. The transportation or importation into any State, Territory, or possession of the United States for delivery or use therein of intoxicating liquors, in violation of the laws thereof, is hereby prohibited.

Section 3. This article shall be inoperative unless it shall have been ratified as an amendment to the Constitution by conventions in the several States, as provided in the Constitution, within seven years from the date of the submission hereof to the States by the Congress.

AMENDMENT XXII [1951]

No person shall be elected to the office of the President more than twice, and no person who has held the office of President, or acted as President, for more than two years of a term to which some other person was elected President shall be elected to the office of the President more than once.

But this Article shall not apply to any person holding the office of President when this Article was proposed by the Congress, and shall not prevent any person who may be holding the office of President, or acting as President, during the term within which this Article becomes operative from holding the office of President or acting as President during the remainder of such term.

AMENDMENT XXIII [1961]

Section 1. The District constituting the seat of Government of the United States shall appoint in such manner as the Congress may direct:

A number of electors of President and Vice President equal to the whole number of Senators and Representatives in Congress to which the District would be entitled if it were a State, but in no event more than the least populous State; they shall be in addition to those appointed by the States, but they shall be considered, for the purposes of the election of President and Vice President, to be electors appointed by a State; and they shall meet in the District and perform such duties as provided by the twelfth article of amendment.

Section 2. The Congress shall have power to enforce this article by appropriate legislation.

AMENDMENT XXIV [1964]

Section 1. The right of citizens of the United States to vote in any primary or other election for President or Vice President, for electors for President or Vice President, or for Senator or Representative in Congress, shall not be denied or abridged by the United States or any State by reason of failure to pay any poll tax or other tax.

Section 2. The Congress shall have the power to enforce this article by appropriate legislation.

AMENDMENT XXV [1967]

Section 1. In case of the removal of the President from office or his death or resignation, the Vice President shall become President.

Section 2. Whenever there is a vacancy in the office of the Vice President, the President shall nominate a Vice President who shall take the office upon confirmation by a majority vote of both houses of Congress.

Section 3. Whenever the President transmits to the President pro tempore of the Senate and the Speaker of the House of Representatives his written declaration that he is unable to discharge the powers and duties of his office, and until he transmits to them a written declaration to the contrary, such powers and duties shall be discharged by the Vice President as Acting President.

Section 4. Whenever the Vice President and a majority of either the principal officers of the executive departments, or of such other body as Congress may by law provide, transmit to the President pro tempore of the Senate and the Speaker of the House of Representatives their written declaration that the President is unable to discharge the powers and duties of his office, the Vice President shall immediately assume the powers and duties of the office as Acting President.

Thereafter, when the President transmits to the President pro tempore of the Senate and the Speaker of the House of Representatives his written declaration that no inability exists, he shall resume the powers and duties of his office unless the Vice President and a majority of either the principal officers of the executive departments, or of such other body as Congress may by law provide, transmit within four days to the President pro tempore of the Senate and the Speaker of the House of Representatives their written declaration that the President is unable to discharge the powers and duties of his office. Thereupon Congress shall decide the issue, assembling within 48 hours for that purpose if not in session. If the Congress, within 21 days after receipt of the latter written declaration, or, if Congress is not in session, within 21 days after Congress is required to assemble, determines by two-thirds vote of both houses that the President is unable to discharge the powers and duties of his office, the Vice President shall continue to discharge the same as Acting President; otherwise, the President shall resume the powers and duties of his office.

AMENDMENT XXVI [1971]

Section 1. The right of citizens of the United States, who are 18 years of age or older, to vote shall not be denied or abridged by the United States or any state on account of age.

Section 2. The Congress shall have the power to enforce this article by appropriate legislation.

GLOSSARY

advisory primaries Primary elections in which the winner does not automatically receive a percentage of the delegates. The primary results serve only to advise the state delegates in their voting. (181)

affirmative action The setting of ethnic and sex quotas for employment and promotion. (505)

agrarianism The Jeffersonian view of land as the principal source of wealth, and of the model American as a yeoman farmer owning his own acres and largely self-sufficient thereon. (70)

Alien and Sedition acts A set of laws that sought to repress tyrannous statements against the government. These laws came to be viewed as a symbol of unacceptable governmental interference with the American political process. (72)

anti-Federalists Members of the political party organized around Jeffersonian principles, which opposed the ratification of the Constitution and sought to preserve the states' rights position. (70)

appellant An individual who appeals a judicial conviction to a higher court. (383)

Articles of Confederation The compact among the thirteen original colonies to form the United States of America. This compact served as the effective constitution of the United States until it was replaced by the present Constitution. (26)

autonomy The right of self government, self-determination, and independence. (22)

ballot A system of registering one's vote. (175)

bill of rights Before the signing of the Constitution, provisions written into the constitutions of the newly independent states guaranteeing to their citizens the traditional English rights as well as certain distinctive colonial rights, which were safeguards against encroachment by the new state governments. (26)

Bill of Rights The first ten amendments to the Constitution, ratified in 1791, ensuring certain rights and liberties to the people. (87)

binding primaries Primary elections in which the winner receives a definite percentage of the state's delegates. (181)

bipartisanship The making of policy without regard to political concerns or party affiliation; close cooperation between the two parties. (477)

bully pulpit An office used to educate and lead the nation; a platform from which to proclaim moral leadership. (56)

bureaucracy Any administrative system, such as a government agency, that is permanent, that operates on standardized procedures, where the jobs performed have formal and specialized descriptions, and where direction and orders come from the top down. (56)

cabinet The secretaries, appointed by the president, who head each of the twelve executive departments. (263)

categorical group A group of people who by nature share basic characteristics but do not necessarily form interest groups. (109)

caucus (system) An informal group of people who meet to nominate a candidate or to discuss ideas relating to party politics. (176).

Central Intelligence Agency (CIA) The federal agency that collects and evaluates foreign intelligence. (339)

change agent The civil servant who is willing to take risks in order to challenge and reform the system. *See also* **orthodox bureaucratic type.** (369)

checks and balances An internal system of government, with separate legislative, executive, and judicial branches that are interdependent in the process of governing, set up by the framers of the Constitution to ensure that their national government could not come under the tyrannical control of one branch. (18)

circuit courts of appeal Courts at the intermediate level of the federal judicial system, in which cases are appealed from lower courts. (379)

civil liberty The legal guarantee of the basic rights of freedom of speech, thought, and action to all individuals. (496)

civil rights Rights belonging to an individual by virtue of his or her status as a citizen or member of a civil society. (496)

Civil Rights Act of 1964 A congressional enactment forbidding racial discrimination in public accommodations and places of employment. (497)

civil service (system) The system of recruitment for government employees, in which candidates are chosen on the basis of their performance on civil service examinations. (344)

closed primary A primary in which voting is restricted to party members. (176)

coalition An assembly of various factions that unite to form a stronger alliance for mutual action. (137)

common law The system (originating in England) of unwritten law based on custom and court decision. (20)

Common Situs A controversial bill before the United States Senate that would permit a single striking union to close down an entire construction project no matter how many other nonstriking unions were involved. (94)

confederation A union of semi-independent states, distinguished from a federation in that the sovereignty of the component states is greater than the authority of the union. (17)

conference committee A committee formed to find a compromise version of a bill when there are major differences between the two versions that have passed their respective houses of Congress. (325)

congressional courts A set of special-purpose courts established by Congress to deal with appeals regarding administrative decisions of the federal government. (382)

constitutional courts The judicial court system established by the Constitution. (382)

constitutional monarchy A system of government in which there are constitutional limitations to the power of the sovereign ruler. (21)

constitutional rights Civil rights and liberties guaranteed under the Constitution and clarified through court interpretation. (497)

constitutionalism The creation of written documents outlining the structure, functions, and limitations of government. (16)

Continental Congress The American colonial government that formulated the principles of the Revolution and directed the War of Independence. (26)

contract An agreement or covenant between two or more persons, in which each party is formally bound by mutual assent. (22)

counterintelligence programs Campaigns of political sabotage conducted by various intelligence agencies such as the FBI and the CIA against persons or groups considered to be dangerous "subversives." (508)

counter-majoritarianism The power of a few men, such as the justices of the Supreme Court, to bind the majority by their decisions. (45)

court of appeal *See* **circuit courts of appeal.**

Court Plan An unsuccessful maneuver by FDR to create a new majority in the Supreme Court that would sustain New Deal programs by proposing that Congress appoint a new justice when any sitting justice failed to retire at the age of seventy. Also known as **packing the Court.** (397)

courts of first instance *See* **district courts.**

crisis of legitimacy A critical period during which all new regimes must demonstrate their authority and establish the power to govern. (52)

Curtiss-Wright case The case in which the Supreme Court broadly interpreted the president's power in foreign affairs, claiming that this power "does not require as a basis for its exercise an act of Congress." (258)

deficit The negative financial position that occurs when the amount expended by the government (for welfare programs, defense compensation, and so on) exceeds the amount it receives in tax revenue. (416)

Democrats During the 1830s, members of the political party that identified with Andrew Jackson, appealing to the small farmers of the rural countryside and reaching out to the working people of the cities. (74)

demography The study of the statistical distribution, density, and backgrounds of the population. (104)

distribution In polling, the extent to which a particular opinion is held among the members of the sample polled. (106)

district courts The lowest level of the federal court system, where trials in criminal cases and civil suits actually take place. (379)

divestiture rule Legislation making it illegal for newspaper publishers to own broadcasting franchises in the same city as their newspapers or for broadcasting stations to own newspapers in the same city. (240)

docketed cases Those cases that have been received for preliminary consideration by the Supreme Court. (388)

due-process clause The provision of the Fourteenth Amendment that correct procedures must be observed by legislatures as they draft laws and by the police and courts as they implement laws. (402)

Economic Opportunity Act A bill sponsored by the Johnson administration and enacted in 1964 that emphasized training and retraining of the unemployed; it targeted on the young, the disadvantaged, and minorities. (427)

electoral college A slate of electors (chosen by the party apparatus in each state) whose function it is to elect the president and vice-president of the United States. (188)

elitist model A model of society that suggests that America is dominated by a small group of people who control economic, political, and military power. (99)

Employment Act A greatly watered-down version of the proposed "full employment act," this bill, passed in 1946, called for the promotion of "maximum employment, production, and purchasing power," and gave the president the responsibility for preparing an annual report on the state of the economy with the assistance of a new executive agency, the Council of Economic Advisors. (229)

employment and training programs The massive body of public service jobs programs and government-sponsored training programs, which were initiated in the 1960s and have continued and expanded ever since. (421)

equal-protection clause The provision in the Fourteenth Amendment that guarantees equal protection under the law to all citizens regardless of race or sex. (504)

Espionage Act Congressional legislation passed in 1917 providing severe penalties for the multiple offenses of obtaining and divulging secret defense information. (514)

establishment clause The provision of the First Amendment that prohibits congressional aid to establishments of religion; this has been interpreted by the court to include churches or religiously affiliated schools. (502)

Executive Office of the President The special group of federal agencies created to provide the president with the necessary resources and expertise to perform his duties. (337)

executive privilege The doctrine that prevents the courts from ordering the president to divulge private communications with close advisers. (377)

expansionism The policy of expanding a nation's territory or sphere of influence to incorporate new land and more people. (461)

faction A group of persons forming a cohesive minority within a large group; partisanship. (42)

fairness or equal time rule Legislation requiring a broadcast station that endorses or opposes a candidate for public office or attacks the "honesty, character, integrity, or personal qualities of an identified person or group" to give the other side a chance to reply on the air at no charge. (240)

favorite sons Individuals who are popular in their home states and are nominated for the presidency even though they are not seriously competing. (182)

Federal Communications Commission (FCC) The federal agency formed in 1927 to issue broadcast licenses; in recent years, this agency has become a means of greater governmental control over the media. (240)

Federal Elections Campaign Act Congressional legislation that sought to limit and alleviate corrupt financing practices by setting limits on campaign contributions and spending and by providing for public financing in presidential races. (207)

Federal Reserve Board An independent federal agency responsible for regulating the supply of money in the economy. (434)

federal system The division of power and functions between the colonial governments and the central government in London. (15)

federalism A system of government in which power is divided between a central and regional governments. (17)

The Federalist A series of essays urging the adoption of the Constitution. (34)

Federalists Members of the political party organized around the Hamiltonian principles of strong central government and commercial republicanism. (70)

feudalism The political system prevailing in Europe from the ninth to about the fifteenth centuries, characterized by homage of vassals to lord with all land held in fee and service of tenants under arms. In England, it also involved an institutionalized struggle for political power. (20)

fluidity In polling, the changeability of an opinion, often occurring over an extended period of time. (107)

foreign policy The sum total of words spoken and actions taken by one government in relation to other governments. (458)

Fourth Estate A term used to describe the press, implying that with its power to inform, criticize, expose, and prod, it constitutes a vital force in the political process. (218)

franchise The right to vote; suffrage. (84)

Freedom of Information Act Legislation passed in 1966 making all records of federal agencies public,

unless the material falls within one of the nine exempted categories of information. (519)

freedom of speech The right, guaranteed under the First Amendment, of all individuals to express themselves: (500)

free-exercise clause The provision in the First Amendment that prohibits governmental interference with the free exercise of someone's religion. (502)

freeholders Those individuals who owned land in the colonies. (22)

full employment An ideal situation in which a job exists for every able-bodied individual seeking work. (415)

government corporation A government agency that functions like a business corporation except that its revenues remain as operating expenses and are not considered "profits." (342)

Great Compromise The political compromise that provided for a two-chambered Congress, with the Senate based on the equality of the states and the House of Representatives based on population. (32)

Great Society A term used to describe the series of domestic programs enacted during the Johnson administration, featuring aid to education, Medicare, strong civil rights legislation, urban renewal, and job-training programs. (148)

Gross National Product (GNP) The total dollar value of all goods and services produced and purchased in a given year. (417)

group think A psychological mechanism by which members of small groups reinforce the consensus arrived at within the group by cutting off much of reality outside the group. (272)

imperial presidency A term used to describe an office of executive power that has assumed autocratic proportions, with none of the usual constraints (congressional, constitutional, political) proving effective. (276)

in-and-outer The bureaucratic employee who has been recruited from the private sector to fill a particular area of expertise; these individuals remain loyal to the administration that chooses them, and serve in Washington for limited periods of time. (369)

incrementalism The theory that public policy decisions emerge from piecemeal adjustments within the system—slight shifts in policy that, over time, result in a fair degree of change. (430)

incumbent The individual holding an indicated office or elective position. (300)

independent regulatory commission A government commission that is responsible for regulating or controlling a specific aspect of national life and that is not subordinate to either executive or congressional directives. (343)

indirect democracy A system of government (representative democracy) in which the people do not exercise governmental power themselves but authorize a relative few to exercise power over them. (84)

inflation The sharp and continuing rise in price levels for goods and services. (416)

inner cabinet Those cabinet secretaries who handle national security. (266)

institutionalization The process by which organizations and procedures acquire value and stability. (53)

intensity How strongly people hold an opinion; size is not the critical factor, for a small group holding an opinion intensely can have more impact than a major group with undefined views. (108)

interest group A collection of people who share a common concern and work together politically to promote that concern. (108)

interposition The ability of a state(s) to interpose its authority between its citizens and the commands of the national government if it determines that those commands are unconstitutional. (80)

isolationism A policy that opposes involvement in foreign commitments. (461)

issue-activists Those individuals who are active in party politics and emphasize issues and sharply distinct ideologies. (141)

Jacksonian democracy A political philosophy that reached out to the small farmers as well as the immigrant workers of the city, emphasizing the political competency and participation of the common people. (84)

judicial activism A judicial style that maintains that judges do and should play an active role in shaping public policy. (399)

judicial construction Rights and liberties decreed or proceeding from court interpretation. (497)

judicial review The power of the Supreme Court to declare the acts of Congress, the president, or the states void as unconstitutional. (40)

laissez faire An economic philosophy that values a free, uncontrolled market; interpreted politically to limit the regulatory power of the state and federal governments. (395)

latency In polling, the potential for additional people to join a particular opinion group; as public consciousness and awareness is aroused, there is an "upside potential" for more individuals to join a cause. (107)

legislative oversight The overseeing by Congress, through its committee structure and power to tax and appropriate money, of the massive federal bureaucracy. (307)

legislative reapportionment The Supreme Court decision that the "one man, one vote" rule would apply to both houses of state legislatures. (395)

legislative vetoes Devices allowing Congress to quickly correct, by joint resolution, mistaken interpretations of statutes that agencies make into rules. (348)

legitimacy The perceived acceptability of various organizations and operations, an important component in establishing the authority of a new regime. (55)

libel (slander) Written or spoken defamation of a person's character or reputation. (500)

liberal tradition The movement toward representational forms of government; policies that favor the freedom of individuals to act or express themselves in the manner of their choosing. (30)

line agencies The agencies of the federal government that perform line functions, that is, agencies with operational or administrative duties. (337)

lobbying Any intentional effort to influence legislation. (122)

loyal opposition A role of the media that suggests an overall support of the system, yet potent criticism of wrongdoing at any level. (218)

majority leader of the Senate The leader of the majority party in the Senate, whose role is to schedule activity on the floor of the Senate, to be the first speaker heard on the floor as each session opens, and to determine the Senate agenda. (315)

majority rule A political doctrine by which the numerical majority of voters holds the ultimate power to make decisions binding on all voters. (26)

manifest destiny The nineteenth-century doctrine that the continued expansion of the United States throughout the North American continent was its natural right and duty. (461)

media Channels of mass communication, such as newspapers, magazines, television, or radio. (214)

media events Strategic events tailored for media coverage of sufficient duration and impact to qualify as "entertainment." (223)

monarchy A system of government controlled by a sovereign ruler; in an absolute monarchy, there are no constitutional limitations on the monarch's power. (12)

most favored nation A foreign nation enjoying trading advantages with the United States. (464)

multinational corporation A company that has plants in many countries and tremendous impact internationally. (481)

National News Council A council founded to receive, examine, and report on complaints concerning the fairness and accuracy of news reporting and to defend the press against attacks on its freedom. (241)

National Resources Planning Board A specialized bureaucracy within the executive office of Franklin Roosevelt that was involved in the struggle to use the federal budget as an instrument in achieving full employment. (445)

National Security Council An organization composed of the president, the vice-president, the secretaries of state and defense, and the Chairman of the Joint Chiefs of Staff that meets to determine national security policy. (339)

National Security Study Memorandums (NSSMs) A series of documents prepared by the National Security Council that specify the various choices or options available to the United States in national security matters. (469)

natural rights The inherent rights of humanity, such as life, liberty, and the pursuit of happiness. (25)

neutrality A state of impartiality in disputes and nonparticipation in war. (459)

nonpartisan primary A primary election in which all voters are free to participate and candidates are not required to declare their political affiliation. (178)

office column ballot (Massachusetts ballot) A ballot that groups candidates by office, with the party label following the individual candidates. (175)

Office of Management and Budget (OMB) An agency within the Executive Office of the President whose principal function is to supervise the preparation of the annual budget of the federal government. (339)

oligarchy A system of government controlled by a small faction; government by the few. (18)

ombudsman A freewheeling intermediary between the individual citizen and the many federal bureaucracies. (310)

open-ended poll An opinion survey format in which interviewees are simply asked for their opinion, without specific choices. (205)

open primary A primary election in which any qualified voter may participate. (177)

opinion makers Certain individuals within the public at large who carry weight with their peers. (101)

original jurisdiction The situation where a legal case originates before the Supreme Court, rather than as an appeal. (68)

orthodox bureaucratic type The civil servant who works within the machinery of government, taking a long-range view of problems and few risks. *See also* **change agent.** (369)

outer cabinet Those cabinet secretaries who are responsible for domestic concerns. (266)

packing the court *See* **Court Plan.**

Parliament The supreme legislature of Great Britain, consisting of the Crown, the House of Lords, and the House of Commons. (20)

party column ballot (Indiana ballot) A ballot that lists candidates in rows under their party affiliation. (175)

party platform The document that delineates the party's stand on specific issues. (150)

patronage The awarding of political jobs and positions on the basis of favor or service. (136)

petrodollars Funds invested in the United States by Arab oil producers. (474)

Phillips Curve A graphic theory showing the relationship between unemployment and inflation; the lower unemployment falls, the higher is the tendency toward inflation. (436)

pluralist model A model of society suggesting that the political system is composed of a variety of groups actively influencing public policy; political and economic power is therefore widely diffused and dispersed throughout society. (100)

plurality The largest number of votes, but less than 50 percent. (178)

political socialization The process by which individuals are exposed to and conform to the dominant political values and perspectives; various institutions such as schools, the family, and the mass media transmit these values and ideologies. (97)

political strategy A plan or method set up either to win a political election or to create a favorable image for a politician already in office. (253)

polling Measuring public opinion by means of a survey; when conducted scientifically, polls have been found to have considerable predictive value. (102)

potential electorate The vast numbers of American citizens that are eligible to vote. (191)

precedent A previous legal decision serving as an authoritative rule or justification in subsequent judicial cases of similar nature. (20)

president of the Senate A largely ceremonial position filled automatically by the vice-president of the United States. (315)

president pro tempore The chair of the Senate, usually the senior senator, during the many expected absences of the vice-president. (315)

primary A special preliminary election in which voters directly nominate the candidate of their preference. (176)

prior restraint The requirement that prior approval, generally in the form of a license or permit, must be obtained before information may be communicated. (518)

Privacy Act Legislation restricting the methods by which the government may obtain and retain information about American citizens. (521)

public opinion The opinion of a variety of special publics; as V. O. Key notes, public opinion consists of "those opinions held by private persons which governments find prudent to heed." (95)

public service jobs Federally funded programs for jobs in the public sector, designed to improve the condition and quality of the national community. (421)

pure democracy Government by the people in which the ultimate authority is retained and exercised by the people directly. (13)

radicalism The doctrine that advocates sweeping, often revolutionary, changes in social, political, or economic organization. (23)

ratification The act of officially confirming or sanctifying something such as a treaty or constitution. (32)

rebate The return of part of an amount given in payment. (440)

recession A decline in economic activity and slowed economic growth. (418)

referendum The submission of a proposal to a direct popular vote. (84)

Regulation of Lobbying Act A law intended to make it a matter of public record who is a lobbyist and the amounts spent on lobbying activity. (126)

rights of Americans The body of constitutional, statutory, and administrative rights of all American citizens as formally specified in writing by the government. (499)

runoff A special election held when no candidate receives a majority of the vote, usually among the top two or three vote getters. (178)

saliency In polling, the relevancy of an opinion. (106)

secession The act of withdrawal by a state(s) from the Union. (80)

security adviser Head of the National Security Council; usually an important channel through which the president perceives the international arena. (339)

security classification system The process of designating material and documents as secret and available only to authorized persons. (514)

segregation The practice of imposing social separation of races, particularly evident in public school facilities and public accommodations. (504)

seniority system Until very recently the traditional system used in Congress, under which the chairship of committees automatically goes to the committee member of the majority party with the longest continuous service to the committee. (320)

Shays's Rebellion An agrarian revolt led by Captain Daniel Shays in 1786, which brought into focus the need for a better organized central government to handle civil disorders and support state authority. (29)

slander *See* **libel.**

Speaker of the House The leader of the majority party in the House. Working closely with the majority leader in the Senate, the Speaker appoints members of the Select and Conference Committees and directs floor activity and discussion. (317)

special committees Committees formed to consider special issues falling outside the well-defined subject areas of the standing committees; these committees allow Congress to react to or investigate dramatic, current problems. (322)

spoils system A system first developed under Andrew Jackson's administration in which federal employment was awarded on the basis of political favors and appointments. (345)

staff agencies The special agencies that function to support, inform, and aid the president. (337)

standing committees The established committees in Congress designed to consider specific issue areas; there are twenty-two standing committees in the House and seventeen standing committees in the Senate. (319)

states' rights A political doctrine advocating the limitation of federal prerogatives to those powers specifically provided in the Constitution, and reserving to the states all powers not expressly forbidden to them. (18)

statutory civil rights Rights and liberties defined and protected through legislative enactment. (497)

strict constructionism A judicial philosophy that favors judicial restraint, reflected in the reluctance to make new interpretations of the Constitution. (406)

structure In polling, the distribution of an opinion; for example, whether it is prevalent throughout the general public or whether it appears more randomly, without any clear pattern of concern. (106)

structured poll An opinion survey format in which specific questions with choices are asked. (205)

subpoena A legal writ requiring appearance in court to give testimony. (377)

suffrage The right to vote. (192)

Supreme Court review The power of the Court to review decisions of lawsuits and criminal convictions made in the lower courts. (384)

third parties Parties of principle and ideology that provide an alternative to the accommodationist two-party system. (155)

Third World Those underdeveloped nations of Asia, Africa, and South America that remain unattached to either the Communist or Western nations. (482)

Tories The colonists who were loyal to the British Empire and opposed the break from England. (24)

two presidencies theory The theory developed by Aaron Wildavsky that there are two aspects of executive control—the domestic presidency and the foreign policy presidency. The theory maintains that presidents enjoy greater success in controlling defense and foreign policy related issues than they do in dominating domestic policy making. (262)

tyranny A government in which a single ruler is vested with absolute power, especially when this power is used arbitrarily, unjustly, or cruelly. (41)

volatility In polling, how rapidly an opinion changes; a volatile opinion is one that changes rapidly and may even reverse itself. (107)

War Powers Act Legislation passed in 1974 that limited to sixty days the time an American president could commit troops overseas without congressional approval. (477)

Whigs A nineteenth-century party of commerce and nationalism, but without the aristocratic cast of the earlier Federalists; Whig leaders organized for democratic electoral politics and reached out to the expanding electorate. (74)

whips Members of Congress who assist the majority and minority party leaders in communicating with their rank-and-file colleagues and getting votes for important legislation. (319)

White House Office The most important of the separate organizations that make up the Executive Office of the President, composed of the president's closest aides. (338)

"winner-take-all" provision A provision within the electoral college system that the candidate receiving the most popular votes gets all the state's electors. (188)

wire services A news agency that sends out syndicated news copy by wire to subscribers; United Press International and Associated Press are the two major wire services providing information to the national news chains. (238)

writ of certiorari An order issued by the Supreme Court to a lower court to send a case up. (390)

writs of mandamus Orders issued by the Supreme Court to public officials either to perform required legal functions or to prohibit some form of action. (66)

INDEX

Page numbers in italic refer to illustrations.

Year	Candidates	Party	Popular Vote	Electoral Vote
1884	**Grover Cleveland**	Democratic	4,874,986	219
	James G. Blaine	Republican	4,851,981	182
	Benjamin F. Butler	Greenback-Labor	175,370	
1888	**Benjamin Harrison**	Republican	5,444,337	233
	Grover Cleveland	Democratic	5,540,050	168
1892	**Grover Cleveland**	Democratic	5,554,414	277
	Benjamin Harrison	Republican	5,190,802	145
	James B. Weaver	People's	1,027,329	22
1896	**William McKinley**	Republican	7,035,638	271
	William J. Bryan	Democratic; Populist	6,467,946	176
1900	**William McKinley** (**Theodore Roosevelt**, 1901)	Republican	7,219,530	292
	William J. Bryan	Democratic; Populist	6,356,734	155
1904	**Theodore Roosevelt**	Republican	7,628,834	336
	Alton B. Parker	Democratic	5,084,401	140
	Eugene V. Debs	Socialist	402,460	
1908	**William H. Taft**	Republican	7,679,006	321
	William J. Bryan	Democratic	6,409,106	162
	Eugene V. Debs	Socialist	420,820	
1912	**Woodrow Wilson**	Democratic	6,286,820	435
	Theodore Roosevelt	Progressive	4,126,020	88
	William H. Taft	Republican	3,483,922	8
	Eugene V. Debs	Socialist	897,011	
1916	**Woodrow Wilson**	Democratic	9,129,606	277
	Charles E. Hughes	Republican	8,538,221	254
1920	**Warren G. Harding** (**Calvin Coolidge**, 1923)	Republican	16,152,200	404
	James M. Cox	Democratic	9,147,353	127
	Eugene V. Debs	Socialist	919,799	
1924	**Calvin Coolidge**	Republican	15,725,016	382
	John W. Davis	Democratic	8,385,586	136
	Robert M. LaFollette	Progressive	4,822,856	13
1928	**Herbert C. Hoover**	Republican	21,392,190	444
	Alfred E. Smith	Democratic	15,016,443	87